A Princely Impostor?

A Princely Impostor?

THE STRANGE AND UNIVERSAL HISTORY OF THE KUMAR OF BHAWAL

Partha Chatterjee

PRINCETON UNIVERSITY PRESS

PRINCETON AND OXFORD

Library of Congress Cataloging-in-Publication Data

Chatterjee, Partha, 1947–
A princely impostor? : the strange and universal history of the Kumar of Bhawal /
Partha Chatterjee.
p.   cm.
Includes bibliographical references and index.
ISBN 0-691-09030-0 (cloth : alk. paper) — ISBN 0-691-09031-9 (pbk. : alk. paper)
1. Roy, Ramendra Narayan, Raja of Bhowal, 1884?–1946.   2. Roy, Ramendra
Narayan, Raja of Bhowal, 1884?–1946—Trials, litigation, etc.   3. Impostors and
imposture—Bangladesh.   4. Identity (Psychology)   5. Nationalism.   I. Title.

CT9981.R69 C47   2002
954.92′2035 — dc21   2001038752

British Library Cataloging-in-Publication Data is available

This book has been composed in Janson Typeface

Printed on acid-free paper. ∞

www.pup.princeton.edu

Printed in the United States of America

1   3   5   7   9   10   8   6   4   2

To the memory of my father,

_____

who loved to tell this story

CONTENTS

ILLUSTRATIONS

PREFACE

THIS IS A BOOK of narrative history. Its subject is an unusual trial that created a sensation in Bengal in the 1930s, enough to be noticed and written about in many other parts of India. The trial involved a prominent landed family of eastern Bengal, now Bangladesh; it entangled in its enormous net doctors and bureaucrats, priests and prostitutes, soldiers and artists, professors and holy men, besides hundreds of peasants, not to speak of lawyers and judges. The witnesses came not only from Bengal but also from places as far as Nepal and Punjab, and included large numbers of Europeans, mostly Scotsmen and Englishmen, who were part of the white expatriate community that still dominated the governing institutions of late colonial Bengal. The crucial event whose reconstruction formed the core of the dispute in court had taken place in 1909, and the judicial process of trial and appeals was completed in 1946. My history of the trial is thus set against the background of the larger history of Bengal in the first half of the twentieth century.

This is also a book about narrative history. Following upon the valiant labors of at least three generations of historians to reform their craft in order to supply the academic marketplace with products that would match the analytically more rigorous but rhetorically simpler standards of the social sciences, the wheel appears to have turned full circle in the last couple of decades. Historians are now persuaded by the arguments of critics such as Hayden White or Michel de Certeau; they know they are only fooling themselves by pretending to be innocent about the role of rhetoric in even the most analytical historical prose. This newfound self-awareness, curiously, has lulled some into a lazy scepticism that refuses to see any distinction between history and fiction. History writing, they say, is an activity akin to and of the same species as fiction writing because, like the latter, it relies on the power of rhetoric to produce the effect of truth.

Of recent historians, Carlo Ginzburg has attempted most vigorously to reestablish the use by historians of proof as opposed to rhetoric and to reassert the claim of history to knowledge as distinct from representation. He does not do this in a spirit of naïve and obstinate positivism. Rather, he is concerned to mark out a ground on which the historian could, in a self-conscious practice of his or her trade, persuade (rather than fool) the reader to accept the truthfulness of the account by using methods that are not the same those of the novelist. In particular, Ginzburg has often compared the methods of the historian with those of the detective and the judge; all three take on the job of finding the truth and, having done so, are required, by an appropriate exposition, to prove their case.

I will have occasion in this book to comment on Ginzburg's arguments, which I do not fully accept. But more prominently, I will need to compare the judicial with the historical method of arriving at a true reconstruction of past events. The judges in the Bhawal sannyasi case were faced with the problem, familiar to historians, of deciding which of the conflicting accounts presented before them represented the truth. Can the historian judge the judges? Could I, more than half a century after the law lords delivered their final judgment in London, agree to hear the arguments all over again and act, as it were, as another court of appeal? Ginzburg would say, "Yes," and I would not disagree. To facilitate such a hearing, and in the spirit of an impartial evaluator of evidence, I have reduced the authorial interventions in my narrative to a minimum. The story here is constructed entirely out of information that can be attributed to definite sources; all gaps in information have been left unfilled, and speculative remarks have been appropriately flagged. All of the basic rules of positivist historiography, I dare say, have been scrupulously respected.

The result, I hope to show, is a narrative in which the truth turns out to be undecidable. To anticipate a question that I know will be asked of me by every reader, let me say at the beginning that after having spent more than four years working through the massive records of the Bhawal case, and although three courts of law ruled in favor of the plaintiff, I remain an agnostic. I do not know if the sannyasi who appeared in Dhaka in 1921 was in fact the second kumar of Bhawal who, as far as was known at the time, had died in Darjeeling in 1909. I say this after having applied to the evidence all the tests of truth that I know and after having evaluated, in as reasonable and transparent a manner as I can, the procedures adopted by the judges of the three courts who heard the case. This predicament—of being left without the truth—is, I feel, directly attributable to my methods. Had I been writing a novel based on the Bhawal case, I would have had greater freedom to construct a more consistent plot and a more satisfactory conclusion to the story. On the other hand, I feel greatly relieved not to be in the position of the judge. Unlike the historian, he does not have the luxury of indulging in irony: he must pronounce whether or not the case has been proved!

My story also addresses the philosophical problem of identity, but not in the hypothetical mode preferred by analytical philosophers. Rather, it confronts the abstract universalism of philosophical analysis with the narrative density of a "true story." In the course of this encounter, I will at times come close to affirming the radical plea of a philosopher such as Derek Parfit who asserts, contrary to our ordinary, culturally formed common sense, that

identity does not matter. At other times, though, I will need to acknowledge the enormous power of governmental technologies to mold, catego-
rize, and authenticate our identities. The truth of identity, in my story, is
not just a matter of philosophical inquiry but of forensic knowledge. The
courts had to determine whether or not the plaintiff was the person he claimed
to be. I will thus find it necessary to match the analytical criteria suggested
by philosophers against a cultural history of truth.

This story deals with relatively unimportant historical characters who do
not usually merit much individual attention from professional historians.
Although the Bhawal case was widely written about by journalists, pam-
phleteers, and bazaar writers, this is the first full-length book of academic
history to deal with the case. However, there are certain larger historical
processes that I show to be at work in the particular progression of my story.
The twin processes of nationalism and decolonization are especially important. I hope to demonstrate that the historical event of the transfer of
power from British India to the two sovereign states of India and Pakistan,
which is usually treated in political history as the result of constitutional negotiations between British officials and Indian political leaders during and
immediately after World War II, actually has a secret history within the organs of the colonial state. The decade leading up to the war was one in
which a generation of Indian practitioners of the art of government—in this
case, of the administration of justice—had fully worked out the discursive
and institutional premises of national self-governance. The Bhawal case, I
argue, was resolved the way it was because it became caught up in this secret history of nationalism and decolonization.

I will also have occasion to point out the ideological limits of this nationalist construction of the task of self-government. In particular, the limits of gender and class are important for my story. The Bhawal case provoked a large popular literature in the 1920s and 1930s that took up a
completely different perspective from that of the judges. In addition, my
story is peopled by several women who played roles quite different from
those depicted in the judicial discourse. These provide alternative perspec-
tives, outside the domain of the elite and of the law, from which the story
can be told.

Faced with the facts of the momentous consequences on individual lives
of the decisions of governmental authorities, the historian cannot, I agree,
remain indifferent to the question of the truth. Whether he can always find
it is, of course, another matter.

Although I have seen most of the twenty-six volumes of evidence of the
Bhawal sannyasi trial, of which exactly twenty copies were printed before
the hearings in the High Court, I was unable to copy them or consult them

at leisure. Fortunately, the trial was exhaustively reported in the Bengal press. The *Amrita Bazar Patrika*, in particular, carried three or more broadsheets—more than twenty full columns—of reports on each day's hearings; these are available in the newspaper reading room of the National Library in Calcutta. I supplemented these with reports from *The Statesman* of Calcutta and from the *Ḍhākā prakāś* preserved in the University of Dhaka Library. Full texts of the judgments delivered in the Dacca district court and the Calcutta High Court were published at the time; the pavement book stalls on College Street in Calcutta are still a goldmine for such rarities. I found the largest collection of pamphlets on the Bhawal sannyasi affair in London in the India Office collection of the British Library. The official archives, however, did not yield much. The Court of Wards had collected all relevant papers relating to the administration of the Bhawal estate for the use of its lawyers, and some of these papers were produced in court. The files that did not reach the lawyers, fortunately, have now been brought together in a special collection at the National Archives of Bangladesh.

The photographs included in this book were either among the exhibits in the Dhaka trial in 1933–1936 or published along with the judgments of the Calcutta High Court in 1940, and are in the public domain.

In the course of working on this book, I have received the generous help of many people in many parts of the world. In Dhaka, Dr. Sharifuddin Ahmed and Mir Fazle Chaudhuri guided me through the holdings of the National Archives of Bangladesh and Mayezuddin through the University of Dhaka Library. Mamun-ur Rashid, Secretary, Statistics Division of the Government of Bangladesh and formerly of the Court of Wards, was extremely generous with his time and knowledge. Professor Muntassir Mamoon of the University of Dhaka shared with me his enormous store of information on the history of Dhaka. Dr. Binayak Sen and Mrinal Roy spent hours walking with me through the streets of Dhaka. Shireen Huq, Zafrullah Chaudhuri, and their wonderful family gave me a home in Bangladesh; it is hard for me to repay my debt to them.

I am grateful to the staff of the Oriental and India Office reading room of the British Library in London. The bulk of my work there was done in the old reading room on Blackfriars Road before the collection shifted to the new building at St. Pancras.

I found interesting bits of material in the libraries of the University of Michigan in Ann Arbor, the University of Chicago, and the Law Library of Columbia University in New York.

In Calcutta, I have used the National Library and, as always, the library of the Centre for Studies in Social Sciences. Abanti Adhikari was an enthusiastic and enormously reliable research assistant. The late Nirmalya Acharya was my guide to the mysterious alleys of College Street publishing; his untimely death has left a huge void in my life. Gautam Bhadra continues to supply me with nuggets from his inexhaustible fund of historical information. Siladitya Banerjee, Aniruddha Bose, Sajeda Momen, and Saugata Roy helped me in various ways. Anjusri Chakrabarti prepared the maps for this book, and M. Iqbal Shaikh edited the scanned photographs for publication. My colleagues at the Centre for Studies in Social Sciences, Calcutta, have commented on earlier drafts of this work and have unfailingly helped and encouraged me in the research; my thanks to them all. I am particularly grateful to Manjula Banerjee, T. K. Basu, Aditi Mukherjee, and Sunil Mukherjee for talking to me at length about their memories of the Bhawal sannyasi affair. My thanks to my wife Gouri for much valuable assistance.

Rukun Advani, Nicholas Dirks, Amitav Ghosh, and Gyan Prakash read the penultimate draft of this book and offered numerous detailed comments that were invaluable in shaping the final version; I am immensely grateful to them for being so generous with their time, wisdom, and encouragement. Muzaffar Alam, Janaki Bakhle, Richard Bernstein, Akeel Bilgrami, Dipesh Chakrabarty, Mechthild Guha, Ranajit Guha, Tapati Guha-thakurta, V. Narayana Rao, Carol Rovane, and Sanjay Subrahmanyam read and commented on different parts and versions of the manuscript. Among my students at Columbia University, Jennifer DeWan was a wonderful research assistant, Uma Bhrugubanda prepared the index, and Arjun Mahey, Vishnupad Mishra, and Ravi Sriramachandran offered valuable help. My colleagues in the Subaltern Studies collective have been my intellectual companions for many years; their encouragement and criticism sustain my work in many ways. Mary Murrell, Fred Appel, Tim Sullivan, and Margaret Case of Princeton University Press and Rukun Advani of Permanent Black have been enthusiastic supporters of this book; their help was crucial for its publication. The final manuscript of the book was prepared during my term as a Fellow of the Wissenschaftskolleg in Berlin; my discussions with colleagues there were both entertaining and informative, and the friendly and helpful staff and excellent facilities proved to be especially timely and valuable.

As this book was ready to go to press, I discovered that the original box of photographs produced as evidence in the trial had been retrieved from a London auction house in 1997 by Ebrahim Alkazi and placed in his collection of photography in New York City. Unfortunately, the discovery came too late for me to make full use of this astonishing collection. I am extremely grateful to Mr. Alkazi and to Esa Epstein of SEPIA International Inc. for their generous help in making copies of these photographs for my use, and also to Anupama Rao for leading me to this source. The frontispiece and figures 3, 5, and 8 appear courtesy of the Alkazi Collection of Photography.

The Roman transliteration of Bengali words is a matter of much confusion and controversy. Resisting the prevailing fashions, I have chosen a path of convenience rather than consistency. Bengali and Sanskrit words have been romanized with diacritics in citing book titles. Personal names have been transliterated without diacritics in the currently standard form, except when it is known that the person concerned used a different romanized spelling. I have used the most familiar current spelling for place names. This has sometimes produced a discrepancy between my spelling and the one used in the sources: thus, for example, Bhawal and Bhowal, Jaidebpur and Joydebpore. The capital city of Bangladesh is now most commonly known as Dhaka; I have used this spelling when talking about the city, but have retained the old spelling of Dacca to refer to the district and division going by that name in British Bengal. It is foolish to pretend that the legacies of colonialism can be consistently erased without a trace.

ABBREVIATIONS

ABP   *Amrita Bazar Patrika*, Calcutta

Basu, *J*   Judgment of Pannalal Basu, First Additional Judge, Dacca in *Ramendra Narayan Roy v. Bibhabati Debi and others*, Title Suit 38 of 1935, in *Bhowal Sannyasi Case: Full Text of the Judgment* (Dhaka: Bosen, 1936)

Biswas, *J*   Judgment of Justice C. C. Biswas of the Special Bench of the Calcutta High Court in *Bibhabati Debi and others v. Ramendra Narayan Roy and another*, Appeal from Original Decree 1 of 1937, in S. C. Das Gupta, ed., *The Bhowal Case: High Court Judgments* (Calcutta: S. C. Sarkar, 1941)

Costello, *J*   Judgment of Justice L.W.J. Costello, ibid.

GB   Government of Bengal

ICS   Indian Civil Service

Lodge, *J*   Judgment of Justice R. F. Lodge, in Das Gupta, ed., *The Bhowal Case*

NAB   National Archives of Bangladesh, Dhaka

OIOC   Oriental and India Office Collections, British Library, London

WBSA   West Bengal State Archives, Calcutta

A Princely Impostor?

MAP 1. Some relevant locations in Dacca district. Based on information in S.N.H Rizvi, *East Pakistan District Gazeteer*

Chapter One

THE FACTS OF THE MATTER

Bʜᴀᴡᴀʟ was an estate—a zamindari —in the eastern district of Dacca in British Bengal. The zamindar's house, a large mansion, was in Jaidebpur, a small town located a little to the north of the present capital city of Bangladesh. Zamindaris in Dacca were notoriously small, the region having been a classic example of what agrarian historians of Bengal call subinfeudation—that endless multiplication of rent-collecting interests that brought about a massive fragmentation of landed estates in the nineteenth century. By Dacca standards, however, Bhawal was a very large estate, with an annual rent income of about Rs.650,000 in the early twentieth century. The family was regarded as the premier Hindu zamindar family of the district; the zamindar was locally called the raja, and the estate as the Bhawal raj.

In 1909, when our story begins, the estate was owned by three brothers with equal shares. They were known as kumars, princes. The eldest was twenty-seven years old, the second twenty-five, and the third twenty-two. All three brothers were married and lived in the family mansion—the Jaidebpur Rajbari. Three married sisters also lived in the house at this time, together with their respective husbands and children.

On April 18, 1909, Ramendra Narayan Roy, the second kumar, left Bhawal for Darjeeling by train, arriving at the hill station on the twentieth. He was accompanied by his wife Bibhabati, Bibhabati's elder brother Satyendra, and a retinue of twenty-one servants. Ashutosh Dasgupta, the family doctor, was also in the party. The reason for the visit was Ramendra's health. The second kumar had contracted syphilis about three years before, and now ulcers had broken out on his legs and arms. The hills, it was thought, would be a good change for him, and his brother-in-law Satyendra had already made a scouting visit to Darjeeling and arranged a house for him to rent. It was somewhat surprising that Bibhabati was not accompanied by any other woman of the family, for it was not customary in families of the standing of the Bhawal Raj for young wives to travel alone with their husbands. But later, when this question was raised, it was explained that Satyendra had thought the house in Darjeeling too small to accommodate a large party.

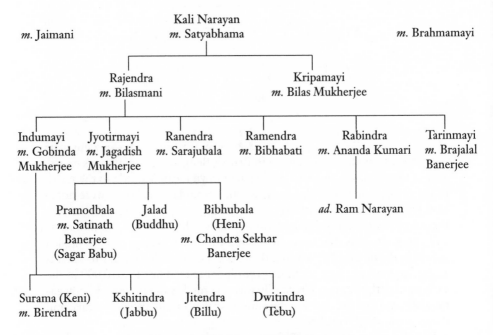

FIGURE 1. The Bhawal Raj family tree

The first few days of the second kumar's visit passed without incident. On May 6, however, he fell ill: a telegram arrived at Jaidebpur the next morning from one of the clerks in the Darjeeling party saying that the kumar had a fever. The following morning, a telegram arrived with the news that he was much better. But another, which arrived late in the evening, brought alarming news. "Kumar seriously ill," it said. "Frequent watery motion with blood. Come sharp." Early next morning, the youngest kumar set out from the Rajbari to catch the mail train to Darjeeling. As he was approaching the station at Jaidebpur, a man stopped his carriage and handed him a telegram which said that the second kumar had died. Three days later, the second kumar's party returned from Darjeeling to Jaidebpur, bringing back the young widow Bibhabati.

The prescribed religious rites were performed for the dead kumar on May 18, the customary eleven days after death. It was said later that there was a proposal to burn a *kuśaputtalikā* before performing the *śrāddha* ceremonies (homage to the deceased performed as a supplement to the funerary rites), since there were disturbing rumors about the way the kumar's body had been cremated in Darjeeling. The kuśaputtalikā, in Brahminical funerary rites, is a grass effigy that is symbolically burned when the body of a dead person, for whatever reasons, has not been or is supposed not to have been cremated. It was established later that no such symbolic cremation was performed at the second kumar's śrāddha in Jaidebpur, and many people maintained that no such thing had even been suggested.

Nevertheless, some rumors were afloat about the circumstances of the second kumar's death in Darjeeling and the manner in which his body had been cremated. Sharif Khan, an orderly who went to Darjeeling with the kumar's party, brought back the dramatic story of how, when he had been asked to help shift the kumar's bed, the ailing kumar had suddenly vomited, and so corrosive was the ejected fluid that some drops that fell on Sharif Khan's clothes actually made holes in them. More persistent was a rumor that although the kumar's body had been taken to the cremation ground in Darjeeling, it had not been cremated.

It is hard to know whether any members of the family took these rumors seriously at the time. The evidence suggests that people in Jaidebpur were stunned by the sudden death of the second kumar. His śrāddha was a lackluster affair without any of the pomp that might be expected of a śrāddha at the Rajbari.

Soon afterward, Bibhabati's elder brother Satyendra Banerjee began to intercede on behalf of his sister in order to protect her interests in the property. There seems to have been a proposal to take out a deed to exclude her from the management of the estate in return for a monthly allowance, and Satyendra rushed to Calcutta to seek legal advice to stall the move. Later, it was suggested that the idea was not so much to exclude the second rani as to prevent her brother from meddling in the affairs of the raj. In any case, nothing came of this proposal. Satyendra now moved from Calcutta to Dhaka, rented a house, and began to live there with his wife and mother; he tried to persuade Bibhabati to move out of the Jaidebpur Rajbari. For several months, Bibhabati resisted. In November 1909, however, she formally appointed Satyendra her agent and claimed Rs.30,000, which was the value of a life insurance policy taken out by the estate in the name of the second kumar.

Dark days seemed to descend upon the Bhawal Raj. The eldest kumar, Ranendra Narayan, died in September 1910. Soon after, Bibhabati went to live with Satyendra's family in Calcutta, not to return to Jaidebpur for the next twenty years. She received a monthly allowance of Rs.1,100 and took out more than Rs.35,000 from her share in the estate, besides the insurance money, with the help of which her brother bought a house on Lansdowne Road in Calcutta. In April 1911, F. W. Needham, the British manager of the estate, informed the second rani in Calcutta that the management of her share was being taken over by the Court of Wards, the government department responsible for looking after zamindari estates that did not have owners who could manage them properly. In May that year, the share of the third kumar was also taken over because he was deemed unfit to manage it. In May 1912, when the share of the eldest rani was taken over, the entire estate came under the jurisdiction of the Court of Wards. In September 1913, after a brief illness, the third kumar died. Suddenly, the premier Hindu zamindar family of Dacca was reduced to three childless widows, none of whom was in charge of her property. Soon after her husband's death, the third rani also left Jaidebpur. Six years later, she adopted a son.

For several years after Ramendra Narayan's death, rumors surfaced periodically—not just that the second kumar's body had not been cremated, but that he was still alive, living as a sannyasi. Apparently, only a few months after Ramendra's death, a wandering sannyasi, on being told in Jaidebpur about the second kumar's death, remarked that he had seen a Bengali—a rich man's son—traveling with a group of sadhus who had found him in Darjeeling. Some relatives were sent out to northern India to make inquiries. Jyotirmayi, a sister of the kumars, who often went to Benaras, made it a habit to ask at that great meeting place of religious people if anyone could give her any news. She later said that from what she heard from various sources, she became convinced that her brother was alive. In 1917, a sadhu who had taken a vow of silence arrived in Jaidebpur and wrote on a piece of paper that the second kumar was alive.

After this, the rumors became particularly strong, because Rani Satyabhama, the aged grandmother of the three kumars, who was then living alone in the Jaidebpur Rajbari, wrote to the maharaja of Burdwan asking if he could confirm that the second kumar's body had indeed been cremated eight years previously, since she knew that the maharaja had been in Darjeeling at the time. She was hearing rumors, she said, from places all over eastern and northern Bengal, that her grandson had been seen wandering about in the company of mendicants. In reply, the maharaja wrote that he did remember having been told one day in Darjeeling that the second kumar of Bhawal had died and he had asked his staff to send the holy Ganga water and tulsi leaves that would be needed at the funeral. More than this he could not say.[1]

The rumors and speculation persisted. Many years later, Ronald Francis Lodge, judge of the High Court in Calcutta, would remark that the strength of the rumors showed "how the people of the locality were ready to believe that Ramendra Narayan Roy was alive. They were in a mood to accept a claimant, and if any one was inclined to put forward a claim, he must have realised from the experience of that year that an impostor bearing any resemblance to the late Ramendra Narayan Roy would have a reasonable chance of success."[2]

THE SANNYASI

The Buckland Bund was in the early part of this century an embankment on the Buriganga River, a popular promenade for the inhabitants of the city of Dhaka. Today, it is the approach to the Sadarghat launch terminal and one of the most congested streets of the city. As one trudges through the slush and garbage, negotiating the fruit and vegetable vendors and an endless stream of rickshaws, one's view of the river blocked off by an ugly wall and with no trees in sight, it is hard to imagine that the road had been built as an attractive riverfront boulevard. But older residents of the city still remember a time when they could take a leisurely evening walk on the bund.[3] Sometime in December 1920 or January 1921, a sannyasi appeared on the Buckland Bund. He had matted hair and a long beard, wore only a loincloth, and his body was covered with ashes. For about four months, he sat on the bund in front of Ruplal Das's mansion (which still stands in a state of crumbling magnificence as an ineffectually protected heritage site). He sat there night and day, rain or shine, impervious to the weather. He attracted a lot of attention, because he was, as one of the witnesses said later in court, "a beautiful fair man with a fine and noble stature. . . . I do not remember having seen such a handsome, fair *jaṭādhārī* sannyasi [with matted hair] at Dacca."[4] Often a small crowd would collect around him, and people would ask him where he was from or if he would give them medicines. He spoke in Hindi. Some later said that he told people that he was from Punjab and had left home when he was a child. Others said that he spoke of having left his parents and wife. He apparently complained of the climate and the water in Bengal. To those who asked for medicines, he sometimes offered a pinch of the ash with which his body was always smeared, but refused to give amulets.

It seems that fairly soon after his arrival on the Buckland Bund, word began to spread that the second kumar of Bhawal had come back as a sannyasi. People now came to the riverside in Dhaka to see for themselves if this was true. They would stand around him and ask him questions. Most of the time, the sannyasi would remain silent; when he did respond, he would say in his rustic Hindi that he was a renouncer and had no home or family. Many went back convinced that the rumors were baseless. Some even said that the man was an impostor, although no one had heard the sadhu make any claims at all about who he was. Yet, as the crowds jostled around him under the pale winter sun on the Buckland Bund, the whispers were clearly audible: "This is the mejo (second) kumar! The second kumar of Bhawal!"

The first person from the Bhawal Raj family who went to see the sannyasi on the bund was Buddhu, the son of Jyotirmayi, an elder sister of the kumars. He went from Jaidebpur accompanied by some gentlemen from Kasimpur, a neighboring village, and returned not knowing what to make of his visit. The sadhu certainly had, he thought, a strong resemblance to the second kumar, but whether he was in fact his uncle, returned from the dead after twelve years, he could not say. It was then that the gentlemen from Kasimpur decided that an attempt should be made to bring the sannyasi to Jaidebpur.

On April 5, 1921, Atul Prasad Raychaudhuri, a younger member of the zamindar family of Kasimpur, brought the sannyasi to his house. Atul Babu had known the second kumar well, and the two families were on close terms. It was later suggested that the sannyasi was taken to Kasimpur not because anyone suspected that he might be the kumar of Bhawal but because it was hoped that he might be persuaded to do a *putreṣṭi yajña*, a sacrificial rite performed in order to get a son, since Sarada Prasad, the head of the Kasimpur family, had none. The sannyasi, it seems, said flatly that he knew nothing of such rites. In any case, he stayed in Kasimpur for about a week, living under a tree. On April 12, he was sent on an elephant to Jaidebpur, arriving there at about six in the evening.

The elephant stopped at the Rajbari. The sannyasi got off and went to sit under a kamini tree near Madhabbari, a building within the Rajbari complex that served as a resthouse for travelers and mendicants. None of the family now lived in the Rajbari, as the three sisters had moved a few years before to their own houses in a neighborhood about a quarter of a mile from the Rajbari. Rani Satyabhama, now nearly eighty years old, usually lived with one of her granddaughters. Some distant relatives and employees of the estate, however, came to see the sannyasi that evening. One of them, Radhika Goswami, a nephew of Satyabhama, recalled later that he looked at this man, naked except for his loincloth, and tried especially to observe his hands and feet. He could not be sure that he was the mejo kumar.

The next morning, Rai Saheb Jogendra Nath Banerjee, secretary to the Bhawal estate, along with his younger brother Sagar, who was married to Jyotirmayi's daughter, came to see the sannyasi. They found him sitting on the southern verandah of the building known as the Rajbilas. Sagar Babu observed him very closely. "He looked at us as we stood facing him. I could see the colour of his eyes. It was brownish. I observed his build, his style of sitting, and the way he looked—his way of looking. I suspected he was the Second Kumar. I told Jogen Babu what I thought. He said the matter looks serious. I asked him what he thought. He said: Don't make a row. Let's wait and see him further."[5]

A little later, Buddhu arrived to say that his mother would like the sannyasi to be taken to her house. When asked, the sannyasi said that he would go in the afternoon.

Jyotirmayi saw the sannyasi for the first time in her house that evening. He had been brought in a dogcart (known all over India as a tumtum) a few minutes before, and when she came out on to the verandah, she found him seated on a mat, surrounded by members of her family. The sannyasi sat with his head bowed, looking through the corner of his eyes. "That reminded me of Mejo's way of looking at people. It excited my suspicion. I started looking at him, scrutinizing his features, eyes, ears, lips, figure, hands and feet, the contour of his face."

She asked him how long he would stay. He replied in Hindi that he would go the next day to Nangalbund for the Brahmaputra bath. She gave him some fruits and cream to eat. He ate the cream. Soon after, he left. "I noticed his gait—it was that of the second kumar. I noticed his height, but he seemed slightly stouter, a shade stouter."[6] After he had left, they all talked about the sannyasi. It was decided that they would ask him to come for a meal the next day when they could observe him in the daylight.

The next morning, the sadhu was seen walking along the verandah of the Rajbilas, which used to be the main living quarters of the family, looking through the shutters of the second kumar's room, going into the adjacent bathroom and washing under a tap. At noon, he went to Jyotirmayi's house in a carriage belonging to the estate. This time, he went into the front room and sat on a chair. Gobinda Mukherjee, Indumayi's husband, sat on a chauki, a flat wooden divan, while Satyabhama and Jyotirmayi sat on chairs. Everyone else stood. "The sannyasi," Jyotirmayi said later, "asked my grandmother in Hindi to sit on the chauki." She moved and sat on the edge of the divan. The sannyasi asked her to sit up and helped her move to a more comfortable position. He said, "Buḍikā baḍā dukh hai" (the old woman is very unhappy). Then he pointed to Jyotirmayi's daughters and asked who they were, and then in turn he asked about her son and her sister Indumayi's sons. "Pointing to Keni, my sister's daughter, he said: 'Yeh kaun hai?' (who is this?). I said, 'She is the daughter of my elder sister.' As I said that, the sannyasi burst into tears. Tears trickled down his cheeks. Keni was then a widow."[7]

Tebu, Indumayi's son, showed the sannyasi photographs of the kumar. Seeing them, he began to weep uncontrollably. Jyotirmayi asked him why he was crying when he had taken the vows of a renouncer. The sannyasi said, "Ham māyāse rotā hai" (I cry because of *māyā*, my sense of attachment). Jyotirmayi asked, "Māyā for whom?" She then told him about her brother who was said to have died in Darjeeling, and how some said that his body had been cremated, while others said it had not. Even before she had finished, the sannyasi said, "No, no, that is not true. His body was not burned. He is alive." Jyotirmayi looked directly into the sannyasi's eyes and said, "Every bit of your face looks like my brother's. Are you he?" "No," the sannyasi said, "I am nothing to you."[8]

However, he agreed to have a meal that day in Jyotirmayi's house.

> I noticed his index finger sticking out as he was taking his food, and he was putting out his tongue a bit. I noticed his features. I noticed his adam's apple. I noticed his hair was red; *kaṭā* eyes, brownish. I noticed his teeth: they were those of the Second Kumar, even, smooth and beautiful. I noticed his hands and fingernails—every one of the fingernails. I noticed the palm and back of the hand. I noticed his leg, feet and toes. How could I forget? We had lived together from infancy. His whole body—arms, legs and face, and even the eyelids were smeared with ashes. His hair was long. He had a beard now. The Second Kumar did not wear a beard when he went to Darjeeling. His utterance on this day was indistinct. His voice was that of the Second Kumar.[9]

Jyotirmayi now had a very strong suspicion that this was indeed her brother. She wanted him to stay a few more days so that she could check whether he had the old marks on his body. But the sannyasi was anxious to go back to Dhaka and would not stay any longer.

For the next week or so, he was not in Dhaka—when Buddhu, on Jyotirmayi's instructions, went to look for him, he was not to be found. He had apparently gone to visit Chandranath, a shrine in Chittagong district. On about April 25, however, he was back at his usual spot on the Buckland Bund. On that day, Buddhu took the sannyasi to the house of a relative in Dhaka, where Jyotirmayi had arranged for her younger sister Tarinmayi to meet him.

On April 30, the sannyasi was once again taken to Jyotirmayi's house in Jaidebpur. This time, several relatives and people from the town collected to see him. Jyotirmayi tried to persuade him not to cover his body with ashes when he came back from his bath. For two days, the sannyasi refused. On the third day, however, he came back from the river without the ashes on his body. Jyotirmayi later said, "Then I saw his complexion. It was the Second Kumar's complexion as of old, and seemed brighter still on account of *brahmacarya* [celibacy]. Then, looking at his face, cleaned of ashes, he looked like Ramendra himself. I noticed his eyelids darker than his complexion. I saw the mark left by the carriage wheel, and I saw the rough and scored skins at the wrists and at the instep. The relatives I already named, my grandmother and the rest also saw him, and recognized him, just as I did."[10]

The next day, May 4, early in the morning, the sannyasi allowed Buddhu, acting once again on instructions from his mother, to inspect him closely for various marks on his body. Jyotirmayi explained later that she did this because "the matter was very serious and we wanted to be dead certain, so that no question could ever arise in our minds." By late morning that day, large crowds were collecting outside the house. Jyotirmayi decided to confront the sannyasi: "Your marks and appearance are like those of my second brother. You must be he. Declare your identity." "No, no," the sannyasi said, "I am not. Why do you annoy me?" "You must say who you are," Jyotirmayi insisted.

DECLARATION

She asked Buddhu to go out and tell everyone that all the marks on the second kumar's body had been found on the sannyasi's. By this time, there were already several hundred people, mostly tenants from the estate, who had collected outside Jyotirmayi's house, wanting to know more about the sannyasi. Jyotirmayi said to the man she was now convinced was her brother that she would not eat until he had made a public declaration of his identity. It was twelve years, almost to the day, since her brother was supposed to have died in Darjeeling.

That afternoon, the sannyasi appeared before the assembled crowd of some two thousand people. Someone asked him, "What is your name?"

The sannyasi said, "Ramendra Narayan Roychaudhuri."

"What is your father's name?"

"Raja Rajendra Narayan Roychaudhuri."

"Your mother's name?"

"Rani Bilasmani Debi."

Somebody then shouted, "But everyone knows the names of the raja and the rani. Tell us the name of your wet nurse?"

The sannyasi answered, "Aloka."

Hearing this, the crowd broke out into cheers: "*Jay!*" they said. "Victory! Victory to the second kumar!" The women started ululating. The sannyasi seemed to go into a faint. Jyotirmayi and a few other women came out from behind the screens and started to fan him and sprinkle rosewater on his head. A few minutes later, he was taken into the house of Tarinmayi, the youngest sister. The crowds tried to follow, but after much persuasion, they were made to desist.

The next day, May 5, Needham, the manager of the Bhawal estate, sent a confidential report from Jaidebpur to Lindsay, collector and district magistrate of Dacca.

My dear Lindsay,

A very curious and extraordinary thing is happening here which has created a tremendous sensation throughout the Estate and outside.

About 5 months ago a fair complexioned mendicant came to Dacca, it is reported, from Hardwar and stayed on the river side just opposite to Rup Babu's house, whence he was taken to Kasimpur by Babu Saroda Prosad Roy Choudhury, Zemindar of Kasimpur. He halted there for a few days. On his way back to Dacca he halted at Madhabbari at Jaidebpur, as other mendicants used to do. During his stay at Madhabbari he was taken to the house of Srj. Jyotirmoyee Devi. Srj. Jyotirmoyee Devi began to shed tears finding in the sadhu some likeness of her late 2nd brother (Kumar Ramendra Narayan Roy of Bhowal), and the sadhu too burst into tears. This raised some suspicion in the minds of the inmates of the house. After a photo of the 2nd Kumar was presented to him, he began to shed tears profusely; this strengthened the suspicion already created. He was then questioned by the inmates of the house as to who he really was, but without giving any answer he abruptly left for Dacca. For a few days nothing was heard of the sadhu.

A week ago the sadhu was again brought to the house of Srj. Jyotirmoyee Devi by Babu Atul Prosad Roy Choudhury, zemindar of Kasimpur, and since then he has been staying here. On seeing the sadhu who is here now an impression has been made upon the minds of the people who are visiting him daily in hundreds that he is the late 2nd Kumar. Tenants from different parts of the estate, and also outsiders, are daily coming in large numbers, visiting the Sadhu and giving out that he is the 2nd Kumar. His presence has created a very great sensation in the locality.

Late evening the sadhu, being questioned and hard-pressed by several hundreds of tenants, at last gave out that his name is Ramendra N. Roy and his father's name was Rajendra N. Roy and his nurse was Aloka Dhai. After this the Sadhu fainted, and the numerous people present began to utter "Hullu-dhani" and "Jay-dhani". All the people who were present at the time were convinced that he was no other than the 2nd Kumar, and the tenants present gave out that even if the estate could not accept him, they would stand by him and maintain his position. Finding the gravity of the situation, the inmates of the houses of late Srj. Indumoyee Devi and Jyotirmoyee Devi informed Mohini Babu and Mr. Banerjee that the sadhu had given out such and such things. They forthwith proceeded to the house of Srj. Jyotirmoyee Devi and enquired about the matter. The sadhu did not meet them. They went there this morning again, but the sadhu sent intimation that he would see them this afternoon. The inmates of the house threatened the sadhu that he was incurring great responsibility by expressing in words and by conduct that he is the 2nd Kumar, and that he cannot leave the place without giving the full particulars about his identity and past history. Under the circumstances a sifting enquiry about the sadhu is urgently needed. From morning crowds of people have been flocking to see the sadhu, and the excitement and sensation is so great that the matter may take a serious turn unless necessary steps are taken promptly.

I am awaiting your instructions in the matter.[11]

Copies of the letter were forwarded to Bibhabati Debi, the second rani, in Calcutta as well as to the other two ranis for their information.

Four days later, on May 9, there appeared in *The Englishman* of Calcutta the following letter to the editor:

Sir, you published on Saturday morning a report sent by the Associated Press from Dacca under the heading "Dacca Sensation" to the effect that a person has suddenly appeared who claims to be the Second Kumar of Bhowal, who died twelve years ago.

The late Kumar was attended in his last illness by Lieutenant-Colonel Calvert, the then Civil Surgeon of Darjeeling, and the death certificate was given by Mr. Crawford, Deputy Commissioner of Darjeeling.

I was personally present at the time of the death of the late lamented Kumar and attended the funeral service along with numerous friends and relatives of the deceased who were then present in Darjeeling. The Rani of Bhowal, the widow of the Second Kumar, who is my sister, is still alive. Yours etc., S. N. Banerjee.

Meanwhile, in Jaidebpur, streams of people converged every day upon the grounds in front of Jyotirmayi Debi's house to get a glimpse of the sadhu who had now declared himself as Ramendra Narayan, the second kumar of Bhawal. He had dispensed with the appurtenances of a mendicant, and wore ordinary clothes, although his hair and beard were still long. Each day he would sit on a chair in front of the house, talking to people who came up to him, answering questions, sharing old memories and often weeping. The daily register kept at the Jaidebpur police station has the following entries for these days:

10–5–21. 3 p.m. No rain during the past 24 hours. The Sadhu who declared at Jaidebpur Rajbari that he was the Second Kumar of Bhowal is still staying there. Large numbers of men are coming to see him from far and near. Most of the general public believe that he is the Rajkumar.

11–5–21. . . . A Sannyasi has come to Jaidebpur. Large numbers of men are coming and going from various parts to see him, and 15 annas of the people [that is, fifteen out of sixteen; 16 annas = 1 rupee] are expressing the opinion that he is the Second Kumar, Ramendra Narayan Chaudhury.

13–5–21. 2–30 p.m. Information has been received that a big meeting will be held on Sunday next of the general body of the tenantry to accept as the Kumar the Sannyasi who declared his identity as the Second Kumar.[12]

The police information was correct. An open meeting was called for Sunday May 15, to be held in front of the Jaidebpur Rajbari. That day, people started coming in from early morning from distant parts of Dacca and

Mymensingh districts. The railway company even ran special trains to Jaidebpur, and still people were hanging from the footboards and windows. By the afternoon, well over ten thousand people had collected; some said later that there were as many as fifty thousand. The meeting began with Adinath Chakrabarti of Barishaba, a prominent talukdar (tenureholder under a zamindar) of Bhawal, in the chair. He explained in detail the background of the present sensation, recounting the story of the second kumar's death, the rumors concerning his cremation, the recent appearance of the sadhu in Dhaka, his visit to Jaidebpur, the questions that were put to him by his sisters and other relatives, the marks on his body, and his admission a few days ago that he was indeed the second kumar. Everyone who had seen and spoken to the sannyasi, Adinath asserted, was convinced that he was Kumar Ramendra Narayan Roy. Only a few of his relatives, for their own selfish reasons, were still resisting this idea. But the talukdars and tenants of the Bhawal estate were united in their conviction that their beloved second kumar had returned. They must now come forward and declare their belief in public. Adinath asked everyone who believed that the sannyasi was the second kumar to raise their hands. Thousands of hands went up in assent. He then asked if there was anyone who doubted the identity of the sannyasi. Not a single hand was raised. Purna Chandra Chatterjee then moved a resolution in the name of the assembled talukdars and tenants of the Bhawal Raj that they had recognized the sannyasi and were convinced that he was Kumar Ramendra Narayan Roy, the second son of the late Raja Rajendra Narayan Roy. The resolution was passed without any dissent. It was decided that copies would be sent to the governor, the Board of Revenue, the divisional commissioner, and the district magistrate. As the summer sun began to descend toward the horizon, the man everyone had come to see was brought to the meeting seated on an elephant. Slowly, the elephant circled the dais, to the accompaniment of cheers from the crowd. "Jay, Madhyam Kumar ki jay!" they said. "Victory to the second kumar!" Suddenly, a huge storm started to blow, as it was liable to do at this time of the year, followed by torrential rains. The meeting broke up, but by then everyone had had their fill of the excitement.

A few days later, an association was formed under the name of the Bhawal Talukdar and Praja Samiti to raise funds "to establish the Kumar in his legal position by legal means." The association was presided over by Digendra Narayan Ghosh of Harbaid, a prominent talukdar of Bhawal.

On May 29, 1921, some three weeks after his declaration of identity, the former sannyasi now claiming to be the second kumar of Bhawal came to Dhaka and, accompanied by two lawyers and a local zamindar, appeared before Lindsay, the collector, in his house. After he left, Lindsay made the following record of the interview.

The sadhu came to-day about 11 A.M. with Babu Sarat Ch. Chakrabartti, Babu Peari Lal Ghosh and, I think, the Kasimpur Manager. He said he wants some arrangement made about his estate so that the tenants could be benefitted. I explained that the Board of Revenue must hold him not to be the Second Kumar as they have carried on the work of the estate on that assumption for many years. I said he could prove his identity in court in a suit, or if he pre-ferred to produce his evidence before me I was willing to record it. He agreed to the latter procedure, and the pleaders said they would file a petition to-morrow for such an enquiry. They asked that the Board might pay the expenses and I replied that if they put in a petition to that effect I would get orders on it.

In reply to my questions the sadhu (Second Kumar) told me that he had been ill for 2–4 days of pneumonia before he lost consciousness in Darjeeling. He could not remember the name of the house in Darjeeling where he lived, he went from Jaidebpur to Darjeeling, that he was not ill at Jaidebpur except from a boil just above his right knee which occurred within 10 days of his going, there was no special cause of this boil, he did not remember when he was in Calcutta before that, that he recovered his senses in the jungle in the hills in the presence of one sadhu who has since been his Guru, that the sadhu said he had been senseless for 3–4 days, that the sadhu told him that he had found him lying on the ground as if he had been thrown there and that his body was wet with rain as it had been raining before he found him, that the sadhu did not say whether he found him in the day or at night.

The sadhu agreed that the rents should be collected as usual by the estate officers and the pleaders urged that the tenants would have less objection to paying if the receipts were given in Bibhabati's name leaving out that of her dead husband.[13]

On the margin of this report, Lindsay also made the following observation: "The sadhu appeared to be an up-country [man] with a beautifully clear skin with no sign of syphilis."[14]

Five days later, on June 3, the following public notice was issued in Ben-gali in the Bhawal estate.

All the tenants of the Bhawal estate are hereby informed that the Board of Rev-enue has got conclusive proof that the dead body of the second kumar of Bhawal was burnt to ashes in the town of Darjeeling twelve years ago. It fol-lows therefore that the sadhu who is calling himself the second kumar is an im-postor. Anyone who will pay him rent or subscriptions will do so at his own risk.

With the permission of the Board of Revenue, J. H. Lindsay, Collector, Dacca.[15]

Officials and employees of the Bhawal estate were instructed to publicize this notice as widely as possible and not to do or say anything that might add to the belief that the second kumar had returned. On June 10, a week after it was issued, when the notice was sought to be announced in public at a place called Mirzapur, the assembled crowd protested in a somewhat less than orderly fashion, forcing the police to open fire; a man called Jhumar Ali was shot to death.

The battle lines had been drawn. People were making up their minds on whether or not they believed that the sannyasi was really Ramendra Narayan, the second kumar of Bhawal. For the next twenty-five years, as events would unfold around this sensational case, there would be few in the whole of Bengal, regardless of region, class, gender, or social status, who would not come to hear of the Bhawal sannyasi and his claim. Most would also have an opinion on whether the sannyasi was really the second kumar of Bhawal.

Chapter Two

AN ESTATE CALLED BHAWAL

The district of Dacca in British Bengal was divided into two natural regions. The more familiar topography, typical of eastern Bengal, was to be found in the low alluvial lands toward the eastern and southern parts of the district, which was bounded by the great rivers Padma and Meghna and crossed by the Dhaleswari and the Sitalakhya (or Lakhya). This was a densely populated and fertile region, inundated for most of the rainy season; it yielded flourishing crops of rice and jute as well as the many fruits and vegetables for which the district was famous. British officials did not like the scenery here; they thought it "very tame and dull," a "dismal country," and the people, they observed with astonishment, were "almost amphibious in their habits." Officers on tour sometimes reported such extraordinary scenes as a grey-bearded patriarch swimming toward the district magistrate from across the flooded fields to hand him a petition. One reason for the colonial official's antipathy toward this part of the district was, of course, that the natural environment made his work more difficult. "In the height of the inundation no land is to be seen and all travelling has to be done by boat, a state of affairs which is not unfavourable to commerce, but . . . adds largely to the difficulty of the administration of the district."[1]

We need not spend time worrying about the rainwater in the Dacca lowlands, however. Our story comes from the other part of the district, the highland toward the northwest known as the Madhupur jungle. This is an elevated tableland rising about forty to fifty feet above the low plains, intersected by ridges and winding depressions. The land in the depressions, locally known as *bāid*, was used for cultivating rice, whereas most of the higher land was covered by forest, although, by the early twentieth century, some of it was being cleared for growing jute or winter crops. The staple tree of the Madhupur forest was the *gajāri*, an inferior variety of the robust *śāl* tree that was a favorite of colonial forest officials elsewhere in India. There were no large rivers and few streams in this part of Dacca, which was generally regarded by the people as an unhealthy area. In British eyes, however, it was an attractive place. "[F]or any lover of the picturesque it possesses many charms. In place of the dead level of the alluvial plain there are rolling uplands covered with short grass or dark green forest which dip towards the basins."[2]

The Bhawal estate was situated in the Madhupur forest region. The main town, Jaidebpur, was three stations and twenty-two miles north of Dhaka city on the East Bengal Railway line running from Narayanganj to Mymensingh. Today, Jaidebpur is best reached by the Dhaka-Mymensingh highway. What remains of the Madhupur forest is protected as the Bhawal National Park. But in the early years of the twentieth century, most of the land in this region north of Dhaka city was part of the Bhawal estate. It was, as we have said, one of the largest zamindari estates in Dacca; it spread over 579 square miles and 2,274 villages, and contained in 1921 a population of around 500,000. Outside Jaidebpur, in the *mufassil* (countryside), the estate was divided into 44 *dihi* or revenue divisions, each in charge of a *naib*. But unlike most large zamindaris of eastern Bengal, Bhawal was a compact estate, with most of the land falling within a single *pargana* or revenue district.[3] Much of the land was uncultivated, and in general the area was regarded by outsiders as poor; there were few occupations besides growing rice and jute and collecting forest produce. It was often pointed out, for instance, that there were relatively few upper-caste Hindus or high-born Muslims living in Bhawal and that, apart from poor Muslim and lower-caste Hindu peasants, there was a sizable number of Rajbangshi and Koch in the area—people regarded as hovering on the borderline between caste and tribal societies—besides a group called, with unconcealed contempt, the Banua (meaning "wild" or "of the forest"). Muslims comprised nearly 60 percent of the population of the area.

THE RULERS OF BHAWAL

Like many of the larger zamindaris of Bengal, the estate of Bhawal also claimed a long and eventful history. The imagination of the local literati in Bengal seldom shies away from identifying its presence in a name or a place mentioned in the ancient epics. In Bhawal, those who knew of such things took pride in claiming that their land was none other than the kingdom of Chedi ruled by the legendary King Śiśupāla, whose exploits are described in the *Mahābhārata*. The kingdom then was extensive, they said, including within its borders the present city of Dhaka and extending some two hundred miles north toward Kamakshya in Assam. The ruins of Śiśupāla's palace and fort could still be seen at Dighalir Chhit by those adventurous enough to walk into the tiger-infested forests.[4] More careful historians suggest that the Śiśupāla of Dighalir Chhit was probably a member of a later local branch of the Pāla dynasty that ruled in parts of eastern Bengal after the collapse of that ancient kingdom.[5]

Coming to a period more easily, even if uncertainly, located in historical chronology—the period before the Mughal conquest of Bengal in the sixteenth century—one hears the story, perhaps no less legendary than that of Śiśupāla, of the twins Pratap and Prasanna, born of a low-caste Chandal mother. The Bhawal literati record this episode with some distaste: "With the passage of time, the kingdom of the great and ancient Hindu rulers was eclipsed and Bhawal came to be dominated by men from the inferior classes."[6] The twins had been blessed by fate and possessed exceptional powers. Rising above the disabilities imposed by their low status, they obtained an education, and by a combination of political skill and armed force established their dominance not only in Bhawal but also in neighboring Chandpratap and other areas. They adopted the title Ray and built a capital at a place still known by the name Rajabari (the royal abode) not far from Jaidebpur. Some sources claim that they followed the Buddhist faith and had taken a vow to rid the Bhawal area of Brahmins, but this claim cannot be corroborated.[7] Judging by the oral tradition that goes under their name, Pratap and Prasanna Ray seem to have done some radical things. Not only had they established a Chandal kingdom, they also upset the social hierarchies even further by trying to teach peasants to read and write. For this purpose, they devised a simplified script called Chasa Nagari (literally, the peasant's script) which, it seems, some of the oldest inhabitants of Bhawal could still read until a few years ago. In the end, of course, the Brahmins had their revenge. One day, Pratap and Prasanna Ray invited the Brahmins of their kingdom to a feast. The Brahmins insisted that, in accordance with tradition, they could only accept a meal cooked by the queen herself. This started an altercation between the twins as to whose wife should have the privilege of being called the queen of Bhawal. The fight went from bad to worse until, in the end, Pratap and Prasanna killed each other. Needless to say, the story reflects all of the prejudices of Brahmins about the unfitness of men from the lower castes to become good rulers. But it also appears to carry the memory of an interesting episode in the social history of eastern Bengal, where landed proprietors from the low and even untouchable castes were not uncommon even in the modern period.

As one moves to the period of the annexation of Bengal into the Mughal Empire, Bhawal finds a more prominent place in the recognized historical sources. It was the name for the area north of Dacca, which was dominated in the late sixteenth century by Bahadur Ghazi, one of the twelve great warlords (*bhuiya*) of Bengal who had combined to resist the Mughals. He is mentioned several times in the *Bahāristān-i-Ghāybi* of Shitab Khan, better known as Mirza Nathan, as the zamindar of Chaura, a village not far from present-day Kaliganj.[8] Bahadur, along with his nephew Anwar Ghazi, another member of the Twelve Bhuiyas, was at this time a follower of Isa Khan of Bikrampur, and after the latter's death in 1599, of his son Musa Khan. Bahadur Ghazi, who possessed a large fleet of warboats that were especially effective in campaigns in the riverine tracts of east Bengal, was a major collaborator of Musa Khan in his fight against the Mughal armies sent by the Emperor Akbar to subdue and annex Bengal. Until Akbar's death in 1605, most of these areas of east Bengal were still holding out against the imperial power. In 1608, Emperor Jahangir appointed Islam Khan, grandson of the famous saint Salim Chishti of Fatehpur Sikri, as governor of Bengal. Mughal historians give Islam Khan the main credit for subjugating the recalcitrant warlords of those godforsaken frontier regions of east Bengal where no Mughal general wanted to be sent. By a judicious combination of military force and diplomatic tact, Islam Khan managed to overcome or neutralize the chiefs who were resisting Mughal power in northern and central Bengal. In 1611, he launched a campaign against Musa Khan in Dacca. Ably assisted by his general Mirza Nathan, Islam Khan and his imperial forces inflicted a series of defeats on Musa. Bahadur Ghazi, whose warboats were a crucial part of Musa's tactical plans, decided that the game was up and surrendered. Islam Khan seized his boats but spared his zamindari.[9]

The Ghazi family of Chaura continued to be zamindars of Bhawal under the Mughal dispensation. Bahadur Ghazi was recognized as the zamindar of five parganas—Chandpratap, Kasimpur, Talipabad, Sultanpur, and Bhawal. A year after his submission to the Mughals, he and his forces joined the imperial expedition to Kamrup and a few years later to Tippera. Soon after the successful Kamrup expedition, Islam Khan, who hated the climate of Bengal, was seeking some distraction in a hunt in the forests of Bhawal, where he met with an accident that led after a few days to his death.[10]

In the 1640s, Daulat Ghazi, Bahadur's grandson, was the zamindar of Bhawal and with him the history of the estate took a dramatic turn. There are two distinct versions of the story, which reflect, as we can now see, very different political points of view. The dominant version is to be found in most written histories of Bhawal and is summarized in the official gazetteers of the British period. According to this, Daulat Ghazi was either incompetent or oppressive or both. Prosperous farmers and traders were fleeing the estate, and the zamindar's coffers were empty. Imperial officials from Dhaka served Daulat Ghazi with a notice for huge amounts of unpaid revenues, and the beleaguered zamindar made a desperate appeal to the Mughal viceroy Prince Muhammad Shuja, then residing in Rajmahal on the borders of Bihar. At this time, a young scribe working in the imperial establishment, either in Dhaka or at the viceroy's court in Rajmahal, came to the Bhawal zamindar's aid. Kushadhwaj Roy was descended from a Brahmin family of the famous Bajrajogini village in the Bikrampur region of Dacca and had made a name for himself at the provincial capital as an astute revenue functionary. His efforts won Daulat Ghazi a reprieve. As a reward, the zamindar invited the Brahmin to settle down in Bhawal and take charge of the administration of the estate. The Roy family began its career in Bhawal as diwan or minister to the Bhawal zamindar.[11]

After the death of Kushadhwaj, his son Balaram took over his father's responsibilities, but the complaints about the Ghazi family's wayward and oppressive ways continued. The tenants refused to pay rent and the estate became unmanageable. The Mughal authorities finally decided to settle the
zamindari with Balaram Roy and two other Hindu officials of the estate.
Balaram's son Srikrishna was confirmed as zamindar of Bhawal by an imperial order of 1683. The chronicles are very definite about the date of this
order—6 Zilhajj 1088 A.H.—and the *sanad* (grant) was still in the possession of the Bhawal Raj in the early twentieth century. The Ghazi family
contested the settlement, but in a judgment of 1704 the imperial government finally rejected its claims.

It is difficult to know how much of this history is tainted by the stereo-
type, common in the nineteenth century, of the country being put to waste
by a dissolute and tyrannical Muslim nobility, only to be rescued by wise
and efficient Hindu officials.[12] What we do know, however, is an alternative version of the story, still told by elderly residents of the Bhawal area. In
this version, the Ghazis were valiant and well-meaning soldiers, not particularly interested in the mundane intricacies of revenue administration,
which they left in the charge of their Hindu diwan. Daulat Ghazi, we are
told, had gone on pilgrimage to Mecca when, during his absence, Balaram
Roy and the other Hindu officials hatched a conspiracy to defraud him of
his estate. On his return from the hajj, Daulat Ghazi discovered that his zamindari was gone. He tried hard to get it back, but his political skills were
no match for the intrigues of the wily Brahmin. The Ghazis were ousted as
the ruling family of Bhawal. Today, the town of Jaidebpur has been renamed
Gazipur and it is now the headquarters of the Bangladesh district of the
same name. Whether or not we accept this as a just historical retribution,
there is no doubt that the Ghazis were for a long time a dominating presence in the history of Bhawal.

Bhawal under British Rule

When the English East India Company acquired the diwani (revenue administration) of Bengal in 1763, the Bhawal zamindar was Lakshmi Narayan Roy, sixth in descent from Balaram. By this time, the family had set up
its residence at Pirabari, renamed Jaidebpur after Jaydeb Roy, Balaram's
grandson. The chronicles speak of this time as marked by the depredations
of tigers and other fierce animals and of people trying to move to safer
places. It is possible that there was a decline in cultivation and an expansion
of waste lands and forest. In the last decades of the eighteeenth century, we
read of a new form of estate management marked by the creation of intermediate tenures called *taluk*. Respectable families from the three high

castes—Brahmin, Kayastha, and Baidya—were brought in to the Bhawal region as talukdars to act as intermediaries in the collection of rents from the tenants.

In the early nineteenth century, Bhawal still had a reputation of being an inhospitable and fearsome place. The Madhupur forest was said to be infested not only by wild animals but also by dangerous humans. There was only one road passing through the area from Dhaka to Mymensingh. There were sparse settlements along the road and the few grocers and shopkeepers who offered food and lodging to travelers themselves turned into robbers at night. There were even *thug*s (thieves) from northern India who came into this area; the famous Lieutenant Sleeman, pursuing his targets, arrived in Dacca in 1835 and set up thugee offices in the district.[13] Curiously however, the forest and its notoriety proved to be a blessing in at least one respect; unlike many of the other great zamindaris of eastern Bengal, Bhawal and its adjacent estates were spared the attention of property dealers and speculators who, in the early nineteenth century, recklessly bought and sold shares and intermediate rights in zamindari estates, leaving them fragmented and hopelessly enmeshed with dozens and even hundreds of cosharers. As one revenue official commented: "Bhawal, Kasimpur and Talipabad owed their salvation to the dense jungle, which proved a complete deterrent to would-be adventurers."[14]

In 1794, the zamindar Lok Narayan Roy died, leaving behind his wife Siddheswari and an infant son. Siddheswari is one of several remarkable women from the Bhawal zamindar family who will figure in our story. A young widow with property was a familiar target of family conspiracy in zamindari circles. Siddheswari and her son Golok Narayan were driven from their home by the machinations of their relatives. But she fought back, made representations to the government and to the courts, and recovered her property. Golok Narayan, however, grew up to choose a life of religious meditation and refused to involve himself in the affairs of estate management. Siddheswari thus continued to run the Bhawal estate. It was at this time that indigo farming was spreading in Bengal, and several European planters were buying intermediate rights in land in order to force tenants to cultivate indigo instead of foodcrops. The most prominent indigo planter in Dacca was James Wise. He is sometimes confused with Dr. James Wise, the man who put together the first collection of popular myths, legends, and proverbs of east Bengal. But our James Wise was an indigo planter and zamindar—a wealthy man whose name still appears on shop signs at Wise Ghat in old Dhaka.[15] As a planter, Wise was vicious, and even the official records describe him as "a landlord notorious for his encroaching propensities."[16] Wise began to entice or coerce the smaller cosharers and intermediate tenureholders of the Bhawal estate to part with their holdings. He set up his own collection offices within the estate and tried to push cultivators to grow indigo. The tenants were at their wits' end and appealed to Rani Siddheswari to come to their aid. Siddheswari, with the help of her grandson Kali Narayan, then a young man of twenty, mobilized a troop of Koch warriors under the leadership of a wrestler from Dhaka by the name of Bhagirath Pathak. In 1838, the rani's men met a team of armed guards from Wise's estate led by the fearsome Panju Sardar. At the end of a fierce battle on a field north of the great tank near Wise's collection post at Tararia, Panju's men were defeated and Wise's "encroaching propensities" suffered a setback. Nevertheless, he continued to hold a part of the estate.

Rani Siddheswari died in 1845. Upon hearing of his mother's death, Golok Narayan returned from his spiritual travels, renounced his claims to his property, and formally handed over the estate to his son Kali Narayan. The title deed signed by Golok Narayan is preserved in the National Archives of Bangladesh. For a few years, things were quiet until, in 1849, the conflict with James Wise blew up again. Golok Narayan was greatly concerned by this development and decided to sort out the matter once and for all. He intervened, sought a meeting with Wise and told him that it was not proper that their quarrel should be inherited by the boy Kali Narayan, and that to settle matters Wise should either buy the whole of the Bhawal estate or allow Golok Narayan to buy up the Englishman's shares. Wise did not take the proposal very seriously and said that he could sell his shares if he was paid Rs.100,000 for every sixteenth part that he held. (Shares in zamindari estates were calculated by the anna share or the sixteenth part; sixteen annas equaled one rupee.) This was an outrageously high price, but to everyone's astonishment Golok Narayan accepted the offer. Kali Narayan and the other estate officials tried to dissuade Golok Narayan, but he would not listen. Arrangements were made to pay Wise the huge sum of Rs.446,000 for the 4¾ shares he held in the Bhawal estate. To the planter's credit, he cleared out of Bhawal and turned his attention elsewhere. The chronicles record that the indigo troubles were finally over in Bhawal.

The deal put a huge financial strain on the estate. In addition, Golok Narayan had been lavish with his charities and good deeds. Some of these, admittedly, had added to the luster of Jaidebpur, such as the huge tank to the west of the palace, the market, several temples, and indeed the palace itself. But all of these also contributed to the debts incurred by the estate. Nevertheless, Kali Narayan proved to be an able manager of his properties. Unlike his father, he relished the worldly skills of estate administration. In a few years, he was able to pay off his debts, after which he turned his attention to expanding and improving his estate.

According to British officials of the nineteenth century, there were two kinds of Bengal zamindars. One lot was inefficient, wasteful and dissolute in their habits, factious, profligate in matters of entertainment and ostentatious spending, and oppressive in extracting rents and illegal surcharges from their tenants. The other kind was cautious and law-abiding in managing their estates, careful not to run up debts, usually educated in English, and sociable but deferential toward colonial officials. Kali Narayan belonged to the second category. As a young boy growing up under the care of his grandmother, he caught the attention of Walter, the district magistrate of Dacca. Kali Narayan had lost his mother when he was a child. His father, uninterested in worldly matters, had gone away on pilgrimage, no one knew where. Walter arranged for the boy to be taught some Persian and some accounting. Kali Narayan was more interested in riding and hunting, and Walter did not disapprove of these gentlemanly pursuits. Apparently, he had his own son staying with him in Dhaka, and the two boys, more or less of the same age, struck up a friendship and went riding together. When Rani Siddheswari died, Walter, it seems, helped trace Golok Narayan, who was immersed in his spiritual quest somewhere in Assam. This was when Golok Narayan arranged to hand over the ownership of the estate to his son.

In managing his properties, Kali Narayan was supported by colonial officers, but he clearly knew how best to use this support. He began to buy up shares in neighboring zamindaris and considerably expanded the rental base of the Bhawal estate. He was particularly successful in clearing up legal disputes over the property and obtaining judicial decisions in his favor. He also introduced certain new methods to increase the area under the estate and the amount of rent collected, though some of these methods were not exactly nonviolent. Thus, he systematically tried to regain possession of tenures given out earlier, by first acquiring a fractional share in the tenure and then using "the power of the Raj" to collect the entire rent. He also had the land surveyed every eight years—such frequency was extremely rare—and divided the land into eleven or twelve classes by quality, each class subject to a different rate of rent. It was found by government survey officials in the early twentieth century that through these surveys, "the land has shown a constant, though impossible, tendency to ascend to a superior class."[17] Needless to say, the rents collected increased as well.

Besides administering the estate more effectively, Kali Narayan renovated and expanded the family residence in Jaidebpur; it now became an impressive mansion. He built a guesthouse in the European style for his English visitors, who now began to come quite frequently, especially on hunting expeditions into the Madhupur forest. The stables at Jaidebpur began to grow, with new elephants and horses procured every year. When it was proposed that the Buckland embankment be built in Dhaka, Kali Narayan contributed Rs.20,000 toward the construction fund. Not surprisingly, the government rewarded him with the honorific title of Rajah Bahadur, and the Bhawal estate was accorded a high rank among zamindaris in the district, second in precedence only to the Nawab Bahadur of Dacca.

Kali Narayan adopted several elements of the lifestyle and activities of progressive zamindars in nineteenth-century Bengal. Apart from sprucing up the town of Jaidebpur, he tried to introduce to Bhawal society something of the new cultural life of the educated bhadralok, the emerging middle-class elite of Bengal. He patronized literary gatherings and musical soirees. In 1865, he sponsored a society for the welfare of tenants in his estate that to some extent formalized a channel of communication between the zamindar's establishment and the representatives of at least the more prosperous and articulate sections of tenants. This was also the time when, in the wake of tenants' revolts in many parts of Bengal against indigo planters and oppressive zamindars, the government was pushing for some protection for tenants against eviction and illegal rents and surcharges. Kali Narayan apparently decreed that surcharges extracted by talukdars in Bhawal for the holding of religious festivals and for payments to mullahs and priests be stopped. Another of his forays into social reform was formally to allow men from the Koch and Rajbangshi communities on his estate to wear the sacred thread. This was probably an early sign of the well-known movement of social uplift in northern Bengal, later to be led by the Rajbangshi reformer Panchanan Barman, which was opposed and ridiculed for the most part by upper-caste bhadralok.[18] It is interesting that Kali Narayan, a Brahmin zamindar, should have made this gesture of approval toward the movement.

Kali Narayan had one shortcoming that he greatly regretted: he had been unable to learn English. He resolved to rectify this by sending his only son Rajendra Narayan to an English school in Dhaka, and later by starting an English high school in Jaidebpur. He also appointed an Englishman named Bedford as manager of the estate and tutor to his son; Bedford died a few years later. At this point, Kali Narayan made another momentous decision that would leave a permanent mark on the history of Bhawal. He sought out and persuaded Kali Prasanna Ghosh, then a minor clerk in the Dhaka court, to come to Bhawal as manager of the estate. Kali Prasanna had already made a name for himself as founder-editor of *Bāndhab*, the most prestigious literary journal published from eastern Bengal, and as a leading orator in literary and debating societies in Calcutta and Dhaka. He was a man of both ability and vision, and by bringing him to Bhawal, Kali Narayan ensured that the estate would continue to enjoy the prominence and reputation he had acquired for it. Kali Prasanna was assured that he would be free to go to Dhaka as often as necessary in order to look after the publication of *Bāndhab*. As it happened, things did not turn out as he expected. In 1878, a year after Kali Prasanna Ghosh moved to Bhawal, Kali Narayan died. Rajendra Narayan was then a boy of seventeen. He signed a power of attorney in favor of Kali Prasanna, giving to the latter the authority to act on his behalf in managing his estate. The pressure of work on Kali Prasanna made the publication of *Bāndhab* quite irregular, until in 1888 it was suspended, to be resumed only after his retirement from the Bhawal estate thirteen years later.

It is said that after handing over the affairs of the estate to Kali Prasanna, Rajendra Narayan, secure in the knowledge that his properties were being well looked after, took to a life of comfort and pleasure. He had been introduced to an education in the Western style, although he was not what one would understand by the term "educated man" in elite Bengali society in the late nineteenth century. He wrote letters in English, and even if the zamindari chronicle exaggerates when it says that he spoke English "with the ease and fluency of Englishmen," he certainly mixed socially with officials and other Europeans. He frequented the clubs and restaurants of Dhaka and Calcutta and invited European guests to visit Bhawal for hunting parties. He was fond of music, played the tabla very well, employed professional musicians to teach him and play for him, and patronized musicians and dancers who came and stayed in the precincts of the Jaidebpur Rajbari. The presence of Kali Prasanna Ghosh had secured for Bhawal a prominent place on the cultural map of Bengal. The literary society started by Kali Prasanna and financed by Rajendra Narayan arranged for visits by many eminent writers and scholars from Calcutta, gave away prizes and awards, and published books and journals. Rajendra Narayan also had a special regard for Sanskrit studies and was the principal patron of the Dhaka Saraswat Samaj, the most important society of Sanskrit scholars in eastern Bengal. He succeeded quite easily to the place of prominence to which his father had risen in official circles in Dhaka and was duly honored with the title of Rajah Bahadur.

Rajendra Narayan died in 1901, leaving behind his wife, three sons, and three daughters. The estate had been for nearly twenty-five years in the charge of Kali Prasanna Ghosh, who ran it like an autocrat. Not everyone was happy with his style; there were persistent complaints that he was arrogant and arbitrary, and that even minor functionaries of the establishment were high-handed and oppressive in dealing with the tenants. The charges were brought up with particular vehemence by another well-known poet of Bhawal, Gobinda Das, who published in a Calcutta journal a satirical account in verse of the oppression and lawlessness in the Bhawal estate.[19] Kali Prasanna went to court with a suit of libel against the editor of the journal, who apologized. But Kali Prasanna persuaded Rajendra Narayan to prohibit Gobinda Das from entering the estate. The younger poet, whose station in life was far more modest, was able to return from his banishment only after Kali Prasanna had left Bhawal.[20]

There is evidence to suggest that a great deal of resentment had built up among some members of the zamindar family against the power wielded by Kali Prasanna. Rajendra Narayan had paid little attention to the administrative side of his zamindari. More significantly, he had neglected to devote the same care to the education of his sons as his father had tried to do for him. Critics later alleged that the moral atmosphere of the Jaidebpur Rajbari had been corrupted and that, despite the towering presence of Kali Prasanna Ghosh, none of the intellectual and cultural qualities associated with him percolated to the younger members of the raj family. Rajendra Narayan had appointed his wife Bilasmani as trustee on behalf of his sons. But soon after Rajendra Narayan's death, Jaidebpur was rife with conflict and intrigue over who was to run the estate. There were allegations that Kali Prasanna had diverted the funds of the estate for his own private ends. The second kumar, Ramendra, it seems, was particularly vociferous against Kali Prasanna. Once, when the latter was away in Dhaka, Ramendra arranged to have the tank adjoining Kali Prasanna's house searched by divers who found, or so it is said, several valuable papers of the estate hidden under the water in sealed boxes.[21]

Five months after Rajendra Narayan's death, Rani Bilasmani dismissed Kali Prasanna Ghosh from the position of manager and brought a suit against him for misappropriation of funds to the tune of over a million rupees. In his place, Surendra Nath Matilal, father-in-law of the eldest kumar and a lawyer at the Calcutta High Court, took charge of the estate for a year until Rani Bilasmani appointed H.C.F. Meyer as the new manager. Kali Prasanna returned to Dhaka to resume the publication of *Bāndhab*. After a while, the lawsuit was settled out of court.[22]

The Court of Wards

In June 1904, a year and a half after he came to Bhawal, Meyer wrote a long letter to Rankin, the collector of Dacca, complaining against Rani Bilasmani who, he said, was wasting money and interfering in his work.

> What is required is some authority to whom I could appeal, at present there is no one. The two younger Kumars are helpless as far as business is concerned. They have next to no education. The eldest Kumar is a very good-hearted lad and as long as I am at his elbow, I can make him see things in the proper light; he has a business capacity.
>
> He himself has acknowledged many times that his mother is ruining the Estate and things are getting worse but when I try and get him to assert himself and try and put matters right, he will do nothing. He means well and if he had charge of the Estate as *Kurta* under my guidance he would do well.
>
> . . . I feel it my duty to let you know what is happening here and unless some steps are taken by Government, the affairs of the Estate will, day by day, get worse.

At the end of the letter, there was a one-line statement signed by Ranendra Narayan, the eldest kumar, certifying "the above-mentioned facts to be correct."[23] The letter is interesting in that Meyer, a nonofficial, was complaining to the seniormost government official of the district against his own employer on the ground of sharing, as a European, the concerns of the government about the inefficiency and profligacy of native landlords. Meyer, it seems, was Irish with a trace of Indian blood in his ancestry, and in the intensely race-conscious official circles of white men and women of those times, he was known to be an aggressive supporter of British dominance in India.[24]

It is also necessary to remember here that from the second half of the nineteenth century, British officials in Bengal had become particularly concerned about the proper management of zamindari estates. The revenue collected from the landed estates formed a very large part of the government's income, and although the estates were the private property of the landlords who were obliged, under the threat of draconian penalties, to pay the annual revenue to the government on time, they often failed to do so because—or so at least the government believed—of the inefficiency and corruption of the zamindari establishments. By the late nineteenth century, the government spared no opportunity to bring the management of the zamindaris under official control by insisting on the appointment of European managers or by having the estates taken over by the Court of Wards.[25]

The Court of Wards was a curious institution. It functioned directly under the Board of Revenue in Calcutta, but in the districts was headed by the collector, the highest administrative official responsible for revenue collection as well as law and order. Depending on the size and number of estates under its charge, the Court of Wards would have its own offices and staff to collect rents from tenants, manage the property, and arrange for the education of the sons of the zamindars (in the theoretical hope that they would grow up to take back their estates and run them properly). The usual situation when a zamindari estate was taken over by the Court of Wards was that a proprietor had died, leaving minor sons. But acting on reports from the collector, the Board of Revenue was also empowered to disqualify proprietors on the ground that they were unfit to manage the property. The Court of Wards could then take over the property and run it on behalf of the proprietors, who would then become the "wards" of the court.

Soon after receiving the complaint from Meyer, therefore, Rankin asked the Board of Revenue in Calcutta to disqualify the rani and allow him to take over the estate "in order to save the property from the ruin which was likely to result from gross mismanagement and the tenants from oppressive and illegal and extortionate proceedings." The board, however, took the view that since the rani was only a trustee and not the proprietor, it would be reasonable to wait until her sons were old enough to take charge of the property.[26] Rani Bilasmani rightly concluded from all this that a conspiracy was afoot to take over the estate and, in September that year, dismissed Meyer. Immediately after this, Ranendra, who had just reached twenty-one years of age but was clearly under the influence of Meyer, made a formal application to the government declaring himself "disqualified" to manage the estate. Within days, Rankin received orders from the Board of Revenue to take over the Bhawal zamindari. On October 6, Rankin, along with Milligan, an assistant magistrate, and Meyer, and followed by a posse of policemen, arrived at the Jaidebpur Rajbari and announced to the rani that the estate had been put under the Court of Wards and that he was giving her ten minutes to put all the ladies of the house into one room so that he could proceed to search the palace for the papers and the money that he believed had been concealed. The rani denied that she had concealed anything and, in the middle of the altercation, suffered a fainting spell. The rooms were searched for three days and, according to Rankin, some missing papers were found hidden in a cellar. On the third day of the search, the rani finally handed over Rs.36,000.

Bilasmani did not relent. She went to Calcutta and tried to mobilize opinion in her favor. She approached officials and prominent persons and had articles published in nationalist newspapers criticizing the takeover of the Bhawal estate. A question was asked in the Legislative Council by the Congress leader Ambika Charan Mazumdar, to which the minister of land revenue had to make a reply justifying the government action. The action, the minister said, had been made necessary by repeated reports of mismanagement of the estate and especially by the application of Ranendra Narayan Roy, who disqualified himself and sought a takeover by the Court of Wards. Rankin, the collector, had acted with judgment and restraint. He had taken the dismissed manager Meyer with him to Jaidebpur to help find the missing papers, and the police constables were required to guard the estate treasury. It had not been confirmed whether the rani had indeed fainted during the search, but it was reported that she had been fasting that day. The minister refused to lay the papers of the case on the table of the council.[27]

Having exhausted the possibilities of influencing the government to change its decision, Rani Bilasmani filed a suit in the High Court of Calcutta against the Court of Wards, claiming possession of the estate. Almost immediately, in March 1905, the Court of Wards released the estate. Officially, it was recorded that the Bhawal zamindari had been "surrendered under an arrangement made with all the family."[28] But there is little doubt that the circumstances in which the takeover had been carried out made the government's case extremely shaky. There was enough evidence for Rani Bilasmani's lawyers to argue in court that the established norms had been violated and that the government had acted directly against the proprietor's intention.[29] The Board of Revenue chose to swallow its pride and return the estate to its proprietors. Ranendra Narayan now became the zamindar of Bhawal, holding the shares of his younger brothers in trust until they came of age.

ZAMINDARS AND TENANTS IN EASTERN BENGAL

In theory, as laid down by the so-called Permanent Settlement instituted in Bengal by the British in 1793, zamindars were only meant to collect rents from their tenants and pay a fixed annual revenue to the government. In practice, they often wielded the powers of sovereign overlords within their estates.

Through the nineteenth century, as more and more land was brought under cultivation in east Bengal, and both production and population increased, the zamindari structure acquired greater and greater complexity. To facilitate the collection of rents in often far-flung estates, zamindars created intermediate tenures, generally referred to as *talukdari*s. (In fact, there were specific names to designate particular rungs in the rent-collecting hierarchy; there could be as many as fifteen or more rungs of intermediate tenures between the zamindar and the tenant.) The proliferation of intermediate tenures was practical and viable as long as new lands were brought under cultivation and an increasing rent could be supported. Toward the last decades of the nineteenth century, however, "high landlordism" of this kind was becoming distinctly oppressive in eastern Bengal and was beginning to evoke protests from tenants.

Faced with a potentially dangerous peasant unrest, the colonial government tried to set legal limits to rent increases and put legal checks on the eviction of tenants by landlords. Innovative and enterprising landlords nevertheless managed to continue to extract increasing amounts from their tenants, as we saw in the case of Raja Kali Narayan and, following him, of Kali Prasanna Ghosh. Centralization of the rent-collecting apparatus by replacing the earlier *mandal*, who was both leader of the village community and local rent collector for the zamindar, with the salaried *tahsildar* was one method. Others were to create new tenancies and settle them at a higher rent, or to raise rents after the purchase of an estate, or to alter the standard of measurement. Still other methods involved a straightforward exercise of superior force. These were the so-called *abwab* or illegal cesses imposed over and above the rent.

In Dacca district, the "ceremonial abwab" was a widespread custom. Tenants were expected to pay the zamindar in money or produce or services (in addition to their regular rent) on various festive occasions such as religious ceremonies, marriages, births, the beginning of the sowing season or the end of the harvesting season, and so on. There were professional charges (entirely illegal, of course) imposed by zamindars on barbers, cobblers, mid-wives, and prostitutes. When the income tax was levied, zamindars immediately shifted the burden to their tenants by imposing—blatantly—an "income tax *kharcha* [expenses]"; when government officials visited the estate, the entertainment expenses were reimbursed by imposing a *rasad kharcha*.[30] In addition, there was the *begar* or unpaid labor that tenants and the members of their families had to provide on the lands and in the household and properties of the zamindar. The abwab in Dacca was said to amount to as much as 30 per cent of the rent.[31] It was not just the extra money or services that was at issue; a British district officer reported that many zamindars had told him "that the delight of the *abwab* is in the arrogation of sovereignty."[32]

Besides the abwab, there were fines and punishments that zamindars imposed on tenants for a wide variety of infringements ranging from failure to pay the rent to insubordination and disobedience. "Illegal evictions, false criminal prosecutions, fortuitous fires and the open destruction of homesteads by means of elephants are the ordinary methods of procedure in such cases."[33] Most of the larger zamindari establishments consisted of a considerable number—sometimes half or more of all estate employees—of armed men, called *jamadar, mridha, peyada, paik*, and so on, who were used against recalcitrant tenants. The usual procedure was for the defaulting or disobedient tenant to be locked up in a cell next to the collection office. If this was not enough, there were more violent methods such as beatings, harassment of the women of the tenant's family, setting fire to his house, bringing criminal charges against him, and so on.[34]

Not all zamindars or talukdars had the means to oppress, of course. By the close of the nineteenth century, most zamindaris in Dacca had been so fragmented that the average estate paid an annual revenue of no more than Rs.300. Most zamindars and talukdars had neither the resources nor perhaps the inclination to extract by force what they could not get by right. Indeed, this was the social stratum that was now turning decisively to urban literate occupations. The historical tendency was both overwhelming and irreversible; rent incomes from landed property would no longer be the chief means of livelihood or enrichment for the new educated middle class emerging out of the ranks of the impoverished zamindars and talukdars.[35]

But Bhawal, as we have seen, was not an estate that fell in this category. It was the second largest estate in the district and, even under the somewhat lackadaisical reign of Raja Rajendra Narayan, more than compensated for by the skill and astuteness of his manager Kali Prasanna Ghosh, it retained the character of a powerful zamindari. There were many stories that circulated of the oppressions of the Bhawal rajas and their dreaded *amla* (estate officials). Perhaps the Bhawal zamindari was no more oppressive than other large east Bengal zamindaris, but there is no reason to believe that it was any less so.

Another aspect of landlord-tenant relations that would acquire significance in the early twentieth century was the cultural world in which they were embedded. Although the largest zamindari in Dacca—the Nawab estate—was owned by a Muslim family, and there were a few other large Muslim zamindaris such as the Haturia estate, most zamindars in the district were upper-caste Hindus. Moreover, even in Muslim zamindaris, the estate officials or amla tended to be upper-caste Hindus. On the other hand, most of the tenants were Muslims or low-caste Hindus. As a result, even though the bureaucratic discourse of zamindari administration continued to be carried out in a language that was still predominantly Persian—persisting since the time of the Mughal revenue system—the cultural discourse of zamindari power was framed largely within an upper-caste Hindu, indeed Brahminical, ethic. There was a strong rhetoric of paternalism derived from old notions of Hindu kingship, in which the king was meant to protect and look after his subjects as though they were his children. But the king was also the sovereign, the wielder of *daṇḍa* or punishment, and to exercise that power was not only his right but in fact his duty, because daṇḍa was the foundation of justice, order, and right conduct in the social world.

Like any other feudal order, east Bengal zamindaris welded together in their ceremonial and administrative practices the coercive as well as the consensual aspects of power. Tenants would come to visit the Rajbari on ceremonial occasions and feel gratified by being allowed to touch the feet of the raja. They could be punished for disobedience or default, but if the raja was satisfied that someone was truly unable to pay the rent, his dues might be remitted altogether. Justice was personalized, often arbitrary, but there was an unmediated and theatrical quality to it that made it seem almost palpable, and hence accessible to those seeking it.

Although the government relinquished control of the Bhawal estate after running it for only six months in 1904–1905, it put on record its assessment of the zamindari. It was found, the government said, "in a condition of chaos and . . . grossly mismanaged." Out of a total annual rent and cess demand of nearly ten lakhs of rupees (1 lakh = 100,000), more than seven lakhs were in arrears, and in the period during which it was under the Court of Wards, only a little over one lakh of rupees could be collected "mainly due to the opposition of the Rani." The extent of debts owed by the estate was estimated at Rs.450,000. The report also said that the estate maintained a large number of armed men, apparently kept only to harass the tenants. There were also as many as four hundred *lambari* or peons who were not paid at all but who roamed the countryside like "roving locusts" and "lived and even flourished by oppressing the tenantry."[36]

The colonial government was desperate at this time to introduce order and efficiency in the running of the zamindaris. It was interested in improving agricultural production, but even more keen to stem what seemed like a growing peasant discontent against oppresive rents and illegal exactions by landlords. But there was little it could do if the legitimate owners of the property insisted on running it themselves. Besides, with a nationalist agitation brewing among the educated middle classes in the cities and towns of Bengal, the loyalty of the zamindars could turn out to be crucial for the government in future political battles. In 1905, the three sons of Rajendra Narayan took over as proprietors of the Bhawal estate, with Ranendra—the eldest kumar—acting as the legal head of the family. All three kumars were young men in their twenties. Not even Rankin, the irrepressible Scotsman, could have foreseen that in five years, the estate would be back in the hands of the Court of Wards.

Chapter Three

ON HUNTING AND OTHER SPORTS

Horatio Herbert, Lord Kitchener of Khartoum, had been appointed commander-in-chief of the Indian army on the express recommendation of Lord Curzon, viceroy of India. At the time, Kitchener was a hero of the British Empire because of his exploits in the Sudan, where he had defeated the rebel forces of the Mahdi and "avenged," as the British press described it, the killing of Governor Gordon a few years before. Kitchener was said to be a stiff and socially awkward soldier, not very popular with either his officers or politicians. The famous recruitment poster for the First World War, with an automaton-like Kitchener announcing "Your country needs you," has been much parodied. His image as an imperialist general, however, methodically and ruthlessly crushing the enemies of the British empire, was impeccable. After the battle of Atbara in which the rebel Sudanese forces were decimated, Kitchener marked his victory by riding through the town on a white charger with the rebel commander Mahmoud dragged behind him in chains. After his final victory at Omdurman, he ordered the dead Mahdi's body to be dug up and the skull presented to him ceremonially. His biographers say that he had the skull polished as a decoration for his desk, and his successor in Khartoum actually used it as an inkpot.

Kitchener spent his tenure in India carrying out an ambitious scheme of redesigning the Indian army for modern warfare. He was a general who had changed with the times and knew that the days of the cavalry charge were over. Warfare was becoming hugely technical, and sappers and engineers would now decide the fate of battles. In pushing ahead with his plans, however, he demanded more powers than any commander in India had ever enjoyed. He began a battle of his own against Curzon, the viceroy, which he fought singlemindedly through the corridors of power in London until Curzon was forced to resign. It is clear that Kitchener himself had set his eyes on the viceroyalty, but this ambition was to remain unrealized.[1]

In 1909, Kitchener was at the pinnacle of his career in India. He toured the country assiduously, inspecting every aspect of the military establishment with his famous attention for detail. On his tours, usually accompanied by members of his staff, he often accepted the hospitality of Indian princes and magnates, and is said to have enlarged his remarkable collection of antiques and art objects by helping himself to the possessions of his hosts, not always with their consent.[2] In January 1909, he was in Calcutta, as indeed was most of the official elite and Indian notables, for that was the festive and ceremonial season in the imperial capital. In February, we have the following brief entries in his tour diary:

Feb. 12. Leaves Calcutta for shooting trip in Dacca district.

Feb. 23. Returns to Calcutta.[3]

We know from other sources that the shooting trip was actually in Bhawal and that it had been arranged in Calcutta only a few weeks before, when the kumars were on a visit to the city. As soon as the program was fixed, it was arranged that the Bhawal family would return to Jaidebpur to prepare for the commander-in-chief's visit. Kitchener's trip to Bhawal was a private one but, needless to say, all of Dacca officialdom from the governor downward saw to it that every detail had been taken care of. Kitchener arrived at Jaidebpur on the afternoon of February 14 by special train from Narayanganj, accompanied by Colonel W. R. Birdwood (later Field Marshall Lord Birdwood), who had been on Kitchener's staff in the Boer War in South Africa, a Captain Fitzgerald, and an English doctor. The party was received at the station by Ranendra Narayan and the other kumars, dressed in durbar regalia. They were driven to the Rajbari in a silver-mounted brougham. They stayed in the European-style guesthouse known as the Baro Dalan, where they had dinner catered by a team sent out by Peliti, the famous Italian restaurant of Calcutta. The next morning, they went out shooting in the part of the Madhupur forest called Bagbari. Lord Kitchener and the other Englishmen were on elephants and they were guided by Ramendra, the second kumar, riding his favourite elephant, Phulmala. It was not a particularly successful shoot, since the commander-in-chief of the Indian army bagged only a single deer. He and his party returned to Jaidebpur and left for Dhaka the same evening.

It was only natural that of all the members of the Bhawal family, Ramendra Narayan should have accompanied the distinguished English visitors on their shikar. From a young age, the second kumar had spent a lot of time riding and hunting and was known to be very good at them. He gave a great deal of attention to the horses in the Rajbari stables and the elephants in the *pilkhānā* and, even as a boy, had started a menagerie on the Rajbari grounds that grew into quite a decent collection—two tigers, two leopards, two bears, one white fox, one ostrich, three partridges, and two orangutans. The menagerie had been closed down and the animals and birds sold off in 1904 during the six months that Bhawal came under the charge of the Court of Wards—one of the consequences of the government's drive to cut down on frivolous and wasteful expenditure on the estate.

Although Ramendra was always keen to learn what the mahouts and syces had to teach him about hunting and riding, he had no patience at all for the more conventional disciplines of reading and writing. Indeed, all of the three kumars showed a marked resistance to schooling. They were first given some lessons by two local tutors in Bhawal, and were then sent to the Collegiate School in Dhaka. After a few months, all three of them stopped going to school. Their education ended completely when their father died. Rani Bilasmani once engaged an English tutor named Wharton, who resigned after a few months of futile effort. He had been encouraged, he said, in his resignation letter to the rani, by senior government officials to take up the position "in the hope that I might be able to induce them [the three kumars] to attend to their studies, and to learn how to behave as gentlemen under my tuition." Unfortunately, he said, he had made no headway. Ramendra, in particular, was the most troublesome. He had put a kitten inside Wharton's solar topee where the little animal had made a mess; Wharton didn't realize it until he had put on his hat! Ramendra had also filled his tutor's inkpot with urine. "Not only have your sons neglected their studies in every possible way, but they have in no way attempted to reform their deplorable bad habits, and it is quite in evidence to me that they have no intention whatever of taking my advice or of accepting my tuition."[4]

The efforts at educating the kumars clearly did not succeed. All that Ramendra was ever capable of, it seems, was to put his signature on documents. Later, when the question of the second kumar's competence in reading and writing came up in court, no one was able to produce a single page of written matter composed by Ramendra—no notebooks, exercise books, diaries, not even a letter (except some that were proved to be forgeries). All his interests were in sports and animals. He was growing up into a strongly built young man, robust and full of energy. Indeed, compared to his brothers, he was always regarded as the most turbulent and wayward. But there was one feature he shared with his brothers: like them, he had an exceptionally fair complexion, and the color of his eyes and hair were described by an Englishman as "auburn" and by most local people as kaṭā (not black). Everyone agreed that the appearance of all three kumars was quite unlike that of the usual Bengali, and that they would stand out in a crowd.

In May 1902, at the age of eighteen, Ramendra's marriage took place in Jaidebpur to Bibhabati, then a girl of thirteen. Bibhabati's mother was born in a branch of the famous Uttarpara zamindar family, but she had been widowed at a young age and lived with her brother in Uttarpara, a few miles north of Calcutta. The Bhawal zamindars were Srautriya Brahmins, a degree lower than Kulin Brahmins who were at the top of the hierarchy among the Rarhi Brahmins of lower Bengal. Following a classic pattern of hypergamy, the Bhawal family had used its wealth and power to marry its daughters into Kulin families of Dacca and have the sons-in-law live in the Jaidebpur Rajbari. With Rajendra Narayan and Bilasmani's sons, the move was made to bring brides from the new and enlightened world of Calcutta. Ranendra's wife Sarajubala came from a lawyer's family of Calcutta, and now Ramendra's match had been made with a girl from a Kulin Brahmin family of Uttarpara. Notwithstanding the association with the famous Uttarpara zamindars, however, Bibhabati's family was clearly not regarded as a social equal of the Bhawal Raj, because the bride's party had to come to Jaidebpur for the wedding instead of the usual procedure of the groom going to the bride's house.

The marriage did not bring about any noticeable change in Ramendra's lifestyle. He lived in a suite of rooms at one corner of the ground floor of the main residential bloc of the Rajbari. The women's quarters were upstairs, and strict purdah was maintained. Ramendra's companions shared his interests and were described by many witnesses as men "of a low sort." They called themselves his "clerks," but it later transpired that only one of them was actually employed by the estate and paid a salary. They were young men, some from bhadralok backgrounds with some education, such as Harendra, Birendra, and Mukunda; others were locally called "Bengali sahibs," meaning Indian Christians—Anthony Morel, Cabral, Edwin Fraser, and Macbean. They surrounded him most of the time, eating and drinking in his rooms, accompanying him on shikar and on his trips to Dhaka. They fitted perfectly the classic description of the *musāhib* who would flock around a rich young man, flattering him, egging him on in his extravagant pursuits, and generally fleecing him. Ramendra and his friends were attended to by a batallion of about twenty personal servants and cooks exclusively assigned to the second kumar.

Rani Bilasmani died in 1907. For six years, she had held the estate in trust on behalf of her sons. Now, according to the terms of Rajendra Narayan's will, the three kumars became the owners of the estate in equal shares and were required to manage the estate jointly. Ranendra, the eldest kumar, became the *kartā* or head of the family.

Dhaka had in the meantime been promoted to the status of a provincial capital, following the partition of Bengal in 1905 by the viceroy, Lord Curzon. Bhawal was now located within the new province of Eastern Bengal and Assam. The partition, of course, provoked a major agitation protesting the colonial attempt to divide the linguistic community of Bengali speakers. Called the Swadeshi movement, the agitation was in many ways the first nationalist mass movement in India, developing and deploying for the first time some of the most powerful slogans and techniques of mobilization that would become the hallmark of Indian political movements in subsequent decades.[5] The predominantly upper-caste Hindu bhadralok were in the forefront of this movement, and in eastern Bengal in particular there was much patriotic fervor among the landowning bhadralok families of the district towns. In the end, the Swadeshi movement was successful in overturning the partition decision and, after a brief life of a little over five years, the province of Eastern Bengal and Assam was dismantled. Bhawal, along with the rest of east Bengal, was reinstated in 1912 within a single province of Bengal with its capital in Calcutta.

It does not appear that Ranendra Narayan, the zamindar of Bhawal, was in any way touched by the patriotic spirit of Swadeshi. He had stepped into a prominent place in the official circles of Dhaka, reserved for a scion of one of the leading landed families of the district. From 1906 on, in fact, those circles were no longer located on the civil lines of a district town; they had been raised to the status of the governing institutions of a province of British India. Ranendra Narayan had earlier attended the Delhi Durbar of 1903 and was waiting to have the title of Rajah conferred upon him, as it had been on his father and grandfather. He was a member of the Governor's Council and was regularly invited on formal occasions to tea with the governor in Dhaka. It seems he was not as comfortable as his father in these gatherings, and preferred entertainment of a somewhat less elevated kind. He drank heavily, and although a young man in his twenties, he had been examined medically for various complaints caused by excessive consumption of liquor.

Ramendra, the second kumar, did not drink. His sporting prowess was now widely known, because in 1907 he challenged Nawab Salimulla to a tumtum (dogcart) race on the Dhaka race course for a wager of Rs.1,000, and won. A kumar of Bhawal, the second largest zamindari of the district, getting the better of the Nawab Bahadur of Dacca, the largest zamindar, must have caused something of a sensation in Dhaka, even if the contest was only a friendly sporting event. The following year, he won the newly instituted Viceroy's Cup in Calcutta, riding his own horse.

It is unclear whether Ramendra also played polo, although there was a polo ground in the Rajbari complex and polo instructors were brought over from Manipur. It seems that when riding, the second kumar preferred to hold the reins with his right hand, and this may have discouraged him from the game, in which it is mandatory to hold the reins with the left hand and the stick with the right. But we do know that he raced his polo ponies on the Dhaka race course.

Ramendra was, however, utterly reckless when riding or driving around town, and on more than one occasion he hit passers-by on the street. No one, of course, dared complain against a kumar of the Raj family. His bravado was also the talk of the town. Once he heard a report that some people had been punished by the railway authorities for fishing from the tank adjoining the Jaidebpur railway station. Ramendra assembled a group of men from the estate, went to the station tank, and had fishing nets thrown in the water. The English station master came out to protest, at which Ramendra pulled out his gun and chased the terrified official into his cabin. Locked inside, the station master sent a telegram to Dhaka: "Station surrounded by Joydebpur Kumar's men. Send help urgent. Life in great danger." Ramendra and his men kept vigil outside the cabin until the evening train brought four armed constables. Emboldened, the station master came out with a peace offer. Ramendra's men would be allowed to fish in the tank if the kumar would support the station master in keeping other people away from government property. Ramendra agreed, but only after he had gotten the official to send another telegram saying: "All arranged amicably. No danger."[6]

It does not appear that Ramendra involved himself in any way with the affairs of the estate. He was content to let his elder brother, the "baro kumar," and the estate officials take care of business matters. He would appear for the annual *puṇyāha* ceremonies, of course, when tenants would pay the first instalment of the annual rent, signifying their loyalty to their raja by making a tributary presentation of *nazar*. On such occasions, Ramendra and Rabindra would flank the baro kumar, a silver canopy held over their heads and armed guards standing to attention, as tenants would prostrate themselves before them, touch their feet, and be blessed. Ramendra was also an enthusiastic listener at theatrical and musical performances at the Rajbari. The Natmandir (performance hall) there was the pride of Jaidebpur, with its high, elegantly carved wooden ceiling, and beautifully patterned wrought iron columns. With his brothers, Ramendra would naturally sit at the center of the audience, surrounded by distinguished talukdars, estate officials, and relatives in a carefully assigned order, while the women of the Rajbari would watch from the upstairs balconies, secluded behind latticed screens. Ramendra was also an important participant at the annual Janmastami procession in Dhaka, celebrating the birth of Krishna. Organized by the Basak traders of the city, it was famous for its pomp and splendor and for the presence in it of all the great zamindars and notables of the district as well as all sections of Dhaka's inhabitants, irrespective of religion.[7] Ramendra himself chose the elephants that would be sent from Jaidebpur, and rode one himself; the Bhawal Kumars, after all, were exceeded only by the Nawab Bahadur of Dacca in terms of pride of place in the *misil* (procession).

By this time, Ramendra had also developed an interest in women. At the time of his marriage in 1902, when he was eighteen years old, he was apparently besotted by the charms of a dancer called Elokeshi, and created a scandal by putting her up in a room inside the Rajbari premises. He later arranged for her to move to a house in Dhaka, and visited her regularly. Elokeshi was probably his first mistress, but there were several after her. As his boisterous circle of hangers-on expanded, they would often accompany him on his visits to prostitutes in Dhaka or on wild parties on boats. On one of his annual trips to Calcutta, Ramendra had to borrow Rs.10,000 over and above his allowance, all of which he spent on a courtesan called Malika Jan. (It is very likely that this was the same Miss Malika Jan who was a famous professional singer and early recording artiste.)[8] On another Calcutta trip, he took a fancy to an Anglo-Indian woman and showered her with expensive clothes and jewelry.

By 1905, when Ramendra was twenty-one, it was known that he had contracted syphilis. He was treated for it from time to time, but by all accounts it did nothing to change his habits. In 1909, just before Lord Kitchener's shikar trip to Bhawal, Ramendra was told by Dr. S. P. Sarbadhikari in Calcutta that his illness had gotten worse and that the ulcers that were breaking out on his arms and legs were caused by syphilis. This was the principal reason for the decision that he should go to Darjeeling in the summer.

BIBHABATI

When Bibhabati first came to Jaidebpur as Ramendra's bride, she was thirteen. She had been brought up in the enlightened circles of the Calcutta middle class. Unlike the women of the Bhawal Raj family, she had gone to school. Her mother, Phulkumari, had herself imbibed the atmosphere of the nineteenth-century cultural renaissance. As a young widow, she had had to raise her children in the midst of considerable hardship, but she had shown much care and wisdom in dealing with her situation. One of her daughters, Malina, was married into the family of the Bengali prime minister of Jaipur state in Rajasthan. Her son Satyendra was preparing to study law. Bibha was now married into a leading zamindar family of east Bengal.

Not surprisingly, considering her age, Bibhabati spent most of her time in the women's quarters of the Rajbari playing with the large collection of dolls that had accumulated there over the years. She was treated with kindness by the older women of the Rajbari, especially her mother-in-law and sisters-in-law. But she felt very lonely and found the strange ways of the zamindari household oppressive. Her only moments of consolation were the times when she could read the letters her mother wrote her. Phulkumari kept up a regular correspondence, comforting her unhappy daughter and guiding her with detailed instructions on how to cope. One of the first letters we have is from January 1903, less than a year after Bibha's marriage.[9] Appearing through the conventional phraseology of Bengali letter writing is Phulkumari's concern to teach Bibhabati what she was not being taught at her in-laws' house.

Bibhu, my treasure,

I had become extremely anxious about you, but was relieved to a certain extent yesterday on receiving a letter in your own hand. . . . You are well aware, dear, how much I am pained and distressed even at the most trivial illness or the slightest of your troubles; and how can I control myself if I find you suffering from a disease or when I contemplate that you will lie bed-ridden for the whole of your life? . . . I can obtain some peace of mind if I know that you are well and happy, but because of the serious disease which unfortunately has seized you, your memory is getting weakened and your understanding is getting dimmed for which reason you cannot write me letters as fully and frankly as before. . . .

It is not necessary for me to enlarge on the fact that your mother-in-law is a most amiable person. . . . Just as she loves you as her daughter, I hope you will also do your duty by showing her corresponding devotion and respect and try that her love for you may increase further. Although this time you have written many things in your letter, I have not derived the slightest satisfaction from it as you have said nothing about Ramendra. . . . I am anxious to know whether you meet Ramendra every day and the nature of his love for you. You have said that your heart pines and wanders because there is nobody in the house, but don't you at all meet Ramendra or have a chance to talk to him during the day? I know that these things are regarded as the height of shamelessness in your father-in-law's family, but in my judgment there is nothing wrong or immodest in them. If husband and wife are together, the minds of both remain happy and their love for each other is heightened. So from now on you must see that Ramendra spends long hours in your company in the day time.

One ought to exercise one's body regularly every day. So you will take a walk regularly for one hour in the morning and one hour in the evening. You will get up in the morning after 7 o'clock, put on some warm clothing, shoes and stockings and take strolls in the verandah. Very severe cold has set in now, so in the weak state of your health there is a chance of your catching a chill. So you will wear a chemise of flannel underneath and wear your clothes over that. Otherwise, if you expose yourself to the cold, there is a risk of your rheumatism being aggravated.

. . . I am in great anxiety because of your disease; whoever falls a victim to it becomes deranged and loses [his/her] memory altogether. I have read a great deal about this disease and it appears to me that the only medicine for it is cheerfulness. As far as I have seen, nothing cheers and braces up the mind so much as instrumental music; so if you take up playing on the harmonium, your mind will remain cheerful and you will experience great peace of mind. So you will speak to your mother-in-law and get a lady tutor engaged. What more shall I write? We are all well. Make me happy by writing soon of your wellbeing.[10]

Bibhabati had been complaining for some time of weakness and exhaustion. It is not clear what conclusion her mother had drawn from this, although she seemed to be thinking of some specific and serious illness. There was a suggestion later, although denied by Bibhabati herself, that she had epileptic fits. Whatever it was, Bibha's conjugal life hardly matched up to her mother's ideal of the companionate marriage. Bibha spent all her time in the women's quarters on the upper floor of the Rajbari. Ramendra lived in his own rooms downstairs, surrounded by his courtiers. At night, Bibha would sometimes be sent for by Ramendra. On those occasions, she would come down a winding staircase and join her husband in his bedroom.

Social historians of Bengal have spoken generally of the practice of child marriage prevalent at this time. There was also a spirited social reform literature in the late nineteenth century that talked of the terrible dangers, both physical and mental, faced by young, often prepubescent, girls married to older, sometimes middle-aged, men. But there are almost no contemporary sources that describe the sexual and emotional experiences of girls in their early teens married to wealthy, frequently debauched, husbands. Manoda Debi, describing the marriage of her elder sister in 1885 into a zamindar family in Dacca district, remembers how her grandmother wept as she told her grandfather that it was well known that these zamindars had their wives tied to the bedpost while they slept with the servant-women on the bed. To this, her grandfather had replied, "Don't worry. This boy is young and smart. I will bring him here and educate him myself."[11] Haimabati Sen gives a chilling description of a night when, as a girl of nine or ten in Khulna, she had gone to sleep in her middle-aged zamindar husband's room and woke up in the middle of the night to find her husband in playful conversation with another woman. "Then they spread a mat on the floor, sat down, and began to drink. And after that—good heavens! When I saw what was going on I began to quake with fear and lost consciousness."[12]

It is clear that the stories about Elokeshi reached Bibhabati soon after her marriage; that could have been the time when she stopped writing to her mother about Ramendra. One can also be sure that the older women of the Rajbari liberally supplied the fourteen-year old with all their accumulated wisdom on how to retain the attentions of a wayward zamindar husband. Bibha even got instructions by mail from her elder sister Malina, who had come from faraway Jaipur to visit her mother in Uttarpara.

I hear that you have been acting like a great idiot since your illness; you don't take proper care of your health and you don't think at all of anything that may be good for you. Before you were the one who was the most intelligent of us all. Now we are sorry for your acting in this way. All of us are very glad that Ramendra's leg is all right. You should stay with him always, and you should always try so that you may be dear to him. If he sleeps in the outer apartment, then you too should sleep with him. To sum up—dear sister, it is the husband's love which is the supreme happiness in our lives, and to guide him in the proper path is our principal duty. Hence please don't be unmindful at any time in this matter. Always keep him happy with sweet smiles and sweet words. You should also dress well in order to please him.[13]

But despite the concern and advice of her wellwishers, Bibha's married life did not improve. Ramendra continued with his old ways. Bibha complained about her health. In 1906, she was taken to Calcutta for treatment. It would be surprising if her mother had not heard by this time of Ramendra's disease. The doctors examined Bibha and said that she had not been infected, but that she was suffering from anemia. The following year, Rani Bilasmani fell ill and was taken to Calcutta. She died there from an attack of cholera. In the Bhawal household, Indumayi, Bilasmani's eldest daughter, took charge of the inner quarters. Rani Satyabhama, Kali Narayan's wife, was still alive, but she was only the indulgent grandmother, not the mover and shaker of household affairs.

In May 1908, Satyen Banerjee, Bibha's elder brother, received his B.A. degree and also was married in Uttarpara. Bibhabati and Ramendra traveled to Calcutta to attend the wedding. In October that year, Satyen went to Jaidebpur and stayed for several months. Although he had enrolled in Calcutta as a law student, he was under some pressure now to find a job. He tried to get Ranendra, the baro kumar of Bhawal, to use his influence in official circles in Dhaka to find him a government job in Shillong. By this time, Bibha's mother had clearly decided that the situation in the Bhawal Rajbari was beyond repair, because she repeatedly remonstrated with Satyen not to waste his time there. "[C]ome back home—and don't try to fool me with random and flimsy excuses. I can stand everything, but I cannot stand anyone fooling me. I am not really so foolish and ignorant as you suppose me to be—I can see through all your pretenses. I hear a new thing today, that you are unable to come because of Ramendra's illness. No one has made the slightest mention of it so far! I know that whenever you go to Jaidebpur, you don't feel inclined to come back. But how will you find a livelihood if you give up your studies and sit idle? . . . I am exasperated by the constant taunts and ridicule I have to suffer here for your sake."[14] We should remember that Phulkumari Debi was still living with her brothers and was anxious that her son, now a married man, should find a stable source of income and relieve her from her dependence on relatives. She must also have greatly disliked the idea that Satyen might be looked upon as another hanger-on at the Bhawal Rajbari. She was quite forthright in her letter to Bibhabati.

> I do not at all understand where your brother is or what he is doing. That scoundrel does not even write a letter, and you too do not give me any news about him. But can't you even understand how anxious I am for him, and don't you know why I don't like to send him to Jaidebpur? Tell him that he need not try for jobs any more. . . . I can no longer stand his pretence of seeing Sahebs. If he tries to get a job in the way he has been doing at Jaidebpur, he will not get one in his whole life. He need not look for jobs any more. Send that worthless fellow here as soon as you can. . . . Some day, I fear, I may have to atone for the great sin of bearing a bad son in my womb by committing suicide.[15]

A week later, she wrote again to her daughter.

> On considering the matter a second time, I think it is not good for your brother to stay there a single day more. That he has stayed so long has been considerably injurious to him. So do not let him stay there any longer but send him as soon as you receive this letter. Judging from your ways and circumstances, I do not think you can come out of Jaidebpur soon. . . . I am dumbfounded at your silliness. If Ramendra is so ill now, what were all of you doing so long? Even your clever brother who has been vegetating there for a month wrote nothing to me about this matter. Now that I want him to come back, you make a pretext of having to bring Ramendra. If you had tried, you could certainly have come to Calcutta by now.[16]

THE CALCUTTA VISIT

In early December 1908, all three kumars, along with their wives and, needless to say, a large retinue, went to Calcutta in two parties and stayed in three rented houses. The reason for the visit was Ramendra's illness. The ulcers had now broken out in different parts of his body, and his arms and legs were in bandages. He was examined by several doctors in Calcutta, and by Colonel S. P. Sarbadhikari in particular, and it was confirmed that his syphilis had gotten worse.

Bibhabati, too, was not well. In fact, her mother was very concerned about her daughter's health, and feared that no one was giving her the attention she needed. She wrote frequently from Uttarpara to Bibha in Calcutta and gave her detailed instructions.

> Your body has become so weak and bloodless that I was greatly alarmed to see you. Particularly, I have become greatly worried at your carelessness and indifference in all matters. . . . if for your sake I now have to suffer mental anguish, I will never bear that shock. So please abandon all thought of causing your mother's death and attend to preserving your own health.

The Doctor Saheb has asked you to take four ounces of "raw meat juice" both in the morning and in the evening everyday. Arrangements have also been made to bring it to you, but who can help you if you do not care to take it, or if you throw most of it away? Your disease is anemia and so you will get no benefit from these tonics unless you take them regularly. Your servants and maidservants are always busy with the children, so it is possible that they may forget. Therefore you should yourself remember to take your medicines at the proper time every day. The red medicine which the Saheb has prescribed for you before meals is, I have heard, a very good medicine. The quantity of blood in your body will increase if you take this medicine. You are eating the local bazaar bread because you refuse to eat the bread from European hotels. But I know very well that you can never digest the local bread. It is made of very inferior flour. So please give up these prejudices and begin to follow the straight path. You must not set up any further excuses or objections and take Mellin's Food mixed with milk as many times as possible. Keep a spirit stove in your room to prepare it. . . . Khoka [Satyen] cannot go to see you every day because of his studies, but I will send him whenever you want to see him. Apply the thermometer two or three times every day and see if you get fever. If you cannot write to me every day, you must write every other day.[17]

The letter made no mention of Ramendra or of the state of his health. In another letter written only a few days later, she was more insistent.

Please give your eldest sister-in-law my sincere blessings and tell her that your food should be cooked both in the morning and evening in an earthen pot with fuel wood. Food cooked in a brass pot will not suit you now. Please convey to her this earnest request of mine. . . . Of course, you must ask the cook beforehand to prepare those things which you feel like eating. Only boiled rice and boiled potatoes will not do. . . . Don't eat such things as lobsters, large fish or curries made with spices and peppers. It is wrong that nothing is prepared for you separately and that you either have to eat things that are not good for you or else starve. I have been much pained by this. When you have to spend all your life in that house, how can you afford to be so timid? By this senseless timidity, you are ruining your health. So give definite instructions on what suits your taste. Your life depends on nutritious food. You can never be well again if you are indifferent and unmindful about your food.

. . . I have explained this to you many times, but if you don't follow it I will have no alternative but to commit suicide. I have experienced many troubles and mental worries in life and have borne them all by myself, but I am now living only for your sake.[18]

As already mentioned, the entire party from Bhawal returned to Jaidebpur in early February, a few days before Lord Kitchener's shikar visit. In the middle of March, Satyen Banerjee arrived in Jaidebpur. The Calcutta doctors had advised Ramendra to avoid the summer heat and move to the hills

FIGURE 2. Ramendra, the second kumar

for a few months. The choice was between Mussoorie and Darjeeling and, after consultations with Satyen, Ramendra chose the latter. Satyendra was asked, along with Mukunda Guin, who was acting as clerk to the second kumar, to go to Darjeeling to find a suitable house. The two returned a week later after making arrangements to rent a house called Step Aside, close to

FIGURE 3. The Kumar after a hunt

the central Mall area of the hill resort. It was then decided that the second kumar, the second rani, and their party would leave for Darjeeling by train on April 18.

Apart from the sores on his body, Ramendra was not unwell at this time. He kept up his usual activities. Only a few days before leaving for Darjeeling, he went on a shikar and bagged the second tiger of his life. Satyendra, it seems, accompanied his brother-in-law on this shoot but had to return midway because he was too frightened. One evening before the trip, Ramendra also went to have dinner at the house of Dr. Mahim Dasgupta, the family physician to the Bhawal Raj, where it was suggested to him that given the state of the second kumar's health, he should be accompanied in his party by Ashutosh, the doctor's son who had just obtained his licentiate certificate. Ramendra, it seems, laughed at all the fuss that was being made about his health, but agreed to let Ashutosh join his entourage.

Several years later, when Jyotirmayi, the second sister of the kumars, recalled the scene of the party setting out for their holiday in the hills, she remembered Ramendra "leaving with a smile on his face." There was little indication then that things were about to take a dramatic turn.

Chapter Four

WHAT HAPPENED IN DARJEELING?

A<small>FTER</small> the "self-declaration" by the sannyasi in May 1921, Bhawal was agog with excitement. In spite of all its claims to being a place of historical importance, nothing as sensational had ever happened there. Hundreds of people flocked daily to Jaidebpur to get a glimpse of the man who many now believed was the second kumar, returned from the dead after twelve years. This in itself was a miracle, a sign that there was some supernatural or divine agency at work. Then again, here was a holy man, a renouncer, who had spent many years going through the rigorous spiritual exercises required of a sannyasi, a man who until the other day was taken to be, so to speak, a fully certified member of the community of holy men who were the objects of reverence and faith for millions of people all over the country. And suddenly, it transpires that the sannyasi was actually a wealthy zamindar, scion of a ruling family, a prince who had returned as a renouncer (see Figure 3). What was the significance of all this?

Durganath Chakrabarti was a prominent member of the association of talukdars and tenants of the Bhawal estate. He was also an amateur poet (Bhawal had several members of this numerous Bengali tribe, as we will soon find out). Durganath played an important role in organizing the various public meetings held to felicitate the second kumar on his miraculous return and also to press his claim to his property. A few weeks after the self-declaration by the sadhu of Buckland Bund, Durganath composed and published a long panegyric in verse as "a devotional offering to the Exalted Young Sannyasi Ramendra Narayan Roy Chaudhuri Bahadur."[1] Who was this holy man who had appeared before the people? What was the purpose of his appearance? Durganath narrated the story as follows.

Moved by the dictates of his conscience, a king decided one day to relinquish his throne in order to visit, without giving up his life or his body, the kingdom of death. Never before had such a thing happened. But God in his wisdom decided that in this age of Kali, an event such as this was required. So the king died. But his life did not leave his body. Only now he came back to his kingdom dressed in loincloth and ashes. It was as if Yama, the messenger of death, had made a mistake and later corrected himself. It was like a magician's trick. Perhaps it was only to show that there was a life indestructible in this impermanent and transient world that such a miracle had been staged. Now the word was on every lip: "The second kumar of Bhawal had never died! He is still alive!" This was the time, Durganath declared, for people to show their loyalty to their true ruler. It would mean resisting fears and threats and rising above petty interests and enticements. But it was at such moments of crisis that one was required to go through the test of integrity and commitment. The tenants of Bhawal, he assured the "young sannyasi," would not fail that test.

THE PAMPHLET WAR

Durganath's pamphlet was only the first of a series of publications of remarkable spread and persistence. For more than twenty-five years, as the drama of the sannyasi of Bhawal would unfold in Dhaka, Calcutta, and London, the propaganda war would be carried out in Bengal in the form of little booklets, varying in length from eight to sixty-four pages, some written by persons close to the sannyasi, others by local publicists or writers eager to make a mark on the local literary scene. Some would be factual, argumentative, laying out a case. Others would be in verse, composed as ballads, or in the form of the popular *kabigān*, meant to be set to tune and sung. Mostly printed at small presses in Dhaka, Barisal, Bogra, or Mymensingh and costing a few annas each, they would be hawked by itinerant booksellers in village marts and fairs and even from house to house in the districts of eastern Bengal. Some copies would presumably also be distributed by the author or his patrons among influential persons who they might want to bring around to their cause. In addition, the pamphlet became a form of putting on public record a statement or a viewpoint on behalf of or against the claims of the sannyasi. At a time when the daily newspaper in Bengali had still not become an item of everyday consumption even among the literate middle class in eastern Bengal, the pamphlet was a potent form of propaganda and opinion building in the public arena, especially in an affair with such sensational dramatic possibilities as the Bhawal sannyasi case.

Soon after Durganath's wondrous and somewhat incredulous poetic effort, a series of booklets appeared in the district of Dacca that began to address the two questions of fact that would be central to the whole affair. First, was the sannyasi the second kumar of Bhawal? Second, if so, what had happened to the kumar in Darjeeling twelve years before? The answer to the first question would take the form of listing the number of people who had known the second kumar and who, after meeting the sannyasi, had declared that they had recognized him as the person they had known. The weight of the evidence here would lie in the number of such people, especially those who had known the kumar intimately, who were now persuaded by the appearance of the sannyasi or by little details from the past that the sannyasi would recall in the course of their conversations that he was indeed the second kumar. On the second question, the crucial account would obviously have to come from the sannyasi himself: how did the kumar manage

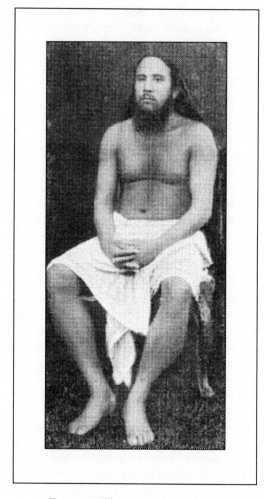

FIGURE 4. The sannyasi as claimant

to survive his death and why did it take him so long to return home and declare his identity? The pamphlets began to offer answers to both of these
questions.

A typical pamphlet from this time is the one published from Dhaka by
Maulavi Muhammad Fazlul Huq and Sri Sultan Kabiraj.[2] It listed a large
number of people who had recognized the sannyasi as the second kumar.
They included, as was now well known from the huge meeting in Jaidebpur
in May, his sisters and other close relatives as well as many talukdars and
tenants of the Bhawal estate. In addition, the pamphlet mentioned the large
number of prominent zamindars from other parts of Bengal and close
friends and acquaintances of the kumar who, on hearing of his sensational

return, were coming to Dhaka to meet the sannyasi and verify for themselves if what they had heard was true. Thus, the *Herald* of Dhaka had reported that two leading zamindars of Mymensingh—Jagat Kishore and Sashikanta Acharya Chaudhuri—had met the sannyasi and had come away convinced that he was indeed the second kumar of Bhawal. Birendra Kishore Raychaudhuri, zamindar of Gauripur, had gone to Calcutta to consult with Maharaja Manindra Chandra Nandi of Cossimbazar and other important landlords of Bengal to persuade the government to accept the sannyasi as the legitimate claimant to the zamindari of Bhawal. Edwin Fraser, who in his youth had been one of Ramendra Narayan's companions, came to Jaidebpur to see the sannyasi and was immediately spotted by the latter from out of the crowd that was jostling in front of him. The sannyasi spoke to Fraser, asked that he be given some snacks and also indicated that a spoonful of ghee be put on the side of his plate because that was the way Fraser liked it. Needless to say, Fraser was completely persuaded about the real identity of the sannyasi. The redoubtable Mr. Meyer, who had once been the manager of the Bhawal estate and had conspired many years before to have it taken over by the government, came to Jaidebpur from Dhaka, where he was now the manager of the Nawab estate, and after an intense conversation went back convinced that the second kumar had indeed returned to Bhawal. The matter of recognition was not confined to humans. The elephants of the stable at the Jaidebpur Rajbari—belonging to the species renowned for its phenomenal memory—had shown definite signs of recognition when the sannyasi patted them and later went for a ride.

More interesting details were offered on the question of what happened in Darjeeling twelve years before. The pamphlet opened the topic by noting the many rumors that had circulated in Bhawal about the circumstances of the second kumar's death and the way in which his body had been cremated. For the first time, it was suggested in print that there may have been foul play. The sannyasi had said, the pamphlet reported, that he had fallen unconscious after the last dose of medicine had been administered to him in Darjeeling. When he regained consciousness four or five days later, he found himself in the midst of a group of Naga sannyasis. He had lived and traveled with the sannyasis ever since, and even had the name of his guru Dharamdas Naga tattooed on his left arm. The question was: what sort of medical treatment had the Kumar received in Darjeeling? What medicine had Ashutosh Dasgupta, the doctor in the Kumar's party, given to him? If indeed the Kumar's condition had deteriorated so severely, why had not Dr. Pran Krishna Acharya, the famous Calcutta doctor who was then staying in Darjeeling only a few houses away from the Kumar's, not been consulted? And what had Dr. Calvert, the civil surgeon, stated in the death certificate that Satyen Banerjee was supposed to have in his possession? The pamphlet also mentioned that Mukunda Guin, who had served as clerk to the second kumar in Darjeeling, had recently come to Jaidebpur from Tripura, where he was now a police inspector, and had said that he had come away from the cremation of the second kumar in Darjeeling when he saw Birendra Banerjee, another clerk in the kumar's party, performing the last rites. Why had Birendra Banerjee, completely unrelated to the second kumar, performed the last rites?

Another pamphlet reported at greater length on what had happened at the cremation ground in Darjeeling.[3] "It was being said by some people in Bhawal," the report stated, that when the kumar's body was brought to the cremation ground in Darjeeling, there was a sudden cloudburst and hailstorm during which the persons accompanying the body had left to take shelter under a shed some distance away. When they returned to the cremation ground, they found that the kumar's body had disappeared. After searching in vain for some time, they had set fire to the empty pyre and returned to announce that the cremation had been performed. What had actually happened was that a group of Naga sannyasis who were passing the cremation ground had heard a groaning sound coming out of the pyre. Coming closer, they had discovered that the body lying unattended on the pyre was of a young man who was still alive. They had taken him away, treated and looked after him, and brought him back to health. The young man had then become a disciple of Dharamdas Naga and had lived and traveled with his group. Three or four years previously, this group of Naga sannyasis had come to Dhaka and a photograph was taken of them. It is clear from the photograph that the same young sannyasi was then roaming around the country in the company of sadhus. No one had then suspected him to be the dead kumar of Bhawal.

Some of the pamphlets tried to bolster their case by citing the English newspaper *Herald* of Dhaka or the Calcutta daily *Dainik Basumatī*, which had also reported in May 1921 these stories circulating in Bhawal.[4] The pamphlets also recounted the now well-known story of the rumors surrounding the sadhu of Buckland Bund, his reluctant journey to Jaidebpur, the examination carried out by Jyotirmayi Debi, the final declaration by the sadhu of his true identity, and the massive public meeting in Jaidebpur. Several pamphlets mentioned the curious fact that even after his declaration, the sadhu continued to speak in Hindustani, claiming that, as he had not heard or spoken Bengali for many years, he had forgotten his native tongue. One pamphlet speculated that there might be some strange mystery behind this peculiar matter, as well.

OFFICIAL POSITIONS

We have already mentioned the first official report on the declaration by the sannyasi of his identity in the letter of May 5, 1921, by Needham, manager of the Bhawal estate, to Lindsay, the collector and district magistrate of Dacca. That afternoon, probably on instructions from the collector's office in Dhaka, Needham asked his officers in the estate to make further inquiries about the sannyasi. Needham, incidentally, was not entirely in the good graces of the district administration. Two years before, S. G. Hart, the then collector, had complained about the inefficient and lackadaisical style of management in the Bhawal estate. The commissioner had specifically remarked that "the whole trouble about the Bhowal Estate is due to the fact that the Manager will not give his personal and active supervision to the affairs of the Estate. Everything is left to the office subordinates." Hart had suggested that a younger person—an energetic deputy collector, for instance—be appointed to shake up the estate administration. The commissioner did not think that would serve any purpose, because "the Manager, a European on Rs.1500/- will not like an Indian Dy. Coll. on Rs.300/- to interfere with his work and over his head, even though armed with the support of the Collr." Needham was given a warning to mend his ways, but in view of "the prestige attached to the post and to a European holding it," he was left in place.[5] Two years later, as the affair of the sannyasi began to unfold, Needham still appeared unaffected. His letters and reports were still drafted by his subordinates, and Lindsay, the collector, who had little faith in the alertness of the manager, had to issue direct instructions on how to handle the admittedly unusual situation in the estate.

Mohini Mohan Chakravarty, assistant manager of the Bhawal estate, had drafted Needham's first report to Lindsay on the declaration by the sadhu. On the afternoon of May 5, he was able to interview the sannyasi and submitted the following report to Needham:

In obedience to your verbal order I went last afternoon to the house of Sj. Jyotirmoyee Devi with Mr. Banerjee, Special Officer, Forest Officer, Head Clerk and other estate officials to make further enquiry about the sadhu who has been posing as the late second Kumar. We tried our best to get some definite statements from him as to his identity, but he declined to answer concerning his previous history. The sadhu definitely informed . . . that his name is Ramendra Narayan Roy, that his father's name was Raja Rajendra Narayan Roy and that his elder brother's name was Ranendra Narayan Roy, but he did not give reply to any question put to him concerning some past events in the life of the second Kumar. This refusal to reply is very significant. Matters have come to such a pass that the sadhu must establish his alleged identity, or steps should be taken to prosecute him for false personification. It is needless to say that if the sadhu be allowed to pose falsely as the late second Kumar with impunity, it will tell very seriously on administration of the estate, as the sadhu has by this time been able to establish the sympathy of the tenants who seem to be thoroughly convinced that he is no other than the late second Kumar. Under the circumstances your kind instruction is solicited as to what steps should be taken.

It is reported that he has given out that he will prove his identity, if necessary, when time will come before the higher authorities.[6]

There was clearly a crisis of authority in the Bhawal estate. The tenants were veering to the side of the sannyasi and if the government did not make a decisive intervention, the administration of the Court of Wards would collapse.

After receiving these reports from Jaidebpur, Lindsay, the district magistrate, prepared a long report on May 10, 1921, for the eyes of his superiors in Calcutta, in which he listed the pros and cons of the alternatives before the government.

CONFIDENTIAL

Report on the claims of a certain sadhu to be the second Kumar of the Bhowal Estate
This sadhu has been in this neighbourhood for about a couple of months and appears from the first to have been an interesting man, for he held conversations with people like the Government Pleader and the Chairman of the District Board. To them he said that he had been following the life of a sannyasi from the time when he was 12 years of age. Like other sannyasis, he paid a visit to Kashimpur and visited Jaidebpur on his return journey to Dacca. While there some of the old servants noticed a likeness to the second Kumar, and from his behaviour when a photograph of the Kumar was shown to him, the suspicion in their minds was confirmed. The rumour spread rapidly that the second Kumar had returned and is now almost universally believed by the tenants of the Estate and even by respectable gentlemen in Dacca. To understand one reason why this curious story could gain credence, it is necessary to recall a story of events at the Kumar's death. It is alleged that when the dead body was being taken to be cremated at Darjeeling where the death occurred, a very severe storm came on, which drove away the servants from the body on the funeral pyre. When the storm subsided and the attendants returned, the body was gone, but in spite of this they set fire to the wood and returned, saying that they had burnt the body. I have got copies of the medical certificate given by Colonel Calvert certifying to the death of the second Kumar on the 8th May, 1909, after an illness of three days, a certificate of his death by Mr. Crawford, then Deputy Commissioner of Darjeeling, a certificate signed by Satyendranath Banerjee and C. J. Cabral that the Kumar's body was cremated in their presence, and similar certificates by Sasi Bhusan Banerjee, clerk of the P.W.D. Sub-Division, Darjeeling. There is no doubt whatsoever that the man is dead and that the Court of Wards has been perfectly justified in acting on the assumption of his death ever since it took charge of the estate.

2. The people of this country, however, are all very fond of miracle, and the tenants resent as blasphemy any doubt as to his identification. My first proposal was that he should be prosecuted under section 419 I.P.C., but in a consultation at Jaidebpur between the Superintendent of Police, the Government

Pleader and the Manager, it was thought that the offence of cheating had not yet been completed, and so it would be worse than useless to lodge an information at this time. It would only arouse resentment, which will be all the greater if the prosecution fails. On the 6th instant, the sadhu publicly declared that he was the second Kumar, and many tenants agreed to support him and pay their rents to him, but so far he has not asked that any rent should be so paid. It seems he is being tutored by the inmates of the houses of Jyotirmoyee Devi and the late Indumoyee Devi, who are sisters of the second Kumar, and who, of course, would be only too pleased if he re-appeared. On the 7th, the Sub-Divisional Officer, the Superintendent of Police and other officials visited him, and I understand he was not able to tell the S.D.O. the nickname of the second Kumar's wife. The sadhu speaks only Hindusthani and appears to be ignorant of both Bengali and English languages, which the second Kumar knew well. He told the Superintendent of Police that he wanted the Commissioner, the District Magistrate and the leading gentlemen of Dacca to convene a meeting at which he would satisfactorily establish his identity. On the 8th, many hundreds of gentlemen came from Dacca and many pressed the sadhu to speak in Bengali, but not a word was uttered in this language. On each of these days he was visited by 2 or 3 thousands of tenants, who were greatly delighted at the return of the second Kumar.

3. Yesterday, the non-co-operators took a hand in the game, as this is an excellent opportunity for them to give trouble to the government, and they have publicly sworn in the name of Allah that they are determined to die for the sadhu, though Government may not recognise him as the second Kumar. The non-co-operation parties throughout the Estate are taking the matter up. Such is the situation at present, and there is no fear of a breach of the peace so long as no action is taken against the sadhu.

4. I had a consultation with the Superintendent of Police, the Manager and the Government Pleader this afternoon in which we came to the conclusion that it was better to let the sadhu commit himself more definitely, put himself completely under the law by a clear offence before any action should be taken. If he takes no further action, people may get tired of the new excitement. On the other hand, it seems to me that it would be wrong to call any meeting to establish or dis-establish the identity of the sadhu. If his identity is to be established, it must be done in a proper legal manner before a Court of Law where the evidence both ways would be submitted to trained minds. The Government Pleader will go to Calcutta tomorrow to tell Mr. Lees about the present situation and to take his advice, and I am also asking him to take the best legal opinions about the legal position of the sadhu.[7]

As far as Lindsay was concerned, then, his mind was made up on the issue of the sadhu's identity: the man was an impostor. The only question now was the political one—how best to deal with the crisis of authority caused

by the fact that a credulous mass of tenants had been manipulated into believing that the second kumar had returned. He knew that decisive administrative steps would be necessary, but the legal ground for it needed to be
prepared, because the sadhu's cause had been taken up by prominent people who had access to powerful legal brains. Besides, there were the political agitators of the non-cooperation campaign who had taken up the cause
of the sadhu. This had the potential for considerable mischief, and Lindsay
was determined to be watchful and firm. On May 28, he instructed Needham to issue a warning to all employees of the Bhawal estate that they must
not do or say anything to encourage the belief of the tenants that the sannyasi was the second kumar. If they did so, they would be considered to be
acting against the Court of Wards and would invite punishment. It was also
clarified that the Court of Wards alone would decide on the identity of the
claimant.[8]

The Non-cooperation Parties

In fact, the agitations over the demands of the Khilafat and Non-cooperation movements were just beginning to assume serious proportions in east
Bengal.[9] The Khilafat movement had made headway in this area even before the Nagpur session of the Indian National Congress in December 1920
saw the acceptance by Chitta Ranjan Das and the Bengal Congress of
Gandhi's plan for non-cooperation with the British government in India.
From September 1920, leaders such as Muniruzzaman Islamabadi and
Akram Khan had launched an effective anti-government campaign among
the Muslim peasantry, especially in the northern and eastern districts of
Bengal. They were aided in this by leaders of the militant Fara'izi sects, such
as Badshah Mian of Faridpur and Abdullah al-Baqi of Rangpur. The agitations were initially to protest against the treatment by Britain and its allies
of the Ottoman emperor, defeated in the First World War. Soon, however,
it took on the character of a peasant resistance against government authority. From early 1921, when the Congress under C. R. Das organized itself
at district levels to conduct non-cooperation, the Khilafat committees became the most prominent campaigners for the Congress program in the
east Bengal districts. The most worrying aspect of this campaign from the
point of view of the government was the nonpayment of local taxes, which
soon threatened to turn into the nonpayment of rents to the zamindar. The
few European-owned estates, such as the Midnapur Zamindari Company
with extensive lands in several districts, were an obvious target. By January
1922, the Government of Bengal would officially report: "The situation remains volcanic . . . below there is a strong under-current of disorderly elements, mainly Muhammadan, which is steadily carrying the whole mass towards violence."[10]

In May 1921, of course, much of this was still in the future. But the rumblings had been heard. If peasants could be mobilized to stop paying taxes to the government, then they could just as easily be told not to pay rents to an estate administered by the Court of Wards, especially if they were made to believe that the estate was being unfairly held back from its legitimate proprietor.

INQUIRIES

Just before the first meeting between the sannyasi and Lindsay on May 29, a petition was submitted to the district magistrate by Gobinda Chandra Mukherjee, husband of the late Indumayi Debi, and Jyotirmayi and Tarinmayi, the two surviving sisters of the kumars. Lindsay wrote to his superior officer, the commissioner of the Dacca division, seeking his advice on how to proceed:

> [T]hey state that the sadhu who is living with Jyotirmoyee is Ramendra Narayan Roy, the second Kumar, and that he has been identified by many persons as such. They have learnt that enquiry is being made about him, and they wish to produce evidence to prove his identity. They further wish that the evidence already recorded should be shown to them and that they should be allowed to cross-examine the witnesses. Obviously they have no right to see the evidence already recorded or to cross-examine the witnesses, and I have verbally told them as much. The question remains whether they should be allowed to produce evidence before me, and if so, whether the Estate should bear the expenses of these witnesses. One reason in favour of recording the evidence is that it should allay the feelings of the tenants who are much excited and who all believe the sadhu to be the second Kumar. Further, if this were done, I would then have ample justification in issuing a notice to the tenants that there is no necessity for them to pay subscriptions to any body to enable the sadhu to run a suit in the civil court to prove his identity.
>
> On the other hand, the mere fact that I have consented to record such evidence might lead the people to believe that I think there is a reasonable probability of the sadhu being the second Kumar and might thereby encourage the agitators in his favour. There is something to be said for both points of view, so your instructions on this matter are solicited.[11]

Lindsay also began to pursue other lines of inquiry. One of these was to try and establish the true identity of the impostor. If it could be proved who the impostor actually was, his claims could be countered more effectively. Before the end of May, he sent Mamtazuddin Talukdar, a police officer, and Surendra Kumar Chakrabarty, an officer of the Bhawal estate, all the way to Punjab to trace Dharamdas Naga, supposedly the guru of the sannyasi. The two officers managed to track down Dharamdas, showed him a photograph, and had him record a statement before an honorary magis-trate. Dharamdas identified the photograph as that of his *chela* (disciple) Mal Singh of Aujla, who after initiation as his disciple had taken the name of Sundardas. The result of this police inquiry seemed to clinch for Lind-say and the government the question of the identity of the sannyasi—he was a Punjabi sadhu posing as the second kumar of Bhawal.

The other line of inquiry was regarding the medical circumstances of the death of the kumar. Lindsay wrote to Calvert, the civil surgeon who had treated the kumar in Darjeeling, and received the following reply.

> I remember the second Kumar of Bhowal who came on a visit to Darjeeling in May, 1909. He was suffering from "Gallstone". His death made a consider-able impression upon me at the time, as I thought that had he only listened to our advice, he need not have died. On the day of his death he was seized with a severe attack of biliary colic. An injection of morphia would have relieved him almost immediately of his pain. He refused to have any subcutaneous in-jection, because his mother when *in extremis* had died after receiving a hypo-dermic injection, and he attributed her death to the injection, instead of to the illness which necessitated the treatment. Owing to vomiting and purging, opium by mouth and rectum was not retained. The severe pain being unre-lieved, brought on collapse from which he died. I cannot now be certain whether I was present at the moment of his death, but I saw him shortly be-fore it in a state of profound collapse. On my last visit his Bengalee medical practitioner was present and arrangements made for the late Colonel Macrae, I.M.S., then I.G.C.H., Bengal, to see him in consultation in the morning. Col. Macrae had been Civil Surgeon at Dacca and knew the Kumar's family. The Kumar, however, did not recover from the collapse and died the same night.[12]

These findings must have strengthened the official belief that there was now enough material evidence to act against the sannyasi. As we have noted before, the impostor notice was issued by Lindsay on June 4, 1921, after he received instructions from the Board of Revenue in Calcutta. He also took the administrative step of prohibiting the sannyasi from entering the Bha-wal estate.

Soon after this, Lindsay went to Jaidebpur and, along with Needham, had a meeting with Gobinda Mukherjee, the late Indumayi's husband. Lindsay made it clear that now that the Board of Revenue had concluded that the sadhu was an impostor, there was no use making further representations to the government on this subject. The only way left for establishing the sadhu's claims was through the courts. He asked whether the sadhu's sup-porters were prepared to take that step. Gobinda Chandra replied that there were many people who had recognized the sannyasi as the second kumar and were prepared to testify before any court of law. He also said that there were persons willing to testify that the kumar's cremation had not been car-ried out in Darjeeling. He said that Bibhabati, the second rani, was not pre-

sent at the cremation ground and could only have heard about the cremation from her brother. How could she be certain that her husband's body
had been cremated? Her opinion on this matter could not be taken to be
decisive. Lindsay said that Needham was soon going to Calcutta with his
wife, and that Mrs. Needham might inquire about this matter from the second rani.[13]

The visit to Jaidebpur might have also made Lindsay somewhat concerned about the attitude of the estate employees, because on June 13 another warning was issued to them: "The Board of Revenue has found that
the sannyasi who says he is the second Kumar is an impostor. All the servants of the Bhowal Court of Wards are hereby informed that if they are
found directly or indirectly espousing the cause of the sannyasi, they will be
liable to summary dismissal."[14] Orders were also issued by the Bhawal estate manager to the naib or deputy in charge of a local rent collection office to explain why he had taken part in a meeting held in support of the
sannyasi. Another circular was sent to all naibs to send confidential reports
with names of prominent suporters of the sannyasi among the tenants.
There were repeated circulars instructing estate employees to persuade tenants not to be misled by the propaganda that was being carried out on behalf of the sannyasi and to warn them that by paying rents or subscriptions
to an impostor, they were risking their rights to the land because the government could seize their property for nonpayment of rents.[15]

Supporters in Law

Violent reactions to the impostor notice soon made it clear that the tenants
of the Bhawal estate were in no mood to accept the government version of
the story. For almost a year after the sannyasi's declaration, subscriptions
were collected on his behalf by the Bhawal talukdar and tenants' association. It was reported that more than Rs.150,000 was collected. It was also
apparent that the sannyasi's claims might in the end be pursued in court.
One of his principal supporters now was Ananda Chandra Roy, a famous
lawyer and social reformer of Dhaka, who seemed to be organizing a plan
of action for persuading the government to accept the sannyasi's claim. He
had known the Bhawal family for a long time and was convinced that the
sannyasi was indeed the second kumar and thus the rightful claimant to the
Bhawal property. Ananda Chandra also became a leading figure in the public campaign that had now grown in support of the sannyasi.

Another lawyer of Dhaka who would stay as a legal advisor to the sannyasi for the next two decades was Surendra Nath Mukherjee.[16] He too had
known the kumars of Bhawal. When the story broke of the sannyasi's declaration in Jaidebpur, he visited the sannyasi and was convinced that this was
the second kumar. He proceeded to verify the facts, especially those that

were being asserted on behalf of Satyen Banerjee and the government. Realizing that the crucial mystery lay in the story of the death and cremation of the kumar in Darjeeling, he made a trip to Darjeeling, spoke to many people connected with the affair, and returned to Dhaka to start a vigorous campaign on behalf of the sannyasi. He spoke at public meetings organized by the talukdar and praja association, giving what he believed were the facts of the case, and published a long interview in a pamphlet in which he said that his only concern was to uncover the truth of this bizarre case.[17] He warned, however, that he was not revealing all of the details, because if the government did not relent, the sannyasi might be forced to go to court to prove his case.

There were political leaders, too, who were keen to associate themselves with the public clamor over the sannyasi. In July and August 1921, Razaur Rahman Khan, Fanindralal De, and Indu Bhushan Dutta asked questions in the Bengal Legislative Council about the Bhawal incidents. They asked what proof the government had of the sadhu's identity to justify the impostor notice and what the explanation was for the shooting incident at Mirzapur. They also asked if it was true that some people had approached the government on behalf of the sadhu demanding an inquiry and wanting to present evidence on his identity. The Maharaja of Burdwan, minister of land revenue, replied that the Board of Revenue had advised the collector of Dacca to issue the impostor notice on the basis of information secured by the Court of Wards. The government was not prepared to place any of these papers on the table of the house, since the matter of dealing with the claimant must rest with the Court of Wards. He said that a judicial inquiry had been ordered into the Mirzapur incident.[18]

INQUIRIES IN DARJEELING

On June 7, 1921, the Board of Revenue prepared a note entitled "The Story of the Sadhu" and forwarded it to the deputy commissioner of Darjeeling with instructions to put certain questions concerning that story to a list of persons living in Darjeeling.

THE STORY OF THE SADHU

The sadhu says that he is the second Kumar of Bhowal—Kumar Ramendra Narayan Roy. His story is that on the midnight of the 8th of May, 1909, the doctors thought that he was dead and declared him to be so. The body was then removed to the burning ground where it was placed on the funeral pyre and before it was set on fire, heavy storms and rain came on which drove away the attendants, that the rains subsiding the attendants returned to the burning ground but found that the body had gone; they, however, set fire to the wood and returned home with the story that the dead body of the Kumar had been

cremated. The story further is that when the attendants had run away, a sannyasi who was close by came to the funeral pyre, perceived that the life was not
extinct, removed the body to his quarters and by the application of some charm
the body was brought back to life.

The above story is considered absurd and untrue, and it is necessary to obtain the statements of persons (Bengalees) who were present in Darjeeling then
to ascertain the real state of things. Some interrogatories are attached herewith indicating the line in which the witnesses are to be questioned. The
Kumar was a man of very fair complexion, of stout build, of strong physique,
with brownish hair. He was 27 years of age when he died in Darjeeling in a
house called 'Step Aside' below the Mall. There were with him at the time his
wife, her brother, a few officers and some menial servants. The rainfall report
of the time shows that there was no rain either on the 8th or on the 9th in
Darjeeling.

The attached list of questions that were to be asked was as follows.

1. (a) Did you know the second Kumar of Bhowal?
   (b) Did you see the Kumar in life?
2. Were you present at the death or with funeral procession or at the cremation of the body of the Kumar?
3. Did you see the dead body? Give a description of the dead body as far as
   you can recollect—what was the complexion; was he a thin or a stout man?
   Can you remember the colour of his hair; and any other description that
   you can remember?
4. What was the weather like during the cremation—was it fair or was it
   raining?
5. Were you present till the end of the cremation—was the body completely
   burnt?
6. Can you remember any incident either at the house before the procession
   started or during the procession or during the cremation?
7. Was anything done during the procession?
   (N.B. Whole rupees and small bits of coin were scattered and given to the poor
   during the procession.)

A list of persons who were to be asked these questions was also attached.
They were all Bengali bhadralok employees of the government secretariat
in Darjeeling.[19]

The Countercampaign

When he went to Darjeeling, Suren Mukherjee, a principal supporter of
the sannyasi, discovered that a team of government officials from Dhaka
and Satyen Banerjee himself had already visited the hill station and had

propagated there the government version of the story. This version, as it now stood, was that the sannyasi was an impostor and that his appearance in Dacca was the result of a conspiracy by certain interested parties. The conspirators knew that as long as the Bhawal estate remained under the management of the Court of Wards, it would be of no benefit to them. They had bided their time, found a person with an apparent likeness to the second kumar, prepared him for the part and, with the connivance of the kumar's sisters and the political leaders of the non-cooperation movement, had now ignited this mass frenzy in support of the sannyasi's preposterous claim.

The countercampaign also identified the sannyasi as a man from Punjab. In one of the first public statements against the sannyasi's claim, a letter appearing under the signature of M. C. Dutt in the English weekly *The Bengalee* and the Bengali monthly *Nāyak*, both published from Calcutta, ridiculed the sannyasi who could speak no language other than Urdu and when asked about his earlier life could only weep and say he had no *yaad* (memory) of those days. Girish Chandra Ghosh, a lawyer of Dhaka, pointed out in the *Herald* that this M. C. Dutt was a certain Manindra Chandra Dutt, a young man no older than eighteen who had worked for a time as a compounder to Ashutosh Dasgupta, the doctor who had accompanied the kumar on his fateful trip to Darjeeling. What M. C. Dutt had said about the second kumar could only have been hearsay, because at the time of the latter's alleged death in 1909, Dutt was a child. Girish Chandra claimed that it was not true that the sannyasi could speak nothing but Hindustani. Many had heard him speak in Bengali in the same way that people of the Bhawal area spoke it.

The countercampaign against the sannyasi did not, however, cease when these objections were raised in the Dhaka press. In fact, it was stepped up. In June 1921, Kedarnath Chakrabarti, editor of the *Rāyat*, published in that journal a series of articles, later released as a pamphlet, that made an elaborate presentation of the argument that the sannyasi was a fraud.[20] This was the first major public presentation of the case against the sannyasi, taking him on in the same print medium in which he had so far had virtually unchallenged success.

Kedarnath started by pointing out that Ramendra Narayan's death in Darjeeling in May 1909 was a settled fact. His *śrāddha* had been performed in the Bhawal Rajbari, his property had been legally transferred to his wife, his life insurance had been paid to her—all to the satisfaction of the concerned authorities and without anyone having objected. Why all this fuss now, twelve years after the event? There was no mystery in the kumar's death. The real mystery lay in the sudden appearance of a claimant and the attempt to arouse the passions of a gullible public. A similar case had occurred in Bengal a hundred years before, when the impostor Pratapchand had claimed the zamindari of Burdwan and had managed to incite the people in his support. Ordinary people are instinctively drawn to romance and improbable tales. But the authorities who defend the law cannot allow themselves to be swayed by these irrational emotions. On that occasion, they had rejected the claims of the pretender Pratapchand, just as they were doing so now with the pretender kumar of Bhawal.[21]

In Kedarnath's story, the center of attention is the Bhawal Raj family after the death of the kumars. In the absence of a *kartā* (head), the household comes under the effective charge of Indumayi and Jyotirmayi, the sisters of the kumars. The three widowed ranis feel dominated and mistreated by their sisters-in-law. The youngest rani complains to the Court of Wards, which decides that the sisters should move out of the Rajbari. They are now left with no leverage at all in the affairs of the Raj. Still, there is one ray of hope—none of the ranis has children. In the normal course of things, the sons of Indumayi and Jyotirmayi would inherit the properties of the Bhawal Raj. This hope was cruelly dashed when, in May 1919, the youngest rani adopted a son. Many objections were raised to the adoption, but they were overruled. On top of this, when Kripamayi, the widowed sister of Raja Rajendra Narayan died in April 1920, her share of the property was taken over by the Court of Wards instead of being transferred to the surviving daughters of Rajendra Narayan. This, according to Kedarnath, was the last straw. The sisters then decided to stage the return of their dead brother.

How did the people react to this move? Kedarnath analyzed the reaction among the tenants of the Bhawal estate in the context of the Court of Wards administration. The rule of the zamindars—Kali Narayan, Rajendra, or Ranendra—was in the traditional mode. It was oppressive, often arbitrary, but at the same time personal, capable of being paternal and caring. Tenants could be fined or punished for little reason, but they could also be rewarded by grand gestures of benevolence. More significantly, although the zamindars were keen to squeeze the last paisa out of the tenant, their collection machinery was lax and inefficient. As a result, there was much room for tenants to evade the arm of the administration and do as they pleased. The regime of the Court of Wards was the exact opposite. It was cold, impersonal, ruthlessly efficient. There was no escape from its clutches. This was particularly so in relation to the extensive forests in the Bhawal estate, where tenants believed they had customary rights that the zamindars had never questioned but that the new administration refused to recognize. The forests of Bhawal were now swarming with armed guards, and the villagers had no access to the forest produce unless they could afford to bribe the estate officials. In other words, all sections of tenants had some grudge or the other against the government administration of the estate. Needless to say, they were greatly excited when a sannyasi showed up declaring that he was their legitimate zamindar, prepared to assert his claims before the government.

Not only that. Kedarnath pointed out that in several published reports of the sannyasi's declaration, it was said that the claimant was actually reluctant to enjoy the fruits of his property. He was a renouncer who had no love of material wealth. He was making his claim only in the interest of truth. Once that was established, he would take steps, as the *Basumatī* had put it, "to dispose of his property." Many had taken this to mean that he would give away his lands to his tenants. Kedarnath saw in this a tactic reminiscent of Mark Anthony after the assassination of Julius Caesar. Anthony wants to incite the crowds to take revenge on Caesar's murderers. So he waves a piece of paper before them and says, "Here is Caesar's will. He has given away all his possessions to you, the people of Rome. And there go the killers of Caesar!" The crowds are inflamed, they pour their wrath on the senators, Anthony's task is accomplished. After that, who asks about Caesar's will?

Having uncovered this Machiavellian trick, Kedarnath now engaged in a bit of Machiavellian persuasion himself. Did the tenants of Bhawal really stand to gain by supporting the sannyasi's claim? Not a chance! The government was unlikely to concede the sannyasi's claim in a hurry. In the end, he would have to go to court. How long would that take, and how much would it cost? Showing an uncanny prescience that no one could have noticed at the time, Kedarnath predicted that it would take twelve to fourteen years for the case to be settled in the courts, since neither party would give up before reaching the final court of appeal in London. That would cost several millions of rupees for which a fund had already been started among the tenants of Bhawal. But to what end? Even if the sannyasi succeeded in pressing his claim, the Court of Wards would still retain its control over two-thirds of the estate, the shares of the two other ranis. And it would stay in charge of the administration until the adopted son of the youngest rani came of age. That would be another fifteen years. Until then, the tenants would not be rid of the Court of Wards, whereas in fifteen years the Court of Wards would leave in any case. What did the tenants stand to gain by spending their effort and money in the cause of the sannyasi?

Kedarnath conceded that the agitators on behalf of the sannyasi had made some headway in gaining the attention of the populace. They had aired their claims in public, staged a drama, and swayed the popular opinion in their favor. The government and the Board of Revenue, too, had inquired into the matter and had satisfied themselves that the sannyasi's claims were false. Unfortunately, this evidence had not been laid before the public. The only communication that had reached the people from the government side was the impostor notice, which did not elaborate on how the government had come to the conclusion that the sannyasi was an impostor. Not surprisingly, in the face of the continuing barrage of propaganda from the sannyasi's side, the people were unaware of the evidence on the other side. Kedarnath now proceeded to lay these down.

The crucial question of fact was the cremation. Had the Kumar's dead body been set to fire and burnt to ashes? The sannyasi's claim was that the body had been left unattended at the cremation ground during a sudden hailstorm and had been recovered by a wandering Naga sadhu. When had the body been taken to the cremation ground? At night, or in the morning? From all the published accounts of the sannyasi's story, it seemed that the storm came at night. But this was contrary to the facts of the case. The Kumar died at night and his body was taken to the cremation ground in the morning in a procession of more than a hundred people. There were many witnesses to the cremation and it was an occasion well remembered by people in Darjeeling. Did it rain that day? Or on the previous night? The *Calcutta Gazette* publishes reports of the daily weather in Darjeeling. The relevant gazette for May 1909 shows clearly that for three days up to the time of the Kumar's death and for four days afterward, there had been no rain in Darjeeling. So what was this story of a hailstorm in the night?

As for witnesses, there were many respectable and reliable people who were present at the time of the cremation of the kumar on the morning after his death. Nibaran Chandra Mukherjee of Narayanganj had recently written to his friend Phani Bhushan Banerjee of Jaidebpur as follows.

I hear one Shanyashi has been able to throw dust upon your eyes and he is preaching himself as the 2nd Kumar of Bhowal Raj. His statement is absolutely unfounded and he must be a bogus "Kumar".

I was one of the Shasanbandhus of the 2nd Kumar and I can swear that his dead body was perfectly and properly burnt to ashes. I know everything about his cremation, condolence meeting etc., perfectly well. I made a somewhat elaborate statement last night with regard to this matter to Babu Surendra Nath Mukherjee, Pleader, Dacca, who I believe is taking an interest in this case. I also requested him to show you my statement. Now, I request you not to come to any conclusion or decision with regard to this important matter without hearing everything from me.

Kedarnath then turned to the question of the kumar's medical treatment and the allegation that he had been denied the attention of senior physicians and instead had been left in the hands of the inexperienced Ashutosh Dasgupta. In reply, Kedarnath quoted a letter written by Dr. Calvert, civil surgeon of Darjeeling, to Ranendra Narayan Ray, the eldest kumar of Bhawal, on May 10, 1909, two days after the second kumar's death.

My dear Kumar,

Please accept my most sincere condolence in the great loss which you have sustained through the death of your kind-hearted and amiable brother. I am afraid his sudden death must be attributed to a little over-confidence on his part regarding the nature of his illness and its probable termination. The morning I was called in he felt so much better that he declined the treatment I proposed; even the earnest solicitation and exhortation of his private secretary and friends who were most solicitous concerning his condition failed to move him. Later in the day he had a relapse, the colic coming on in a most intense form. His Secretary with praiseworthy zeal himself went around the station until he had found me on my rounds and secured my attention to the case. This time he listened to the advice of the Secretary and his friends and allowed me to adopt the right treatment. The colic quickly ceased under hypodermic medication, but unfortunately the system had received such a shock in the interval that he sank and died from collapse in spite of all our endeavours. All that was possible was done to save your brother's life and he received the greatest care and attention from those about him. It would have been a great boon if he could have had his friends around him, but the exacerbation of his illness came on so suddenly and terminated so quickly that it was not possible. He had had milder attacks of this nature before and it was his recovery from these which prevented him realising the serious nature of the last one before it was too late.

Yours sincerely,

J. T. Calvert

It was completely untrue, therefore, wrote Kedarnath, that the kumar had not received proper medical attention; in fact, he had received the best that was available in Darjeeling. J. N. Ghosh of Calcutta had recently published a letter in *Nāyak* stating that Dr. Nibaran Chandra Sen, the most renowned Indian doctor of Darjeeling, had been retained for three days to attend full time to the second kumar, and that Dr. Calvert had consulted him when deciding on the treatment.

Kedarnath also quoted as an appendix to his pamphlet a certificate signed by Dr. Calvert.

> Certificate A
> Policy No. 74789
> Life—Kumar Ramendra Narayan Roy
> Claimant—Rani Bibhabati Devi

CITY OF GLASGOW LIFE ASSURANCE COMPANY

Certificate of Death

To be granted by the Medical Practitioner who attended deceased in his last illness

I, John Telfer Calvert, Lt.-Col., I.M.S., Civil Surgeon, Darjeeling, do hereby solemnly declare, that I have known Kumar Ramendra Narayan Roy for 14 days and have been his consulting Medical Attendant for 14 days; that I attended him in his last illness; that he died aged about twenty-seven years at

Darjeeling at 11–45 o'clock P.M. on the 8th day of May, 1909, after an illness of 3 days; that the cause of his death was collapse following upon an acute attack of biliary colic (gall stone).

The above was inferred from symptoms and appearances during life; that the symptoms of the disease which caused death were first observed by me on May 6th, 1909; and the attack became acute on the morning of the 8th and he died the same evening.

Signature—J. T. Calvert

Designation—Lt.-Col., I.M.S., Civil Surgeon

Place—Darjeeling

Declared before me this seventh day of July, 1909.

Signature—W. M. Crawford,

Justice of the Peace, and District Magistrate, Darjeeling[22]

Having presented his evidence on the medical treatment and cremation of the kumar, Kedarnath's articles turned to the matter of the recognition of the sannyasi. He raised doubts about the alleged statements by prominent persons in east Bengal that they were convinced that the sannyasi was the second kumar. He quoted a letter from a maternal uncle of the kumars stating that although there were some similarities between the sannyasi and the second kumar, the dissimilarities were so strong that it was impossible to conclude that he was Ramendra Narayan. Kedarnath also reported that a parallel meeting had been held in Jaidebpur of talukdars and tenants who disputed the resolutions adopted in the more publicized meeting in support of the sannyasi's claims. Among those who organized this parallel meeting were Phani Bhusan Banerjee and Mukunda Guin.

Kedarnath referred once more to J. N. Ghosh's letter in *Nāyak* in which he had claimed that he was in possession of many documents that had been examined by the Board of Revenue in its investigations. It was possible that the whole matter might end up in court, in which case the evidence would be presented there. Ghosh also maintained that the stories circulating about the Rajbari elephants having recognized the second kumar were totally false. All of Ramendra Narayan's favorite elephants—Gunda, Rebecca, Phulmala, Bird, Nachbhari, and so on—were dead. Even Meyer, who was supposed to have recognized the second kumar, had now stated in the newspapers that he was by no means fully convinced.

Kedarnath's pamphlet also published in full a letter by Mukunda Guin in the *Ḍhākā gejeṭ*. He had been private secretary to Ramendra Narayan at the time of his Darjeeling visit. Mukunda stated that the kumar had died sometime near midnight of May 8, 1909. At about eight or nine the next morning, the body was taken through the town in a procession that many gentlemen of Darjeeling had joined. Mukunda was present at the cremation ground when the last rites and *mukhāgni* (putting fire in the mouth of the deceased) were performed, but had to leave to make other arrangements and was told later that the cremation had been duly completed.

Mukunda then disputed the assumption that the sannyasi's physical appearance resembled that of the deceased second kumar. The sannyasi, he said, was at least six inches taller than the kumar. His lips were wider and his nose much wider. It had been suggested that the nose might have become wider because of the yogic exercise of *prāṇāyam* which the sannyasi had practiced regularly in the last twelve years, but Mukunda did not know if this was a credible explanation. In any case, he was certain that if an expert were to compare the sannyasi's appearance with a photograph of the second kumar, he would detect the differences immediately.

In his manners, the second kumar was aristocratic, dignified, proud, careful not to act too familiar with people lower in social rank. The sannyasi seemed only too eager to make use of what others offered him. He was willing at the slightest suggestion to remove his clothes and show the marks on his body, and was particularly servile toward men who appeared to be in positions of authority. This was totally contrary to the way in which the kumar carried himself.

Mukunda Guin related his conversation with the sannyasi and cited several instances in which the sannyasi's replies to questions about the kumar's life were unsatisfactory. Mukunda had asked him about Lord Kitchener's shikar. At first, the sannyasi did not even know the name, then claimed to recall going on a hunt with a certain "Kitchen sahib," thought the elder kumar had gone too (he had not), and that they had shot a couple of tigers (no tigers were sighted on this hunt). He was unable to say anything about the violent disputes with the Senbari zamindars in which the second kumar had been deeply involved. He was unable to name the high school at Jaidebpur, called Rani Bilasmani High School after his own mother. Even in the matter of recognizing people, just as he is supposed to have recognized some, he had failed to recognize many others. This had created a strong suspicion that the sannyasi was being coached.

As the debate raged in Dacca over the sannyasi's true identity, one persistent claim made by his supporters was that Dharamdas Naga, the sannyasi's spiritual guru, would soon come to Dhaka and set all doubts at rest by examining the sannyasi and announcing whether or not he was the person he had rescued from the funeral pyre in Darjeeling and taken under his protection as a disciple. It was said that Jyotirmayi Debi's son-in-law had managed to find Dharamdas in Hardwar and was trying to persuade him to come with him to Dhaka. At the end of August 1921, Dharamdas did come to Dhaka and stayed for three or four days at Jyotirmayi's house. But before making any pronouncements, he suddenly left. The sannyasi's supporters alleged that the police had bothered him incessantly and tailed him everywhere he went. Scared and disgusted, Dharamdas had left. Needless to say, his sudden departure compounded the rumors on both sides about whether Dharamdas ever met the sannyasi in Dhaka and, if so, what he had concluded.[23]

The most perplexing thing about the sannyasi was that he only spoke Hindustani. Was it credible that a lapse of twelve years could cause someone to forget his mother tongue? Nagendranath Ray of Armanitola, Dhaka, wrote in the *Hindusthān* that the police story that the sannyasi was actually a man from Punjab was quite plausible. All sorts of explanations were being given of why the sannyasi was unable to speak Bengali. Some said that the part of his brain that activated his knowledge of Bengali had been damaged. Others said that the sannyasi believed that Bengali was a spiritually impure language. Still others had claimed to have heard the sannyasi speak fluent Bengali. Yet he was unable to sign his name in that language. Nagendranath asked the question: if so many responsible and wealthy persons were so convinced of the sannyasi's identity, why were they not going to court to establish his claim? Was it because the sannyasi was such a bad learner of languages?

It was also being said that Rani Bibhabati's conduct in not agreeing to meet the person claiming to be her husband was strange. But why should it be so? If, Nagendranath argued, her husband had died in her presence twelve years ago, why should she give credence to these stories? Most ordinary people have no conception of the intense animosities and suspicions that flourish in aristocratic families. If Rani Bibhabati was certain that the sannyasi's appearance was the result of a conspiracy hatched by her sister-in-law Jyotirmayi, why should she condescend to pay the sannyasi a visit?

The question of the sannyasi's ignorance of Bengali as well as of details of the kumar's life continued to bother many people. Jagadish Chandra Chowdhury, a lawyer of Dhaka, wrote as follows to the *Amrita Bazar Patrika*.

> Many people are anxious to know why I have so abruptly given up the cause of the Bhowal Sannyasi after having been so long his staunch advocate.
>
> I worked for the Sannyasi for over two months. For the first month I was always busy with Babu Ananda Chandra Roy and did not care much to go in close contact with the Sannyasi. But gradually a suspicion arose in my mind and so I began to test him more closely. . . . The Sannyasi can not speak Bengali. He understands Bengali just as you and I understand his Punjabi. His attempt to speak Bengali is most ludicrous. His appearance does not tally with that of the late kumar in most vital points. He is thoroughly ignorant of the life story of the late kumar and his ignorance of Bhowal is profound. He does not know much of what a Bengalee ought to know. I shall commit no wrong if I speak in general terms that so far as I know of the evidence on the

cremation, it is a treasure of trash, inconsistent and absurd. I have known from the most authentic source that his Guru Dharmadas Naga has cursed him and called him a cheat.

I was just consulting with some of my friends and members of the Association to decide the line of action, when the guardians of the Sannyasi's camp took alarm and began to preach that I was a traitor and that I have been bribed. God alone knows what bribe I have taken.

The battle lines were being drawn. Already there was talk of camps. And indeed, camps there were, judging from the way opinions had hardened both for and against the sannyasi. There was also violence in the air, with accusations of threats and intimidations. Matters took a grisly turn in September 1921, when Mukunda Guin was stabbed to death on a Dhaka street. His dying declaration, given to the police, was that he had written many things against powerful people. It was never known who killed him.[24]

A FINAL EFFORT

The sannyasi's camp was, however, still hesitant to give up its efforts to persuade the government to recognize his claim. In July 1922, when Lindsay had been succeeded by J. G. Drummond as the district magistrate of Dacca, a letter was sent to him over the signature of Satyabhama Debi, grandmother of the kumars. She had seen the sannyasi first when he came to Jaidebpur in May 1921. Since then, he had been prohibited from going there. Satyabhama had recently come to Dhaka and was now living in the same house as the sannyasi. "Acting on your suggestion," the letter said,

> I have taken the trouble to come down to Dacca and meet the sadhu. I have seen him every day at Jaidebpur during his stay there. After coming here I have seen him daily. I have come to the conclusion that he is no other than my second grandson Kumar Ramendra Narayan Roy.
>
> You have informed me that the fullest possible enquiries were made about the sadhu, and it was established beyond the shadow of doubt that his claim to be the Kumar is a bogus one. As to this, allow me to say that an enquiry or enquiries in which the very near relations of my grandsons are not confronted with the sadhu cannot be regarded as full or complete. In particular, I beg leave to mention that the wives of my 1st and 2nd grandsons were never brought to Dacca and asked whether they recognise the sadhu as the second Kumar of Bhowal or not.
>
> There was rumour of poison having been administered to my 2nd grandson at Darjeeling, and there was a deep mystery regarding the alleged death of my 2nd grandson in Darjeeling. As far as my information goes, his body was never

cremated. There was some discussion on the point at the time of the *sradh* at Jaidebpur. There was also a persistent rumour afloat not only in Bhowal but in several parts of Bengal that my 2nd grandson was alive and moving with the sadhus.

In the case of the death of a sonless Hindu, the proper person to put the first fire into the mouth of deceased is the wife, and Rani Bibhabati Devi who was at Darjeeling at the time of the alleged death of the second Kumar did not attend the cremation ceremony and did not perform act of putting the first fire into the mouth of the deceased—an act which is important in the estimation of a Hindu and one for which every Hindu is very anxious. Evidently Rani Bibhabati is relying upon the statement of her brother Babu Satyendranath Banerjee about the story of the cremation. Satyendra accompanied the party of the second Kumar to Darjeeling, and his conduct in connection with the alleged death of my 2nd grandson is not free from suspicion. His subsequent conduct is also highly suspicious. . . .

As a *pardanashin* lady in an advanced stage of life it is not possible for me personally to examine all the evidence that the Revenue authorities may have got in this connection and on the basis of which the Board of Revenue has thought fit to declare my 2nd grandson to be an impostor.

The enquiries were made in the time of your predecessor Mr. J. H. Lindsay, I.C.S., and I am not aware which portion was made by him personally and which portions by others. I shall be obliged if you will kindly supply me with a statement of the nature of the enquiry that has been made, and also with a copy of evidence that has been obtained or elicited at the enquiry. I propose to have the evidence examined by six eminent lawyers, if possible by one lawyer from each of the six different High Courts of India. These lawyers will be persons unconnected with the Bengal Court of Wards or any member of the Bhawal Raj family. I will communicate to you the result of their examination from my own private funds. I also desire to engage one or two retired honest officers of the Detective Department to find out the truth in this case. For I am sure that if I can convince you about the identity of the sadhu with my 2nd grandson Kumar Ramendra Narayan Roy, your sense of justice will induce you to recommend to the Honourable Board of Revenue to reconsider and alter their decision.

I have been informed and believe that several old officers of the Bhowal Raj Estate who are now serving under the Court of Wards are quite ready and willing to admit the sadhu as the second Kumar of Bhowal, and they do not do so openly for fear of losing their appointments. If they are given the assurance that they run no risk in telling what is true, then you will be able to ascertain the true state of things from several of them. . . .

To be sure that in this old age of mine there is no defect in my vision and that my eyes do not deceive me, I got myself examined by the present Civil

Surgeon of Dacca. He tested me about my eye-sight and found my vision good and certified that I can recognise faces. This certificate is a recent one and was signed on the 2nd instant. The recognition by me of my 2nd grandson cannot, therefore, be regarded as an illusion.

If Mrs. Drummond will kindly condescend to come over to my place on some evening which is the most convenient time for me, she can see me and report to you about my physical condition.

I am in good health. With my prayer to God for your happiness and prosperity, I remain, yours sincerely,

Rani Satyabhama Devi

As far as the records show, no reply was sent to this letter from the district magistrate's office.

Satyabhama's letter indicates the extent to which the women of the Bhawal Raj family were prepared to go to present their claims in a form that would be credible to officals of a colonial government. She attached to her letter a medical certificate from a British doctor to establish that her eye-sight was still good; she suggested that the wife of the district magistrate might come and visit her to verify her condition, since the customary rules of purdah would not allow the district magistrate himself to meet her. A year later, in August 1923, when Sayabhama was dead, Jyotirmayi sent a petition to K. C. De, member of the Revenue Board, then visiting Dhaka, seeking an appointment with him so that she could present her case regarding the claims of the sannyasi. De, an Indian member of the colonial civil service, responded in Bengali. "I have received your letter of the 29th Sraban. You have expressed a desire to come and see me at my *bāsā* [residence]. You are a lady belonging to a very high family and I do not think it proper that you should come and see me at the Circuit House. You can send your son-in-law on Thursday next at 8 A.M. and instruct him to tell me all that you have to say. I shall hear him in full and pass suitable orders."[25] It is apparent that there were differences in the way British and Indian officers of the colonial government negotiated the requirements of law and bureaucracy with the demands of native cultural practice. These differences were important. As the case of the Bhawal sannyasi would move through the corridors of government and the judiciary, those very differences in assumptions and orientations would become a significant factor in deciding the fate of the case.

As it happened, K. C. De met Chandra Sekhar Banerjee, Jyotirmayi's son-in-law, and told him that nothing could be done by the Board of Revenue unless the sannyasi himself put up a petition stating his claims. So far, all petitions had been made by others claiming to have an interest in the welfare of the Bhawal estate, but nothing had been heard directly from the claimant himself. De advised Chandra Sekhar to persuade the sannyasi to make a direct representation to the Board of Revenue. It seems there were a lot of consultations with lawyers on this issue, and the advice given was to go ahead and make the representation. But it was not until December 1926 that a memorial was formally presented to the Board of Revenue on behalf of the sannyasi.

Before that, there were other developments in this strange story.

FIGURE 5. Jyotirmayi Debi, the Kumar's sister

Chapter Five

FIRST BRUSH WITH THE LAW

The Defamation Suit

Among the pamphlets published in support of the sannyasi's claim was one composed in verse under the title *Phakir beśe prāṇer rājā*, which roughly translates as "The Prince of Our Heart in the Garb of a Fakir." It began to circulate in the Dacca region sometime in July 1921. It was published under the authorship of Purna Chandra Ghosh of Harbaid, the son of Digendra Narayan Ghosh, president of the Bhawal talukdar and tenants' association set up to fight for the sannyasi's cause. About one thousand copies were printed from the Jagat Art Press, Dhaka.

In this pamphlet, the story of the second kumar's visit to Darjeeling was dramatically described as a conspiracy in which he was deliberately taken away from his natal family in Bhawal in order to be poisoned and killed. Satyendra Banerjee, the kumar's brother-in-law, by now widely referred to as Satya Babu, was portrayed as the brain behind the plot, and Dr. Ashutosh Dasgupta, generally known as Ashu Doctor, as the executioner. Mukunda Guin, the secretary, and Sharif Khan, Jamini and Akhila, attendants, were named as accomplices.

> To hear the story sends shivers down the spine;
> Yet this poet must now narrate their feats.
> He was trusted by the kumar, Ashu Doctor was his name,
> Respectable in his looks, but a blackguard in deed.
> By his side Satya Babu, brother-in-law,
> Champion of intrigue, the villain of the piece.
> One more accomplice, his name Mukunda,
> Black sheep of Bhawal, hailing from Mansurpur.
> With them the orderlies Jamini and Akhila,
> The guard Sharif Khan, and a few others.
> Together they plotted, worked out a plan,
> And took the second kumar with them to the hills.
> What was the drug that Ashu Doctor fed
> That caused the second kumar to collapse senseless?

Ashu Babu, he was a friend of the kumar:
Trusting him, the kumar swallowed the dose....
Satya Babu of Calcutta, a man of many parts,
Knew he had to cover up any way he could.
The kumar unconscious—they were jumping with joy!
Quickly they took the body away and laid it on the pyre.
But they couldn't set it alight: a hailstorm came down!
They left the body behind and ran for shelter.[1]

What was being whispered ever since the sannyasi's declaration had now appeared in print. Ashutosh Dasgupta, in fact, had been in the eye of the storm from the very moment when the sannyasi made his declaration in Jaidebpur. He was now working on the Bhawal estate in a charitable dispensary. On May 5, 1921, he had written as follows to Sailendra Nath Matilal, brother of the eldest rani, in Calcutta.

An extraordinary thing, such as one has not read in a romance, has happened at Bhowal. A Sannyasi Sadhu has arrived here in the house of Buddhu Babu. He has declared that he is the Second Kumar and his name is Ramendra Narayan Roy. He has given also the name of the nurse, Aloka. The tenants will raise by subscription two lakhs of rupees, and recover his property. 5 or 6 thousand people are coming to see him every day and some of them paying 'nazar'. Every man and woman is firmly convinced that he is the Kumar, that there can be no doubt about it. The affair has caused a great sensation. As I came and said that it [the sannyasi's claim] was false, a hundred thousand people of Bhowal have been blaming me. I am passing my time in great trouble.[2]

Ashutosh Dasgupta had now been publicly blamed in a printed booklet. In September 1921, the doctor filed a suit for defamation in the subdivisional court of Sripur against Purna Chandra Ghosh, author and publisher of the pamphlet, Satish Chandra Ray, printer, and Ramlal Sil, bookseller. At last, the sannyasi's story was going to be put to the test of the law.

The suit came up for hearing in Sripur in the court of Sarada Prasanna Ghosh, deputy magistrate. This itself was a curious coincidence, because Sarada Prasanna was the son of Kali Prasanna Ghosh, who was once the all-powerful manager of the Bhawal estate. S. P. Ghosh decided to deal with the charges against Ramlal Sil separately, and proceeded with the trial of the other two accused. Appearing for the prosecution was government pleader Sasanka Coomar Ghose. On the side of the accused were Peari-mohan Ghosh and Surendra Nath Mukherjee. When the time came for the crucial hearing of Ashutosh Dasgupta's evidence, the proceedings became extremely heated. The magistrate refused to allow a series of questions asked by the defense that sought to open the matter of the kumar's relations with his brother-in-law and the details of his medical treatment in Darjeeling. After agitated arguments, the lawyers for the defense declined to ask any further questions or call any more witnesses. In April 1922, Sarada Prasanna Ghosh delivered a judgment pronouncing Purna Chandra Ghosh and Satish Chandra Ray guilty of the charges brought against them. Purna Chandra was sentenced to three months' imprisonment.

The accused appealed the judgment. The district sessions judge found irregularities in the trial and ruled that the two accused should be tried again, this time separately. This order was appealed against from Ashutosh Dasgupta's side, but the Calcutta High Court upheld the retrial order. The case against Purna Chandra Ghosh began again in Sripur in the court of Sarada Prasanna Ghosh. Soon after, Sarada Prasanna came up for promotion, and the case was transferred to the court of Birendra Mohan Ghosh, deputy magistrate.

THE EVIDENCE IN COURT

The argument made on behalf of Ashutosh Dasgupta was that he had accompanied the second kumar to Darjeeling at the latter's request, that he had acted as the full-time medical attendant to the kumar in Darjeeling, that the kumar had been treated there by Dr. Calvert and Dr. Nibaran Sen, and that Ashutosh had only acted under the instructions of those renowned doctors. By suggesting that he had joined a conspiracy to poison the kumar, the pamphlet had maliciously defamed him in public. On Purna Chandra Ghosh's side, the defense was that he sincerely believed what he had written to be true, that he had published the pamphlet in good faith for the good of the public, and that he had no malicious intent. The issue of bona fide good faith became the crucial question in the trial. Was there enough evidence for someone like Purna Chandra to believe that there had been an attempt to poison the kumar?

The defamation case was the first time that a large volume of material evidence was produced on the kumar's medical condition in Darjeeling and the treatment he had received. Dr. Calvert's death certificate mentioned "biliary colic" as the illness from which the kumar had collapsed and died. This certificate was, however, made out in a printed form supplied by the Glasgow Life Assurance Company, and was clearly meant for the purpose of supporting the claim for the kumar's life insurance. The magistrate refused to accept this certificate as a public document. On the other hand, Ashutosh Dasgupta had said in his evidence that the second kumar had suffered from biliary colic two years before his death, but in the intervening period, despite several medical examinations prompted by other complaints, this was not a disease that had been reported by any of the kumar's doctors, even Dr. Dasgupta.[3] When the Kumar had consulted Dr. S. P. Sarbadhikari in Calcutta in December 1908, which was when the kumar was advised to go to the hills in the summer, Dr. Dasgupta was with the kumar but had not thought it necessary to inform Dr. Sarbadhikari about the biliary colic from which the kumar had once suffered.

More significantly, evidence was produced in court of the various prescriptions that had been administered to the kumar in Darjeeling. T. Cleare, manager of Smith, Stanistreet and Company, appeared in court with a huge ledger book for the year 1909 in which all prescriptions served by their pharmacy in Darjeeling were copied.[4] This record showed that the first prescription made out for the kumar was on the morning of May 6, when Dr. Calvert was called in for the first time.

℞

Spt. Amon Aromat	ʒiii
Sodi Bicarb	ʒi
Tinct. Card Co.	ʒvi
Spt. Chloroform	ʒiss
Aqua Cinnamon	ad ℥ vi
M ft.—mixt.	
ʒi—one mark every 2 hours	

℞

Lint opii	℥ ii
For external application	

Sd./ J.T.C.[5]

On the following day, May 7, there was one prescription, as follows.

℞

Quinine Sulph	Gr.iv
Aloin	Gr.½
Ext. Nux Vomica	Gr.⅓
Euonymin	Gr.i
Acid Araimor (Arsenius)	Gr.1/100
Ext. Gent.	Grs.
M ft. Pill (silver) 1 T.D.S. P.C.	

Sd./ A. T. Das Gupta

It was argued from the side of the defense that this prescription, made out by Dr. Ashutosh Dasgupta, did not contain any drug that could have been meant for the treatment of biliary colic. Instead, it contained drugs that should never be prescribed to a patient suffering from severe diarrhoea, which was one of the kumar's symptoms. Not only that, one ingredient of the mixture—Acid Araimor (arsenius)—was a small dose of arsenic. Among the kumar's symptoms recorded on May 8 were severe pain in the abdomen, irregular pulse, bloody stools, perspiration, severe diarrhoea, thirst, and collapse, all of which were known signs of arsenic poisoning. That day was, in fact, the day of crisis, because a series of prescriptions made out by Dr. Calvert and Dr. Sen were served that day by the pharmacy. Could it not be legitimately concluded that the drug administered by Ashutosh Dasgupta had caused the rapid deterioration in the kumar's condition on May 8?

The question of the cremation also became an issue. Had the kumar's body been cremated? Some witnesses testified that a body had been taken out from the house called Step Aside at night. Some said they had heard at the time that the kumar's body had disappeared from the pyre at the cremation ground, although no one actually claimed to have been part of the cremation party at night. One witness said that he was present during the morning procession to the cremation ground and described how the body was completely covered at all stages of the cremation, suggesting that it might not have been the kumar's body. It was also suggested that the dead body of "a stout and fair-complexioned Lepcha called Pengumche" had gone missing from Victoria Hospital in Darjeeling that night, and it was this body that was taken out in procession and cremated on the morning of May 9. Moreover, witnesses were produced who testified that they had actually seen the second kumar a few days after his alleged death in the company of a sadhu. Jogesh Chandra Roy, a railway employee, deposed as follows.

> On following Monday Sala Babu [brother-in-law, that is, Satyendra Banerjee] and the party left Darjeeling by the 9–44 A.M. down train. . . . Ten or twelve days after, I saw the Kumar in the garb of a sannyasi, coming down Darjeeling in a train, with a sannyasi. I recognised him to be the Kumar of Bhowal. I was on the platform. Rabindra Nath Sanyal was also on the platform. The head of the Kumar was then shaven. Probably his cloth had a border. I knew the other sannyasi. He was Aghori Baba. I went forward to the Kumar in order to speak to him, but he turned his face downwards. At that time I was called by someone and left the place. There was rumour at Darjeeling that Aghori Baba picked up dead bodies and was convicted once. Hence we used to fear. . . . From his complexion, eyes, lips, face, I recognised him to be the Kumar of Bhowal.

And Rabindra Nath Sanyal testified as follows.

> Ten or twelve days after Sala Babu's departure from Darjeeling, one day I saw the Kumar of Bhowal in the dress of a sannyasi in an old third class trolley carriage by the 9–44 (A.M.) train. I saw him sitting there. His head was clean shaved. He had a *geruā* [ochre] dress and a *kamaṇḍalu* [brass or copper jar carried by sannyasis] in hand. I watched him for about 8 or 10 minutes from a distance of 2 or 3 cubits. I recognised him and observed him carefully. I recog-

nised him to be the Kumar of Bhowal whom I had seen on the platform some days back. Another tall sannyasi was with him. When he had gone for tickets I went near the trolley and observed the Kumar carefully. . . . When the tall sannyasi was absent, I cried out: "You all, come and see the Kumar of Bhowal, the newly made sannyasi." At this the Kumar moved his head showing an angry mood towards me. Hearing my cries, 7 or 8 Pahari coolies and two of my peons came and saw him.[6]

THE JUDGMENT

Birendra Mohan Ghosh, deputy magistrate, concluded from the evidence of the prescriptions and of authoritative medical texts that it was by no means clear that the kumar was suffering from biliary colic in Darjeeling. The medicine that Dr. Ashutosh Dasgupta had administered to the kumar was harmful for him. It contained arsenic, and the symptoms recorded on the day of the Kumar's death tallied with those mentioned in several standard medical texts as the symptoms of arsenic poisoning. The magistrate also found that sufficient efforts had not been made by Dr. Dasgupta and the other companions of the kumar during the morning of May 8, 1909, to treat his condition of severe diarrhoea. It followed that there was enough ground for any prudent and reasonable man to believe that there was a conspiracy carried out in Darjeeling in which Ashutosh Dasgupta had participated to poison the kumar and bring about his death. The magistrate judged that the pamphlet had been written and published in good faith, and in May 1923 dismissed the charge of defamation.

THE APPEAL

The government appealed to the High Court against this judgment of the lower court. Clearly, much more was at stake here than the alleged defamation of a doctor from a rural charitable dispensary in Dacca. The appeal came up in December 1924 before a bench consisting of Mr. Justice Greaves and Mr. Justice Panton of the Calcutta High Court. Appearing before them were some of the luminaries of the legal establishment of Calcutta. The team of lawyers on the government side was led by the acting advocate general B. L. Mitter; appearing for Purna Chandra Ghosh was John Langford James, a renowned barrister of the Calcutta High Court (who unfortunately died a couple of years later, cutting short a distinguished career); and for Ashutosh Dasgupta was Sir Binod Mitter, another celebrated barrister and son of the famous Sir Ramesh Chandra Mitter.[7]

Arguing for the government, B. L. Mitter made four points. First, there was not enough evidence to establish that Ashutosh Dasgupta had himself administered medicines to the kumar. Second, the conclusions drawn from the evidence by the lower court were wrong. Third, there was no proof that at the time of publication of the pamphlet, Purna Chandra Ghosh was aware of the existence of all of the evidence that had been produced on his behalf in court. And finally, there was no satisfactory reason for the publication of this pamphlet twelve years after the death of the kumar.

Langford James began his argument by remarking on the extraordinary fact that the government had found it necessary to appeal against a judgment of a lower court in Dacca district dismissing a charge of defamation brought by an ordinary medical practitioner against the publisher of a little-known pamphlet. This was the first time that the government had ever appealed against such a judgment in a private suit. The advocate general had stated that the appeal had become necessary because it was feared that the tenants of the Bhawal estate might refuse to pay rent to the Court of Wards. Was this a valid reason for the government to take sides in a private suit?

Turning to the substance of the case, James said that there was enough evidence to show that Ashutosh Dasgupta was the full-time medical attendant to the kumar during his stay in Darjeeling and that he had himself prescribed the drug that could have been harmful to the kumar, given his medical condition on the morning of May 8, 1909. The lower court judge had drawn a reasonable conclusion based on the evidence and the expert medical knowledge available to him. The appellate judges would only have to determine if such a conclusion was reasonable and possible, not whether the opposite conclusion was also reasonable and possible.

Standards of Truth

Sir William Greaves and E.B.H. Panton, I.C.S., were not, however, persuaded by James's arguments. The judges held that the reasoning of the lower court and its conclusions were faulty. They said that there was not enough evidence to prove that Ashutosh Dasgupta had himself administered a harmful drug to the kumar which had caused him to lose consciousness; had he done so, it would have aroused the suspicions of the two other senior physicians attending to the kumar. They also accepted the government contention that there was no proof that at the time he published the pamphlet, Purna Chandra Ghosh knew all of the medical evidence that had been produced in court. Finally, the High Court found the attempt by the lower court magistrate to pronounce on the medical evidence presented before him to be completely invalid. "[F]or a Magistrate untrained in medicine to attempt, largely without trained assistance, to ascertain what certain medicines were prescribed for and what should be prescribed for biliary colic by reference to medical books was entirely unsound and the conclusion was valueless. Again the assumption that the amount of arsenic contained in the prescriptions would produce arsenical poisoning, collapse and unconsciousness was a conclusion impossible to support without expert evidence."[8] The high court upheld the government appeal and sentenced Purna Chandra Ghosh to one month's simple imprisonment and a fine of Rs.1,000.

Proofs: Legal and Popular

One round of legal battles had been fought. The government had won. Even though the sannyasi himself was not a litigant, those representing his side had lost. Whether the sannyasi was really the second kumar of Bhawal was not the immediate issue in this case but, of course, that was the question that had produced the context in which a public debate had arisen. To establish the truth of the sannyasi's identity, one would have to answer the question: what happened in Darjeeling? What the British judges of the High Court established were the standards of proof that would have to be met for that question to be answered properly in the public sphere. It was not enough, as Birendra Mohan Ghosh of the lower court had done, to take the evidence of the prescription made out by Ashutosh Dasgupta and tally it against the knowledge commonly available in medical textbooks. The necessary conclusions could only be drawn by experts. Indeed, someone like Purna Chandra Ghosh could not be said to have acted like "a prudent and reasonable man," as the law required, if he had not, before making his charges in print, first satisfied himself that trained experts in medicine might think there was enough ground for suspecting that the kumar might have been poisoned in Darjeeling. The truth of this case would have to be established by the methods of science as practiced by authorized experts. Until then, the truth that must prevail in the public domain was that which the institutions of the state had publicly accepted.

Although the first legal battle had been lost by the sannyasi's supporters, the war was by no means over. This was signaled by a new round of propaganda launched on behalf of the sannyasi. Suren Mukherjee, who had been one of the legal advisers to the sannyasi from the very beginning, published a pamphlet soon after the High Court judgment, reiterating the claims on their side.

There was no doubt, he said, that Satyen Banerjee and Ashutosh Dasgupta had accompanied the kumar on his trip to Darjeeling, that no one knew of any illnesses that the kumar was suffering from at the time, that the kumar died following a mysterious illness that lasted only three days, that the medicines prescribed by Dr. Dasgupta had nothing to do with the disease to which the kumar is supposed to have succumbed, and that on the morning of the fateful day, while the kumar was going through a spell of severe diarrhea, he received no medical attention until late in the afternoon. The public at large was still in the dark about what had caused the kumar's death.

On the question of the kumar's cremation, too, the public was in the dark. There was clear evidence that a body had been taken from the house Step Aside to the cremation ground on the night that the kumar died. Whose body was it? If it was the kumar's, then the body cremated on the morning of May 9 could not have been his. Soon after the appearance of the sannyasi in Jaidebpur, Satyen Banerjee had announced in the newspapers that there were many relatives and friends of the kumar who had witnessed his cremation in Darjeeling. So far, apart from Satya Babu himself, none of these relatives and friends had come forward.

On the other hand, the people of east Bengal had welcomed with open arms their beloved kumar. The entire Bhawal zamindar family and kin, the family priests, the Brahmins of Jaidebpur, other zamindars of the region, and all talukdars and tenants of Bhawal had accepted the sannyasi as the second kumar.

> Since the people of the country have already accepted Kumar Ramendra Narayan, no further proof of his identity is necessary. The people have realized the true state of affairs. The country was now under the rule of the English government; the people know that if a theft occurs even in the dead of night, the thief cannot hope to get away. And here we find a supposed impostor openly claiming to be Kumar Ramendra Narayan, moving around freely in the city of Dhaka, accepting money and contributions from the people, and still the police, despite their best efforts, have failed to find out his true identity. The people cannot accept this to be the case. They have rightly concluded that this man is none other than Ramendra Narayan Roy, the second kumar of Bhawal.[9]

Not only that. About two years before, in December 1922, Rani Satyabhama, grandmother of Ramendra Narayan, had died in Dhaka. Although old, she was a woman of keen eyesight and hearing. She had recognized the sannyasi as her grandson soon after his arrival in Jaidebpur. Before her death, she specifically requested that her grandson perform her funerary rites, which Ramendra Narayan had done, both at the cremation and at the śrāddha held in the presence of three thousand people representing the cream of Dhaka society. A few days previously, Ramendra Narayan had also performed the annual śrāddha of his late grandmother. "In the eyes of a Hindu, and judged by the laws of the Hindus, these are not matters of small consequence. Is this not proof? The people will make their own judgment."[10]

Chapter Six

THE HOUSE ON LANSDOWNE ROAD

The Sannyasi as Second Kumar

Forbidden by the administration from entering the Bhawal estate, the sannyasi settled down in a rented house in Armanitola in Dhaka city and lived there from June 1921 as a member of Jyotirmayi Debi's household. He moved around the city in a tumtum, driving it himself as the second kumar had done, visiting relatives and acquaintances, attending social events in the aristocratic circles of Dacca. He was, as already noted, the central figure at the lavish śrāddha ceremonies of Satyabhama Debi, where he seemed to be accepted as the second kumar of Bhawal by all of Dhaka society, except for the officials. He received countless visitors at home, some still curious to find out for themselves if what they had heard was true, others completely convinced of his identity and paying him the respect and deference due to his aristocratic status.

He moved to Calcutta in the middle of 1924, when the defamation case appeal came up before the Calcutta High Court. He rented a house on Harish Mukherjee Road in Bhawanipur and lived there for the next five years. Jyotirmayi and some members of her family came to live with him in Calcutta.

Two interesting things happened soon after his arrival in Calcutta, both of which were reported in the many pamphlets that kept appearing on the subject of the defamation suit. The first was his visit to the eldest rani, Ranendra Narayan's widow, who now lived in her father's house on Madhu Gupta Lane in north Calcutta. It was widely reported that the sannyasi had instantly recognized Sarajubala Debi. Not only that, he had also recognized her mother, sixteen years after the second kumar had last seen her.[1] The *Herald* of Dhaka described the incident as follows.

> The eldest ranee (widow of the eldest Kumar) lives in Calcutta in her father's family in which several ladies and gentlemen had seen the Mejho [second] Kumar while alive. Though the Sannyasi had been strictly prohibited from visiting the Mejho ranee, to the family of the Bara [oldest] ranee he got access easily. The result is that he is now acknowledged almost universally there . . . as Kumar Ramendranarain. The Sannyasi is visiting the family quite frequently and is cordially received as a near relation as would be the case if he

were Ramendranarain himself. It is said that the mother of the Bara ranee herself put a test and was satisfied and after that all doubts of the family have disappeared.[2]

The other development was that a few weeks after his arrival in Calcutta, the sannyasi was instructed by officers of the Bhawanipur police station that he should not make any attempt to visit the neighborhood of Lansdowne Road, where the second rani lived in the house of her brother Satyendra Banerjee. If he did, he was warned, he could be arrested. *Dainik Basumatī* of Calcutta reported that its correspondent had spoken to the sannyasi for over half an hour (in Bengali, the report was careful to mention) during which he had given this information. The sannyasi also said that the second rani had seen him a couple of times driving down Lansdowne Road in a phaeton.[3]

So far, although the government authorities in Dhaka and Calcutta had been approached a number of times on the issue of the sannyasi by various members of the Bhawal Raj family or by persons having an interest in the affairs of the estate, no formal representation had yet been made by the sannyasi himself claiming his position or his property. As we have seen, K. C. De, member of the Board of Revenue, had advised Jyotirmayi Debi in 1923 that this ought to be done. Although many lawyers had given the same advice, it was only in December 1926 that a memorial was presented by the sannyasi to the Board of Revenue asking for an inquiry into his identity and the withdrawal of the impostor notice. The board gave his lawyers, led by Langford James, a formal hearing in Calcutta and rejected his plea in April 1927 on rather curious grounds. The determination of his identity, it said, would not serve any useful purpose because if it was found that the sannyasi was in fact Ramendra Narayan Roy, the board was not empowered to return his property to him without going through proper legal procedures in court. On the other hand, if it was found that he was an impostor, it would all be a waste of time.[4]

Even though the sannyasi was denied formal recognition of his claim by the government, he did manage to obtain considerable social recognition as the second kumar of Bhawal in the elite circles of Calcutta. He became a member of the Bengal Landholders Association, the premier body of Bengal landlords, in the name of Kumar Ramendra Narayan Roy, zamindar of Bhawal. He bought shares in a steamship company called the Bengal Flotilla Service and became its director. He attended receptions and parties thrown by other zamindars and notables. At one such party, he was even introduced to Lord Lytton, the governor of Bengal, as the kumar of Bhawal. All this time, he was living in Bhawanipur along with Jyotirmayi's family, apparently receiving funds and subscriptions from his supporters in Dacca.

Not once did he visit his wife, who lived with her brother's family on Lansdowne Road. Indeed, as we have noted before, he had been warned by the police not to try to do so.

SATYA BABU, OR MR. BANERJEE

Lansdowne Road in the early twentieth century was one of the new thoroughfares going southward from the predominantly European part of Calcutta. The old heart of the "white town" was then situated in the well-laid-out quarters just south of Park Street. But by the turn of the century, as the city had grown as the premier administrative, mercantile, and industrial centre of the Indian empire, the European residential areas had expanded south toward Ballygunge, while the successful Bengali professional groups moved away from the congested "native town" in the north of the city and built new houses in Bhawanipur. Lansdowne Road separated Bhawanipur from Ballygunge and soon acquired the stamp of the new lifestyle of the modern Calcutta bhadralok, freed from the constrictions of the large extended family mired in orthodox ritual, confidently engaged in the making of a new urban culture that could participate in the modern world and yet assert its vernacular identity, self-assured and relaxed in the company of the European elite.

Nineteen Lansdowne Road was a spacious two-storied house typical of the lifestyle of this new professional upper-middle class. It was much smaller than the city residence of the maharaja of Natore across the street, center of many a glittering musical soiree at this time, or even of the house of Sarat Chandra Bose at Woodburn Park, just off Lansdowne Road, which would be a gathering place of nationalist political leaders from all over the country. Next door to it were the grounds of the St. John's Diocese, where soon a school would be built for the daughters of the Bengali middle class of south Calcutta, and well known as the Diocesan School. Nineteen Lansdowne Road was the house of Mr. S. N. Banerjee, a lawyer of the Calcutta High Court and now an honorary magistrate and justice of the peace, whom we have met earlier in our story as Satya Babu, brother-in-law of the second kumar of Bhawal. In another of those coincidences that seem to be strewn across the narrative of this extraordinary case, Nineteen Lansdowne Road was actually the house where the second kumar had stayed in the winter of 1905–1906 during one of his pleasure trips to Calcutta; the young bride Bibhabati was in Jaidebpur at the time.

After Bibhabati left Jaidebpur permanently in 1910, following Ramendra Narayan's death, she came to Calcutta to live with her brother's family in a house off Harrison Road. There was some question as to how much of her husband's life insurance she would get. On November 15, 1909, F. W. Needham, the chief manager of the estate, was writing to Ranendra Narayan, the eldest kumar as follows.

> I have received a letter from the late second Kumar's widow, saying that she has instructed her brother, Babu Satyendranath Banerjee, to realise the money due on her late husband's Life Insurance policy with the City of Glasgow Insurance Co. She is evidently under the impression that the whole amount of the insurance money belongs to her; but this is not the case, as the premium was always paid by the Estate; and accordingly, I think she is entitled by law only to a $\frac{1}{3}$rd share of the same, as heir to her late husband's property, after deducting the loan of Rs.10,000/- (Rupees ten thousand) with the interests on the same, which was given to your late brother by the Insurance Co. on his policy and which is entered in the list of the Bonded debts. However, if you and Rabindra Sahib are willing to forego your shares of this money in her favour, you will kindly let me have a note to this effect; and I will then do the needful, and apply to the Insurance Co. for the money and will credit the same to Srimati Bibhabati Devi Choudhurani's account, and she can draw the same whenever she wishes to do so.[5]

It appears that the two surviving kumars did forego their claims, and Bibhabati received Rs.30,000 against her husband's life insurance. She was also getting a monthly allowance of Rs.1,100 from the Bhawal estate. The allowance rose rapidly over the next few years, as the incomes of the estate increased under the Court of Wards' management. By 1919, Bibhabati was getting a monthly allowance of Rs.7,000. Her brother used her money to buy the house on Lansdowne Road and settle down to a life of genteel comfort on the fringes of official elite society. He had in the meantime received his law degree and enrolled as an advocate at the Calcutta High Court. Slowly, he acquired the honors and titles that were bestowed on those whom the colonial officials recognized as native gentlemen of note. He frequented the elite clubs, attended official receptions, and clearly had access to important persons in government.

The secure calm of daily life must have been greatly disturbed in Satyen Banerjee's house when the news reached him in May 1921 of the sannyasi's astonishing declaration of identity. Satyendra immediately went and saw Lees, the member of the Board of Revenue, at Writers' Buildings and arranged to have a letter published in *The Englishman* refuting the claims of the sannyasi. Subsequently, he kept in regular touch with M. H. B. Lethbridge, the secretary to the Board of Revenue, and supplied him with many of the documents that would substantiate the government's claim that the second kumar's body had been properly cremated at Darjeeling and that the sannyasi was a fraud. Among these was Calvert's medical certificate obtained from the life insurance company. Within a week after the sannyasi's declaration, Sasanka Coomar Ghose arrived in Calcutta with Lindsay's report on "the claims of a certain sadhu" and, accompanied by Satyendra Banerjee, went to Darjeeling to meet Lees. More documents were collected by this team in Darjeeling, including the rain reports for May 1909, and sent to Lindsay in Dhaka. As mentioned before, various witnesses from among the Bengali residents of Darjeeling were examined at this time by N. K. Roy, deputy magistrate.

BIBHABATI IN CALCUTTA

Bibhabati was now settled as a young widow living with her brother's family. The role was a familiar one in high-caste Bengali domestic life. Indeed, her own mother had been put in a similar position, with the added responsibility of having to bring up four children. It is difficult to say whether Bibhabati regarded having to leave the Jaidebpur Rajbari as an unmixed disaster. The life of a Brahmin widow, forced by customary practices to forego many of the basic material comforts to which she would have been used as a woman married into a wealthy household, would have been painful for her. Many of those rigors were probably relaxed or overlooked in the more modernized lifestyle of her brother's house in south Calcutta. As a young bride, she did not like the life she had to live in the Bhawal Raj family. Returning to the enlightened middle-class circles of Calcutta, the cultural gulf with the life she had left behind must have seemed enormous. Besides, we know enough about her married life and the sexual habits of her husband to infer that she could not have thought of him as fulfilling the highest expectations of love and companionship. Was she secretly relieved that she would no longer have to suffer the ignominies of such a married life? Of course, everything in her upbringing would have taught her to accept all the disappointments and humiliations and remain steadfast in her role as dutiful wife and daughter-in-law. Following the sudden and utterly unexpected death of her husband, she behaved exactly as a young widow in her position would have been expected to behave. She was stunned at first, then overwhelmed by grief. Witnesses later described how, in Darjeeling, she wept uncontrollably when the conch-shell and iron bangles, markers of her married status, were removed from her hand and ritually broken. Arriving in Jaidebpur, she is said to have remarked how she had first been made queen in the royal household, only to be brought down to the status of a beggar. Was she happy to be away from the Rajbari and its decadent lifestyle?

Many years later, she was asked in court about her relationship with her husband.

> *Q.* When you came to Jaidebpur after your marriage, did you feel that you had fallen into the hands of an illiterate and debauched man?
>
> *A.* No.
>
> *Q.* Can you swear that you did not feel terribly hurt because your husband would not sleep with you?
>
> *A.* No, I did not feel hurt.
>
> *Q.* Do you remember if your mother ever sent word to you that "Bibha should try to see that her husband sleeps with her in the same bed"?
>
> *A.* It is possible that she did.

And again:

> *Q.* If it is suggested that before the trip to Darjeeling, the Kumar was a man of loose moral character, would that be a correct statement?
>
> *A.* He was my husband. I don't want to make any remarks on his character.
>
> *Q.* Would you say the same thing about the character of the Eldest Kumar?
>
> *A.* He was a respected elder. I don't want to make any remarks on his character either.
>
> *Q.* And would you say the same about the Youngest Kumar?
>
> *A.* I don't want to make any remarks on anyone's character.

And again:

> *Q.* Are you suggesting that your husband could not stay without you even for a few days?
>
> *A.* I have never said such a thing.
>
> *Q.* Did the Kumar miss you very much when you were apart?
>
> *A.* I will not try to explain to you.
>
> *Q.* Was the Kumar someone who was very fond of his wife?
>
> *A.* I have never noticed him being interested in that subject.
>
> *Q.* Some married men go to great lengths to please their wives. What was your husband like?
>
> *A.* I cannot make comparisons with others.
>
> *Q.* Did your husband act on your advice?
>
> *A.* Not always.
>
> *Q.* Have you ever felt that your husband's main concern was his wife?
>
> *A.* No.[6]

During the years before the sadhu's appearance in Dhaka, when the Rajbari would often be abuzz with rumors that the second kumar had been seen at various places in the company of religious men, word would certainly have reached the second rani in Calcutta about these speculations. It is known that Jyotirmayi Debi, during one of her visits to Calcutta, told Bibhabati about these rumors and about Jyotirmayi's attempts to find out more about the matter from religious centers in northern India.[7] Bibhabati herself went on at least two long visits to Benaras and other places of pilgrimage with her brother's family during this time. It does not appear that she gave much credence to these rumors about her husband roaming around religious places in the company of sadhus.

When the news reached the Banerjee household of the sannyasi's appearance and declaration in Jaidebpur, it was Satyendra who came forward to defend her sister's interests. But of course, the sadhu's story cast serious aspersions on Satyendra's role in the alleged death and cremation of the kumar in Darjeeling. Soon, as the popular press and oral media began to churn out their own sensationalized versions of the sadhu's story, "brother-in-law Satya Babu" came to figure in them as the principal conspirator and villain.

Bibhabati steadfastly refused to entertain the possibility that her husband might be alive. The more the clamor reached a fever pitch in Jaidebpur, the more rigid she became. Satyabhama Debi, the kumars' grandmother, wrote Bibhabati a letter. Bibha had already heard that Satyabhama had accepted the sadhu as her grandson. She refused even to open Satyabhama's letter, suspecting that it would be an attempt to persuade her to come to Dhaka to meet the sadhu. Had she opened the letter, she would have read the following:

> Infinitely blessed Bibhabati Debi,
>
>   Ramendra Narayan, the second son of my son Rajendra Narayan, is alive.
>
>   The man who came to Dacca a little over one year ago in the garb of a sannyasi and whom numerous tenants of Bhawal and many bhadralok of Dacca acknowledged to be the Second Kumar—I have seen him carefully. I saw him first at Jaidebpur and for the last few days have been seeing him every day at the rented house in Dhaka. There is no doubt in my mind that he is my second grandson, Ramendra Narayan Roy. Though I am old, my sight, I think, is still good, and you know very well how at the *śrāddha* after his alleged death there was a proposal to hold *kuśaputtalikā*, and why it was not held.
>
>   It is my conviction that you need only come and see him and no doubt will be left in your mind. Since his arrival at Dacca none of you have seen him with your own eyes. May be you only heard things from people, and read things from the papers.
>
>   I therefore affectionately invite you to come in order that the truth might be declared. Do come therefore, see things with your own eyes, and save the honour and fame of the family of my distinguished husband by doing what you conceive to be your duty according to justice and religion.
>
>   Sri Satyabhama Debi

Satyabhama could not write herself. The letter was written for her, and she put her signature on it.[8] Bibhabati had correctly guessed the contents of the letter; she did not read it. During all the hulabaloo, she firmly refused to go to Dacca.

She did see the sadhu, though—not once, but a few times. This was when he came to live in Calcutta in 1924. Although he had been warned by the police not to try and visit Bibhabati, he did drive down Lansdowne Road a few times. Bibha saw him once from a window, and then on another occasion from the terrace above the front portico of the house, partly hidden behind a krishnachura tree. Both times, Buddhu, Jyotirmayi's son, was in the phaeton with the man who claimed to be her husband. She saw him on other occasions, too. Once, near the new Victoria Memorial, his carriage passed hers and he was only a few feet away. She saw him clearly that time. She also saw him on the Strand, where he was sitting in a taxi with an open top. All of these sightings took place in the early evening when she had gone out on a drive. No word was ever exchanged between them.

Were these sightings purely accidental? Is it possible that they had been arranged, possibly through the mediation of someone like Buddhu? It would have been extraordinary if Bibhabati did not at least have the curiosity to see for herself who this man was who was claiming to be her dead husband. What did she conclude after she had seen him at least half a dozen times? She was asked this question endlessly, perhaps until the last day of her life. She always said, without fail, that the man had no resemblance at all to her dead husband. She saw no similarity between the two, none at all.

BENGAL 1925–1930

On June 16, 1925, the house called Step Aside in Darjeeling where the second kumar of Bhawal had allegedly died in 1909 entered the history of Bengal. Staying in the house that summer was Chitta Ranjan Das, whom Gandhi himself had hailed as "the uncrowned king of Bengal." He was the unchallenged political leader of the province. On that day, following a brief illness, Das died. His body was taken by train from Darjeeling to Calcutta. The cortege that accompanied the body from Sealdah station to the cremation ground at Keoratola has gone into the city's folklore as the biggest procession ever seen until then.

The death of C. R. Das marked a watershed in the politics of Bengal. As the leader of non-cooperation in Bengal, he had effectively welded the powerful Khilafat committees, especially in the eastern and northern districts, with the Congress organization. It was a stupendous achievement to bring together within the same organizational ambit the mass agitators of Khilafat, who were urging the peasantry to rise against the evil British government that was bent on destroying Islam, and the revolutionary groups allied to the Congress, who were almost exclusively upper-caste Hindu in composition, skilled in factional maneuver and intrigue, and deeply distrustful of the masses. In 1923, moving away from Gandhian non-cooperation, C. R. Das took his Swarajya Party into the Bengal legislature and won the elections to the Calcutta Corporation. Seeking to confront the principal bone of contention between Hindu and Muslim political leaders, he devised a formula, called the Bengal Pact, by which a majority of local political offices and government jobs in the predominantly Muslim districts would be reserved for Muslims.

Following Das's death in 1925, the entire edifice of Hindu-Muslim fraternity within the Bengal Congress fell to pieces. The Hindu leaders refused to respect the Bengal Pact, and Muslim leaders began to withdraw from the Congress. From 1926 a series of conflicts between Hindus and Muslims began in different parts of Bengal. That year, Muslim leaders in Dhaka announced that no Muslims should participate in the great Janmastami procession, perhaps the biggest collective festival in the city. The boycott call led to provocative slogan shouting and stone throwing by Hindu processionists, which culminated in violent clashes and six deaths. It was the beginning of a process that would reach its nadir twenty years later in the Great Calcutta Killings.[9]

The Situation in Bhawal

The estate of Bhawal had been under the control of the Court of Wards ever since the death of Ranendra Narayan, the eldest kumar, in 1910. One of the standard complaints against zamindari establishments in east Bengal was the exaction of illegal cesses of various kinds from the tenants by the zamindar and his officers and the liberal application of *zulm* or forcible methods to extract these payments. After taking over the Bhawal estate, the government reported that as much as 2½ annas in the rupee (about 15.6 percent) were paid by every tenant over and above the rent as a cess out of which 1½ annas (or 9.4 percent) were appropriated by the estate officials. The Court of Wards announced in 1912–1913 that it had put a stop to these exactions.[10] Needless to say, the government also claimed to have improved the machinery of rent collection and cut down on wasteful expenditure.

Following the declaration of identity by the sadhu, there was clearly a crisis in the estate. The tenants were agitated; the association of talukdars and tenants formed in support of the sannyasi was active. Presumably acting on legal advice, the sannyasi never formally claimed that the second kumar's share of the rent be paid to him rather than to the Court of Wards. But tenants did frequently refuse to pay the rent to the estate. After the government moved decisively against the sannyasi, declaring him an impostor and prohibiting him from entering Jaidebpur, the estate began to take tough measures against tenants who refused to pay the rent. Legal steps were taken against them to impose penalties and then begin the dreaded "certificate procedure" by which their lands could be taken away and settled with others. Although the association of talukdars and tenants continued to be active in its support for the sannyasi's cause and raised subscriptions for his legal expenses, it appears that the resistance to paying rents began to wane after 1923–1924. In 1927–1928, the collections were quite high and the attempt to recover arrear rents seemed to be proceeding well, because the government reported an annual collection of 114.4 percent on current demand.[11] By this time, the scene of action had, of course, shifted to Calcutta, where the claimant was busy exploring various official channels to pursue his case.

In 1929, however, having gained some social recognition of his presumed position but having failed entirely to move the government, the former sannyasi appeared to make a crucial decision. He moved to Dhaka and began to collect rents from the tenants of the Bhawal estate against his share of one-third of the property. That year, he also celebrated for the first time the *punyāha* festival in his Dhaka residence to mark the beginning of the tenancy year—a characteristic ritual in eastern Bengal symbolizing the ties between landlord and tenant. Now, it seemed, the sannyasi had made up his mind to make his claims where it mattered most—in the Bhawal estate— and, if need be, to confront the government head on.

The district administration did not remain silent. In April 1929, O. M. Martin, the district magistrate, served on him an order in which he was referred to as "Sundar Das alias the Bhowal Sannyashi," and which said, "Whereas it has been made to appear to me that you intend to go to Joydebpore and whereas your presence there would cause obstruction and annoyance to persons lawfully employed, i.e. the officers of the Bhowal Court of Wards Estate, and possibly a disturbance of the public tranquility, I do hereby forbid you to enter the jurisdiction of Joydebpore Police Station."[12] For the moment, the sannyasi did not make any attempt to violate the order. But he lodged a formal protest against it. In his oral statement before the district magistrate, he said: "I claim the Bhowal Estate. The property belonged to my father. I left Jaidebpore in the year 1316 B.S. I came back to Jaidebpore after 12 years. . . . I got Nazar [gifts, tribute] from the tenants. They gave it to me voluntarily, then as now. Even now I get Nazar. They come themselves and give Nazar. They come to Dacca and give it. All the tenants believe me to be the Kumar. They are willingly paying me rent. I am not forcing them to make any payment. . . . I am not willing to give up my claim to my paternal property. I am not willing to stop receiving rent."[13]

The former sannyasi had now made his intentions clear. He continued to live in Dhaka, playing out his socially prescribed role as Kumar Ramendra Narayan Roy of Bhawal. His supporters were active within the estate. In 1929–1930, the government reported that rent collections had fallen dramatically to 73.9 percent: the collection process had been "greatly hampered on account of the agitation started by the impostor Sadhu."[14] Bignold, the estate manager, wrote to Sarajubala Debi in Calcutta, "it is true that many tenants are refusing to pay rent to the estate and I hope that as some of these tenants are approaching you, you will be good enough to use your own influence with them to pay up their due and have nothing to do with the impostor. It is earnestly requested that you will not encourage them to refer to the impostor as 'our dear Ramendra Narayan Roy'."[15]

It was at this time that Bibhabati Debi went to Dhaka, and then to Jaidebpur, to persuade tenants not to be misled by the propaganda being mounted from the other side. She told them that the government had rejected all of the sannyasi's claims and had declared him an impostor. They would only get into trouble if they listened to his supporters. It is not clear whether the second rani's visit was organized by the government to counter the sannyasi's new initiative, or whether she had been advised to go to Jaidebpur to protect her own interests.

The Suit

In 1930, a suit was filed in the court of the first subjudge of Dacca district in the name of Kumar Ramendra Narayan Ray, son of the late Raja Rajendra Narayan Roy of Jaidebpur. In it, the plaintiff asked for a decree from the court declaring that he was Kumar Ramendra Narayan Roy and that he was entitled to a one-third share in the properties of the Bhawal Raj. He gave a short account of the now-familiar story of his illness in Darjeeling, his supposed death and cremation, the rescue by a group of Naga sadhus, and his arrival in Dhaka after twelve years. He claimed that after the great meeting in Jaidebpur in May 1921, he was widely acknowledged as the second kumar and was paid his share of the rents by the tenants of the estate. His wife and her brother had conspired to induce Lindsay, the collector, to issue the impostor notice against him. He alleged that his wife, prompted by evil counsel and the prospect of gain, had been denying his identity without seeing him at all and had been interfering in various ways with his possession. Bibhabati Debi was made the first defendant in the suit, in which she was legally represented by E. Bignold, manager of the Bhawal estate under the Court of Wards. The second defendant was Sarajubala Debi, the eldest rani, who, although she had personally acknowledged his identity, was also legally represented by the manager of the estate who was hostile to the plaintiff. The third and fourth defendants were Ram Narayan, the adopted son of the third kumar, and Ananda Kumari Debi, widow of the third kumar. They had not expressed any opinion as to his identity, but since they were also wards of the manager of the estate, they too had been made parties to the suit.

The suit was filed on April 24, 1930. Earlier in the month, the Indian

National Congress had declared Civil Disobedience, and Gandhi had made his historic march to Dandi on the Gujarat coast to violate the salt laws. All over India, the colonial government was preparing to launch a severe crackdown on the movement. At the opposite end of the British Indian empire—in Chittagong on the far eastern coast of Bengal—on April 18, 1930, during the Easter holidays, a group of revolutionaries calling themselves the Indian Republican Army, Chittagong Branch, had, in deliberate emulation of the Easter Rising in Ireland, launched a daring attack on two police armories and various European official establishments.[16] All of east Bengal was trembling with excitement and apprehension. The colonial government seemed to be under attack from several fronts. How would it respond to the challenge to its authority?

On May 22, 1930, some Hindu boys playing with tops on the Nawabpur Road in Dhaka caused an "accidental injury" to a Muslim boy. This led to a fracas that blew up overnight into a major communal clash. Two Muslim men were apparently stabbed to death that night. The following day, when a procession was taken out with the dead bodies, Hindu young men threw stones and jeered at the processionists. For the next four or five days, there was mayhem in the town. Crowds of men, armed with sticks, knives, and iron rods, attacked the houses and shops of wealthy Hindu merchants and zamindars. Dhirendra Chandra Ray, a zamindar living in Armanitola a few houses away from the Sannyasi-kumar of Bhawal, recalled that as one such crowd rushed across the Armanitola park toward his house, he stood on the roof with his gun pointed at the advancing men and dared them to come forward. Taken aback by the sight of a rifle, the crowd stopped and moved away.[17] But not everyone had a gun, and judging by what would happen later in communal clashes in Bengal, the level of physical violence had still not reached its peak; the killings were estimated in the dozens and not in the hundreds. In fact, what is significant is that the attackers, mostly the urban poor, seemed more intent on looting than on killing. There was a rumor, it was said, going around in the town that the Nawab of Dacca had declared that for six days the poor Muslims could help themselves to whatever they wanted and that the police would not stop them. The looted property was often ceremonially distributed or sold at throwaway prices. In many cases, it was reported that the attackers searched for account books, bonds, deeds, and other papers and burned them. Clearly, what was happening was not simply "communal": it was a case of the poor seeking some sort of instant justice against wealthy Hindu zamindars and traders.[18]

But the moment was significant. With the nationalists stepping up their campaign through unarmed Civil Disobedience and armed uprisings and assassinations, and peasants and the urban poor becoming increasingly restive, the question was beginning to emerge, even if in outlines that were still rather hazy: was the authority of the colonial gevernment beginning to erode?

BRITISH LAW IN THE DISTRICTS

To understand what this authority meant in the east Bengal districts in the early half of this century, it would be instructive to turn to the memoirs of a British civil servant who spent many years representing the Raj in those inhospitable places: "Power, loneliness, hard work and an acquiescent public seemed to be ordained as one's natural setting. One struggled with poor success to maintain a life of some comfort and elegance in the face of insistently hard conditions. The facts of life were raw and bleak. There was no ice, food had little nutriment, lighting was with oil lamps and primitive punkhas flapped overhead. Life was like an expedition. . . . But there was one overriding satisfaction—one was master of everything that went on around one."[19] The district officer was master, ruling over a population that lived, at least as it appeared in his supremely arrogant eyes, little above the level of animals. "Most of the population is extremely poor. The poor man is almost without exception totally illiterate. . . . His sexual morals are those of animals—a Hindu landlord once described to me his Muslim tenants as mindless combinations of stomachs and testicles. The small man's morality consists in an admiration and a fear of anti-social chicanery and petty violence."[20] It was in this situation that the official power structure representing colonial authority had to be established and worked: "The higher district authorities, no less than the humble investigating police officer, had to accept the rural set-up as it exists. But the district authorities, in the last resort, have powers which can quell and dominate, among which are powers of arrest and prosecution. In the District Authorities, the community recognises, resides the ultimate power. If the power of the District Magistrate is thought to wane, then the power of the rich man, the landowner and the educated man will wilt and weaken."[21]

A. J. Dash, from whose memoirs of his life as administrator in the east Bengal districts in the period 1927–1935 we are quoting, even considers the interesting possibility of a challenge to the colonial official's authority from a local landlord, especially in the new context of the 1920s and 1930s, when there were more and more Indian officers in the higher civil service.

> Should a big and powerful landlord pay a call of respect on the District Magistrate? It is expected of him and he knows in his heart that it is in his own interest to do so.
> Perhaps he may be tempted to show to himself and the public that he is not

subject to the suzerainty of the District Magistrate either by not paying his respects, or by offering him such hospitality when the District Magistrate visits
his estate as to show that he has him in his pocket. Such disregard might seem
to offer enhancement of the landlord's influence and power. If this was in his
mind, he would soon find his mistake. A Bengali District Magistrate would
react instantly and strenuously. A British District Magistrate might not. But
his Bengali staff would because they feel themselves to be units in a power system overriding the power system of any individual in the district, however pre-
sumptuous he might be. Such an insolent landlord might soon find himself suffering first from pin pricks, not actual indignities. The men he used to uphold
his power might be picked off steadily and made to feel that the arm of the law
was more powerful than the protection system of their master. (The rural
power system in fact employs methods which are contrary to the law of the
land.) Then he might find himself without any means of operating his power
system except very desperate ones. And he might find himself under arrest.[22]

The official "power system" that Dash so confidently writes about was,
however, undergoing a rapid change, especially through the 1920s and
1930s. For old hands like him, firmly rooted in long-established traditions
of district administration, the changes were too subtle and the new currents
too unfamiliar even to register in their perception. Later in our story, we
will encounter dramatic evidence of how the aura of absolute power surrounding the district officer was actually disappearing, even within the
"power system."

What about the judicial system—the courts, the judge, the rule of law?
If the population lived virtually like animals, it was obvious that they could
hardly have any regard for the law.

The illiterate poor man does not understand the principles behind the British
Indian legal system or how, unaided, he can activate its processes to make them
conform usefully to the legal problems of his rural life. Every village is therefore infested with "touts" whose function is to manage this activation of the
legal system. If perjury is needed to further this activation, why should one object to perjury or treat it otherwise than just one of the various necessary methods by which the British system of law can be made use of. There is a general
feeling that perjury and forgery are merely interesting exercises in human in-
genuity which quite often supply a real public need. . . .

The tout has excellent working contacts with all the village toughs, petty
burglars and bad characters. He had to be approached by all who have or want
to have disputes with their neighbours and want them resolved somehow. . . .

The courts require evidence which may not be available in the right form
or at all. Touts will provide it and present it in usable form. To follow the correct legal procedure may be inconvenient or expensive. Touts provide means
by which it may be made more convenient or better serve the purpose of the

applicant. Discreet perversion may perhaps be needed but no question of moral principle arises in these operations.

No one is willing to give evidence in courts of law if he can possibly avoid it and then only when he can see clearly that his own interest will not be adversely affected. So when some dispute or accident takes place which might lead to action in the courts, touts at once come into action and in collaboration with them, the landlord's local agent (naib) and perhaps some of the local "educated" elite, decide what case, if any, should be put forward and what evidence shall be arranged.[23]

We should also note here that at the lower rungs of colonial government in the districts and subdivisions, the executive and judicial branches were not entirely separated. The collector and subdivisional officer were also magistrates. The district judges, it is true, belonged to the judicial branch, but they were often recruited from the same Indian Civil Service, and there was always a whiff of doubt surrounding their abilities, because they were thought to have been found unsuitable for the rough and tumble of the real job of administration and shunted aside into the more sedentary judicial service. There was no question that the requirements of administration enjoyed the greatest priority, greater even than the rule of law. Rabindra Chandra Dutt, beginning his career in the 1930s as a young ICS officer in east Bengal, found out that when the local police charged persons suspected of being "bad characters" without "an ostensible means of livelihood," and tried to prove their case in court with tutored witnesses and trumped-up evidence, the magistrate was expected to convict. "'No conviction, no promotion' was an adage, for instance, nowhere prescribed in writing, but nevertheless well understood by the magistracy. A Magistrate who displayed his independence, insisted on a stricter standard of proof, and consequently acquitted large numbers of accused in police cases, had to reconcile himself to stagnation in his career."[24] As a recent historian of British colonial law has summarized the issue: "The supposed autonomy of the judiciary was an illusion, perpetuated by colonial legitimating ideology, and the law was a department of the executive."[25]

We have quoted at such length from these accounts of the judicial system in the east Bengal districts in order to provide an indication of the attitudes and presumptions of the colonial establishment regarding plaintiffs, defendants, witnesses, counsels, and so on who appeared before them in the district courts. Without a knowledge of these attitudes and presumptions, it would be impossible for us to explain what happened within the judicial system after the person claiming to be Ramendra Narayan Roy filed his suit in the Dacca district court.

The district judge of Dacca at this time was Alan Henderson. In his reminiscences for the year 1931, Henderson writes as follows.

A suit which was to become famous as the Tichborne case of India was getting to the stage at which it would be ready for hearing. It was concerned with the very large *zamindari* known as the Bawal [*sic*] Raj. . . . The plaintiff was a *sadhu* who had been in Dacca for some time and suddenly proclaimed that he was the second Raj Kumar. The wife denied that he was her husband, but his case was taken up with the greatest enthusiasm by the Hindu public generally. . . . The Government Pleader came to see me and said that no Hindu judge sitting in Dacca would dare to decide the case against the plaintiff, and suggested that a young European officer should be appointed as a special subordinate judge to try it.[26]

Evidently the race and even, or so it seems, the religion of the judge could come into play in deciding the truth in a case that involved the beliefs and sentiments of the population. Even the much-vaunted objective and impersonal procedures of British rule of law were not seen to be immune from the corrupting influence of native prejudice and irrationality, particularly when the system was required to depend on the irresolute character of Indian judges. The native mind, it was feared, was far too susceptible to the power of superstition and miracle.

Chapter Seven

A FONDNESS FOR MIRACLES

T HERE WERE, of course, many racial and cultural stereotypes that contributed to the deep-rooted suspicion of colonial officials about the motives of their Indian subjects in matters of property and pecuniary gain. Stories of domestic feuds and harem intrigues were legion in every local history of "notable families" compiled by district officials during the nineteenth century. Added to this was the supposed proclivity of the Indian mind to be seduced by the most improbable and unnatural stories about miraculous events that could not be explained by rational knowledge. Even Indians who were otherwise perfectly well educated and reasonable were liable, in the same way as uneducated peasants, to fall for these absurd stories.

To take the case of scions of aristocratic families supposedly returning from the dead, there were several stories that were known in British India in the nineteenth century. Some of these cases even came up in court. Here is a sampling.[1]

THE SOI-DISANT RAJA PRATAPCHAND

Let us begin with the famous story of the alleged impostor Pratapchand.[2] This story relates to the Burdwan Raj, one of the largest and most prestigious zamindari families in British Bengal, at the time when the East India Company ruled over Bengal—that is to say, before India was directly brought under the administration of the British crown following the suppression of the great revolt of 1857–1858.

The zamindars of the Burdwan Raj were Punjabi Khatris, a trading caste. By the late sixteenth century, many Khatris had entered administrative service under the Mughals. The founder of the Burdwan Raj family, Abu Rai, was *kotwal* (chief of police) of Burdwan town in the middle of the seventeenth century. By the end of the century, the family had acquired a small zamindari. By the middle of the eighteenth century, at the time of the English conquest, Burdwan was one of the largest and most influential landed estates in Bengal.[3] Following the drastically new revenue systems introduced by the English in the late eighteenth century, when most of the great ancient zamindaris of Bengal fell apart, the Burdwan Raj managed to maintain its lands by devising an ingenious system of tenures and sub-tenures.[4]

In 1817, the zamindar was Raja Tejchandra, an old man fond of cards, dice, birds, charity, and young wives (he went on to marry as many as eight times). His lack of attention to matters of state was legendary. For a long time, the most powerful person in the zamindari had been his mother, Rani Bishnukumari, a remarkably strong-willed and independent woman who fought and won many legal and administrative skirmishes with the English authorities and whose name was romantically linked with her legal advisor Ramkanta Roy, grandfather of the famous social reformer Rammohan Roy. By 1817, however, Bishnukumari was long dead. The estate was managed by officials. In spite of his many marriages, Tejchandra had only one son, Pratapchandra, who was now a young man fond of wrestling, swimming, riding, and gymnastics. Pratap was said to have a penchant for getting into fights with British officers, to whom he often handed out a solid thrashing.

The trouble began with Pranchand Kapur, who was known in Burdwan as Paran Babu. He had come to Burdwan from Lahore and became prominent as the elder brother of Kamal Kumari, to whom Tejchandra took a fancy and made his seventh wife. Pranchand was clearly an ambitious man who worked his way into the maharaja's confidence. Soon, his influence over the affairs of the zamindari began to grow rapidly. Needless to say, Kumar Pratapchand did not get along well with Pran Kapur, who must have seemed to him a greedy and meddlesome interloper. But he was much too preoccupied with his sporting activities to care about the zamindari. He was a happy-go-lucky young man, riding about town on his fancy horses, surrounded all the time by friends and hangers-on.

Sometime in 1820, however, a sudden change seemed to come over the demeanor of the young kumar. He appeared withdrawn and depressed. He refused to join his friends on their usual pursuits. The English painter George Chinnery was then in Burdwan doing a portrait of Pratapchand. The kumar had been enthusiastic about the painting, but now he sat infrequently, and even then he seemed distracted. Sanjibchandra Chattopadhyay, in his classic telling of the story, makes only a cryptic reference to what was going on: "Until a few days before, every afternoon, he would stand on the terrace of the outer buildings and look through his binoculars towards Nilpur. Suddenly, out there, the gates would open and a buggy would streak out: he would stand and watch. Now he had stopped going to the terrace; he does not touch his binoculars."[5]

We know from other less inhibited sources what was really going on. Pratap had had a liaison with his stepmother Kamal Kumari. It would be later alleged that he had been trapped into this illicit relationship by Pranchand, who wanted to destroy the kumar's reputation with the maharaja.

But suddenly, Pratap was bitten by pangs of conscience and began to see himself as a sinner of the worst kind. After several days of depresssion, he came down with high fever. His favorite physician, Hakim Asgar Ali, began to treat him, but with little success. An English doctor called Coulter was called in. He prescribed leeches on the patient's forehead, which the patient firmly refused. Pratapchand's condition deteriorated. The following day, he asked to be taken to the banks of the Ganga. This was the ultimate step, because death beside the Ganga was supposed to ensure a smooth passage to heaven. He was taken to the riverside at Kalna, where a tent was put up and the whole area screened off to keep out the crowds. The old maharaja went with his dying son, but none of the other members of his family accompanied him, not even Pratap's two wives. That night, Pratapchand died. His body was cremated at about two o'clock. At three in the morning, Maharaja Tejchandra left for Burdwan.

About two or three days after his death, rumors began to float that Pratapchand had not died at all: he had run away. It is not known how Tejchandra reacted to these rumors. But afterward, for several years, he refused every suggestion to adopt a son, saying, "My Pratap will return. I know he will return." Rational people described this as the raving of an old man, devastated by the death of his only son.

After Pratap's exit from the scene in 1821, Pranchand's power over the zamindari became unchallenged. In 1826, he managed to persuade the maharaja to adopt a son. It is said that Tejchandra was ill at this time and Pranchand virtually put him under arrest to extort the consent. The boy adopted was given the name Mahtabchandra, but he was, not surprisingly, Pran Kapur's own son. Not satisfied by this, Pranchand also arranged in 1827 the marriage of his twelve-year-old daughter Basant Kumari to the sixty-two-year-old Maharaja. Pranchand's hold over the future of the Burdwan Raj was now total: the only two surviving ranis were his sister and daughter, and the sole male heir was his biological son. His plans were fully realized when Tejchandra died in 1832.

Two years after the old Maharaja's death, a sannyasi appeared in Burdwan. He walked into the grounds of the palace, looked around for a while and sat down near the gates. Someone passing by stopped and stared at him, and after a few moments shouted: "Chhota Maharaj! This is our Young Maharaj, he has come back!" Soon the clerks and officials were clamoring around the sadhu. Most seemed convinced that this was indeed Kumar Pratapchand. The news reached Pran Kapur. He sent armed guards to drive away the sadhu from the palace grounds. But wherever the sadhu went in town, the crowds would gather. The guards finally drove him out of town and across the Damodar River.

Now the sannyasi, who went by the name of Alok Shah, dropped his pretence. He announced that he was indeed Kumar Pratapchand. As a young man, he had led an undisciplined and dissolute life and had committed many grave offenses forbidden by religion. His spiritual preceptor had advised him to change his ways and undergo a penance. He had faked his illness and organized the death scene on the banks of the Ganga to escape from his sinful life in Burdwan. For fourteen years, he had purified himself through spiritual discipline and pilgrimage. Now he was ready to resume his responsibilities in the world.

The pretender proceeded to garner political support. He knew from the start that Pran Kapur was in total charge of the Burdwan zamindari and enjoyed the full confidence of the officials of the East India Company. He wrote letters and paid visits to the other zamindars of Bengal, especially those in Manbhum and Bankura districts in the neighborhood of Burdwan, presenting his case and asking them to intercede on his behalf. He found sympathetic listeners in the rajas of Panchet and Bishnupur, who had lost a lot of their lands in auction sales to the Burdwan Raj. It seems the "fake Pratap" disclosed his plans to raise a hundred thousand men to fight the English, promised to restore the Bishnupur Raj to its former glory, and assured the rajas that Maharaja Ranjit Singh of Punjab would soon send his troops to Bengal to help Pratap's cause. More importantly, wherever he went, he attracted followers. In January 1836, he went to Bankura, presumably on the advice of Raja Kshetra Mohan Singh of Bishnupur, to put his case before the English magistrate of the district. The English had had troubles with minor tribal uprisings in this area. This time, the Company officials were determined to nip any disturbance in the bud. The district magistrate led a surprise attack on the alleged Pratap's camp at night and arrested him along with a hundred followers. The magistrate later reported that the sannyasi Alok Shah had marched through Bankura town with 4,500 armed men brandishing their swords. He added that "the lower classes in these parts have been most thoroughly deceived by this man by reason of the countenance he has received from the respectable (so-called) families and . . . would to a man have risen" if the sadhu had not been arrested.[6] The sannyasi had, however, managed by this time to gather some support among influential Indians in Calcutta, who sent an English lawyer to Bankura to defend him. When he made inquiries about why his client had been arrested, the lawyer was told by the magistrate that these legal niceties were best reserved for Calcutta; in the districts, the officials did not need a warrant to arrest a troublemaker, nor was it customary to reveal the charges!

Eight months later, the alleged impostor was put on trial in Hugli on charges of "assembling a tumultuous body of armed men and setting at defiance the Constituted Authorities." Once again, an English lawyer was sent up from Calcutta, but the judge ruled that no lawyer could represent the accused. The sannyasi was sentenced to six months in prison.

When he was released from prison in Hugli in February 1837, there was a carnival in town. Numerous distinguished people came from Calcutta to meet the man they believed was Raja Pratapchand, wrongfully jailed by the English. The rajas of Panchet and Bishnupur came, and the wealthy men of Hugli organized bands and processions. He was invited to stay in the house of one of the wealthiest merchants of the town.

The pretender waited for a whole year before making his next move. He decided to go up to Burdwan by boat. By this time, he had been accepted by many as the maharaja of Burdwan and had gathered a large retinue. A flotilla of forty-eight boats sailed up the Bhagirathi River in April 1838. In a few days, the boats reached Kalna, where Pratap had either died or disappeared more than seventeen years before. For more than a week, the boats stayed offshore, while large crowds assembled on the banks. Kalna itself was tense, and both Ogilvie, the district magistrate of Burdwan, and Pran Kapur, the real power behind the Burdwan Raj, had their spies reporting to them on what was going on. One morning, the man calling himself Raja Pratapchand came ashore and rode through the town with some of his followers. He stopped from time to time, spoke to the people assembled on the streets, and after a couple of hours, returned to his pinnace on the river. An English missionary called Alexander, who was sending daily reports to Ogilvie, wrote: "Protap Chund has just gone on board his boat, after parading the whole length of Kalna in a Tonjohn [*tanjām*, a sedan or chair carried like a palanquin by bearers] with a drawn sword in his own hand, attended by upwards of a hundred swordsmen and double that number of stickmen. The concourse was altogether 6 to 8,000. He appeared to be intent on the Rajbarry. But your active Darogah prevented him. The aspect of things, I think, threatens an affray if he is not checked soon."[7] It so happened that a platoon of the Company's troops was then marching from Calcutta to Burdwan. Ogilvie, the district magistrate, sent word to the troops to march to Kalna. That night, Ogilvie himself arrived in Kalna, and a few hours later, the platoon under the command of Captain Little. In the early hours of the morning, the troops began to fire on the boats. There was no resistance from the alleged raja's followers. Most jumped into the river and were arrested, but several were killed. The former sadhu managed to escape to the opposite bank and from there to Santipur. There he was arrested the next day and sent to custody in Hugli. The sadhu's English lawyer, W. D. Shaw, who came to represent him, was also arrested. When he asked what his offense was, he was told, "Treason!"

It was Shaw's arrest, and Ogilvie's refusal to produce him in court, that turned the attention of the English press of Calcutta to this case, and in turn to the state of the rule of law in the districts. Shaw's friends brought charges in court against Ogilvie. The *Hurkaru* wrote that "The British inhabitants of Bengal will now look with intense anxiety to the course which Sir Edward Ryan may adopt on this occasion. On him will depend in great measure the degree of protection for life and property and freedom Europeans not in the service may expect. If it be once ruled that a company's servant can hold a writ of Habeas Corpus at arm's length, no man is safe."[8] "No man" here meant "no European man." No one writing in the English papers of Calcutta was much concerned about whether the alleged impostor Pratapchand was being given the legal protection due to him. In fact, in those early days of English rule, it was by no means obvious that men like the sannyasi had any legal rights at all. If the officials of the Company decided that he was trouble, then every procedure of English rule could be justifiably used to put him down.

Ogilvie actually was brought to trial in Calcutta for the shooting incident in Kalna. The supposedly fake Pratap, now a witness for Shaw, deposed against Ogilvie. Many soldiers of the Company's platoon present at Kalna that night deposed on whether they had heard Ogilvie give the orders to fire. Ogilvie himself claimed he had given no such orders, and that the troops had fired by mistake. The jury—all white, needless to say—returned a verdict of "not guilty." The judge, Sir J. P. Grant, dismissing the charges against Ogilvie, said: "You now stand quite free from all charges and imputations, and if there has been a little error of judgment, you are still most clearly proved to have had no participation whatever in the act itself, which resulted so fatally, and to have acted throughout by no feeling or motive other than becomes a gentleman."[9] To save the face of the "rule of law," Ogilvie was later prosecuted in Calcutta for having wrongfully arrested and confined the lawyer Shaw. Chief Justice Ryan sentenced him to a fine of Rs.2,000 and added: "The Court will not however cause you to suffer imprisonment; because, we must suppose, that you have been actuated by motives arising from erroneous information and a mistaken zeal, but also an ardent wish to preserve peace and good order in your district."[10] The rule of law, in other words, was conditional upon the preservation of peace and good order. Even judges of the highest courts in the Company-ruled province recognized this.

The trial of Pratapchand for "fraudulent personation" began at Hugli in September 1838. (This was the same district where, some thirty years later, William Herschel would introduce, for the first time in the world, the use of fingerprints for purposes of identification.)[11] Samuel, the district magistrate, had built up a case that the alleged raja was actually a well-known confidence trickster called Krishnalal. The magistrate marshaled many witnesses to testify to this theory. His methods can be judged from the following letter he wrote to the famous Dwarkanath Tagore of Calcutta, who had shown some sympathy for Pratap's cause. "I was disappointed by your non-arrival, as I think you could speak decidedly than any of the other witnesses to the man's non-identity, but it is not of much consequence. I have no objection to make a bargain with you. I will let you off altogether, if you will procure me the names of half a dozen good respectable witnesses from Boranagore, who know him as Kristolall. . . . Remember I must have the evidence from Boranagore within a week or so."[12] On the question of recognition, there were witnesses on both sides. Many who had known the young Kumar Pratapchand well claimed that the accused was not Pratap. On the other hand, there were others, including some Europeans—the educationist David Hare, for instance—who said that this was the same Pratap they had known. A "mute witness" was Pratapchand's portrait done by Chinnery. "The prosecution certainly seemed to have unwittingly subpoenaed in this portrait a rather hostile witness . . .long odds in favour of the Rajah and no takers," wrote the *Hurkaru*. It added: "Poraun Baboo is quite a dark horse however; and may prove a winner."[13]

The crucial evidence, however, was on the question of Pratap's death and cremation in 1821. There were fifteen witnesses—all long-time employees of the Burdwan Raj—who claimed they had personally witnessed the kumar's death and cremation in Kalna eighteen years before. The accused alleged that these witnesses were wholly under the control of Pran Kapur. In his testimony, he also claimed that he had faked his illness and death and that a simple exercise of hatha yoga had been enough to fool the doctors who had been attending him.

On the question of whether the accused was in fact a man called Krishnalal, the evidence was ambiguous. The judge decided that since the evidence on Pratap's death and cremation "appeared to be conclusive," and since the story of the accused having faked his death was incredible, there was only one conclusion possible.

> Combining all their testimonies, I cannot avoid the conclusion that the prisoner's identity is sufficiently established by a preponderance of evidence above whatever has been adduced to impeach it. . . . It is true that in the main point the Law-Officer rejects the evidence on the grounds that there are several discrepancies, which I admit, in the averments made by the witnesses who swear to the prisoner's identity with Kristo Lal. . . . [I]t appears to me the identity is established by tolerably good, or I may say, sufficient evidence, although it may not be so satisfactory and decisive as the testimony to the Rajah's death. But I have a remark to make on this subject. After the prosecutor had proved the death and cremation of Rajah Protap Chund, it was, I think, in no way incumbent on him to show who the prisoner really is. So long as the death, cremation, and non-identity remain, as I regard them firmly established, it would have been a matter of no moment to the case had he failed to prove that the prisoner is Kristo Lal.[14]

At this time, it was still customary in the Company's lawcourts for a qazi (Muslim judge) to rule in criminal cases. In this case, the qazi ruled that the evidence presented against the accused on the question of impersonation was not weightier than that presented in his favor. As long as the correct identity of the accused was not established, he could not be punished for impersonation. The judge had to refer this difference of opinion to the Nizamat court in Calcutta. The qazi of the Nizamat court gave his verdict that under Muhammadan law, it was a punishable offense to impersonate with the motive of personal gain. Since it was established that by using the name of Raja Pratapchand, the accused stood to gain, it was legitimate to punish him for this offense even if his true identity was not established. The Nizamat court sentenced "the prisoner Alok Shah, alias Protap Chaund, alias Kristo Lall" to a fine of Rs.1,000 or a jail term of six months.

It would appear that this was a light sentence, compared to the commotion that had been created and all the accusations of sedition and waging war on the government. But the claimant's fate was actually sealed by a subsequent order of the Nizamat court. The prisoner appealed against the judgment, seeking legal clarifications. Justice Braddon and Justice Tucker of the Nizamat court rejected this petition, remarking that as "they have judicially pronounced the petititoner not to be the Moharajah Protap Chund, they cannot, in future, receive any petitions or applications from him under that name and title."[15] Regardless of his true identity, therefore, the claimant could not take any further legal steps to establish himself as the maharaja of Burdwan.

The sadhu passed the rest of his life as a religious cult leader of sorts. He had a following in several parts of western Bengal, especially a large following of women. Those who knew him in his later life were struck by the range of his interests and knowledge. He practiced advanced yoga exercises and was conversant with the metaphysical subtleties of several schools of Indian philosophical thought. He acquired a command of English and made himself something of a specialist in European politics.[16] But he moved from village to village, and his religious practices with women followers were often looked upon with suspicion by the local people. He died in penury in Calcutta in 1852 or 1853.

Is it possible that he really was Raja Pratapchand, wrongfully denied his claim by a colonial government that was suspicious of miraculous returns and, most of all, anxious to deny all claims that might unsettle the established order? The popular opinion of the time seems to have been hugely in favor of the claimant. Ordinary people were convinced that he had been denied justice by the high-handedness of the English officials and the machinations of Paran Babu. Sanjibchandra Chattopadhyay, himself a functionary of the colonial judicial system, while writing the history of the *jāl* (false) Pratap affair in the 1880s, did not hide his scorn for the colonial rule of law or his sympathy for the supposedly fake Pratap. A more recent historian draws the following conclusion.

Is it possible that Pratap, confounded by Pran Kapur, confused by alcohol and a sexual encounter with his stepmother, and guided by religious advisers, actually did stage his own death and then returned, only to find that most of the people who knew him were afraid or unwilling to identify him? It may be that this is what happened. By this time, though, it mattered little who occupied the gadi. The zamindari bureaucracy, supported by the British judicial system, would gather the revenue while the raja would carry out his familiar role as enabler of ritual, embodying the beneficent but generally powerless and sometimes dissolute faces of authority. The Jal Pratap episode suggested that there was no shortage of people who welcomed the notion that "the English reign is over" but there were few people of influence whose sentiments were so unambivalent that they would risk much to end Company rule.[17]

Many Indians of influence, especially those whose interests were tied with the new structures of colonial power, clearly hesitated to take the side of a man whose claims the colonial officials were determined to oppose. Dwarkanath Tagore was the clearest example: disregarding his early sysmpathies for the claimant, he testified in court against him. It appears that he was persuaded to change his stand mainly because of the fear that his business interests, closely linked to those of the Company and private European traders, would be at risk.[18]

A hundred year later, when the case of the Bhawal sannyasi would come up in court, the political conditions would be vastly different. But then, as in the Pratapchand case, the determination of identity would once again become related to the political conditions in which the truth is produced.

A CASE FROM MIDNAPUR

Another case of a Bengal zamindar returning from the dead was reported in the mid-nineteenth century.[19] This case has certain astonishing resemblances with the Bhawal story.

The plaintiff in this case claimed to be Rudra Narayan Ray, zamindar of Ghar Basdebpur belonging to the Jalamutha estate in the Contai region of Midnapur district. He was the eldest son, born of the first wife, of his father, Raja Naranarayan Ray. The late raja had a second wife, Rani Krishnapriye, who had borne him two sons. On the death of Naranarayan Ray, following the family custom, the eldest son Rudra Narayan had been anointed as the new raja and a formal petition was made to the district collector to officially recognize him as the zamindar. The claim was contested by Rani Krishnapriye on behalf of her two minor sons. She alleged that Rudra Narayan was hostile toward her, and demanded separate recognition of the claims of her sons. Her appeal was rejected by the collector and later by the divisional commissioner.

The plaintiff's story was that in 1833, having failed to dislodge Rudra Narayan from the zamindari, the rani arranged to have him poisoned. The body of the dead raja was taken to the riverside for cremation. Suddenly, a huge thunderstorm broke, forcing the cremation party to run for cover, leaving the dead body unattended. However, two sannyasis happened to be in the vicinity. They noticed that the man on the pyre was not dead. They took him away, gave him medicines, and revived him. Rudra Narayan now realized what had happened and decided it was not safe for him to return to his family. He stayed on with the sannyasis and traveled with them to various places in northern India. In the meantime, the Company's administration recognized Rani Krishnapriye as holding the property in trust on behalf of her minor sons.

After two years, the plaintiff returned to Midnapur. The news went around that Raja Rudra Narayan had come back. Officials from the estate came to see him with gifts and *nazar*. Even as he was making his formal application to the district magistrate seeking recognition as the zamindar, Rani Krishnapriye had him arrested. He was released following the intervention of other sympathetic zamindars of the area.

The plaintiff's case was heard in the Sadar Amin's court in Midnapur. He produced forty-five witnesses to support his claims. The suit was dismissed. The plaintiff appealed to the Sadar Diwani court in Calcutta, where A. J. Mills, officiating judge, upheld the decision of the district court.

It was clearly not easy to come up with stories of miraculous returns from the dead and hope to upset the settled order as constructed by the new political rulers of the country.

THE LANDHAURA CASE

This is a case not from Bengal but from northern India in the late nineteenth century. Apart from being typical of such cases involving the determination of identity, it is also relevant because an article describing the case appeared in 1903 in the famous Bengali periodical *Prabāsī*, then published from Allahabad.[20]

Landhaura was a very large estate in the Saharanpur-Meerut region of what is now western Uttar Pradesh. It had been formed by a Gujar chief in the eighteenth century, and when the area came under British occupation in 1803, it was ruled by Raja Ramdayal Singh.[21] The Gujars were in general an economically depressed people with a reputation for violence and lawlessness, and were treated by the British as a "criminal tribe." But the

Landhaura rulers were regarded as the most important Gujar family of the region.

The *Prabāsī* article began by pointing out the "criminal" proclivities of the Gujars and suggested that Ramdayal Singh had acquired his large zamindari by various questionable means. This was confirmed, in the opinion of the people of the area, by the fact that none of his successors had been able to enjoy for long the fruits of the property he had accumulated, in spite of the fact that Raja Ramdayal had generously endowed many religious institutions and guesthouses along the pilgrimage route to Hardwar and Hrishikesh. After Ramdayal, all male children in the family had been short-lived, and the zamindari had been dominated by widows.

In 1850, Ramdayal's grandson Harbans Singh, like his father, died at the age of twenty, leaving behind his wife Kamal Kunwar and an infant son, Raghubir Singh. The estate came under the Court of Wards and after a few years, Raghubir was sent to the newly established Wards' Institute in Benaras to be educated. In 1866, at the age of eighteen, Raghubir returned to Landhaura, and the following year, took over as proprietor. All this time, it was his mother, Rani Kamal Kunwar, who had been running the family establishment with the assistance of her brother Sahib Singh. Now Raghubir married and took over some of the responsibilities. But only a year later, in 1868, Raghubir died of tuberculosis.

"It is well known," said the *Prabāsī* article, "that if someone in an aristocratic family dies at a young age after a brief illness, there are bound to be rumors of all sorts. This is exactly what happened here." It was alleged that Raghubir Singh may have been poisoned, and a few complaints even reached the district officials. The official gazetteer of Saharanpur noted many years later that Raghubir "died under somewhat suspicious circumstances."[22] A few months after Raghubir's death, a son was born to his wife Dharam Kunwar, but the child died the following year. The estate now came under the management of Rani Kamal Kunwar, Raghubir's mother, and Rani Dharam Kunwar, his wife. The elder rani persuaded Dharam Kunwar to adopt a son, but this child too died within a couple of years.

In 1874, there was a great sensation in the region when a fakir appeared near Roorkee and declared himself to be Raja Raghubir Singh. He claimed that he had been poisoned, but fortunately had managed to escape from the scene of his cremation. His declaration created enough commotion to induce the district magistrate to have the man arrested. But complaints were lodged on behalf of the fakir to the High Court in Allahabad, which appointed Joint Magistrate Markham to go to Saharanpur for a judicial investigation into the matter. Markham conducted an inquiry, recorded the evidence, and concluded that the man posing as a fakir was actually someone called Mahal Singh hailing from Hoshiarpur in Punjab. The alleged

Raghubir Singh was jailed for "cheating by false personation." The sentence was upheld on appeal to the higher court.

But the fakir was a persistent man and clearly had resourceful supporters as well. Even as he was serving out his prison term, he filed a civil suit in the Saharanpur court claiming proprietorship of the Landhaura estate. The officials were by now distinctly worried about the impact of the popular mood on the judicial proceedings. The High Court ordered that the case should be heard in the Meerut district court rather than in Saharanpur. The trial began in January 1877 in the court of subjudge Kashinath Biswas and lasted a year and a half. The defendants were the two ranis—Kamal Kunwar and Dharam Kunwar. Both sides brought in famous barristers and advocates from Allahabad; clearly the fakir's case had been taken up by wealthy patrons.

The plaintiff's story was that when he returned to Landhaura from school in Benaras, he discovered that his mother was involved in a scandalous and sinful relationship with her own brother. He confronted his mother with this and the atmosphere within the royal household became extremely bitter. Kamal Kunwar and Sahib Singh, who until then had been in total control over the affairs of the family, began to plot against Raghubir. When Raghubir fell ill, he was given medicines that caused him to lose consciousness. The plaintiff claimed that his body was taken to the riverside at Kankhal near Hardwar and, instead of being cremated, was simply thrown into the Ganga. This turned out to be a stroke of good fortune. Some distance downstream, a washerman saw the floating body and had it pulled ashore. He discovered that the man was still alive although his mouth was stuffed with cottonwool. The washerman took the assistance of a Brahmin *goswami* (priest) who immediately slit the drowned man's throat to help him breathe and then slowly nursed him back to health. For the next few weeks, Raghubir stayed with the goswami.

One day, Raghubir saw a horseman wearing the uniform of the Landhaura estate come to the goswami's house and speak to him in a low voice. Raghubir decided to make a clean breast of it. After the horseman had gone, he told his protector of his identity and of the plot laid against him. The Brahmin listened to his story and then proceeded to read his palm and draw up astrological charts. After a lot of calculations, he finally told him to wait for a while before returning to Landhaura. He said the next seven and a half years were not an auspicious time for the raja, since the stars were against him. It was best not to reveal his identity during that time. Raghubir listened to this advice and spent nearly eight years visiting religious places in Kashmir and Punjab. After the inauspicious period was over, he had returned to Landhaura to reclaim his social position and property.

Needless to say, there were witnesses on both sides who either claimed to recognize the plaintiff as Raja Raghubir or denied that there was any similarity between the two. Among Raghubir's relatives, two aunts of Rani Dharam Kunwar claimed to recognize him. Another important witness in his favor was Kedarnath Raychaudhuri, a former teacher of the Wards' Institute of Benaras. The plaintiff himself was subjected to a grueling cross-examination in which he provided much detailed information on the royal household of Landhaura and on his mother Rani Kamal Kunwar and his wife Rani Dharam Kunwar. He even claimed to know the exact size and position of moles and marks on various parts of Dharam Kunwar's body. On the defendants' side, there were many respectable witnesses who refused to accept the plaintiff as Raja Raghubir Singh. Both Kamal Kunwar and Dharam Kunwar took the stand, looked at the plaintiff, and declared that he was not Raghubir Singh.

In May 1878, Kashinath Biswas delivered his judgment, in which he declared the plaintiff's story as astonishing, imagined, and utterly incredible. He dismissed the suit. The judgment was appealed in the Allahabad High Court, but the judges upheld the decision of the Meerut court. The *Prabāsī* article ended with a cautiously noncommital remark: "There have been two attempts in India to capture an estate by fraud: once by the fake Pratapchand in Burdwan and again by the fake Raghubir Singh in Landhaura. It is to be hoped that in both cases, the truth prevailed."[23]

Miraculous Returns

Without pushing the case too strongly for a structural analysis of these stories of the miraculous return of dead princes, it may nevertheless be useful to list some of the elements that seem to recur in them. First, in several of the stories, there is the suggestion that the prince had led a morally degenerate life, or at least had committed some sinful act, before his supposed death and subsequent return. The period of disappearance then seems to signify a penance or a change of heart. In some of the stories, the noble family itself is described as degenerate, marked by intrigue, suspicious deaths, and loose sexual morals including incest. Second, the prince is invariably the victim of a conspiracy, and the favorite means of attempted murder is poisoning. Third, the conspiracy usually involves strong female figures, who are often malevolent or, in other cases, acting at the behest of male conspirators. Fourth, there is invariably a botched cremation that provides the opportunity for the prince to escape or to be rescued. In one sense, this is a necessary nodal point in the narrative, since it creates the crucial possibility for the supposed death and cremation to be explained as events that had not actually taken place. But it also shows the limits of the "miraculous" in these stories. Nowhere is it claimed that the physical identity of the claimant with the original is irrelevant; indeed, it is strenuously asserted that they are physically one and the same person and that the identity can be narratively explained and established. This is important in view of the fact that we are dealing with stories that were expected to pass the test of the law, even though they may have been constructed or appropriated by the popular imagination.

Fifth, the prince usually returns as a holy man. At one level, this signifies the moral strength of his claim—the fact that he has been purified of the sins and corruptions of the aristocratic lifestyle, and that he now has an aura of renunciation. Moreover, a period of living in disguise and in exile has been, ever since the *Rāmāyaṇa* and the *Mahābhārata*, a well known trope of ordeal in the lives of exemplary rulers. But at another level, it also helps explain the period of disappearance in the narrative. The life of the mendicant is a life outside society. It allows the missing prince to hide his real identity without getting into any new social entanglements. Finally, following his return, the colonial government opposes his claim to his identity. Invariably, then, it becomes a matter of finding the right legal methods to persuade the government to recognize his claim. Lurking below the surface of the legalese, however, is the popular dream, now clinging to the extraordinary figure of the raja as a fakir, to see justice and truth prevail over intrigue and oppression.

Speaking of miraculous returns, it is also necessary to mention a novel that was cited in the pamphlet wars over the Bhawal sannyasi as proof of the continuing fascination of the Bengali public with the *jāl* Pratap theme. Prabhatkumar Mukhopadhyay, a leading writer of fiction in Bengali and a barrister of the Calcutta High Court by profession, serialized a novel called *Ratna-dīp* [The Jeweled Lamp] in the journal *Mānasī* between 1912 and 1914, and published it as a book in 1915. It was to be his most successful novel, and would be produced on stage in 1940 and later on film in 1953. It was written three years after the second kumar's death—long before the sadhu's appearance and declaration in Jaidebpur—but Kedarnath Chakrabarti, writing in the *Rāyat* against the sadhu's claims, expressed regret that even a writer of Prabhat Babu's standing had been unable to resist the temptation of indulging in such colorful fantasies.[24] Prabhat Mukhopadhayay's plot builds on the possibilities of mystery and romance in a story about the return of a man presumed to be dead. It is a thoroughly secularized romance, with no hint of miraculous happenings or supernatural interventions.

The story is about a railway stationmaster posted in a small out-of-the-way place in Bihar who suddenly hears that his wife, whom he had left behind with his parents, had disappeared. He goes home to make inquiries and finds out that his wife, who was unhappy living with her in-laws, had probably left with another man. Crushed by the discovery, he returns to his station to find that the railway company was going to suspend and probably sack him for having left without leave. With nowhere to turn, he is contemplating desperate measures. That evening, a train makes an unscheduled stop at his station and the body of a dead sannyasi is unloaded. The sannyasi, a passenger on the train, had apparently had a seizure and died. The station master has to arrange for the body to be guarded at night until the police would arrive in the morning. Sitting alone at night in his office, he is attracted by a large sack that was the sannyasi's only possession. Unable to restrain his curiosity, he opens the sack and finds, among other things, a large amount of money in silver coins and a set of notebooks. For the next few hours, the station master is completely engrossed because the notebooks contain the extraordinary life story of the sannyasi.

He was the son of a well-known Bengal zamindar. Like many other young men of his class, he had led an intemperate life and had gotten into trouble. He had left home and announced his own death in order to lead the life of a sannyasi. But now he had read of the death of his father, and having atoned for his sins, felt that he should return to claim his rights and responsibilities. He had already informed the estate that he was still alive and had decided to return. It was on his way back home that the sannyasi had apparently died of a stroke.

The next morning, when the police arrived to take away the body for a postmortem examination, the stationmaster made his second astounding discovery. It was one of the railway porters who first commented that the sannyasi looked remarkably like their station master. Soon several others crowding around the body were making the same observation. That evening, the stationmaster made the decision of his life. No one except him knew of the sannyasi's true identity. The people on the estate were expecting their lost kumar to come back. Having read the sannyasi's memoirs, he now had a fair idea of the kumar's household, the main characters, the family history, and other details. The next morning, the stationmaster was not to be found. He was on his way to the estate in Nadia, where he would appear as the new zamindar.

Prabhatkumar's story does not claim any identity between the dead man and the claimant. On the contrary, it is set up as a story of impersonation, with direct allusions to the *jāl* Pratapchand affair as a historical precedent. On the surface, the tension builds within the narrative over the attempt by a brazenly villainous character to expose the impersonating hero. But the real conflict is an internal one—about the ethics of impersonation. This is brought out when the hero finds himself falling in love with his presumed wife who, needless to say, believes that the return of her dead husband is a gift from the gods. The impersonator realizes the enormity of his deceit and finally confesses. In the end, the rational and just order is restored: the former stationmaster is reunited with his real wife who, it turns out, had been duped by a procuress; the rani returns to widowhood because, after all, her "real" husband was "really" dead.[25]

The Tichborne Case

All of these cases were items in the background, as it were, of the Bhawal sannyasi affair as it moved forward into the courts of law. The Pratapchand case was mentioned several times in the popular press. The others may have been in the minds of those who suspected that it was easy for impostors and tricksters to sway a gullible Indian public by fabricating a story of conspiracy and miraculous escape. But the one case that was repeatedly referred to as the most relevant legal precedent was the Tichborne trial of the 1870s in England.[26] It is interesting to compare the Tichborne case with the Bhawal affair, because it shows that the "fondness for miracles" was not limited to the Indian peasant, nor was the perception of British justice unaffected by considerations of class and wealth. The legal conclusions in the two cases would, however, be completely different.

Roger Tichborne was the son of Lord Tichborne, baronet of the Tichborne estate in Hampshire. As a young man, he was interested in a military career in the East India Company, and joined the army in the hope of being sent overseas. When this did not come to pass, he quit the army and left for South America in 1852. Two years later, he was traveling from Rio de Janeiro to Jamaica when his boat was reported lost. Roger was presumed dead. Arthur Tichborne, a cousin, succeeded to the Tichborne estate.

In 1867, a man arrived in England from Australia and claimed to be Roger Tichborne. He had already corresponded with Lady Tichborne, Roger's mother, from Australia and she had helped him with funds for his trip to England. His story was that after the shipwreck, he had been rescued by a fishing vessel bound for Australia. He had arrived there and had taken up a job in a farm in New South Wales under the name of Thomas Castro. For twelve years, he had not had any contact with his family in England. Only recently had he come to know of the death of his father. It was then that he had decided to write to his mother, seeking her approval for his plan to return home.

Lady Tichborne immediately welcomed the claimant as her lost son. He settled down in the family home and was given an allowance for his personal expenses. His cousins and other relatives were, however, suspicious from the very beginning. Soon they mounted an inquiry into the antecedents of Thomas Castro and found evidence from Australia that he had also called himself Arthur Orton. The demeanor of the claimant seemed to suggest that he had had little education and was unfamiliar with the ways of the highborn. But Lady Tichborne would hear none of these quibbles; she was thoroughly content with having her son back.

In 1869, Lady Tichborne died. The claimant had now lost his benefactor and he had no independent means. He filed a suit claiming recognition as Roger Tichborne and title to the family property. Although the local gentry was thoroughly against him, he had considerable support among the tenants. His supporters devised a novel way of raising funds for the claimant: they issued bonds that would be redeemed when the claimant won his suit and acquired his property. Large sums were actually raised by this means. The civil trial began in 1870 in Westminster. It created quite a sensation, and the popular mood among the working classes all over the country was in favor of the claimant. The plaintiff was examined especially on his educational attainments and on certain physical marks of identification which Roger Tichborne was supposed to have had, including tattoo marks and "an extraordinary peculiarity in his private parts." The jury dismissed the plaintiff's case and recommended that he be committed for perjury. The judge agreed.

The claimant now decided to take his case to the country. He traveled from one town to another. Public meetings were organized for him, and the working classes in particular were everywhere favorable to his cause. They felt that he had been hounded by the gentry because of his social failings, which were the result of his having spent so many years as an honest working man in Australia. In spite of having been born into the aristocracy, Roger Tichborne was really one of them.

Criminal proceedings were started in 1873 against Arthur Orton alias Thomas Castro. The trial was held in Westminster Hall and became the longest criminal trial in British judicial history. Most of the funds for the defense were raised by public subscriptions. At the end of it, the Tichborne claimant was sentenced to fourteen years in prison for perjury. But the public denunciation of the trial and the sentence lasted for quite a while in the popular press.[27]

THE JUDGE

When Henderson, the district judge of Dacca, was urged that he arrange to appoint a European judge to try "the Tichborne case of India," he was put in a quandary. His reminiscences suggest that he shared the doubts of other British officials in Dhaka about the ability of an Indian judge not to be swayed by the public campaign. But the technical procedures of circumventing the normal order of assigning cases were exacting, and it was not at all certain that the High Court would agree. "[T]he theoretical and practical difficulties would have been insuperable, and I did not think it worthwhile to forward the suggestion to the High Court."[28]

In the normal course of things, then, the case came up for hearing in the court of Pannalal Basu, subordinate judge of Dacca district. In 1933, when the hearing opened, Basu was fifty-one years old. He had been in the judicial service since 1910, before which he had taught philosophy for a few years at Bangabasi College in Calcutta and at St. Stephen's College in Delhi. As a student, he had distinguished himself in philosophy and had obtained a first class M.A. degree in that subject from the University of Calcutta.[29] It is unlikely that he ever thought that his academic training in philosophy would one day have to be mobilized in deciding the most celebrated and, as it turned out, final case of his career as a judge.

Chapter Eight

THE IDENTITY PUZZLE

WHAT constitutes the identity of a person? This is the sort of question that philosophers ponder. Indeed, this specific question has produced a large philosophical literature in the Western world at least since the seventeenth century, following the landmark effort by René Descartes to posit a duality between mind and body and to locate the self in consciousness, that is, in the faculty of knowing that is independent of the knower's bodily organs, including the brain. Western philosophers have since puzzled over numerous intricacies concerning the precise role of physical and mental properties in the constitution of the identity of a person. Most of these debates, especially the ones in recent Anglo-American academic philosophy, completely bewilder us ordinary mortals. But for our present purposes, it is necessary to get a sense of what the theoretical issues are in determining the identity of a person. The matter is not merely academic. During the entire course of the Bhawal sannyasi case through the lawcourts of Dhaka, Calcutta, and London, references would often be made by lawyers, judges, and witnesses to philosophers and philosophical treatises that address the question of personal identity. We need not struggle to keep up with the endless hairsplitting that is the philosopher's normal professional practice; we will be concerned with what philosophers might have to tell us, not with what they say to one another.

The recent locus classicus on the subject is Derek Parfit's *Reasons and Persons*. A renewed debate has been carried out by Anglo-American academic philosophers in the last fifteen years over the issues raised by Parfit concerning personal identity.[1] We will look at some of these recent debates in order to emphasize what is at stake today in our retelling of the story of the Bhawal sannyasi. But of course these were not philosophical discussions that Pannalal Basu, subjudge of the Dacca district court, could have known about in 1933. He would have known, from his academic training, the tradition of British philosophy from John Locke and David Hume to early twentieth-century philosophers such as J.M.E. McTaggart. We should, therefore, also take a look at this tradition.

WHAT IS IDENTITY?

What are the issues involved in determining the identity of a person? Let us begin with some preliminary distinctions.

When two things are identical, they must obey what is called Leibniz's law. This law says that if x is identical to y, then whatever is true of x must be true of y, and vice versa. Referring to our case, if the second kumar and the Bhawal sannyasi are identical, that is, if they are the same person, then if the second kumar was five feet five inches tall, the Bhawal sannyasi must also be five feet five inches tall.

This sort of identity is called numerical identity, where the identity of x and y means that they are one and the same thing. There can, however, be another kind of identity, where two things may be exactly similar without being one and the same thing. If I pick out two new tennis balls from a box, one ball could have exactly the same properties as the other, but they would still be different balls. This sort of identity is called qualitative identity, where x and y are exactly similar because they belong to the same type but they are not numerically identical. If the second kumar had an identical twin, for instance, who disappeared for a few years and returned as the Bhawal sannyasi, then despite having exactly the same features, the second kumar and the Bhawal sannyasi would still not be the same person. In the matter of the social and legal identity of a person what we usually look for is numerical identity and not mere qualitative identity.

In our examples above, we have, however, skirted around the crucial question of change over time. To introduce this dimension into the problem, we must make the further distinction between synchronic identity and diachronic identity. If x and y are synchronically identical, then they are numerically identical, that is, they are one and the same thing at a given time t. Thus, James Hamilton Lindsay and the collector of Dacca are synchronically identical in the year 1921. If x and y are diachronically identical, then the relation of numerical identity must hold between them over time. That is to say, they would be the same temporally enduring thing observed at different points of time. Thus, the boy Ramendra who played pranks with his teacher Wharton and the young man Ramendra who accompanied Lord Kitchener on his hunt were one and the same person at different stages of life.

We can now see where the difficulties would crop up in deciding on numerical identity over time. In a world where things change with time, how can we decide that in spite of observable qualitative changes, a thing is still the same? The problem has been posed for Western philosophers from the time of the Greeks. There is the famous example of the ship of Theseus, whereby different parts of a ship—made of wood in those days—are gradually repaired and replaced over time until one day every part has been replaced; nevertheless, it still remains the same ship. If we think of the human body, every cell in it is replaced over time, so that it may be true to say that no human adult has the same physical body with which he or she was born. But it does not follow that I-as-a-child and I-as-an-adult are not the same person. How can we find the proper criteria for determining the diachronic identity of persons? Clearly, a lot will depend on how we choose to define the "person-ness" of persons.

Derek Parfit has listed the questions that have to be asked about the nature of persons and of personal identity over time.[2] These are: First, what is the nature of a person? Second, what is it that makes a person at two different times one and the same person? Third, what is necessarily involved in the continued existence of each person over time? Parfit also introduces a moral or value aspect to the discussion by adding a fourth question: What is in fact involved in the continued existence of each person over time? The answer to the third question would be only part of the answer to the fourth, since what is *necessarily* involved in the continued existence of a person need not exhaust what is *in fact* involved in it. Thus being happy, for instance, is not necessarily involved in our survival, but it may well be part of what is in fact involved. The introduction of the moral or value dimension also opens up the distinction between the objective aspects of identity, those that a person may possess because of his or her biological and social location, and the subjective aspects, those that he or she may value or identify with. This dimension is important for our discussion, since we will be deeply concerned with the social and legal issues of identity.

PHYSICAL CRITERIA OF PERSONAL IDENTITY

There are two sorts of criteria that are talked of in deciding questions about the diachronic identity of persons: physical criteria and psychological criteria.

The simplest physical criterion is drawn from static objects that continue to exist over time. Thus, the Jaidebpur Rajbari is the same house where the second kumar once lived, even though today it accommodates a variety of government offices of the Gazipur district of Bangladesh. The criterion here is the physical continuity of an object in space and time. In the case of some objects, there can be physical continuity despite considerable physical changes. A butterfly, for instance, can be said to have a continued physical existence from an egg to a caterpillar to a chrysalis to a butterfly: in this case, the distinct physical forms are seen as stages in the continuous life of a single organism.

It is important to clarify what is involved in applying Leibniz's law to physical criteria of diachronic identity. While researching the story of the Bhawal sannyasi, I recently read old issues of the weekly *Ḍhākā prakāś* preserved in the library of the University of Dhaka. The journal now exists in bound annual volumes, the newsprint is yellow, many pages are torn, and the margins are frayed. I had to turn the pages with great caution because the paper almost crumbled to dust under my fingers. Six or seven decades ago, the same issues of the journal must have had crisp white pages, and they were not bound in annual volumes. How can I say that what I was reading was an issue of *Ḍhākā prakāś* from 1934? Surely, applying Leibniz's law, it is not correct to say that everything that was true of the issue of the journal in 1934 is true of it in 1999. If we think it through, however, we will realize that this would be a misapplication of Leibniz's law. If x has the property of being white and crisp at time t_1 and y is yellow and crumbling at time t_2, then it could still be the case that x is identical to y. This is because Leibniz's law only requires that for x and y to be identical, if x is white and crisp at t_1, then y must also be white and crisp at t_1, not at t_2. In other words, the requirement here is that of synchronic identity. To apply it to diachronic identity, we must decide whether it is possible for the crisp white pages of x in 1934 to become yellow and crumbling in 1999, that is, at a later stage in the life of the same x. If I am satisfied that there is physical continuity of the copy of *Ḍhākā prakāś* over space and time from the hands of an avid reader of the hearings of the Bhawal sannyasi case in 1934 to the almirah of the old periodicals collection of the University of Dhaka library in 1999, then I accept that what I have read in 1999 is diachronically identical to the journal that was published in 1934.

Can the same thing be said of the copy I have of a pamphlet propagating the sannyasi's story? The pamphlet was printed at Gendaria Press in Dhaka in 1921. I first read it in 1995 in a bound volume of "vernacular tracts" in the Oriental and India Office Collections of the British Library in London. The copy now lying in front of me is a print taken from a microfilm of the original pamphlet. I am reasonably certain that the copy that I saw in London in 1995 was physically continuous with what was printed in Dhaka in 1921. In any case, the copy was in much better shape than the volumes of *Ḍhākā prakāś* at the university library in Dhaka, undoubtedly because the number of people who have handled such material in London in the past six or seven decades is only a small fraction of the number in Dhaka. But the print taken from the microfilm is clearly not physically continuous with the original pamphlet. No question of numerical identity can arise here, even though we might be able to argue for some measure of qualitative identity.

Can there be diachronic identity if there are gaps in the physical continuity of an object? I still possess a radio that works on tubes, not transistors. We have had it in the house for about fifty years. It has had to be repaired a few times, and I distinctly remember having seen it once at the mechanic's shop completely taken apart; it must have been in that state for at least a week. Does the radio have a history of continued physical existence over the last fifty years? Some philosophers would say, no, since it was not a radio at every point in its spatio-temporal path. Others would say, yes, since even during the week when the radio was taken apart, each of its separate parts continued to have uninterrupted physical existence. Still others would say, it doesn't matter if the radio was taken apart and put back together, because even when it was disassembled, it continued to exist as a radio.

Applied to persons, the physical criterion of identity is physical continuity over time of the same body and brain (brain here being taken as a physical entity). "Same" body and brain cannot, of course, mean exact similarity at two points of time, for that would be to ignore normal and natural processes of change. What is necessary is not the continued existence of the whole body, or even of the whole brain. It is possible to think of a person continuing to exist even after losing several parts of his or her body. What is minimally required is the survival of enough of the brain to be the brain of a living person. This is what physical survival *necessarily* involves; the continued existence of other parts of the body is strictly not necessary. The physical criterion lays down, then, that x at t_1 is the same person as y at t_2 if and only if enough of x's brain survives at t_2, and has the capacity to support a full human consciousness, and is now y's brain; and if no other person z exists at t_2 who also has enough of x's brain to support a full human consciousness.[3]

We should emphasize that philosophers who accept the physical criterion of personal identity actually mean by it the continued existence of the brain as a physical entity. They do not regard other parts of the human body as equally significant, because those could change or even cease to exist without necessarily disturbing the continued existence of the person. In the physical sense, then, the essential attribute of personhood lies in the brain.

It is also necessary for us to note that the way in which the physical criterion has been defined in the philosophical discussion makes it very difficult to think of external checks to verify whether or not the criterion is being met in a particular case. This is because the entire debate over personal identity has taken place around the question of "the self." As we will see below, the typical form of posing the problem has been: "If my brain is transported or transformed in such and such a way, then what would be the implication for me as a person?" This does not, however, give us a practical criterion for deciding a problem such as that of the Bhawal sannyasi. How could anyone verify if a substantial part of the second kumar's brain survived in the sannyasi? It is not difficult to see why, when the question of physical resemblance between the kumar and the sannyasi came up in court, it was not the physical brain but various physical features and marks on the body that were offered as criteria. Each of these was hotly debated, because the question could always be asked as to whether a particular physical feature might not change over time without destroying the continued physical existence of the person. In a fundamental sense, then, the philosophers are right: apart from the survival of enough of the brain, the continuity or otherwise of other parts of the body does not give us a necessary physical criterion of personal identity. Nevertheless, it is not hard to see why the common sense of ordinary people would seek such resemblances in order to decide whether or not the sannyasi was really the second kumar.

Psychological Criteria of Personal Identity

We have observed before that a key question that comes up in the application of Leibniz's law to the diachronic identity of persons, that is, their identity over time, is what we take to be the essential nature of persons. In other words, we have to provide some answer to the question, "What constitutes the person-ness of persons?" A large number of answers that have been suggested by philosophers concerns the mental or psychological properties of human beings. Clearly, there is a strong tendency here to seek the essence of the human person in his or her rational, moral, and affective faculties, which are seen as being integral parts of his or her mental or psychological attributes.

The classic formulation of the mental or psychological criterion of personal identity in modern Western philosophy was made by John Locke in his *Essay Concerning Human Understanding* (1690).

> [T]o find wherein personal identity consists, we must consider what person stands for; which, I think, is a thinking intelligent being, that has reason and reflection, and can consider itself as itself, the same thinking thing in different times and places; which it does only by that consciousness which is inseparable from thinking, and, as it seems to me, essential to it. . . . For since consciousness always accompanies thinking, and it is that which makes every one to be what he calls self, and thereby distinguishes himself from all other thinking things; in this alone consists personal identity, i.e. the sameness of a rational being; and as far as this consciousness can be extended backwards to any past action or thought, so far reaches the identity of that person; it is the same self now it was then; and it is by the same self with this present one that now reflects on it, that that action was done.[4]

Locke's criterion of personal identity is, therefore, the possession of an uninterrupted flow of self-conscious awareness, that is to say, memory. But Locke makes a distinction here between "person," which refers to the bearer of a rational and reflective consciousness, and "man," which is a biological entity. The criterion for determining the identity of a person is not necessarily the same as that for determining the identity of a man. He illustrates this with one of his most-quoted examples, which is in some ways a precursor to the "thought experiments" of later philosophers writing on the subject.

> [S]hould the soul of a prince, carrying with it the consciousness of the prince's past life, enter and inform the body of a cobbler, as soon as deserted by his own soul, every one sees he would be the same person with the prince, accountable

only for the prince's actions; but who would say it was the same man? . . . I know that, in the ordinary way of speaking, the same person, and the same man, stand for one and the same thing. . . . But yet when we will inquire what makes the same spirit, man, or person, we must fix the ideas of spirit, man, or person in our minds; and having resolved with ourselves what we mean by them, it will not be hard to determine in either of them, or the like, when it is the same, and when not.[5]

It should be clarified that in locating the essence of personal identity in the uninterrupted existence of self-conscious awareness, Locke is not endorsing the Cartesian idea that persons are essentially disembodied souls. In fact, Locke specifically contradicts the Cartesian formulation, without explicitly denying—perhaps to ensure the safety of his own bodily life—the immortality of souls. Using another oft-quoted example, he says that if the mayor of Queensborough happens to have what was once the soul of Socrates, but has no memory of being Socrates and of having his experiences, then, soul or no soul, the mayor is not the same person as Socrates. This is because we have no way of attaining any knowledge of the soul; it is beyond our consciousness and cannot constitute the essence of rational and thinking persons. Unlike Descartes, therefore, Locke is not claiming that human consciousness or memory resides in some indestructible thinking substance that makes up the soul. Whereas Descartes would say that memory could only discover the identity of a person that is constituted by the soul, Locke is saying that consciousness or memory is constitutive of personal identity. If there is no memory, there is no identity.

Locke's theory gives us a simple and verifiable criterion to decide questions of identity. It is easy to show that, in this simple form, it is not a very reliable criterion, however. What does it mean to say that for x at t_1 to be the same person as y at t_2, y must have the memory of having the experiences of x at t_1? Surely, if I am asked to remember my experiences on a certain date some twenty-five years ago, it is very likely that I will not remember a single thing. Even if I were asked about something more recent, such as which time of the day I wrote a particular paragraph a few pages earlier in this book, I might still be unable to remember. By Locke's criterion, I would have to concede that I am no longer the same person that I was twenty-five years ago, or even last week!

When we say, following Locke, that to be the same person one must have the memory of one's past experiences, we cannot mean all of one's past experiences. That would be to insist that one cannot forget anything. The difficulty is to decide how much can be forgotten without losing one's identity. If the Bhawal sannyasi claimed that because of the passage of years he had forgotten everything of the experiences of his life as the second kumar, would that be credible? Supposing we were to relax the requirement and say that he ought to remember at least some of those experiences, how much would be enough to establish identity? If his memory of the particular events that he did remember were to be probed by cross-examination, and if he claimed that his memory was confused or uncertain, would that destroy the case for identity?

The trouble is that Locke's criterion is not supple enough to tackle the complexity of the psychological processes of memory. Recent philosophers have attempted to improve on Locke's effort. Parfit has proposed a concept of psychological connectedness that is more complex than the simple notion of the memory of past experience. I may be able to remember today some of the experiences that I had twenty-five years ago. These would be direct memory connections that would meet Locke's criterion. But even if I did not have any such direct memories, there could still be continuity of memory over these twenty-five years. This would be the case if there was an overlapping chain of direct memory connections. Thus, from one day to the next, most people remember some of their experiences on the previous day. Between a time-point t_1 and, let us say, a time-point t_{100}, a person at t_{100} may forget everything that he experienced at t_1. But he would have remembered many of those experiences of t_1 at t_2 (let us say, the following day); many of his experiences of t_2, he would have remembered at t_3; and so on to t_{100}. So there could be an overlapping chain of memories from t_1 to t_{100}. Between one time-point and the next, say one day and the next, there could be many direct connections or very few. Parfit suggests that if at least half the number of direct connections that hold over every day in the lives of most actual persons are preserved until at least the next day, there is strong connectedness. He then defines psychological continuity as the holding of overlapping chains of strong connectedness. The psychological criterion of personal identity can then be stated as follows: x at t_1 is the same person as y at t_2 if and only if x is psychologically continuous with y, and with no other person z at t_2.

It is interesting to note that in Parfit's scheme, strong connectedness itself cannot be the criterion of identity. The person y today may be strongly connected to herself yesterday, when she was strongly connected to herself the day before, and so on. But this does not mean that she is strongly connected to herself twenty-five years ago. Does this mean that y today is a different person from y twenty-five years ago? To draw that conclusion would be to repeat the error involved in Locke's simple criterion. Parfit avoids the error by making psychological continuity rather than connectedness the criterion of personal identity.

How is psychological continuity maintained? Taken in the narrow sense, psychological continuity can only have a normal cause. Thus, if I seem to remember having an experience only after it was suggested to me that I had that experience, then I did not actually remember it in the normal way. That is to say, my apparent memory is not causally dependent on my past experience but rather on the suggestion that I had that experience. In the narrow interpretation, there is no psychological continuity here. The same goes for changes in character. If the Bhawal sannyasi displays a radically different character from the second kumar, then it would have to be shown that this was the normal consequence of having led a radically different life for twelve years; otherwise, there would be no psychological continuity. Even if someone were to display extraordinary lapses of memory about one's past experiences, this could be because of the normal consequences of a condition such as amnesia. In that case, even the absence of memory may be regarded as not threatening psychological continuity, and hence personal identity, as maintained by normal causes. As we will see later, amnesia was a major point at issue in the Bhawal sannyasi case.

If we accept the narrow interpretation of psychological continuity, the psychological criterion coincides in most cases with the physical criterion. The normal causes of psychological continuity essentially imply the continued physical existence of the brain. Even when a person is suffering from amnesia, it is a consequence of the malfunctioning, caused by injury or disease (neurosis) or decay, of his brain. We could say then that a test of psychological continuity might serve just as well as an indicator of physical continuity. Questions of memory and character would figure very prominently in the hearings and arguments of the Bhawal case.

In the wider interpretations of psychological continuity, not only normal causes but any reliable cause, or indeed any cause, is considered acceptable for maintaining psychological continuity, and hence for establishing personal identity. The examples philosophers use to pose the choice between the narrow and the wide interpretations usually involve "thought experiments" where drastic confusions arise in matching brains with bodies. We will look at some of these cases presently. But the implication of the choice is that in the wider interpretation, even if psychological continuity lacks a normal cause, any other cause, so long as it can be established as a cause, would be considered just as good. Thus, if the Bhawal sannyasi's loss of memory of large parts of his alleged life as the second kumar does not appear to have a normal cause, then any other cause, such as a shock with unknown consequences or the mysterious medicines given to him by the Naga sadhus who rescued him, would be considered acceptable for establishing psychological continuity. Clearly, it would make a lot of difference which interpretation of the psychological criterion is accepted. The choice, as we will now see, hinges on certain ethical or value considerations surrounding the issue of personal identity.

Does Identity Matter?

To get a flavor of how the moral-philosophical problems of identity are posed and analyzed, let us consider a famous "thought experiment" described by

Bernard Williams.[6] Suppose two persons A and B undergo an experiment in which their entire memories, character traits, and other mental characteristics are recorded and then switched. All of the mental properties of A's brain are now realized in B's brain, and vice versa. What was once A's body now has a brain with B's memories and characteristics; what was once B's body now has a brain with A's memories and characteristics. Let us call the first the A-body person and the second the B-body person. The question is: who should we consider the same temporally continuous person with A— the A-body person or the B-body person?

To analyze the question, Williams adds a twist to the experiment. Let us also suppose, he says, that before the operation, A and B are told that one of the postoperation persons would be paid a large sum of money and the other tortured, and that A and B could choose which person they would like to be rewarded and which tortured. It is plausible to argue that since A and B know that their minds and bodies will be swapped, A would choose that the B-body person be rewarded and the A-body person tortured, and B would choose the opposite. Now suppose the experimenter goes ahead with the operations and then rewards the A-body person and tortures the B-body person. The B-body person, now having the memories of A, will then justifiably complain that his choice was not respected, while the A-body person, having the memories of B, will thank the experimenter for having acted according to his wishes. We can then conclude that the B-body person is the same person as A and the A-body person the same person as B.

Now consider another thought experiment: I am captured by a mad neuroscientist and told that my body would be subjected to torture, but before that my mind would be erased of all my memories and character traits and replaced by the memories and traits of another person. How would I feel? Would I not be afraid of being tortured? But why should I, since the person who will be tortured would have somebody else's mind? That would probably actually increase my anxiety, because not only would I be afraid of being tortured but would also worry about the strange things that will be done to my mind. Most crucially, during all of these traumatic moments before the operation, I would remain convinced that everything that would happen both during and after the operation would happen to *me*.

This produces an antinomy. The second experiment is actually only an alternative description of the first experiment, the difference being that instead of a neutral third-person account, it is narrated in the first person. But whereas the first experiment convinced us that the preoperation A and the postoperation A-body person were different persons, the second experiment seems to persuade us that, operation or no operation, it is still me that will undergo the trauma of torture.

A great deal has been written about the dilemma posed by Williams, and many suggestions have been made to resolve it.[7] We need not spend time here going into the mind-boggling complexities of this literature, which seems to reserve a special place for the mad neuroscientist and his endless attempts to duplicate, split, or otherwise manipulate brains and swap their locations in different bodies. For our purposes, it will be sufficient to note, first, that on the moral implications of the question of personal identity, there are two broad approaches called the reductionist and the nonreductionist; and second, that cutting through that debate, there is Derek Parfit's radical suggestion that what really matters is *not* personal identity but psychological continuity with *any* kind of cause.

The reductionists basically uphold some version of the physical and/or psychological criteria we have described before. They maintain, in other words, that personal identity involves the continued physical existence of enough of the brain and/or psychological continuity with the right kind of cause. Parfit, as we have already noted, prefers to modify this position by holding that any cause is sufficient. In contrast, nonreductionists do not accept that personal identity can be reduced to certain facts about physical or psychological continuity. They insist that the identity of a person must involve a further fact. This could be a separate entity from his or her brain and body, such as a Cartesian spiritual substance, for instance, or a separate physical entity not yet recognized by science, or at the very least, something beyond the sum total of elements comprising the body and brain of the person.

Parfit attempts to show that no matter how carefully we define physical and psychological continuity, it is always possible to imagine situations in which personal identity will be indeterminate and undecidable according to the reductionist criteria. He concludes from this that what matters is not personal identity but continuity of a person in some form, that is, the person's survival. Thus, if there was some technology that could record the exact state of all of the cells of my body and brain and reproduce those cells in an exact duplicate of me, that duplicate would be exactly like me both physically and psychologically, with an exactly similar body and with the same memories and personality traits. Now, if it was suggested to me that the original "I" be destroyed and the duplicate survive, would I mind? Parfit argues that nothing would be lost if that was to happen. Whether or not *I* survive in my original body, my physical and psychological continuity would be maintained just as well in my duplicate.

Though avidly discussed, Parfit's suggestion has not been widely approved. To many, it has seemed too radical a proposal that goes against the grain of conventional assumptions. Once again, if we shift the perspective from a first-person account to a third-person account, the moral choices appear to become very different. Peter Unger asks us to imagine how he would feel if it was suggested to him that his wife Susan be replaced by an exact duplicate. Unger says that like most other people, he would refuse to accept any such proposal. "Evidently, I do not just care about the very many highly specific qualities my wife has. . . . Quite beyond any of that, I care about the one particular person who is my wife; I care about Susan and, as well, I care about the continuance of my particular relationship with her."[8] Unger, therefore, is insisting that what matters in survival is not just physical and psychological continuity in some manner or form but the identity of the particular individual that we value and identify with. It is not true that in our actual and ordinary preferences, we are indifferent between having a relationship with a particular person and his or her exact duplicate.

We have now come to a crucial point in our discussion of the moral and philosophical issues surrounding the Bhawal sannyasi case. The dominant tendency in the legal approach to the question of identity, as we have already noted, is the narrow one that insists on physical and psychological continuity based on normal causes that can be demonstrated and verified by scientific methods. Could there also be a Parfit-like view that places less emphasis on the demonstration of identity and treats more seriously the question of survival? Recall that the question was actually posed after the decision of the Calcutta High Court on the appeal in the defamation suit. Suren Mukherjee, a prominent lawyer in the sannyasi's camp, had declared that it did not matter if the court decided that the sannyasi's story had not been borne out by sufficient scientific evidence. Most of the kumar's relatives and all of the prominent people as well as the peasants of Bhawal had accepted the sannyasi as the second kumar. If we put this in the philosophical terminology we have introduced in this chapter, we could say that the sannyasi had succeeded to most of the social relationships of the second kumar, and that the physical and psychological continuity of the kumar had been accomplished, whatever the cause. In other words, the kumar had survived in the sannyasi.

There could, of course, also be an Unger-type objection to this claim, an objection that would come quite close to a nonreductionist argument. With a slight twist of the philosophical imagination, we could think of Bibhabati, the second rani, as putting forward exactly this objection. What did it matter to her if all of Bhawal thought that the second kumar had survived in the sannyasi? She only valued the particular relationship that she had accepted with the particular person who was her husband. An exact duplicate, to continue with our philosophical usage, was simply not good enough.

What about the government? This question demands a more complicated answer. The British officials, both in the administration and in the judiciary, would certainly have insisted on a clear demonstration of physical and psychological continuity under normal causes verified by scientific methods. They would have been appalled by the suggestion that the survival of the person by "any" cause was sufficient. That, to them, would have meant granting a token of approval to the native fondness for miracles. But an important change was taking place in the very composition of the administration and the judiciary because of the rapid induction of Indian officers and judges in the 1920s and 1930s. These were men who were not only well trained in British administrative and legal doctrines and practices but also deeply imbued with the ideas of Western modernity that they had encountered in their school and university education. But they had also grown up with the rising tide of nationalism. Would that have any effect on what they would regard as the right criteria and the acceptable evidence of identity? Let us make a note of this question; we will answer it later.

Before we move on, we should also note that in the Anglo-American philosophical literature on personal identity, Parfit is regarded as a radical. This is because by undermining the importance given to the issue of identity, he launches into a trenchant critique of the utilitarian assumptions of individual self-interest on which most of English-language moral philosophy rests. To the charge that his claim is counterintuitive and contrary to conventional usage, Parfit would reply that that is because conventional usage is based on false and irrational beliefs. "The truth is very different from what we are inclined to believe," he declares.[9] The attempt to assert a nonreductionist position against Parfit, such as that by Unger, thus becomes an avowedly conservative project, namely, to describe and defend the actual values and beliefs of ordinary people regarding identity and survival.

These "actual" values and beliefs of "ordinary" people are, of course, deeply bound to particular cultural conditions. This is something that is entirely unrecognized in the Anglo-American philosophical literature, tied as it is to a universalist style of argumentation, even when it seeks to do a phenomenology of everyday life. When it is asserted that ordinary intuition places an irreducible value on personal identity and on particular relationships with particular persons (in the overwhelming number of cases, the examples given are those of relations within the immediate nuclear family), it is easily forgotten that in other cultures, everyday common sense might well attribute very different values to those identities and relationships. It is not a coincidence that Parfit's radically antiutilitarian ideas are explicitly influenced by Buddhist doctrines of selfhood, from which, however, he draws entirely universalist conclusions.

> I believe that my claims apply to all people, at all times. It would be disturbing to discover that they are merely part of one line of thought, in the culture of Modern Europe and America.
>
> Fortunately, this is not true. I claim that, when we ask what persons are, and how they continue to exist, the fundamental question is a choice between two views. On one view, we are separately existing entities, distinct from our brain and bodies and our experiences, and entities whose existence must be all-or-nothing. The other view is the Reductionist View. And I claim that, of these,

the second view is true. . . . *Buddha would have agreed.* The Reductionist View
is not merely part of one cultural tradition. It may be, as I have claimed, the
true view about all people at all times.[10]

It is clear that even radicals within the Anglo-American tradition of philosophy would steadfastly resist the idea of a cultural history of truth.

Narrative Identity: Sameness and Selfhood

The French philosopher Paul Ricoeur, who comes from the European phenomenological and hermeneutic tradition, has recently attempted to transcend the impasse posed by the reductionist and nonreductionist approaches to the question of identity by introducing the concept of narrative
identity.[11] Ricoeur focuses on two very different senses of the term identity. The first is identity as sameness, which is derived from the Latin *idem*.
Both numerical and qualitative identity refer to this sense of the term. In
fact, the entire reductionist approach in all its variants may be seen as a way
to determine personal identity in the sense of sameness. But there is another sense in which the word identity is used in the European languages.
This is the sense of selfhood, deriving from the Latin *ipse*. The puzzles and
paradoxes posed in the Anglo-American analytical literature from the time
of Locke and Hume are, says Ricoeur, the result of conflating one sense of
identity with the other. When nonreductionists talk of identity that cannot
be reduced to the body and brain, they mean selfhood in a sense that is not
just sameness. The two senses must be distinguished if one wishes to avoid
the confusing antinomies that come up so frequently in the literature. Yet,
although sameness and selfhood must be distinguished, they clearly occur
in tandem, closely connected to each other. How are we to distinguish them
and still hold on to the idea that they are two senses of the notion of personal identity?

Ricoeur suggests that sameness and selfhood come together in narrative.
The criteria of sameness over time have to be flexible enough, as we have
seen, to accommodate changes that do not destroy the essential physical or
psychological continuity of a person. This means that there is operating
here an idea of structure, something that endures over time, while changes
are registered and explained in terms of events. This is precisely what narratives do—describe the continuity of structures through a sequence of
events. In the case of personal identity, the relevant narrative forms are life
history and fiction, in both of which the two senses of identity—sameness
and selfhood—come together in the idea of character. Character consists
of "the set of distinctive marks which permit the reidentification of a human
individual as being the same."[12] As is clear from narrative strategies, this

reidentification depends not only on numerical and qualitative identity but also on an understanding of uninterrupted continuity and permanence in time. When a character is established, "the sameness of the person is designated emblematically." That is to say, it "designates the set of lasting dispositions by which a person is recognized. In this way character is able to constitute the limit point where the problematic of *ipse* becomes indiscernible from that of *idem*, and where one is inclined not to distinguish them from one another."[13]

The concept of character embedded in narrative gives stability to personal identity. A character inevitably has a history in which it acquires new traits and dispositions, often brought about through a sequence of events that induces the character to innovate. These innovations accumulate and leave a sediment in the character, which thus acquires a permanence by which it can be reidentified despite changes brought about by events. It is here that sameness and selfhood overlap. When one thinks one knows the set of permanent traits that belong to a character, one can reidentify it as the *same* person and, from the same evidence, also argue that those traits constitute a further fact, designating the *self*, not reducible to the body and brain of the person.

To locate the problem of identity in narrative is a crucial move, because it shifts the focus from experience and memory to accounts of events. The issues of physical and psychological continuity would of course remain, but now the narrative of events in the history of our real or fictional character would seek to *explain* changes in character as caused by the impact of those events. Not only that, Ricoeur also points out that no narrative is morally neutral. Even as it describes the actions of its characters, a story invites the reader or listener to *judge* those actions. The functions of description, persuasion, and prescription are fused together in narrative.

It is not difficult to see why the move to narrative identity becomes relevant for us in dealing with the material of the Bhawal sannyasi case. We have pointed out the difficulty in applying the physical or psychological criteria of identity to the case of the sannyasi. How on earth could anyone verify if enough of the second kumar's brain survived in the sannyasi for him to have remembered over every day between 1909 and 1933 at least half the number of things that most people normally remember over each day? Inevitably, then, the procedure would end up in comparing physical features, identifying bodily marks, matching character traits, and setting tests of memory to serve as indices of physical and psychological continuity. Apparent discrepancies would be explained precisely by describing a narrative of events that would causally link the changes in physical or psychological character to those events. Those proclaiming the truth of the sannyasi's story would narrate the events in such a way as to preserve the integrity of the character of the second kumar, asserting its continued existence into his life as a sannyasi and then as the plaintiff, despite all the changes brought about by his eventful life Those denying the truth of that story would attempt to show that the changes were too drastic to be accommodated within the life history of the same character, that the proffered explanations stretched the narrative beyond the limits of the credible.

What we can expect then are rival narratives. They will differ not because they will be different descriptions of the same events. Rather, by offering different causal connections between events and physical or psychological change, and by asserting different constructions of the selfhood of the character, these rival narratives would present very different emplotments of events over time. Not only that, they could also appeal to different criteria of what is plausible or credible in a narrative. None of these can be assumed.

Despite Ricoeur's attempt to bring together the reductionist and nonreductionist claims within a dialectical conception of the narrative, the puzzles posed by the philosophical literature on identity are not by any means removed. Ricoeur is able to attribute a certain stability to the concept of the character, evolving through time by a cumulation of sedimented change that qualifies and enriches it without destroying its permanent structure, largely because he assumes the stability of the position of the narrator who "knows" the story. To a certain extent, this results from Ricoeur's concern with fictional narrative, both literary fiction and science fiction, as providing an important corpus of "thought experiment" accounts that throw light on the problems of determining personal identity. But what about situations in which the narrator does not have control over his narrative? Think of our situation with the story of the Bhawal sannyasi. Who is our character? Do we even have a name for him? Ever since his return to Jaidebpur in 1921 and his subsequent claim to the personhood of the second kumar, we have had to narrate his story under the sign of a question mark. This is because we have chosen to respect the conventions of historical narrative and not arrogate to ourselves a control over the destiny of our characters that is not warranted by the evidence before us. How can we speak persuasively of the continuity of the kumar-sannyasi character when we, as historians of his life, cannot avoid confronting the undecidability of his identity?

We can also see that despite the facility afforded by the narrative conception of identity, the challenge posed by Parfit's radical suggestion—personal identity is not what matters—cannot be easily answered. Even after Ricoeur's valiant attempt to integrate a nonreductionist view of the self with the reductionist emphasis on sameness, he concedes that in some of the limiting cases described in literary accounts, identity does become undecidable. Should we not say then that Parfit is right? Ricoeur resists this move. But he does accept that the moral foundation of selfhood in the "ownership" by a person over his or her memories, actions, and feelings is flawed. "In a philosophy of selfhood like my own, one must be able to say that ownership is not what matters. What is suggested by the limiting cases produced by the narrative imagination is a dialectic of ownership and dispossession, of care and carefreeness, a self-affirmation and self-effacement. Thus the imagined nothingness of the self becomes the existential 'crisis' of the self."[14]

Does this help us in our narrative predicament? Can we speak about the problems of determining the identity of the sannyasi as an existential crisis of the self? To begin with, direct accounts of the sannyasi explicating the inner workings of his self are miniscule. The overwhelming bulk of the sannyasi's story is in the form of narratives constructed by others—relatives, friends, associates, supporters, witnesses, and lawyers. Given what is available to us as evidence, we have to admit that a speculative exercise on the existential crisis of the self of the kumar-sannyasi is not the most interesting historical task before us. We must not, however, forget that the question of self-regarding and other-regarding criteria of identity has been already introduced into our case. One plank of the sannyasi's story was the claim that he had been recognized and accepted as the second kumar by his relatives, his friends and acquaintances, and by the tenants of his estate. The second kumar, as he was regarded by others, had survived in the sannyasi. So why bother any more about identity? Of course, it was objected that his wife, the second rani, had not recognized him and had refused to accept his story. But this, the sannyasi's supporters said, was because of her narrow self-interest. She was refusing to accept what everyone else had recognized because it was in her interest to maintain the legal status quo.

Can we accept this? Is it fair to say that whereas the sannyasi's story put forward a plausible case for going beyond the limits of individual interest to recognize the collective wisdom of a larger community of people who, so to say, constituted the site for locating the social persona of the kumar, the rani was bent on obstructing this course because of her narrow self-interest? Did she not constitute a crucial part of the "others" of the kumar? Should we not recognize that it is possible for a collective consensus to be oppressive and unjust for some? What are we to do when the collective body of "others" is marked by radical conflict? It is not a situation that integrative theories such as Ricoeur's can handle very well. As for us, preparing to unfold the story of the trial and its sensational conclusion, we have to accept for the time being the fact that the problems posed by the case of the Bhawal sannyasi remain deeply puzzling.

IDENTITY AND RECOGNITION: INDIGENOUS NOTIONS?

There is one more aspect of this philosophical matter that we should consider, because it will have a bearing on some of the legal debates that arise later in our story. We have so far spoken only of the modern Western philosophical discussion on identity. This was justified, since that is the ground on which the principles and procedures of British Indian law were founded. But is there a different philosophical tradition in India that treats these questions differently? Could these ideas have molded, through language and cultural practices, the actions and testimonies of people involved in the Bhawal sannyasi affair? We should say immediately that unlike many European philosophers and jurists, Indian philosophical authority was almost never cited in the trial we are about to describe. Nevertheless, the question of culturally embedded assumptions, transmitted through language, ritual, and social practices, does remain relevant. They did become subjects of controversy in the legal battles over the sannyasi.

It will be useful to make two general points about Indian philosophical discussions on identity and recognition. First, although a great deal of Indological scholarship since the nineteenth century, both in the West and in India, has focussed on the *ātman* of the Upanishads as "the Indian notion of the self," this is by no means the whole story. The Upanishadic ātman is spirit or consciousness for which the world is object. It is universal, disinterested; its knowledge is objective, valid for everyone. To say "my ātman" or "your ātman" in the same way that one says "my self" or "your self" would, in fact, be meaningless. This is not a notion of selfhood that would yield, for instance, the narrative identity of a character as described by Ricoeur. But although the concept of ātman as subject is certainly a very prominent idea in Indian philosophical thought, it is not true to say that the concept of person as a concrete, bodily entity that calls itself "I" does not exist. The person, as distinct from the ātman, is a *kartā* (agent) and a *bhoktā* (enjoyer). He or she relates to objects in the world not as objects of knowledge but as objects of affect or desire. Objects are attractive or repulsive, to be acquired or avoided. The person lives in a mundane world of interests; his or her knowledge of this world both determines and is determined by the life of interest. Such knowledge produces desire (*icchā*), which in turn leads to appropriate action (*pravṛtti*), which, if successful, gives pleasure, and if not, pain. This mundane, empirical person is what branches of knowledge such as law, medicine, or social ethics have to deal with.

This concept of the person, when it appears as a philosophical idea, is, as J. N. Mohanty notes, a "weak concept."[15] That is to say, it does not give us, like the nonreductionist view of identity, an irreducible and unanalysable unity that we call *the* person. On the contrary, the person as a legal or social agent is reducible to the psychophysical body that acts and enjoys. This is a complex of bodily senses, ego, and intellect that, obviously, is not quite the same as Parfit's physical continuity of the brain (not even in the case of the Buddhist philosophers) but nevertheless implies a kind of reductionist view of the person. But the Indian philosopher would also say that this person—the legal or social agent—who is nothing other than the psycho-physical body, is not self-conscious, for this empirical person could act without knowing it, unselfconsciously. Self-consciousness comes only when the psychophysical body is united with the objective consciousness called ātman.

Thus, although there is definitely a concept of the concrete person that acts in the empirical world and is reducible to a physical-psychological entity, it occupies an inferior position in the hierarchy of Indian ideas of selfhood. Ideas of the knowing subject with objective and universal consciousness have much greater philosophical, and one might say, cultural, value. Contemporary social historians of India might argue that this hierarchy of ideas of selfhood probably reflects the cultural dominance of Brahminical values in Indian intellectual life.[16]

Second, coming to the problem of recognition, it is necessary to note that no school of Indian philosophy recognizes memory (smṛti) as a source of true cognition (pramāṇa).[17] There are many reasons given for this. For instance, it is said that whereas perception makes its object known without reducing it to other causes, memory can only reveal its object by awakening traces (saṃskāra) of past experience. This always leaves room for doubt (saṃśaya). Other philosophers say that memory cannot yield knowledge of any kind, because the past experience that is its object is no longer there—it does not exist. If we leave aside these extreme views, it remains a fact that even those schools that grant some role to memory consider it an imperfect and inferior mode of knowledge.

To consider a problem that is directly relevant for us, let us look at the logical treatment by the Nyāya philosophers of pratyabhijñā or recognition. Recognition, they say, is different from memory. Memory is a revival of a past experience and takes the form of a representation of ideas and images in the same form and order in which they were experienced in the past. Recognition, on the other hand, is a qualified perception that is brought about by the direct cognition (anubhava) of an object but also involves an element of representation in the form of traces of past experience (saṃskāra). Recognition, therefore, unlike memory itself, could yield some sort of qualified true cognition.

Let us first examine memory. The reason why memory awakens a past experience is because latent impressions or traces of that experience are retained in the soul (ātmā). (It is significant that the place where impressions are retained is the soul, which most schools of philosophy accept as indestructible; this means that impressions may be transmitted from one biological life to another, which allows some people to remember some experiences from a past life.) There are many specific causes that might revive the impression of an original past cognition (pūrbānubhava), such as, for instance, association, repetition, similarity, lakṣaṇa or characteristic mark, and so on. But memory can be valid (yathārtha) as well as invalid (ayathārtha).

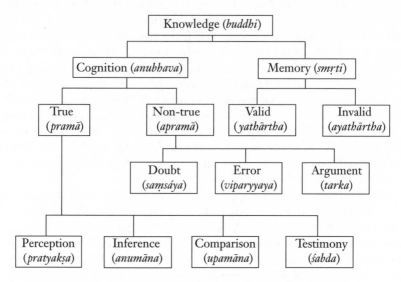

FIGURE 6. The Nyāya classification of knowledge

The validity depends on whether the original cognitions were true. If so, the memory is in accord with the real nature of the objects remembered and so is valid; if not, it is not in accord with the objects remembered and so is invalid. (The question here is not whether we have remembered correctly but whether the memory is that of an original true cognition.) Thus, I may remember having met someone in my childhood who spoke to me in Chinese, but in actual fact she was only speaking gibberish, which I took to be Chinese. My memory is invalid because it did not revive a true original cognition. The Nyāya philosophers speak of dreams, for instance, as necessarily invalid memory. But even when a memory is valid and awakens a true past cognition (for instance, my memory of being caned at school), it is not in itself *pramā* or true cognition, since the object of cognition is not present and the cognition does not arise out of the object itself. (It might be a cause of relief to me that the headmaster is not standing behind me with his cane, but I would still have to deny myself a true cognition.)

Recognition or pratyabhijñā means knowing a thing as that which was known before. It is not only knowing that a thing is such-and-such (as in perception) but also that it is the same thing that we saw before. To repeat the most frequently quoted example here (which is exactly relevant to our problem), I meet a man called Devadatta in Benaras. "This is Devadatta," I say to myself. Seeing him, I remember meeting someone called Devadatta in Mathura many years ago; "this is Devadatta," I had said to myself then.

There is a true cognition now, there was a true cognition in the past, there is an awakening of the trace of a past experience. But this is still not pratyabhijñā or recognition. That happens when I now say to myself: "This is the same Devadatta that I saw in Mathura."[18]

What sort of cognition is this? The Buddhist philosophers say it is a combination of perception and memory. It is not perception, because it relates to a past object with which there cannot be a sense-contact. I have no perception (*pratyakṣa*) of the Devadatta I saw in Mathura. But it is not pure memory, which can only refer to the past, whereas recognition refers to a present object: "This Devadatta is the same as that Devadatta." It is also not a fusing of perception and memory, since the former arises out of sensation and the latter out of imagination and the two could not be fused into a single product. Pratyabhijñā, say the Buddhists, is a dual cognition, including both perception and memory and referring respectively to the two aspects of an object as "this" and "that," that is, as present and past.

The Nyāya philosophers claim, however, that pratyabhijñā is a single psychic act because it refers to one and the same object. There is a unique cause (*karaṇa*) of the phenomenon of recognition that is constituted by the senses and by the traces of past experience. Recognition gives us knowledge of an object as existing in the present and as qualified by its relation to the past. A thing's relation to past time or a past experience is a character that qualifies its present existence. To know this is to know that we have perceived it before, that is, to recognize it. Thus, there is an element of representation that takes the form of a definite recollection of some past experience of an object and that modifies its present perception. But it is nonetheless perception, albeit qualified, because it is brought about by a sense-object contact.[19]

It is not necessary for us to recount the abstruse, though often quite fascinating, arguments and counterarguments made by Nyāya, Vaiśeṣika and Mīmāṃsa philosophers on this point. One important feature of this debate is the persistent concern with the possibility of doubt (*saṃśaya*) about the knowledge produced by recognition. When I say "This Devadatta is the same as that Devadatta," what is the "that-ness" (*tattā*) here? If it is said, for instance, that it is the combination of past qualities known to me from past experience, the contemporary Nyāya philosopher will reply: "Suppose I have seen five black pens in the past of which one is mine, and I see one black pen before me now. Is this *that* pen that belongs to me? I am certain about the past qualities, but cannot eliminate doubt about that-ness."[20] When I ask, "Is this Devadatta that Devadatta?" there can be many reasons for doubt about whether my perception of "this-ness" (*idantā*) qualified by the knowledge of "that-ness" (*tattā*) has yielded a true cognition. This Devadatta, I see, is fat, whereas that Devadatta was not; but then, the "fatness" may be a consequence of the passage of time. Then again, that Devadatta had long black hair, this Devadatta is bald; that too may be a change brought about by time. We are back, once more, to the problem of diachronic identity; the Nyāya philosophers are ever watchful for the presence of doubt, and the possibility of error, in the knowledge produced by recognition. The qualified perception of pratyabhijñā cannot have the same certainty as pratyakṣa.

Indeed, it is a general characteristic of the Nyāya theory that for noninferential knowledge, especially of a kind that does not fall into the class of the familiar, truth is never apprehended from the beginning. There is always the scope, and indeed the need, for further validation or correction.[21] One might say that whereas the primacy of perception in the Nyāya philosophy gives it a realist bent, its questioning of the other modes of knowledge makes room within it for a large measure of scepticism.[22]

Another relevant feature of these debates is that even when knowledge is proved to be invalid, it is not necessarily wholly false. Thus, walking on the beach, I see a piece of silver. Picking it up, I realize it is a seashell. My earlier perception is proved to be erroneous. But, the Nyāya philosopher will say, it was not entirely false, because the seashell does have some of the qualities of "silverness." Of course, although false knowledge is not always wholly false, true knowledge must be true in all respects.[23]

Two final points about memory and its role in recognition. The Vaiśeṣika philosophers argue that when one remembers, the trace or impression (saṃskāra) of past experience that is awakened is immediately destroyed, but a new impression is then created. If I remember something frequently, the saṃskāra is also frequently renewed. Second, the passage of time can destroy a saṃskāra if there is no memory that revives it. Some diseases, such as those of the mind, can destroy saṃskāra. Death destroys saṃskāra; even the most learned man will not remember his learning in his next life. But neither time nor disease nor death will destroy all saṃskāra. Sadly, it is impossible to tell which impressions disappear and which survive; "only the Supreme Lord knows that," the philosophers will say.[24]

One more form of knowledge is relevant to the next part of our story of the Bhawal sannyasi, and that is testimony or śabda. True verbal testimony is accepted by the Nyāya philosophers as true cognition (pramāṇa). In fact, it is pointed out that a very great part of the knowledge we have (the philosophers obviously mean learned people like themselves) is not from our own perception of objects but from our perception of the words and sentences we hear from our teachers or read in books. True cognition produced by śabda consists of our understanding of the statements of trustworthy persons. Śabda or verbal tetimony is of two kinds: the vaidika or Vedic is divine testimony and therefore infallible; the laukika or human testimony is true only when it comes from a trustworthy person.

Not all philosophers accept that verbal testimony is a distinct source of true cognition. The Cārvāka philosophers say that if a testimony is accepted as true because it comes from a trustworthy person, it is only an inference (*anumāna*) from his character to the truth of his statement. There is no independent source of knowledge here. The Buddhists add that if from a testimony we seek to prove that there are actual facts corresponding to the statement, we reduce it to perception (*pratyakṣa*). Here too there is no independent source of knowledge. The Nyāya philosophers, however, insist that śabda is neither inference nor perception, because the validity of the knowledge produced by testimony depends not on the validity of the statement or of the facts corresponding to the statement but on the trustworthiness of the utterer. Being realists, the Nyāya philosophers were, we can guess, only attempting to theorize the fact that we accept on trust by far the greater part of what we hold to be true. It is only a question of trusting the right authorities. But they were also emphasizing the specific mode of knowledge involved in deciphering the meanings of words and sentences required for an understanding of verbal testimony. Śabda cannot be reduced to inference, they say, because we do not have to know the meanings of words to infer fire from the sight of smoke. But we cannot gain any knowledge from a lecture on physics if we do not understand the meaning of the words and sentences being spoken by the lecturer.[25]

Several of these knotty philosophical issues will crop up in the legal debates over the trial of the Bhawal sannyasi. Let us go there without further delay.

Chapter Nine

THE TRIAL BEGINS

THEY WERE both barristers of the Calcutta High Court, both from Lincoln's Inn. Although one was called to the bar three years before the other, it is likely that as students in London their paths had crossed.

Bejoy Chandra Chatterjee was in his early fifties and at the peak of his eminence as a nationalist lawyer. He had returned to India in 1905 and had immediately joined the agitations against the partition of Bengal. He was married to the daughter of Surendra Nath Banerjee, the foremost political leader of Bengal of the time. As the rift developed within the Congress between moderates and extremists, Bejoy Chandra found himself caught in the middle. His youthful convictions might have pulled him toward the more extreme wing of the party, but his personal association with Surendra Nath inevitably tied him down to the moderate constitutionalists. The conflict took an ugly turn at the Surat session of the Indian National Congress in 1908. There Bejoy Chandra tried to mediate between the two sides, but to no avail. The session ended in a complete fiasco, with the rival sections literally going for each other's throats. Disgusted, Bejoy Chandra withdrew from party politics and concentrated on his legal career. He quickly established himself as one of the most prominent young barristers of the High Court. He simultaneously continued his political activities as a liberal constitutionalist, staying away from Non-cooperation and C. R. Das's Congress. But as a lawyer, he became celebrated for his legal defense of several nationalist revolutionaries. In 1931, there was a particularly nasty incident of shooting on political prisoners inside the Hijli detention camp in Midnapur. The government, determined to crack down on the growing civil disobedience and terrorist movements, tried to cover up the incident. When a citizens' committee was set up to conduct a public inquiry, B. C. Chatterjee offered his services as chief counsel for the people.

By this time, B. C. Chatterjee had joined the Hindu Mahasabha, set up to champion the cause of the Hindus in the increasingly sectarian negotiations and conflict over constitutional reforms in India. In 1932, Gandhi ended his fast against the demand for a separate electorate for the Depressed Classes (the lower castes) and signed the Poona pact with B. R.

Ambedkar and other backward caste leaders to have reserved seats for them within the general Hindu electorate. The Hindu Mahasabha leaders in Bengal were particularly agitated by this because the representation of upper-caste Hindus in the provincial legislature would be further reduced. B. C. Chatterjee was particularly vocal on this subject and wrote a string of pamphlets condemning the Poona Pact and its acceptance by Prime Minister Ramsay Macdonald as a principle for the forthcoming constitutional arrangements of provincial government. In 1933, Chatterjee went to England and tried to canvass British official opinion in defense of Bengali Hindu interests. He made a strong argument that unlike other regions of India, in Bengal there were no political disabilities suffered by the depressed castes, and there was no reason why the Poona Pact should be imposed on the province.[1] He pointed out to the Muslim leaders of Bengal that "the better mind of England" was with the Hindus and not with them and pleaded: "Let them not be dazzled by the transient glamour of immediate advantages at the real cost of India as a whole."[2] He warned that now when the former revolutionaries were prepared to join constitutional politics, handing over the province to a mandatory Muslim-majority government could turn Hindu youths against Muslims. "The *Anandamath* which is the Bible of the [revolutionary] party preached a patriotic and holy war against Muslims. The very conditions imagined by Bankim [Chandra Chatterjee] in that book would become an incandescent reality were the scheme of the [Macdonald] Award to go through."[3]

Chatterjee's views were by no means untypical of nationalist Hindus in Bengal at the time.[4] He was no rabid Muslim-baiter, nor was he a fire-eating extremist. He was thoroughly wedded to British legalism and its constitutional tradition and thought of educated Bengali Hindus as its most accomplished spiritual heirs. "I am one of those many millions of Hindus," he wrote, "who are held to England by ties of a moral and spiritual discipleship whose snapping and ceasing will mark a calamity in history. My final prayer is that England may proceed as cautiously as she pleases and give as little as she likes, but that the little she does give must be a definite unmistakable step towards fitting India for responsible government."[5] Chatterjee wrote this just before he arrived in Dhaka in November 1933 to become the counsel for the plaintiff, Ramendra Narayan Roy, now known throughout Bengal as the Bhawal sannyasi. Perhaps he did not foresee that his involvement in the case would keep him away from politics for quite a while.

Among those assisting B. C. Chatterjee was Surendra Nath Mukherjee, the Dhaka lawyer whom we have met before as one of the key persons in the sannyasi's camp ever since his declaration of identity in 1921. Given his unparalleled familiarity with the details of the case as it had developed from that time, Suren Mukherjee was chosen to go to England from the plaintiff's side to cross-examine the several defense witnesses who deposed there in commission. When the hearing opened in Dhaka, there were at least a dozen other lawyers of Calcutta and Dhaka assisting B. C. Chatterjee in the plaintiff's team, of whom Arabinda Guha would play an important part in the plaintiff's affairs for many years to come.

Counsel for the defendants was Amiya Nath Chaudhuri, known universally as A. N. Chaudhuri. He had a law degree from Cambridge and was called to the bar in 1902. He was the youngest in a line of distinguished lawyer brothers. The eldest, Sir Ashutosh Chaudhuri, was a famous barrister who ended his career as a judge of the Calcutta High Court; Jogesh Chandra was founder-editor of the leading law journal *The Calcutta Weekly Notes;* Pramatha, also a barrister, was better known for his literary pursuits; Kumud Nath, once again a barrister, was a famous hunter who lost his life when he was attacked by a tiger in a forest in central India. It is said that Durgadas, the father of the Chaudhuri brothers, was once slighted by a high British official who thought he had come to seek a job for one of his sons. Durgadas resolved that day to send each of his sons to England to become a barrister, because that was the only respectable profession in which one did not have to serve the British.[6]

If B. C. Chatterjee had a reputation as a nationalist barrister, A. N. Chaudhuri was his exact opposite. He was extravagantly westernized in his lifestyle and belonged to that exclusive social set of Calcutta in which white expatriate businessmen and officials dominated. He was married to Millie, a daughter of the barrister Sir W. C. Bonnerjee. She had the rare distinction in Calcutta of having been educated at the Sorbonne in Paris. Their son, Joyanto Nath, had just joined the Indian army; he would one day become its commander-in-chief. A. N. Chaudhuri was approached by the Board of Revenue to act as counsel for the defendants. It was not normal for A. N. Chaudhuri to accept a case in a district court, but then this was not a normal case.

On the government side, Sasanka Coomar Ghose, government pleader of Dacca, was the key person preparing the case for the defendants. From the time the suit was filed in 1930, he was in communication with the Board of Revenue through the commissioner of the Dacca Division. In July 1930, E. J. Bignold, manager of the Bhawal estate, prepared for the board a "statement of facts" in which he reiterated the government case that the second kumar had died around midnight on May 8, 1909, that Calvert and Crawford had certified his death, that the board had thoroughly investigated the identity of the sadhu who appeared in 1921 claiming to be the second kumar, and that there was conclusive evidence that he was "a Rathor of Aujla in the district of Lahore." To this, Ghose had appended his opinion that "the suit should be defended along the lines set forth" in Bignold's statement.[7] In August 1931, it was decided that Ghose should travel to England to instruct the counsel who would examine the defense witnesses

Calvert, Lindsay, and Crawford, all of whom had retired from service and returned to Britain.[8] At first, it was suggested that F. W. Maitland, who had retired from judicial service in India, would be the counsel, but later the board decided that J. M. Pringle, a former ICS man who had been in Dacca in the 1920s and knew the case, would be a better choice.[9]

As for the expenses, it was reported that "the Second Lady has arranged for Ghose's passage." In fact, it was in connection with the arrangements for Sasanka Ghose's trip to England that the Board of Revenue put on record that it "adheres to the decision of 1923 that the 2nd Lady's share will be liable for the whole cost of the declaratory suit."[10] Sarajubala, the first rani, had declared at the outset that the Court of Wards should not file any statement on her behalf, and that no expenses should be incurred on the suit out of her share of the estate.[11] It was from Bibhabati's share of the revenues of the Bhawal estate, then, that the government case would be fought through the next fifteen years. There was at this time no estimate, and possibly not even an inkling in anyone's mind, of the total amount of money that would be spent in defending the government's authority and reputation against the claims of an alleged impostor.

We should also note that in the run-up to the actual hearings in the Dacca district court, a row was developing between government officials and the judge. Part of the case on the plaintiff's side was an attempt to show that the district officials of Dacca were prejudiced against the plaintiff and had acted at the behest of Satyen Banerjee, brother of the second rani. To prove this, the plaintiff's lawyers had in July 1931 called for a set of documents from the divisional commissioner's office in Dacca. In August 1931, the commissioner informed the court that he was unable to produce the documents. Pannalal Basu then issued summonses to various officials of the district calling for the papers. In May 1932, Sasanka Ghose, the government pleader, gave his opinion on the judge's summons:

> The Subordinate Judge trying the Bhowal Impostor's Declaratory Suit has, at the instance of the Impostor, issued summonses in spite of our protest calling . . . for Registers of confidential communications between the Bhowal Estate and various officials relating to the Impostor in 1920 and 1921. . . . [T]he Commissioner perhaps will consider it highly undesirable to produce such registers in Court. . . . I am of opinion that the demand of the court to produce registers of confidential communication is unreasonable and their production should be refused on the ground that it is not in the interest of state to produce communications made under official confidence and they are privileged.[12]

On the basis of this opinion, B. M. Ghosh, the district collector, suggested to the commissioner that "we may inform the Court our objections and request him not to compel us to produce the documents." Nelson, the commissioner, was more peremptory in his orders: "Reply that it is not in the public interest that confidential communications should be disclosed and that I do not propose to produce the documents referred to."[13] Despite the government's unambiguous stand, however, the matter would not end there, as we shall see later.

Incidentally, the administration of Bengal had now been placed under a new and demonstratively tough regime. Sir John Anderson, who was sent out as governor of Bengal in 1932, had built up a reputation as one of the most capable administrators in Britain and had shown his mettle in Ireland in 1919–1921 by clamping down ruthlessly on the revolutionaries by using the "Black and Tans" police. Coming to Bengal, he decided to tone up the police administration and especially the intelligence branch, and to present an image of a government that would not yield an inch to agitational and seditious activities. His regime was paradigmatic of what has been described as a state of "civil martial law." British district officers in Bengal, demoralized by the mass support for Civil Disobedience and the terror tactics of the revolutionaries (three successive district magistrates had been assassinated in Midnapur), were especially encouraged by the arrival of the no-nonsense Scotsman as the new governor of the province.[14]

INITIAL PROCEEDINGS

The proceedings began in Pannalal Basu's court on November 30, 1933, with an initial statement by B. C. Chatterjee presenting the plaintiff's case. The records of the testimonies of J. C. Calvert, civil surgeon of Darjeeling at the time of the second kumar's illness and alleged death; Sarajubala Debi, the elder rani of Bhawal; and Dr. Prankrishna Acharya, the famous Calcutta physician who was present in Darjeeling at the time of the kumar's alleged death—all three of whom had been earlier examined in commission—were then placed before the court. Calvert had retired from service and returned to England, where he was examined by Pringle under instructions from Sasanka Ghose. Sarajubala pleaded her inability to come to Dhaka, and was examined in Calcutta by Sir N. N. Sircar, advocate-general of Bengal. Dr. Acharya, too, had been examined in Calcutta.

We will have occasion later to talk at length about Calvert's testimony, because it would become a major point of contention in the trial. Dr. Acharya, in his testimony, said that he well remembered being called early one morning in May 1909 in Darjeeling by a nurse who asked him to come and examine whether the kumar of Bhawal was really dead, because that is what was feared. He went to Step Aside at about 6:00 A.M. and saw a body lying on a cot covered from head to foot. When he attempted to remove the cover to examine the body, he was told by those standing around that since he was a Brahmo, he should not touch the body. Dr. Acharya was greatly annoyed by this and left the place immediately. He was unable to see the body at all. Answering a question from the defense counsel, Dr. Acharya said that in all of forty years of his career as a doctor, there had not been a single other occasion when he had been prevented from touching a body, alive or dead, on the ground of his religion. If he had been allowed to examine the body, he might have been able to tell when the person had died.[15]

Sarajubala Debi, the first rani of Bhawal, described how, three years after the appearance of the sannyasi in Dhaka, when he came to her house in Calcutta, she had recognized him instantly. From that time on, the plaintiff had visited her regularly when he was in Calcutta, about two or three times a month. It was not true, she said, that she had given the plaintiff any money to fight his case in court. Cross-examining her, N. N. Sircar suggested that Sarajubala's interest in the plaintiff was related to her steadfast opposition to the adoption of a son by the third rani. The first rani had never accepted the adoption because she had wanted her brother's son to be adopted by her youngest sister-in-law. For a long time, the second rani had joined her in her opposition to the adoption. In 1929, however, when a suit filed by Tarinmayi Debi's sons came up for hearing, Bibhabati suddenly supported the third rani. It was at this time, argued Sircar, that the first rani decided to go over to the plaintiff's side. Sarajubala denied this and said that she had recognized the plaintiff long before 1929 and had declared her belief on many occasions. In fact, her attitude toward the plaintiff was well known to the government. For instance, in 1925, when she had offered to present some portraits of her father-in-law and husband to Northbrook Hall in Dhaka, J. H. Drummond, the collector, had written to her, "I am afraid however that in the present situation it is impossible to expect His Excellency to unveil the portrait. Were he to do so, it would appear as if he approved of your attitude towards the Sadhu. . . . It is time the Government's attitude is made clear and that no shadow of countenance is given to the claim which certain people put forward in the Sadhu's behalf (though he seems quite disinclined to make any claim himself)."

During cross-examination, she was also grilled on the background to her first meeting with the plaintiff in her house in Calcutta. Had she made up her mind before seeing him?

Q. Before you saw him, did you get any information from your brother, Sailendra Matilal, about the Kumar being alive?

A. My brother went to Dacca in connection with a case; on his return, I asked him, "What did you see?" He replied, "I saw the same man."

Q. How many days before you saw him yourself did you get this information from your brother?

A. I don't remember exactly: it might be two or two and a half years.

Q. Was there any more doubt about the Kumar being alive when you got the information from your brother?

A. I went on hearing from my brother—that was all.

Q. If you try to avoid answering the question by saying, "I went on hearing," we shall be forced to submit a petition to the court; I am asking you again, did you have any doubt after hearing from your brother? (*Objected to*)

A. I could not decide anything on any one's word until I saw him myself.

Q. Did you have any doubt that the information of your brother might be a mistake?

A. My brother saw him and he was convinced; until I saw him myself I could not decide anything.

Q. So long as you will not answer this question, I shall be compelled to ask this question again and again. I am asking you again, was there any doubt in your mind that your brother's information might be correct?

A. My brother does not lie to me.

On the actual meeting, the questioning was on similar lines.

Q. Did he enter your room without giving you any intimation?

A. One evening there were some gentlemen in the house. He came and sat there. I sent for him through a servant.

Q. Could you see those gentlemen and the plaintiff from inside your room?

A. No, they could not be seen from inside the room.

Q. Then how did you know that the plaintiff had come?

A. I heard that he had come. All the gentlemen of the neighbourhood came to see him.

Q. What did you hear? Surely you did not hear that he was the plaintiff?

A. I heard that the sadhu Kumar of Bhawal had come.

Q. Do you remember who came and gave you the information?

A. I was then in my evening prayers. Such talk was going on outside; I heard them.

Q. Had there been any doubt in your mind that he was not the Kumar, then you could not have called a stranger into your room. Can I take it for granted that you had no doubt in your mind? (*Objected to*)

A. My brother on coming back said, "He is that man." Then he came. I called him into my room. I said, "Bring him upstairs, I will see him."[16]

Clearly, Sir N. N. Sircar was trying to establish that Sarajubala was already predisposed to believing that the plaintiff was the second kumar. One should not, he was suggesting, attach much value to her evidence that she had recognized him at their first meeting.

Another relative who, in these early proceedings, testified to having recognized the plaintiff as the second kumar was Kamal Kamini Debi, his aunt. She said that after the second kumar's alleged death in Darjeeling, when she had asked Bibhabati how her husband had died, the second rani had cried and said that she had not been allowed to see her husband in his last moments. She had been told that all sorts of important people were coming to see the kumar and she could not go out to the front room. After the plaintiff's appearance in Dhaka, Kamal Kamini had met Bibhabati again, when the second rani asked her how she had recognized the kumar. Kamal Kamini then told her the story of how Rani Satyabhama had recognized the second kumar and how he had performed the funeral rites after Satyabhama's death. There could be no doubt in anyone's mind that the plaintiff was indeed Kumar Ramendra.[17]

The Plaintiff Speaks

As the first witnesses from the plaintiff's side began to recount before the judge how they had recognized the plaintiff as the second kumar, the question that was in everyone's mind was when the man himself, sitting there in court, would come to the box. A. N. Chaudhuri, the defense counsel, brought up the point during the first few days of the hearing. The suit had been filed, he said, nine years after the appearance of the plaintiff. During this time, the plaintiff had had the chance to discuss the story of the second kumar's life with all of his relatives. To keep back the plaintiff from the witness box at this stage would make the court's task even harder. B. C. Chatterjee replied that there was no intention to keep back the plaintiff. There had been a recent bereavement in his family—Jyotirmayi Debi's son Buddhu had died a few weeks previously. As soon as the ritual ceremonies were completed, he would be put in the witness box.[18]

Soon, the day came. In the second half of December 1933, on every working day, the courtroom of Pannalal Basu overflowed with eager spectators. The man who claimed to be Kumar Ramendra Narayan was being examined.

Guided by his counsel, the plaintiff narrated the story of his—the kumar's—childhood and youth. His hands and feet were small in proportion to the rest of his body, he said, as was the case with his mother, his brothers, his sisters, and some of his nephews and nieces. Like several other members of his family, his hair was reddish and his eyes were brown. He had a broken tooth caused by a carriage accident in his youth. He had marks on his right arm left by the claws of a tiger from the Rajbari menagerie that had once attacked him. He had the marks of a carriage wheel that had passed over his foot at the time of the third kumar's wedding.

He then went through the now well-known story of his Darjeeling trip, his illness, and his falling unconscious sometime during the day on May 8, 1909. He had been well for about two weeks after his arrival in Darjeeling. His illness began with flatulence at night. "That night I spoke to Ashu

FIGURE 7. The plaintiff

Doctor. The next day, a European doctor came. He prescribed a medicine. I took it. On the third day I took the same medicine. It did no good. That night at 8 or 9 pm, Ashu Doctor gave me a medicine in a glass. It did me no good. As I took it, my chest burnt, and I vomited and became restless. These symptoms appeared 3 or 4 hours after I took the medicine. I began to scream. No doctor came that night. . . . The next morning, I passed blood stools—the motions were in quick succession. My body got feebler. Then I fell unconscious."

When he regained consciousness, he was under a tin shed in a forest on the top of a hill, surrounded by three or four sannyasis. He was very weak and the sannyasis told him not to talk. He stayed there with them for about two weeks. He then accompanied them to Benaras, where they stayed for about four months. From there, they went to Amarnath in Kashmir, where he was given the mantra by his guru Dharamdas. Until then, he had no recollection of who he was or where he had come from. After receiving the mantra, he sometimes had vague recollections about his past. When he mentioned this to his guru, he told him to be patient; he would return home at the proper time.

For the next few years, he traveled with the sannyasis all over northern India and Nepal. When he was at Brahachatra, he seemed to remember that he was from Dacca. Dharamdas told him to go to Dacca, locate his family, and decide for himself if he wanted to stay there. Otherwise, he could return to his guru at Hardwar.

He took a train to Dhaka from Assam. On arriving in the city, he made his way to the bank of the River Buriganga and stayed there for about three months. Many people would come and talk to him. They spoke in Bengali, but he always answered in Hindi, because his guru had warned him not to disclose his identity until he was completely sure that he wanted to.

He then described his visit to Jaidebpur with Atul Prasad Roy, whom he had recognized but to whom he refused to say who he was. There was a flood of recollection when he arrived at the Rajbari: everything was familiar. He described his visit to Jyotirmayi's house, where he met his grandmother, his sisters, and their families. He still spoke only in Hindi and Jyotirmayi, when she asked him who he was, also spoke in Hindi. He continued

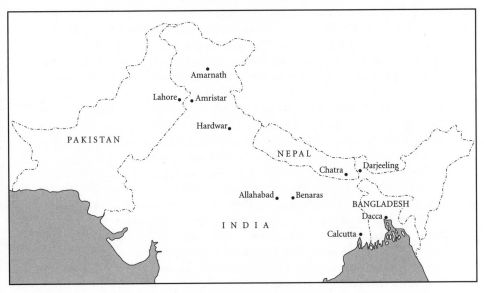

MAP 2. Some locations in the plaintiff's story

to insist that he was a renouncer with no family ties and refused to reveal his true identity.

It was clear that the cross-examination of the plaintiff would be crucial; it could make or break the case. A. N. Chaudhuri made a major decision of strategy not to examine the plaintiff on his memory of the life of the kumar. He probably decided that everyone had had plenty of time—twelve years since the sannyasi first made his appearance in Dhaka—for the plaintiff to have been thoroughly coached in the life history of the second kumar. Even if he tripped up on a few points, it could always be put down as a normal failure of memory. On the other hand, every time the plaintiff succeeded in passing a memory test, it would add to the credibility of his story. Chaudhuri, therefore, decided to test him on whether he fitted the type to which he was supposed to belong. Was it possible to believe that this man in the witness box was actually a Bengal zamindar?

Could he read either English or Bengali in print? No. Could he read handwriting? No, except for his own signature. He could sign his name in both English and Bengali. Did he read newspapers? No. Had he heard of the *Amrita Bazar Patrika?* No. Was he aware of the fact that Kumar Ramendra Narayan subscribed to the *Amrita Bazar Patrika?* It is possible, the plaintiff said, that there was a subscription in the name of the kumar, but the paper would have been read by the estate employees, not by him. Sometimes his staff would explain to him in Bengali the news that appeared in the English paper. Did he remember going to the Dacca Collegiate School? Yes. He was twelve years old then. Did he remember which class he was in? No. Did he know which was the lowest class in school? No. Could it have been the Eighth Class? It could have been. He did not know what the Eighth Class was. Did he know Shyama Charan Master? Yes, his name was Shyama Charan Guha. Did he know Arithmetic? No. Did he know the names of any of the English or Bengali books he read in school? No. He never read any books. He always looked out of the window, watching the horses and carriages on the street. He preferred to spend his time at school playing with the other boys, drinking tea, and munching biscuits. Did he take a slate or paper with him to school? Yes. Did he write on them? No. Not even a scratch? Why should he scratch on paper? Was he a tiger?

The plaintiff appeared prickly and irritable. Yet A. N. Chaudhuri and Sasanka Ghose were not getting anywhere with his education. Clearly, he was not even pretending to have had one. The cross-examination moved to another tack. Could the plaintiff recognize the signatures on these letters? Some of them, said the plaintiff, looked like his, but the others were clear forgeries. Sasanka Ghose then read out the letters in court: they were written by Kumar Ramendra to his wife, he said. The plaintiff replied that he had never written these letters; they were forgeries.

Did the plaintiff ever suffer from syphilis? Yes, four or five years before he went to Darjeeling, he had syphilis. He was first treated by Dr. Elahi, a physician on the estate. At that time, he did not know that syphilis was a serious disease. Later, he found out that it could do a lot of harm. He was gradually cured. "God has cured me." The sannyasis saw the marks of syphilis on his body, but he could not say if they gave him any medicines for it.

Was the mark on his right arm left by a tiger's claws? Yes. Could it have been a cat's claws? No. Did he know that a tiger's paw and a cat's paw were the same? No, he did not know that. He knew that he had been clawed by a tiger with all the claws. How many claws did a tiger have on its paw? He did not know.

When he was in Darjeeling with the sannyasis, he did not know if they were Bengalis or not. He spoke to them in Bengali, they spoke to him in Hindi, but he was not aware at the time of the difference between Bengali and Hindi. When he regained consciousness, he asked, "Where have I come?" He did not understand that the sannyasis were different from him. In the state he was in, he was not capable of understanding the difference. He did not have the capacity to understand if the sannyasis were Bengali or Hindustani or Punjabi or English. While he was lying under the tin shed in the forest, he did not have any consciousness of his past life or family. "I was like a baby just born." The sannyasis spoke to him in Hindi and he understood them. But he did not have any consciousness at the time that it was Hindi rather than Bengali. He was not even conscious of whether he was a man or a ghost. He was not conscious whether he was on a mountain or in the ocean. He could not tell the trees from the skies or from the clouds. He did not know whether the place was in heaven or in hell. This condition lasted until he went to Benaras. He did not know if he went to Benaras by train or on foot. He had no memory of that journey. He did not know how the sannyasis addressed him at the time—whether as a baby or an old man, as a man or a dog. He could not distinguish between cows and calves, horses and elephants; he could not recognize them. He could not recognize food.

His consciousness returned after he received the mantra from his guru. But he did not remember anything of his earlier life. For the next five years, as he traveled from Benaras to Punjab with the sannyasis, he did not have any consciousness of whether he was a Bengali or a Hindustani. The sannyasis did not give him a name at that time. It is only after he came to Dacca that he realized that he was a Bengali. His guru did not know his home or his family. Had he known, he would have sent him back to his family.

On arriving at the railway station in Dhaka, things began to seem very familiar. "As I got down at the station, I remembered that I had come here many times." He saw familiar faces and recognized people he had known. But he still did not know he was a raja's son. But soon he noticed that people were gathering around him, whispering "This is the Bhawal kumar. This is the mejo kumar." There, sitting on the Buckland Bund in Dhaka, with a circle of curious people surrounding him, his memory began to come back. He remembered he was from Dacca, remembered his home and family, remembered his brothers and sisters. Every time he saw something familiar, he remembered.[19]

Standing in court, he also explained that he was not truly a sannyasi. He had never taken the vows of renunciation in which the sacred thread is thrown into the sacrificial fire.

A. N. Chaudhuri, counsel for the defense, launched into a searing cross-examination on the plaintiff's knowledge of Bengali. He asked him about his inability to correctly pronounce certain sounds and his often indistinct enunciation. The plaintiff replied that he had a tumor under his tongue that had appeared sometime during his travels with the sannyasis. This prevented him from pronouncing certain sounds. He had always known Bengali, but had chosen not to speak it until his self-declaration in Jaidebpur in May 1921. Could he count up to one hundred in Bengali? No, because he was not a shopkeeper. Did he know the months of the year in Bengali? Yes. Did he know them in Hindi? No. Did he know the meaning of *śveta varṇa*? Yes, it meant white. *Svara varṇa*? He did not know. *Rakta varṇa*? Red. *Vyañjan varṇa*? The color of aubergine. (At this, there was a ripple of laughter in the courtroom. *Svara varṇa* and *vyañjan varṇa* meant vowel and consonant, respectively. The plaintiff had probably guessed—incorrectly—that *vyañjan* was the Sanskritic form of *bāygan*, the name for aubergine in the Dacca dialect. No one who had not studied grammar at school could be expected to know *svara varṇa* and *vyañjan varṇa*.) Did he know *śukla pakṣa*? *kṛṣṇa pakṣa*? *uttar pakṣa*? *pūrva pakṣa*? (The former were the fortnights corresponding to the waxing and waning of the moon, the latter the two sides in a debate between logicians.) No, he did not know because he was not a pundit. He did not know a single word of English. He did not know what "athletics" was. He had never played cricket. He did not know lbw or mid-off or square leg, which anyone interested in cricket would know. He did not know if billiard balls were made of wood or rubber. He had never played billiards; his elder brother had. Oh yes, the only time he had tried to play the game, he had torn the cloth on the table.[20]

He was asked about racing. The plaintiff said he may have gone to a few races, but he did not remember. Could he remember the name of any horse that won the Viceroy's Cup? He had won it himself, but he did not remember in which year. He rode his horse himself. The race was at Tollygunge in Calcutta. "I don't know what the Tollygunge races are called. I don't know what is meant by steeplechase. The race I won might have been a hurdle race. I don't remember the name of the Cup. I got the Cup, not any money along with it." In a race, if a rider was put at 8 and another at 7–

12, could he say what that signified? No, he couldn't say. Could it be 8 maunds? No, but he didn't know.

The plaintiff claimed he was a shikari. A. N. Chaudhuri put to him numerous questions on the technicalities of hunting and on firearms and ammunition. The plaintiff did not know the answers to most of the questions. B. C. Chatterjee pointed out to the judge that the questions were being framed by using English technical terms and the witness had declared that he did not know any English.[21]

In the matter of knowing English and Bengali, A. N. Chaudhuri himself was put into a bit of embarrassment during his cross-examination of the plaintiff. He asked if the plaintiff's nose might have become blunt (*bhotā*) because of having performed for many years the yogic exercise of *kumbhaka*. Before the plaintiff could answer, B. C. Chatterjee intervened and asked the judge to please note the term *bhotā*. Chaudhuri corrected himself: "Perhaps I don't mean *bhotā* [blunt] but *motā* [thick]." There was a roar of laughter in the court.[22] Of course, Chaudhuri might have argued that the ignorance of Bengali in an English-educated Bengali gentleman such as he was not of the same type as that in a Punjabi peasant claiming to be a Bengal zamindar.

The plaintiff was also questioned on his knowledge of local political history. Who was the lieutenant-governor in 1309 or 1310 (1902–1903)? He didn't know. Who was Lord Minto? He had heard the name but didn't know who he was. Who were the commissioners and collectors of Dacca between 1309 and 1316? He didn't know, except that Rankin was collector first and later commissioner. Did he know Mr. Garth? Yes, he was manager of the Nawab estate. Which years? He didn't know, but Garth died before he left for Darjeeling. Did he know Bankim Chandra Chatterjee? He was from Calcutta. Who was he? He had written books. Which books? Never read any of his books. Anyway, he was dead. Could he remember any song he had heard before 1909? He could not. Could he not remember a single line? No.[23]

Answering questions about his relations with his wife Bibhabati, the plaintiff claimed to know of various marks on her body which no man other than her husband could know. She had, he said, "on one side of her private parts" a mark left by a cyst. She had the mark from before her marriage.[24] A. N. Chaudhuri did not ask too many questions about the plaintiff's memory of the kumar's life. The ones he did ask, the plaintiff answered, except for the name of the husband of Bibhabati's sister. As the correct answers began to accumulate, Chaudhuri suddenly exclaimed, "The witness has been tutored to answer these questions." B. C. Chatterjee exploded: "If he is going to cast any imputation against my honesty, then I tell him there will be bloodshed." Pannalal Basu had his hands full trying to calm the two barristers, who were fighting the case of their lives.[25]

Chaudhuri also questioned the plaintiff on his motives for coming to court for recognition of his identity. What would he do with the property if he got it? The plaintiff at first said that he had no use for it; it might come of use to others. "So you do not claim the property for your own use?" "No, not for my sake; for the sake of all others." Chaudhuri decided that this line of questioning was risky and wanted to withdraw the question. Chatterjee protested immediately, saying he would rather leave the courtroom than argue with the defense counsel on such an outrageous request. Left with no alternative, Chaudhuri continued: "Do you claim your inherited property for your own enjoyment?" The plaintiff too seemed to decide that enough was enough. "Yes," he said. "How will you spend your money?" "The way rich people spend their money." "On liquor and women?" "Yes, on women, elephants and horses." "Do you still have a taste for those things?" "I have no money now. How should I know if I have the taste?" Chaudhuri decided to call it a day.[26]

RECOGNITION

One of the main strategies decided upon by the plaintiff's lawyers was to produce as many witnesses as possible who had known the second kumar and who would testify in court that they had recognized the plaintiff as the kumar they had known. Apart from his relatives, these witnesses would be friends of the kumar, employees of the Bhawal estate, and talukdars and tenants. It is not clear if the lawyers decided from the very beginning that the way to drive home the recognition point was to demonstrate the sheer number of people who claimed to recognize the kumar. As the hearings continued, the number of such witnesses from the plaintiff's side kept mounting, making the Bhawal case one of the longest trials in legal history.

Several of the early witnesses were employees or former employees of the estate. They described how they had known the kumars in their childhood or youth. All of them testified that the second kumar could not really read or write, and could only sign his name in Bengali and English. When shown samples of his signature, some of them said they were the signatures of the second kumar. Most said that they first saw the sannyasi at the public meeting in Jaidebpur in May 1921. Many saw him later at closer range and spoke to him. The sadhu spoke to them in Bengali with a Hindustani intonation. His speech seemed to be impeded and was often indistinct. When asked about this, the sadhu explained that his tongue had been affected by poisoning. They were convinced that he was indeed the second kumar. Several of these witnesses also said that the Court of Wards had acted against them because they had shown a sympathy for the sadhu. Some had lost their jobs, others had proceedings brought against them on the tenancies they held on their land.

Harish Chandra Nandi, who first joined the service of the Bhawal Raj as a menial servant and rose to become a clerk, said that when he first spoke to the plaintiff, the latter recognized him instantly and addressed him by his nickname. Radhika Mohan Goswami, who had once worked for the estate, said that he was distantly related to the second kumar through his grandmother, and the plaintiff was able to describe the relationship at their first meeting after his arrival in Jaidebpur. Kumud Mohan Goswami said that the plaintiff addressed him at their first meeting as "Sadhu Kaka," just as the second kumar did. The plaintiff spoke to him in Bengali with a *paschima* (western) twang. Clarifying, he said it was not a *merua* (colloquial for Marwari) acccent, but more like what was spoken in Benaras. Suresh Chandra Mukherjee said that he had closely observed the bare-bodied sadhu in Jyotirmayi Debi's house and was convinced that the sadhu had the same marks on his body as the second kumar. Ramesh Chandra Ghosh, who had worked on the estate for twenty years, said that when he first went to meet the plaintiff and asked him if he recognized him, the plaintiff had said, "Of course, you are Ramesh Babu, naib [deputy rent collector] of Kurmitola." Kailash Chandra Chakrabarti testified that the second kumar was very fond of birds and animals. When Kailash Chandra went to meet the plaintiff in Jaidebpur, the latter said, "You are the person who gave me a white jackal." Ganga Charan Banerjee said that he used to play with the kumars when they were young, and used to be called "Master" because of his studious manner. He knew of the marks of injury on the second kumar's arms and legs. When he saw the plaintiff in Jyotirmayi's house, he saw that the marks were still there. Even before Ganga Charan had spoken, the plaintiff said to him, "Master, where were you so long?" He also said, "Don't you wear the watch I once gave you?" Jitendra Banerjee said that soon after the sadhu's arrival in Jaidebpur, he had seen him ride Buddhu Babu's tumtum. He held the reins in his right hand and the whip in his left, just as the second kumar had done. The next day, he went riding on an elephant. Passing a palm tree, he pointed it out and said, "Isn't that where we caught a snake?" Jitendra remembered the occasion many years ago when the second kumar had seen a huge snake lying under the tree and had it caught and taken to the Rajbari in a packing case.[27]

Basanta Kumar Mukherjee was a brother-in-law of Raja Rajendra Narayan, and had been employed on the estate first as a forest inspector and then as naib. When he first went to see the sadhu after his arrival in Jaidebpur, it seemed to him that the latter did not recognize him. He asked the sadhu if he knew who he was. Suddenly, his face seemed to light up and he said, "Are you Basanta Dada?" Then he sat him by his side and asked him many questions. "Where is Buri? Is she married now?" Buri was Basanta Kumar's daughter. "How is Batasi Tha'ran?" meaning his wife. "How is Kali Tha'ran?" meaning his sister-in-law. Basanta Kumar had no doubt that this was Ramendra.[28]

Raimohan Goswami was a well-known singer and had sung *kirtan* (devotional songs) with his troupe at the Bhawal Rajbari from the days of Raja Rajendra Narayan. He knew the second kumar well and thought he had a good ear for music. When he met the plaintiff in Jaidebpur, the latter had recognized him and asked, "Raimohan Babu, how is your voice these days?" Umanath Ghosal was one of the most famous *jatra* (traveling show) actors in eastern Bengal and had performed regularly at the Jaidebpur Rajbari. When he visited the plaintiff in his Armanitola house in Dhaka, he had asked if the latter could recognize him. The plaintiff had smiled and said, "Ghosal Mahasay, the jatra king." Umanath was most famous for acting in the role of the king in his plays. Jamini Kumar Mitra's father had been diwan or manager of the Rajbari for fifty years. In his youth, Jamini had often played on the palace grounds and knew the kumars well. When he went to meet the plaintiff and asked him if he could recognize him, the plaintiff had asked, "Is Diwanji still alive?" The plaintiff had also recognized Upendra Datta, who had played and taken elephant rides with the kumars in his youth. Upendra, along with some other witnesses, was asked how he would feel if a Punjabi impostor sat on the *gadi* (ruler's seat) at Bhawal. He would be appalled, Upendra said, and would not accept it for one moment.[29]

Prafulla Kumar Mitra, a lawyer by profession and perhaps the most famous sportsman of his time in the Bhawal region, having played for the Mohun Bagan Club in Calcutta and founded the East Bengal Club, testified that the second kumar was fond of riding and hunting and, to the best of his knowledge, had never played football or cricket or tennis. V. T. Stephen, an Armenian jute merchant of Dhaka, testified that he had met the kumars a few times, once at an official reception at the Shahbagh gardens in Dhaka, and noticed that although the eldest kumar seemed to understand English, the two younger kumars did not understand it at all. Stephen always spoke to the kumars in Hindustani. Jamini Kishor Chakrabarti, who had worked in the estate in various clerical and managerial positions, said that he had never seen the second kumar write in Bengali or heard him speak in English. He used to sign his name as "R. N. Roy." After the appearance of the sadhu, Jamini Kishor had long conversations with him. The sadhu spoke in Bengali. He put many questions to the sadhu, trying to test his memory. The sadhu seemed to remember everything, and Jamini Kishor had no doubt that he was indeed the second kumar.[30]

Rebati Mohan Ghosh had once been employed as a tutor to the second kumar. Like others before and after him, Rebati Mohan too had failed to give Ramendra any lessons in reading or writing, even though he met him two or three times a week for three years and tried to teach him some English words through conversation. The second kumar had a bad temper, he remembered, and he had been warned not to offend him. When Rebati Mohan went to see the sadhu in Jyotirmayi's house, there were many people who surrounded him all the time. Everyone was keen to check for themselves if the sadhu was really the second kumar. Once Rebati Mohan saw the sadhu get angry with those who had come to see him. "Are you animals?" he shouted. "Why do you come and paw my body like this? I don't want to be a raja." The angry look in the sadhu's eyes was exactly like the kumar's. The sadhu spoke in Bengali but with a Hindustani accent. Rebati Mohan had asked the sadhu about the peculiar impediment in his speech. The sadhu had shown him the tumor under his tongue because of which, he said, he could not pronounce all the words correctly.[31]

Bhagaban Chandra Gope, whose family had supplied milk to the Rajbari for generations, said that the second kumar had patches of rough skin near his ankles, which he had noticed when he bent down in obeisance to touch the kumar's feet. The plaintiff had the same rough skin on his feet. He also said that he had paid rent to the plaintiff for the last three years, even though the Court of Wards had brought certificate procedures against him for not having paid his rent to the estate office. Sibchandra Mandal, who supplied fodder for the Rajbari cows and deer, said that the second kumar used to call him "Jata" because he had matted hair. When he saw the plaintiff in Buddhu Babu's house soon after his reappearance, he recognized him and called him "Jata." Harachandra Malo, who had fed the birds on the estate and was also the punkha-puller of the second kumar, saw the plaintiff in Buddhu Babu's house and asked him, "Maharaj, do you recognize me?" The plaintiff replied, "Aren't you Hara Malo? Is your mother still alive?" Harachandra's mother, who also worked in the Rajbari, had died a few years before.[32]

Dilbar Jamadar, a Pathan from Punjab, was the mahout of the Rajbari and had looked after the second kumar's elephants. He was on the kumar's elephant during the *jangi lat* (literally, the Soldier Lord) Kitchener's shikar. When he went to see the sadhu in Buddhu Babu's house, he recognized him instantly. How could he not? He was constantly with him in the old days. The plaintiff too recognized him and said to him that his elephant was in the Rajbari pilkhana, but the secretary of the estate was unwilling to let him ride it. Dilbar said, "I have eaten your salt for so many years. If you want an elephant to ride, I will get one for you." So he went to the zamindar of Ulusara and borrowed an elephant and then to the babus of Kasimpur and got the howdah. The plaintiff went on a ride along with Buddhu Babu. The next day, as the giant meeting was taking place in Jaidebpur, Dilbar took the plaintiff to the meeting on his borrowed elephant.[33]

Pratap Chandra De, who had worked as *khansama* (attendant) to the kumars and claimed to recognize the plaintiff as Ramendra Narayan, said that he had never seen the second kumar study. He remembered the Englishman Wharton and had seen the kumars riding with him but not studying. He also said that he had never seen the second kumar sleep upstairs in the women's quarters, even after his marriage. Prabhat Chandra De, another personal servant of the second kumar, said that when he first went to meet the plaintiff in a crowded room in Jyotirmayi Debi's house, the sadhu had recognized him within minutes and asked him, "Prabhat, where do you live now?" The former khansama also said the second kumar went riding dressed in a lungi or in loose pyjamas. He only wore European clothes when there were important European visitors, such as Lord Kitchener, or when he went to Dhaka.[34]

Chandranan Singh, a Manipuri rider who used to work in the Rajbari stables at Jaidebpur, said that the second kumar used to spend a lot of time with syces and mahouts. Although he trained with Chandranan Singh for a few days, the second kumar did not take up the game of polo. It was the youngest kumar who was the polo enthusiast. When he heard of the sensational return of the second kumar to Dacca, Chandranan came all the way from Agartala in Tripura to see the plaintiff in his Armanitola house in Dhaka. After a few minutes, the plaintiff recognized him and said, "Manipur Thakur, how are you?" That is what the second kumar used to call him.[35]

Krishnalal Basak had been an assistant to Cabral, who was a tailor employed at the Jaidebpur Rajbari and part of the second kumar's circle of disreputable friends. When Krishnalal met the plaintiff in his Dhaka house and introduced himself, the plaintiff recognized him. In the course of the conversation, Krishnalal asked the plaintiff if he remembered the occasion when the estate manager Meyer met with an accident. The plaintiff answered, "Yes, of course. The coachman Hamid was hurt very badly and had to be taken to hospital."[36]

Nand Kishor Tewari, who had been the personal guard of the second kumar, said that the plaintiff had recognized him when he went to see him in Jyotirmayi Debi's house. The sadhu had said: "You are Paresh Thakur's son-in-law." Nand Kishor's father-in-law had also been employed by the Bhawal Raj. After his meeting with the sadhu, Nand Kishor had been called up by Jogen Babu, the estate secretary, and told that the second rani had said that all employees who were sympathetic to the sadhu must quit her service. Nand Kishor had said that he was convinced that the second kumar had returned and that he could not betray him. He lost his job.[37]

On cross-examination, the usual tactic of the defense was to show that the employee was disgruntled and bore a grudge against the Court of Wards administration. Sometimes, it would try to establish that the witness was personally indebted to one or another of the close associates of the plaintiff, especially those like Jyotirmayi who were the most active in his cause. Invariably, the question would be raised as to who had asked them to come to court and testify and who was bearing the expenses. The idea was to show that this was an organized attempt to bolster the plaintiff's story and that the witnesses either had a personal interest in seeing him installed as the proprietor of the estate or had been paid to testify in his favor.

Of the tenants of the Bhawal estate who came to testify on behalf of the plaintiff, all said they had recognized him as the second kumar. Many said that they paid rent and *nazar* to him in 1921 and were given receipts. They had certificate procedures brought against them for not having paid their rents to the Court of Wards office. It appears that they did not pay him rent again until the *punyāha* festival in Dhaka in 1929. Most of these witnesses said that they had been paying the plaintiff the second rani's share of the rent in the last three or four years. He had received these rents personally and had given them receipts in his name.

Shariatulla Haji said that both he and his father were fond of hunting and used to accompany the kumars on shikar. Once, he said, a tiger had killed a cow and he had come to the Rajbari with the news. Hearing about the incident, the second kumar told Shariatulla to accompany him into the forest because the tiger had to be killed. They had gone on two separate elephants, and Shariatulla managed to kill the tiger. The second kumar had given him a bakshish of eighty-five rupees. When Shariatulla went to see the sadhu after his appearance in Jaidebpur, he at first did not recognize him because he had matted hair and a beard. It took him a little time to realize that this was indeed Kumar Ramendra.[38]

As far as local hunters in the Bhawal region were concerned, these figured prominently in the early hearings because they were the second kumar's companions. Umed Ali Bhuiyan, aged eighty-five and a tenant on the estate, had been an enthusiastic shikari. He was asked by B. C. Chatterjee if he knew of "target," "magpie," "cat's eye," "bull's eye," "cordite," "breach loader," "dumdum bullets," or "softnose bullets." Umed Ali had never heard those words. Nor had he ever heard the second kumar using those words. There were, he said, numerous illiterate shikaris in the Bhawal area, and the kumar went into the forest in their company. This was confirmed by Basanta Kumar Mukherjee, an official of the estate with an interest in shikar. Although an educated man, Basanta Kumar did not know many of the English technical terms associated with hunting, and instead knew local terms used by shikaris in the Bhawal region.[39]

Narendra Mandal, another tenant and a cowherd by occupation, said that after the sadhu appeared in Jaidebpur, he went to see him and recognized him as the second kumar. Since then, he had written many songs about the second kumar and had gone around from village to village singing them. He did not sing for money, nor had he published his songs in a book. Ranjan Ghani was the leader of a band that had played at the Rajbari on ceremonial occasions. He had recognized the plaintiff, had paid rent and *nazar* to him, and even took his band to play at the *puṇyāha* ceremony held by the plaintiff in Dhaka.[40]

INTIMIDATIONS

The stakes were getting higher; much was happening outside the courtroom to affect what might happen inside it. Wasimuddin Fakir, a tenant from the estate, said that after he had attended the plaintiff's *puṇyāha* in Dhaka, he was called by Phani Babu, one of the estate officials, and told to sign a piece of paper. They had closed the doors of the office and he was too scared to refuse. He signed the paper without asking what he was signing. Rahim Baksh, another tenant who was paying rent to the plaintiff, claimed that after he had come to Dhaka to give evidence in this case, he had been approached by Ram Babu, brother of the estate secretary Jogen Babu, and told not to testify.[41]

Hafiz Habibur Rahman, vice president of the Mymensingh Praja Samiti, the new political movement of tenants that was developing all over eastern Bengal, testified that the Court of Wards in Bhawal put up every obstacle it could to prevent tenants from expressing their support for the plaintiff. Hafiz Abdul Rahman testified that tenants had been harassed by officers of the Court of Wards if they publicly expressed their sympathy for the second kumar.[42]

An even more dramatic revelation took place during the testimony of Sibchandra Malakar, who used to do painting work at the Rajbari and decorations with *śolā*, the light pith of the water plant *aeschynomene aspera* that was most famously employed for making the solar topee—essential equipment of the colonial official. After the diffident Sibchandra testified to having recognized the plaintiff as the second kumar, A. N. Chaudhuri produced a piece of paper in which Sibchandra had made a statement to the effect that the plaintiff did not resemble the kumar and that Sibchandra was convinced that the plaintiff was an impostor. Sibchandra agreed that the signature on the statement was his. B. C. Chatterjee objected that the signature could not prove the contents of the statement. While the rival lawyers launched into yet another shouting match, the witness requested the judge for permission to explain the matter. Sibchandra then said that the estate officials had repeatedly pressured him to sign the paper until finally, in the Nalgola house of the Bhawal estate in Dhaka, he was told that he would never get another order from the Rajbari for his sola and painting work. While he hesitated, he was put into a dark room and locked inside. Sibchandra feared for his life and obtained his release by signing the paper.[43]

Ashutosh Banerjee was a retired station master of the East Bengal Railway and was posted at Jaidebpur at the time of Lord Kitchener's visit to the

Bhawal estate. He had recognized the plaintiff when he came to see him in Jyotirmayi Debi's house. The plaintiff, too, recognized him and asked, "Ashu Babu, where is your beard?" Ashutosh did have a beard when he was in the railways. He also said that when he was coming in the morning to testify in court, he was stopped by a man outside his house and told that the officer of the Kotwali police station wanted to see him. Ashutosh said that he would go to the station on his way back from court. He was stopped by another man outside the courtroom who said he had been flown in on an aeroplane by the government to ask him not to depose in this case. He said that as a government pensioner, Ashutosh was duty-bound to obey the order of the government. Ashutosh said that he would obey if he was shown the order. The man then told him to go home and he would be shown the order there. "Don't forget," he said, "that you have children to bring up. If you depose against the government, it will go very much against you."[44]

In early February 1934, when Rajendra Nath Roy, a talukdar, was in the witness box, B. C. Chatterjee said to the judge that Bibhabati Debi had reportedly visited Jaidebpur and had been urging the talukdars and tenants not to testify in support of the plaintiff. A. N. Chaudhuri replied that the plaintiff's party had spread a rumor that Bibhabati Debi had died and a certain Dhaka newspaper had even published a report on this. The second rani had felt it necessary to personally visit Jaidebpur in order to persuade everyone there that she was not dead. Upendra Chandra De, a pharmacist of Jaidebpur, however, testified that only the previous week, the second rani had called him and said, "Have all of you people gone mad? My husband is dead. I know it. What are you doing, behaving in this way like mad men?" Upendra had asked the rani to take a look at the plaintiff, as he had done, and then decide for herself whether he was the kumar or not. Nabin Chandra Gope and Aminuddin Khan, tenants of the estate, also said that they had been sent for by the second rani a few days ago. "An impostor has come to Dacca," she had said from behind the screen in her Rajbari quarters, "and you people are calling him the Kumar. He is not the Kumar. I won't have you calling him the Kumar." Nabin Chandra had said, "But how can we disown him? We know he is the Kumar." Digendra Sarkar, a former employee, testified that after the rani had spoken to them, they were told by Jogen Banerjee, the estate secretary, that if, in spite of the rani's warning, they gave witness in court in support of the plaintiff, they would get into a lot of trouble. Although Digendra knew that a big landlord could make trouble for the tenants, he believed he would commit a very grave sin if he betrayed the kumar, whom he had recognized and who had asked for his support.[45]

Bibhabati also appeared to have had meetings with talukdars of the Bhawal estate in which she urged them not to support the impostor. In his testimony, Surendra Mitra described one such meeting at the Rajbari at which some talukdars again requested the second rani to meet the plaintiff and decide for herself if he was the kumar or not. The rani did not reply. Later, Jogen Banerjee told the talukdars that they had heard what the rani wished them to do; they should act accordingly and not testify in support of the plaintiff. Ahmed, another talukdar, testified that it was Dr. Ashutosh Dasgupta who arranged one such meeting between the second rani and a group of talukdars.[46]

SOCIAL PEERS

Apart from employees and tenants of the estate, there was also a large number of zamindars, talukdars, and educated gentlemen who were brought in to give evidence on behalf of the plaintiff. Most asserted that they had recognized the plaintiff as the second kumar, and gave details of what they knew of the kumar's physical and cultural characteristics. Manindra Mohan Bose, a brilliant young man from the Bhawal area who was now a lecturer in Indian vernaculars at the University of Calcutta, recalled that he often visited the Rajbari in his youth and had met the second kumar many times, especially when he started the football club at Jaidebpur with the financial help of the second kumar. Manindra Mohan remembered that when he spoke to Ramendra Narayan in the mixed Bengali and English that educated Bengalis often use among themselves, the latter would not understand him. In fact, Manindra got the impression that the Bhawal zamindar's second son had mental abilities that were below normal. He also knew nothing of the rules of football, even though he agreed to help in setting up the club.[47]

Several other witnesses confirmed that the second kumar did not know any English. Charuchandra Dasgupta, a former schoolteacher, said that although he had heard the eldest kumar use English phrases and even sentences in conversation, he had never heard the second kumar do so. Jogesh Chandra Roy, another former schoolteacher, said that as a young man, Ramendra's mental age seemed to be like that of a child of three or four. Later, when Jogesh Chandra met the plaintiff, the Hindi accent in the latter's speech was not very prominent; what was far more striking was the impediment in his speech.[48]

An interesting testimony on the language question was given by Ram Ratan Chibba of the Bengal Telephone Corporation, who was a neighbor of the plaintiff on Harish Mukherjee Road in Calcutta from 1925 to 1929. Chibba spoke to the plaintiff in Hindi, but he knew that the latter's Hindi was Bengali-accented whereas his own was Punjabi-accented. He avoided Urdu words when speaking to the plaintiff because he discovered that the latter did not understand them. Chibba himself was from Ludhiana district in Punjab and he was certain that the plaintiff was not a Punjabi passing off as a Bengali: if he was, Chibba would have known.[49]

Hemendra Kishor Acharya Chaudhuri, of the famous Muktagachha zamindar family of Mymensingh, had been friendly with Ranendra Narayan, the eldest kumar of Bhawal, and had visited the Jaidebpur Rajbari many times. His impression was that Ramendra was completely uneducated, even though he was by no means an imbecile. When he went to see the plaintiff in his Armanitola house in Dhaka, the latter recognized him as soon as he entered the room and addressed him as "Hem-dada," as Ramendra used to do.[50]

Jatindra Nath Lahiri, a lawyer of the Calcutta High Court who was related to the Natore Raj family, had known the eldest kumar of Bhawal and met the second kumar in Calcutta in the winter of 1908–1909. The second kumar had visited him in his Lansdowne Road house along with a certain Digen Babu. They had driven in a tumtum; and the kumar was dressed in a lungi and shirt. He appeared to be extremely restless and could not sit at one place for more than a couple of minutes. He told Lahiri that he was staying in a rented house on "Wellish Istrit" but would now drive to Uttarpara in his tumtum. Digen Babu clarified that the house was on Wellesley Street. Lahiri thought the second kumar was a young zamindar with no education or culture. Later, when in 1933 the plaintiff came to see Lahiri in his new house on Harish Mukherjee Road, accompanied by his lawyer Suren Mukherjee, he said that was not the house where they had first met because that house was near the Natore Maharaja's house. Lahiri found him to be the same man, although he had gained weight and his face had filled out. Lahiri asked the plaintiff if he remembered who he was with at their first meeting, and the plaintiff replied that it was either the barrister J. N. Roy or Digen Banerjee.[51]

Not everyone who came to testify in favor of the plaintiff reported that the latter had recognized them. Haladhar Roy of the wealthy Bhagyakul zamindar family recalled that he had become friendly with the second kumar of Bhawal during a steamer ride on his way to Calcutta from Dhaka. Later, when he heard of the plaintiff living on Harish Mukherjee Road in Calcutta, Haladhar Roy went to see him and thought he looked exactly like the second kumar. When he asked the plaintiff if he could recognize him, he said he couldn't. After he had introduced himself, however, the plaintiff said, "But I know Muralidhar Babu, your elder brother. We borrowed a lot of money from him." The Kumars of Bhawal had indeed once borrowed fifty thousand rupees from Muralidhar Roy of Bhagyakul.[52]

Subodh Kumar Basu was a former member of the Bengal Legislative Council and moved in the circles of officialdom in Calcutta. In his youth, he had been a champion wrestler. Once he was visited by Rai Saheb Jogen Baner-

jee of the Bhawal estate in the company of a young man who seemed to be
as fair as any Englishman. The young man was introduced to him as the
second kumar of Bhawal, and he seemed to be interested in sports. He asked
Basu if he thought he had the physique to take up wrestling and invited him
to Jaidebpur, where he offered to teach him to ride. Many years later, Basu
went to see the plaintiff in Calcutta. In the meantime, the news had spread
of the kumar's sensational return, and Basu was curious to find out what it
was all about. He went unannounced and recognized the plaintiff as the second kumar. After he had introduced himself, the plaintiff asked him, "Did
I once come to see you with Jogen Babu?"[53]

   N. K. Nag, a barrister of the Calcutta High Court and, in his youth, a
friend of the second kumar in Dhaka, was a sceptic when he went to see the
plaintiff in Calcutta in 1925. Nag had read about the sensation in Dacca
caused by the sudden appearance of the Bhawal sannyasi, but after the government had declared the sadhu an impostor, Nag did not think twice about
the matter. He went to see the plaintiff because his name had been included
among the invitees to a party thrown in honour of Raja Srinath Roy. Nag
was an organizer of this party, and someone had objected that the plaintiff
had been declared an impostor by the government and should not be invited. When Nag went to the Harish Mukherjee Road house to inquire, he
did not announce himself. "As I entered, I found two gentlemen talking
with a third on the ground floor. I saw the faces of the two gentlemen, not
of the third they were talking to. As I entered, one of the two gentlemen
whose face I could see asked what I wanted. The third gentleman then
turned round and looked at me in the face, while I looked him in the face.
Then he, the third gentleman, rose from his chair, and said, 'Are, Naga'
[Hello, Naga]. Saying this, he caught hold of my hand and put me in a chair
and said, 'Saheb hayechhis, bilat giyechhili?' [You've turned a sahib. Been
to England?]." Ramendra used to call his friend "Naga hala" or "Naga
beta." Nag, however, persisted and asked him how he knew who he was.
The man asked back, "But aren't you Naga?" Nag said, "You can't answer
a question with a question." The plaintiff then named Nag's father, his
uncle, several relatives, and an array of common friends. Nag then asked
the plaintiff if he could mention an incident that was known only to him
and Nag's father. The plaintiff said, "Yes, once I went to your house very
late in the night to borrow money from your father." He then narrated the
incident in detail. Nag was convinced that this was none other than Ramendra, because that was the only time he had come to his house and the
whole matter had been kept a secret. Everyone, including Nag's father,
knew why the second kumar needed the money so urgently that night. It
had to be because he had to pay off a dancing girl or visit a prostitute. Nag
had come to see the plaintiff with a sceptical mind, but discovered that
he had found a friend he had believed to be dead.[54]

Another friend of Ramendra who knew about his escapades with women was Abdul Mannan, now a building contractor in Dhaka. When Mannan met the plaintiff in Dhaka in 1921, the latter had asked him about the ring he had once given Mannan. It took Mannan some time to remember the incident in Calcutta when the two friends were going from the house of Krishnabhamini, the actress, to that of Malika Jan, the singer. Ramendra had given Mannan his gold ring because, he said, if Malika Jan saw it, she would want it.[55]

Jadab Chandra Basak had become so friendly with the second kumar that they used to visit each other's mistresses. Kusum Khemtawali of Zindabahar Lane in Dhaka was then Jadab Chandra's mistress. It was in her house that he first met the second kumar. A few days later, Ramendra took Jadab Chandra to Elokeshi's house in Begumbazar. In the period 1903 to 1908, Jadab Chandra visited Ramendra regularly—at the Nalgola Rajbari in Dhaka as well as in Jaidebpur. After the appearance of the sannyasi in Jaidebpur, Jadab Chandra went to see him in Jyotirmayi Debi's house a day before the mammoth meeting in May 1921. Jadab Chandra recognized the sadhu as his friend Ramendra, but he did not have a chance to talk to him that day. A few days later, he saw him again in Dhaka. The plaintiff addressed him as Jadab and asked him if he had left his old habits. To test him, Jadab Chandra took out a photograph of Elokeshi that Ramendra had given him and asked the plaintiff if he knew who the woman was. The plaintiff recounted the entire incident during which he had given him the photograph and went on to talk about many other incidents. None of these stories could have been known to anyone else. Jadab Chandra had no doubts any more that this was Ramendra.[56]

P. C. Gupta, an engineer in Calcutta, was another acquaintance of the second kumar in his youth. Gupta was interested in riding and hunting and often visited the Jaidebpur Rajbari with his father. Gupta got to know Ramendra particularly well. "He was not polished as one would expect a Raja's son to be. He would not rise to receive a gentleman—that sort of thing I would not expect of him. He was shy of bhadraloks and tried to avoid them." Gupta especially remembered a ride in the Rajbari car. This was sometime in 1907. When he saw the plaintiff in Dhaka in 1921, he asked him about the car. The plaintiff immediately said, "You mean the car with the door in the back?" Gupta put several other questions to the plaintiff and was convinced that this was none other than Ramendra.[57]

A striking fact about the official inquiries into the whole affair, from the time of the appearance of the sannyasi in 1921, was that the alleged impostor was never tested on his memory of the kumar's life. This appeared to be a conscious strategy adopted by the defendants' lawyers in the trial. But even earlier, when there was so much controversy about the sadhu's identity, there was no official interrogation of the claimant. The only occasion when there was something approaching a test of memory was on May 5, 1921, the day after the first admission by the sadhu that he was Ramendra Narayan Ray. On this day, directed by Needham, the estate manager, Mohini Chakrabarty, Jogen Banerjee, and a few other estate officials went to interview the sadhu in Jyotirmayi Debi's house. Some of those present at this interview had later said that the sadhu was asked various questions about the second kumar's life, most of which he refused to answer. One of these was about an incident during the Kumar's Darjeeling visit. Gauranga Kabyatirtha, then subregistrar of Jaidebpur and an accomplished Sanskrit scholar, testified in court on this incident. He was present at this interview and said that Dr. Ashutosh Dasgupta, also present there, asked the sadhu in mixed Hindi and Bengali: "On the cornice of the house in Darjeeling, there was a bird. Who had shot it and why did you rebuke him?" Before the sadhu could answer, someone said, "Let Ashu Doctor give the name to Gauranga Babu before the question is answered." Ashu Babu whispered to him, "Birendra Banerjee." The sadhu's answer was "Hari Singh." Ashutosh immediately said, "But Hari Singh didn't go to Darjeeling at all. The answer is wrong." Then Birendra Banerjee was sent for. He came in and said that it was Hari Singh who had shot the bird. Birendra couldn't handle a gun.[58]

THE NAUTCH GIRL

It was well known that at the time when he married Bibhabati, Ramendra had a mistress by the name of Elokeshi. The defendant's lawyers for a long time attempted to contest this fact. As we will see later, the defense case initially was to present an image of the second kumar as a cultured aristocrat, utterly inconsistent with the illiterate sadhu who appeared in Jaidebpur twelve years after the Kumar's death. Accordingly, the idea that the second kumar was a wayward young man of uncouth habits and dissolute morals was resisted. During the plaintiff's examination, he had been shown a photograph which he identified as that of Elokeshi. Still the defense maintained that Elokeshi was a fiction; the second kumar did not have a mistress.

In December 1934, more than a year after the hearings had begun, Elokeshi Khemtawali, now fifty years old, herself came to court to give evidence on behalf of the plaintiff. She was shown a photograph that she identified as her own, taken in her house in Begumbazar in Dhaka by a professional photographer engaged by the second kumar. She was about twenty years old then, in the full bloom of her youth, which was why her skin looked so much lighter. At that time, the second kumar used to spend most of his time with her. She had met him first in Jaidebpur when she had gone there to sing and dance at the festivities organized to celebrate the birth of a son to the eldest kumar. Ramendra had fallen in love with her and had kept her for almost a month in a building called the Dewankhana within the Rajbari complex. Before she came back to Dhaka, he gave her Rs.300 in cash, a shawl, and a pair of fine Dhaka sarees. About a month later, he took her back to Jaidebpur, putting her up this time in a house called the Hawakhana. She lived there for a year and a half, during which time Ramendra got married. Elokeshi did not see him for four days, but he came to her on the day after his wedding. Sometime later, the second rani came to know about the affair and one day, accompanied by Jyotirmayi, she came to Elokeshi to rebuke her. Elokeshi insisted on leaving Jaidebpur. The second kumar arranged for a rented house in Begumbazar in Dhaka, where she stayed for two and a half years. After that she moved in with her mother into a house in Chandni Ghat. During this time, her relationship with the second kumar was close. Except when he was in Jaidebpur, he spent most nights with her. They stayed in her house, a few times in the Nalgola Rajbari, at times in a houseboat on the river.

Once, the second kumar went to Jaidebpur and did not return for five months. When he came to her next, he said that he was suffering from sores and bubo caused by syphilis. She insisted that she had never had that disease. This led to an altercation after which the second kumar went away. The relationship came to an end. Sometime later, Elokeshi became the mistress of Sarat Babu.

When the second kumar died in Darjeeling, Elokeshi heard the news. Later, she also heard rumors that his body had not been burned. After the sadhu made his sensational declaration in Jaidebpur, Elokeshi heard the news that the second kumar had returned. She went to see him in his house in Armanitola. There were a lot of poeple there, but she clearly recognized him. She did not speak to him that day. She saw him again at Nanak Shah's *akhara* (monastery) where there was a religious gathering organized by Sikhs. She looked at him long and suddenly their eyes met. The plaintiff came up to her and asked, "Elokeshi, how are you?" She saw him a few times after that. She had no doubt at all that he was the second kumar.

Elokeshi also said that Surendra Pattanayak, officer-in-charge of the Kotwali police station, had called on her three days ago and told her not to testify in this case. He said it was a case against the government and by appearing as a witness she would get into a lot of trouble. He also offered her fifty rupees for not appearing in court.[59]

JYOTIRMAYI'S TESTIMONY

The most important witness among the kumar's relatives to testify on behalf of the plaintiff was Rajkumari Jyotirmayi Debi, the kumar's elder sister. In the summer of 1934 in Dhaka, every day for almost three weeks, the

court of Pannalal Basu convened in the house of Jyotirmayi Debi who, as a
lady used to purdah, pleaded her inability to appear in an open courtroom.

B. C. Chatterjee led Jyotirmayi through the history of the Bhawal Raj
family and the childhood of the kumars. She said that there were private tutors at the Rajbari who taught the children. She herself read with the tutors
until the age of sixteen, when her second child was born. She was able to
read and write Bengali and also knew some English. But her brothers,
especially the two younger ones, had not had any education at all. This
was because their grandmother Satyabhama Debi interfered every time a
teacher tried to impose some discipline. Satyabhama was extremely indulgent toward her grandsons, and said that no harm would be done if they did
not become learned men. Although the kumars were sent to the Collegiate
School in Dhaka, they did not persist with their studies and after the death
of their father, the attempt at giving them a formal education was practically given up. Jyotirmayi also said that all the brothers and sisters could
speak some Hindi because there were many Hindustani servants in the Rajbari. Jyotirmayi and her elder sister Indumayi could speak the refined Bengali of the educated bhadralok, but the two younger kumars spoke, she said,
"like low-class people."

Shown some letters, produced as exhibits in court, said to have been written by the second kumar to his wife Bibhabati, Jyotirmayi examined them
closely and said they could not have been written by Ramendra. Ramendra
never wrote a letter to his wife. Indeed, he could not write at all. If there
were formal letters that had to be written for official purposes, he would
simply put his signature to something written for him.

Whenever there were European guests at the Rajbari, the eldest kumar
would attend to them. The two younger kumars would go and meet them
briefly but would never stay for meals. There was a polo ground at the Rajbari, and the eldest kumar and later the youngest kumar were enthusiastic
polo players, but the second kumar never played the game. He also did not
play football, cricket, tennis, or billiards.

Jyotirmayi had *kaṭā* (brown) eyes, the same as the plaintiff. The brownish tinge was unusual among Bengalis, but it was a family trait. She also
had small hands and feet like the plaintiff and this too was a feature shared
by many in her family. The skin near her wrists and instep was rough—
another family trait. Her complexion, like that of her brothers Ramendra
and Rabindra, was very fair, often described as European. European ladies
visiting the inner quarters of the Rajbari had commented on her complexion. She and her two younger brothers also had brown hair.

In the summer of 1909, she noticed that Ramendra was wearing bandages
on his arms and she was told that he had eczema. She also heard that Ramendra would be going to Darjeeling because of his sores. Ramendra had
asked her and their grandmother to accompany him and his wife to Dar-

jeeling and, after some hesitation, Jyotirmayi had agreed. But Satya Babu, Ramendra's brother-in-law, said that there would not be enough room in the house at Darjeeling. Jyotirmayi had then asked why it was necessary for Ramendra to go to Darjeeling to cure something as simple as eczema. Satya Babu told her that Ramendra was suffering not from eczema but from "a bad disease".

After Bibhabati, Satya Babu, and the rest of the party returned to Jaidebpur from Darjeeling, Jyotirmayi heard from some of the servants the story of how the kumar's body had not been cremated. She gathered this particularly from the accounts given to her by Birendra Banerjee and Sharif Khan, although she thought Sharif Khan's story was highly exaggerated. A month later, an anonymous letter was received by Ranendra, the eldest kumar, that the second kumar was alive. Ranendra was about to make inquiries when Satya Babu said that he would get certificates from Dr. Calvert, the civil surgeon of Darjeeling. After the certificates arrived, the eldest kumar did not proceed further in the matter.

Although Bibhabati left Jaidebpur for Calcutta, her relations with Jyotirmayi remained cordial until the arrival of the plaintiff. Of all her brothers' wives, Bibhabati was the closest to Jyotirmayi. The second rani often wrote to Jyotirmayi's daughters, and they met whenever Jyotirmayi was in Calcutta. Bibhabati was very fond of Jyotirmayi's son Buddhu. Whenever he went to Calcutta, he would stay with Bibhabati. She gave away some of Ramendra's European clothes to Buddhu. These were later given to the plaintiff, and they fitted him reasonably well. Buddhu also had several pairs of Ramendra's boots and these fitted the plaintiff perfectly. Jyotirmayi identified for the court some of the second kumar's clothes that had been presented as exhibits, including his durbar dress, which had been given to Buddhu by Bibhabati.

Jyotirmayi then narrated in detail the now well-known story of the sadhu's arrival in Jaidebpur, her questioning of him, and his admission of his identity. Some people who later turned against the plaintiff, such as Jogendra Banerjee and Phani Bhusan Banerjee, were at this time convinced that the sadhu was indeed the second kumar. The plaintiff recounted many incidents of the second kumar's life before his going to Darjeeling. He recognized many people, although sometimes he also failed to recognize them.

It was only after she was convinced that he was her brother did Jyotirmayi let him live in her house. She was very careful about this, which is why she insisted on the elaborate questioning and tests. After the declaration by the plaintiff, she and her sister Tarinmayi held a *bhāiphotā* ceremony to anoint their brother ritually and wish him health and a long life.

When tenants paid nazar to the plaintiff, he would give the money to Jyotirmayi. Whenever he needed money, he would ask her for it. She remembered that at one time in Calcutta, she had with her Rs.12,000 of nazar in cash, but pursuing her brother's case had ruined her financially. She had incurred a debt of Rs.20,000 on account of the plaintiff and did not know how much more she would have to borrow. Her annual income from her property was no more than Rs.1,200.

Not unexpectedly, Jyotirmayi's cross-examination by A. N. Chaudhuri was severe. As far as the government side was concerned, this was a conspiracy to instal an impostor, and Jyotirmayi was the chief conspirator. Much would be gained if this witness could be broken. Although she was being examined in her own house, the grilling combined with the July heat proved to be too much. One afternoon, the hearing had to be adjourned for the day because the witness fainted.

During cross-examination, Jyotirmayi Debi said that after the arrival of a sannyasi in Jaidebpur who wrote down on a piece of paper that their brother was alive and living as a sadhu, she and her grandmother were convinced that the second kumar had not died in Darjeeling. She had heard many rumors and had made many inquiries, especially in Benaras.

After the declaration of identity by the sadhu, he began to speak in the Bhawal Bengali that everyone spoke. Sometimes he used Hindi words, but Jyotirmayi never thought he was speaking anything but Bengali. She insisted that she had never said to anyone that Satya Babu or anyone else had attempted to murder her brother. All she knew was that Satya Babu had arranged the kumar's trip to Darjeeling and had come back to announce his death.[60]

OTHER RELATIVES

Jitendra Chandra Mukherjee was more familiarly known in Bhawal as Billu Babu. He was the son of Indumayi Debi, the eldest sister of the kumar. In his childhood, Billu had studied with the kumars in the Rajbari. In his testimony in court, he confirmed what was now already known about the inattentiveness of the two younger kumars in academic matters and that they gave up studies altogether after the death of Raja Rajendra Narayan. Shown some letters allegedly written by Ramendra to his wife, Billu Babu said that it was impossible for the second kumar to have written such letters. He also said that the second kumar had tried to play polo for a few days, but he held the reins with his right hand and the stick with his left. He was unable to strike the ball properly and, disgusted, he threw away his stick one day and never played again. Ramendra also sang loudly, and out of tune, while he bathed, but he never sang in public.

In his younger days, Billu Babu had taken only a casual interest in hunting. But he knew that even the expert hunters of the region did not know the various English terms used in the sport. The hammer of a gun was called *ghora;* they sighted the target with the *machhi;* when they killed a wild boar, they said that a *jangli suar* had been killed. He also said that English table manners were completely unknown in the Jaidebpur Rajbari. He did not know what a "cupboard" was, or a "dessert spoon," even though he knew what spoons and forks and knives were. When asked if he knew a "salt cellar," Billu Babu said it would have to be a man who sold salt; if not, he did not know what it was. He had read some English, and he was certain that if there were English expressions that he did not know, it was impossible for the second kumar to have known them.

Billu Babu recalled how the decision was made for the second kumar to visit Darjeeling. Billu had wanted to join the party, but Satya Babu had explained that chickens would be cooked in the only kitchen in the rented house there, and Billu, who was not used to eating chicken, would not find that acceptable. He also said that Billu would have to miss school. The second kumar had intervened and said that Billu could come and join them after his school closed for the summer.

He distinctly remembered the morning when the news came of the second kumar's death. The eldest kumar read the telegraph message aloud and it said that the second kumar had "expired at dusk." Sometime later, another telegram arrived either from Uttarpara or from Darjeeling saying that Satya Babu was intending to take the second rani straight to Calcutta. The eldest kumar immediately asked Jogen Banerjee to rush and intercept the mail train at Poradah station and bring Bibhabati to Jaidebpur.

After the party returned from Darjeeling, Billu was told by Birendra Banerjee that the kumar's body was taken to be cremated at night. But when the storm came, they had to take shelter at a place some distance away from the cremation ground. When they returned, the body could not be found. He had the same story from Sharif Khan. From his conversations with the second rani, who was very fond of Buddhu and Billu, he gathered that she had not been allowed by her brother to see her husband in his final hours. About a month and a half after the śrāddha ceremonies of the second kumar, two anonymous letters came to the eldest kumar saying that his brother was still alive. After this, the rumors began to circulate.

Asked if he did not have a material interest in the plaintiff's case, Billu Babu said that if he knew that the plaintiff was a swindler who could deceive the whole of Bengal, then he would not be wise to trust him to look after his interest after he had gotten his property. No, he was supporting the cause of the plaintiff because he was convinced that he was his uncle Ramendra.

At present, the plaintiff did not eat meat or fish and indeed could not stand their smell. He spent long hours every day in prayers and meditation. He ate both rice and chapati. Not surprisingly, Billu Babu was saying, the years spent as a renunciator had affected his uncle's lifestyle.[61]

Chandra Sekhar Banerjee, son-in-law of Jyotirmayi Debi, confirmed what had been said by others about the second kumar's character and the arrival of the sadhu in Jaidebpur. Chandra Sekhar had never seen the second kumar read or write, except for signing documents prepared for his signature. Ramendra could not speak English and avoided situations where he might be asked to converse in that language. Once when they were traveling together to Narayanganj by train, two European passengers who were in the same first-class compartment said something to the second kumar. He muttered a few sounds, turned to Chandra Sekhar and said that he would travel in the second class. They moved to another compartment.

After the self-declaration of the sadhu, he began to speak in the Bhawal dialect, although he had a slight Hindi accent. More significantly, he spoke with the local tribal people called Banua in their language. The second kumar used to spend a lot of time with the Banua because he would go into the forests with them. Most people in the Bhawal region could not understand the Banua language. On hearing the sadhu speak that language, Chandra Sekhar was completely convinced that he was none other than Ramendra.[62]

Satinath Banerjee, better known as Sagar Babu, was the younger son-in-law of Jyotirmayi Debi. He was with Rabindra, the youngest kumar, on the way to the Jaidebpur railway station on the fateful morning when the telegram arrived announcing Ramendra's death. Sagar Babu claimed to remember the exact words of the message: "Mejo Kumar expired in the evening." This telegram was never found in the records of the Bhawal estate. They came back to the Rajbari, where they met Jogen Banerjee, the secretary, and gave him the news. Jogen Babu said he had heard the news at night in Narayanganj on his way back from Barisal.

After her return to Jaidebpur from Darjeeling, the second rani stayed in her own room, crying most of the time. Billu and Buddhu were the only ones she talked to. Sagar Babu remembered that for many days she refused to talk to her brother Satya Babu.

Sagar Babu was present in Jaidebpur when the sannyasi came there in 1921. He and his elder brother Jogen Banerjee, the estate secretary, examined the sadhu very closely. Sagar Babu was convinced that this was the second kumar. Jogen Babu too had an open mind until he was upset by some allegations made against him by Gobinda Babu, Indumayi's son-in-law. From that time onward, Jogen Babu cooperated with the government.

Under cross-examination by A. N. Chaudhuri, Sagar Babu, like other relatives, was also asked about the kumar's education and habits. He confirmed Jyotirmayi Debi's description that the second kumar did not read or write, and did not care much for the refined ways of genteel folk. He denied that the second kumar had a dining room in his quarters at the Rajbari or that any of those rooms had a dining table or a sideboard.[63]

Sarojini Debi was an aunt of Bibhabati. Her husband had arranged Bibhabati's match with Ramendra, and Sarojini Debi remembered very well the wedding at Jaidebpur. Sarojini saw Ramendra several times—in Jaidebpur at the time of the wedding and later in Calcutta and Uttarpara during Ramendra's visits there—and grew quite fond of the new *jāmāi*. She first heard of Ramendra's death when her husband came home one evening in Uttarpara and said that a telegram had arrived with the news. She had other relatives in Darjeeling at the time and, in the course of the next few months, she heard many stories about the confusion regarding the cremation. She also heard rumors that the kumar was alive. She was on good terms with Bibhabati after her return to Calcutta and met her regularly. After the appearance of the sadhu in Jaidebpur, Sarojini had a great desire to see him, but her sons told her that the government had declared him an impostor. They said that if indeed he was the real kumar, she would get a chance to see him later. She never spoke to Bibhabati or Satyen about the return of Ramendra because she did not want to hurt their feelings. About a year ago, a visitor came to see her in her house in Uttarpara. When she saw him for a few seconds, she knew it was Ramendra. They spoke for about half an hour. Ramendra said that if she was sure she had recognized him, would she agree to testify in court? She said, "Yes."[64]

The Plaintiff in Public

Meanwhile, in the middle of its regular and extensive coverage of the trial, the *Ḍhākā prakāś* also reported from time to time stories of the plaintiff visiting other places in east Bengal. In July 1934, for instance, it quoted the Mymensingh periodical *Cārumihir* to report on the visit to Mymensingh of "the Bhawal sannyasi, well known throughout the country." The sannyasi-kumar, it seems, put up in a rented house in town where numerous men and women visited him every day. Brajendra Kishor Raychaudhuri, the famous zamindar of Gauripur, came to hear of this and immediately arranged for him to stay at one of his palatial houses. "He is being received everywhere like a prince. . . . Many zamindars and distinguished gentlemen are sympathetic to his cause. There is a visible excitement in the town," the *Cārumihir* said.[65] Of course, as Judge Pannalal Basu had reminded himself, this public acclaim of the plaintiff was not necessarily a point in his favor in this trial.

Chapter Ten

DARJEELING: THE PLAINTIFF'S CASE

THE TIME OF DEATH

THE plaintiff's case was that his alleged death had occurred in Darjeeling on May 8, 1909, in the evening. Since by Brahminical custom the body could not be kept overnight, arrangements were made to take it to the cremation ground later that evening. There were no male relatives of the kumar in his entourage. Thus, although there were many clerks and servants, there was a shortage of "respectable gentlemen," especially Brahmins, who could make up a funeral procession appropriate for a prominent zamindar, even when his death was so sudden and unexpected and in a place far away from home.

Thus, the plaintiff's side had to prove that the kumar's death had occurred in the evening and that there was an attempted cremation that night. Among their key witnesses on this point, the most prominent was a group of professors from Calcutta. They were on holiday in Darjeeling at the time, staying at the Lowis Jubilee Sanitarium, which had been originally set up as a hospital for tuberculosis patients but had been converted into a hotel patronized especially by the Bengali middle class of Calcutta. (There were two sanatoria set up in the 1880s for tuberculosis patients in Darjeeling—the Eden and the Lowis Jubilee—and both were called "Sanitarium.")[1] Satyendra Nath Maitra of the Indian Education Service, who had retired as principal of the Dacca Intermediate College, testified that he had stayed with his wife at the Sanitarium in Darjeeling between April and June 1909. He remembered that one evening at around eight o'clock, when he was sitting in the common room with his friends Professor Radha Kumud Mukherjee and Professor Haran Chakladar, a man came in with the news that a kumar of Bhawal had just died and that he had been sent to bring some people to carry the body and join the procession. Professor Maitra himself did not go for the cremation. On cross-examination by A. N. Chaudhuri, Maitra said that he did not remember seeing any funeral procession the following morning. He also had no definite recollection of a condolence meeting for the kumar held at the Sanitarium, but said that it was possible that he attended it. He vividly remembered the man coming in with the news, because the effect was dramatic, and the usual evening gathering in the common room dispersed immediately. He did not go to the cremation and indeed did not take an interest in the death because he did not know the kumar of Bhawal personally.[2]

Professor Radha Kumud Mukherjee, head of the Indian History Department at Lucknow University and author of many well-known scholarly books on ancient Indian history, said that

> While at the Sanitarium . . . I got no news of the Kumar of Bhowal, except that one evening when we were in the common room, the news of the passing away of a Kumar of Bhowal was delivered to us. . . . As far as I can recollect, only one man came and asked for help to carry the corpse. But I may say that I have no definite recollection of the number of men who came, but I definitely remember that the news came. It came before we had our dinner according to the bell. The dinner bell used to be struck at 8 or 8.30 pm, not before 8 pm. I never came to the common room after dinner, as I felt cold and could not go out of my room. I did not go to the cremation ground—it was too far below, and my health did not permit me.[3]

Professor Hiralal Roy of the Jadavpur Engineering College in Calcutta was a graduate of Harvard University and held a doctorate in engineering from the University of Berlin. He too was staying at the Sanitarium at the time. Roy remembered the evening of May 8 exactly as Professors Maitra and Mukherjee had done. They were assembled at about eight o'clock in the common room, where they were usually entertained with songs by Professor Maitra and a certain Ajit Babu. That evening, they all dispersed after the man arrived with the news about the kumar's death. Professor Roy did not go to the cremation, but he remembered attending the condolence meeting at the Sanitarium a few days later. At the time, he had no reason to suspect that the kumar had not been cremated or that he might still be alive.[4]

The Night Cremation

The kumar's alleged death had taken place in Darjeeling in the summer of 1909. Summer in Darjeeling was very special in those days. Indeed, one might say that Darjeeling came to life as a place only in the summer. Following a routine that was truly imperial in its conception, the higher levels of the administration of the province of Bengal moved from Calcutta to Darjeeling in April and returned only in July. In the days before motorized transport, it was not easy to move so many people and so much paper all the way from sea level to an altitude of eight thousand feet. But the railway engineers worked a miracle, and a line was laid all the way up to the hill station. A guidebook from the turn of the century cheerfully announced: "The trip to Darjeeling is now-a-days accomplished with the greatest comfort and ease, under circumstances very different from those ruling in the early years of the popularity of the station, when the long winding ascent had to be made by dâk palkies, hill ponies, or tonga carriages. Twenty-one and a quarter hour's easy railway travelling transports the traveller from Calcutta to Darjeeling."[5]

The climate was described as European. The air was healthy, utterly different from that of the steamy plains. "It is incredible what a few weeks of that mountain air will do for the Indian-born children of European parents; they are taken there sickly, pallid or yellow, soft and flabby, to become transformed into models of rude health and energy."[6] Or, more lyrically,

> Civil Surgeon's Digests read,
> 'Tend Darjeeling's Schools, and heed;
> Not a major ill of sorts,
> One can learn from such Reports;
> *No* complaints through heat or chills,
> *No* pains, potions, powders, pills.[7]

After a few years of careful tending, the immediate surroundings were turned into something resembling the Scottish highlands. And on a clear day, the view of the mountains was breathtaking. "'See Darjeeling and die!' has become a familiar aphorism now; and well it may, for how can one ever hope to be able to describe the awful beauty of the snowy range from this spot? . . . Truly earth is here decked in Nature's most sumptuous garment, and the fairest and noblest works of God are seen in perpetual alternation, constituting it an earthly paradise."[8] So they came to Darjeeling in the summer, to take in the air, view the mountains, go for long walks, write bad prose or worse poetry, and generally to recreate an ambience of European living high above the stifling tropical plains. The officials of empire, relieved at having escaped the summer heat, relaxed in their clubs along the Mall. Their clerks and minions, huddled in cramped and insanitary temporary quarters around the bazar, cursed their luck at having been chosen to make the trip.

It was because it was summer that there were so many Bengali gentlemen in Darjeeling at the time of the supposed death of the second kumar of Bhawal. Most were clerical staff in government offices in Calcutta who had accompanied their bosses along with their files and papers. Madhusudan Mukherjee worked in the Political Department of the Bengal Secretariat at Writers' Buildings in Calcutta. In the summer of 1909, he was staying at Bhutia Basti Villa in Darjeeling along with other employees of the government. One evening, he recalled in court, Surya Narayan Mukherjee came to their mess and asked Anukul Chatterjee, a fellow resident, to accompany him to the cremation of the kumar of Bhawal. Anukul asked

Madhusudan to come with them, but since Madhusudan was not on friendly terms with Surya Narayan, he did not go. Madhusudan remembered that Anukul returned from the cremation late at night drenched from head to foot. They did not discuss the cremation, and Madhusudan did not hear at the time that anything was amiss. Both Surya Narayan and Anukul were now dead.[9]

Jnanendra Nath Banerjee, who worked in the Public Works Department in Darjeeling, was also an enthusiastic actor in the amateur theater. He remembered two persons coming to his house at about 7:30 or 8 o'clock one evening to ask him to attend the cremation of the kumar. Since he did not wish to miss his rehearsals, he did not go. As he was returning home from the rehearsals sometime after midnight, he met Anukul Chatterjee, who also worked in the Public Works Department. Anukul Babu was drenched. When Jnanendra asked him where he had gone at that hour of the night, Anukul said that he had gone to the cremation of the kumar of Bhawal, but since the body had disappeared, he had come away. Jnanendra did not believe him, since Anukul Babu had a reputation for telling tall stories. Jnanendra did not remember if it had rained that night. Early next morning, he had gone to Kurseong, along with a large group of Brahmin gentlemen, to attend the *śrāddha* ceremony of the raja of Kakina. When he returned to Darjeeling that evening, he came to hear about the funeral procession of the kumar of Bhawal that had been taken out that morning. It struck him as odd, especially after what Anukul Babu had told him the previous night. In 1921, he had given a statement to N. K. Roy when he was asked about the cremation. At that time, he could sense that there was some controversy about the death of the kumar of Bhawal. It was only a few days later that he read in the newspapers about the appearance of the Bhawal sannyasi. In his statement to N. K. Roy, he did not mention what Anukul Chatterjee had told him because it was only hearsay and he himself had not been present at the cremation.[10]

Ranjit Singh was head clerk and accountant of the Darjeeling Club. In 1909, he was fourteen and studying at the Government High School. He lived with his parents in the police barracks at Darjeeling. He was fond of singing and dancing, and had joined the Nripendra Narayan Public Hall, where he often appeared on stage. On the evening of Saturday May 8, he was at the hall rehearsing for a show when two men came in to announce that a certain raja's son had died at Step Aside. Some of the Bengali gentlemen present there left soon after. That night at about ten o'clock, as he was going home, he heard the sound of "Hari bol" near the Chowk Bazar and saw a procession with a dead body and about thirty Bengali gentlemen. He did not recognize any of the gentlemen, but it was a foggy night and he could not see clearly. That night, there was a storm and it rained quite hard.

He remembered this because he had to go to Kurseong early next morning and was concerned about the weather. He did not notice when the rain stopped because he had fallen asleep. The next morning, he took the train to Kurseong, where he was part of a group that had been invited to sing songs at the śrāddha of the raja of Kakina. Many Bengali gentlemen were present there.[11]

Ashraf Alam, a clerk at the superintending engineer's office in Darjeeling, said that in 1909, he became acquainted with Sharif Khan, one of the members of the Bhawal staff. One evening, Sharif Khan came to him with a Bengali gentleman and said that the kumar bahadur had died. They asked Ashraf Alam for his help in buying fuel and other articles that would be needed for the cremation. Ashraf took them to Ram Khilan's shop, where they bought all the necessary things. Later that night, after he had gone home, he saw the funeral procession with about thirty people, several of them carrying lanterns. Lakshmi Chand, who in 1909 was an assistant in Ram Khilan's grocery store in Chowk Bazar, remembered Ashraf Munshi coming to the shop one day with a Bengali babu and some porters and saying that the raja of Bhawal had died and that they needed to buy articles for the cremation. Lakshmi Chand supplied them with ghee, kerosene, incense, rice, earthen pots, and other things that were carried away by the coolies. Later that night, he saw the dead body being taken past the bazar in a procession.[12]

Kiran Chandra Mustafi worked in the Bloomfield tea estate between 1907 and 1928 and lived in the gardens just below the police barracks. That evening in May 1909, he was taking a walk in the Mall where he met his friend Nanda, who taught at the Government High School. Nanda told him that a kumar of Bhawal had died at Step Aside. As they were walking toward the house, they saw the procession with the dead body. There were about twenty-five men in the procession and they joined it. After reaching the cremation ground at about ten o'clock, the charpoy with the dead body was placed on the ground and some people began looking for a suitable spot to build the pyre. Within fifteen minutes of their arrival at the ground, a storm broke out, followed by rain. Mustafi, along with eight or nine other people, took shelter under a shed at a slaughterhouse about a quarter of a mile away. There did not seem to be any other shelter nearby. They were there for almost an hour. When the rain stopped, they went back to the cremation ground and found that the charpoy was there but not the body. A few people were walking around with lanterns. When he asked what had happened, somebody said that the dead body was missing. Mustafi and Nanda waited for some time and then left. Mustafi did not know any of the people at the cremation ground, nor did he know the family of the dead kumar. He reached home that night at about 1 A.M.

Cross-examined, Mustafi said that the body on the charpoy was covered with a shawl and he could not say whether the body was tied to the charpoy. He did not know if all the people had left the cremation ground to avoid the storm and rain or if some had stayed back. Since he did not know anyone, he did not ask whether anyone was with the dead body or how the body had disappeared. He heard later that the body was cremated in the morning. He assumed that the kumar's body had been found and cremated. He had no reason to think anything else until many years later he read in the newspapers about the return of the second kumar of Bhawal.[13]

Bireswar Mukherjee, who in 1909 was posted in Kurseong, used to go to Darjeeling on most weekends, and stayed with his elder brother there. One particular Saturday, he had gone in the evening to the Nripendra Narayan Club, where he was told by his friend Sanjib Lahiri to come with him to Step Aside, where a kumar of Bhawal had died. When they reached the house, they found a dead body on a charpoy, covered in something like a shawl tied to the four corners of the cot. Soon afterward, the procession set out with the dead body. Bireswar and Sanjib took their turns in carrying the body. Bireswar assumed that the processionists included members of the Bhawal Raj family, although he did not know and did not ask. When they reached the cremation ground, it began to rain. Bireswar had to return to Kurseong the next morning, and so came away without waiting for the cremation. By the time he reached his brother's house, it was raining heavily.[14]

The evidence of Jatindra Chandra Chakravarty, who worked in the Darjeeling Municipal Office in 1909, was more or less the same. Nothing much had happened at the cremation ground before the storm because the fuel to be used on the pyre had not arrived. After waiting at the shed for about an hour, Jatindra along with others had returned to the cremation ground when the rain stopped. They found an empty charpoy with a wet shawl lying on the ground, and the body nowhere to be seen. Various people, lanterns in hand, were searching the place. Jatindra joined the search for a while, but after some time, came away and went home. The following evening, he heard that the cremation had taken place in the morning. He assumed that the body had been found in the night, but since there were not enough people to help, it had been brought back and taken out again in the morning. On cross-examination, Jatindra said that on their return to the cremation ground after the rain had stopped, he had asked various people he took to be part of the Bhawal Raj party, including one person who said he was the dead kumar's brother-in-law, how the body had disappeared. No one seemed to know.[15]

Chandra Singh used to work in the revenue office in Kalimpong in 1909, but often visited Darjeeling, where he owned property. That summer, he came to Darjeeling in the last week of April and stayed for a few days. He remembered seeing a man who looked like a European wearing a red lungi and yellow kurta. He was told that he was the kumar of Bhawal. A few days later, Chandra Singh was walking near the Sanitarium at about eight in the evening when he met two Bengali gentlemen from the engineer's office who asked him if he had heard that the kumar of Bhawal was dead. They asked him to accompany them to Step Aside. Chandra Singh went with them to the house, where he found a dead body lying on a mattress on the floor of an upstairs room. He asked the doorman how the kumar had died. The doorman said that he had "passed blood stools." A little later, the body was brought down to the ground level, laid on a charpoy, and tied to it with ropes. A white sheet was thrown over the body and on top of it a shawl whose corners were tied to the legs of the charpoy. The body was then taken out in a procession of about twenty-five people. When they arrived at the cremation ground, there were about thirty-five people there. This was the old cremation ground in Darjeeling. They had decided to stop there because the new one was further away and the footpath leading to it was difficult to negotiate at night. Soon a strong wind began to blow and, within minutes, it started to rain. Chandra Singh, along with about fifteen others, ran for shelter to the slaughterhouse a short distance away. When the rain stopped, they went back to the cremation ground and found some people, lantern in hand, moving about. A tall gentleman who was also present at Step Aside was very agitated and was shouting, "Where is the body?" The people were still searching when Chandra Singh came away. He was afraid that if the man was found to be still alive, anyone who had touched him would have to spend thirteen nights at the cremation ground, for that was the Gorkha custom. He came home, bathed, and went to sleep. He was unwell the next day and did not go out at all.

During cross-examination, Chandra Singh said that after he came back to the cremation ground, he saw the shawl covering the body lying on the ground and the white sheet at one corner of the charpoy. The ropes with which the body had been tied were loose, but they were still hanging around the charpoy. The charpoy was not in the same position that it had been put when they first arrived at the cremation ground.[16]

Why had it been necessary for the processionists to move away from the cremation ground to take shelter from the rain? Was there no shed at the cremation ground? Manimohan Sen had been assistant secretary of the cremation ground committee in Darjeeling between 1905 and 1908. He reported that in 1905, the old shed at the cremation ground was in a dilapidated state. It was decided to lay out a new cremation ground a little distance beyond the old one. The plans were prepared and approved by the municipality in 1907 and the new cremation ground started functioning at the end of that year. The residents of Darjeeling continued to use the old ground for several years after the new one was opened, however. The shed at the old ground had been pulled down and only the plinth remained.[17]

THE MORNING CREMATION

The plaintiff's side did not deny that there was a funeral procession taken out on the morning of May 9 that passed through the town of Darjeeling going down to the new cremation ground. It also did not deny that there was a cremation. But whose body was it?

Dr. Pran Krishna Acharya was the first witness to raise doubts about the covered body lying at Step Aside on the morning of May 9. Although he had been called in because it was feared that the kumar was dead, he had not been allowed to examine the body. Basanta Kumar Mukherjee of Darjeeling testified that on that morning, Jagat Mohini, a nurse working at the Victoria Hospital, came to his house to ask him to attend the cremation of the kumar. Jagat Mohini was known to the women of Basanta Kumar's family. He went to Step Aside at about eight in the morning and found a body lying there fully covered. He could not see the face of the dead person, nor any other part of the body. "In our country, dead bodies are never left untouched. But no one was sitting next to this body with a hand on the arm, although there were people moving around." About half an hour later, the body was taken out in a procession. As they were leaving the house, Basanta Kumar saw a young lady standing on the upstairs balcony, weeping. He was told that she was the wife of the kumar. The procession passed through town and finally reached the new cremation ground, where it was placed on a pyre. Normally, Basanta Kumar said, the dead body of a Hindu is bathed and the body rubbed with ghee before cremation. Nothing of the kind was done here. In fact, the body remained covered all the time. A young boy was asked to perform the mukhāgni. He was crying. No ceremonies were performed before mukhāgni. Basanta Kumar had never seen a Hindu being cremated that way before. He thought it very strange, although he did not suspect any wrongdoing or foul play.

In 1921, Basanta Kumar had answered questions put to him by N. K. Roy, deputy magistrate, regarding the cremation of the kumar. In that statement, he did not say anything about the strangeness of the cremation ceremonies because he had not been asked about them. During cross-examination, Basanta Kumar added that he did not notice the face of the dead person at the time of the mukhāgni. He could not say whether the body that was cremated was that of the kumar or not.[18]

An important witness for the plaintiff was Ram Singh Subba, a tea planter whose house was next to Step Aside and who looked after the property on behalf of its owner, Mr. Warnsey and later Sir N. N. Sircar. He described how in 1909 some officers of the kumar of Bhawal met him with a proposal to rent Step Aside for the summer. Everything was arranged, and the kumar arrived with his party. Subba met the kumar a few times and they spoke to each other in Hindi. One day, when Subba went to Step Aside to inquire if everything was all right, he was told by "Sala Babu," that is, Satyen Banerjee, that the kumar was ill. The next day, Satyen Banerjee told him that the kumar was suffering from hill dysentery. That Saturday, when Subba went to Step Aside at about 7:30 in the evening, he heard sounds of weeping. He went upstairs and found the kumar lying on a mattress spread on the floor. Dr. B. B. Sarkar, Dr. Ashutosh Dasgupta, and Satyen Banerjee were standing next to him. Subba was told that the kumar had died. He could see that in the next room, the rani was lying in bed, crying very loudly. Subba went home feeling very sad. Sometime in the middle of the night, he was awakened by his servant Srilal, who said that there was some trouble outside and that he was going out to look. Subba went back to sleep and did not know what had happened. Early next morning, he went to Step Aside, where Satyen Babu asked him to arrange for a new charpoy and to send some ghee, earthen pots, and other things to the cremation ground. There was a dead body in front of the house covered from head to foot with a shawl. Some time later, a procession of about twenty-five people left with the body for the cremation ground. Subba accompanied the procession all the way. He saw the body being put on the pyre. At that time, the cloth covering the body slipped to one side and Subba could see part of the left side of the body, including some black marks. No one could see the face of the dead person. About two weeks after the cremation, Subba heard a rumor that the Kumar's body had been taken to be cremated at night but, because of a storm and rain, it could not be burned.

Cross-examined by A. N. Chaudhuri, Subba said that he was about fourteen feet away from the charpoy at the cremation ground and could not say if the marks on the body were natural or not. They looked very strange and he had never seen marks like that on a human body. He did not ask anyone about the marks.[19]

Lal Chand, who owned a pan shop on Hill Cart Road in Darjeeling, said that one night in 1909 he saw a funeral procession passing his shop. There were several Bengali gentlemen in the procession and one of them came to his shop to buy a packet of cigarettes. He asked him who had died and was told that it was the raja of Bhawal. A little later, it started to rain heavily, and Lal Chand decided to close his shop. The next morning, there was another funeral procession and this time too he heard that it was the raja of Bhawal. Lal Chand was puzzled by this and asked the guard of the nearby hospital why the raja's body was taken out twice. The guard did not know. Later, Lal

Chand heard the story about the raja's body having gone missing from the cremation ground at night.[20]

Swami Omkarananda Giri, who became a sannyasi in 1929, had been an officer of the Darjeeling municipality from 1901 to 1927. He recalled that in May 1909 he was asked one morning by the nurse Jagat Mohini to attend the cremation of the kumar of Bhawal who had died the previous night. He went to Step Aside and saw the body being taken out of the house. He joined the procession and also carried the bier for part of the way. As the body was being put on the pyre, the cloth covering it slid to one side and he saw that the complexion of the dead man was very fair. He found the cremation quite extraordinary because most of the usual rituals were not performed. The body was kept covered the whole time until it was completely burned. He was unable to see the face of the dead man.[21]

THE NAGA SANNYASIS

The Darjeeling story was narrated vividly by Darshandas Naga, also known as Gopaldas, who claimed to be one of the Naga sannyasis who took away the second kumar from the cremation ground. Darshandas was from Ludhiana in Punjab and had left home at the age of twenty, finally to become a disciple of Harnamdas, his guru. Although people took him to be a Naga sannyasi, he was not really a sannyasi but only an *udasi* (member of the Udasi sect). He was not an educated person and did not know the religious texts. Dharamdas, who was the plaintiff's guru during his exile, was also a disciple of Harnamdas. Darshandas and Dharamdas, along with four or five other udasis of their sect, traveled all over northern India for several years, going from one shrine to another.

They had gone to Darjeeling to visit the temple of Mahakal. The bazar area of the town was too crowded, and they did not want to stay there. They walked down the hill and found some caves near the cremation ground. They decided to spend the night there. Sometime that night, Darshandas heard the chanting of "Hari bol." He had never been to Bengal before and did not know what that sound meant. He, along with Lokdas, another sadhu in their group, went out to look and saw several people at the cremation ground with lanterns. Darshandas and Lokdas went back to their caves. Soon it started to rain, and the chanting stopped. Lokdas asked Darshandas to go and see what was happening. Darshandas came out and heard a peculiar sound coming from the cremation ground. Darshandas shouted to Lokdas to bring out the lantern. They went to the cremation ground and found a man lying on a charpoy. Darshandas held the lantern as Lokdas loosened the ropes with which the man was tied to the charpoy. Lokdas then removed a cloth that was tied to the charpoy and another cloth with which the body was wrapped. He then looked very closely at the man and said that he was breathing. Darshandas ran back to the caves and called Dharamdas and Pritamdas. The four of them carried the man back with them to the caves. Darshandas noticed that the man was shivering and groaning. Once inside, they removed the wet clothes from the man's body and covered him with dry clothes and a blanket. In the meantime, Pritamdas came and said he had found a tin shed a little way below that would be drier and warmer than the caves. They carried the man there, but found that the shed was locked. Lokdas said that it was raining and there was no time to search for the key. Using the pair of tongs that sannyasis always carried, they wrenched open the chain tied to the padlock and went in.

The next morning, Dharamdas called in a barber and had the man's head shaven. Lokdas went and brought some small fruits that were crushed, and the juice was applied on the man's head. He was still unconscious. Some-time later, a Bengali babu came to the shed and said that since they were holy men, he would like to feed them. Dharamdas said that they did not need food. But they had a sick man with them who needed a blanket. The babu went and brought them a blanket and also said there was a larger shed a little distance away where he could arrange for all of them to stay. They moved to the new shed in the afternoon.

Three days after moving to the new shed, the man regained conscious-ness. He looked around him and asked where he was. Lokdas told him not to speak. He was administered some medicines—Darshandas did not know what they were. They stayed in the shed for about fifteen days, during which time the man recovered a little. He spoke to them in a language Darshan-das did not understand.

They went by train from Darjeeling to Siliguri. By this time, the man was able to walk, but he had to be helped. From Siliguri, they made their way to Benaras, stopping at many places. At one place, a sannyasi came and asked Darshandas where they had found the man who was traveling with them, because from his speech he seemed to be a Bengali. Darshandas avoided answering the question. In Benaras, they stayed at the Bara Akhara Udasin in Assighat, a major center of their sect. From there, they traveled to many places in Punjab and Kashmir. Sometimes, they met Bengalis who talked to the man and asked Darshandas and the other udasis who he was. They did not tell anyone how they had found him because they feared they might get into trouble.

For a long time, the man did not have a name; he was simply called the *brahmachari* (initiate). After a few years of being an initiate, Dharamdas gave him the mantra and he was named Sundardas. By this time, Sundardas would speak in Hindi. In the course of their travels, when they came to Nepal, Sundardas suddenly seemed to behave differently. It appeared as though he had something on his mind that was troubling him. Dharamdas asked him what it was. Sundardas said he seemed to remember things from his past and that it was very likely that his home was in Dhaka. Dharamdas asked him if he would like to go and look for his family. Sundardas said he would do so if Dharamdas told him to. Dharamdas said that now that he had a suspicion that he was from Dhaka, he should go and look for his family. After that, he should make up his mind whether he wanted to return to domestic life. If he chose not to stay with his family, he could come back and rejoin his guru in Hardwar. Dharamdas and Darshandas thought that Sundardas had now recovered his *purna gyan* or full consciousness, because he could remember his home. They took leave of Sundardas at Brahacha-tra and went to Hardwar, and subsequently met their guru Harnamdas at Nankana Sahib.

Darshandas did not meet Dharamdas again for quite a while. One day, his guru told him that he had met Dharamdas, who said that Sundardas had apparently gone back to his family. The guru asked Darshandas to go to Bengal. He was not to try to meet Sundardas because then the police would be after him. This was about eleven years ago. Darshandas came to Bengal and visited many places, including Dhaka. He went to Jaidebpur, where people told him about the second kumar who had returned as a sannyasi. He said nothing, because his guru had forbidden him to say anything about Sundardas.

He met the plaintiff in his house in Dhaka about a year ago. By then, the hearings had begun in court and Darshandas had heard about the plaintiff's testimony. He went all the way back to Nankana Sahib in Punjab to ask his guru what he should do. After hearing the whole story, the guru said that Darshandas should now testify in court in favor of the plaintiff.

Cross-examined by A. N. Chaudhuri, Darshandas said that he first heard that Sundardas was actually the raja of Bhawal from his guru Harnamdas, who had heard it from Dharamdas. He did not know how Dharamdas had heard this news. This was when Harnamdas had instructed Darshandas to go to Bengal. Although he was curious to see Sundardas again, Darshandas did not try to meet him because his guru had told him not to. In Jaidebpur, he had met Billu Babu and Jabbu Babu, who knew him as Gopaldas. They asked him if he knew the sadhu who had now been recognized as the raja of Bhawal. Gopaldas said, "No."

Asked why they took away the man they had found at the cremation ground instead of trying to find his family, Darshandas said that they were delighted that they had found such a *satvastu*—a blessed thing—as a dead man who had come alive. They did not stop to think if the man's family knew that he was alive or whether they might come and demand him from them. They had found a miraculous thing, and it was their duty to nurse the man back to health. For quite a while after they found him, they did not understand his language. They inferred from his movements what he wanted. In fact, until they came to Brahachatra, it seemed as though the man did not recover his full personality.

Q. Did it occur to you that these people who had come to cremate him would be glad if they saw the man alive?

A. No. We were glad we had got him. It did not occur to us that the other party would be glad.

Q. It did not occur to you that these people might be friends and relatives and might be glad to find him alive and might also be pleased with you?

A. If they were like that, they would have nursed him better at home and not left him at the *sasan* [cremation ground].

Q. Finding him alive, you thought they had come to cremate a living man?

A. We did not know whether they had brought him knowing he was dead or knowing he was alive. We did not know.

Q. Did it occur to you that there was *dushmani* [enmity] in their conduct?

A. Such a thought did not occur to us at the time.

Q. Why were you afraid of their coming back?

A. We did not know with what object they had brought him, and they might come and say: "Why have you touched him?" and they might take us to task.

Q. You thought they might beat you?

A. They might put us to trouble, but we did not think what exactly they would do. We only thought their coming would mean no good to us. There was no time for us four to take counsel then—at that moment, all we thought of doing was to remove him as quickly as possible, there would be time for thought afterwards. We did not think that the other party might snatch the man from us—no time to think all that. Our object was to hide him and not tell anybody about him—we have got a dead man living, it was a *satvastu* and had to be cherished tenderly.

Reexamined by B. C. Chatterjee, Darshandas said that he would never forget the first words uttered by the man after he regained consciousness. He said, "Āmi kothāy?" When he heard them, Darshandas did not know the meaning of those words. Later, he found out that it meant "Where am I?" But he was thrilled to hear a dead man speak. The memory had stayed with him ever since.[22]

Girija Bhusan Roy, who used to work as manager of a blanket factory and later as a contractor in Darjeeling, corroborated part of Darshandas's story. He said that one morning, he received a message from the guard of the workshop of the blanket factory. He went to inspect and was told that some sannyasis had broken open the door of one of the sheds. He found four sadhus there with a sick man lying on a charpoy. He asked the sadhus why they had broken into the place. They said that they were worried about the condition of the man with them and that if they were allowed to stay in the shed for a few days, they would be very grateful. Girija Babu asked them if they

FIGURE 8. The plaintiff as a Bengal zamindar

needed medicines. They said they would be happy to get a blanket for the sick man. Girija Babu asked them if they needed food, but they said they had what they required. Girija Babu arranged for a blanket to be sent, and also instructed the guard to see to it that the sadhus got what they needed.[23]

In early 1935, Pannalal Basu was routinely promoted to the position of first additional district judge of Dacca. The Bhawal sannyasi trial was now transferred to his new court and was renumbered Title Suit No. 38 of 1935. All this was, of course, a matter of formal procedure; the trial went on as before.

Chapter Eleven
_____

EXPERTS ON RECOGNITION

THE SPIRIT OF RATIONAL INQUIRY

"I⊤ IS perfectly clear," Judge Pannalal Basu would remark when pronouncing his judgment on the Bhawal case, "that the public sympathy is on the side of the plaintiff. One could see that from the crowds that would come to Court, and listen to the proceedings."[1] The case had indeed become the greatest legal sensation in Bengal's recent history. The pamphlet press kept churning out poems, songs, plays, skits— virtually all possible literary forms were mobilized to give vent to the popular excitement about this case. Most of the opinion was in favor of the sannyasi-prince. But this, as Pannalal Basu reminded everyone, was "of no avail to the plaintiff. The point will have to be decided on the evidence before the Court, not upon opinion, public or otherwise. This public sympathy for the plaintiff is rather a circumstance against the plaintiff in the sense that the Court will have to look closely at the evidence of the witnesses who speak to his identity."[2] The judge did not, however, mean this as an insensitive and obtuse statement on the passionlessness of the law. He was keenly aware that the excitement that had been aroused by this case was not irrelevant to an intelligent understanding of the issues involved. "When, however, it is said that this opinion which Mr. Chaudhuri often referred to as the opinion of the mob is itself a circumstance against the plaintiff it is difficult to agree, as though the true Kumar, if he has really returned would excite no enthusiasm, or would be left in the cold shade of neglect. . . . It is, therefore, a case in which one must proceed in a spirit of rational inquiry, and try to draw an inference from the evidence adduced."[3]

THE VISUAL SCIENCES

S. C. Chowdhury was a handwriting expert who had retired from service with the Criminal Investigation Department of the Bengal Police. He had been a recognized handwriting expert for almost twenty years. He testified that in 1932 he had been asked by Sasanka Coomar Ghose on behalf of the Court of Wards to compare the signatures "Romendra N. Roy" of the second kumar of Bhawal with those of the plaintiff. On April 8, 1932, he had submitted a report in which he had concluded, after careful examination of the specimens given to him, that all the signatures were of the same hand. In coming to this conclusion, he had considered the fact that there was a gap of some twenty years between the two sets of signatures and also that it might be possible that the second set was an imitation of the first, attained by careful practice. His opinion was that the variations between the two sets were more probably the result of change over time, but it was unlikely that the second set had been copied from the first. S. N. Chowdhury had also been approached by a lawyer acting on behalf of the plaintiff and had been asked to compare a set of signatures of the second kumar on a deed of settlement with the signatures of the plaintiff. Once again, Chowdhury had concluded that the two sets of signatures were of the same person.

During cross-examination, Chowdhury was shown certain letters allegedly written by the second kumar to his wife. Comparing these letters with samples of the Bengali signature of the plaintiff, the handwriting expert said that the letters showed greater graphic maturity and forearm movement than the signatures of the plaintiff. That is to say, he thought the letters were written by someone with a greater habit of writing than the plaintiff.[4]

To counter S. N. Chowdhury's evidence, the defense produced its own handwriting expert. He was Charles Hardless, who compared the signatures "Romendra N. Roy" and "Ramendra Narayan Roy" of the second kumar and the plaintiff. He said he had the signatures enlarged before comparing them. His conclusion was that the two sets of signatures were not by the same person.[5]

In August 1935, when the hearing of defense witnesses was well under way, there was a flutter in court when B. C. Chatterjee produced a publication called *Document Investigation*, Volume III, edited and published by Charles E. Hardless. In it, Hardless had advertised the fact that he had been selected by the Court of Wards on behalf of the government to give expert evidence in this suit. Chatterjee said that Hardless had committed contempt of court by advertising himself while the case was still pending and by suggesting that the Court of Wards had selected him on behalf of the Government of Bengal. Added to the advertisement was the following testimonial.

Mr Charles E. Hardless of Allahabad gave evidence as a handwriting expert for the Court of Wards in the Bhowal Sannyasi Case at Dacca. Mr. Hardless spared no pains in making his evidence cogent and convincing. His methods of investigation are scientific and up-to-date. He is not given to exaggeration/partisanship. His services should be of great assistance to courts.

(Sd.) A. N. Chaudhuri, Barrister-at-Law, High Court, Calcutta

This was further contempt of court, suggested Chatterjee. Chaudhuri replied that when he had given the testimonial, he had no idea that it would be published. He had written to Hardless asking him not to publish it any more. Pannalal Basu ruled that he would not take any steps if the advertisement did not appear again.[6]

John Lawrence Winterton was a well-known photographer of Calcutta. He had earlier worked at Bourne and Shepherd, the leading photographic studio in Calcutta, but in 1913 had set up his own establishment called Edna Lorenz (which, incidentally, continued successfully until the 1970s). Summoned by the plaintiff's side, he came to the Dhaka court and was presented with two photographs—one of the plaintiff taken by Winterton in his own studio a few months before and another of the second kumar taken many years previously. Winterton looked long and hard at the two photographs, and announced that in his opinion they were of the same man in different periods of life. The shape of the forehead, eyebrows, eyelids, nose, nostril, mouth and chin, and the lobes of the ear were the same. Owing to age, the hair was much thinner, but it still had the same kink and curl. He was then shown other photographs of the plaintiff. One with a beard and matted hair, he said, was a bad photograph taken with a short-focus lens: the hands and feet were out of proportion with the face. Another had made the face lighter than it should be, so that all the half-tone was lost, as a result of which the nose looked broader. One by one, he examined seven or eight photographs of the plaintiff. They were all of the same man, he said. He was then shown two photographs of Raja Rajendra Narayan. Winterton said that the shape of the ears reminded him of the plaintiff's ears.

Cross-examined by A. N. Chaudhuri, Winterton said that he had been born German but had been naturalized in England. His German name was Winterstein and his friends said that he still had a trace of German in the way he spoke English. He insisted that background stories of identity could never interfere with his technical comparison of photographs: he always compared them minutely, part by part, feature by feature. Presumably, he was also implying that his own mixed identity had made him sensitive to the fact that although cultural identities could be assumed, physical features could not be changed at will. Shown other photographs of the second kumar and the plaintiff, he declared once again that they were of the same person at different periods of life.[7]

An even more celebrated expert witness from the art world was produced in court on behalf of the plaintiff. He was Jamini Prakash Ganguly, vice principal of the Government College of Art in Calcutta and the leading portrait painter of the time. He was shown five photographs—one a recent photo of the plaintiff, another taken in 1925, and three of the second kumar when he was twenty-four or less. After examining them part by part, he concluded that four of them were of the same person. He particularly noticed identities in the forehead, the eyebrows, the eyes, the shape of the nose, the formation of the upper and the lower lips, and especially the peculiar shape of the ears where a lump of flesh twisted outward at the tip. Shown photographs of Raja Rajendra Narayan and of Jyotirmayi Debi, J. P. Ganguly said that the peculiarity of the lower lip in these photographs was the same as in the photographs of the second kumar and the plaintiff. The plaintiff's eyes, Ganguly said, were light brown. To paint them, he would take burnt umber, which was the color of the plaintiff's hair, and mix it with other colors to make it lighter in depth. The plaintiff's ears were large and very distinctive; in all his life as an artist, Ganguly had never seen ears like these. They were not stuck to the cheek but pendant: there was a cleft between the lobe and the cheek.[8]

For the defendants, too, there were distinguished experts offering their opinions on the photographic evidence. Percy Brown was the principal of the Government Art College, Calcutta, and as such, J. P. Ganguly's senior in the college hierarchy. He was the author of several authoritative books on Indian art and architecture. He was also a keen photographer. Examining the photographs of the kumar and the plaintiff, he concluded that they were not of the same person. The kumar's skull and forehead were broader; his hair was wavy whereas the plaintiff's was straight; the outer corner of his eyes were higher than the inner corner, whereas the plaintiff's eyes were horizontal. The plaintiff's nose was wider; his earlobes stuck out whereas the kumar's were pendant.[9]

M. Musselwhite, managing partner of Bourne and Shepherd, the premier photographic establishment of Calcutta, also appearing for the defendants, said that the photographs of the kumar and the plaintiff were not of the same person. He said that the ears were of different shape and that the top of the ear in relation to the eye was higher in the kumar's photos than in the plaintiff's. The kumar's nose was sharp, the plaintiff's was flat and distended. The kumar's eyes were brighter, larger, and spoke of an open and frank contenance; the plaintiff's eyes were narrower. He agreed, however, that all the photos of the kumar had been retouched, whereas those of the plaintiff had not.[10]

INTERPRETING THE PHYSICAL EVIDENCE

One of the surviving medical records of the second kumar came from his insurance papers. The kumar had been examined in Calcutta by Dr. Andrew Caddy in March 1905, when his life insurance policy was made. In it, his height was mentioned as 5 feet 5 inches and the identifying marks were noted as "Hair brown, fair moustache. Eyes grey." At this time, the second kumar was twenty-one years old. Curiously, this medical record was not submitted in court by the Court of Wards along with the other insurance papers, even though it was clear that the Board of Revenue had called for and examined it in 1921 immediately after the sannyasi had declared himself the second kumar. The document was procured by the plaintiff's side from the office of the insurance company in Edinburgh and produced in court as late as December 1934, more than a year after the hearings had begun.[11]

Girish Chandra Sen, former agent of the City of Glasgow Life Assurance Company, had sold the life insurance to the second kumar. He recalled in court that one afternoon in April 1905, he had taken the second kumar to be examined by Dr. Arnold Caddy. Girish Chandra translated Caddy's questions into Bengali and the kumar's answers into English. After finishing his examination, Caddy filled out the forms of the insurance company and asked if the kumar had any marks of identification. Girish Chandra replied that the kumar's fair complexion, grey eyes, and brown hair, which were uncommon among Bengalis, would be enough identification.[12]

Another document among the insurance papers obtained by the plaintiff's side was an affidavit by Kali Prasanna Ghosh, the former manager of the Bhawal estate, made out in 1910 as part of the claim for the kumar's life insurance money. "I, Rai Bahadur Kali Prosanna Vidyasagar C.I.E., do hereby solemnly declare that I was for the last 25 or 26 years personally acquainted with Kumar Ramendra Narayan Roy whom I knew from his very birth, that he died aged about 26 years at Darjeeling on the 8th of May 1909; that his personal appearance was as follows: Complexion fair, eyes and hair rather brownish; strong-built, average stature."[13]

Of the visible marks on his body, the plaintiff had on his forearm a tattoo in Urdu script that was transliterated for the court as "Baba Dharam Das da chela naga." Translated from the Punjabi, this was interpreted to mean "The novice-Naga, disciple of Baba Dharam Das."

The plaintiff, when his height was measured in court, was 5 feet 6 inches without shoes.

Dr. MacGilchrist of the Indian Medical Service, appearing as an expert on behalf of the plaintiff, was asked how long a man could grow in height. He said that in India a man could grow upto his twenty-fifth year. Thus, a man who was 5 feet 5 inches at twenty-one or twenty-two could grow to 5 feet 6 inches at twenty-five. The limit was reached when the ossification of certain bones was complete. Dr. Bradley of the Royal Society of Tropical Medicine, also called to court as an expert, said: "Twelve to twenty-one is the most active period of growth in height, other conditions as to food etc. being equal. We generally expect growth to stop at twenty-two or twenty-three, but exceptions occur."[14]

On the other identifying marks, Jyotirmayi Debi had said that the second kumar had thick and scaly skin on the top instep near his ankles, a tiger claw mark on the right arm, an injury mark on the left ankle caused by a carriage wheel, a broken tooth, and an operation mark on the back. When cross-examining her in June 1934, the defense lawyers insisted that there were no such marks on the second kumar. The marks had been found on the plaintiff and were now being imputed to the kumar. In September 1934, the defendants stated their case that the kumar had no carriage accident in which the wheel passed over his ankle, and that he did not have the mark that the plaintiff had on his ankle.

Col. Denham-White, FRCS, professor of surgery at the Calcutta Medical College and resident surgeon of the Presidency General Hospital, appeared on behalf of the defendants. Despite his qualifications as a surgeon, he had built up a "gigantic practice" in Calcutta as a general physician and was referred to by another English member of the medical service as an "incredibly good doctor."[15] Denham-White examined the plaintiff and thought the plaintiff's scaly feet were a condition of hyperkeratosis, possibly due to deficient endocrine secretion. MacGilchrist, the expert produced by the plaintiff, thought that it was ichthyosis or fish-skin, and that it was hereditary. The mark on his ankle Denham-White described as an "irregular scar over the top of the left outer ankle." Until this time, the defense case still was that the kumar had no such mark. When the medical report arrived from the insurance company, however, it was discovered that Dr. Caddy had in 1905 noted as one of the identifying marks of the second kumar an "irregular scar over the left outer ankle." This appeared to be a major piece of evidence in favor of the plaintiff, and the question would be asked why the defense had not produced this medical report in court even though the Court of Wards had a copy of it in its files.[16]

The plaintiff was examined on behalf of the court by a team of three doctors—Lieutenant Colonel Denham-White and Major Thomas representing the defendants and Lieutenant Colonel K. K. Chatterjee representing the plaintiff. They found a swelling on the right side of the bridge of the nose, bony in origin. What was it? Denham-White thought it was traumatic, caused by a blow or an injury. Thomas could not say definitely—it could be an abnormality in the nasal bone or the remnant of an injury. Chatterjee, who was senior professor of surgery at Carmichael Medical College and an acknowledged researcher and specialist on venereal diseases, was quite definite that it was a syphilitic node, caused in the tertiary stage of the disease in which a node that had formed on the nasal bone had ossified. Dr. Chatterjee also pointed out that during the plaintiff's medical examination, Dr. Denham-White had to squeeze the testes three times before the plaintiff winced. A normal man would have screamed at the pressure. The loss of testicular sensation and a fissure on the plaintiff's tongue, Chatterjee said, were the signs of an old syphilitic man.

Dr. Bradley, expert witness for the plaintiff, said that there were several marks on the plaintiff's body that might have been caused by syphilis. "I saw those bleached-out depressions, which might have been caused by syphilis, on the front of the legs and some on the forearms." He also said that if a patient has had tertiary-stage syphilis, he is never cured, even with treatment.[17]

The Cause of Death

Recognition could only be part of the plaintiff's case. What about the supposed death of Ramendra Narayan, the second kumar of Bhawal? How had that occurred?

Colonel J. T. Calvert, former civil surgeon of Darjeeling and later principal of the Calcutta Medical College, was, as we have mentioned, examined in commission in London. Calvert said that the second kumar of Bhawal had died from pain caused by biliary colic when a stone was impacted in the duct. The patient's condition had deteriorated through the day, and he finally collapsed and died at night. Calvert saw the patient die and left the house sometime after the death. There was no sign of pneumonia nor were there any signs of arsenic poisoning. As he had said in his affidavit made out for the insurance company, Calvert maintained that he had attended the kumar for fourteen days in Darjeeling and was assisted by Dr. Nibaran Sen, who was now dead. The patient was suffering from pain caused by biliary colic. "That is what he had when I saw him first, in consultation, after his arrival in Darjeeling. I watched the condition from day to day. So far as I remember, he had some minor attacks off and on, finally culminating in the fatal seizure which we were not anticipating."

Under cross-examination, Calvert said the following.

Q. Did you prescribe any medicine for the pain in the right side of the abdomen when you saw the Kumar first?
A. I wish to protest against questions on immaterial matters, which, in my opinion, after I have stated clearly the facts I know I remember, may lead me, or confuse me, to think that I remember these small details after so long a lapse of time. (*In answer to the question which was repeated, Col. Calvert says*) I do not remember but most certainly I must have done so.
Q. In what form?
A. I treated the condition from day to day, and I can't remember now what I gave him.

He said that he did not remember when he first recorded the time of death. It must have been when the kumar's men brought him the claim on the insurance policy for his signature. He made no notes and did not keep a diary of his treatment. He did, however, remember the case because it made a great impression on him. He felt that the death of the young man was avoidable if only he had agreed to the treatment. He knew the death had occurred around midnight because he had recorded 11:45 as the time of death in the insurance certificate. He would not have written it without first ascertaining the facts. Shown the first prescription he had made out for the kumar on May 6, he agreed that it was a prescription he was "in the habit of giving for stomach troubles." The spirit amonia mixture was "a carminative used in dyspepsia," and the lint opii would "suit local pain of any kind . . . superficial pain." Asked if this was what would be prescribed for biliary colic, Calvert said it was not a question of what treatment was necessary but what the patient would accept. Since the kumar would not accept an injection, this was the next best thing. He was then shown the prescriptions that were administered on May 8, the day the Kumar died.[18]

℞

Mag. carb.
Sodi bicarb
Bismuth Carb
Pulv. Tragacanth Co.   ... aa ʒi
Oil cajuputi   ... m ℥xii
Aqua menth. pip   ... ad ℥vi
     T.D.S.
               Sd./ J. T. C.

℞

Sodi Citrate   ...   ʒi
Aqua Sterilized   ... ad ʒvi
     with milk as directed.

℞

Pep. Powder fresh.
           Sd./ N. C. Sen

℞

Atropia Tab.   ... Gr. 1/100
Strych Tab.   ... Gr. 1/30
Digitalin Tab.   ... Gr. 1/100
Ether Pure   ... 1/2 oz.
Morphia Tab.   ... Gr. 1/8
         Sd./ N. C. Sen

℞

Spt. Ether	...	ʒiv
Spt. Amon Aromat	...	ʒiv
Aqua Camphor	... ad ʒviii	

⅛ for a dose.

℞

Ext. opii

Belladonna

Saponis ... ad Gr. ½

    M. ft. Pill send 6 such

    T.D.S.

Sd./ J. T. C.

℞

Lint Saponis	...	ʒii
Sinapis Co.	... ad ʒii	

    To rub all over the limbs with ginger powder.

℞

Lint Chloroform

Belladonna ... ad ʒii

    To be applied over the stomach.

℞

Spongis Lelini ... 12″ × 12″

Sd./ N. C. Sen

On his first prescription of the day, Calvert was asked if there was anything in it to stop "watery motion with blood." Calvert said that it was not usual for patients to pass watery stools with blood, and to his knowledge that was not the kumar's condition. The kumar was not suffering from diarrhea that morning. He had passed bloodstained mucus with a little free blood, caused by the biliary colic.

Was Calvert present when the kumar died? The doctor said that the collapse was "uniformly downhill" and the end was "sudden." He saw the man dead and left after some time. In cross-examination, he was asked the question again.

Q. Do you remember if Mr. Lindsay asked you if you were present at the death of the Kumar?

A. To the best of my belief, he asked me if I recollected the death of the Kumar. He was writing eleven years after the death took place.

Q. Did Mr. Lindsay ask you if you were present at the death of the Kumar and if you saw the body after death?

A. It is quite possible he may have done so.

Q. If Mr. Lindsay did enquire of you if you were present at the death of the Kumar and if you saw the body after death, what was your answer?

A. My answer was I recollected very well his death, but at the moment I could not remember with certainty whether I was present at the moment of death or not. I don't remember any question being asked as to seeing the body after death.

(Mr. S. N. Mukerjea (plaintiff's counsel) says the witness's answer shows the existence of a letter from Col. Calvert in answer to Mr. Lindsay, and he calls for that letter.)
(Mr. Pringle says that the letter has never been called for, and this is not the time to call for it.) (Letter not produced.)
(Mr. Pringle produces a "brief" copy of a letter which he hands to Mr. S. N. Mukerjea for perusal. Marked for identification "X").[19]

Calvert's reply to Lindsay's letter was, however, later produced in court. In it, in 1921, twelve years after the kumar's alleged death, Calvert had said: "I cannot now be certain whether I was present at the moment of his death." B. C. Chatterjee pounced upon the contradiction and alleged that Calvert had given "transparently false evidence" in England in 1931 when he said that he was present when the kumar died. Besides, why was the defense so unwilling to produce this letter in court? Was it not because it would throw Calvert's testimony into doubt?

Indeed, was Calvert's evidence consistent with the facts represented by the prescriptions, the other medical records, and the testimonies of other witnesses? One of B. C. Chatterjee's principal tactics was to put into question Calvert's death certificate and his assertion that the kumar had died of biliary colic.

A major expert witness Chatterjee relied on was Lieutenant Colonel A. C. MacGilchrist. He had impeccable credentials as an expert on medicine and enjoyed a reputation as a clinical practitioner as well as a research scientist. If someone had to be put up in a British Indian court to challenge the expert testimony of a civil surgeon like Calvert, it would have to be a civil surgeon of even greater eminence. MacGilchrist had just retired from a career in the Indian Medical Service, during which he had been civil surgeon of several Bengal and Bihar districts. He had an M.B. and an M.D. degree from Edinburgh, a D.Sc. degree in pharmacology from the University of London, and was a member of the Royal College of Physicians of London. He had been professor of physiology of the Calcutta Medical College and a fellow of the well-known Royal Society of Tropical Medicine and Hygiene of Calcutta.

MacGilchrist was shown several prescriptions made out for the treatment of the second kumar on May 6, 7, and 8, 1909. He did not think most of them were intended for the treatment of biliary colic. The first prescription of Dr. Calvert of May 6 appeared to be meant for a simple case of indigestion, especially flatulence. The external application of opium would have been useless for biliary colic, since none of the active ingredients would be absorbed. Another prescription seemed to be for diarrhoea or tenesmus. It is possible, he said, that because of a loss of fluids, cramps had set in the muscles that could, in the extreme, lead to death. The prescription for soap, mustard, and ginger powder to be rubbed over the limbs could be meant for cramp of the muscles. These cramps could be caused by arsenic poisoning or by cholera or by acute diarrhoea. He did not think anyone would prescribe it for gall stones. The prescription directing liniment of chloroform and belladonna to be rubbed over the stomach would be useful for pain in the stomach. He would not prescribe it for impacted gall stones. The treatment for biliary colic was hot bath and hot fomentation, and also olive oil. In case of pain, morphia could be administered. If the patient refused injection, morphia could even be administered orally. But MacGilchrist asserted that there was not a single prescription in the entire lot presented as exhibits that prescribed any medicine to be given during the intermission of biliary colic. Rather, there was one prescription that was particularly appropriate for shock and loss of fluid. On Dr. Ashutosh Dasgupta's prescription, he said that it contained quinine, arsenic, strychnine in the nux vomica, and two drastic purgatives—aloin and euonymin. "It could be given as a general tonic in chronic malaria. The doses were within therapeutic limits, but largish for a tonic—a tonic should not purge. The medicine, if taken as directed three times a day, will purge." McGilchrist thought that this prescription conveyed an idea entirely opposite to that of Calvert's first prescription of the previous day. Calvert's prescription was sedative; this one would irritate the stomach. One would not give it for biliary colic or for gastric irritation and flatulence. In cross-examination, he was asked whether the arsenic prescription could cause arsenical poisoning. MacGilchrist answered: "I was not told that there was an attempt to poison the patient by giving him a large dose of As. . . . Nobody told me that 12 of these pills were in fact administered. So far as my information goes, the poisoning might be due to accident—I have already said I had no knowledge as to whether it was due to accident or otherwise."[20]

Another medical expert called by the plaintiff was a Canadian doctor by the name of Bradley who was a fellow of the Royal Society of Tropical Medicine. Asked about the arsenic prescription of May 7, Bradley said that given the symptoms as reported, there could have been an overdose.

Q. What brings overdose in your mind?
A. The picture of arsenic poisoning. I mean, if I had been called and seen the patient in that condition and seen this prescription, the first question that I would ask is: "How many of these have you given him?"

And again.

A. Judging by what we know of the patient it might prove serious in combination with the other ingredients, but I would come to the conclusion that an overdose had been given by mistake, but I should say that this prescription as it stands, one pill three times a day, might itself prove serious under the circumstances as I visualise them, but I should imagine an overdose, when there were so many doctors and nurses, but I put in nurses as I read in Col. Calvert's evidence that there was a nurse on that day and she does not appear again—I should imagine some interference with each other. I should suspect an overdose—the case being muddled up in some way. How can it be otherwise when on three days you have an amazing collection of prescriptions? It is certainly not the etiquette of our profession to administer a medicine to a patient behind the back of the consulting physician. . . .

Q. Are you suggesting that Col. Calvert did not treat the case properly?

A. I did suggest that in view of his statement that there was bright red blood in stools and the collapse and death of the patient. I think that I should add in defence of Col. Calvert that he failed to realise that there was any influence or factor in the case until it was too late. He was too great a physician to make a careless mistake. He was proceeding on the assumption that it was biliary colic until it was too late. I don't want to criticise a man like Col. Calvert. Either he made a mistake or his memory was at fault.[21]

Bradley, in fact, was plainly suggesting that Calvert was unaware of Ashutosh Dasgupta's intervention in the case until it was too late.

Col. Denham-White and Major Thomas, who appeared as experts on behalf of the defendants, also gave their opinions on the Darjeeling prescriptions. Major Thomas agreed that Calvert's first prescription was an alkaline carminative mixture suitable for dyspepsia of any kind. Denham-White said that it was a common or garden medicine. On Ashutosh Dasgupta's prescription of the following day, Thomas said that there might have been suspected malaria—hence the quinine. Aloin and euonymin were purgatives, so that one could guess that the patient was constipated. Nux vomica and arsenic were tonics, and the dose of arsenic was well within range. If the pills were taken as directed, they would not cause arsenical poisoning. Thomas felt that the prescription might have been given purely empirically, "thinking that if there was malaria, it might be treated." In cross-examination, he was asked: "Do you know that in India people wanting to poison by arsenic arm themselves in the first instance with a prescription containing asenic?" Thomas answered: "I should think it very possible that they would do that." On the subject of the prescriptions made out on the day of death, Thomas was asked if he knew that the kumar had diarrhea. He said he did not know that. He had been told that the kumar's stools that day contained mucus and blood, and he would not call that purging.[22]

Shown Ashutosh Dasgupta's prescription, Denham-White said, "I presume the doctor had in his mind a case of chronic malaria, complicated by constipation, or *vice versa*. Quinine and arsenic are common remedies for chronic malaria, and aloin and euonymin are purgatives." The doses were within prescribed pharmaceutical limits. Was it possible that if twelve such pills were trussed up in a solution and given to a patient, it would cause arsenical poisoning? Denham-White said that no human being could be persuaded to swallow twelve such pills, and if administered in a solution, it would be vomited out. On the final day's prescriptions, he said, "It is my opinion that the illness was dysentery but the treatment was not of that."[23]

THE MENTAL SCIENCES

The Ranchi Mental Hospital was a leading center for the treatment of mentally ill patients in British India, and Colonel Berkeley-Hill, superintendent of the hospital, was one of the pioneers of clinical psychiatry in the country. Testifying in court in Dhaka, he said that he had been studying the mental condition of human beings for more than thirty years. He had read the plaintiff's testimony before coming to court. He thought that the story told by the plaintiff about his loss of memory was quite plausible. Given the fact that the kumar was about twenty-five years old when the events in Darjeeling took place, it is very likely that his bodily processes, capacity for reflex action, and mechanical adjustments were unimpaired while he had a complete loss of memory. Was it possible for someone to lose memory for as long as eleven years, as the plaintiff had claimed? Berkeley-Hill said that the longest period he had read about was seventeen years, so that it was by no means impossible. On the question of language, Berkeley-Hill said that it was quite natural for people to acquire an accent when they lived for a long time in another country. He had noticed that English people who lived in America for many years spoke with "a Yankee twang." It was not unnatural at all that the plaintiff still spoke Bengali with a Hindi accent.

During cross-examination, Berkeley-Hill said that the condition described by the plaintiff was called amnesia. It was different from aphasia. If there was aphasia due to cerebro-spinal syphilis, it could lead to death if left untreated. Berkeley-Hill was unwilling to attribute any cause to the plaintiff's amnesia, since he had not examined him medically. On the basis of the account provided by the plaintiff, it was impossible to tell whether the loss of memory was due to physical or mental causes. A possible mental cause that might result in this sort of amnesia was the fear of death. A physical cause could be an injury that produces a shock in the brain resulting in loss of memory. Questioned by A. N. Chaudhuri, he admitted that he had personally never come across a case where a loss of memory had lasted twelve years.

On the side of the defendants, Major Thomas and Major Dhunjibhoy of the Indian Medical Service gave evidence. Major Thomas thought that the condition described by the plaintiff suggested a case of double personality: a man who had forgotten for a period who he was, but was otherwise normal, "dissociated, yet adapted." If that was so, then certain elements in the plaintiff's story were not possible. For instance, if in the first year of his exile, from Darjeeling to Benaras, he was as he describes—"not conscious etc."—then that would indicate a condition of regression which was not consistent with being dissociated and adapted. Regression would be a case where an adult would suddenly revert to being like a child. This could not coexist with simultaneous behavior like that of an adapted adult. Second, when he returned to his primary personality, he could not be expected to remember his secondary personality. Therefore, after regaining his memory of his life as a kumar, it was not possible for him to remember the phase of his being like a child and traveling with the sadhus. Major Dhunjibhoy added that dissociation usually occurred in persons with a neuropathic trait such as hysteria. He also said that regression could not have degrees: one either regressed into the child state or not.

Popular Fantasies

Beyond Death (A Story)
[1]

Don't be startled, I'm a living person.

Even the sight of a messenger of death sent by Yama could not have caused so much panic—Lilamayi froze. She couldn't even scream. The man had matted hair and was dressed in the ocher robes of a sannyasi. Lowering the pistol he was pointing at her, the sannyasi said, It's been a long time—I hope you've recognized me?

Her voice quivering, Lilamayi answered, No—who are you?

Do you really want me to tell you? Are you sure your heart didn't skip a beat when you saw this long familiar face? Remember the day when I stood exactly at this spot, pointing my pistol at you, shouting, Lila! a bullet! That's how I want to punish you! But it was your impossibly beautiful face that stopped me. Remember?

Sannyasi, why have you entered my room like a thief?

Only to tell you that I am still alive. I know you've recognized me, but you won't admit it. No matter, I'll prove it.

Prove what?

That I am your husband and the owner of this zamindari.

My husband died—there was a *śrāddha*—many years ago. What you claim is false.

I see you've reached the last stage of moral decline. If you've recognized me, say so, I could still have mercy on you. But remember, I won't in the future.

I am not worried about the future. You don't mean a thing to me.

I didn't come here to kill you. I wanted to find out your mind—now I know. It won't be right for me alone to punish you for your sins. You must be punished in court, in front of the whole world. Even if you don't recognize me, many of my relatives will.

The sannyasi left. Lilamayi became more and more restless. How incredible! Her husband still alive? This was worse than her worst nightmare. Before the sannyasi appeared, she was riding high with excitement; now suddenly, she seemed to hit a wall. Her heart trembled in fear. The man had been cleverly poisoned and killed. She was now the owner of a huge property and enjoying to the full the pleasures of life. Suddenly he reappears in person—how astounding! Fetid fumes of anxiety seemed to suffocate Lilamayi; she could hardly breathe.

With a loud bong, the clock struck one. Her face white as ash, Lilamayi was pacing restlessly within the room. Suddenly, with unsteady drunken steps, a man entered her room. His face was beaming with pleasure.

Thanks! Dear! I'm not surprised that you are still awake at this hour of the night. I can still feel the intensity of your love.

Oh, stop it! The sword of disaster is hanging over my head. What have you done, Doctor?

Lilamayi's voice sounded abnormal.

Like a passenger traveling comfortably in the Darjeeling Mail when it suddenly meets with a collision, the doctor took some time to recover from the shock. Still dazed, he said, Why, what's the matter?

If he must stay alive, why did we have to take this risk?

Who are you talking about? Who is still alive?

My husband.

That's a lie.

It's true. He was here. He left only a moment ago.

You must have been dreaming.

Lilamayi explained that what she was saying was true. The doctor suddenly realized that the effects of his drink had vanished. Quickly, he took out a bottle from a secret pocket and poured out the liquid into his mouth.

Don't worry, Lila. Don't worry. Even if it's true, he can't do us any harm right away.

May be not right away, but some day he will.

No, not even that. How can he prove anything after so many years? It all happened a long time ago. Who will believe him? Here, drink a little, get rid of all these worries. Don't burden your life with these anxieties.

Pouring out a drink, the doctor held the glass to her lips as Lilamayi drank.

[2]

The story is mysterious. Gaurishankar was the son of a rural zamindar. Despite his best efforts, the father had failed to give his son a good education, because Gaurishankar was by nature boisterous and inattentive to his studies. He was more interested in hunting in the forests than in studying at school. Noticing the signs of waywardness in his son's moral character, Gaurishankar's father decided to get him married to the enlightened, educated, beautiful city girl Lilamayi.

Lilamayi's father was not very well off. He knew the groom was not educated, although he was certainly wealthy and handsome. But Lilamayi decided she did not like her husband. Had Lilamayi not looked down on him because of his lack of education, maybe Gaurishankar's life would have changed. Maybe he would have been completely besotted by Lilamayi's beauty. But the old zamindar's expectations in marrying his son to Lilamayi were not fulfilled. Gaurishankar's character was not reformed. Sometime later, when his father died, Gaurishankar became the owner of the property and turned even more wayward and cruel.

Doctor Dharanidhar was the object of Lilamayi's affections from before her marriage. As a consequence of her free relations with the doctor in her unmarried state, one or two abortions had become necessary and these were duly performed. The attraction between the two was magnetic. Given his indigent conditions, it was not possible for him to marry Lilamayi. When Lilamayi left after her marriage, it broke Dharanidhar's heart. He married sometime later, and that soothed his soul a little. But Lilamayi's rose-petal lips and lotus-stem arms beckoned from afar, "Come, come to me, my love."

Dharanidhar managed to set up practice in Gaurishankar's estate and became the family doctor of the zamindar. Relations resumed between the doctor and Lilamayi. Things went so far and Gaurishankar's suspicions were so aroused that he threatened one day to shoot his wife. But Gaurishankar fell ill and had to be taken to a resort. And who should go with him but the family doctor? The illness got worse. Many famous doctors were called. One day, the news spread that Gaurishankar had died.

Lilamayi had no dearth of money. If one has money, there is no heinous deed in the world that one cannot hire someone to do. Gaurishankar's body was taken to be cremated. But a fierce hailstorm and rain forced the pallbearers to leave the body and run for shelter. When they returned in the morning, the body could not be found. Everyone assumed that the body had been eaten by wild animals. Elated, Lilamayi completed the funerary rites of her husband and resumed her secret romance with Doctor Dharanidhar.

[3]

. . . The whole place was abuzz. The tenants were coming in hordes to see the sannyasi. They said, This is our zamindar. The sannyasi would recognize some of them and ask them about this and that. The tenants were dancing with joy, not because they now had a chance to take revenge on the widow Lilamayi, leading her licentious life in her palace and oppressing her tenants. True, a strange mystery that was for so long only the subject of rumor and gossip was now about to be revealed in public. It was a matter of much idle speculation, but that is not all: people were also interested in knowing the truth. Even if it was true that Lilamayi had, to fulfil her desires, cleverly eliminated Gaurishankar, the tenants could not be her judge. She would have to be judged by the law, in the courts. Guided by the belief that the sannyasi was the real Gaurishankar, the tenants pledged to pay him the rent and to support him in every way to recover his zamindari, . . .

Doctor, do you still say I shouldn't worry?

I have more reason to worry than you do. I just keep it submerged in drink. Here, why don't you drink a little? Don't waste the last drops of pleasure by worrying endlessly.

Lilamayi snatched the bottle from Dharanidhar's hand and smashed it to bits.

Pleasure! Pleasure! I'm about to lose my possessions, lose my life, and you still talk of pleasure?

Why not? You should do so even more than me. Because the danger you face is nothing compared to what I face.

Nothing? My reputation, my life, means nothing?

Nothing compared to what I stand to lose. No one will shed a tear if you die. Think of what awaits my family? My children, my wife—they will be washed away into the sea. I jumped into this business only for your sake. I am far more guilty than you are. Rather than facing punishment in court, it is better for me to kill myself to save my reputation. But no, I have to die in agony thinking of the fate of my children. And you, a princess, will die in happiness. Lila, is this my reward for loving you?

I have loved you all my life. Happiness for me, agony for you—that is not justice in the kingdom of love. I cannot let that happen. I am not a pauper yet. My jewel boxes are still full, I still have a lot of wealth. I'll give all of it to you. With it, your wife and children can live comfortably for the rest of their lives.

Do you really love me so much? Even at the last moment of your life, do you really want to give away all of your possessions to make me an equal partner in your life? I've lost to you, Lila. Tell me, are you really mine?

Yes. Whether I win or lose, whether I live to enjoy the riches of a kingdom or die at the gallows, I am yours, heart and soul.

This is exactly why I said, let us, these last moments of our lives, keep ourselves happy. Silly of you to have broken the bottle. Come, let us get another. Pour a little into my mouth, pour some into yours. Let's forget about the stormy weather and drown ourselves in pleasure.[24]

The Go-between

Manamohan Bhattacharya had worked for many years as personal clerk to the Bhawal estate manager. Appearing as a witness for the plaintiff, he confirmed the now well-known story of the lack of education of the kumars, especially the two younger ones. The second kumar, he said, tended to avoid the company of educated people. He then described in detail the sequence of telegrams that arrived from Darjeeling regarding the second kumar's illness and death. Just before the *śrāddha*, there were rumors that the body had not been cremated and that the kumar was still alive. The eldest kumar was particularly disturbed by this and wanted to start investigations. Satya Babu then said that he was personally present when the body was cremated and that he would get a death certificate from Dr. Calvert. At this, Ranendra Narayan desisted from taking any further steps.

Sometime after the second kumar's death, Manamohan was dismissed from service by Ranendra Narayan. He was then appointed by Bibhabati as her clerk. When there were discussions about claiming the insurance on the second kumar's life, Satya Babu said that the second rani had expressed a wish that the money be given to the Lowis Jubilee Sanitarium in Darjeeling. Hearing this, the eldest kumar said that if that was her intention, he would not claim the insurance. Anyway, nothing was said about this any more. The certificates from Calvert and Crawford arrived, the papers were sent, and the check finally came to Jaidebpur. Manamohan accompanied Satya Babu to cash the check from Chartered Bank in Calcutta, and carried the money back with them to Jaidebpur. On their way back, Manamohan was startled when he found that two women who appeared to be prostitutes were traveling with them on the train. When asked, Satya Babu explained that he was taking them to Dhaka for the two kumars. Manamohan knew that relations between Satya Babu and the kumars were strained and that this was probably his way of pleasing the kumars. When they arrived in Goalundo by steamer, the women were handed over to the steward of the Nalgola Rajbari. Manamohan thought the whole thing scandalous.

Sometime later, when the second rani left Jaidebpur for Calcutta, Satyen Banerjee consulted lawyers to contest the Court of Wards' decision to declare Bibhabati unfit to manage her property. It was pointed out that she was an educated woman and, with her brother's advice, would be perfectly capable of looking after her share of the estate. A petition was filed to this effect, but the government did not change its decision.

Manamohan worked for Bibhabati for about two years. At this time, there were some disagreements between them that he could not reveal in court. He resigned from her service and returned to Dacca. After the sadhu arrived in Jaidebpur, Manamohan went to see him and, after a few minutes, recognized him as the second kumar. When he asked the plaintiff if he could recognize him, the latter at first said "No." Then sometime later, he asked, "Are you the manager's clerk?" Manamohan thought the voice and mannerisms of the sadhu were exactly like those of the second kumar, although he spoke with a Hindi accent and his speech was often indistinct.

Sometime in 1933, when the present suit was coming up for hearing, Bibhabati sent for Manamohan and told him that she would need his help. He explained to her that he was convinced that the plaintiff was the second kumar. Bibhabati said, "But Manamohan Babu, you must not give evidence without asking me." She also said a few other things that Manamohan would not repeat in court. Manamohan pleaded with her to meet the plaintiff and decide for herself. Bibhabati said that there was no point in meeting the plaintiff because the trial would start in a few days.

In September 1934, he was asked by Jogen Banerjee, former secretary of the Bhawal estate who was now acting on behalf of Bibhabati Debi, to meet her in the Nalgola house in Dhaka. When he went to meet her, he found that the third rani was with Bibhabati behind the screen, because she asked Manamohan to help the second rani in her troubles. She then asked him to sign a statement. Manamohan said he could not make a statement against the plaintiff. He also said that a number of letters had been produced in court that were said to have been written by the second kumar to Bibhabati. He knew those letters were forged and he could not say otherwise in court. He pleaded with the second rani to accept a compromise and settle the case out of court. Bibhabati said that there was no possibility of a compromise.

Under cross-examination, Manamohan said that he had tried several times to persuade the second rani to meet the plaintiff. If she had met him and decided he was not her husband, Manamohan would have been willing to help her. If she thought he was her husband, Manamohan would have tried his best to bring about a compromise. But Bibhabati would not agree to meet the plaintiff. After the forged letters were produced in court, Manamohan felt that the second rani was getting herself into further trouble. He told her so when he met her.[25]

Confusion over Bibhabati

A suggestion had been made somewhere that about a year after her marriage Bibhabati had become pregnant. The implication of this information was not clear. It could be used to put a certain construction to Ramendra and Bibhabati's conjugal life. It could raise the question of whether Bibhabati had had an abortion. Whatever the implications, the plaintiff's lawyers were especially concerned to put this speculation to rest. They recalled Jyotirmayi Debi, who testified that it was untrue that Bibhabati had conceived a child; if she had, Jyotirmayi would have known. She was not aware that Bibhabati's periods had stopped for three months when she went to Calcutta in 1904 or that she was examined by Major Sinha when her periods started again.[26]

Dr. Sushila Sundari Dasi, an obstretrician and gynecologist of Dhaka, was also put up as a witness. She said that she regularly attended the women of the Jaidebpur Rajbari until the death of the third kumar in 1913. She had been appointed the lady doctor of the Bhawal Raj by Rani Bilasmani. She had treated Rani Bibhabati once, but she had not heard that the second rani had ever become pregnant.[27]

These were the last witnesses called by the plaintiff's side. The hearings had gone on for more than a year; as many as 1,042 witnesses had been examined for the plaintiff, apart from 27 who had been examined on commission. Judge Pannalal Basu made a classification of the kind of people who deposed for the plaintiff.[28]

Ordinary tenants	473
Relations	18
Old officers	66
Menial servants	33
Personal servants	10
Railway servants posted at Jaidebpur or elsewhere	19
Tradespeople, drummers, musicians, and the like	41
Ordinary bhadralogs, such as teachers, students, priests, old students at Jaidebpur	33
Substantial taluqdars	21
Intimate friends	2
Rich or substantial men of high position, or professional men such as barristers, pleaders, advocates, doctors	58

After an entire year of hearings, only one side of the case had been presented. Even in November 1934, Pannalal Basu had expressed his impatience at the time that was being taken and had asked the plaintiff's counsel when he expected to conclude the hearing of his witnesses. B. C. Chatterjee said that he would be done by the end of December. That had not happened, even though the defense counsel kept insisting that the plaintiff's side close their case. Pannalal Basu later explained that although the hearings had gone on for an extraordinarily long time, he could not legitimately refuse to have witnesses examined as long as the trial went on without interruption.

At one stage of the trial the learned Counsel for the defendants was continually asking the Court for an order requiring the plaintiff to close, i.e. refusing to take evidence on disputed points on which the Court could not form, much less express, any opinion. He opposed without *locus standi* and without success, the issue of summons to witnesses though the Court had no discretion in the matter, so long as the trial went on without interruption. He tried to discuss witnesses, as they stood in Court, ready to be put in the box. He talked of estoppel because the learned Counsel for the plaintiff had mentioned a certain date on which he expected to close. It was obvious that the Court could not refuse to examine witnesses, so long as they were going to speak on material points, and so long as what was happening was not an abuse of the process of the Court.[29]

Finally, in the middle of February 1935, B. C. Chatterjee announced that he had no more witnesses to bring forward. The defense had the chance to present its witnesses.

Chapter Twelve

FOR THE DEFENSE

THE DARJEELING STORY

T HE DEFENSE had clearly decided that instead of taking on the vexed question of recognition, it would have a much stronger case if it could establish that the second kumar had died in Darjeeling and had been cremated there. That would make irrelevant the highly improbable story of the kumar being rescued from the cremation ground and losing his memory for eleven years. It would also obliterate the importance of the recognition issue; if it was clear that the kumar had died in 1909, what did it matter if some people claimed to recognize him in the plaintiff? The plaintiff had to be someone else. The defense, therefore, began by presenting witnesses who would bear out the story of the morning cremation.

Shyamadas Banerjee was a cousin of Rani Bibhabati. He was an accountant in the Bengal Secretariat and was in Darjeeling in the summer of 1909. Testifying in commission, he said that he visited the kumar daily during his illness in Darjeeling. On the day he died, he went to see him at seven in the evening and went home at nine. At about one in the morning, he got a message from Satyendra that the kumar had died at about 11:30. He rushed to Step Aside and was there the whole night. Bibhabati was sitting next to her husband's body, crying. Dr. Nibaran Sen was there for most of the night. In the morning, Shyamadas went out to collect people to accompany the dead body. He took permission from the finance secretary to ask the staff of his department to go to the cremation ground. The cremation was performed according to the prescribed rituals. The clothes were removed from the kumar's body, which was rubbed with ghee and bathed. New clothes were then put on and a new sacred thread hung around the shoulder.

Cross-examined, Shyamadas Banerjee said that he had been asked to give evidence in this case by Mr. MacPherson, secretary to the Board of Revenue. He had earlier made a statement to Lethbridge, who was the secretary to the board in 1921. He admitted that proceedings were brought against him by the government for defalcation of funds. When he paid up the money, he was allowed to take premature retirement.[1]

Jagat Mohini Debi, a nurse and midwife, testified that in 1909 she was in Darjeeling, where she was called in, along with another nurse, to attend to the second kumar on the last day of his illness. She was at Step Aside when the kumar died sometime near midnight. She remembered that Dr. Calvert stayed for half an hour after the death. In the morning, the body was decorated with flowers and taken down. Jagat Mohini accompanied the procession for some distance, but was then called away by Kasiswari Debi, Mahendra Babu's wife, who asked her to go to the Burdwan maharaja's house to get some Ganga water. She went there in a *dandi*, a chair carried by porters, collected the water and sacred thread, and took them to the cremation ground. She found that the body was being smeared with ghee. It was then washed and placed on the pyre. She watched the entire cremation and, after the body was burned, she along with others poured water on the pyre.

During cross-examination, she was questioned repeatedly on her claim that she was a Brahmin widow. It was suggested that she was actually a Muslim woman who called herself Jagat Mohini Dasi when she was a trainee in the midwifery course at the Dacca Medical School. She was asked if she had not been the mistress of a certain Hasan Ali. Jagat Mohini denied all of this. Why did she wear ornaments if she was a Brahmin widow? Because her husband had given her permission. Was it true that she ate meat and fish? Yes, because her doctor had recommended it. When did her husband die? She did not remember the year. Did she remember what rites she had to perform after her husband's death? She did not remember the details. Was she invited to any Hindu social functions? No. The plaintiff's counsel was trying to show that she was not, as she claimed, a Brahmin woman and therefore could not have been asked to carry the Ganga water and sacred thread to the cremation ground. More generally, the attempt was to show that she was an unreliable witness because she was lying about her own identity.[2]

Bipin Bihari De now had a shop in Jaidebpur bazar. As a young boy, he was the personal servant of Rani Bibhabati and went with the Bhawal party to Darjeeling. He said that about four years before his death, the second kumar had suffered from biliary colic, and Bipin himself had nursed him at the time. The kumar died in Darjeeling at midnight. For about four days, he had fever and pain in the stomach. He died in the room next to his bedroom, where he had been moved the previous day. Bipin was present when the kumar died. It was not true that he died in the evening, nor was his body taken to the cremation ground at night. It was also not true that another body had been brought to Step Aside that night. The kumar's body was taken out in the morning. Bipin did not go with the procession. After the body was taken to be cremated, the rani was helped back into her bedroom. She was disconsolate. She began to pull off the jewelry she was wearing and to throw the pieces all over the room. Bipin picked them up and collected them in a pile at the corner of the bed. Kasiswari Debi, the lawyer Mahendra Banerjee's wife, who was known to the family and had come to Step Aside in the morning, took the rani into the bathroom and removed the re-

maining ornaments. He did not remember at what time the Bengali doctor
and the Sahib doctor came to see the kumar and whether they were in the
house when the kumar died. The lawyer's wife came to Step Aside at about
nine in the morning, when the funeral procession was setting out.

Bipin had continued to work for the second rani after the kumar's death.
He went with her to Dhaka and Calcutta and left her service in 1917. Bipin
was sure that the plaintiff was not the second kumar. The plaintiff too had
not recognized Bipin when he saw him in Jaidebpur.[3]

Bijay Krishna Mukherjee, who was in Darjeeling in 1909, said that he
heard about the kumar's death in the morning and went to the cremation.
He saw the body burn to ashes and returned at about four o'clock in the
afternoon.[4] Durga Charan Pal, Nagendra Nath Mukherjee, Mohammed
Nural Huq Chaudhuri, Tejbir Lombu, and Motiwar Rahman Chaudhuri, all
of whom were in Darjeeling that summer, said they had heard of the death
on Sunday morning, visited Step Aside where they saw the dead body on a
charpoy, and saw the funeral procession go through town toward the cremation ground.[5] Kalu Chhatrani, whose husband was the chowkidar of Step
Aside, said that she was woken up by her father at about midnight and told
that the kumar had died. She heard sounds of crying all through the night.
In the morning, she went down and saw the dead body lying on a charpoy.
The face of the body was uncovered and she saw that it was the kumar.[6]

Dr. Srish Chandra Roy, who now practiced medicine in Delhi, was staying at the Lowis Jubilee Sanitarium in 1909. He had seen the second kumar
of Bhawal a few times in Darjeeling that summer, always dressed in European clothes. One morning, when Dr. Roy was having breakfast, he heard
about the kumar's death. He went to Step Aside and saw the kumar's body
being taken out. The face was uncovered at the time, and he clearly recognized it as that of the second kumar. Under cross-examination, Dr. Roy admitted that he had some outstanding debts and that he had secretly married a second time, but he denied he had told anyone that he would gladly
testify in the Bhawal case if he was given a decent sum of money.[7]

Panchanan Maitra, a clerk in the Revenue Department, went with the official train to Darjeeling every summer. He remembered that one morning
in 1909, he heard in the office that the second kumar of Bhawal had died.
He went to the bazar and saw the funeral procession of the kumar passing
down Hill Cart Road.[8]

To counter the evidence of the "professors' group" at the Sanitarium, the
defense produced a professor of their own. Haran Chandra Chakladar was
lecturer in history at the University of Calcutta. In the summer of 1909, he
too was spending his vacation in Darjeeling and was staying at the Lowis
Jubilee Sanitarium. He remembered hearing of the kumar's death early
in the morning. He did not know about any messengers coming to the

Sanitarium with news of the kumar's death the previous evening. He went to Step Aside at about seven o'clock in the morning and accompanied the funeral procession to the cremation ground. The body was bathed, and a relative of the kumar set fire to the pyre. He saw the dead body both before and after it was taken to the cremation ground, and he was sure it was the body of the second kumar of Bhawal, whom he had met once before in Darjeeling. He was present until the body was burned. He also remembered addressing a condolence meeting on the death of the kumar in Darjeeling at which about three hundred people were present. He had met the kumar at the Step Aside, where he had been taken by an acquaintance about five or six days before the kumar's death. He was told that the kumar was suffering from colic but that it was not serious. About ten years before this trial, Lindsay had gone to his house in Calcutta, along with Satyendra Banerjee, to ask him a few questions about the death of the kumar. By then, he had heard of the controversy about the sadhu. He answered Lindsay's questions but refused to make a formal statement. He had told Lindsay that if required, he would testify in court.[9]

A key witness for the defense was Birendra Banerjee, personal clerk to the second kumar in 1909, who had performed the mukhāgni rites at the morning cremation. Birendra testified that the second kumar was suffering from biliary colic and that his condition deteriorated during the day on Saturday. But he did not lose consciousness until about fifteen minutes before his death. In the afternoon, when his hands and feet began to get cold, Dr. Calvert along with the rani and Satya Babu persuaded the kumar to take the injection. The two nurses rubbed a white powder over his body. It was not true that the kumar died in the evening, nor was it true that his body was taken for cremation that night. The kumar's body lay all night in the room where he died. Rani Bibhabati, the two nurses, and the maidservants were in the room. Satya Babu, Mukunda Guin, and Birendra were there from time to time. It was false that the rani was kept locked in the next room when her husband died.

The body was brought down in the morning. The funeral procession left at about 8:30. After reaching the cremation ground, Birendra rubbed ghee on the dead body and bathed it. After putting new clothes and a new sacred thread on the body, it was placed on the pyre. Birendra performed the mukhāgni. He remembered that at that moment Sharif Khan began to cry. The body was completely burned by about 3:30 in the afternoon.

Birendra denied that he had ever told Billu Babu or anyone else that the body had been taken for cremation at night and that it had disappeared. After the plaintiff arrived in Jaidebpur, Birendra had told many people that he could not be the second kumar because Birendra himself had cremated the kumar's body in Darjeeling.

Birendra had also testified in the defamation case. During cross-examination, B. C. Chatterjee pointed out various inconsistencies between his statements in that case and his testimony in this court. He also complained more than once to the judge that the witness was being prompted in his answers by defense lawyer Upendra Nath Banerjee.[10]

Did It Rain That Night?

This was a crucial point in the defense case. As we have mentioned, the clinching evidence for Lindsay when he decided that the sadhu was a fraud was his discovery that the *Calcutta Gazette* of the period had said that there had been no rain in Darjeeling on May 8, 9, or 10. Could this be corroborated? The Reverend Father Peel of St. Joseph's College, Darjeeling, was attached to the meteorological department of the college. From his records, he could say that it had not rained at Darjeeling between May 4 and 11, 1909. He could also say with certainty that if it had not rained between St. Joseph's and St. Paul's Colleges in that time, then it could not have rained between Ghoom, Jalapahar, and the Lebong spur. He did not agree that there could be rain at any time at one place in Darjeeling without it raining elsewhere; there were certain patterns, and a trained and experienced meteorologist could discern them. He said that premonsoon storms had only one cause: cold currents come from the Singgila range down the Darjeeling spur and meet the hot currents coming up the Manchi Valley or further down in the Balisan Valley. In the former case, the rain will be at St. Joseph's and affect north Darjeeling. In the latter case, it will be recorded at St. Paul's and affect south Darjeeling. He also said that the direction and velocity of the winds and the steady rise of the barometer recorded from May 6 to 10 indicated a spell of dry weather.[11]

Rain readings were also made at St. Paul's School, and these were published in the government gazette. The published records show that there was no rain at Darjeeling from 8 A.M. on May 4 to 4 P.M. on May 12. These were the records that persuaded Lindsay that the sadhu's story was false. Readings were also made at the Planters' Club. Manmatha Chaudhuri, then head clerk of the club, said in court that some years previously, two gentlemen had come to the club and taken away the register for 1909. The register was not produced by either party in court. The plaintiff's side produced the rainfall register of the Darjeeling Municipality for 1909. The entry following May 3, 1909 had clearly been tampered with and appeared to be May 13. It was impossible to say what the original entry was. There was also a rainfall register kept at the Botanical Gardens, and this too was produced in court. The clerk who claimed to have kept the register deposed in court. But the register had been kept irregularly and badly, and it was clearly not a reliable document.[12]

OFFICIAL TESTIMONIES

The defense case was, for all intents and purposes, being fought by the government. The basic structure of its argument followed the official line that had been adopted ever since Lindsay had declared the Jaidebpur sadhu to be an impostor. Not surprisingly, the list of defense witnesses prominently featured a large number of former officials who corroborated the government story.

J. T. Rankin was the collector of Dacca and, between 1905 and 1911, and secretary to the Board of Revenue of the Government of Eastern Bengal and Assam. We have met him before as the officer who carried out the raid at the Jaidebpur Rajbari and took over the Bhawal estate from the control of Rani Bilasmani. Rankin had retired from the Indian Civil Service in 1921 and returned to Britain, although his memory was well preserved in Dhaka with a street and a school named after him. In 1935, he came again to India to appear in the Dacca district court in the case of the impostor sadhu.

Rankin spoke of his memory of the kumars of Bhawal. He said he met them often, mostly in Dhaka and a few times in Jaidebpur. He had visited Jaidebpur a few times, especially when Meyer was the manager, and stayed in the Baro Dalan, the European-style quarters where Meyer used to live. After Meyer left the Bhawal estate, Rankin did not go back there because the managers who followed were Indians, with whom Rankin could not stay. He said the two elder kumars spoke to him in English. The third Kumar sometimes appeared not to understand English, which is why Rankin tried out his Bengali on him. He would meet the kumars in garden parties, at public functions, and at the races. Rankin liked to play polo and remembered playing the game with the two younger kumars at Dhaka and Jaidebpur. He also went hunting with the second kumar when he visited the Bhawal estate.

During cross-examination, B. C. Chatterjee asked Rankin if it was the case that when the two younger kumars visited him, they were always accompanied by the eldest kumar. Rankin could not say if that was the case. Could it be that the eldest kumar acted as interpreter? No, he did not think so. Did he remember any specific conversation he had in English with the second kumar? No. Could the second kumar keep up a sustained conversation in English? Probably not. Did Rankin know of Indians who began a conversation in English and after a few words switched to their own language? Yes.

Looking at the plaintiff in court, Rankin thought he did not resemble the second kumar of Bhawal. He was certain that he had not seen the plaintiff before. B. C. Chatterjee asked him if he was comparing the plaintiff with his mental recollection of the second kumar's appearance as he had seen him twenty-five years ago. Rankin said, "Yes." Did he form a mental image then of what the kumar might look like twenty-five years later? No. Then with what image was he comparing the plaintiff? With the kumar as he remembered him. Twenty-five years ago? Yes. He was shown photographs of the second kumar and those of the plaintiff. Rankin did not see any resemblance. Chatterjee said that famous photographers and portrait painters had testified in this court that there were strong resemblances between the two sets of photographs. Rankin confessed he was not an expert in these things. If he was presented with a problem of deciding on the identity of a claimant such as this, what would Rankin do? Well, he might ask a handwriting expert to compare the writing of the plaintiff with samples of the writing of the second kumar. Did he know that a handwriting expert had testified in this court that the two sets of handwritings were of the same person? No, Rankin did not know that.

Chatterjee also asked him about his raid of the Rajbari in 1904. Rankin said he had acted on a report from Meyer. Was he a friend of Meyer? Yes, for a long time. Did he ask Meyer to accompany him on his raid? No. Was it then the deity of chance that had sent Meyer to Jaidebpur at the same time as Rankin? He did not know. Was it the case that he thought of Rani Bilasmani as an enemy because she had dismissed Meyer from her service? No. Did he know that the second kumar had vowed never to have anything to do with Rankin because he thought Rankin had insulted his mother? No, he did not know that. Was his attitude pro-Meyer and against the second kumar because of the experience of the raid? No, he would not say that.[13]

As Rankin was leaving the courtroom after his testimony, he suddenly fell down unconscious and had to be taken to hospital. It was discovered that he had been suffering from cancer for some time. A week later, on February 25, 1935, Rankin died in Dhaka. His death caused a fresh round of sensation. Public memory of his treatment of Rani Bilasmani had been revived by his testimony in Pannalal Basu's court. People remembered that the second kumar in particular had at the time sworn vengeance on the saheb for having insulted his mother. Was this his retribution? Otherwise, why should the civil servant, living a comfortable retired life in Britain, choose to come all the way to Dhaka only to die after testifying against the sannyasi?[14]

J. H. Lindsay, who was collector of Dacca between 1919 and 1922, had now retired from the civil service and was secretary of the School of Oriental Studies in London. He was known to be a "highminded serious Scotsman" who had given up a promising career in the Indian civil service to be in England with his son in his impressionable years.[15] He was examined in commission in London. He said that he interviewed the plaintiff in Dhaka in 1921. They spoke in Hindi. He could not say if the plaintiff spoke or understood Bengali. He had also asked the deputy commissioner of Darjeeling to make a list of all Bengalis who were in Darjeeling in the summer of 1909 and to record statements from them on the basis of a questionnaire. He had seen the *Gazette* of 1909 and decided that the story of the rain and storm was most improbable. In fact, it was the rain reports for Darjeeling in May 1909 that convinced him that the sadhu's story was false. This was the basis of his announcement that the claimant was an impostor. He had also made inquiries into the identity of the claimant through a police officer. He was of the opinion that much harm would be done if the plaintiff was declared the kumar because it was always more difficult to run an estate if there were two rival possessors.

In cross-examination, Lindsay was asked about the memorandum of his interview with the plaintiff.

> *Q.* Did he say he suffered from diarrhoea at Darjeeling?
> *A.* I don't know anything except [this memo]. From this document I see I recorded "pneumonia". I have no recollection of doing so.
> *Q.* Can you swear you did not commit a mistake here?
> *A.* No.
> *Q.* Why did you make this memorandum?
> *A.* I am not sure. I wanted to get the man's own statement of his case as early as possible. I think that was the idea.
> *Q.* I put it to you the memorandum was not made at the time of the interview.
> *A.* I think it was. It was certainly made the same day. I think it was made in my office room at my house.[16]

In the meantime, the plaintiff's side had pressed for the production of official correspondence, especially with regard to Lindsay's handling of the affair in 1921. After several requests from the judge, some papers were handed over to the court, but many were not. In September 1934, Graham, the commissioner of Dacca division, was advised by his office that there were many confidential papers among those asked for by the court. "It may be considered whether these documents should be produced in the open court. The production of these communications may be detrimental to the interest of Sm. Bibhabati Debi, a ward of the Court. But for the sake of justice all these should be disclosed. On previous occasions such communications were not allowed to be produced (vide Mr. Nelson's order)." Graham decided that the court should be informed that "the documents are privileged" and could not be produced.[17] Judge Pannalal Basu did not take a kind view of this assertion of official privilege.

H.C.F. Meyer, former manager of the Bhawal estate, was positive that the plaintiff was not the second kumar. He had seen the plaintiff a few times in Dhaka. In his opinion, the second kumar was most unlikely to turn an ascetic or have anything to do with religion. Meyer had been appointed manager by Rani Bilasmani on the recommendation of Rankin, the collector, and Savage, the commissioner. When he was in Jaidebpur, the three kumars had finished their education. He did not remember seeing the two younger kumars write anything, either in English or in Bengali. The eldest kumar led a dissolute life and had no moral character, although he was kind and charitable. Meyer found the estate in a condition of gross mismanagement. There were serious malpractices and much zulm (oppression) on the tenants. When Meyer started to set things right, there was a plot against him. Unfortunately, the rani fell victim to the intrigue and decided to terminate his contract, even though she had to pay him Rs.15,000 as compensation. On cross-examination, Meyer was shown a copy of the deposition he had made in the Sripur case in 1922. In it, he had said about the sadhu: "Yes, I have seen the man. I have seen the sadhu on the road, and as far as I have seen him, I cannot give a definite opinion as to whether he is the Second Kumar or not, but my impression is that he is not the Second Kumar." Meyer did not confirm that he had said exactly those words, because what he was shown was only a copy of his deposition. Rather, he insisted that he was convinced that the man was an impostor from the time he first saw him in 1921.[18]

Jogendranath Sen, until recently an employee of the Bhawal estate, testified that all three kumars could read and write both Bengali and English. They had been taught English by Mr. Transberry and Mr. Wharton. Jogendranath did not see any resemblance between the plaintiff and the second kumar. He said that the plaintiff's appearance had created problems in the collection of rents on the estate. Earlier, about five hundred rent suits were filed in a year; these days more than five thousand suits were being filed. During cross-examination, Jogendranath admitted that his uncle had embezzled Rs.26,000 from the Jaidebpur Loan Office. He and his father had undertaken to return the money to the Bhawal estate in instalments. The money had now been paid back. He denied that part of the payment had been waived by the estate on condition that Jogendranath testify for the defense in the present suit.[19]

Rai Bahadur Sarada Prasanna Ghosh, member of the judicial service and son of Kali Prasanna, who had been manager of the Bhawal estate for many years, knew the kumars well in their childhood and youth. He was not asked any questions by the defense lawyers about the kumars' education. In cross-examination, when he was asked about it, he said, "When their father was alive, the three kumars did a little reading and writing. Afterwards, sometime after his father's death, [the second kumar] grew very wild. How can I say what he did? His sexual character became very bad after his father's death."[20]

K. C. Chunder and J. N. Gupta, both members of the Indian Civil

Service, testified on various aspects of the working of the district administration and the Court of Wards. When K. C. De began to testify for the defense, B. C. Chatterjee said that his opponents were only trying to influence the court by producing senior members of the ICS. All of these people
were only expressing their opinions on the case; they had no tangible evidence to offer. Why were they being produced one after the other?

K. C. De, who was member of the Board of Revenue between 1921 and
1928, claimed that in 1926 the plaintiff had seen him in Dhaka. This was a
formal interview De had given him. The plaintiff was in ocher robes and
matted hair and was accompanied by a lawyer. De suggested that he submit
a petition to the government, but the sadhu said in Hindi, "Ham fakir admi,
rupia leke kya karega?" (I am a fakir; what shall I do with money?). During
cross-examination, it was pointed out that in 1926, the plaintiff was in Calcutta and could not have met De in Dhaka. Besides, it was well known that
the plaintiff had stopped wearing the matted hair and sadhu's outfit in 1924.
De admitted that he had once met and advised Jyotirmayi Debi's son-in-
law on the plaintiff's claim, and that was probably when the plaintiff also
came along. It was shown from a letter written by him that the interview
with Jyotirmayi's son-in-law was in 1923. It was also pointed out that De
had given a formal interview to the plaintiff in Calcutta in 1924, but at that
time the plaintiff could not have been dressed as a sadhu. De admitted that
he had first met the plaintiff in Calcutta in 1924 and he was convinced from
that first meeting that the man was an impostor. He had suggested a formal
petition because then the sadhu would be pinned down to a signature and
could not run away from his claim. He was also asked if the attitude of the
Court of Wards toward Jyotirmayi had not been vindictive. De admitted
that it had been extremely vindictive. Was there any resemblance between
the second kumar and the plaintiff? "Both are fair, both have blue eyes, but
the Sannyasi is of gross appearance, ill-bred manners, appeared to be the
son of a peasant, not of a Rajah."[21]

Mohini Mohan Chakravarty, subdeputy magistrate of Madaripur, was in
1921 the assistant manager of the Bhawal estate. When the sadhu first arrived in Jaidebpur, Mohini Mohan went to see him because he had heard
he gave medicines. He brought the sadhu home and wanted him to give
medicines for his wife. But the sadhu only spoke Hindi, and since Mohini
Babu's Hindi was not very good, he was unable to explain clearly his wife's
ailments to the sadhu. The sadhu went away without giving any medicines.
About two weeks later, Mohini Babu heard for the first time that the sadhu
had claimed to be the second kumar. He was surprised by this and went to
Jyotirmayi Debi's house, where he was told that the sadhu was tired and
would not be able to see him. He saw him the next day along with Jogen
Babu and other estate officials. Mohini Babu drafted the report on that
meeting, which was sent by Needham, the manager, to Lindsay, the collec-

tor. The officials asked the sadhu various questions, to many of which he did not reply. After a while, the sadhu started sobbing and covered his face with a towel. Sagar Babu and Buddhu Babu asked the estate officials not to annoy the sadhu any more. As they left, Jogen Babu said to Mohini Babu that all the speculation about the sadhu being the second kumar was just idle talk. When Mohini Babu went back the next day, he heard indecent songs being sung about Rani Bibhabati, Satya Babu, and Ashu Doctor, with the sadhu sitting there.

During cross-examination, B. C. Chatterjee put it to Mohini Chakravarty that at first he, like everyone else in Jaidebpur, was quite prepared to believe that the sadhu might be the second kumar. It was only after he knew of the view of the government and the Court of Wards that the sadhu was an impostor that he became a disbeliever. Mohini Babu denied this and said that as early as May 4, when he gave his first report to Needham, he and Jogen Babu had come to the conclusion that the sadhu was a cheat. He thought that even Jyotirmayi Debi and her family did not at that time believe that the sadhu was her brother. Asked to explain various statements in the report sent by Needham to Lindsay, Mohini Babu said he had drafted them as statements of what was being said in Jaidebpur and not as facts whose truth had been verified. He also said that when he drafted his report, he did not know whether it would go in favor of or against the sadhu. Was he fearful of displeasing his superiors? No, but he would do his duty and be loyal to his superiors.

> Q. Would you say that you consider it your duty not to give out your honest belief on a matter simply because it did not coincide with the view of those who are above you?
> A. I would not disclose my honest belief in these circumstances.[22]

A crucial figure in the affairs of the Bhawal estate for almost three decades was Rai Saheb Jogendra Nath Banerjee. He was appointed private secretary to the three kumars in 1904 and became a key person in the estate administration after the death of the kumars. He was given the title of Rai Saheb in 1922. But his official career was dashed in 1934.

On May 8 of that year, exactly twenty-five years to the day after the alleged death of the second kumar of Bhawal in Darjeeling, two Bengali young men dressed in European clothes walked up to the governor's box at the Lebong race course. It was summertime in Darjeeling, and everyone who was anyone in Bengal officialdom was at the races. One of the young men suddenly pulled out a revolver and shot at the governor, Sir John Anderson. He missed, and the superintendent of police, standing next to the governor, shot back at the assassin and brought him down. The other young man then fired at the governor from an automatic pistol. He too missed and was overpowered by one of the guards. The two revolutionaries were

Bhabani Bhattacharya and Rabindra Banerjee. It was discovered that the assassination had been planned in Calcutta and Dhaka and, after investigations, eight revolutionaries, all from Dacca, were accused of conspiring to kill the governor of Bengal. Bhabani and Rabindra were sentenced to death, but the latter's sentence was commuted to fourteen years' imprisonment.[23]

Rabindra Banerjee was the son of Rai Saheb Jogendra Banerjee, secretary of the Bhawal estate. His son convicted of high crime against the state, the Rai Saheb had had to give up his job with the Court of Wards and had now become an advisor to Rani Bibhabati. He was widely known as the chief *tadbirkar* or organizer for the defendants in this case. But the arrest and conviction of his son had left him a broken man. Before he appeared in court, he produced a letter from his doctor requesting the judge that, in view of his health, he be examined for no longer than two hours at a stretch.

Recalling the death of the second kumar, Jogen Babu said he was returning from a trip to Barisal on Sunday night when he heard the news at Narayanganj. It was not true that he heard of the kumar's death on Saturday night. From Narayanganj, he went to Poradah junction and returned to Jaidebpur with the second rani and the rest of the Darjeeling party. After the sadhu announced in Jaidebpur that he was the second kumar, Jogen Babu interviewed him along with Mohini Chakravarty. He also met him separately and asked him why he had not returned home or even written a letter for all these years. The sadhu replied in Hindi that he had been visiting religious places and that sannyasis never wrote letters. When he went to see him again in Jyotirmayi Debi's house, there were a lot of people surrounding the sadhu. One person made a speech saying that they would spare no effort to establish the sadhu as the kumar. Another person recited a poem vilifying the rani, Satyen Babu, Ashu Doctor, Jogen Babu, and several others. The people appeared to be quite excited, and Jogen Babu did not stay long.

He was sure from the very beginning that the sadhu was not the second kumar. His relations with his brother Sagar Babu had deteriorated after the appearance of the plaintiff. It was not true, Jogen Babu said, that he had tried to dissuade anyone from testifying in this case. He was shown a letter written by him to a naib of the estate. In it, Jogen Banerjee had instructed the naib: "Take the statements of the witnesses selected by you for the estate, and send them to me. I am sending herewith a specimen of the statement, but see that the language of each is not the same." Enclosed was the following specimen statement:

Age. . . . I pay . . . as rent to the Raj Sircar. I did a lot of darbar at the Rajbari in the late Second Kumar's time. I knew all three Kumars and they knew me too. The late Second Kumar used to do *bichar* [adjudication] etc. I went to him many times and knew him very well indeed. This sannyasi talks Hindi. The

Second Kumar used to talk to us in Bengali. The sannyasi's speech and appearance do not resemble the Second Kumar at all. . . . Between the death of the Second Kumar and the arrival of the sannyasi, I did not hear a rumour that · he had not been cremated or that he had not died. I do not believe at all that the sannyasi is the Second Kumar.

Jogen Banerjee admitted that he had sent these letters.[24]

To counteract the huge number of witnesses who had claimed to recognize the plaintiff, the defendants also put up nearly four hundred witnesses who knew the second kumar and who claimed that the plaintiff was not the same man. Of these, more than three hundred were tenants or employees of the estate. Their stock response to questions was that the second kumar and the plaintiff were totally dissimilar.[25]

In fact, on the physical resemblance question, the defendants' case was that the plaintiff was utterly dissimilar to the second kumar. This was shown in Jogen Banerjee's specimen statement. It was emphasized by most of the defense witnesses. As the trial progressed, however, it began to emerge that this was something of a trap for the defendants. Even if the plaintiff was a different man, how was it possible that so many thousands of people—acquaintances, tenants on the estate, outside observers—who could not all be conspirators, were led to believe that he was the second kumar if indeed they were so completely dissimilar in their looks? The defense seemed to modify its case in the course of the trial, because later they seemed to be saying that the difference was in the faces of the two men, and even there they probably had the same color of hair. At one point, A. N. Chaudhuri was asked if he thought that all of those who claimed to believe that the plaintiff looked exactly like the second kumar were lying. Chaudhuri replied that those who had a casual acquaintance with the second kumar might be deceived by a certain general resemblance with the plaintiff. "They are not so different that anybody who says they are the same necessarily gave false evidence." But except for this quite vague resemblance, there was total dissimilarity in the specifics, insisted the counsel for the defendants.[26]

BIBHABATI SPEAKS

The principal defendant, Rani Bibhabati Debi, was examined in March 1935. She was the star witness for the defense and, despite the best efforts of B. C. Chatterjee to unsettle her, she stuck to her position, firmly and with enormous dignity.

She was taken through the events leading up to the death of the kumar in Darjeeling. His condition had deteriorated from around noon on Saturday, the day he died. Did the doctors anticipate his death? "His death was completely unexpected to me," she said. Did she know that it was extremely rare for a patient to die from impacted gallstones? She did. Was it not probable, then, that he did not die of gallstones but something else? "How should I know that? Am I a doctor?" Gallstones do not cause blood stools; arsenic poisoning does. Did she not think that her husband might have been given arsenic? "Why should I think that?" Had she thought of the possibility? "I know that is a lie. . . . I did not think about it because it is a lie. I didn't know before what effects are caused by arsenic; I don't know it now." Did she know that Dr. Ashutosh Dasgupta had prescribed arsenic? No. How long had she known Ashutosh Dasgupta? Since her marriage. She knew him to be an honest man. He had done his best to help when the kumar fell ill in Darjeeling. When was the kumar's body brought downstairs on Sunday morning? Between 7:00 and 7:30. Where was the body before that? In the room and on the bed where he died. She was awake the whole night, sitting next to her husband's body until it was taken down. Was she sure that the time was seven in the morning? She was not sure of the exact time, but it was definitely well after sunrise.

Bibhabati also said that she did not believe that Satyabhama Debi had really recognized the plaintiff as her grandson. Satyabhama was old, and Bibhabati knew the influence on her of the plaintiff's supporters. That was why Bibhabati had not even opened Satyabhama's letter to her. She did not know what the old lady had written in it, but whatever it was, it would not have changed Bibhabati's opinion on the plaintiff. She also said that if the kumar's relatives in Jaidebpur had really suspected the sadhu to be the kumar, they would have first informed her. As it was, she was informed much later, after the event had been publicized to the whole world as a fact.

She insisted that when she saw the plaintiff a few times on the streets of Calcutta, they were all chance sightings. B. C. Chatterjee put it to her that when she first saw the man from above the portico of her house on Lansdowne Road, she was stunned and overwhelmed by the fact that he looked so like her husband. The subsequent sightings were all organized for her benefit, possibly by Buddhu. Bibhabati rejected the suggestion. They were chance meetings, she insisted, and, of course, she did not exchange a single word with the man. If it was suggested that the plaintiff and the second kumar were twins, would she agree? Never. Do they have no similarities? She did not see any. Was it possible that she might have forgotten her husband's face? "Is that ever possible?" she retorted.

The plaintiff had said in his testimony that the second rani had three marks of identification. The big toe on both her feet was longer than the other toes, there was a lump of flesh at the corner of her eye and the third mark could only be known to her husband. Did she have these marks? Bibhabati said she did not think the first was very distinctive. The second was true. The third was untrue and she was willing to have herself examined by the court. Judge Pannalal Basu did not think that a physical examination of the rani was called for; there was a claim on one side and a denial on the other, but the point was "of no use."[27]

Why had she told her lawyers that she had once become pregnant? She had told them of the fact that her periods had stopped for three months. Was there much rejoicing at the Rajbari when this fact became known? Her mother-in-law was very happy and used to tell people that the second rani would have a son. It is not entirely clear why the defendants wished to bring up this subject, because it led to the plaintiff's lawyers alleging that the whole thing was hushed up because it was suspected that the father of the child was not the second kumar. Judge Basu would have none of this in his court. He put a stop to this line of questioning, since it had not "the slightest foundation in evidence. I regret the topic was introduced and I condemn the charges it led to."[28]

The Third Rani

Ananda Kumari, the third rani of Bhawal, testified for the defense. She claimed that her husband spoke English and wrote letters in Bengali. She had heard all three kumars speak in English to European ladies visiting the Rajbari. She thought both the second and the third kumars were educated men, although they did not have university degrees. She identified the letters produced by the second rani as having been written by the second kumar. She also claimed that the telegram first seen by her husband announcing the second kumar's death had said that he had died the previous midnight. She denied ever having heard rumors that the second kumar had been poisoned or that he had not been cremated or that he was alive.

Ananda Kumari had seen the plaintiff twice in Dhaka. Looking at him in court, she said that he was not the second kumar. She also said that she did not know that the second rani had objected to her adoption of a son. At this point, B. C. Chatterjee said to the court that there was a specific reason why the witness was deliberately giving false testimony: she was apprehensive that if the plaintiff won his case, the adoption would be overturned. He would therefore like to ask her questions about her moral character to show that her evidence was unreliable. Chatterjee was in fact seeking to reopen an entire line of argument that had been used by Tarinmayi's husband and son, who had in 1926 contested the adoption in a legal suit. The argument was that the third rani had been unchaste during the lifetime of her husband and was consequently, in accordance with the requirements of the Hindu law, disqualified from inheriting her husband's property or adopting a son. Pannalal Basu refused to allow Chatterjee to ask questions about the rani's chastity. The matter of the adoption, he said, was irrelevant to this case.[29]

Popular Commentary

The tenants recognized him; the sister recognized him; not so the second rani;
The first rani said, Yes, I swear, the sadhu is the second kumar.
The second rani said, Well, sister, you're quite a sister-in-law, I see,
Don't I know my husband? That sadhu is not him.
There's some slight similarity, yes, which is why he can pass for the kumar,
That's why he is here in Bhawal—to grab the estate by fraud.
He's a fake sadhu, wants to be my husband, but I'm not so cheap.
The first rani said, Whatever happens, do wear a nice sari;
A new romance between old lovers, don't ever miss the chance;
The husband is at your door, go grab him, don't blacken your pretty face.
The second rani said, Slam a broom on his face; pull out both his ears, I will;
Can't stand his sight, I swear I never will let him in.
The first rani said, I've taken him in as my own dear brother-in-law,
Now I'll take him to your room and wait and watch the uproarious fun.
Furious, the second rani said, Do you want to go to court?
Fine, I'm ready, let's see what fun you get from it all.
So a huge trial began, the two sides locked in deadly war,
Witnesses on both sides, a few more for the sannyasi.
Money raining on both sides, the lawyers feeding to the brim,
The world waits to see what happens: which side will finally win? . . .
They thump the tables in tea shops, the debate is truly on:
Some declare the rani will win, others prefer the sannyasi.
It's the tenants' money going up in smoke, the sannyasi bides his time,
He drinks his milk and eats his ghee and waits for the judgment to come.
If he loses, he makes a run for it, with his *lota* [sannyasi's brass pot] and blanket
    and all;
If he wins, he sits on the throne to which he truly does belong.[30]

Chapter Thirteen

THE CLIMAX

THE KUMAR AS A BENGAL ZAMINDAR

A. N. CHAUDHURI continued to press his point that the second kumar of Bhawal was, after all, a Bengal zamindar. The plaintiff did not fit that role. How could one believe that they were the same person? "Our case is that the Second Kumar was a very much better-looking man, sharp features, sharp nose, large eyes. The setting of the features, the combined effect was that he looked a gentleman. The plaintiff looks a bloated *palwan* [wrestler]. He does not look a gentleman, nor a Bengali."[1]

Phani Bhusan Banerjee, a cousin of the kumars, said he, along with the third kumar, had been taught English by Mr. Transberry. He had played cricket, football, and billiards with all the kumars. He had heard the kumars speak in English with Mr. Wharton, who was appointed their tutor. The second kumar wore European clothes whenever he went to evening functions or to restaurants and theaters in Calcutta. Phani Babu was a key witness in the defendants' case that the second kumar was a polished young aristocrat. A notebook was produced in court, which Phani Babu claimed he had prepared to refresh his memory on the details of the case. Much of the book was in his own handwriting, but a few pages had been written by one of the lawyers for the defendants. The plaintiff's lawyers alleged that it had been prepared as a sort of lesson book for the witness in order to coach him for his examination in court. The book contained various names and terms with explanations, such as sketches of a billiard table, a polo field, a cricket field, a tennis court, and a football field with terms and basic rules. There were lists of perfumes and soaps, European clothes (chesterfield, "frog coat," "loun suit," "nicarpacar," "jodhpur bridge") and European food (roast ham, pigeon grill, fowl). There were table boys and dinner wagons, cupboards and sideboards. It would be suggested that the second kumar was interested in photography—it was known that the eldest kumar was for a short time. So Phani Babu's notebook had a great deal on cameras and developing agents. Under horses, there were numerous English terms with Bengali or local equivalents.

During cross-examination, the plaintiff's counsel suggested that Phani

Babu had been given favorable terms of tenure on a large piece of *miras* land (held in hereditary tenure); the terms could be withdrawn by the estate management whenever it wished. The reason why the estate had allowed remissions and easy instalments was, as Needham, the estate manager, had put it in a note in May 1923, "Phani Babu's faithful and loyal devotion to the estate during the present trouble." Phani Banerjee admitted that his dues had been remitted but denied that this was because of his strong opposition to the plaintiff.[2]

Anutosh Dasgupta, lecturer at Bangabasi College, Calcutta, and brother of Dr. Ashutosh Dasgupta, said that in his childhood he had heard the second kumar speak in English with Cabral and two other Anglo-Indians on the estate staff. He also thought the second kumar was more educated than the third kumar. He had also seen the second kumar play polo, tennis, and billiards.[3]

Saradindu Mukherjee, a zamindar and once an elected member of the Bengal Legislative Council, had known the Bhawal family well and had met the second kumar several times in Calcutta and also during a visit to Jaidebpur. He met the plaintiff in Calcutta in 1931 and had a conversation with him. The plaintiff, he said, spoke a distorted Bengali mixed with Hindi and did not appear to be a Bengali at all. He pronounced Saradindu's name as something like "Sarindu Babu." B. C. Chatterjee asked him about prominent zamindars living in Calcutta and members of the Landholders' Association who had accepted the plaintiff as Kumar Ramendra Narayan of Bhawal. He said he did not know about their opinions. Did he know that A. N. Chaudhuri pronounced Bhawal as "Bow-all"? No, he did not know that.[4]

Rai Bahadur Hemanga Chaudhuri, zamindar of Sherpur in Mymensingh, said that in August 1921 he had gone to see the plaintiff in Armanitola in Dhaka. The plaintiff had come out of his bath and had a towel wrapped around him. He asked him a question to which the plaintiff did not answer. Someone else in the room told Hemanga Babu to ask his question in Hindi. Hemanga Babu then asked the plaintiff in Hindi why he was not speaking Bengali. The plaintiff answered in Hindi that he could not speak Bengali. Hemanga Babu would be very surprised if someone said that in 1921 the plaintiff could speak Bengali.[5]

O. C. Gangoly, attorney and a well-known writer on art and archaeology, said that he met the plaintiff a few times in Calcutta some ten years ago. From his conversation with him, he was convinced that he was not a Bengali. Not only did he speak Bengali with a Hindi accent but he spoke imperfect Bengali, and his stock of words was very limited. On the other hand, he spoke Hindi quite perfectly. Gangoly did not think that a Bengali living for ten or twelve years in a Hindi-speaking region would forget to speak his mother tongue. Asked if he had tried speaking to the plaintiff in the Bhawal dialect, Gangoly said he had not; he did not know if the plaintiff could speak the Bhawal dialect perfectly.[6]

Khan Sahib A. M. Hamid, zamindar, who himself spoke Bengali with his tenants and Urdu at home, said that he knew the kumars of Bhawal. When he met the plaintiff, he only spoke Hindi. Except for his complexion, he did not find much similarity between him and the second kumar. He said he was not aware that many other zamindars of eastern Bengal had recognized the plaintiff as the second kumar.[7]

Lieutenant Colonel O. N. Pulley, chief staff officer of the maharaja of Tripura, had retired from the Indian army in 1919. He was aide-de-camp to Sir Lancelot Hare, governor of Eastern Bengal and Assam, in 1908–1909 and came to Jaidebpur with Lord Kitchener's shikar party. Testifying in court, he said that he had met the three kumars of Bhawal a few times and remembered conversing with all of them in English, since Pulley himself did not know any Bengali. He had met the second kumar five or six times and thought he was an unusually good-looking gentleman with very striking eyes that made a great impression. Looking at the plaintiff in court, Pulley said he did not think he was the second kumar of Bhawal. Cross-examined, it transpired from the exact dates of his stay in Dhaka and Jaidebpur that he could not have seen the kumars before Lord Kitchener's shoot and, therefore, actually saw very little of the second kumar before the latter's departure for Darjeeling. On the kumar's knowledge of English, Pulley explained that he had been told that the kumars had an English tutor and had assumed that they had learned their English from him.[8]

More Popular Fantasies

A Strange Problem (Story)
[1]

I am a widow. Society has ruled that I must stifle all the mad desires of youth and weep for ever in silence. Why? I too have a body of flesh and blood. Is it only because of the crime of having been born a woman that I must bear without protest this oppressive, tyrannical rule of society? My spirit cannot accept this rule, but society will nevertheless press it on me. My lord, is it your wish too that I put a lid on my mad emotions and desires and fling my life into the dark dungeons of repression? I cannot believe that, my lord.

Jharna covered her face with her hands and wept silently. Addressing her dead husband, she said, I know you will never return. You only showed me briefly the joys of married life, and then left abruptly. I know I will never taste those joys again. But the thirst of my youth has not been quenched! Is it your wish that I should pretend to ignore those irrepressible urges of my heart and go around in society as a dutiful *sati* [virtuous wife]?

There was no answer. The dead husband did not return. Only tears and tears—waves of pain and fear dragged Jharna into the deep seas of mourning. Accompanied by the strains of her organ, Jharna's song of loneliness spread across the horizons. . . .

Jharna!

Who's that? Oh, you, sir!

Sir? Will that address never change? Isn't it the same you from childhood . . . never mind.

I know it's painful to hear it. But I was unmarried then. There's a huge difference between those days and now. But I haven't forgotten, Ashok-da. I haven't forgotten those days when I knew you as an elder brother. The memory keeps burning in my heart, it comes back in spasms like a corrosive poison.

Good. At least you remember me. Jharna, I've tried hard to persuade myself. But my heart won't accept that you are not mine. That's why I came one day like a wild gust of wind at your door. Just to look at you from a distance.

Don't stoke the fire, Ashok-da. I don't know if I can control myself. May be I will lose my way.

Who knows which is the right way and which isn't? Everyone wants a little peace of mind. If I get you, maybe the strings of my life will play again. Those colorful dreams of my early youth, a land of fantasy—

A new rhythm—a new tune—a new song will sweep me away. I will drown in it, drown. No, no, Ashok-da. Please, my head is reeling!

Ashok held Jharna in his arms.

[2]

Never admit it, Jharna! He is not your husband.

But it's the same face, the same nose, the same eyes, how can I not admit it, Ashok-da? And yet, I know he died so many years ago. How is it possible that I see him again in front of me, alive? This is stranger than the strangest fiction.

There is some physical resemblance, but the man is definitely a fake. He wants to grab your estate by fraud. We went and cremated your husband, with our own hands. He was burnt to ashes. How can he be alive?

But I still have my doubts. The sannyasi's voice is exactly like my husband's. Tell me, Ashok-da, when he fell ill, it was you who called the doctors and arranged for his treatment. I still don't understand how my husband, who was so healthy and strong, could die from a simple stomach disorder.

The best doctors treated him, but he still didn't survive. What's the point in discussing that now? It's useless to think of these things. That sannyasi means nothing to you.

I feel sure he is my husband. He's been saying things from the past that no one else could know.

Are you going to accept that man as your husband?

How can I not accept the truth?

It'll be the end, Jharna! It'll be disaster! Never admit that he is your husband. Otherwise, you will have to explain his death. It will be proved that you secretly poisoned him.

Was it me or you?

What are you saying, Jharna? Don't you trust me?

How can I trust you? Your face tells me that you were responsible. You were the one who secretly poisoned my husband. Tell me the truth, did he really die? Why do you lower your eyes?

Forgive me, Jharna! I lost my head, I was so desperate to have you. That's why I conspired with the doctor to poison him and make him unconscious. We cleverly removed him and came back after burning another body.

Then it was you who turned my husband into a pauper? I never imagined. . . .

But you do love me, Jharna, don't you? Then why are you displeased?

It was a grave sin to have loved a devil like you. Shame on you! You are despicable! You're supposed to be an educated man, but those who can kill for the mere love of a woman are worse than beasts, they are not men.

I've become a beast only for your sake, Jharna! If you loved me even for one day, don't send me to the gallows. Please, spare my life. . . .

I feel sad, Ashok-da. I really did love you very much. Why did you have to turn into the devil and pour poison into my heart?

Forgive me, Jharna. Please forget.

Fine! If I have loved the devil, let me sink into hell. Don't worry, take my money and arrange to defend ourselves. . . .

Jharna, we tried our best, but perhaps it wasn't enough to save us.

What more can I do, Ashok-da?

Just forgive me. I've reduced you to a pauper and now I'm going to hell. . . .

Ashok took out a pistol and prepared to shoot himself. Jharna caught his hand and said, Shoot me first, Ashok-da!

Why?

I've not accepted him as a husband for so long. Should I now have to go to him as his wife? They'll shout and clap, the whole world. I couldn't face that, never. Better to die. Shoot me, Ashok-da.

I can't. For you I can kill anyone, but not you.

Then I won't let you kill yourself. Since we agreed to defend ourselves, let's try for the last time, whether we can settle this strange problem.[9]

THE GURU, OR SO IT IS CLAIMED

It was the third week of September 1935. The hearings had gone on for nearly two years. Defense witnesses were being produced one after the other, all of them claiming that the plaintiff did not resemble the second kumar or that he was hardly like a Bengali zamindar. Suddenly, there was a new sensation when it was announced that Dharamdas Naga, the plaintiff's guru, who had supposedly rescued him from the funeral pyre, had appeared in Dhaka to testify for the defense. Thousands of people assembled outside the courtroom to see the witness. Who knew—perhaps this was the crucial moment when the impostor would be exposed.

The witness did not know any language other than Punjabi. Major S. L. Patney, superintendent of the Dacca Central Jail, was asked by the court to act as an interpreter. Shown a photograph of the plaintiff, the witness said that it was that of his disciple Sundardas, whom he had initiated at Nankana Sahib. Before his initiation, Sundardas was called Mal Singh, and he was from Lahore. He was a Punjabi Sikh before his initiation and did not know Bengali. Dharamdas pointed to the plaintiff in court and said that was his disciple Sundardas. Dharamdas had never been to Darjeeling and had never saved anyone from the funeral pyre. He did not know any sadhus by the name of Darshandas, Pritamdas, or Lokdas. He knew someone called Gopaldas, who was also a disciple of his guru Harnamdas, but Gopaldas was never called Darshandas. Several years ago, he had made a statement to this effect before a magistate in Amritsar district.

There were huge disturbances outside the courtroom at this time. In fact, the din was so loud that Pannalal Basu decided to postpone the cross-examination of the witness until the following Monday, when special police arrangements would be made to prevent any disturbances. The word that buzzed around the excited crowds was that this guru was a fraud; he was not the real Dharamdas Naga.

Over the weekend, a petition reached the judge that Dharamdas, the witness, had high fever and that he would not be able to appear in court on Monday. Armed with a medical certificate from Major Lynton, the defense lawyers pleaded with Pannalal Basu to examine the witness in the house where he was staying. Basu decided to visit the witness in Nalgola to find out if he was fit to come to court, and instructed Major Lynton to be present there. Lynton explained that he had feared the witness might develop pneumonia, but this morning the fever had subsided. The witness, he thought, could be examined in the house but not taken to court. B. C. Chatterjee, the plaintiff's counsel, said that it would not be fair for him to question a sick man lying in bed. But A. N. Chaudhuri pressed for the cross-examination to begin right away because the court would soon close for the Puja holidays, and the hearings would be further delayed. Chatterjee finally agreed but only after making the point that he thought the witness was trying to avoid cross-examination in an open court.

Chatterjee began questioning the witness, but almost immediately objected that Major Patney was interpreting his questions to lead the witness.

He also said that Major Patney had met the witness Dharamdas during his illness and was accompanied at the time by defense lawyers. He had thus disqualified himself from acting as an interpreter. Pannalal Basu agreed to a change of interpreters. The cross-examination resumed, but after a few minutes Dharamdas claimed that his head was reeling. The court rose for the day.

When the hearings began the next day, Chatterjee asked the witness if he had grown fairer or fatter than he had been fifteen years ago. Dharamdas said he looked the same fifteen years ago. Did he remember his age? Yes, he was sixty. If he was an udasi as he claimed, why was he wearing clothes and sandals? The witness said that he had begun to wear a smock about three years before, when he had broken his arm. He had been wearing sandals since his arrival in Dhaka. Was it true that there was a large swelling on his abdomen, which he was hiding under his robe? He did have a swelling and he had had it for a long time, but he was not hiding it. Then why was it that no one had noticed it during his previous visit to Dhaka in 1921? He could not say if anyone noticed it; perhaps it was because he took his bath very early in the morning.

He did not know the names of the defendants in this case. Arjun Singh Pardesi, who had brought him from Nankana, was paying his expenses. Before initiation, Sundardas was called Mal Singh. Where did Dharamdas initiate Mal Singh? At Nankana Sahib. Could it have been at Aujla, his own village? No. How old was Mal Singh when he was initiated? He was twenty-two. Was Mal Singh of Aujla thin or fat? He was thin. Did he know that witnesses from Aujla had said that Mal Singh was a fat man? He did not know that, but there was a second Mal Singh at Aujla and they might have been referring to him. He remembered that a police inspector and a Bengali gentleman had come to him once about fifteen years ago and had asked him questions about Sundardas. They took him to a magistrate and recorded his statement. If he was sixty now, would he have been forty-five then? Yes. Did he know that the Bengali gentleman who met him in Punjab had sent a report from there to the manager of the Bhawal estate? He did not know that. If the report said that the Dharamdas who had made a statement to the magistrate was aged fifty-five, then he could not have meant the witness, could he? If the report said that Dharamdas had initiated Mal Singh at Aujla, then again he could not be the same Dharamdas. If the report said that Dharamdas had initiated Mal Singh when the latter was fifteen, then once more the witness could not be the same Dharamdas. If the report said that the photo that Dharamdas had identified was a "standing photo" of the Jaidebpur sadhu, then it could not be the seated photograph of the plaintiff that the witness had now identified in court. B. C. Chatterjee then produced in court the report of Surendra Kumar Chakravarty to the manager of the Bhawal Court of Wards regarding his inquiry in Punjab in 1921. He declared that if Chakravarty's report was true, then the entire evidence of this witness was false. There were no crowds, because the court was in session in a private house in Nalgola. But the dramatic tension was palpable as the court adjourned until after the Puja holidays.

The cross-examination continued after the holidays in the regular courtroom. The witness said that when he came from Nankana to Dhaka to testify, he was accompanied by Pankaj Coomar Ghose, a defense lawyer. Arjun Singh, who traveled with him, made all the payments but he thought his expenses were being paid by the government. As far as he knew, he was testifying for the government.

At this point, Sasanka Coomar Ghose, the defense advocate, submitted a statement that he said had been made by Dharamdas Naga in 1921 before the magistrate Raghubir Singh. B. C. Chatterjee pointed out that the document had no signature or thumb impression. He was certain that the statement had not been made by Dharamdas, the plaintiff's guru.[10]

To bolster Dharamdas's testimony, the defense then produced Lieutenant Raghubir Singh, the magistrate who had recorded his statement in June 1921. Raghubir Singh was a wealthy zamindar from Rajasansi near Amritsar and a member of the Punjab Legislative Council. He confirmed that the document produced in court by the defense was the original statement of Dharamdas recorded by him in Urdu.

> Dharam Das, *chela* [disciple] of Harnam Das, by occupation *udasi*, age 45, address Sansara, profession *sebadar* [temple manager]. I reside at mauza Sansara, thana Aujla, district Amritsar. This picture which has been shown to me is that of my *chela* [disciple] Sundar Das. His name was formerly Mal Singh. He used to live in mauza Aujla in the district of Lahore. His cousin [father's younger brother's son] Narain Singh, who now lives at Chak 47 in the district of Montgomery, came to me with Mal Singh at Nankana Sahib. That was 11 years ago, and I made him my *chela* at that time. At that time Mal Singh was 20. Mal Singh's *parwarish* [relations] were his uncles Mangal Singh and Labh Singh of Aujla. Six years ago, Sundar Das left me. The eyes of Sundar Das were *billi* [catlike] and his complexion fair. I saw him four years ago at the Kumbh Mela at Prayag [Allahabad]. I have not seen him again. The *tasbir* (photo) Ex. P1 is the *tasbir* of my *chela* Sundar Das. Read and admitted correct. 27–6–21

It was confirmed that the statement recorded by Raghubir Singh mentioned Dharamdas's age as forty-five.[11]

Mamtazuddin Talukdar, inspector of police, was one of those sent to Punjab in 1921 to track down Dharamdas Naga. He appeared in court to corroborate the defense story. He said that in 1921, when he was officer-in-charge of the Kotwali police station in Dhaka, he had been asked by Lindsay, the district magistrate, and Quarry, the superintendent of police, to go anywhere in British India to find the antecedents of the Bhawal sannyasi. He was given a fee of Rs.500 and a photograph of the sannyasi. Accompanied by Suren Chakravarty of the Bhawal Court of Wards, he traveled to Benaras and Lucknow and then to Hardwar, where some sadhus identified the photograph as that of Sundardas, disciple of Dharamdas, who, they said, might be found in Amritsar. They found Dharamdas in a gurdwara in Sansra near Amritsar. He identified the photograph as that of his disciple Sundardas. Mamtazuddin had him record his statement with a magistrate in Rajasansi. Suren Chakravarty was not present when the statement was recorded. After he returned to Dhaka, the superintendent of police sent him once more to Punjab to record the statements of those who had identified the plaintiff's photo as that of Sundardas. He said the Dharamdas now present in court was the same Dharamdas he had met in Punjab.

Cross-examined by B. C. Chatterjee, Mamtazuddin said they had not made any inquiries about Dharamdas at Sansra. He did not know if Dharamdas was a sadhu or a family man. He had heard that Dharamdas was an udasi. If Suren Babu had said in his report that they had made inquiries at Sansra about Dharamdas, then Mamtazuddin would not say that Suren Babu had sent a false report, although Mamtazuddin too was not giving false evidence in this court. Did he know that Dharamdas had stated in this court that his guru Harnamdas had a white beard? No. Did he know that the Harnamdas who was produced in this court had a black beard? No. Did the Dharamdas he had met in Punjab have a dark compexion? No. Was Suren Babu lying when he said in his report that Dharamdas had a dark complexion? No.[12]

Surendra Chakravarty, employee of the Bhawal estate, then appeared in the witness box and confirmed Mamtazuddin's story. He was shown his report of 1921, in which he had said the following.

> What we came to know about Dharam Das at Sansara is this. He has numerous chelas who wander about to earn money, and send it, and Dharam Das himself wanders about too. He is about 55, complexion black, jata [matted hair] on the head and a beard. Dharam Das told me that 3 or 4 years ago Sunder Das proceeded from Kumbha at Allahabad towards Calcutta. Sunder Das is about 30, with a kata [brownish] moustache and a kata beard.

In a postcript to the report the following was written.

> If the photo of the Sadhu in lengti [loincloth] . . . be that of the Jaidebpur Sadhu, he is certainly Sunderdas.

It was also mentioned in the report that this photograph of the sadhu was a "standing photo." Surendra Chakravarty confirmed in court that this was the report he had sent to the Bhawal Court of Wards, but in it he had made some minor mistakes, especially with regard to the ages of Dharamdas and Sundardas, which had been corrected later in Mamtazuddin's fuller report to the divisional commissioner of Dacca. He identified a photograph as that of the Dharamdas he had met in Punjab and who had appeared in this court a few weeks previously.[13]

The court was also presented evidence given by ten witnesses from Aujla examined in commission in Lahore in October 1933. They said that in 1931, a man called Arjun Singh had shown them a photo that they identified as that of Mal Singh. Mal Singh was a Rathor Sikh from a very poor family. His father died when he was very young, and he went to live with an aunt. When his aunt died, he lived with another uncle, and when he died, he lived with a cousin called Sunder Singh. He left the village when he was sixteen and turned a sadhu. He had been seen at Nankana Sahib sometime in 1918 or 1919.[14]

DOCTOR ASHUTOSH

Although he was widely known as Ashu Doctor—short for Ashutosh—his formal name was actually Anukul Chandra Dasgupta. He had been in the eye of the storm in the defamation case of 1921–1922. Now the spotlight had shifted somewhat to the question of recognition, and the poisoning allegation was no longer at the center of controversy in court. But popular interest still seized upon Ashu Doctor as a key accomplice in a sensational plot that almost succeeded. At the end of November 1935, Ashutosh Dasgupta came to testify.

He said that the second kumar had died at about midnight on May 8. Colonel Calvert and Dr. Nibaran Sen were present at the time. Both doctors had examined the kumar and declared him dead. Dr. Dasgupta also examined the body and found that the kumar was dead. Dr. B. B. Sarkar was not present when the kumar died. It was not true that the kumar had died in the evening. Dr. Dasgupta went to the cremation ground, where the necessary ceremonies were performed, the body was placed on the pyre, and Birendra Banerjee set fire to it.

It was not true that Dr. Dasgupta had given a medicine to the kumar, following which the kumar had cried out, "Ashu, what have you given me?" Had he made out the arsenic prescription on May 7? In the defamation case, he had denied it. He had said then that he did not prescribe any medicine to the kumar in Darjeeling. All prescriptions had been made out either by Dr. Calvert or by Dr. Sen. When Calvert was asked about the arsenic prescription during his cross-examination in London, he said that in the kumar's condition he would not prescribe it. In court in Dhaka, Ashutosh Dasgupta was again asked if he had made out the prescription that bore his signature. He replied: "I wrote a prescription under the advice of doctors. I did not make the prescription, but I was asked to write it, and wrote it. Either Dr. Nibaran or Col. Calvert asked me to write it." Dr. Dasgupta admitted that the prescription could not be given for biliary colic, or for fever if the colic was on. "If the second kumar had diarrhoea and biliary colic on the 7th, I would not prescribe it. In diarrhoea, if he had diarrhoea, the prescription was unsuitable. It would do no harm. It would aggravate diarrhoea, might have done so—there is only mild purgative there. I agree that 'the prescription would not be given to a patient suffering from biliary colic or diarrhoea,' as I said. It could be given in biliary colic. 'Aloin aggravates diarrhoea,' I still say that. I would not give it in diarrhoea. If a man wanted to aggravate diarrhoea, he would give it." He was also asked about his earlier testimony in the defamation case, in which his account of the timings of the kumar's illness and the visits of the various doctors did not agree with his statements here. He said that when he made those earlier statements, he believed them to be true. But now his recollection had improved, after seeing the prescriptions and telegrams sent to Jaidebpur from Darjeeling. Now he knew that his earlier statements were not true. It was pointed out that he had been shown the prescriptions in the earlier trial, as well. He still insisted that what he was saying now was the true account; if his earlier statements did not tally, they were incorrect.[15]

SATYENDRA BANERJEE

In December 1935, there was a palpable sense in the courtroom that the hearings were reaching a climax. Rai Bahadur Satyendra Banerjee took the witness box. Apart from Bibhabati herself, he was without doubt the principal witness for the defense. All of Bengal waited to see what would happen when B. C. Chatterjee questioned him.

Carefully introduced to the court by A. N. Chaudhuri, Satyen Banerjee said that he was an advocate of the Calcutta High Court and a first-class honorary magistrate. After his sister Bibhabati's marriage to the second kumar of Bhawal, he had met the kumars many times in Jaidebpur and Calcutta. Both the second and third kumars were literate, and he had seen them reading and writing both Bengali and English. He had heard the second kumar converse in English with Mr. and Mrs. Meyer, Mr. Wharton, with European doctors, and Anglo-Indian employees. Shown an exhibit, he identified the signature of Ramendra Narayan.

Satyen Banerjee, needless to say, denied that he had, with the assistance of Dr. Ashutosh Dasgupta, caused the death of the kumar in Darjeeling. It was not true, he said, that the kumar had died on the evening of May 8. He went through the now familiar defense story of the kumar's death at around midnight, the funeral procession through town in the morning, and the daytime cremation. Bibhabati had been with the kumar the whole day of the eighth and, after his death, she sat next to his body the whole night. It was not true that she had a hysteric fit during the day and had to be taken away to another room.

Had he seen the telegrams that were sent from Darjeeling to Jaidebpur during the kumar's illness and after his death? Satyen Banerjee said that the first time he saw them was when, after the appearance of the sannyasi in Jaidebpur in 1921, the manager of the estate and the collector of Dacca had written to Bibhabati asking about them. The telegrams were in the possession of Sailendra Matilal, the brother of the first rani. But the one announcing the death of the kumar was not in that collection, and it was never found.

By this time it had become known that a diary kept by Satyen Banerjee had come into the possession of the plaintiff's lawyers. This was a sensational development, because in it Satyendra had written down the details of what had happened in Darjeeling from the time of the kumar's illness. The diary had been produced as an exhibit in court, and there was no doubt that the plaintiff's lawyers would make maximum use of it when cross-examining Satyendra. A. N. Chaudhuri tried to forestall some of the damage by anticipating the opponent's line of attack. Why, he asked his witness, had Satyendra decided to keep a diary? Because, Satyendra said, he smelled a conspiracy against his sister. When the party returned to Jaidebpur, it was suggested that a deed of management would be executed by which Bibhabati would relinquish her share in the management of the estate in return for a monthly allowance. Satyendra, concerned about protecting his sister's rights, decided that he should keep a daily note of all that was happening in the estate. In fact, as an aid to his memory, he decided to write down all that had happened since the kumar's illness in Darjeeling. He began writing the diary—in English—around May 20, noting down the events from May 7, the day before the kumar's death. He stopped writing the diary in December 1909. Around this time, the plan for a deed of management was abandoned, and Bibhabati was restored to her rightful position in the estate. The diary was with him and he had last seen it just before the Court of Wards took over the Bhawal estate in 1912. Some time after that, it was stolen along with a large number of old letters and other papers. He strongly suspected Manamohan Bhattacharya, who had been the personal clerk to Rani Bibhabati, of having stolen the diary and papers, especially because he knew that Manamohan had made over the second kumar's horoscope to the plaintiff's lawyers. The horoscope had been in Satyendra's house along with the same set of papers.

Cross-examined by B. C. Chatterjee, Satyen Banerjee agreed that after the plaintiff's appearance, extensive inquiries were made from European tailors and outfitters in Calcutta to discover records of measurements for the second kumar's clothes and shoes. Banerjee himself was involved in these inquiries. He thought that the plaintiff had larger feet than the kumar, because the latter had unusually small feet. But Banerjee did not know that the second kumar's shoe size was six, which matched that of the plaintiff. Asked if the kumar had a scar on his left ankle caused by a carriage accident, Banerjee said that he did not remember having heard of any such thing. When he was shown a medical report of the second kumar, he agreed that it mentioned a scar on the left ankle, but he said he was seeing the report for the first time.

Satyen Banerjee was asked about Dr. Pran Krishna Acharya's evidence. Why had Dr. Acharya been called in the morning if Dr. Calvert and Dr. Nibaran Sen had already pronounced the kumar dead the night before? Banerjee said that he did not know who had called Dr. Acharya and for what reason. It was possible that Dr. Acharya was passing that way, saw a dead body in front of Step Aside and, curious, wanted to feel the pulse to find out if the man was dead. In any case, Banerjee did not ask Dr. Acharya to come to Step Aside that morning.

Asked about the sequence of events on May 8, 1909, Satyendra Banerjee said that his uncle Surya Babu, who was then living in Darjeeling, had called in Dr. B. B. Sarkar that evening when Calvert and Nibaran Sen were both present. But Dr. Sarkar had left before the kumar died that night. He was shown a page from his diary in which Banerjee had made the following entry:

> Kumar Ramendra expired midnight, Darjeeling "Stepaside". 4 doctors attending, one his family doctor, 2. Rai Bahadur Nibaran Ch. Ghosh, 3. B. B. Sircar, 4. Lt.-Colonel Calvert. They were all attending when he died. His last words to me a minute before life was extinct were—tell Ashu that I feel difficulty in breathing. Bibha began to have fits. The doctors melted away. Only two nurses remained. Sarif Khan was mad. Sent Behara for Sejomama [Surya Babu] who came at about 3 in the morning. Message to Uttarpara and to Jaidebpur. Sent man to the Sanitarium for men to get the corpse removed for funeral.[16]

Satyen Banerjee said that although he had written in the diary that Dr. Sarkar was present when the kumar died, that was a mistake. That calamitous night, he had been upstairs at Step Aside the whole time and came down only at about three o'clock in the morning. From that time until the funeral procession left, he had gone up and down several times. He also said that Bibhabati had "what a Bengalee would call 'fits'. . . a temporary dazed state, a state of temporary speechlessness or perhaps lock-jaw due to sudden shock," but she did not have to be taken to another room.

It was quite impossible that someone had gone from Step Aside to the Sanitarium that evening to announce that the kumar was dead. Banerjee was not suggesting that Professor Radha Kumud Mukherjee was lying when he said that he remembered hearing the news when Professor Maitra was singing in the common room. But it could not have happened that evening.

Shown another page from his diary, Banerjee admitted that when he returned to Jaidebpur from Darjeeling, he was often afraid at night. He was aware of the popular superstition that if a dead Brahmin was not properly cremated, his spirit came back as a ghost to haunt his surviving relatives. It was not because of his fear of the *brahmadaitya* that he had spent sleepless nights after the kumar's death. He was a superstitious man and was afraid of any noise in the night.[17]

ANTICIPATION

Although it took them almost the same length of time—just under a year— the defense put up fewer than half the number of witnesses presented by the plaintiff's side: 433 compared to 1,042. It was one of the longest trials in British Indian legal history. From November 1934 to May 1936, there had been no fewer than 608 days of actual hearing. Before summing up, the two counsels agreed before the judge that the plaintiff would be examined by a doctor with a view to establishing certain marks on the second kumar's body as described by a defense witness and the alleged node on the chin bone described by a witness for the plaintiff.[18]

> Bengal is a country gone mad; its patience strained to the limit:
> The judgment has not yet appeared of the Bhawal trial. . . .
> If it's pronounced that the sannyasi is the kumar, the whole world will stir,
> All the drums will roll in city, town and country.
> Not just the rani, all lettered women will bow their heads in shame:
> Who has ever heard a story as shameful as this?
> In a land where women worship their husbands, whether day or night,
> No matter if he's a drunkard, beast, or rogue, she's at his feet. . . .
> The Bhawal kumar had no learning, his rani had been to school.
> If the kumar is truly alive, then the news is not too good:
> So many years later, if it's proved he didn't die,
> A huge fire of anger will start burning against the rani.
> The Bhawal kumar was, it's true, a bit of a drunkard and a rake,
> And he suffered, it's also true, from a gross and ugly disease.
> But a man with a hundred faults, he still sought the good of his tenants:
> Even the moon has its dark patches, they don't spoil its beauty.[19]

Chapter Fourteen

REASONINGS

THE DEFENSE FINISHED presenting its evidence on February 12, 1936. The next day, A. N. Chaudhuri began his closing argument. The evidence was massive; nearly 1,500 witnesses had been examined. Chaudhuri took six weeks to lay out his case proving that the plaintiff was not, as he claimed, the second kumar of Bhawal. B. C. Chatterjee, on his part, took another six weeks to present his arguments on behalf of the plaintiff. When the court adjourned on May 20, 1936, it was the height of summer in Dhaka.

By the time Judge Pannalal Basu sat down to write his judgment, he knew he would have to set out his reasoning carefully and elaborately. There was every likelihood that his findings would be appealed against in the High Court, and he could not afford to be sloppy. He took three months to write his judgment. Early in the morning, he would go out from his house in Tikatuli, walk briskly for half an hour or so, come back and sit down at his desk. He would not step out for the rest of the day. Across the street from his house, a man would appear punctually at eight in the morning and stay until the evening, strolling on the pavement, sitting on a stool under a tree or at a shop entrance. The members of the Basu household knew who he was—a policeman in plain clothes sent to do duty as a security guard to the district judge trying a particularly sensitive case. It is not known whether Judge Basu noticed the man. During the trial, he had been approached by the district magistrate with the offer of a full-time police guard posted outside his house. The judge had firmly refused the offer.

He also decided not to use the services of a typist. It was too sensitive a case, and he could not trust any of the typists available to him to respect the confidentiality of his judgment until it was finally read out in court. There was too much at stake for too many rich and powerful people. Day after day, month after month, listening to the witnesses in his court, he had seen how far money and influence could go to induce even respectable and otherwise honest people to bend the truth. He first wrote out his judgment in longhand and then, carefully and laboriously, typed out the whole text, all by himself. At night, his study would be locked. The judge slept with the key under his pillow.[1]

FIGURE 9. Pannalal Basu

THE BASIC FACTS

"The principal question raised in this suit," Pannalal Basu began, "is a question of fact. It is in respect to the identity of an individual. It is not outside judicial experience, nor is the suit unprecedented, but it is very extraordinary, and its gravity arises from the magnitude of the property at stake, and from certain personal relations it affects" (1).[2] He then described the main facts of the case, the history of the Bhawal Raj family, and of the three kumars. "The family lived like ordinary Hindu bhadralok," he remarked. "It is idle to impart an English air or impute an English trait to the family or its ways because it kept a *baburchi* [Muslim cook], or because the Rajah, and after his death the Kumars, would put on English clothes when they met sahebs or on ceremonial occasions, and occasionally shikar clothes when they went out to shikar, or because, it may be, the Rajah once stayed in an English hotel in Calcutta" (16).

Of the kumars, the judge noted their lack of education and loose sexual morals. It was clearly established, he said, that the second kumar had a liaison with the dancing girl Elokeshi that continued after his marriage. The kumars had their own rooms on the ground floor, where they spent most of their time. Bibhabati's account that her husband would normally sleep upstairs in the rani's quarters was not true. The more reliable account, the judge felt, had been given by the old servants of the Rajbari. The second rani "would come to her husband only occasionally, and that at night, and only if sent for by the boy khansama Bepin, and this would happen only occasionally." On his own visit to the Jaidebpur Rajbari, the judge had noticed the staircase by which she could come down close to her husband's room. "One fact of significance is that at present this room of the Second Kumar and the said bedroom of the Bara Kumar [on the ground floor] are lighted and incensed at night in their memory, and the furniture there dusted, and the room swept, shewing that it is these rooms that are associated with their memory, no room upstairs" (31–32). This is, as we shall see, one of many instances in which Pannalal Basu would use his position as a cultural "insider" to read the meanings of everyday practices in Bengali society and deploy that knowledge in the determination of the truth within the framework of British Indian law.

On the second kumar's marital life, the judge felt that Bibhabati's attempt in court to paint a picture of marital bliss was untrue. There was little evidence of this, not even a single present that he had given his wife. "On top of this came the syphilis, the risk of infection and the filthy sores. I do not find anything in the short married life of this childless lady to which she could look back with pleasure, nothing, at all event, in the associations that could draw her to her husband's home after she went to live in Calcutta twenty-five years ago" (36). After the second kumar's death in Darjeeling, when the party came back to Jaidebpur, the second rani, however, behaved exactly as one would expect.

> She lay in her bedroom upstairs, weeping, and according to an entry in Satya's diary, seemed "deranged" by grief—could not recognise her brother. The evidence of Jyotirmoyee Debi and Billoo and some elderly ladies—neighbours— who came to see her at this point is that she lay in great grief, and when her brother Satya Babu came to see her, as sometimes he did, she would turn her face away and say, "Don't come to me. You made me a Rani and you have made me a *bhikharini* [beggar] too." Which proves nothing. What is important is that she behaved exactly as a recent widow would, and there has been no suggestion that she knew, or had anything to do with, the conspiracy which it is said led to the poisoning. (47)

After leaving Jaidebpur for Calcutta, she had lived with her brother's family. The estate accounts show that she had received until 1935 a total of nineteen lakhs of rupees. But she had no bank account and paid no income tax. "I keep my own money," she said in court. "Have done so since my husband's death. There is an iron chest upstairs. I keep the key." No accounts or papers were produced, although, as Judge Basu remarked, "you cannot handle such sums without papers of some sort, and I do not believe, looking to Indian habits, that there are no accounts." Satyendra Banerjee could not show any independent source of income, except some investments in shares. "It is perfectly clear," wrote Judge Basu, "that the whole income of the Second Rani has passed into her brother's pocket. She says that 'her will is her brother's will,' but looking to her condition—she could not produce a scrap of paper to shew her control over any part of her princely income—the converse is undoubtedly the truth" (59). It was clear that in the stunned and confused state in which the Bhawal Raj family found itself following the sudden death of Ramendra, it did not quite trust Satyen Banerjee. Judge Basu thought there was good reason for the mistrust. The eldest kumar "was a cavalier sort of man, fond of pleasure and drink," and he was no match for Satyendra who, as his diary revealed, saw in the quarrel between the ranis "a healthy sign." Satya Babu, "an impecunious young man still in college" was, thought the judge, "without a single generous impulse of youth and carried on his young shoulders a head as scheming and as shrewd and as sordid as any you might expect to find in a man of sixty" (46, 53).

The Sadhu

Who was the sadhu who appeared on the Buckland Bund in January 1921 and declared himself the second kumar in Jaidebpur in May? The investigating team of Mamtazuddin and Suren Chakravarty sent out to Punjab claimed to have cracked the riddle. The man was Mal Singh, alias Sundardas, of Aujla. He was fair, with black hair and catlike eyes. The witnesses from Lahore also confirmed this description. But this did not tally with Lindsay's description of the sadhu who, he noted, had "golden brown hair." An attempt was made by the defendants' lawyers to argue that the plaintiff's hair was originally black but had become reddish brown because he didn't oil or wash it regularly. Another argument that was made about the plaintiff was that he was thought to be a sadhu who gave medicines. That is why people crowded around him at Buckland Bund, and when he was brought to Kasimpur and Jaidebpur, it was entirely on his reputation as a medicine man. Once in Jaidebpur, the conspirators hit upon him as a candidate for the role of the second kumar. "This medicine-man theory—that the plaintiff was taken from Buckland Bund to Kasimpur to cure sterility, that he called at the Assistant Manager's to cure a female disease, that he went to Jyotirmoyee Debi's house to cure another case of sterility . . . and that this medicine man suddenly declared himself to be the Second Kumar on the 4th May—this theory continued until, in view of other facts that emerged, it was hardly mentioned during argument. In fact, Mr. Chaudhuri did not, it seemed to me, like to be reminded of it" (77).

But medicine man or not, the defense case still was that a Punjabi who had come to Dhaka in January 1921 and to Jaidebpur in May was declared by the conspirators to be the second kumar and it was only then that people began to call him that. Pannalal Basu had to consider the significance of this possibility.

> On the defendants' case, then, the sannyasi on the Buckland Bund was being taken from place to place as a medicine man, to Kasimpur, to Saibalini's house, to Jaidebpur, suspected by nobody as the Kumar, coming for the second time to treat somebody staying at the house of Jyotirmoyee Debi but in the yard, seen by people calling for medicine, until on the fourth day—the 4th of May—this sannyasi, a Punjabi, talking an unintelligible jargon, looking utterly different from the Kumar, suddenly declared, or was made to declare, or represented as having declared, that he was the Kumar, without knowing whether the Kumar was tall or short, fair or dark, young or old, married or single. If it was his own act, or if it was not his own, the family put him up, despite the widow, despite his absolute illiteracy, despite his tongue, and despite his utter dissimilarity in looks, despite his complete ignorance of the role he was to play; and then placed him in the open to be seen by all comers, in the heart of Jaidebpur, and sent him to interview the Collector of Dacca, and made up their mind to fight the Court of Wards, and against an estate whose rent-roll is something like ten lakhs of rupees.
>
> But the possibility of this too will have to be examined, and the Court will consider, despite the utter dissimilarity theory, whether some resemblance aided by the emotions of women had not produced a trick, and wish had not become father to the thought; nor would the improbability of the thing establish the identity. (84)

Judge Basu wondered why the defense stuck for so long to the theory of "utter dissimilarity," which could only imply "a conspiracy suddenly conceived or conceived in the course of three days." It would have to be a "mad conspiracy" to try and pass off this sadhu as the kumar, "a singular looking individual so difficult to personate," when he "did not know Bengali and not a detail of so difficult a role. . . . That I consider impossible, and I will have to consider why a measure of resemblance, such as could deceive, was not being conceded as an explanation of the direct evidence of identity that has been given. But the other theories, including self-deception, will have to be considered too, and will have to be excluded, before the plaintiff can succeed, for that might explain the singularly impressive and earnest way in which Jyotirmoyee Debi deposed before me" (89).

FIRST REACTIONS IN JAIDEBPUR

The plaintiff was admitted into Jyotirmayi's house from May 4—the fourth day of his visit to Jaidebpur. He slept in her daughter's room.

> He was admitted into the intimacies of family life at once. There were young ladies in the house which had hardly any separate *andar* [inner quarters]. Jyotirmoyee Debi herself was young—she was on the right side of forty and a *purdanashin* [observer of purdah]. She was looking at what was going on from behind the *chik* [curtain]. But directly the plaintiff fainted, she said, quite incidentally, she went out to him, and people made way for her as she came out. No small emotion would expose her to public gaze. And then consider the family and its ways. She was a widow, and the women of the family were extremely orthodox—it was elicited that she would not take pipe-water on grounds of ceremonial purity which such widows affect. Such women would have a horror of having a person of no caste into the house, a man then young and, on the defendants' case, of unknown traits and antecedents. And this person was taken into the house and admitted into the family intimacies on the chance of his succeeding in playing the rôle of the Kumar, though he was a Punjabi, though he knew nothing about the family, and though he was looking utterly different; and she expected this man will fight the Bhowal estate and recover it, and did not foresee that the estate will fight to its last rupee, supposing he was not laughed or whipped out of Jaidebpur, and could go as far as the court, and even then what was the chance of success, and how far its fruits? No one who is not insane would think of doing it, nobody who is not insane would join it. But she did it and has stuck to him, though the plaintiff was compelled to leave Jaidebpur on the 7th June, and she has been an exile from home.
>
> Beyond certain limits, controversy is fruitless. I find that the lady, Jyotirmoyee Debi, did honestly believe that the plaintiff was her brother, and it remains to be seen whether that belief proceeded from a genuine recognition. (91)

Needham's report to Lindsay on May 5 which, as was admitted, was prepared for him by Jogen Banerjee and Mohini Chakrabarty, mentioned that all the people present in Jyotirmayi's house believed that the sadhu was the second kumar. Jogen Banerjee said in court that he accepted what was written in the report. The inmates of the house were convinced that the sadhu was none other than the kumar, and this included Buddhu, Jabbu, and Jyotirmayi. The report did not say that the man looked different or that he spoke gibberish. Jogen Babu knew the second kumar as well as anyone else. He saw that Jyotirmayi was convinced that the man was her brother. He might have believed that the man was a double of the second kumar, looking very much like him but whose mind or speech might turn out to be different, if sufficiently explored. Or he might even have believed that the sister's recognition was mistaken but honest. Yet he said in court that from the very first moment, the sadhu looked to him utterly different. Mohini Chakrabarty said that there was no time for believing or disbelieving, because the matter was too urgent and serious. Pushed on the point, he finally said he did not believe a word of what was said in Jyotirmayi's house on May 4— it was all nonsense. "[He] did not tell Mr. Needham so, and dressed and served this nonsense for Mr. Needham to sign and send up to the Collector of the district as a joke. . . . The report is the report of a believer. Even as the first information to which Mohini Babu would reduce it, it was immediately after the occurrence, given to one who would instantly see its untruth, if any, and who went forthwith to verify it, and satisfied, sat down to compose the report for the Collector of the District" (90).

Needham's report was sent off to Lindsay on May 5. Later the same day, Mohini Chakrabarty, Jogen Banerjee, and other officials of the estate were instructed by Needham to go to Jyotirmayi Debi's house and interview the sadhu. The result was Mohini Chakrabarty's report to Needham of May 6. The interview of the fifth was the only time the plaintiff was actually questioned on his memory of the kumar's life. From the evidence given in court, Pannalal Basu concluded that the sadhu answered several questions correctly. The crucial question was on the bird-shooting incident in Darjeeling, which Dr. Ashutosh Dasgupta and Phani Banerjee claimed the sadhu could not answer. The judge found that Girish Kavyatirtha and Abdul Hakim's evidence on this point were more credible. Mohini Chakrabarty's report of May 6 did not give a correct picture of what happened at the said interview. By then, the attitude of the district administration had been conveyed to Needham and his staff. Mohini Babu's report "was framed to fit the attitude of the Court of Wards on the 6th May, and the later orders which followed leave no doubt on the point" (100).

After this came the mammoth meeting in Jaidebpur.

The acclamation by the crowd does not prove the identity, and the want of it could imperil it. But it absolutely puts an end to the amazing case that the plaintiff had been set up by a few persons of Calcutta or Dacca. It is absolutely displaced by the facts that had gone before, the facts that followed this meeting, and the meeting itself. It is idle to contend that the plaintiff, an utterly different-looking man, has been set up by a few as the result of a conspiracy, and that the tenantry did not know him at all. It will appear below that they paid him large sums as *nazar* and rent. It was probably expected because of an order issued to Naibs to see that no tenant or anybody else deposed for him, and I do not wonder that the defendants began to ask the Court for an order to stem the tide of evidence which this amazing case had provoked by forcing the plaintiff to close. The case of a narrow conspiracy was breaking down. (103)

THE SADHU MAKES HIS CLAIM

For the next few days, the sadhu was there for all to see. He was giving them *darshan* [a chance to see him] and they were coming to talk to him, ask him questions, touch him (often to his annoyance), pay obeisance and often money. Was this extraordinary behavior for a kumar of Bhawal? "Why did he not go quietly to Mr. Needham and demand possession of the estate? Mr. Chaudhuri asked me," the judge noted, "to consider this question. If the Kumar were a well-educated, well-polished aristocrat, . . . there would be much in this account that would be odd, . . . extraordinary, and even incredible." What happened, however, was that Ananda Chandra Roy, the famous lawyer of Dhaka who knew the Bhawal family well, came to see the plaintiff at this time and was closeted with him for an hour. It was then that the alternative modalities of making his claim were probably discussed with the plaintiff. A few days later, the sadhu, accompanied by lawyers, went to see the collector. "[H]e went, unasked and unprimed, to the lion's den, and talked sense, alone with the Collector, though he is by no means astute. In fact, he has been described as a puppet, backed by clever people in the background. I consider this facing the Collector at this point of time an extremely important fact in this case" (108).

Satyabhama Debi, grandmother of the kumars, came to live with the plaintiff in his rented house in Dhaka. "One must consider, quite apart from her statements, what induced this lady, the widow of Rajah Kalinarayan, accustomed to living in a palace associated with her husband's memory, to come and live in a small hired house at Dacca, till the end came." She died in December 1922 at the age of eighty or a little more. The plaintiff performed the mukhāgni at her cremation. Her śrāddha, held in Dhaka because the plaintiff had been banished from Jaidebpur, was a grand affair, attended by most members of the Bhawal Raj family and kin and many distinguished zamindars and gentlemen of Dacca. Once again, the plaintiff performed all the rites prescribed for a grandson. "On the defendants' theory, this *mukhagni* by a Punjabi, or a man of unknown origin, was an enormity, and on their theory known to be such. . . . [The śrāddha] was, on the defendants' theory, another enormity and known to be so by every relation, every gentleman who knew the Kumar. There is no evidence that there was any protest by anybody" (115).

As we have seen when describing the evidence in court, there was hardly any attempt by the defense to probe the memory of the plaintiff. But there was a lot of evidence on his physical characteristics. How was one to judge this evidence? Pannalal Basu considered the alternatives. "[T]he question of identity is primarily a question of the identity of the body. One identifies a dead man [by identifying his body]. . . . But where a question of identity has arisen and there is conflicting evidence on the point, one would look to the mind, as individual as the body and impossible to confound with another, if sufficiently searched. Where, as in this case, the mind is deliberately left unexplored on the theory that tutoring has put into the plaintiff the entire store of the kumar's memory, and no skill could shew it factitious, the body became the principal consideration" (121–22).

First, there was the evidence on recognition. Dozens of relatives, friends, and acquaintances, and hundreds of tenants gave evidence that they had recognized the plaintiff as the second kumar. Under cross-examination, many were not able to analyze exactly which parts of the face or body or voice or manners they found to be similar. Did this diminish the worth of their evidence? "If you see a man not once but often, you retain a generalised image and recognise despite change produced by age or disease or accident. . . . You can recognise a voice without being able to describe it. Features individually not very different from those in another produce collectively an effect which is unique. . . . Few can identify a feature, unless it is very peculiar, as one does not see the features one by one and then join them up for the face. One sees the face" (124).

The witnesses for the plaintiff said they had recognized him as the second kumar after looking at him for a while. The witnesses for the defendants said that the plaintiff was utterly unlike the second kumar. As to the latter, Judge Pannalal Basu considered the known position of the Court of Wards against the plaintiff and especially the proved existence of Jogen Banerjee's instruction to the naibs to organize witnesses for the defendants. His conclusion was "that the defendants' tenant witnesses are the product of those letters, looking also to the fact . . . that they had been sent in batches in the custody of a peon by naibs. The tenants who have deposed for the plaintiff have come inspite of these orders, have braved certificates and what are called 'K.P. suits' which occur in many a document as a weapon to be used against the supporters of the sadhu." Moreover, the tenants who deposed in favor of the defendants were generally "of the poorest description." In comparison, the tenants on the plaintiff's side were "more substantial." The judge implied that there was greater chance that the former lot had been induced or coerced into giving evidence in favor of the ruling powers on the estate. Was it possible that the tenants for the plaintiff were claiming to recognize someone they could not have known or even seen very well because, after all, the kumar was an aristocrat, far removed in his daily life from the peasants? The judge considered this point suggested by A. N. Chaudhuri. He could not accept it, because the evidence from both sides made it clear that the second kumar was a very visible man.

> He was an outdoor man, going everywhere and seen everywhere. He would go to the stables in the morning. He would go to the *pilkhana* [elephant stable]. He would go about on elephants, drive about, ride about, will be seen at the Rath [chariot festival], at the *gan* [musical performance] in the Rajbari, in the maidan [field] in front of the Rajbari, at the *hāṭ* [marketplace], at the railway station, out in the jungle for a shoot. Most of the defendants' witnesses have admitted this. . . . The defendants could not make him invisible by putting a sentry at the gate, or suggesting fixed hours for admission into the *chiriakhana* [menagerie], or putting him in a room at the time of the *gan* in the Natmandir, as though sitting in the Natmandir in the middle of the tenantry . . . . was disreputable. It was nothing of the kind. It was rather a graceful condescension. Tenants certainly kept their distance, . . . but they certainly saw their *malik* [master], an arresting personality, as one witness says, even to strangers. (126, 152)

The judge thought it quite incredible that the defendants should have insisted with such vehemence that the second kumar and the plaintiff were utterly different. From all the evidence amassed in court, this was simply not plausible. On the contrary, the impression created by the plaintiff seemed to have been described most straightforwardly by an old peasant witness: "At first sight, he seems to be the same man" (129).

Of the kumar's relatives who claimed to recognize the plaintiff, the judge particularly mentioned Jyotirmayi Debi and Sarajubala Debi. It was suggested by the defendants that Jyotirmayi had a material interest in having the kumar back because, following the adoption of a son by the third rani, Jyotirmayi's sons no longer had a claim to the Raj property. "A brother might suit her, but one does not adopt a brother on that account." The chances of success of a plot involving a Punjabi double was so remote that only an insane person would have gone ahead with it. Jyotirmayi's evidence, the judge thought, was based on an honest recognition. So was the first rani Sarajubala's. Additionally, the judge found persuasive the evidence of Purasundari Debi, Bibhabati's cousin, and of Sarojini Debi, Bibhabati's aunt, both of whom deposed that they had recognized Bibha's husband. The defense counsel had suggested that Sarojini bore some unspecified grudge against Bibhabati and the very fact that she came all the way to Dhaka to give evidence against her proved this. The judge was not persuaded. "A woman would do a great deal for her niece, but she would draw a line if she thinks that she is denying her husband. That is a matter in which men may but few women would support the wife. I find that this lady told the truth when she said that she had recognized the plaintiff as the Second Kumar of Bhowal" (138).

"Not a relation has deposed for the other side," Pannalal Basu noted, "except Phani Babu and his sister, Saibalini, and the latter's son-in-law, an employee of the estate. What is more amazing, [the second rani's] own people at Uttarpara would not come and disown this alleged impostor, except a cousin, Sukumari Debi" (138).

Of the kumar's friends, there was N. K. Nag, who told the story of the plaintiff recounting the night when he had come to Nag's house to ask his father for money to pay the girls. Nag admitted in court that "he would sometimes associate with the Second Kumar in what Mr. Chaudhuri put to him as 'stolen joys'. The witness is a grave melancholy-looking man, and I do not think that he would publicly disclose this chapter of his life for the sake of a person whom he believed to be an impostor" (143).

The defendants, of course, had produced several officials to depose that the plaintiff was not the second kumar. Of them, Colonel Pulley was clearly mistaken in saying that he had met the second kumar several times, because from the officially recorded dates of his visits to Jaidebpur it was obvious that he could only have met him once, at the time of Lord Kitchener's shikar, and that it was very likely that he was confusing the second kumar with the third. "I do not think that this gentleman thought when he was speaking about Lord Kitchener's shoot, or the discussion with the Kumars before it took place, or the English accent, that he was conveying untruths to Court. He had been told things that would fit 'a well-educated, well-polished aristocrat,' and he, a plain English soldier, had the lofty unfitness of Englishmen to deal with low cunning" (161). This was cultural stereotyping of the most obvious kind, stamping the Other with an essential attribute that presumably explained his behavior. The same thing had been done to the Indian character by countless British writers and administrators for almost two hundred years. One might say that Judge Basu was only paying back the British officials in their own coin. It is unlikely, however, that even a decade earlier, an Indian judge of a district court would have disposed of the evidence of a British army officer in quite these terms. That is the measure of the change that had taken place within the organs of the late colonial state.

K. C. De had also mixed up the timings of his supposed interviews with the plaintiff, on which basis he claimed that he did not think he was the second kumar. "Memory played him a strange trick—this mixing the Sadhu with the 1923 interview and then placing it in 1926, and at Dacca, and then clothing him in *gerua* [ochre robes] and then putting on him the *jata* [matted hair] thing associated with a Sadhu, although it is agreed on all hands that the plaintiff was going about as a Babu, dressed as a Bengalee, before he left for Calcutta in 1924. . . . I believe that in this account too, something of the persuading oneself to believe what one had been told, such as occurred in Col. Pulley's case, had occurred" (164).

Rankin came all the way from England to depose in favor of the defendants (and sadly, albeit dramatically, to breathe his last in Dhaka). But it was doubtful if his opinion on the plaintiff's identity counted for much. "Mr. Rankin saw the plaintiff in Court after nearly 26 years, including the years of his retirement in England which meant loss of touch with India and the fading of his memories. Mr. Rankin never mixed with the Second Kumar, 14 years his junior, in a social way. [The second kumar] would pay formal calls at his house in Dacca, generally with the Eldest Kumar. . . . At Jaidebpur, one would expect that the meetings were less formal, but Mr. Rankin would always see him in English dress which implies considerable limitations" (174). Rankin, in other words, never saw the second kumar as he really was. Pannalal Basu did not think Rankin's evidence amounted to anything on the question of identity.

Lindsay had written down an account of his first meeting with the sadhu, not at the time but afterward. "It would be most unsafe," remarked the judge, "to take this report, not read over to the plaintiff nor taken down in his presence, as correct. For instance, I find it difficult to suppose that Mr. Lindsay knew the Hindi for pneumonia unless the plaintiff used this very word." The judge did not accept the document as a correct record of what was said in the plaintiff's first official interview, and thought that Lindsay "had no independent memory of it at all" (295).

Bibhabati herself had seen the plaintiff a few times in Calcutta—entirely by chance, she insisted. B. C. Chatterjee thought the sightings had been arranged with the connivance of the rani who had, in fact, recognized her husband. The judge did not think the inference was a necessary one. It could have been "the curiosity aroused by an impostor, and on the plaintiff's side an attempt to have a look at her so that he might know her if called upon to do so. A trifle excess in these sights which the Rani admits seems odd even from these points of view, but the conduct at best is ambiguous and aids no conclusion" (297). The rani's evidence could not be read to suggest that she had recognized the plaintiff as her husband.

THE BODY

It was known that a "very exhaustive inquiry" was made by the Court of Wards of tailors, shoemakers, and saddlers of Calcutta—mostly European establishments—to unearth records of physical measurements of the second kumar. Not a single such record was produced in court, which the judge thought "remarkable and a fact of compelling significance." The only time anything was mentioned touching on this information was when A. N. Chaudhuri put it to one of the witnesses that the second kumar's shoe size was six. It seems Chaudhuri thought the plaintiff's feet were larger. It turned out that the plaintiff too wore shoes of size six.

Some evidence on the second kumar's physical characteristics emerged from the medical report attached to his insurance papers. This report, as we have already mentioned, was in the possession of the Court of Wards but not produced in court. It was sought for and obtained by the plaintiff's side from the insurance company's offices in Edinburgh. In it, the kumar's height was recorded as five feet five inches. Medical experts from both sides agreed that it was possible for men to grow in height up to the age of twenty-two or twenty-three, sometimes up to twenty-five. When his height was recorded, the second kumar was twenty-one. "It is thus not only possible," ruled Judge Basu, "but probable that the Kumar's growth in height did not stop before he had just attained the age of twenty-one, so that if the plaintiff had been just 5 feet and 5 inches, it might well have been urged as a circumstance rather against him" (187). One could well imagine that if the plaintiff's height had been exactly the same as the kumar's, the defendants would have argued the improbability of someone, especially a robust young man like Ramendra Narayan, not growing even an inch after the age of twenty-one.

Contrasting him with the second kumar, A. N. Chaudhuri had called the plaintiff "a bloated *palwan* [wrestler]." Pannalal Basu was not impressed by the comparison. The plaintiff, it was true, was fat. But Chaudhuri might well have pointed out, "as a distinction, that the kumar was twenty-five and this man is fifty-two" (189). One was comparing the physical characteristics of a man at two points of time separated by twenty-seven years. One had to take into account the probable physical changes caused by the passage of time. Diachronic identity, the philosopher might say, is what was at issue.

The second kumar's appearance, everyone agreed, was very distinctive. He was extremely fair for a Bengali, had reddish-brown hair and—most witnesses said—*kaṭā* eyes. What color was *kaṭā*? Those who knew English described it variously as brown, grey, hazel, auburn, yellow; some even said blue. The plaintiff's eyes, it was generally agreed, were also *kaṭā*—brown, most witnesses said. So was it the same color as the kumar's eyes? The defendants picked out all of the different English equivalents of *kaṭā* to suggest that the kumar's eyes were of a different color from those of the plaintiff's. Judge Basu took note of the fact that in Bengal, anyone whose eyes were not black was said to have *kaṭā* eyes. There seemed to be only two possible descriptions of the color of eyes: the normal black or *kaṭā*. In east

Bengal, *kaṭā* was also called *pingla*—yellowish. *Kaṭā* eyes were sometimes referred to as *biralchokh*—cat's eyes. In northern India too, eyes were either *mamuli*, ordinary, or *billi*, catlike.

> Now *kaṭā* eyes, though exceptional, and though classed together under one name, must have some colour, and this must vary. But nobody in this country, or in Bengal at all events, and the Punjab, trouble about or notice the colouring, so that nobody refers to *kaṭā* eyes as blue or pale blue or water blue or faded blue, or gray or bluish gray or steel gray, or hazel or violet or tawny or hazel-green or the like. Few of such shades exist in this country, or at all events in Bengal, and those that exist and get classed as *kaṭā* are usually not pleasing shades but discolour, so that *kaṭā* eyes, like *kaṭā* hair, are somewhat disfavoured in this country. . . .
>
> Now when one is accustomed to class all such eyes as *Kaṭā* and has occasion to translate the word, one would use the word 'gray'. The plaintiff said, for instance, that his eyes were *kaṭā*. I took down the word, but put within brackets the word 'gray' as its equivalent. It was, of course, wrong, but the use of the word 'gray' for *kaṭā* is, I believe, common. (199)

The second kumar's eyes had been described as "grey" in Dr. Caddy's medical report and as "brownish" by Kali Prasanna Ghosh. G. C. Sen, the insurance agent, said in his evidence that he was translating between the second kumar and the doctor, who wrote down what Sen told him. Sen, the judge inferred, had made the usual translation of *kaṭā* into "grey." Kali Prasanna, on the other hand, was likely to be much more discerning in his use of English. "Brownish" was specific; the learned Kali Prasanna did not only mean *kaṭā*, but a "brownish" *kaṭā*. It was reasonable to conclude that the second kumar had *kaṭā* eyes that were brown rather than blue.

The kumar's ears were so unusual that they were a mark of identity. J. P. Ganguly and Winterton, experts for the plaintiff, deposed that the plaintiff's ears had the same characteristic—the lobes did not join with the cheeks but were pendant. Percy Brown thought the plaintiff's ears did not have this feature, but agreed that the impression might be the result of his fat cheeks—once again, the vagaries of aging. Pannalal Basu did not shy away from making his own judgment. "After looking at the ears in all the photos of the Kumar and the plaintiff, and looking at the ears in life, and particularly in the two untouched photos . . . , I am satisfied that the ears of both are the same, and they are peculiar ears. And I notice the singular fact that the ears of Rajah Rajendra are similar to these, as Mr. Winterton points out" (216).

The plaintiff had an irregular scar on his left ankle. His case was that it had been left by a carriage accident around the time of the third kumar's wedding. The defendants denied this and said the second kumar had no such scar and that there had been no such accident. Phani Banerjee testified to this, and the second rani claimed not to remember that her husband was walking on crutches when the celebrations took place for the third kumar's wedding. That the second kumar did have a scar at the same place was proved when Dr. Caddy's medical report was produced in court. The second rani's evidence on this point was also put in question when a letter was produced written by her sister Malina three weeks after the youngest kumar's wedding: "We are all glad to hear that Ramendra's leg has healed." Judge Basu found that the scar on the left ankle was a positive mark of identity.

The scaly feet were another distinctive characteristic of the second kumar—said to be a family trait. Only Phani Banerjee denied this, and he, the judge thought, was a most unreliable witness. The judge found the same skin condition "running in the family." One more mark of identity in favor of the plaintiff (227).

The second kumar had syphilis. A specific remedy for syphilis called salvarsan was discovered in 1909, the year the kumar supposedly died. (We are talking of an age before the discovery of penicillin.) Consequently, although the kumar was treated for the disease, there was nothing he was given that could have prevented him from developing sores and gumma. The plaintiff had a bony growth on the bridge of his nose. There was a disagreement among the medical experts on what it was. Colonel Chatterjee was a specialist on venereal diseases, and it was his firm opinion that it was a syphilitic node, corroborated by other features which indicated that the plaintiff was an old syphilitic. Denham-White and Thomas on behalf of the defendants did not subscribe to this, but were unable to suggest an alternative explanation. Judge Basu accepted Dr. Chatterjee's opinion.

The plaintiff also had a scar on his abdomen, which he said had been left when Dr. Elahi had operated on a *bagi* (swelling). The plaintiff thought the swelling had been caused by his syphilis. The medical experts in court did not think it could have been a syphilitic bubo since it was not in the groin, but Major Thomas said that people were often confused about such things. The defendants attempted to deny that there was ever a doctor called Elahi in Jaidebpur, but this was proved conclusively, and also that he was known to have performed a surgery on the second kumar.

The plaintiff had a broken tooth, a claw mark on his arm, and a tiny mole on the penis. Several witnesses testified that the second kumar too had a broken tooth, although no one could give an exact date when he broke it. The plaintiff claimed it was from a carriage accident. The claw mark was caused by a tiger cub of the Rajbari menagerie. The defendants tried to get medical opinion that it could have been caused by something else. Pannalal Basu remarked: "It is difficult for me to understand why if the mark was being falsely imputed, a medically impossible cause should be given" (239). The mole on the penis was confirmed by two old servants of the Rajbari and by Elokeshi, known to have been Ramendra's mistress.

The physical resemblances added up. Several independent marks proved to have been on the second kumar's body were found on the plaintiff's. Judge Pannalal Basu's conclusion was: "The plaintiff therefore must be the Second Kumar himself unless it appears that he had died in Darjeeling, or that his mind is different, or that his handwriting is different, or that he is not Bengali" (243). The judge now turned to discuss these topics.

THE MIND

The defendants' line was not to test the plaintiff on his memory but to show that he did not fit the type—the Bengal aristocrat. "As I pictured the Kumar which Mr. Chaudhuri was presenting," Judge Basu remarked, "I thought that if there was an impostor, the plaintiff was one. But the odd thing about him was that he did not look an astute adventurer—cool, collected and able to play a part. He was raging and fuming under the jeers and taunts his answers provoked, when for instance he said he did not know the term 'cue' or the term 'braces'. But he was not noisy or shifty or afraid, and did not look or behave as though he was posturing and trying to brazen it out. In intelligence, he seemed decidedly below the average, and that apparently led to the contention that he was a puppet" (244–45). The plaintiff was clearly an illiterate man, and most of the cross-examination went over his head. If indeed the kumar was a well-educated aristocrat, it would be insane for any plotter to believe that this man could succeed in fooling anyone. But, of course, thought Judge Basu, the kumar was as illiterate as this man. That gave to the defense strategy of deliberately avoiding the question of memory "a glaring significance." A. N. Chaudhuri tried to show that the plaintiff did not even know about the subjects that were the kumar's favorites—riding and hunting. Pannalal Basu was not persuaded. "Out in the muffosil [countryside], a man can shoot without knowing the reason for the difference between the muzzle end and the breech end, and there is, as the evidence will shew, a local terminology for guns and ammunition. . . . An illiterate man may be a good *shikari* [hunter] without knowing the terms put to the plaintiff, and may be a good horseman without knowing the terms put to the plaintiff."

To show what the kumar might have been if he was alive, Phani Banerjee was put in the box as the kumar's "intellectual double." He had to be coached for the part, as his lesson book revealed. But the difference with the second kumar was that Phani Babu had lived as a zamindar for twenty-six years after 1909. Even then, he had to be coached a great deal to come up to the level of Mr. Chaudhuri's kumar. "That Kumar is not a reality, but a fiction, and the Court will have to consider why truth will not distinguish the plaintiff, but falsehood. Untutored, Phani Babu's word for a 'frock coat' is, for instance, 'frog coat'. The plaintiff's word is 'folat coat'. Untutored,

Phani Babu in the matter of these terms would be very much like the plaintiff, even if you take off his education and later acquisitions" (249).

The fact that Ramendra Narayan Ray was a zamindar proved nothing
about the quality of his mind.

> Learned Counsel frequently asked me to remember that the Second Kumar
> was a 'Rajah's son' and, education or no education, there were certain proba-
> bilities. I shall bear them in mind. But knowledge of English is not a gift of
> fortune. You cannot know the lbw [leg before wicket, a term in cricket] or re-
> member it unless you play or take an interest in the game. As to style, it was
> unmitigated Bengali, despite some ceremonial clothes put on to see high En-
> glish officials on their occasional visits. 'Rajah's son' served some purpose with
> the witnesses. Was he not looking a Rajah's son? Had he not the bearing of a
> Rajah's son? Was not his moustache like a Rajah's son? One peasant with due
> deference spoke of the nose as that of a Rajah's son. The Court will not be mis-
> led by a phrase.
>
> I find that the cross-examination, so far as it goes to explore the mind of the
> Kumar, was exactly what one minded to defeat the true Kumar would design.
> It avoids memory and goes to general knowledge. . . . That a witness has been
> tutored is not a ground for not cross-examining him but a ground for cross-
> examining him the more. . . . Could the combined memories of a thousand
> people, aided by the skill of lawyers and the memory of the wife, think of noth-
> ing which the tutoring could not reach, and is it possible that the whole mem-
> ory of the Second Kumar has been put *en bloc* into this alleged Punjabi peas-
> ant? Mr. Chaudhuri kept to general knowledge and to terminology. Did he
> hand to the plaintiff a gun and ask him to handle it in court? . . . He was afraid
> of falling into a trap. He was afraid of falling into the truth.
>
> . . .[I]f the Kumar was educated, that without more would demolish the
> plaintiff and nobody would trouble about memory or anything else. But the
> Kumar . . . was illiterate . . . , so that all that requires scrutiny . . . is any real
> ignorance that would not occur in the Kumar today, supposing he were living.
> (250–51)

For instance, the Kumar was supposedly a sportsman. On his love of hunting and riding, there was enough evidence. What about other sports? Except for Phani Banerjee, no one who knew him well deposed that Ramendra played tennis or cricket or football or billiards. One witness said that
the second kumar despised tennis as a "woman's game." Pannalal Basu
thought that fitted well with Ramendra's type: "he was that sort of man,
fond of elephants and shikar and horses, and women, without pretensions
of any kind such as make some men take to sports which they do not enjoy
but which it is the fashion to know. I find that the Second Kumar did not
know billiards or tennis and the plaintiff has not shown greater ignorance
than he would have done if he were in the box" (256).

On polo, the plaintiff himself said that he and the third kumar had learned a little of the game, but he did not persist with it. When questioned by A. N. Chaudhuri, it was apparent that the plaintiff did not know, or remember, anything about polo. Pannalal Basu thought this especially significant. Chaudhuri had suggested that his questions on cricket and billiards had not been anticipated by the plaintiff's tutors, which is why he could not answer them. If there were tutors, they should certainly have anticipated questions on polo because plaintiff's witness Chandranan Singh, the Manipuri rider, had deposed that he had tried for a few days to teach the second kumar to play polo. But the plaintiff did not know what a "nearside back hand" was, or a "pelham bit"; he didn't even know "chukker" but knew the Bengali term *baji*. Evidence was presented to show that the second kumar was a member of the Polo Club in Dhaka. Judge Basu did not think the evidence was conclusive that it was indeed the second and not the third kumar. He decided that the plaintiff was no more ignorant of polo than the kumar would have been some thirty years after his brief introduction to the game.

On hunting, the plaintiff clearly did not know the English terminology. But he was not ignorant of the subject. "With the Second Kumar, shikar was not a thing taken up by an educated man as a fashionable pursuit, but a play he had begun in childhood and almost as a daily pursuit." He learned about hunting from the numerous illiterate shikaris of the Bhawal forest with whom he spent a great deal of his time. It also seems that being a "Rajah's son," his servants would load his guns, just as they would bathe and dress him. On hunting as well as on the subject of horses, the plaintiff's ignorance of English terminology was not proof that he did not know something that the kumar knew.

The plaintiff claimed he did not know a single song he had sung in his childhood or youth. This seemed incredible. Even Jyotirmayi mentioned a few songs that the young Ramendra sang—loudly and tunelessly, she said—while bathing: "Jhilimili pāniyā, hā re nanadiyā" was one, "Āy lo ali kusum tuli bhariyā ḍālā" was another. Not only that, there is hardly any Bengali Hindu family in which songs are not sung, and not just on religious or festive occasions. Why did the plaintiff stubbornly refuse to admit he knew any? Judge Basu thought over the matter. "The reason is plain," he wrote.

Among our people, there are few, with the exception of professionals or men who sing well, who would admit that they can sing, and even those who sing well require a lot of coaxing before they will sing in company, and that they would begin in a shamefaced apologetic way. I believe nothing would induce a cultivator or an illiterate man to admit in a Court that he knows a song, much less to give one. It is a shame in a crowd, though it may be solitary pride. Apart from this national trait, there are things that are too silly to be said, but which can be sung; and if the Second Kumar's songs were of the kind in Phani Babu's list—most of them are low and all of love, and mostly of the guilty sort—he would not, unless he was educated, confess or repeat them in Court. He would think it the height of impropriety to utter them in the middle of solemn proceedings in a crowded Court. An educated man will take a song, whatever it is, as a literary phenomenon, just as a surgeon takes certain parts of the body. The Second Kumar would be incapable of that detachment. (265)

On the question of the plaintiff's mind, then, Pannalal Basu's conclusion was the following.

It is enough for me to find now, as I do, that assuming that the Second Kumar was illiterate in 1909 in the sense I stated and allowing for the lapse that might occur in bare literacy, the mind of the plaintiff, so much of it as the defendants cared to reveal to me by their cross-examination, is not different from what would be the mind of the Second Kumar today. The rest of his mind they did not explore, and the only reason that I can think of is not fear of factitious knowledge, but of memory. (269)

His Literacy

If the second kumar was a "well-educated well-polished young aristocrat" in 1909 and the conspirators, whoever they were, had hit upon an illiterate Punjabi to play his part, then it was certainly very strange that they did not, before they went to court, even teach him the alphabet, although they had twelve years to do so. On the other hand, except for some English signatures and one Bengali signature, and a bunch of disputed letters to his wife, there was not a single piece of writing that the defendants produced to prove the kumar's literacy. "If there were any writing of the Second Kumar, it would be treasured like gold," the judge thought. There was evidence from officials who said that the second kumar would attend lunches and parties where conversation would be in English. Pannalal Basu was not persuaded by this evidence on lunches, because "not only Rajah's sons, but Rajahs" were known "to eat them without knowing English."

It is perfectly clear that the Second Kumar did not know English at all, except such words as people ignorant of English pick up. Such words the plaintiff himself used in the course of his deposition, and looking to the English the Second Kumar spoke, if English it could be called, he would be today in the same plight as the plaintiff, particularly if for 12 years out of 24 years that elapsed since 1909 he was in the company of sannyasis, away from Dacca and its local associations. A more elaborate scheme to displace him by a false trait it would be difficult to conceive, but every part of it has been destroyed by facts. (280)

There were nine letters, purportedly written by Ramendra to his wife, which were said to be specimens of his Bengali writing. The second rani swore to these letters in court. They were curious letters, the judge thought. All of them mentioned visits or intended visits to officials such as the commissioner or the district magistrate. For the man who wrote the letters, such visits were apparently an unusual honor. Yet they were supposedly written to a girl of thirteen, married only a few months before, by a husband who had gone away for a day or two to Dhaka, a place hardly twenty miles from Jaidebpur.

> The thing that strikes me as odd is that the Kumar was frequently coming to the Dacca house, an hour's journey from home, and if such correspondence was usual, only such letters as mentioned the officials got preserved. The Rani said of course that there were other letters not fit for production in Court as they are silly, but it is still odd that those not silly are mostly on this topic. Another thing that is odd is that these letters, though spread over six years, shew less variety in topic or writing than one would expect; and I see very little of a boy or youth writing to his wife. (285)

On the official visits, the dates mentioned in the letters did not fit the known facts in two instances. One letter said that the second kumar was to meet the *lat saheb*, that is, the governor, the next day in Dhaka. On that day, August 10, 1902, Sir John Woodburn was presiding over the legislative council in Calcutta and was due to go to Bihar on tour. There was no plan of his coming to Dhaka. Another letter written from Dhaka coincided with a period when the second kumar was known to be in Calcutta. Of the handwriting experts who examined the letters, S. C. Chowdhury for the plaintiff declared that if the known signatures of the kumar were the specimens to go by, these letters were not written by the same person. Charles Hardless for the defendants agreed with the basic principles characterizing the two sets of writings, but was unwilling to draw the conclusion that they were by different persons. "I conclude," the judge wrote, "that the disputed letters under discussion are not genuine, that they had not been written by the Second Kumar. . . . [T]here is complete want of evidence, practically speaking, that the Second Kumar ever wrote anything in Bengali, except his signature, and even that so rarely that few had seen him do it" (287).

In 1932, eight signatures of Kumar Ramendra Narayan Roy and nine of "the impostor posing as Ramendra Narayan Roy" had been sent to S. C. Chowdhury, handwriting expert, with instructions to send his report to Rai Bahadur S. N. Banerjee at Nineteen Lansdowne Road. The instructions also said that "five signatures from each group which are most dissimilar may be selected." Judge Pannalal Basu noted: "Rai Bahadur, when he was composing this letter, must have been trembling. He made no secret of what he wanted and he sent the requisition through the Commissioner of Police.

Mr. S. C. Chowdhury was formerly an Inspector of Police, and his work was handwriting comparison for police cases." Chowdhury noted down all the differences between the two sets of signatures, but said that it was still highly probable that they were by the same writer and the differences were caused by age or disease. "An expert who, upon the kind of requisition aforesaid, could give this opinion, has acquired something of the neutrality of science. The opinion was, of course, suppressed from the Hon'ble Board of Revenue. Satya Babu says that it was not sent as it was inconclusive" (288–89). A few days before S. C. Chowdhury was to appear in Pannalal Basu's court in Dhaka, he was asked by one of the lawyers for the defendants to compare the Bengali letters allegedly written by the second kumar with the Kumar's Bengali signature and the signatures of the plaintiff. Chowdhury reported that the letters were not written by the same person as the author of the signatures, while all of the signatures (he had not been told that some were by the plaintiff) were probably by the same hand.

Chowdhury reiterated his opinion in court. He identified the English signatures of the second kumar and those of the plaintiff as written by the same person. Both sets showed the signs of someone who was unused to writing. The Bengali letters, he said, were written by a person with a much surer hand. Charles Hardless, for the defendants, disagreed. He pointed out many differences between the two sets of signatures, which Chowdhury had also done, but unlike the latter thought they were fundamental. Hardless also did not accept that someone might once learn the alphabet and later forget it. Basu was not convinced by this reasoning. "Knowledge of letters, like every knowledge, may be forgotten, and lapse from a bare literacy to illiteracy is a common and intelligible experience. . . . [I]n a man barely literate, lapse to illiteracy while retaining the ability to sign occurs if he keeps signing, but does no other reading or writing, till the signature becomes a mark, and its components slip from memory, particularly if even this is not written for years. I find that the signatures of the Second Kumar and the signatures of the plaintiff, seen by the two experts, are by the same hand, and that Mr. S. C. Chowdhury is right" (293).

Having assessed all the evidence on the physical and mental identity of the plaintiff, Judge Pannalal Basu concluded: "I have examined so far the body and the mind of the plaintiff, feature by feature, and seen nothing that displaces the identity proved by direct evidence of the kind stated and by a collocation of indisputable features that cannot occur in a second individual. . . . Nothing in my opinion can displace the identity unless it appears that the Second Kumar died at Darjeeling, or that the plaintiff is Mal Singh of Aujla or not a Bengalee at all" (298).

Chapter Fifteen

THE JUDGMENT

DARJEELING

$\mathbb{C}$ALVERT'S certificates were the crucial evidence procured by Satyendra Banerjee when questions were apparently raised in Jaidebpur about the second kumar's death. They persuaded the eldest kumar that there was no need for further inquiries. They were also part of the documents that Satyen Banerjee gave to Lethbridge immediately after the sadhu's arrival in Jaidebpur. On what basis had Calvert written those certificates? In one of them, he said he had treated the kumar for fourteen days for biliary colic. This could not have been true, because the records of Smith, Stanistreet & Co. showed that prescriptions were served only from May 6 and no other prescriptions were produced. Another mistake in Calvert's certificate was the second kumar's age which he said was "about 27 years" when in fact he was not yet twenty-five. The same mistake occurs in all other documents connected with the insurance claim, except for the affidavit by Kali Prasanna Ghosh. "It is a common mistake due to a common cause. I notice," wrote Pannalal Basu, "that in Satya Babu's diary he was making inquiries about the date of birth of the Kumar, shewing that he did not know the exact age" (311).[1] In other words, Calvert had written down the kumar's age as given to him by Satyen Banerjee.

It was commonly accepted among the experts that death from biliary colic was extremely rare. It was also agreed that in a case of gallstone, there is constipation. The only cure for biliary colic is an operation. In paroxysm, the only treatment is to relieve the pain by administering opium, most effectively by an injection of morphia. Dr. Calvert's first prescription on May 6 had nothing to do with biliary colic. Even Calvert agreed in cross-examination that it was probably for dyspepsia. The telegram sent that day to Jaidebpur did not mention any colic.

Ashutosh Dasgupta's prescription of May 7 seemed to suit chronic malaria. It would certainly purge and irritate the stomach. No one, not even Dr. Dasgupta, said it was for biliary colic. Was this the source of an arsenical poisoning that caused the kumar's death? That was not, as far as Judge Basu could see, anybody's case. "Dr. Thomas admits what is obvious, that if anyone were minded to poison anybody with arsenic, he would make or get a prescription that might serve as a cloak and capable of explaining the symptoms which include diarrhoea and blood in stools and arsenic in stools. I have not looked at the evidence going to show alternative or better prescriptions, nor is this a murder or attempted murder trial. I am investigating the matter just to find out whether the Kumar had died, or been taken for dead and carried to the burning ground" (319–20). When faced with this prescription, Ashutosh Dasgupta insisted that it was not his, that he had written it under instructions from a senior doctor, either Calvert or Nibaran Sen. Calvert denied he had ever made this prescription. Nibaran Sen was now dead, but no one had deposed that he ever came to Step Aside on May 7.

> Two facts are, therefore, plain. Neither Col. Calvert nor Dr. Nibaran had come on the 7th May or there will be a prescription over their signatures. . . . The Kumar was in pain—let us call it biliary colic for the moment—that night. . . . Not one of the prescriptions indicate fever except this one made by Ashu doctor. . . . I do not believe a word of this evidence. . . . Even Dr. Ashutosh does not say that the Kumar had malaria and he tried to treat it. He says he did not prescribe it at all, that he would not think of treating the Kumar as he was then a youth and had passed an ordinary medical school examination. . . .
>
> Up to the 7th Dr. Calvert had not seen colic at all, and yet he went on speaking of the pain "off and on" and that he was watching the case from day to day . . . and talked of "intervals" and all that sort of thing, though all that he had seen was flatulence on a single day—the 6th morning—and all that he had done was make a single prescription on that day. (323–24)

There were five prescriptions served on May 8, signed by Dr. Calvert or by Dr. Sen, and they had continuous serial numbers in the books of the pharmacist, which indicated "some quick succession, unless Messrs. Smith, Stanistreet and Co. did no business that day except dispensing these prescriptions." The full set of prescriptions indicated the following sequence of events:

According to Major Thomas for the defendants:
1. Simple dyspepsia.
2. Collapse.
3. Opium pills for biliary colic as a substitute for injection, and rectal condition.
4. Cramp and pain in the abdomen, may be . . .

According to Dr. MacGilchrist and Dr. Bradley:
1. Simple dyspepsia.
2. Collapse.
3. Opium pills for profuse diarrhoea.
4. Cramp and pain in the stomach.

Anything contrary to this said by Ashutosh Dasgupta, the judge would not accept. "I am not going to rely on his former testimony [in the defamation case] as substantive evidence except so far as he admits it correct, but it is enough to discredit him altogether. It is only necessary to read his evidence to do that; to this witness, untruth comes more naturally than truth. He seems to revel in it, though it was a travesty even of falsehood" (332). The judge concluded that the collapse that occurred around noon on May 8 was caused by severe diarrhoea with bleeding. Even the rani admitted this, although she called it biliary colic. There were any number of things, the judge noted, that excluded biliary colic. Not a single telegram sent from Jaidebpur mentioned it. It does not cause diarrhoea, which was the principal complaint of the day. None of the treatment was for biliary colic.

> Biliary colic appeared for the first time in the condolence letter composed by Dr. Calvert on the 10th, and even there it is colic. He had not seen the Second Kumar a single day before the 8th except the 6th, and even on that day he had not seen him in pain, and what he had seen on the 8th is now known—blood-stools and collapse. And yet when he sat down to write the gratuitous condolence letter in which he speaks of biliary colic, and his patient having it off and on, and the exhortation of friends, and his refusal to take an injection, and in his later affidavit he suggests a 14 days' treatment, and this led him to say that he had been watching the biliary colic from day to day, although he had not seen it for a day, on the defendants' own account, until the 7th when in the middle of the pain he is said to have prescribed arsenic and when I find he was not present. It is perfectly clear that somebody wanted this document from him—the condolence letter to hide the real cause of the blood-stools and the collapse and the apparent death—and Dr. Calvert who, as he admits, had never seen a case of arsenical poisoning, had thought of, or accepted the suggestion of, biliary colic as an explanation of what had occurred. . . . Nobody, not even Satya Babu or Ashu Babu, explains how or why this letter was written, to whom it was handed over. . . .
>
> I find that the biliary colic is a fiction, that it could not explain the fresh red blood in the stools, and the treatment was not of biliary colic at all. . . . Eliminating biliary colic, what was the cause of the symptoms on the 8th? . . . If the two doctors [MacGilchrist and Denham-White], one on either side, agree that the symptoms on that date mean an irritant, it is enough for me to find that these were not due to a disease, but an irritant that got into him. The evidence does not disclose any other irritant than the arsenic one finds in the arsenic prescription of the 7th made by Dr. Ashutosh, and grave suspicion attaches to him for making the prescription at all, and then denying it, and trying by perjury to hide it and to fasten it upon another. . . . The giving of this medicine, even if there was no attempt to hide it, would be an extremely suspicious circumstance. But so long as the bare possibility that he gave this medicine like a quack and was frightened at the result remains, I cannot find that he did it

wilfully to cause death. I must find, however, that the irritant was arsenic, as there was nothing else, and nothing else explains the symptoms that appeared the next morning. (338–40)

When did the second kumar die? The second rani claimed that Dr. Calvert came on May 8 at about 2 P.M. and, except for a short period in the evening when he went for dinner, he was at Step Aside the whole time until after the kumar died around midnight. Pannalal Basu found it difficult to believe that Calvert would stay there for so long doing nothing, since there were no prescriptions from the evening. Calvert said in his deposition that as far as he could remember, he was present at the time of death. When he was shown his affidavit of July 7, 1909, he said he did not need to see the certificate to remember that the kumar died at midnight; he had a very good recollection of it since the death made a great impression on him. He had kept no notes or memo, but twenty-two years after the event, he still remembered it. In his letter to Lindsay of August 1921, however, Calvert had written: "I cannot now be certain whether I was present at the moment of his death, but I saw him shortly before it in a state of profound collapse." Clearly, then, Calvert had not remembered the event in 1921 but remembered it ten years later. "He might of course recall it," noted Judge Basu,

after seeing the affidavit, as he was forced to say after this letter was elicited, but when he said he had an independent recollection of it, he was not telling the truth.

I am satisfied that this recollection is no better than his recollection of the "14 days' illness" and "the pain on and off" and his "watching the case from day to day." Both [that he was present at death and that the death occurred at around midnight], in view of his affidavit, he had to speak to as things within his memory. One of them is demonstrably false. The other is equally so. For indisputable facts point to and establish that the Second Kumar "died" or was taken as dead between 7 and 8 pm on the 8th May. (341–42)

From the evidence presented to him, the judge outlined the following sequence of events.

First, there was a near collapse—no pulse, the body being rubbed with ginger powder—all before dusk. Even going by the rani's account, there is no treatment between Dr. B. B. Sarkar's arrival and death.

Second, the last telegram sent to Jaidebpur was at 3:10 P.M., to which an anxious reply from the eldest kumar was received at 6 P.M. The next telegram, which was never found, announced the kumar's death.

Third, Dr. B. B. Sarkar came to Step Aside at around sunset. He was brought there by Surya Narayan Banerjee, Satya Babu's uncle, who was then living in Darjeeling. According to the defendants' version of events, Dr. Calvert and Dr. Nibaran Sen were both present at the time at Step Aside. Dr. Sarkar was then a little-known doctor. Judge Basu thought it impossible that he would dare examine the patient in the presence of Dr. Calvert or that Dr. Calvert would tolerate it for a moment. I do not believe it. I do not think it possible. The very fact that this Dr. B. B. Sarkar was there and saw the Kumar at dusk is proof that Dr. Calvert was not there and that the end was near, or the other two doctors would not be away. This one came as a forlorn hope. Ram Singh Subba told the truth when he said that when he came to this room that day at about 7–30, he found Dr. B. B. Sarkar in the room and the dead body of the Kumar. He [Dr. Sarkar] did not go away in a few minutes. As a Bengalee, he did the decent thing and sat there, apparently till the body was taken away. (343)

Fourth, the telegram announcing the death was never produced. The rest of the telegrams were asked for by Lindsay from the first rani, who had them with her along with her husband's papers. Lindsay did not ask her why the most important telegram was missing. The obvious explanation for this, Judge Basu felt, was that the telegram was all along in the possession of the collector's office. Sagar Babu, who was with the third kumar when the telegram was delivered to him on the morning of May 9, deposed that the message was: "Mejo Kumar expired this evening." Phani Banerjee claimed that it read "died last midnight." Niranjan Roy, signaler at the Jaidebpur station, said that they were all anxious at the station about the second kumar's health because they were following the sequence of telegrams, and if a telegram did arrive at night announcing the kumar's death, it would not have been delivered until the morning so as not to upset the family at night, because it was known that there was no train to Darjeeling until eight in the morning. "The fact remains that a telegram was sent at night, and though on this evidence it cannot be said that it had not been sent after midnight, its real contents are those stated by Sagor Babu that the Kumar had expired in the evening. If these were different, the original which, I find, is in the possession of the defendants would have been produced. The "last midnight" is a piece of false evidence if the telegram was sent at night. The message sent to Uttarpara to the Rani's people has not of course been produced" (346).

Fifth, there was the evidence of the professors staying at the Sanitarium. The judge was emphatic about their reliability: "I consider these witnesses gentlemen of unimpeachable credit." True, they were unable to recall the exact date of the incident, and it was asked that if they could not remember the date, how could they remember the hour?

Mr. Chaudhuri did not see that a date is not seen, but a messenger is seen, and the news of death, if brought by a messenger with a request, sticks, and with it the hour as a part of the thing perceived. If you recall an incident, such as an accident in the street or an unusual visitor, that is to say, if the incident is one that by its frequency has not dissociated itself from any particular time, you cannot recall it without recalling the hour as a part of your perception, although you have forgotten the date which is a matter for the intellect. . . .

I find that these gentlemen did receive the news of death from a messenger in the common room of the Sanitarium before 8 pm. It was contended that their testimony was not evidence but hearsay. It was the death speaking. It was part of the *res gestae*, like sending for an undertaker in England. (347–48)

"If these gentlemen heard the news before 8 pm," asked the judge, "what reason is there to disbelieve witnesses who swear that they had heard it too?" There were several such witnesses. The conclusion then was inevitable and, one might say, decisive for the case as a whole: "The Kumar, I find, apparently died between 7 and 8 pm." Although the rani and the nurse Jagat Mohini tried to fill out the period from dusk to midnight, it is clear that there was no treatment at this time, no prescriptions, although senior physicians such as Dr. Calvert and Dr. Sen were supposedly waiting in the house. "Dr. Ashu puts into this period an injection. He cannot say what was injected, for he could not very well say that morphia was again injected during collapse, after the pain had ceased." The rani and Jagat Mohini's account "was cut through by the fact that the Rani was having fits, though she denied it, and by the fact that she appeared before nobody except women." Several witnesses for the defendants, including Satya Babu and Ashutosh Dasgupta, deposed that there were doctors and other men present at the time of the kumar's death. If they were present, the rani could not have been in the room.

"If, then, it is a fact that the Second Kumar apparently died between 7 and 8 pm," continued Judge Basu, "it is almost inconceivable that he was not taken to the burning ground in course of the night. . . . There is a prejudice against *basi mora* [stale corpse] and the thing is not done, and though Mr. Chaudhuri referred to the case of public men like Sir Ashutosh Mukherjee or C. R. Das . . . , the exceptions are of recent origin and public men stand on a different footing" (350–51). The body was taken to the old cremation ground, not the new one. The old ground did not have a shed at the time. Did it rain that night at the cremation ground? The records at St. Joseph's and St. Paul's show that there was no rain that day or night or the next day in Darjeeling. The Planters' Club records had been removed. The Municipality records had been altered. The Botanical Gardens records were hopelessly unreliable. Many witnesses said that it was perfectly possible for it to rain at one place in Darjeeling and not at another. But Father Peel claimed there were definite patterns and from these it was possible to "predict tendencies." Judge Basu found the Reverend Father's reasoning "somewhat obscure." "[Y]ou cannot exclude rain on a given day which the witnesses remember by metereological data which are too complex to permit prediction. . . . I am not satisfied that the rain on that day can be excluded on such general grounds" (360–61).

What about the morning cremation? The defendants argued that this was the only cremation—there was no attempted cremation at night. The plaintiff's case was that the body cremated in the morning was not the kumar's body at all; some other body was procured during the night, completely covered up and carried in a procession, and burned without performing the usual rites. The defendants argued that the kumar's body was upstairs at Step Aside all night, the rani sitting next to it. The body was brought down in the morning, taken through town and cremated with all the prescribed rites. The rani at this time was with Kasiswari Debi, Mahendra Babu's wife. The rani was beyond herself with grief. She threw away her jewelry, and Kasiswari Debi helped her change into a white sari and took her away to her own house. The rani came back to Step Aside after everyone had returned from the cremation.

The judge could not accept the defendants' version of the events on the morning of May 9. The evidence showed, he thought, that the rani came to Mahendra Banerjee's house not with Kasiswari Debi, who was home, but with her uncle Surya Babu, who was Mahendra Babu's tenant. Surya Babu did not have his family with him in Darjeeling and so took the bereaved rani to the women in Mahendra Babu's household. Gita Debi, Mahendra Babu's daughter-in-law, deposed that the rani came wearing an ordinary servant's dhoti. Kasiswari Debi asked her why she had taken off her jewelry so soon, before the men had come back from the cremation. The rani kept saying, "No one says no to me today." Pannalal Basu found Gita Debi's description convincing. "I believe every word of this evidence. It has the ring of truth. There is no mistaking it. Whoever concocted the tale about Kasiswari Debi and laid it at the Step Aside that morning knew nothing about women. The very fact that the rani threw away all her ornaments and came dressed like a servant is proof that there was no other lady there [at Step Aside]" (373).

Judge Basu also did not believe the evidence of Jagat Mohini, the nurse. Apart from the question of being Hindu or Muslim, "if she were what she appeared at Darjeeling—a nurse in nurse's uniform—it is impossible that any Hindu would choose her to carry the sacred water, or that she, a nurse, would be so asked and would go to the *sasan* [cremation ground]." And if all the ceremonies were performed, who was the priest? All sorts of conflicting stories were given about Ambika, the cook in the kumar's party, acting as the priest and of Sashi Babu of Darjeeling chanting the mantra. Birendra, who performed the mukhāgni admitted that he did not bathe before the ritual. "Nothing is impossible, of course, any more than it is impossible for a clergyman to perform a burial service in shirtsleeves and shorts." But the judge was unconvinced. He found that "the body was covered up, carried in procession and burnt as quickly as possible without a single rite" (374).

If the morning cremation was a fake, how was that fact kept a secret? "Every one of the Darjeeling party must have known what was happening, but believing that the death was a fact, they did not mind a faked cremation to save themselves from reproach at Jaidebpur. They could hardly face the family and say that the Kumar had not been cremated. But apparently they talked and thus arose, I find now, the talk of *kuśaputtalikā* at the Sradh, and unless this happened, it is hardly likely that the Rani Satyabhama Debi would write to the Maharajah of Burdwan to inquire in 1917 and mention the fact in the letter of 1922 to the Second Rani" (377).

Returning to the main question of identity, then, Judge Basu took stock of his reasoning.

> My conclusion on this topic is that nothing repels the conclusion touching the identity of the plaintiff with the Second Kumar. That rests upon evidence, including marks which I have set forth, and which are admitted or incontrovertible. The Kumar's apparent death occurred between 7 and 8, his body was taken to the *sasan* at about 10, and this body was never cremated. It is nobody's case, and Satya Babu says that it is not a fact, that this body was found and brought back and carried to the *sasan* the next morning. If the identity has been proved with mathematical certainty, it cannot be displaced by the cremation in the morning of a substituted body. Everybody appreciates its extreme improbability, but it cannot displace the identity, and the facts connected with it, and the lies told about it . . . the fact that less than 10 days after the declaration of identity by the plaintiff, Satya Babu goes to Darjeeling to pin the witnesses down shew that it was not a normal funeral at all. . . .
>
> The fact that the body was left at the *sasan* during the rain, and disappeared, is no proof that it was alive. The real proof of that is that the plaintiff is the same man, looking to his body, its features and marks, and to the evidence of people who say that he is the same man. (378)

Amnesia and Exile

The plaintiff's story about being rescued by the Naga sadhus and his complete loss of memory for several years sounds absurd, "but no more so," reminded the judge, "than some of the cases observed, studied and recorded in authoritative books by scientists; and after the War there came to be established hospitals for treatment of such cases, designated as cases of war neurosis. No mystery whatever attaches to them, any more than it does to smallpox or itches, and they cannot be rejected on the short ground that to what is called "robust common sense" they are impossible" (384).

Of the experts who gave evidence on this point, Major Thomas on behalf of the defendants argued that the plaintiff's account of his condition in Darjeeling was impossible because regression cannot coexist with dissociation. One cannot be in the baby-state and at the same time act like an adult who has forgotten his past. Looking through the plaintiff's story, the judge did not think that was an accurate description of his condition. "The plaintiff does not say he was in the baby-state. He says what that state was and calls it unconscious, and says also he was cognisant of objects, and such complex objects as hills and trees and sannyasis and *khats* [beds], but he has no recollection of this portion of his experience—Darjeeling to Ashighat." The judge then quoted several instances of amnesia cases from Taylor's *Readings in Abnormal Psychology* to show that long periods of loss of memory were not unknown. "Mr. Chaudhuri reasonably asked why it should be supposed that in the plaintiff's case unusual features occurred. The answer is that from Darjeeling to this point [his return to Jaidebpur], the inquiry is not to establish identity, but to see if anything excludes identity being established by other facts. If that is proved, there is nothing from Darjeeling to his arrival at Dacca that could shake the conclusion. Given the identity, there will be no reason to reject it on the ground that it involves a breach of a law of nature. It involves no such breach" (386–87).

Mal Singh?

Finally, was the plaintiff really Mal Singh of Aujla, picked to play the part of Ramendra Narayan Roy? First of all, if this was the defense case, the judge thought it "extraordinary" that the plaintiff was not asked a single question about Mal Singh. The crucial evidence the defendants relied on was by the man claiming to be Dharamdas, backed up by the evidence of Lieutenant Raghubir Singh. The judge had no doubt that the statement recorded by Raghubir Singh in June 1921 was made by *a* Dharamdas after seeing *a* photo marked P(1), which was not produced in court because it was missing. The witness Dharamdas's description of his disciple Mal Singh did not tally with the recorded descriptions in the police reports or in the 1921 statement. Why was that?

> It is perfectly clear what has happened. The statement before Lt. Raghubir Singh bears no signature or finger impression of the maker. It has no meaning apart from the photo shown and that bore Lt. Raghubir Singh's Ex. P(1) and his signature and in all probability a finger impression of the maker. . . . The photo bearing the Ex. P(1) must be the photo of somebody, not the plaintiff at all, or it bears the signature or fingerprint of somebody, not the D. W. 327 Dharam Das Naga at all, and this man could not pass as the maker of the statement, or the statement could not affect the plaintiff, unless the photo Ex. P(1) is withheld and false evidence made with another photo. . . .
>
> I do not believe that the photo marked P(1) is missing. That was not said even on 25–9–35. . . . It came to be said later, not by any witness, but by learned Counsel, that it was missing, though Inspector Momtajuddin said that the statement and the photo were made over by him to Mr. Lindsay, and it is

known that every paper connected with the Sadhu has been kept in special files. The statement remains, but the photo is gone. I consider this not merely a trick of the worst kind—this substituting another photo for the one shown—but fraud. (393–94)

Could there be another reason for not producing the photo P(1)? Judge Basu thought it quite possible that the photo shown to the Dharamdas who made the statement before Raghubir Singh was not that of the plaintiff at all, but some other photo. That was probably the origin of the name Sundardas that was put on the plaintiff. In any case, Basu's conclusion was clear.

I find that the man Dharam Das Naga might be anything, . . . might even be called Dharam Das, admittedly a common name in the Punjab, but he is not the man who had made the statement in 1921 before Lt. Raghubir Singh. It follows on the defendants' case that he is not the man who is the *guru* of the plaintiff who came to Dacca in 1921, even if there were not the evidence, which I accept, that the Dharam Das who came to Dacca in 1921 was different and had not the protuberance on his abdomen. . . . It turns out therefore that the much vaunted discovery of the name Sunder Das that the Court of Wards came to fasten upon the plaintiff was the result of a report accepted without examination, and of a statement evoked by somebody else's photo which has naturally been withheld. One seldom comes across anything more nefarious, but the scheme must have been the idea of somebody who wanted a quick report to convince the Court of Wards. . . .

I find that it has not been proved that the plaintiff is Mal Singh of Aujla. (397–98)

Even then, there was the question of his indistinct speech, which was not that of the second kumar. Since it was not proved that the defect was congenital, Judge Basu did not think it had to be explained if identity was to be established. "If it were impossible for such a thing to appear, it will go to identity. But I do not see how it could not possibly appear, looking to the cyst, the syphilis, the furrow on the tongue, and may be some other cause of which everybody is ignorant" (400).

ANTICIPATION

Through the summer of 1936, as Judge Pannalal Basu worked on his judgment in his Tikatuli residence, and all of Bengal waited with bated breath, was there an apprehension in official circles in Dhaka that there might be an adverse judgment? At the end of June, Arabinda Guha, a lawyer for the plaintiff, wrote "under instructions from my client Kumar Ramendra Narayan Roy" giving notice to the Commissioner of the Dacca Division "not to

pay any money from the Bhowal Estate (Dacca) to Sreejukta Bibhabati
Devi, wife of the said Kumar Ramendra Narayan Roy, till the disposal of
the Bhowal Declaratory suit pending judgment in the court of Mr. Pannalal
Bose." To this, Fawcus, the commissioner, did nothing more than write a
curt marginal note: "No notice need be taken of such a pleader's notice."[2]

But he had a more serious matter in his hands. The costs of fighting the
suit had mounted astronomically. True, the revenue collections had also improved because Sir Douglas Stewart, celebrated for his abilities as a rent
collector (he had been knighted for his skills!), had been sent to Jaidebpur
as the estate manager. The previous year, the government had commended
him for having "further enhanced his reputation as a successful rent collector in spite of the grave embarrassment caused by the interminable drag-
ging on of the Sanyasi case."[3] But the financial constraints were proving to
be too much even for him. On a petition from Sarajubala Debi, the government had had to agree that no expenses for the suit would be met out of
the first rani's share in the estate. The estate had had to approach the Imperial Bank of India for a cash credit advance to meet its payment schedules. The government had lent a helping hand. In August 1935, Sachse,
member of the Board of Revenue, had quietly told the Imperial Bank that
the government revenue to be paid by the Bhawal estate would be held in
abeyance for a while. Stewart was grateful: "if I am allowed say 6 weeks time
for this payment," he wrote to Nelson, the commissioner, "I think I can
manage without taking any loans. . . . I do not want to go to the Bazar for
accommodation."[4]

In February 1936, Sasanka Ghose, the government pleader, applied for a
raise in his fees. The estate manager reported: "he gets fees on an average
for 22 days a month, at the daily rate of Rs.50, i.e. Rs.1100 a month. Besides he gets a retainer of Rs.1100 a year. Thus he gets Rs.1200 a month
from this Estate. His son, Babu Pankaj Kumar Ghosh, has also been engaged as a conducting pleader in this suit. There seems to be no case for reconsideration. The case is now at the argument stage." To this, Nelson, the
commissioner, added: "The Estate also cannot afford lavish expenditure
now. On appeal by the 1st Lady, government has ordered that no part of
the cost of the suit should be paid from her share of income. As such the
balance available for defraying the cost of the suit will be much reduced."[5]

But the situation was actually grimmer than this. A. N. Chaudhuri, barrister and counsel for the defendants, had written from Darjeeling, where
he was enjoying a well-earned vacation after concluding the longest and
most strenuous trial of his career, that he had not received any payment
from the Court of Wards for four months and that his outstanding fees from
the case now amounted to Rs.190,000. Fawcus, the commissioner, must
have spent some time drafting a careful reply. "My dear Chaudhury," he
wrote,

I must ask you to wait for a definite reply till the result of the claimant's suit is known. As you know, we have no reason to anticipate an unfavourable verdict but having regard to all possible consequences including in particular the very large sum that would be immediately necessary should an appeal have to be filed, it seems wise to await the result of the case to take stock of the financial liability of the Estate and then to make arrangements for meeting them. As you know, you need have no anxiety whatever for the ultimate payment of your dues and I only report that the very unusual circumstances of the Estate make it necessary to ask you to agree to this temporary inconvenience to yourself.[6]

As he wrote this, the commissioner would have remembered that Sasanka Ghose, who had worked closely with A. N. Chaudhuri on the trial, had just put up a note warning the Court of Wards that at least Rs.70,000 would have to be raised to meet the costs of filing an appeal should the plaintiff's case succeed. Ghose had mentioned that it might be possible to take an overdraft or a bank loan. But he suggested as an alternative the possibility of mortgaging the share of Ram Narayan Roy, the adopted son of the third rani, since "he was interested in the case and the whole estate would fall to him eventually if the plaintiff's case fails." But U. N. Ghosh, the new manager of the estate, had strongly objected to the latter suggestion. He said it would "spread a rumour which will be very much prejudicial to the prestige and administration of the estate."[7] The correspondence continued through the months of June and July 1936. Why was Sasanka Ghose so concerned about arranging for the money to file an appeal? He was present at the trial virtually every day. Did he have a sense that things had gone badly for the defendants?

On August 17, 1936, the proposal for taking an overdraft or a bank loan was put up to Fawcus. He directed that the papers be "filed for the present. It is understood that Judgment of the Declartory Suit will be delivered on Monday next."[8]

BASU'S JUDGMENT

August 24, 1936. Some people had been camping in front of the courthouse through the night. By early morning, the entire square in front of the district court buildings thronged with people. As the trial had progressed, the Calcutta newspapers had sensed the news value of the story and had used the telegraph to have daily despatches sent by their Dhaka correspondents to be published the next morning. On this day, however, *Ananda Bazar Patrika* and *Basumati* had arranged for their reporters to telegraph the judgment immediately after it was delivered so that they could bring out a special edition that afternoon in Calcutta—a first in Bengali journalism. In

Dhaka, the trial had seen the birth of a new daily tabloid—*Cābuk* (The Whip)—which, priced at one pice, devoted itself for its entire lifetime almost exclusively to news of the Bhawal sannyasi case.[9]

The proceedings in Pannalal Basu's court were scheduled to begin at eleven o'clock. By then, the entire stretch from Sankharipara at one end to the church at the corner of Victoria Park at the other was chock-full of people. Shopowners at the market on Johnson Road could not reach their shops; the market remained shut the whole day. At Jaidebpur, the estate offices and the Rajbari were put under police protection, in case there was trouble.[10]

"I have considered the whole evidence in the case," Judge Pannalal Basu read out, "with the utmost care, and the very able argument of learned Counsels on either side has missed, I believe, nothing material that could be argued for and against the identity." His judgment, typewritten, had come to 525 pages. His conclusions, however, were succinct.

> I believe the direct evidence in support of the identity. It is the evidence of honest men and women, of all ranks and conditions of life, including nearly all the relations, and among them the sister, the First Rani, the Second Rani's own aunt and her own cousin. The witnesses include a great many men of education and position, grave, elderly men whom one would not suspect of romance, who are as afraid of ridicule as anybody, who have nothing to gain or lose and who could not possibly mistake the Kumar. It is impossible that these would commit perjury to support an impostor.

The judge mentioned in particular the "incontrovertible situation" of May 4, 1921, when the plaintiff declared his identity for the first time in Jyotirmayi Debi's house. Even Jogen Banerjee had to admit that those who recognized him that day were honest in their recognition. "Another test, in itself conclusive, is the identity of the body, proved to demonstration and with mathematical certainty by the bodily features, all exceptional, and by the bodily marks, all exceptional, which rest on nobody's credibility. These, in their totality, cannot occur in a second individual, and even if half of the marks go off, the scaly feet, and the irregular scar on the top of the left outer ankle, coupled with the bodily features, will be enough to sustain the identity with equal certainty. . . . Nothing in the mind of the plaintiff shakes this conclusion."

Was the declaration of identity by the plaintiff the result of a conspiracy? "Nothing before the 4th May, 1921, suggests a conspiracy nor anything in the conduct that followed. Since that date down to the date of the suit, he was not hiding for a day." He went and saw the collector, and asked for an inquiry. In 1929 and 1930, he began to collect rents and brought the estate to a virtual standstill. Yet he was neither questioned nor prosecuted. Rather, immediately on the plaintiff's declaration of identity, Satyendra Nath Banerjee rushed to the government and asked that the evidence of death be saved. Lindsay, persuaded that the kumar had died in 1909, declared the plaintiff an impostor.

> Few impostors would survive this declaration. It created the notion, shared by many witnesses, that the issue was not between the first defendant [Bibhabati Debi] and the plaintiff, but between him and the Government. . . .
>
> Mr. Chaudhuri, with some disregard of these facts, was pointing out the delay in instituting the suit and suggesting that time was needed to fit the plaintiff to play the rôle. The plaintiff had himself asked Mr. Lindsay for an inquiry, 24 days after he had declared his identity, and his sisters had sent up a petition for inquiry even earlier. He was prepared to be faced and questioned then, as always, and the inquiry, as I said, was never refused, and he was not told until 1927 that the Court was open. . . .
>
> Conduct speaks and it cannot lie. One sees the dread of the Sannyasi even on the 6th of May, 1921, two days after he declared he was the Kumar, that sends Satyendra Babu *post haste* to Mr. Lethbridge to save the evidence of death; the dread that sends him to Darjeeling before the 15th May to pin down the witnesses to a cremation; the dread of the insurance doctor's report bearing the Kumar's bodily marks. It was seen in July 1921. The defendants do not seize upon it to destroy the impostor. They do not call for it, and hope it will lie safely lodged in the company's office in Scotland. It is the alleged impostor who calls for it and seizes upon it with alacrity just as he seized upon every other document that gave any personal detail. (406–11)

It was nearly noon on August 24 when Judge Pannalal Basu read out the decisive sentence of his judgment: "I find that the plaintiff is Ramendra Narayan Roy, the second son of the late Rajah Rajendra Narayan Roy of Bhowal."

He considered whether the fact that the plaintiff was roaming around for many years with sannyasis disqualified him from the title to his property.

> Renunciation of the world, when absolute, amounts to civil death, under the Hindu Law. The passage does not say that he had been initiated to *sannyas*, or that he had absolutely retired from all earthly interests, and the passage also adds that the life he led was the result of loss of memory. Retirement into religious life must be a voluntary act to have the effect of death. . . .
>
> I should add that there is no evidence that the plaintiff was initiated into *sannyas* and had undergone the essential ceremony that makes him dead to the world. . . .
>
> There will be a decree declaring that the plaintiff is Kumar Ramendra Narayan Roy, the second son of the late Rajah Rajendra Narayan Roy of Bhowal,

and directing that he be put in possession of an undivided one-third share in the properties in suit—the share now in the enjoyment of the first defendant—jointly with the other defendants' possession over the rest. . . .

The plaintiff will get his costs from the contesting defendants, with interest at 6 per cent per annum. (411–13)

Regrouping Forces

That afternoon and late into the night, there were celebrations on the streets of Dhaka. The house in Armanitola where the plaintiff lived, and all around it, was a sea of people. Processions were taken out with fireworks. In Jaidebpur too, there were processions celebrating the victory of the second kumar: "Jay! Madhyam Kumar ki jay!" According to *Ḍhākā prakāś*, Jyotirmayi Debi fell unconscious when she heard the news of the judgment. So apparently did Dr. Ashutosh Dasgupta. Two palmists, Shyamlal Goswami and Parmeshwar Dwivedi, had supposedly declared in 1921 that the plaintiff was of noble birth; their business was now likely to boom. An astrologer was predicting that there would be no appeal against the judgment and that the second kumar would ascend the *gadi* by November.[11]

> c/o The Superintendent of Police
> Darjeeling
> The 29th August 1936
>
> Dear Frl. Schenkl,
>   . . . During the last few days our papers are full of a sensational case in which judgement has been delivered by the judge, after a hearing lasting about 3 years. The facts of the case are so fantastic that one can very well say that 'truth is stranger than fiction'. Since you are in the habit of writing articles, I am sending you some cuttings from which you will get material for writing an article. I believe magazines like Das Magazin, Wiener Magazin or even Sunday editions of Neue Frei Presse or Wiener Tagblatt would welcome such an article for the entertainment of their readers about the 'exotic East'.

This was Subhas Chandra Bose, leader of the Indian National Congress, writing from house internment in Kurseong to Emilie Schenkl in Austria. Subhas Chandra had met Emilie in Vienna in 1934 and kept up a regular correspondence with her from India, even when he was in prison or under internment, until in December 1937 he secretly married her during a trip to Europe. This letter, like others, passed through the official censors. In five long paragraphs, Subhas Chandra summarized for Emilie the story of the sannyasi and the sensational judgment of the court.[12] Little did he know then that one day he himself would become the character around whom equally sensational stories of mistaken deaths and look-alike sannyasis would excite the popular imagination in Bengal.[13]

Those officials of the Court of Wards directly involved in the trial might have steeled themselves against an adverse judgment in the Dhaka court. But British officialdom in general was stunned. Henderson, the district judge whose fate it was to have assigned the case to Pannalal Basu, wrote as follows in his memoirs.

> The Raj Kumar had been a well-known sportsman and racing man. Lord Kitchener had stayed with the family and been taken out shooting in the jungle. When under cross-examination about racing, shooting and billiards, the plaintiff cut a very sorry figure and obviously knew nothing about any of them: in fact a leading member of the Calcutta Bar told me that he would have dismissed the suit then and there. When the lengthy trial came to an end, Sachse, who had now become Member of the Board of Revenue, was living with me during the hot weather: he nearly fell over backwards when a telegram arrived from the Commissioner to say that the suit had been decreed.[14]

Less than a week after the judgment, W. H. Nelson, the commissioner of the Dacca division, wrote to the collector. "There is certain to be an appeal against the Judge's order declaring the Sannyasi to be the Second Kumar of Bhawal and entitled to possession of one-third share of the Bhawal Estate. The appellant will apply for stay of execution pending appeal and the Court will pass orders for the custody of the property till the appeal is decided. . . . Any application by the successful claimant for registration of his name as proprietor should be kept pending till the orders of the High Court are received.[15]

On September 4, 1936, Nelson issued a public notice.

> There has been some excitement among tenants about who is to collect the one-third share of the rents for which the Bhawal Sannyasi has obtained a decree identifying him as the Second Kumar. Some newspapers have reported that the Government has directed the Court of Wards to immediately release one-third share of the estate to the plaintiff as decreed. The Government has publicly notified that these reports are completely false. . . .
>
> Until such time that the plaintiff legally takes over the aforesaid share from the Court of Wards, it cannot be released and shall remain in the custody of the Court of Wards and shall be administered by it in the interests of the estate. . . .
>
> Accordingly, the Court of Wards shall as before continue to collect the entire rent from tenants and the receipts issued by it for such collections shall be legally valid and enforceable.[16]

As we have seen, the estate was in trouble financially. Ever since the suit began, there was an arrangement with the Imperial Bank for the estate to operate a cash credit account of up to Rs.1,20,000. On September 4, 1936, the agent of the Imperial Bank at Dhaka wrote to the manager of the Bhawal estate that "in view of the recent judgment in the Declaratory suit, which has changed the entire aspect of the business, the Bank cannot see its way to granting additional advances to the Estate until the position clarifies."[17] In the meantime, instalment payments against earlier advances plus interest were also due. U. N. Ghosh, the manager, wrote plaintively to the commissioner pointing out that "on account of the decree in the said suit against the 2nd Lady, the position has been very much obscured" and seeking direction on "how these obligatory payments are to be made on due dates." The commissioner advised that everything be held in abeyance until orders were received from the High Court on the question of the custody of the property pending appeal.[18]

In the middle of September, Nelson, in a letter to the collector, clarified the government position.

> The Court of Wards is still in charge and will remain in charge till at least 15 days after a duly promulgated order under Sec. 65 of the Court of Wards Act. Change in the ownership of property does not actually take effect till the deed is executed and the Court releases.
>
> The Court of Wards continues to be responsible for current expenditures of the whole estate especially the heavy items of revenue cases and cost of management. So it is not fair that there should be any stoppage of collections. There is of course no fear that any of the funds of the disputed share will be misapplied and it is possible that for this reason the successful plaintiff may be in no hurry to execute his decree. . . . It is obviously to the interest of all connected with the Estate that the practical management should go on exactly as before.[19]

Nelson had spoken too soon, at least in his remark that the plaintiff was in no hurry to claim his property. A month after the judgment, the commissioner received a letter from Arabinda Guha, the plaintiff's lawyer. "My client is at a loss to understand why you have not yet intimated to him your decision to make over to him possession of his one third share of the Bhowal Estate. . . . [I]n view of the fact that the Court of Wards appears to be rather dilatory in the matter of performing its duty in this behalf, I call upon the Court of Wards on behalf of my said client to recognise its obligation to release my client's share of the Estate from its charge by virtue of the mandatory provisions."[20]

Meanwhile, the expected decision was made by the government to appeal against the judgment of Pannalal Basu in the Calcutta High Court. The appeal was formally presented on October 5, 1936 on behalf of Bibhabati Debi, Ananda Kumari Debi, and her adopted son Ram Narayan Roy. Since they were all wards of the Court of Wards, the appellants were represented

by the manager of the Bhawal Estate as their "next friend or guardian."[21]
The plaintiff Ramendra Narayan Roy and Sarajubala Debi, who had supported the plaintiff, now became the respondents. The High Court, in dealing with the appeal, would issue directions on how the disputed share of the estate was to be held and managed. Until then, the Board of Revenue gave this undertaking to Judge Basu: "the Court of Wards undertakes to hold the income of the property in suit . . . less administration and other necessary costs including payment of rent and cess and such litigation costs which management requires, in its own hands, and not to pay any money out of the income of that property to or for the benefit of the Defendant No.1, Sj. Bibhabati Devi, till 21st November 1936 and thereafter without further orders from the Court and the Appellate Court."[22] The ironies of the law! The property was now the plaintiff's who had won his suit. The Court of Wards had appealed against the judgment. But the costs of the appeal in the High Court would be paid out of the same one-third share that was now the plaintiff's because the estate would continue to be managed by the Court of Wards and the appellants were still its wards!

In April 1938, Ramendra Narayan Roy returned to Jaidebpur for the first time since he was banished from his estate in 1921, twenty-nine years since he left it as the second kumar in 1909. We know of this from a folk poet of Bhawal.

> It's good times for the tenants of Bhawal, their sorrows are over,
>   The second kumar is now the new ruler.
> It happened in the month of Baisakh, the year 1345,
> The tenants rushed merrily to see him.
> They saw him and they cried—tears of happiness—
>   They were meeting after a full thirty years. . . .
> The poet asks, second rani, why the tears in your eyes?
>   You didn't affirm when you needed to,
> You could have stayed a queen; now live like a beggar.
> Everyone swore they knew him, only you refused.
> Now don't pretend you are chaste, your dalliances are known. . . .
> Oh the alluring powers of desire—
>   It hasn't any shame, any limit,
>   It's indestructible, ever shrewd.
>   It robs the sense of *dharma*
>   Of those who fall in its trap.
> Brother and sister have done the deed—
> It'll stay indelible as long as the world exists,
>   No one will ever forget.
>
> A. K. Ghani says, Sisters,
> Whether Hindu or Musalman,

> You could do the same misdeed,
>   So I beg of you, dear sisters,
>   I touch your feet and plead,
> Pay attention to your husbands, nourish their precious lives,
> Your lives as women will be fulfilled, and when you die
>   You will achieve life indestructible.[23]

JUDGE BASU RETIRES

When Pannalal Basu got down from his carriage and walked into his modest rented house in Tikatuli, perhaps there was a touch of weariness in his steps. That evening, he spoke to his wife about his resolve to quit the judiciary. He was fifty-three years old and still had several years of service ahead of him. But the Bhawal case had to be his last. What were his apprehensions? He must have anticipated that there would be an appeal against his judgment. He might also have felt that senior officials of the government might not take kindly to his forthright criticism of the bureaucracy's role in the Bhawal affair. Did he perhaps feel that he might face problems in the judicial service?

Whatever the motivation, Pannalal Basu chose to be independent. He resigned from the service and was released by the end of the year. Two years later, he took up the position of manager of the estate of Panchet, on the forest-lined border of Bengal and Bihar. It was far away from the din and intrigue of the city.

Incidentally, a hundred years before, a principal supporter of the pretender Raja Pratapchand was the raja of Panchet.

Chapter Sixteen

THE APPEAL

THE HIGH COURT of Judicature at
Fort William in Bengal—that was the official name. The building was one
of the sights of the city: an impressive red brick and stone structure, one of
the few Gothic-style buildings of British Calcutta, built in the 1860s by the
architect William Granville. There is a familiar scene in Calcutta folklore
of the rustic from the mufassil (countryside), typically the *bangal* from east
Bengal, standing in front of the High Court with his mouth wide open—
awestruck by that massive edifice symbolizing the incomprehensible mysteries of the colonial judicial process. Our plaintiff, Ramendra Narayan
Roy, whose claim to identity had been upheld by the district court of Dacca,
was literally the bangal who was now being shown the High Court. But
then, the bangal in the apocryphal folk story is a figure of foolish obstinacy.
Overcoming his initial panic, he feigns an apparent nonchalance, even a little bravado, and walks away, claiming he has seen it all before.

Even by the admittedly impressive standards of legal loquacity in India,
the volume of evidence produced in the Bhawal case was unprecedented.
Sir Harold Derbyshire, chief justice of the Calcutta High Court, ordered
that all the evidence given at the trial be printed for the use of the appellate
court, and that the job be done within a year and a half. It was not an easy
deadline for the government press to meet, and a special staff was assigned
for the task. The entire material—the so-called "paper book"—came to
twenty-six volumes: a total of 11,327 printed pages of text and three volumes of photographs. It cost the appellants Rs.80,000.[1]

The appeal was to be heard by a special bench consisting of L.W.J. Costello, C. C. Biswas, and R. F. Lodge. Before being appointed a judge of the
High Court in 1926, Sir Leonard Costello had had a career as a barrister in
London and in the Midlands Circuit. His European colleagues in Calcutta
appear to be a little reticent about him. One of them says in his memoirs
that he was nicknamed "the lion-faced marmoset"; whether the sentiment
behind the naming was affection or sarcasm is unclear.[2] Charu Chandra
Biswas, unlike A. N. Chaudhuri or B. C. Chatterjee arguing their cases before him, was entirely homegrown. He was an outstanding student of English and law and began his career in 1910 as a *vakil* (Indian advocate) in
the High Court. Apart from building up a huge reputation as a lawyer, he
had become a prominent figure in the public life of the city; he was a major

personality in the affairs of the University of Calcutta and of the Calcutta Corporation, the municipal body that looked after the city. In 1930, he became a member of the central legislature in Delhi and was appointed a judge of the High Court in 1937. Lodge, on the other hand, was not from the legal profession. He was a member of the Indian Civil Service and had been in judicial positions in the districts before being appointed to the High Court in 1936.

The counsels for the two sides were, as in the Dacca trial, Chaudhuri and Chatterjee. But now they had many more prominent members of the bar on their teams. A. N. Chaudhuri, counsel for the appellants, was assisted by, among others, Phani Bhusan Chakrabarti, an already well-established advocate, and P. B. Mukharji, a young barrister, both of whom would later end their careers as chief justice of the Calcutta High Court. B. C. Chatterjee for the respondents had on his team an array of nationalist lawyers— Bankim Mukherjee, who was associated with the Hindu Mahasabha; Atul Chandra Gupta, a nationalist intellectual and well-known writer on political subjects; and J. C. Gupta, a Congress member of the Bengal legislature.

The hearing of arguments in the case eventually began in the High Court on November 14, 1938, two years after the appeal had been filed. It went on continuously until August 14, 1939—a total of 164 working days.

In the meantime, there had occurred a minor revolution in Bengal's politics. The peasants' movement, or more accurately, the tenants' or *praja* movement, had spread rapidly in east Bengal; the demand was abolition of the zamindari system and reduction of peasant debts. In 1936–1937, when elections were held under a still restricted electorate that nevertheless included a section of the better-off peasants, the east Bengal districts returned a large number of legislators from the Krishak Praja Party led by A. K. Fazlul Huq, who represents the mainstream of the tenants' movement. Huq's party was fiercely opposed by the United Muslim Party, a small group of Muslim landlords led by the Dacca Nawab family, which claimed to speak on behalf of Bengal's Muslims and was aligned with Mohammed Ali Jinnah's Muslim League. After the elections, Huq opened negotiations with the Congress to form a ministry, but the national leadership of the Congress refused to allow a provincial unit to enter a coalition. Frustrated, Huq chose to form a coalition ministry with his erstwhile enemy, the United Muslim Party. Several of the radical demands of the Praja movement had to be shelved for the moment. But the defense of peasant interests now became tied, often indistinguishably, with the pursuit of the communal demands of Muslim political leaders in Bengal. Zamindari estates were not immediately abolished, but many legal and extralegal privileges of landlords were, and special boards were set up to write off the debts of peasants—the creditors being, in most cases, Hindu landlords.[3] As the hearings opened in November 1938 in the High Court on the appeal in the Bhawal sannyasi case, there were unprecedented and bitter debates across the street in the Bengal legislature, where it must have seemed to many pillars of the establishment that the impossible was happening—peasants from east Bengal were threatening to barge into the citadels of power in Calcutta.

THE APPELLANTS' CASE

A. N. Chaudhuri, needless to say, launched into a trenchant criticism of the judgment of the lower court. That judgment was based, he said, on a fundamentally erroneous method. He conceded that the crucial question was that of identity between the plaintiff and the second kumar. If that was proved, nothing else mattered. But what if the evidence was not conclusive enough to prove identity? In that case, the evidence on what happened in Darjeeling would have to be assessed independently of the question of identity, and a judgment made on whether the plaintiff's account of the Darjeeling incidents had been established beyond doubt. This, according to Chaudhuri, the trial judge had failed to do. He had accepted what he called the "direct evidence" on identity, overlooking the mass of contradictions in that evidence and the entire body of evidence on non-recognition offered by the defendants. Having, on that basis, decided that identity had been established, he had treated the Darjeeling episode as a secondary matter, not requiring any independent examination.

If, on the other hand, the evidence on the Darjeeling events was evaluated on its own merits, independently of the question of identity, then the following questions would have to be answered on the basis of that evidence:

1. Did the second kumar really die or was he merely in a comatose condition when his body was taken to the cremation ground?
2. When did the death or apparent death occur—in the early evening or at midnight?
3. Was the second kumar's body taken to the cremation ground on the night of May 8 and was it cremated?
4. Since the cremation of a body on May 9 was admitted, was that body that of the second kumar or was it a substituted body?
5. Is the plaintiff's story of his rescue by sannyasis and his loss of memory during his travels with them credible and true?[4]

Chaudhuri's contention was that the judge had not arrived at a conclusion of fact on these questions. Rather, he had evaded a finding by saying that whatever the evidence might be on the defendants' side and whatever the improbabilities in the plaintiff's story, they did not displace identity. In other words, having decided that identity had been established, he did not think it necessary to come to a positive conclusion on the Darjeeling events; he had accepted the plaintiff's version of those events on the basis of his finding on identity.

On the first question of death or apparent death, for instance, the judge had remarked: "The fact that the body was left at the *sasan* during the rain and disappeared is no proof that it was alive, and the real proof of that is that the plaintiff is the same man." Reviewing the evidence to show that the body was alive, he says: "Nobody will accept this evidence, or accept it as proof of identity, if it were not otherwise proved; but granted the identity, there would be no reason to reject it." This showed, Chaudhuri argued, that the ground of the judge's finding was identity alone and not any independent evidence that the body was alive.

On the crucial question of the time of death, the judge had disregarded the evidence on the fact that the old cremation ground was no longer in use, that there were no shelters in the neighborhood of the cremation ground to which people could have run to escape from the alleged storm and rain, and that there was no rain in Darjeeling on May 8 or 9. Instead, he had declared that these facts "do not discredit the account given of what happened at the *sasan* on the night of the 8th May, if the body of the Kumar was taken there at night, as it must have been if he had died at about dusk. The positive evidence that it was so taken is not discredited by these facts." Moreover, Chaudhuri alleged, the judge had ignored, on the question of the time of death, the evidence of Bibhabati Debi who, it was admitted, was not part of any conspiracy, as well as the documentary evidence of the telegrams sent from Darjeeling to Jaidebpur. Ignoring this positive evidence and the many discrepancies in the evidence of the plaintiff's witnesses on the hour of death, the judge seems to have reasoned as follows. Since the plaintiff is the same person as the second kumar, he could not have been cremated. Therefore, he must have escaped from the cremation ground, which he could have done if he was taken there at night and left unattended for some time. But he could not have been taken to the cremation ground at night unless he had apparently died earlier in the evening. Hence, the apparent death must have taken place at dusk. Once again, argued Chaudhuri, the judge had based his finding on the time of death on his previous conclusion on identity.

On the failure of the evening cremation, the judge says that the account given by the plaintiff's witnesses, "however consistent, will sound like a tale. Its real security is the death at dusk and the fact that the body was taken to the *sasan* that night." Referring to those who claimed to have seen or participated in the evening funeral procession, the judge says: "they would not be believed if death at dusk was not a fact; and if that was a fact, there would be no reason to disbelieve them." It was identity again that was the final ground of the judge's findings on this question.

Was the body that was burned on May 9 a substituted body? There was very little direct evidence presented by the plaintiff to establish this case, and the judge himself admitted that it was "extremely improbable." Yet, without drawing a conclusion from this inadequate evidence, the judge had gone on to reiterate that the kumar's apparent death had taken place at dusk, the body was taken to the cremation ground but it was never cremated. "It is nobody's case, and Satya Babu says that it is not a fact, that this body was found and brought back and carried to the *sasan* the next morning. If the identity has been proved with mathematical certainty, it cannot be displaced by the cremation in the morning of a substituted body. Everybody appreciates its extreme improbability, but it cannot displace the identity." The judge's conclusion, Chaudhuri argued, was simply that since the plaintiff was the same man as the second kumar, the body burned on May 9 must have been a different body.

On the plaintiff's story of his rescue by sannyasis, the judge said: "His account reads like a fairy tale, and if the plaintiff needed it to establish his identity, he would fail. . . . [B]ut given the identity, otherwise proved, the account is clear and consistent. . . . I cannot say that the account is excluded by any fact clearly proved, or that anything in it displaces the identity, though it will not prove it." About the plaintiff's story of his life with the sannyasis, the judge had said: "It discloses nothing that shakes the conclusion otherwise reached, and not on the strength of this account, that he is the same man as the Kumar. . . . [F]rom Darjeeling to this point [the plaintiff's arrival in Dhaka], the inquiry is not to establish identity, but to see if anything excludes it, the identity being established by other facts."

If indeed, Chaudhuri argued, identity had been established "by other facts," there would be no ground to quarrel with Judge Pannalal Basu's method. Because, in that case, irrespective of what may have happened in Darjeeling, the plaintiff would be the same person as the kumar and that would be the end of the matter. But the appellants' case was that identity had not been established. The trial judge had reduced the question of identity to certain physical similarities of the body and had relegated the mind to a secondary position. And even with respect to the body, had identity been established? The appellants' contention was that it had not.

One lot of evidence on the identity of the body was given by tenants who claimed to have recognized the plaintiff as the second kumar. Of them, the judge says: "It would be impossible to rest one's conclusion upon their testimony, unless the identity otherwise appears." On recognition by relatives, except for Jyotirmayi Debi and Satyabhama Debi, the judge says: "Fortunately, the court will not have to decide between this mass of evidence and what evidence the other side have produced by the credibility of the witnesses alone. There are the marks on the plaintiff's body and there are the photos." The examination of photographs had given the judge only a list of similar features: "the photographs prove no difference in features, except a difference in the nose." That could not affirmatively establish identity. Finally, there were the marks on the body. Here, Chaudhuri's allegation was that the judge had assumed what he was required to find, and having assumed them, had concluded that identity was established. The only "direct evidence" that the judge had found to affirm identity was recognition by Jyotirmayi Debi and Satyabhama Debi; there was nothing else to establish identity.

On the identity of the mind, the trial judge had commented that the cross-examination of the plaintiff "was just what a person minded to defeat the Kumar would design" and that the defendants were "afraid of falling into the truth." A. N. Chaudhuri alleged that the judge had not considered the appalling ignorance the plaintiff had shown on matters such as sports that the second kumar undoubtedly knew. If the plaintiff had been put up, the judge had asked, why could not his sponsors have taught him a little reading and writing when they had twelve years in which to do it? The judge had overlooked the fact, said Chaudhuri, that it would have been dangerous to teach the plaintiff to write because he would have developed a handwriting of his own. On innumerable occasions when questions of memory were put to the plaintiff, he would say that he had forgotten. This alleged loss of memory, Chaudhuri said, was an extremely important feature of the plaintiff's case that required close examination. But except for referring to some cases of shell shock, the judge had not even considered the probability of such a loss of memory. The defendants had pointed out that the so-called impediment of speech from which the plaintiff allegedly suffered was confined only to speech in Bengali and did not occur when he was speaking Hindi. The judge had not considered this matter at all and had jumped to the conclusion that the faulty pronunciation and Hindi intonation did not "displace the conclusion on identity otherwise reached."

A. N. Chaudhuri's overall contention was that the only ground the trial judge had given for reaching his conclusion on identity was the evidence on recognition by Jyotirmayi and Satyabhama, which the judge had accepted. He had said: "I have examined so far the body and the mind of the plaintiff, feature by feature, and seen nothing that displaces the identity proved by direct evidence of the kind stated, and by a collocation of indisputable features that cannot occur in a second individual." It was obvious, Chaudhuri pointed out, that the judge did not regard identity as proved by the bodily and mental features of the plaintiff, but only that he had found nothing in those features to displace identity as proved by direct evidence. What was this direct evidence that was independent of the mind and the body of the plaintiff? It could only be recognition, and the only recognition that the judge had accepted as valid was the recognition by Jyotirmayi and Satyabhama. In sum, therefore, the judge's method ended up as a vicious circle:

first, recognition was to be proved by identity of mental and bodily features; second, those features could not prove identity but only corroborate identity otherwise proved by direct evidence; and third, the only valid direct evidence was recognition by Jyotirmayi and Satyabhama.

Even with regard to these two, since Satyabhama Debi was dead, it was really the evidence of a single witness—Jyotirmayi Debi—that was the sole foundation of the entire judgment of the trial court. The judge had completely ignored the twofold onus that lay on the plaintiff. He had, first, to prove that the kumar was not dead and, second, to prove that the body that was cremated on May 9 was not that of the kumar but of someone else. The two questions were in fact entirely related, and if the plaintiff's case was that there was a failed evening cremation, he could not avoid having to prove that the morning cremation was that of a substituted body. The judge had not imposed this requirement on the plaintiff's case. All that the plaintiff's witnesses had done was suggest that things were not what they seemed. But they had not even tried to explain how it was possible to procure a substituted body that night and to persuade everyone attending the morning cremation that it was the kumar's body. In fact, there were many witnesses for the defendants who swore that they had seen the body at the morning cremation and were sure that it was that of the second kumar, whereas none of the witnesses for the plaintiff had any definite evidence that it was someone else's body.

The plaintiff's story was full of fantastic and utterly improbable events—the "apparent" death, the rescue, the loss of memory, the cremation of a substituted body. Yet the judge had accepted that story and rejected the defendants' case on the ground that a conspiracy to run an impostor was improbable. What was the balance of probabilities on the two sides? The trial judge, said A. N. Chaudhuri, had erred in his judgment. The appellate court should now set that judgment aside.[5]

The Response

B. C. Chatterjee rose to defend the judgment of Pannalal Basu. A. N. Chaudhuri, he said, had given far greater importance to the identity question than the judge had done. The trial judge had first reached his finding on the question of identity and then, regardless of that finding, had proceeded to evaluate the evidence on the Darjeeling events on its own merit. He had adopted a far stricter attitude to the evidence than Chaudhuri was doing. Had he done what Chaudhuri was suggesting, he would have decided the suit in the plaintiff's favor as soon as he had reached his finding on identity.

The judge had not, as Chaudhuri was alleging, decided on the identity question merely on the basis of recognition by a few persons. The chief basis of his decision was the physical identity of the plaintiff's body with that of the second kumar. These identical features, the judge observed, "in their totality, cannot occur in a second individual, and even if half of the marks go off, the scaly feet and the irregular scar on the top of the left outer ankle, coupled with the bodily features, will be enough to sustain the identity with equal certainty."

The judge had definitely not based his finding of identity on the evidence of Jyotirmayi Debi alone. In fact, he had clearly said: "Honest belief even in a sister is not conclusive, though it demolishes the utter dissimilarity theory. It undoubtedly carries the plaintiff a great way, but a single point of difference, like death itself, or a different mind, or proof that he is not a Bengalee, might displace him altogether." The judge had indeed considered these other possible points of difference on their own merits, independently of the identity question. This became obvious if one cared to read the judgment of the lower court as a whole, and not pick out sentences and phrases out of context, as A. N. Chaudhuri had done.

The trial judge's findings on the kumar's illness and the hour of death or apparent death, for instance, were based on a detailed examination of the evidence offered on both sides. He had also carefully considered the evidence on the old and new cremation grounds, the shelters, and the rain—the points raised by the appellants—and had come to independent findings on each of them. Even on the morning cremation, Chatterjee argued, the judge had considered the evidence "on the footing as if these facts [of identity] have not been found." Thus, he had examined the evidence on the route of the morning procession, the covering up of the body, the question of whether the body was upstairs or downstairs at Step Aside, the presence or otherwise of Kasiswari Debi at Step Aside, and the coming of Dr. Pran Krishna Acharya.

B. C. Chatterjee argued that it was perfectly possible to take the Darjeeling section of the judgment and put it before the section on identity; it would do no violence to the judgment as a whole and would take away the ground of A. N. Chaudhuri's criticism. At the conclusion of the Darjeeling chapter, the judgment could still read as follows: "the Kumar's apparent death occurred between 7 and 8, his body was taken to the *sasan* at about ten, and this body was never cremated. It is nobody's case . . . that this body was found and brought back and carried to the *sasan* the next morning. If the identity [is] proved with mathematical certainty, it [could] not be displaced by the cremation in the morning of a substituted body. Everybody appreciates its extreme improbability, but it cannot displace the identity." The judgment would then go on to consider whether identity was proved by the evidence.

The judge had, in fact, decided the identity question on the basis of the physical marks. He had also considered the matters of the loss of memory and the speech impediment. On the former, he had come to the definite conclusion that the plaintiff's story could not be ruled out as unnatural. On the latter, the fact was that the plaintiff had a cyst under the tongue which the doctors agreed could cause the speech impediment. The plaintiff believed that the cyst was caused by the poison that he had been allegedly administered. Whether or not this was the correct explanation could not affect the finding that the cyst was causing the plaintiff's speech impediment. The judge had also considered all the evidence on recognition and had duly noted that the plaintiff could recognize some people but not others. He had relied on the evidence of the photographs only to establish certain points of similarity; he had not relied on it to establish identity.

In sum, and as expected, B. C. Chatterjee disagreed with the appellants' criticism of the judgment of the lower court and argued that the appeal should be dismissed.

THE PECULIAR POSITION OF COSTELLO

The hearings concluded on August 14, 1939. Justice Costello had decided that he would add two weeks' leave to the usual long vacation of the court in order to go to England for a holiday and return in November to deliver his judgment. While he was on the boat, Europe plunged into darkness. World War II had begun.

The three judges did, of course, discuss various points of the case while the hearings were on. But they did not have a chance to discuss their positions as a whole. Biswas, as it turned out, wrote a long and exhaustive judgment, longer even than Pannalal Basu's. But Costello was unable to come back to Calcutta. In April 1940, Germany attacked Denmark and Norway; in May, it overran Belgium and the Netherlands; in June, France fell. In August, the Luftwaffe began the Battle of Britain, bombing cities and industrial targets with a ferocity never before seen in human history. That Costello would soon find a way of getting back to his court was out of the question.[6]

It was a year since the hearings of the appellate court had ended. Justice Biswas and Justice Lodge decided that it would not be proper to wait any longer. On August 20, 1940, Charu Chandra Biswas began to deliver his judgment. He began with a dramatic announcement.

> Before proceeding to deliver judgment in this appeal, I deem it my duty to state that the senior member of the Bench which had heard the appeal, the Hon'ble Mr. Justice Costello, is now on leave in England, and unable, therefore, to be present in court to pronounce judgment personally. He has, howeever, sent in a written opinion from England, which I propose to read in open court in due

FIGURE 10. Charu Chandra Biswas

course. A Rule has recently been framed by this court . . . which authorises any judge of the High Court to pronounce the written judgment or opinion of any other judge signed by him when such judge continues to be a judge of the court, but is prevented by absence or any other reason from pronouncing that judgment or opinion in open court.

I ought to add that neither my learned brother Lodge, J. nor I have so far seen the judgment of our learned colleague, and we are not, therefore, aware of the decision he has recorded. (3)[7]

The Judgment of Biswas, J.

Biswas moved directly to A. N. Chaudhuri's central criticism of the judgment of the lower court—that the judge had decided on the events at Darjeeling on the basis of his conclusion on identity. Biswas was forthright: "it is a complete misreading," he declared,

of this part of the judgment to say . . . that in dealing with what may not inappropriately be called the Darjeeling chapter, the learned judge allowed himself to be swayed by the opinion he had already formed on the question of identity. The passages on which learned counsel for the appellants relied in support of this line of criticism show no more than this—that the learned judge was merely attempting to relate the happenings at Darjeeling to the substantive case on the issue of identity. . . . I do not understand the learned judge as having said anywhere that he must reject the defendants' evidence regarding any of the Darjeeling events as untrue, merely because he had already come to a finding in the plaintiff's favour on the question of identity. On the other hand, as it strikes me, the learned judge subjected the Darjeeling evidence to an independent examination as if identity had not been established. . . . [E]ven if it be supposed that the learned judge's finding on the Darjeeling chapter did not amount to a positive acceptance of the story put forward by the plaintiff in this behalf, it cannot be denied on a fair reading of the judgment that he intended to hold and held that the defendants had wholly failed to prove their case that the Second Kumar had actually died or that his body had been burnt to ashes. (7)

The logical requirement was as follows. If death at dusk, the attempted evening cremation, and rescue were proved, then the morning cremation necessarily had to involve a substituted body, unless the kumar's body was found at night, brought back, and taken out again in the morning, which no one had claimed. Therefore, if the plaintiff succeeded in proving the former set of facts, he did not have to show that the body burned in the morning was a substituted body; it would simply follow from the proved facts as the only possible conclusion. The only way this case could be demolished was by the defendants proving that the body cremated in the morning was without doubt that of the second kumar. The judge had clearly found that the defendants had been unable to establish this case.

Biswas did not agree with Chaudhuri's criticism of Pannalal Basu's order of treatment. The criticism would only be valid if identity was a matter not susceptible to proof in a court of law—that is to say, if it was necessarily undecidable. But that is clearly not the case, since there had been numerous cases of mistaken identity decided in court, including the famous Tichborne case referred to by both sides in the present trial and appeal. So the question was not whether identity was in principle decidable, but whether the judge, on the basis of the evidence presented to him, had decided correctly on identity. "On the assumption of a correct finding by the learned trial judge on the question of identity, Mr. Chaudhuri's attack on the Darjeeling chapter of the judgment would thus appear to be wholly without point" (12).

B. C. Chatterjee had said in his argument that it would make no difference if the order of treatment followed by Judge Basu were reversed. Biswas took up the suggestion and dealt with the Darjeeling events first.

He also noted the present case of the defendants on the alleged conspiracy to put up an impostor. According to this case, Jyotirmayi Debi was the de facto plaintiff in this suit. It was not as though she had arranged for the sadhu to be procured from somewhere, brought to Dhaka, and made to sit at the Buckland Bund to watch the public reaction. Rather, it was on the sadhu's first visit to Jaidebpur in 1921 that she supposedly noticed a superficial physical resemblance to the second kumar and thought of the plan of putting him forward. She arranged another interview with him in her sister Tarinmayi's house in Dhaka and then had him brought to Jaidebpur again for the elaborately staged "self-declaration" meeting. The sadhu was reluctant at first to go along with the plan but his resistance was finally broken.

If this was the defendants' case, it would have to include some description of Jyotirmayi Debi's motive in doing all this, including her invitation of a total stranger into her immediate family. She had no hope of advancing her son's prospects of gaining a share of the Bhawal property by reviving a dead brother. In fact, the adoption of a son by the third rani had put to rest any such hopes. Was there a secret agreement between Jyotirmayi and the plaintiff on sharing the spoils should her outlandish plot succeed? Nothing of the kind had even been hinted at by the defendants. "Was she, then, minded, through malice or malevolence, to inflict harm on the second Rani by foisting a husband upon her, or to deal an indirect blow at the third Rani by imperilling her adopted son's reversion? The evidence is, and it is not disputed by the defendants, that till the arrival of the plaintiff, Jyotirmoyee Devi was on excellent terms with either Rani. I am not at all surprised that learned counsel for the defendants had no answer to give to the pertinent comments made by the learned judge in this connection" (16).

Justice Biswas then went on to endorse Judge Basu's observation that after the sadhu's declaration in Jaidebpur, it was Satyendra Banerjee, with the help of Sasanka Coomar Ghose, who rushed to Calcutta with a letter from Lindsay; Satyendra was instrumental in supplying the Board of Revenue in Calcutta and the Court of Wards in Dacca with the relevant papers, information, and plans to deal with the matter, and went to Darjeeling himself to secure statements from witnesses. Pannalal Basu had also been critical of the way in which the district administration had handled the affair, not only by terrorizing estate officials and tenants but also by resisting the submission of official documents to the court. Biswas went a step further; he launched a searing indictment of the colonial bureaucracy, and of J. H. Lindsay in particular. From the very beginning, when the story broke of the sadhu's declaration, Lindsay had convinced himself, "on whatever materials it might have been," that the man was a fraud. Not only did he refuse the inquiry that the plaintiff had asked for, the records make it clear that he never had any intention of holding such an inquiry. Yet when the sadhu first came to see him, Lindsay gave him the impression that the government would be willing to hear his case. "[I]f Lindsay's memorandum of this incident is to be relied on, . . . there can, to my mind, be no escape from the conclusion that Lindsay was here misleading the plaintiff." In fact, Lindsay had said so in his own deposition.

> Q. Was there anything that stood in your way to prevent you from holding an impartial and sifting enquiry in this matter?
> A. I don't know. Except my own conviction that he was not the Kumar and that the claimant could do what he has done now, namely, attempt to prove that he was the Kumar in open court.

When he wrote in his memo that the plaintiff was suffering from pneumonia in Darjeeling, was he sure he had understood the plaintiff correctly? Could the plaintiff have said diarrhea instead of pneumonia? Lindsay wasn't sure except that his memo said "pneumonia." Could he swear he had not made a mistake? "No." Why had he made a marginal note that the sadhu had a clear skin with no signs of syphilis? Why had he not asked him directly? "It seems to me quite clear that Lindsay did not attach any importance whatever to this interview. . . . I have no hesitation in coming to the conclusion that Lindsay's memorandum is a document on which it would not be safe to place any reliance." Lindsay was also asked in cross-examination what "conclusive proof" he had when issuing the impostor notice. "The reply he gave was characteristic: 'I do not know, beyond the death certificate and the absence of rain.'" How did Lindsay know that the plaintiff's case was that his body had been left unattended in the rain at

Darjeeling? Until that time, the plaintiff had not said this in any of his recorded statements.

> If such a story did not come from the plaintiff or his camp, is it to be supposed that the defendants were taking such pains by lucky intuition to meet a case which was still in the air. . . ? Or would it not be more reasonable to hold that there was a much deeper and more certain basis, a basis in human nature it-self—in 'conscience which makes cowards of us all'? To my mind, the sugges-tion of the rainfall story, first to Lindsay, and then in the statement purport-ing to give the story of the sadhu, . . . betrays a guilty mind which knows the facts as they had happened, and had, therefore, a clearer perception of the case which would have to be encountered. And on the materials on record, to none else could this be ascribed but to Satyendranath Banerjee.

According to Justice Biswas then, Lindsay had swallowed Satyen Banerjee's version of the Darjeeling events, possibly as communicated to him by Sa-sanka Ghose. It was regrettable, Biswas said, that many official records were not produced in court. "The result is that an important witness like Lind-say, who was evidently called by the defendants because he could throw light on many a vital point in the case, is reduced to the position of having to say that he does not remember even such facts as, for instance, that he received a report from Needham on or about the 5th May, 1921." Sasanka Coomar Ghose, another crucial figure on the government side during the entire pe-riod from 1921 to the trial, was also not available for examination. "His po-sition in this respect would indeed appear to have been very much like that of a solicitor engaged in collecting materials for the preparation of his client's case. One cannot help regretting, therefore, that by his acceptance of a brief as one of the defendants' lawyers at the trial, the court was de-prived of the valuable assistance he might have given from the witness-box."[8]

    C. C. Biswas also considered that curious object—Satyendra Banerjee's diary. What was the intention behind those few months of diary writing in 1909? It could not have been meant to be produced as a public evidence in support of his version of the events of that year. He could not use his own statements in his favor, and he had named many others in the diary who could contradict him. "It seems to be more reasonable to hold that Satyen-dra was writing for himself, *but not altogether without an eye to the future.*" He was not manufacturing evidence in anticipation. "[H]is object was no more than keeping a memorandum for his own use of the story he should make and have to adhere to in future, in case any questions came to be raised. . . . One does not always go out of one's way to keep notes about a true story, but if a person is minded to make a false case . . . , it is often safer to reduce it to writing. . . . All this, it may be said, is mere speculation, but what else is left when the only person who could give the real answer to the question before the court does not give it?" In fact, although the plaintiff may have got hold of this diary "by means that were not fair," there was no question about the authenticity of the documents. The defendants had complained about the missing pages in the diary which, they said, were being withheld by the plaintiff because they might not suit his case. Justice Biswas observed that overall, it was the defendants who were really guilty of withholding documents and had "demonstrably failed to come up to the standard of straight dealing." Strictly speaking, it should have been for the defendants to produce the diary if it was relevant to their case, and not have to admit it under pressure.[9]

The Cause of Death

Was there a conspiracy to poison the second kumar in Darjeeling? The trial judge had found that there was "a bare possibility" that Dr. Ashutosh Dasgupta had given the arsenic pills "like a quack," but he could not find that the doctor had done so "wilfully." "Whether this really amounts to a finding *against* conspiracy, as Mr. Chaudhuri contends, is more than doubtful: it is one thing to say that the court cannot find there was conspiracy, and it is quite a different matter to hold that there was none." B. C. Chatterjee, arguing before the appellate court, had said that he thought the evidence did not show that there was an accidental poisoning and it was still his case that there was a conspiracy to poison the kumar (70–71).

A crucial figure in this episode was Dr. Ashutosh Dasgupta who, unfortunately, had changed his story so many times from his first deposition in the defamation suit that it was impossible to rely on his word. For a long time, he denied that the arsenic prescription was his and tried to pass it off as the work of Dr. Nibaran Sen which, as Justice Biswas remarked, "meant a slander on the professional reputation of a doctor who was then dead. The desperate struggle which this witness makes in his present evidence to get round his former statements is indeed a shameless exhibition of perjury which would not be believed if it was not a fact" (91).

A. N. Chaudhuri had suggested that the plaintiff needed the story of the poisoning in order to explain the cyst under his tongue, which supposedly caused his speech impediment. Arguing before the High Court, Bankim Mukherjee, junior counsel for the plaintiff, said that the plaintiff was not making a case that his cyst was caused by an attempted poisoning. From this, Justice Biswas concluded: "Whether any inference should be drawn against the plaintiff from the fact that he was abandoning in this court a case he is supposed to have made at the trial is another matter, but this shows quite clearly that neither the cyst nor the impediment in speech was a circumstance which necessitated a false case of poisoning being made. . . .

Personally speaking, I am not at all satisfied that it was essential for the plaintiff to have made a story of arsenical poisoning, if it was not a fact, in order to bolster up any material part of his case" (102).

Calvert too had to struggle to reconcile his prescriptions with the supposed disease of biliary colic. He was asked if he knew of any authority that suggested that fresh red blood, which was the kumar's symptom on the morning of the fatal day, might occur as a result of biliary colic. He said, "I do not know of any authority on gall-stone diseases in India, but I am not prepared to accept the authorities of other countries." Was his first prescription that morning intended to stop the passing of blood? "I was not concerned in stopping the haemorrhage which in itself was trifling, but in attacking the cause of all his troubles, when the haemorrhage would naturally cease." Justice Biswas was merciless: "Was he attacking the 'cause' by his stomach-soothing mixtures? One feels sorry for a physician of such eminence as Calvert reducing himself to this level!" Nobody could accuse Calvert of being a quack; yet he had talked of diarrhea and tenesmus in biliary colic, and of fresh red blood in stools being caused by "great strain and spasm due to an impacted stone," which all experts had agreed was impossible. Satyen Banerjee too attributed to Calvert the view that "frequent watery motions with blood" was caused by biliary colic: "I have heard these are the symptoms of biliary colic. I heard it at Darjeeling from Col. Calvert." Justice Biswas commented: "this must either make Calvert a liar or brand the witness [Banerjee] as such" (95, 111, 119).

Major Thomas too, on behalf of the defendants, tried to reconcile the symptom of blood in stools with biliary colic. "I would say the pus might come down through the ducts and enter the intestines and in passing down the large intestine set up an inflammatory condition there, or re-awaken or re-exacerbate an old dysentery, a latent dysentery I should prefer to say." Having made this "fantastic explanation," as Justice Biswas called it, Thomas ended up by saying, "I should prefer dysentery as explanation to any other." Biswas's comment: "Would it be wrong to apply to this expert by Mr. Chaudhuri's own token the remark which he chose to make regarding this class of witnesses on the other side—'experts who, we know, can come and support a case provided the remuneration is sufficiently large'?" In the end, Major Thomas had agreed that "you must suspect arsenical poisoning if there is blood in the stools" (111–12).

Then there was Calvert's letter of August 1921 to Lindsay, in which the doctor had said that he was not sure if he was present at the time of the kumar's death. The defendants had tried to suppress this letter and it was produced by the plaintiff, but long after Calvert's examination in commission in England in 1931. "It is difficult," said Justice Biswas, "not to agree with Mr. Chatterjee that no comment against Calvert could be strong enough for his having agreed to give evidence in suppression of the facts he himself had related in this letter, and then given his evidence contrary to its tenor" (117).

The first telegrams sent from Darjeeling to Jaidebpur had mentioned fever. There was no evidence that this was malaria, although Ashutosh Dasgupta tried to suggest this but later retracted. The only telegram that suggested a serious illness was sent on the afternoon of the fatal day—it mentioned "frequent watery motions with blood." "[I]t passes my comprehension," remarked Justice Biswas, "how any one, doctor or layman, can possibly trace in it the remotest indications of biliary colic. On the other hand, the 'frequent watery motions with blood', coupled with stomach pain, might conceivably, if not necessarily, point to arsenical poisoning, at any rate to enteritis" (135).

Calvert's condolence letter to the first kumar was "unusual." "It does seem to be extraordinary that a consulting physician like Calvert should go out of his way to write such a letter for no ostensible reason of his own. It is obvious that the letter must have been procured from Calvert, and that for a definite purpose." A. N. Chaudhuri argued that it was not Satyen Banerjee or Ashutosh Dasgupta who asked Calvert for the letter, but Mukunda Guin, the private secretary, long dead. Justice Biswas thought

> the purpose was to get a statement from Calvert which would reassure Baro Kumar that 'all that was possible had been done to save his brother's life' and that the patient had 'received the greatest care and attention from those about him'. In other words, the object was to get what might look like an unsolicited testimonial from Calvert, not for the Private Secretary alone, but also for the 'friends' of the second Kumar 'who were most solicitous concerning his condition'. . . . In order to reject Calvert's condolence letter as possessing little or no evidentiary value, . . . it is not necessary to hold that in writing this letter he was acting from corrupt motives, for . . . taking the letter as an honest document, it by no means follows that the statements therein contained represented the real state of things. . . . Calvert might naturally have believed that the Kumar had died, and there need be no reason to suspect the *bona fides* of the statement he made in this behalf. It is the plaintiff's own case that the Kumar did pass into a condition which might be, and was in fact, mistaken for death.[10]

As far as the records are concerned, biliary colic or gallstone arises for the first time as the definite cause of death only in Calvert's certificate for the insurance claim. This was two months after the supposed death of the kumar. Justice Biswas did not think that this was suggested by anyone soliciting certificates on behalf of Satyendra Banerjee; it had to be Calvert's own idea. Why had he thought of biliary colic when his entire course of treatment did not suggest it at all? It was, Biswas said, an attempt on his part to give a definite shape to what was really nebulous in his own mind. . . . Not to have been able to particularise the cause of death to the insurance company would have argued a degree of incompetence which no doctor, far less one in Calvert's position, would be prepared to face. On the other hand, if a physician of his standing mentioned a particular illness as the cause of death, there need have been no fear that his statement would not be unquestioningly accepted. . . .

As to the further point made [by A. N. Chaudhuri] that no suggestion of dishonesty or corruption was put to Calvert in cross-examination to discredit his condolence letter or certificate of death, all that need be said is, in the first place, that for the purposes of the plaintiff's case it was not necessary to ascribe dishonesty or corruption, and secondly, that even if this was the underlying suggestion, I see no reason why it should have been directly put to him so long as the plaintiff was able to establish that the documents in question could not be relied on at all. (153)

The insurance papers also included a death certificate from W. M. Crawford, district magistrate of Darjeeling in 1909.

Crawford was admittedly nowhere near the second Kumar when he is supposed to have died, and yet he gives a certificate of death as if the facts noted in it were within his personal knowledge! Crawford said in cross-examination: 'I do not know who asked for it. I do not remember at all the circumstances under which I gave the certificate, nor how the details came to be in it.'

[H]ere was, on the defendants' own showing, another person, who, though not a doctor, was still a responsible officer, and to boot a Justice of the Peace, giving a death certificate without pretending to know anything about the death! This only shows, say what Mr. Chaudhuri might, how easy it must have been for his clients to procure certificates and affidavits to order, and he must forgive the plaintiff if the plaintiff invites the court not to attach to these documents the sanctity which they might superficially appear to possess. (155)

The indictment was clear. The allegation was not of corruption or even of incompetence. The indictment was of a despotic order in which senior colonial officials, especially those belonging to the ruling race, were unaccountable to anyone except their own kind. Over the years, they had developed their own criteria for deciding who among the natives they should trust and who they should treat with suspicion. Within the vested networks of loyalty, they were frequently lax about procedures, indulgent enough to allow a certain degree of bending of the rules and totally assured that their word would never be questioned. Lindsay, Calvert, Crawford—their lapses were not the result of corruption but of the habitual wielding of unchecked autocratic power. The criticisms made by Justice Biswas, as indeed by Judge Pannalal Basu before him, were typical of the new nationalist consciousness in India, by now mature enough to think of the need to replace the colonial despotism with a national political order subject to the democratic will of the people of the country.

THE FAILED EVENING CREMATION

The defendants had alleged that the plaintiff's story that the kumar's body had been left unattended in the rain was most improbable because it would have been "unnatural" and "grossly inhuman" for the processionists to have run away leaving the dead body behind. "What should have been the correct conduct on their part?" Justice Biswas asked.

> Should they have run about hither and thither with the *charpoy* [cot] over their shoulders, or carried it to a shelter which they did not yet know where to find, or should they have left somebody at the spot to keep vigil over the body till the others returned? Would there be any point in their doing so? None of them had the gift of prophetic vision to have been able to foresee the danger to be guarded against, and the dead did not require the same protection from the weather as the living. So long, therefore, as no disrespect to the 'deceased' was intended, and so long as there was no question of abandoning the 'dead' body to its fate, one fails to see either improbability or impropriety in the conduct of those who ran away, expecting to return as soon as the rain held off. (238)

As far as the Darjeeling rain records were concerned, the difficulties in arriving at a firm conclusion were discussed by the trial judge. One of those records—kept by the Darjeeling Municipality—had been clearly tampered with. B. C. Chatterjee had argued that the register had originally said that there was rainfall on 8–5–09 (or 9–5–09), but the date "8" or "9" had been erased and "13" overwritten. A. N. Chaudhuri claimed that the original date must have had two digits, otherwise it would be out of alignment with the figures in the succeeding entries. With the consent of both parties, the register was sent to Scotland Yard in London for examination to see if the original entry could be deciphered. Justice Biswas gave in his judgment the report from the Metropolitan Police Laboratory, Hendon, which, until then, neither party had seen.

> The entry "13–5–09" has been heavily erased mechanically and any underlying figures have been almost completely removed. An examination of the inks present suggests that all the alterations were made some time ago and the diagonal stroke through the erased "13" was written before the document was erased to its present condition. An infra-red photograph shows signs of ink which suggests that there has been a figure "6" underneath the erased figure "3". The photographs enclosed indicate this point.

It is suggested that the procedure was as follows:

A figure, probably "6", was written on the page. This was partially erased and overwritten with a "3". A "1" was placed alongside it. It was then crossed through, a figure "13" put above and then at some later time it was further erased.

. . . Unfortunately in the process of erasure a hole was worn in the paper and it is therefore impossible to say with certainty what the original entry was.

The report, concluded Biswas, goes in favor of the plaintiff inasmuch as the original date was not 13. It was probably 6, but it could have been 8 or 9. Biswas also commented on the lack of transparency on the part of the defendants in not calling for and producing this register, even though they had a certified copy with them. It was the plaintiff who had produced it, even though, at least on the face of it, the record went against his case.

I cannot help observing that his action in calling for and producing this tampered record, even at a late stage of the case, seems to me to furnish only one more illustration, not only of his [the plaintiff's] willingness, but of his anxiety to face all documents that came his way—in marked contrast to the secretive and selective tendencies so strikingly characteristic of his opponents.

On a careful consideration of all the facts and circumstances, it is my definite conclusion that the tampering of the Municipal rainfall record was done in the interest of the defendants.[11]

A Substituted Body?

Justice Biswas reiterated that if the plaintiff was able to show that there was an attempted cremation on the evening of May 8 at which the kumar's body was not burnt, he did not need to further prove that the morning cremation was held with a substituted body. The onus was on the defendants to prove that the body burned in the morning was that of the kumar.

Mr. Chaudhuri says, you cannot first find the evening cremation and then displace the morning cremation by it, but by parity of reasoning, you cannot first find the morning cremation or assume it to be a fact and on that ground seek to destroy the evening cremation.

. . . The burden of proving that the body [in the morning cremation] was that of the Kumar will be on them [the defendants], and in my opinion they cannot hold themselves discharged from it merely because the plaintiff is not in a position to establish affirmatively the negative of their case. . . .

Supposing the plaintiff proved the evening cremation and its failure, and no further, and no evidence was given on either side regarding the morning cremation, would his case about the non-cremation of the Kumar fail? Assuredly not. How then could it be argued, merely because the plaintiff gave some evidence of the morning cremation, that the burden was shifted on to him to prove that the body taken out for that cremation was not that of the second Kumar? . . .

With all respect, the whole of Mr. Chaudhuri's argument is a piece of finely wrought sophistry which fails to carry conviction. (225–26)

What was the evidence put forward by the plaintiff on the morning cremation? The most vital witness was Dr. Pran Krishna Acharya, whose evidence "effectively disposes of the story . . . that the body was that of the second kumar, and that it lay at Step Aside with the face exposed till it was borne away to the *sasan* some time after 8 A.M." Dr. Acharya was told that he should not touch the body because he was a Brahmo, which, A. N. Chaudhuri had argued, was a quite natural response from a Brahmin family. Justice Biswas disputed the claim that this was customary. After all, Calvert had been presumably allowed to examine the body: "one wonders if by their standard the touch of a Brahmo, though still a Hindu, would pollute, but that of a non-Hindu would purify!" Why was Dr. Acharya called, anyway? "If he came on a professional visit, it would almost make it certain that the body he saw was not that of the second Kumar, for supposing the Kumar had died at mid-night, no one would think of getting a new doctor the next morning to examine *his* body, specially as the defendants say Calvert and Dr. Nibaran Sen were both in attendance at the time of death." The other possibility suggested was that he was called to join the procession to the cremation ground. This was even more unlikely, if there was, as claimed, such a prejudice about a Brahmo touching the dead body of a Brahmin. In any case, why should a mere processionist be allowed to go upstairs, stethoscope in hand, to inspect the dead body?

> Look at the matter from any point of view one may, there is to my mind no possible escape from the conclusion that the summoning of Dr. Pran Krishna Acharyya to Step Aside was not and could not have been a casual act, but had a definite purpose behind it, a purpose, however, which Nemesis caused to miscarry—that which was designed to serve as valuable evidence in their favour turning out to be the most damning circumstance against those who had planned this ingenious move. And it is this that accounts for the studied reluctance of the defendants through their witnesses to admit the visit, far less to face it, though it could not be denied in the cross-examination of the witness himself.
>
> . . . The real object must have been to create independent evidence after the *fiasco* of that night, not of the presence of a dead body, but of the presence of *the* dead body of the second Kumar, and this could be easily and effectively achieved if Dr. Acharyya could be made to give a death certificate.[12]

(It may be worth mentioning here that in 1909 it was still not required by the municipal authorities in Bengal, as it is today, for a death certificate to be produced from a doctor before a body could be cremated in a public cremation ground.) Dr. Acharya's evidence clearly established, argued Justice Biswas, that he came to Step Aside at about six in the morning, that he saw a dead body fully covered, and that the body was downstairs. That the body was covered was not in itself unusual. "As it occurs to me, the very fact that one would not normally expect a dead body to be kept lying in the house with the face exposed, specially when for some reason or other the cremation was delayed, might itself have been a circumstance which Satyendra and his confreres banked upon to ward off suspicion on the part of bystanders regarding the identity of the body. A person coming to a Hindu house of death and seeing a corpse laid on a bed, fully covered over, ready to be taken away, was not likely to ask any questions about it" (294). What Biswas found extremely suspicious was the regularity with which all witnesses for the defendants said that they had seen the face of the dead man uncovered. "One wonders in fact what should make these witnesses, almost without exception, remember this little detail, as if this was a matter of tremendous significance at the time. . . . I cannot help the conclusion that it is tutored evidence" (296).

One defense witness, for instance, was Jagat Mohini, the nurse, who claimed to have taken the Ganga water and the sacred thread to the cremation ground. In her professional life, she used to call herself "Dasi," but when she came to court, "she becomes a 'Devi' from a 'Dasi', and unblushingly makes herself out as a Brahmin widow." But no Brahmin widow would call herself 'Dasi.' "not even, I may add, to hide the fact of having taken to a nurse's life." Justice Biswas did not believe Jagat Mohini was a Brahmin, or even a Hindu.

> To me it is perfectly obvious that this attempt, disingenuous as it was, to pass off the witness as a Brahmin had a definite object behind it, namely, to fit her into the role she was intended to play in the story of the sacred thread and the Ganges water, a story which was a very necessary part of the defendants' case, and was designed to serve the double purpose of ensuring the performance of full othodox rites at the *sasan* to the minutest detail enjoined by the *shastras*, and of securing the presence of Kasiswari Devi at Step Aside which, it was rightly felt, would at once dissipate all suspicion regarding a substituted dead body.
>
> In her anxiety to make her evidence as circumstantial as she could, this woman thought it right to add a small but realistic detail that as soon as she carried the news of the Kumar's death to the Government Pleader's house, his eldest son Balen started calling up people on the telephone, but neither she nor the defendants could foresee that this court would obtain from the Post

Master General a list of the telephonic connections at Darjeeling at the time and find out that there was none at Balen Villa. (301–4)

Another defense witness was R. N. Banerjee, familiarly known as Bebul, who was now a barrister in Calcutta. He claimed to have accompanied the body to the cremation ground and watched the cremation to the end. But he is not mentioned in Satyen Banerjee's diary or by any of the earlier defense witnesses. This was surprising, thought Justice Biswas, because Bebul and his brother claimed to have carried the dead body "in trousers and coat"—"a sight which must have been quite an unusual one at a Hindu cremation even at Darjeeling." There is no mention of this important witness in any of the investigations before 1932. The evidence produced in court shows quite clearly that on the day of the cremation, Bebul Banerjee was not in Darjeeling at all; he was in Kurseong attending the *śrāddha* of the raja of Kakina. He also said with great certainty that he had been to the new sasan in Darjeeling in 1905 and saw it ready for use, shed and all, whereas the records produced by him showed that it was not in existence at the time. He even claimed to have seen the second rani and spoken to her at Step Aside on the morning of May 9, not knowing that the rani strictly adhered to the Bhawal Raj rules of purdah and would never appear before strange men. The trial judge had rejected Bebul Banerjee's evidence, which had prompted A. N. Chaudhuri to accuse the judge of bias. What could one say of a witness like Bebul Banerjee who gave evidence directly contradictory to the records he was himself offering? "Here was a member of the English Bar speaking, and speaking with no halting accents, and I cannot help remarking that Mr. Chaudhuri might well have reserved his indignation for his own witness rather than for the trial judge." The simmering antipathy between England-trained barristers and homegrown vakils was hardly concealed here. "I do not believe a word of [R. N. Banerjee's evidence], the information notwithstanding which he volunteered that he was a daughter's son of Rai Jagadananda Mukherjee Bahadur, a well-known citizen of Calcutta of his time who had been honoured with a visit to his house at Bhowanipore by His late Majesty King Edward VII as Prince of Wales."[13] Biswas would certainly have remembered that Rai Bahadur Jagadananda was mercilessly lampooned by the Bengali press and in the Bengali theater in 1876 as "Gajadananda," the abject toady, who had "displayed" the women of his household to the famously lecherous prince.[14]

To support Bebul Banerjee's evidence, the defendants put up Gita Debi, whose husband, a police officer in Calcutta, was known to Satyen Banerjee.

Speaking for myself, I cannot imagine a worse form of bringing undue pressure to bear on a Hindu pardanashin woman than the tactics which were employed by the defendants to get this lady to depose on their behalf when she was not willing to do so herself. The husband simply allowed himself to be turned into a conscripting agent to procure the evidence. . . . It is little to be wondered at that Gita Devi should have unconsciously failed the party who had pressed her into their service in this way. Even on points on which she was expected to speak, she gave herself away by the manner in which she volunteered her answers before the questions were put.

When asked to describe the arrival of the second rani at her house on the morning when the kumar's body was taken away for cremation, she said her mother-in-law, Kasiswari Debi, asked the rani: "Child, why have you taken off your ornaments so soon?" It was clear, as the trial judge himself had noted, she could not have asked the rani this question if she was with her at Step Aside earlier that morning and had herself brought her to her house. According to Gita Debi, her mother-in-law also asked the rani, "What was the Kumar suffering from?" and "Weren't the brothers informed?" An involuntary witness, Gita Debi had given herself away because, Biswas seemed to suggest, of an honest woman's natural adherence to the truth.[15]

Justice Biswas concluded that the defendants had failed to establish that the kumar's body was upstairs the whole night or that it had its face exposed. There was a body in the house in the early hours of the morning, but it was downstairs and it was covered from head to foot. The rani was upstairs, "having fits." "All she saw on the next morning was a covered body downstairs while she was on the upper floor."

The morning procession was accompanied by much pomp and publicity. "[T]he whole object of staging a second funeral would have been lost unless the widest advertisement was given to it." But, significantly, the second rani was not taken to the cremation ground to perform the last rites, "which was at once her duty and her right by preference under the Hindu shastras." She was not physically unfit, because she was fit enough to go to Kasiswari Debi's house. Her absence was even more significant because there was "no relation, agnatic or cognatic" available in Darjeeling to take her place. Birendra Banerjee, who performed the mukhāgni, was no kinsman of the kumar except in the way "that one touch of nature would make the whole world kin. . . . In my opinion Birendra Chandra Banerjee had as much right to perform the Kumar's *mukhagni* as the *sala babu* Satyendra Nath Banerjee might be supposed to have. Birendra purported to do the act no doubt, but this was because he could be easily passed off as a kinsman. The main object must have been to keep Bibhabati off the scene, though, as stated above, she should have been the person to perform this last rite to her husband" (337–38).

The full panoply of Brahminical funerary rituals takes a long time to perform. Since the defendants were insisting that all prescribed rites were carried out, they deposed that they came back from the cremation in the evening. Satyen Banerjee said this in his examination. His diary entry gave him away; in it he had written "Returned at about 2 P.M." Asked if 2 P.M. might mean 2:15, he said, "May be 3 or 4 P.M. . . . Between 3 and 4 P.M. I would call afternoon today. I do not say I could call it evening when I wrote my diary at Jaidebpur—at that time my knowledge of English was not as good as now." Justice Biswas commented: "There could be no stronger condemnation of this witness than the lying quibbling he indulges in with reference to this entry in his diary." His conclusion on the morning cremation: "It was a hurried cremation, sure enough, with no useless rites to delay the operations, but, on the other hand, with a plentiful supply of buffalo-ghee, if not of kerosene oil, to feed the fire for an expeditious ending" (344).

The Rescue

The evidence of Darshandas was crucial here. A. N. Chaudhuri said that the witness was a fake because he did not appear until quite late in the trial. Justice Biswas, on the other hand, thought that that was a clear indication that the plaintiff's side waited until they were able to locate the right man. If they wanted to put up a fake, they could have done so much earlier. Chaudhuri's suggestion, he thought, came "with ill grace from those who put forward a bogus Dharam Das in the box without notice" (358). Reviewing the evidence on the rescue, Justice Biswas concluded: "I hold without hesitation that the second Kumar did not die at Darjeeling, and that his body was not cremated. I hold further—and in doing so, I recognise I go beyond the trial court—that he was the person who was rescued by Darsan Das and his companions from the cremation ground of Darjeeling" (362).

Was it relevant to show what happened in the intervening years from 1909 to 1921? Biswas was categorical: "In the view I take, in order to establish the plaintiff's identity as the second Kumar, it should be sufficient for him to show that the man who was rescued at the Darjeeling *sasan* in 1909 was the sadhu who turned up at the Buckland Bund about 12 years later, and any enquiry as to what was the state of his mind during the intervening period, or whether he had any sufficient excuse for not returning earlier, would be wholly immaterial." A. N. Chaudhuri's argument was that if the so-called loss of memory was not established, then it would have to be the case that the sannyasi knew who he was, and knew further that he had been taken for dead, and still went about roaming all over the place for twelve years before suddenly deciding to come home. This was an absurd story. To avoid it, the plaintiff had thought up the ruse of a loss of memory and it was incumbent upon him to prove it. Otherwise, identity would fail. Biswas did not agree with this view. The history of the period from 1909 to 1921, including loss of memory, was not essential to any finding on identity. But it could supply "almost conclusive evidence on identity." Because if it was shown that the second kumar was rescued by the sadhus and that he was moving around with them for twelve years before returning to Dhaka in 1921, it would be established "with mathematical certainty" that the plaintiff was the second kumar. Biswas, we can see, was insisting on a broadly reductionist view of identity as sameness—nothing else is necessary because there is no further fact—but also making the gesture toward narrative identity as something that would persuade our common sense. But he was not too excited about the contribution of abnormal psychology on this point. "I consider a discussion of the expert evidence on this subject futile and unnecessary." Abnormal psychology was still a very imperfect science, and merely because the stories told by the plaintiff or by Darshandas did not fit any known case discussed in the standard treatises was no ground to reject them as impossible. If the plaintiff is to be believed,

> he must have undergone nothing short of a revolutionary transformation in his mental make-up from which he did not recover till many years after, and the surprise is that he is able to say as much as he really does, not that he cannot say more, or say it with the art and finish of a tutored liar. It would baffle even a normally constituted person to recall with precision the state of his mind during, say, a temporary fit of delirium: how much more difficult would it naturally be for a man whose mind had been literally turned upside down to say years afterwards how exactly he had felt or reacted to his surroundings at any particular stage of his abnormal life! (365)

The defendants pointed out that the plaintiff's story of loss of memory was not mentioned at all in his memorial of 1925 to the Board of Revenue. Asked about this in cross-examination, the plaintiff had said quite frankly: "I can't say what my lawyers wrote in my memorial to the Board." Justice Biswas pointed out that the purpose of the memorial was not to make a claim or to explain why the plaintiff had not returned for twelve years; it was simply to induce the government to cancel the impostor notice. The absence of any mention of loss of memory in that document could not be held against the plaintiff. Loss of memory, thought Justice Biswas, was established as a fact, whatever be its cause, and it explaincd the wandering life of the plaintiff with his sannyasi companions for twelve years.

IDENTITY

A. N. Chaudhuri, thought Justice Biswas, merely picked out a number of isolated passages from the judgment of the lower court to make his case that the judge had not come to any independent finding on identity but had relied solely on the evidence of recognition by Jyotirmayi Debi and Satyabhama Debi as sufficient proof of identity. This was "an elaborate piece of casuistry. . . . No grosser perversion of the true perspective of the judgment could in fact be presented. . . . [O]ne has only to study the scheme of the judgment as a whole to find out how logically and fairly the learned judge has in fact dealt with the question of identity, leaving out not a single test, physical or mental, in arriving at his conclusion." Jyotirmayi's recognition was not based merely on an impression of similarity between the second kumar and the plaintiff. There was an actual verification of the physical marks. But there was also the "revelation of mental identity through long and intimate association with him in the course of his living in their midst as a member of the same family." Biswas added the following comment.

This last fact is indeed one of overwhelming significance, the effect of which the learned judge does not appear, however, to have fully realised, as furnishing undoubtedly the best and most convincing evidence of identity, bodily and mental, assuming of course honesty on the part of the relatives.

In my opinion the defendants have signally failed to show that the act of recognition by the sister and other relatives was or could be dishonest. . . . If, then, her conduct was *bona-fide* to start with, as I hold it must have been, I for one refuse to believe, supposing she afterwards found out she had made an honest error, that she should still persist in it and cling to the impostor as her own brother. That might have been Lindsay's idea, but is certainly not mine. Lindsay, it will be remembered, . . . actually suggested that the sisters of the second Kumar having "openly supported the cause of the sannyasi," it would be "very difficult for them to withdraw from the position they had taken up," but then Lindsay never believed that these ladies had acted honestly at any stage or could have any sense of honour left in them, though they would have nothing whatever to gain by being a party to such a monstrous fraud. (376)

To assess the significance of the evidence of recognition, one must remember, Justice Biswas said, that in the Tichborne trial, all the members of the family except the mother denied the identity of the claimant.

In this case, all the relations, except only a few, gave evidence supporting the identity of the plaintiff. . . . Unlike the claimant to the Tichborne estate, the plaintiff here kept himself open and accessible to all, no prior appointment being necessary for an interview with him: he was freely mixing with people, attending parties and functions, and in fact inviting and challenging recognition all around without restraint, and yet while the evidence from the plaintiff's side came flooding in till the tide had to be checked by a voluntary effort, the defendants, on the other hand, found themselves almost landed high and dry on barren sands of half-truths and untruths.

A. N. Chaudhuri had complained that the trial judge had allowed his court to become a place where "gross and baseless allegations of drunkenness, illicit amour and sodomy" could be flung around at will. As a result, decent and respectable people were reluctant to come forward as witnesses. "All that I can say is that no viler or more unfounded accusation could be made from the Bar against the Bench, and I am amazed that counsel of the position of Mr. Chaudhuri should have forgotten himself to this extent. . . . A counsel who uses slander and vituperation of the judge as a weapon to defend his clients only betrays the weakness of the cause he is out to support" (383).

Arguing against the bulk of the recognition evidence offered by the plaintiff, Chaudhuri had said that true recognition must be spontaneous, "a kind of intuitive impression made upon the mind through a perception of identity." An inference from a comparison of common points was not genuine recognition: it has no independent value at all. Biswas disagreed. "I should have thought that recognition when it was founded on reflection and judgment possessed a much higher value than mere casual impression from physical appearance. . . . Mr. Chaudhuri forgets that it is such 'spontaneous' recognition which in fact is more liable to error, however honest it may be. . . . If spontaneous recognition is thus not always a very safe ground for deducing identity, 'spontaneity' of non-recognition must be even less reassuring as evidence of non-identity" (384). Most of the defense witnesses on nonrecognition gave evidence that fell into this category. We may, in fact, recall here the arguments of the Nyāya philosophers on recognition: memory is a doubtful source of knowledge, they said, and must be corroborated by direct perception.

The crucial witness on nonrecognition was, of course, the second rani herself. But "she had committed herself irrevocably to the position that her husband had died and his body had been cremated at Darjeeling, and she could not but regard any other person claiming to be the second Kumar as an impostor, however overwhelming the physical resemblance might be between the two." She saw the plaintiff in court, and before that in Calcutta at a few chance encounters, and never heard him speak. She had already made up her mind: "to her the question was not an open one at all, and not only did she not have any use for investigating the matter for herself, but she studiously abstained from all enquiry. . . . Conduct like this would doubtless be just as one should expect of a Hindu lady who knew of a certainty that her husband was dead, but then it would rob her statement that the plaintiff was not her husband of any independent value which it might otherwise be supposed to possess" (387).

As far as the plaintiff's witnesses were concerned, A. N. Chaudhuri had argued in each case that the evidence was not of genuine and spontaneous recognition.

Listening to his long and elaborate arguments, I often wondered what was the nature of the evidence which would have satisfied Mr. Chaudhuri on the question of identity, or whether he thought that where the question was raised after many years of absence, identity was by reason of that very fact really incapable of being proved in a court of law. So deeply obsessed was he with his own notions as to the inherent infirmity of the plaintiff's evidence that he seemed to forget that the evidence of identity falling under the different heads had a cumulative significance, apart from the value, positive or negative, attributable to each such head taken by itself. Another obsession, equally strong, which took complete possession of his mind, . . . was the idea, bordering very nearly on conviction, that the learned judge had somehow or other led himself to believe that the plaintiff was the second Kumar, and was accordingly determined to find identity at all costs, irrespective of the evidence. . . . [T]here could be no grosser perversion of the learned judge's attitude. (411–12)

During the trial in the lower court, the defendants had insisted that there was no similarity between the plaintiff and the second kumar. In his argument in the High Court, A. N. Chaudhuri made a concession and said that those who did not know the kumar well could think that there was some resemblance with the plaintiff, but in the eyes of those who knew him intimately, there was no similarity at all. Pressed by the Bench to explain why he had insisted on the "utter dissimilarity" argument, Chaudhuri said, "with astonishing frankness,"

that he was not going to give the learned judge in the mofussil anything to catch hold of—for, [Chaudhuri said] "if you made an admission, it would only be tied round your neck and you could not get away from it"! . . . Whatever one might think of this unconcealed contempt for the mofussil court, there seems little reason to doubt that learned counsel must have felt that an admission of some resemblance, however slight, would be a halter round the neck which would strangle his clients.

In point of fact it is not the admission, but the theory of utter dissimilarity, the absurdity of which it was sought to mitigate by the admission, that must prove the death of the defendants' case. (393)

It was not the admission of resemblance but the insistence on utter dissimilarity that, for the defendants, turned out to be a halter round their necks, "and if it should suffocate them to death, they ought to know whom to thank for it. . . . Mr. Chaudhuri's suggestion that strangers might be deceived, but not those who had known the Kumar intimately, only lends support to the plaintiff's case that the near relations who said they had recognised the plaintiff could not possibly have made a mistake" (396).

Arguing before the High Court, A. N. Chaudhuri had ridiculed the eloquent passage in Pannalal Basu's judgment on the subject of Jyotirmayi's recognition as the work of the "Dacca Shakespeare." Justice Biswas bristled with anger. "[I]t was far easier for counsel, a Bengalee as he was, to carp at the language of a fellow-Bengalee than to assail the truth of [the judge's] facts or the force of his logic. Be it said, however, to the credit of the 'Dacca

Shakespeare' that whatever his English might have been, it was better than the bad language and worse manners of his critic at the Bar, who thought it fit to speak of the judge as 'floating by the skirts of Jyotirmoyee', when all else sank into the 'morass', parodying with vulgar wit an observation of the judge himself—'the rocks in this apparent morass' (408). Biswas's indignation carried with it the entire burden of the wholesale delegitimation that had occurred by then in middle-class Bengali society of the imitative yet arrogant culture of the colonial elite. A. N. Chaudhuri, demonstratively a saheb in his manners and attitudes, had to face the full blast of Justice Charu Chandra Biswas's cultural rage.

The trial judge had not, as alleged by the defendants, ignored the mind of the plaintiff and looked only at physical similarities. Biswas pointed out that the judge had said very clearly that it was only because the defendants had "deliberately left unexplored" the mind of the plaintiff that it became necessary to give "the principal consideration" to the body. It was a fact that the defense did not cross-examine the plaintiff on his memory. "I do not pretend," said Biswas, with some acid in his words, "to know much about the art of cross-examination, and have no right to pit my little or no experience in this line against the acknowledged authority of learned counsel for the defendants, but it does seem to me to be curious, as it did to the trial judge, that the supposed tutoring of a witness should be deemed a ground for withholding cross-examination." The result was that Chaudhuri put himself into an absurd position: "the plaintiff had been fully coached and tutored—that is the excuse which counsel gave for not questioning him on many points, and still in the matter of reading and writing, he had been left untouched, in order that at the very first touch of the cross-examiner he might stand exposed in all his bareness, the illiterate Punjabee peasant he was!" (420–22) Another "outstanding fact" was that the plaintiff "gave his evidence in Bengali, Bhowali Bengali as it was, in the presence of a Bengalee judge, and with a Bengalee counsel pitted against him who was only too alert to have forgiven a single lapse on the part of the witness" (425).

After this—an accumulation of 300,000 words—Justice Biswas's conclusion contained no surprise.

> I concur with the learned trial judge in his findings. . . .
>
> I have read and re-read his judgment several times over, and it is no small tribute to the care, thoroughness and vigilant attention he brought to the consideration of the case that I was unable to trace a single error of fact in his statements. . . . When I think of the time I have taken in preparing my judgment, I cannot but be filled with admiration for the learned judge who was able to produce his in less than half that time, and be it remembered, was able to do so without the exceptional facilities of the printed record which were available to this court. (429)

Chapter Seventeen

RAZOR'S EDGE

Fifteen years before, when a lower court had found in the defamation case that there was enough ground for someone to reasonably believe that the second kumar had been poisoned in Darjeeling, the judges of the High Court had overturned the judgment. There was clearly an expectation among the defendants as well as the officials of the government that a similar thing would happen in the declaratory suit as well. They were looking in particular to the two British judges on the special bench hearing the appeal.

Ronald Francis Lodge had been for many years in the judicial wing of the Indian Civil Service. His first posting was in Dacca in 1913 as additional magistrate and collector. In 1921, when the sadhu made his declaration in Jaidebpur, there were eight members of the ICS serving in the district of Dacca; of them, Lindsay was collector and Lodge, a young man of thirty, was the additional district and sessions judge.[1] (This was a position that Pannalal Basu would occupy in 1935. Of course, Basu would be fifty-three years old when he would be promoted to the position.) It is certain that Lodge was familiar with the affair of the Bhawal sannyasi when it first exploded and was part of the inner official circle in Dhaka that must have discussed the matter in the evenings over whiskey and bridge. Nineteen years later, he was delivering his judgment on the case in the Calcutta High Court.

The Atmosphere at the Trial

Lodge began with a series of comments on the conditions in which the trial was conducted in the Dhaka court. "[T]he precincts of the court were crowded daily with a mob of enthusiastic supporters of the plaintiff who made no attempt to hide their approval or disapproval of each piece of evidence as it was given: hostile demonstrations against counsel for the defence and the defence witnesses were of frequent occurrence: news sheets were printed daily in the town of Dacca, and these sheets often contained offensive lampoons on the supporters of the defendants. . . . It is clear that such an atmosphere was not conducive to a calm judicial determination of the issues involved. Passions were aroused, and feelings ran very high."

As if this was not enough, there was also the mass of witnesses on both

FIGURE 11. R. F. Lodge

sides whose evidence on recognition or nonrecognition had no significance whatever. Lodge was particularly critical of the fact that hundreds of tenants were examined on both sides. "This accumulation of unnecessary evidence has merely added to our difficulties in coming to a proper conclusion." In addition, there was the pressure created by the Court of Wards on the employees and tenants of the estate to stop them from deposing in favor of the plaintiff. "Conduct of this nature merits the severest condemnation." Lodge, however, was quick to point out where he thought the Court of Wards was entirely within its rights. "The suggestion, however, that the estate was not justified in dismissing from service those employees who openly supported the plaintiff . . . seems to me quite unreasonable. I cannot understand the argument that an employer of labour is morally bound to retain in his service an employee who openly supports a pretender and who acts against the interests of his own employer. Nor can I understand the argument that a tenant who has the money with which to pay his rent, but who gives that money to a pretender to the estate and then defaults in payment to the owner in possession, is entitled to any consideration from the latter."

The plaintiff's side was also guilty of creating obstacles to a proper trial. They repeatedly insulted defense witnesses, charging them recklessly with "sodomy, lechery and conspiracy to murder." "The inference is that there was a deliberate attempt by these means to deter witnesses from deposing for the defendants" (437–39).[2]

BASU CRITICIZED

"Where one of two parties puts forward a story which is outside the ordinary course of human experience, and the other party maintains that things happened in a perfectly ordinary normal manner, the mere improbability of the one story may justify its rejection. But, where the alternative to one improbability is another equal, or even greater, improbability, the mere strangeness of the story is not sufficient reason for its rejection." The judge in the lower court had accepted Jyotirmayi as an honest witness because otherwise her whole behavior would have seemed strange and improbable. He did not compare with this the improbability of the plaintiff's story, which was even stranger. In fact, he did not sufficiently examine the conduct of Jyotirmayi from 1909 to determine whether her acceptance of the plaintiff was honest or not.

Second, in setting a measure by which to test the character of the plaintiff, both sides were guilty of adopting false standards, "in one case too high, in the other too low—and adduced false evidence to prove their case." But the judge had treated the two sides differently.

> Proved perjury on the part of some defence witnesses was held to justify suspicion regarding the veracity of other defence witnesses. But similar proved perjury on the part of some witnesses for the plaintiff was regarded as an inexplicable phenomenon; not only did it furnish no justification for suspicion

regarding the veracity of other witnesses for the plaintiff, it did not even affect the credit of the witnesses who committed the perjury.

This difference in treatment . . . is noticeable throughout the judgment, and detracts considerably from the value of the learned judge's estimate as to the reliability of the various witnesses. (440–2)

Lindsay and Calvert Defended

The trial judge had questioned Lindsay's knowledge of Hindi. Lindsay was not asked in cross-examination how good his knowledge was of that language. He did make a remark in one of the documents that he was waiting for Quarry, the police superintendent, to come back to Dhaka before questioning the plaintiff further, because Quarry's Hindi was excellent. But this remark did not justify the judge's conclusion that Lindsay must have misunderstood the plaintiff. As far as "pneumonia" was concerned, English words such as this were "commonly used in India by all classes."

J. H. Lindsay was a responsible officer. It is true that he had made up his mind before the interview took place that the plaintiff was an impostor, and that to this extent he was biassed. But, in spite of this, I am unable to believe that he was capable of deliberately ascribing to the plaintiff statements which the latter had not made, nor do I think it possible that he misunderstood *everything* that the plaintiff said. I believe that Lindsay's note is a substantially accurate record of the interview; and it follows from this that I believe that the plaintiff, in the first account he ever gave of his alleged experiences at Darjeeling, gave a version materially different from that given by him in the witness box. (447–48)

It is useless to ask if Lodge felt compelled to defend Lindsay strictly on the basis of the evidence recorded at the trial. The fact that he knew Lindsay well and probably admired him as a senior member of the civil service could not have been irrelevant to his general assessment of the credibility of "a responsible officer."

Calvert too, Lodge felt, had been unjustly accused of giving false evidence that he had treated the kumar in Darjeeling for fourteen days. Calvert said repeatedly that he did not remember when he first examined the kumar. That there were no prescriptions before May 6 "proves nothing," and when he said that he was treating the patient from day to day, it was only "a general answer not intended to convey any idea as to the number of days on which Dr. Calvert treated the patient." Given the circumstances, Lodge argued that Calvert's statements were "probably true"; in any event, Calvert could not be accused of making out a case for a fourteen days' illness.

As to the condolence letter to the eldest kumar, Lodge thought that

Calvert wrote it at the behest of Mukunda Guin, the kumar's private secretary, who needed it to protect himself from possible accusations of negligence during the kumar's illness. The plaintiff's counsel had suggested that that the letter's phraseology was un-English. Lodge did not know what to conclude from that suggestion, because Calvert had clearly written the letter in his own hand and therefore its contents had to be "substantially true or deliberately false." In the letter, Calvert had said: "The morning I was called in he felt so much better that he declined the treatment I proposed." This treatment was a hypodermic injection of morphia. B. C. Chatterjee alleged that it was absurd for Calvert to propose a morphia injection when the patient was not in pain, so that the whole story of biliary colic and paroxyms must have been an afterthought. Lodge could not accept this. "It must be remembered that when writing that letter Dr. Calvert was not attempting to describe accurately and in detail the course of the illness: he was writing a difficult letter to a person whom he had never seen. I am of opinion that the very fact that this story of the mother dying after an injection remained in Dr. Calvert's memory, is a strong indication that an injection was recommended and refused until too late" (459–63, 468).

THE CAUSE OF DEATH

Lodge began by saying that the plaintiff's evidence on this matter was "wholly unreliable" because "he or his advisors" had made out at least three different cases—once before Lindsay, then in the defamation suit, and finally in the trial. As far as deliberate arsenic poisoning was concerned, this was not credible, because the prescribed drugs were well within admissible doses and there was no need to use it as a cloak. Lodge indulged in a bit of ethnology himself:

> Among Brahmins and other high caste Hindus in this country, it is the custom to cremate the dead body within a very short time of death. There is no custom of keeping the body in the house for several days; nor is there any custom of burying the dead; nor is any medical certificate required before the body can be burned at the cremation ground. Therefore, if a caste Hindu is poisoned and no suspicion is aroused at the time, it is almost certain that the body will be cremated and all evidence of poisoning destroyed. . . . It seems to me, therefore, that in a case of acute arsenic poisoning such a cloak as a prescription containing a minute quantity of arsenic, is either so obviously unnecessary or so obviously useless that no murderer is likely to think of employing it. (465)

Curiously enough, when B. C. Chatterjee had cross-examined Major Thomas about the arsenic prescription, he had asked quite specifically if he knew that "in India" poisoners often armed themselves with a prescription, to which Thomas had said that that was quite possible.

Lodge, however, was clear that the arsenic prescription did not show any criminal motive. "It would have been natural for Dr. Ashutosh Das Gupta to prescribe a laxative. Instead he prescribed a drastic purgative. This purgative would have been harmless at ordinary times. Though it was in fact not suited to the occasion, I do not think that the administration of this medicine shews any criminal intention: it is a medicine which an inexperienced and rather incompetent medical student might have thought to be suitable" (469). On the basis of Dr. Bradley's evidence on behalf of the plaintiff, Lodge thought that the kumar's symptoms on May 8 could occur even in a case of biliary colic "if the patient had taken the drastic purgative prescribed by Dr. Ashutosh Das Gupta." But in general, Justice Lodge was sceptical of the value of the opinions of the medical experts.

> These doctors may reasonably be regarded as experts in medical matters, but they are not necessarily experts in appraising the value of oral evidence. They are competent to give expert opinion on a given set of facts; but they are not necessarily competent to determine from a mass of contradictory evidence what those particular facts are. Therefore, their opinions as to the significance of the prescriptions made and of the symptoms that are known to have occurred are entitled to respect. But any opinion expressed by them, based on a perusal of the oral evidence of a witness [Calvert] and without a clear statement of the facts which they consider to have been established, seems to me of little value. (475)

Justice Lodge thought that the findings of Judge Basu on the cause of death were inconsistent.

> The learned trial judge was not satisfied that there was a conspiracy to kill, nor even a deliberate attempt to murder Ramendra Narayan Roy: yet at the same time the learned judge held that the telegrams sent during the course of the illness were deliberately false, that the watery stools with blood were deliberately hidden from Dr. Calvert and thereby the latter was prevented from applying the proper treatment, and Dr. Calvert was subsequently induced to write a letter full of falsehoods and give a deliberately false certificate of death. I am unable to reconcile these findings. The learned counsel for the plaintiff who based the whole of the rest of his argument on the findings of the judge, challenged this finding and argued that there must have been a conspiracy to kill.

Reviewing the evidence, Lodge found, like Basu, that it did not prove that there was a conspiracy to poison the kumar. His conclusion, however, was quite different. "I am convinced that there could not have been any conspiracy to murder Ramendra Narayan Roy, and, therefore, that there was no reason why Dr. Calvert should write deliberately false letters or give a false certificate. For these reasons I hold that Dr. Calvert must have diagnosed biliary colic and must have treated Ramendra Narayan Roy for that complaint; and I hold further that the symptoms which appeared on May the 8th must have been due to the biliary colic, aggravated possibly by the pills of the prescription *Ex. 51(a)*, and that these pills were administered to Ramendra Narayan Roy in all good faith" (474–77).

The Time of Death

Calvert's death certificate mentioned the time of death as 11:45 P.M. but also said later that "the attack became acute on the morning of the 8th and he died the same evening." Lodge thought that Calvert was "careless" in using the word "evening" because he had clearly specified the time of death.

An important witness for the plaintiff who said he saw the kumar's dead body at Step Aside on the evening of May 8 was Ram Singh Subba. His evidence seemed to Lodge "to bear clear indications that the witness is a deliberate liar." He claimed that he was woken up at night by his servant who said there had been some *golmal* (trouble) with the dead body, but he did not inquire about it then or in the morning when, instead, he made arrangements for a cot to be supplied for the cremation. He did not ask anyone about what happened at the cremation at night. "The whole story is too silly to merit serious consideration. I am satisfied that this witness is wholly unworthy of credit; that he gave false evidence and was coached in the false evidence he was to give."

Regarding Dr. B. B. Sarkar's visit, on which the defense witnesses had been silent, Justice Lodge detected a particularly devious strategy on the plaintiff's side. Since they were in possession of Satyendra Banerjee's diary, they knew from the beginning of the trial that it mentioned Dr. Sarkar as one of the doctors who had attended the kumar. As far as the defense case was concerned, Dr. Sarkar's visit had no special significance. "It was natural for the defence witnesses to omit any reference to it, if they remembered it: it would not be surprising if they had forgotten the visit." For the plaintiff's advisors, on the other hand, since they knew of the visit from the diary, "it was easy to instruct Ram Sing Subha to depose about it." What was one to make of Dr. Sarkar's visit?

It has been argued with some force that a junior doctor like Dr. B. B. Sarkar could not possibly have examined the patient in the presence of or to the knowledge of a doctor of the standing of Dr. Calvert. Dr. Calvert was one of the leading physicians in the province. Dr. Sarkar was an ordinary doctor with little or no practice. . . . It is an admitted fact that Dr. Sarkar did not prescribe for the patient, nor did he interfere in any way with the treatment. I am not satisfied that it is impossible for Suryyanarain to have brought in his own doctor and for that doctor to have examined the patient and given an opinion to the relatives regarding his condition, even though the case was in charge of Dr. Calvert. I think this may have been done at a time when Dr. Calvert was not in the room, but it does not follow that it was done at a time when Dr. Calvert had given up the case. . . . I do not think, therefore, that the visit of Dr. Sarkar establishes that Dr. Calvert and Dr. Nibaran had given up the case as hopeless.[3]

It was suggested on the basis of the evidence of Niranjan Roy, signaler at the Jaidebpur railway telegraph office, who said he had heard some excited talk at the station at about ten o'clock at night on May 9 that the second kumar was dead, that the death telegram must have arrived at Jaidebpur at that time. The trial judge had accepted Niranjan Roy's statement as true. Justice Lodge strongly doubted the evidence.

> To my mind, this story is too fanciful. I cannot believe that a telegram received before 10 P.M. would be withheld by the Telegraph Office in order that the family of the recipient should not be upset. The Telegraph Rules require that a telegram received at the Railway Station should be immediately despatched by a messenger. The position of the Bhowal family at Jaidebpur is such that it is certain that these instructions would be strictly followed in their case, and that there should be no neglect or delay in the delivery of important telegrams addressed to them. I am satisfied that the evidence of this witness is false evidence, and I am satisfied that the telegram must have been delivered immediately after it was received, and that, therefore, the telegram was not received in Jaidebpur until 8 A.M. at the earliest. (493)

The crucial evidence that the trial judge had relied on in finding that the kumar died in the evening was that of the "professors' group." Justice Lodge agreed that these were men of unimpeachable honesty. B. C. Chatterjee had, in fact, regaled the otherwise grave custodians of justice with apocryphal stories of the legendary honesty of Brahmo professors. It was said, for instance, that Professor Maitra was once walking down Cornwallis Street near the theater district and was asked by a passer-by if he knew the way to the Star Theatre. Professor Maitra, a man of strict Brahmo morals, thoroughly disapproved of the theater and instinctively replied, "No, I don't." As soon as he said it, he realized that he had uttered an untruth. He stopped, turned around, called the man back and told him, "Please forgive me. I lied to you. I do know the way to the Star Theatre. But I won't tell you."[4] Lodge was prepared to accept that these men were telling the truth. But were their statements reliable? Professor Maitra, for instance,

> was a man of culture and a resident of Calcutta, interested in intellectual subjects, whereas Ramendra Narayan Roy, a man of Eastern Bengal, a man who

shunned society, judging from Mr. Chatterjee's description, he was an unlettered oaf who spent his days with stable boys and his nights with harlots. It is obvious that there could have been no community of interest between him and Mr. S. N. Maitra. . . . It is obvious that he was not particularly interested in the person of Ramendra Narayan Roy that he should remember the news, and it is obvious that he had no reason to think of this incident for many years after. It has been assumed in the course of the arguments that when a witness of undoubted honesty deposes regarding past events his evidence must necessarily be accurate. It is assumed in the argument that a person of Mr. Maitra's acknowledged probity would state that he did not remember an incident if, in fact, he did not remember it accurately. But this seems to me contrary to everyday experience. It frequently happens that people of undoubted honesty, when attempting to reconstruct incidents from the distant past, reconstruct them quite wrongly, and often describe incidents of which they have no knowledge or describe incidents of which they have knowledge in a manner quite the opposite of the truth. It is obvious that it was a curious freak of memory that made Mr. Maitra remember this particular incident at all, and it does not seem to me to follow necessarily that his memory is reliable.

As far as the other professors in the group were concerned, Justice Lodge doubted that their evidence was independent of that of Professor Maitra. Their memories had been refreshed by a reading of his deposition. "Mr. S. N. Maitra's reputation of strict truthfulness was such that these witnesses would naturally accept his statement without question. I do not regard the evidence of these witnesses as adding any value to the evidence of Mr. S. N. Maitra. Their evidence is a testimony to their confidence in Mr. S. N. Maitra's truthfulness and adds nothing to the value of his evidence."

Justice Lodge then went on to make a curious reversal of an argument made by Judge Basu. The latter had said that the Maitra group consisted of undoubtedly truthful persons who did not have any interest in the fortunes of the plaintiff and, being disinterested, their testimony had to be correct. Lodge argued that the testimony was suspect precisely because it was disinterested. "It was easy for them to make a mistake; and in my view, the fact that the incident which they described was one in which they were not personally interested, makes it all the more probable that they were mistaken in their recollection. . . . These gentlemen were not interested in Ramendra Narayan Roy. They did not go to his cremation. They did not do anything as a result of the message which they said they had heard." Not only that, how was it that they did not give any evidence of an evening funeral procession?

A cremation is a public affair; that of a wealthy man who certainly behaved as an independent prince and, therefore, a person of great consequence would necessarily be accompanied by considerable display. When the morning cremation took place, there was admittedly considerable display. Armed orderlies went at the head of the procession with arms reversed, crowds collected and the body was taken to the cremation ground with cries of "*haribol*", "*haribol*"; and coins were scattered. In other words, every attempt was made to attract attention; and we might naturally expect that there would be the same publicity at the time of the evening cremation. . . . In my opinion, the argument should, therefore, be on these lines. If an evening cremation is proved to have taken place, it must follow that the evidence of S. N. Maitra and his companions is not only honest but accurate. If, on the other hand, it is shown that no evening procession took place, it must follow that the evidence of these gentlemen is incorrect. (494–98)

Lodge obviously did not give much credence to the arguments made by Basu, and in greater detail by Biswas, on the difference in the circumstances of the two cremations.

Lodge considered in particular how far the story of the evening cremation was a "probable story"—"probability" was certainly one of the puisne judge's favorite concepts. There was a new cremation ground with a shelter and better facilities only a little way beyond the old one. It was reported that the supplies required for the cremation had been sent to the new ground. Why should the cremation party stop at the old ground, especially if the weather was threatening? Perhaps they were only foolish. But what happens after they find that the body is missing? They are supposed to have found another body from somewhere, taken it back to Step Aside, brought out another procession in the morning, and cremated the substituted body. This was "an essential part" of the plaintiff's story. The reason for this "extraordinary conduct" was that those who had taken the kumar's body for cremation "became so apprehensive that they would be censured for their conduct on their return to Jaidebpur that they decided to do something to avoid scandal and to avoid rebuke." This was hardly probable.

> They might easily have returned to "Step Aside" and simply stated that they had burnt the body, though they had not done anything of the sort. . . . On the other hand, if the people in Jaidebpur were likely to hear the rumours current in Darjeeling [that the body had gone missing], no possible conduct on the part of the funeral party could serve to prevent the people in Jaidebpur learning about an abortive attempt at cremation and the abandonment of the dead body. . . . If, however, . . . it was essential to burn a body, if a body was available, it is difficult to understand why they should not take the body to the cremation ground that night and burn it at once. . . . By taking the body back to "Step Aside" they were advertising the fact that the first attempt at cremation was unsuccessful. They were running the risk of discovery, because it may be safely assumed that the people who did not leave the "Step Aside" were not parties at that stage to any proposal to substitute another dead body for that of the missing Ramendra Narayan Roy. . . . It is conceded that there is a strong

superstition in this country against taking a body back into the house from which it has once been taken out for the purpose of cremation. It seems to me, therefore, that the motive for taking a substituted dead body back to "Step Aside" is most unconvincing.

Besides, what was the probability of finding another dead body in the space of two or three hours in the middle of the night? "Dead bodies do not lie about in public places and are not ordinarily available on demand. . . . Is it conceivable that these persons would know where the graveyard was to be found? or that they could defile themselves by handling a corpse which they had disinterred from a grave merely for the purpose of avoiding censure and rebuke on their return to Jaidebpur? It seems to me that the whole story bristles with improbabilities, and the story is so nearly impossible that it could not be believed except on absolutely unimpeachable evidence."

Then again, consider the probability of there being rain and storm that night at the cremation ground but none at either St. Paul's or St. Joseph's. Justice Lodge thought it unreasonable to reject all of Father Peel's evidence. He was right in suggesting that "there was probably no rain at Darjeeling on May the 8th, and there was certainly not a heavy storm which spread all over Darjeeling, and reached Lebong, as some of the witnesses say. . . . It seems to me incredible that a storm so violent as is described by the plaintiff's witnesses should come to a sudden termination before it proceeded half a mile beyond the cremation ground." The storm had to be quite violent because the old cremation ground was not close to any human habitation and the funeral party would have had to go quite a distance to find shelter. "In my opinion, it cannot be stated with certainty that not even a shower fell on the cremation ground, but it can be said with fair certainty that there was no such heavy storm at Darjeeling on that night as would drive the funeral party away and compel them to abandon the body."

Then there was the curious feature that most of the witnesses for the plaintiff who claimed to have joined the evening cremation had not been personally invited to do so. B. C. Chatterjee had suggested that this was nothing unusual, especially among people of east Bengal. "It seems to me that if there were any truth whatever in this assertion, it would still be difficult to believe that such enthusiasm would not be chilled on a cold Darjeeling night at 10 P.M. when rain was either threatening or already falling." One witness, Padmini Mohan Neogy, said that he joined the funeral party because he expected a big feast. Justice Lodge thought this was " merely ridiculous," especially because the witness did not later inquire whether such a feast was held. Jatindra Chandra Chakravarty, who claimed to be present at the attempted night cremation, said that he did not inquire about the morning cremation because he "dared not talk about matters offending a Raja." Lodge thought this was "merely silly."

Where were the shelters to which the cremation party is supposed to have gone during the storm and rain? The trial judge had concluded that these were the huts along the edge of Morgenstern's property. Lodge disagreed. "I am unable to believe that the living quarters of malis and servants could be the sheds described, or that these people could take refuge in such living quarters without knowing that they were dwelling huts and without the knowledge of the inmates of those huts. The inference drawn by the learned trial judge seems to me wholly unjustified." Lodge's conclusion was that "no cremation could possibly have taken place on the night of May the 8th."[5]

The Rescue

In the defamation case, it was said that the plaintiff had been rescued by *one* sannyasi who was known by the name of Aghori Baba. Lindsay's record of his interview with the plaintiff also says that he was rescued by "one sadhu who has since been his Guru." Various pamphlets were published containing this story of his rescue, and some of them were appended to the plaintiff's memorial to the Board of Revenue in 1926. Justice Lodge agreed that the plaintiff could not be held responsible for all of these stories, but it was nevertheless a fact that earlier he had given out a different story of his rescue from the one he had given in the trial.

The chief witness for the plaintiff on the episode of his rescue was Darshandas, whose evidence the trial judge accepted because he had not broken down under cross-examination. Justice Lodge thought, on the contrary, that his evidence bore "every indication of being false evidence." He gave the following reasons. First, "there is no reason whatever to believe that any such cave as was described by the witness existed near the cremation ground at that time." There was none at present, and J. E. Morgenstern, who owned property in the area, said that there was none that he remembered. Second, there was a shed at the new cremation ground that was visible from the old one, and "the sannyasis, if they had been there, would have stayed at the new cremation ground and not in this cave." Third, "I find it difficult to believe that a person who had passed out to arsenic poisoning would be able to moan with such vigour when rain fell upon him that his voice would be heard above the storm by a group of sadhus in the cave in spite of the fact that he was wrapped in a cloth from head to foot." Fourth, there was the story of why they took away the man without trying to find his relatives: "a more unconvincing explanation of their conduct is difficult to imagine. But having behaved in this extraordinary manner, the witness proceeded to say that they had no interest in finding out the identity of the man they had saved. They made no enquiries in the Bazar as to who was taken to the *sasan*. They did not feel any interest in the matter at all. This too seems to me highly improbable." Finally, although the witness came to Bengal several times between 1921 and 1933 and was known as Gopaldas, and not Darshandas, he never made any attempt to see the plaintiff or to tell any one his story of the rescue until he was suddenly persuaded by some lawyers and babus to depose in court in the name of Darshandas. His only explanation for this was that his guru had told him not to see the plaintiff or else he might get into trouble. This explanation, thought Lodge, was "unconvincing" and the evidence as a whole "unconvincing in the extreme. . . . From a consideration of the evidence offered in support of the rescue of the plaintiff I am satisfied that the story given is a false story and that no rescue was effected in the manner described by these witnesses. It is interesting to note that the learned trial judge was not really impressed with this evidence, for he says with reference to Gopal Das' evidence that 'his account reads like a fairy tale, and if the plaintiff needed it to establish his identity, he would fail, for it can no more be found on this testimony than it can be found upon his testimony that he is the Kumar.'"[6] Whatever one might think about Justice Lodge's disbelief in the story of the rescue, one can hardly say from his reading of Basu that his understanding of rhetoric was sophisticated.

The Morning Cremation

An important witness for the plaintiff was Dr. Pran Krishna Acharya. In 1921, he had answered a questionnaire sent to him by J. H. Lindsay. Lodge discovered that the answers Dr. Acharya had given then did not always tally with what he said at the trial—especially, he did not mention earlier that he had seen the body fully covered. "[H]is evidence shows that even with a witness whose honesty is above suspicion, there may occur contradictions of the most glaring description. In other words, when witnesses are referring to an event of the distant past, the most glaring contradictions are still consistent with absolute honesty. But when a witness's recollection changes so completely as that of this witness, it is impossible to attach much value to that recollection." Since he did not remember the details of the incident well, it was impossible to set store by Dr. Acharya's evidence that he had seen the body downstairs and not upstairs. The suggestion that the doctor had been called in to give a death certificate without examining the body seemed to Lodge "fantastic in the extreme." He believed that "in all probability through mistake he was called merely to assist in carrying the body to the cremation ground" (536–40).

Of the plaintiff's witnesses on the morning procession, Khetra Nath Mukherjee said that he had noticed the cloth covering the dead body slip for a moment to expose the skin. "I refuse to believe," declared Justice

Lodge, "that a witness after 25 years remembers such an insignificant little detail . . . and refuse to believe that from such an accidental exposure, any person at a cremation ground immediately builds up in his mind a picture of the dead man as stout, strong and fair-complexioned. The explanation of this witness convinces me that the evidence given in court was intentionally and deliberately false." Basanta Kumar Mukherjee had said that he thought the dead body was that of a man taller than himself. "If . . . the body was covered from head to foot so that no part of it could be seen, it is incredible that he should have formed the impression that the body was that of a man taller than himself, unless it so happened that the dead body was that of a man most exceptionally taller. Whether the witness's evidence in court is honest or otherwise, it seems to me clear that his present recollection cannot be relied upon, and his evidence is, therefore, of no assistance to the plaintiff."

The trial judge had concluded that the defense witnesses could not be relied upon because they had given contradictory evidence on who acted as the priest at the morning cremation. Justice Lodge did not accept the argument.

It is conceded that there was no regular professional priest present at the cremation. . . . In the circumstances, it seems to me not unnatural that persons who were present at the cremation should have forgotten who functioned as the priest and should have given contradictory evidence on the subject. . . . I do not think that the contradictions regarding the identity of the person who functioned as priest indicate that any of the other witnesses were giving false evidence in the matter. With regard to the suggestion that rites and ceremonies were not performed, it should be borne in mind that Satyendranath Banerjee and other men of Ramendra Narayan Roy's party were young men less than 30 years of age and were all strangers to Darjeeling. They had sought and obtained the assistance of a number of Brahmins and other gentlemen present in Darjeeling, and these strangers had accompanied the party to the cremation ground to assist in the cremation. . . . It seems to me unlikely that a group of Brahmins would stand quietly by, while some inexperienced young men performed a cremation ceremony in direct defiance of the customary rites and ceremonies. The fact that there was no protest from anybody and no interruption convinces me that there must have been, if not strict observance of ceremony, still sufficient observance as to pass muster with the crowd of stranger Brahmins who assembled there. Our attention has been drawn to the evidence of Birendra Chandra Banerjee that he did not bathe before performing *mukhagni*, . . . nor did he bring water for the purpose of cooking the *pinda* [ceremonial offering of rice]. We are asked to draw the inference that there was no cooking of *pinda* and no observance of any ceremony at the cremation. This sort of evidence by Birendra Chandra Banerjee given 26 years after the event does not, in my opinion, justify any such inference.

Justice Lodge also disagreed with Judge Basu when the latter said about the morning procession that it was strange for there to be so much pomp and ceremony for the funeral of a young man, no matter how rich, who had died a "sudden, strange, calamitous death." Lodge retorted: "It should be remembered that apart from the widow Bibhabati and her brother, Satyendranath Banerjee, the other persons at 'Step Aside' were members of the family of Ramendra Narayan Roy. They behaved throughout their stay at Darjeeling as servants of very rich men and as though Ramendra Narayan Roy was an independent prince, and it seems to me by no means strange that when his body was taken to the cremation ground, it was taken in public procession with as much show as they were capable of making."[7] It has to be said that on this point at least, Justice Lodge's ethnographic knowledge was sadly deficient. It is also evident that he found it especially galling that Ramendra Narayan should have gone about as though he was "an independent prince."

The trial judge had also concluded, from the fact that the second rani had taken off all her jewelry before the cremation party returned home and from Gita Debi's account of her mother-in-law Kasiswari Debi's conversation with the second rani, that Kasiswari could not have been with Bibhabati at Step Aside earlier that morning. Justice Lodge disputed that it was a general practice not to allow widows to shed the signs of matrimony before the processionists returned from the cremation.

> Even assuming on the strength of the learned judge's own experience, that there is such a custom as he describes, it does not necessarily follow that the custom is observed in all parts of the country and in all families. At "Step Aside" there were no elderly ladies of the family of Ramendra Narayan Roy so far as we are aware. Bibhabati certainly behaved at the time as though she were absolutely frantic with grief. It would not be surprising if she flung all of her own ornaments away in the manner described. It does not seem to me impossible that Kasiswari Debi realised that it was wiser at the time not to thwart Bibhabati, and to allow her to have her own way until the first urge of grief had subsided. To my mind, therefore, there is nothing intrinsically unreasonable in the story.

The trial judge's inference from Gita Debi's evidence was also not justified. "In the first place, it is doubtful whether Gita Devi now remembers exactly what conversation took place. But, even if it be assumed that the conversation recorded is exactly the conversation that occurred, it does not, in my opinion, justify the inference drawn from it. I can find nothing strange in Kasiswari Devi's assisting Bibhabati to tear off her ornaments in the first urge of grief, and still attemping to console her with such questions and conversation. I can see nothing in the evidence to justify the inference that Kasiswari Devi was not present at 'Step Aside' on the evening of May the 9th."

It was true that there were many contradictions in the evidence given by defense witnesses regarding the morning procession and cremation. "I have stated," said Justice Lodge, "that, in my opinion, contradictions in the evidence of these witnesses are natural, even such glaring contradictions as appear in the evidence of Rabin [Bebul] Banerjee, and I do not think that such contradictions justify an inference that the witnesses who made them were not present at 'Step Aside' that morning, nor that they have given false evidence."[8] Lodge did, of course, make exactly the same inference in the case of many witnesses for the plaintiff.

In one case, that of Haran Chandra Chakladar, who was present at Lowis Jubilee Sanitarium and disputed the evidence of the Maitra group, Lodge even went to the extent of upholding his statement by declaring Lindsay's record of his interview with Chakladar in 1921 "inaccurate." "[I]t should be remembered that Lindsay made his note from memory and not immediately after his conversation with Haran Chandra Chakladar. It is, therefore, by no means impossible that J. H. Lindsay was inaccurate. . . . There is indeed a contradiction if Lindsay's record of the conversation is accurate. But when we remember the contradictions occurring in the statement of a witness of admitted honesty like Dr. Pran Krishna Acharyya, it is obvious that this sort of contradiction does not indicate untruthfulness on the part of the witness" (560). Strangely enough, Lodge had earlier refused to admit that Lindsay might have been inaccurate in recording the sadhu's statements in his interview with him in 1921.

Justice Lodge also considered the probability that those who were handling the kumar's cremation would take the huge risk of parading in broad daylight a substituted body in a public procession through town.

> [I]t is admitted that there was no attempt to restrict the invitation on the morning of May the 9th. The people at "Step Aside" could not possibly know that the same people who had attended the cremation on the night of May the 8th would not be present at the cremation on the morning of the 9th. It seems to me almost incredible that they would have run the risk of taking any body other than that of Ramendra Narayan Roy to the cremation ground on the morning of May the 9th and expose it to public view. . . . The fact remains that Ramendra Narayan Roy had moved freely in Darjeeling for a week or 10 days before he was ill. He had been seen by many, and he was obviously a conspicuous figure. He was attended by armed followers; he and his brother-in-law were very noticeable, and he appears to have comported himself almost as an independent prince. . . . I find it difficult to believe that the people at "Step Aside" would have risked exposing the body of another man to the public, any of whom might have seen Ramendra Narayan Roy a few days earlier and remembered his features. At the least breath of suspicion their conspiracy would have been exposed.

Lodge concluded that the morning cremation was "an ordinary cremation" and that was "almost conclusive proof that the body burnt was the body of Ramendra Narayan Roy" (561).

THE INTERVENING YEARS

The plaintiff claimed that he had lost his memory after the aborted cremation. Dr. Berkeley-Hill, an expert appearing for him, had said that loss of memory was possible if the plaintiff had suffered a physical or mental shock. There was no evidence produced in the trial of such physical or mental shock. But this, thought Justice Lodge, was not enough reason to conclude that loss of memory was not possible: "medical science has not yet advanced to the stage where we can say with certainty that such a story as advanced by the plaintiff is impossible." Nevertheless, the question was not really one that necessarily had to be decided by recourse to medical science. "[T]o admit that the story of loss of memory is a possible story is not the same as to accept the story as true. Loss of memory is a fact susceptible of proof like any other fact, and if, indeed, the plaintiff lost his memory as he says, that fact can be proved by evidence in the ordinary way." But the plaintiff's side had not made any attempt at all to prove the story of the loss of memory, except by advancing the uncorroborated evidence of the plaintiff himself. One witness who claimed to have spoken to the plaintiff at Jhalki and another at Rangpur said that on being asked directly if he was the second kumar of Bhawal, the sadhu had sighed, and when asked if he planned to return home had replied, "I can't say." This, noted Lodge, did not indicate that the sadhu did not know who he was. (Interestingly, Lodge walked into a logical trap here. If the sadhu at Jhalki or Rangpur did indeed know that he was the second kumar of Bhawal, then identity was confirmed, amnesia or no amnesia. If, on the other hand, the sadhu was someone else, then his response to the question would not indicate anything about the state of mind of the second kumar if he was still alive.)

> The plea of loss of memory is obviously an extremely convenient one for a person coming forward to claim the identity of a man long supposed to be dead. It helps him to avoid answering questions, and it helps to explain ignorance of the past which would be otherwise inexplicable. It seems to me that the plaintiff's failure to prove by reliable evidence that he had, in fact, lost his memory is sufficient to rouse the gravest suspicion regarding the truth of his story. If the plaintiff did not lose his memory, then we are left without any explanation why he made no attempt to return to his family after recovering consciousness. We have no explanation why he made no attempt to communicate with his family and relieve their anxiety. (568–71)

After the second rani returned to Jaidebpur from Darjeeling, there was an attempt to exclude her from the management of the Bhawal estate. Satyendra Banerjee suspected a conspiracy to defraud his sister, and finally persuaded her to entrust him with the management of her property.

> There can be no possible doubt that Satyendranath Banerjee has attained wealth through his control of his sister's estate. But the mere fact that he has prospered in this way is not, in my opinion, sufficient to justify the assumption that his conduct in detaching Bibhabati from her brothers-in-law was necessarily dishonest. It is clear that he believed that her brothers-in-law were determined to cheat her and appropriate her property to themselves. It is further clear that the atmosphere at Jaidebpur was by no means the right atmosphere for a young widow like Bibhabati. Bibhabati was the daughter of cultured parents, even though they were poor. The letters of her mother show clearly a standard of education to which Jaidebpur zamindars could not lay claim. The elder of the two brothers-in-law was a drunkard, and the younger was a drug addict according to the plaintiff's witnesses. Both were uncultured, both were immoral to a degree. There can be little doubt that anybody with the best interests of Bibhabati Devi at heart would have attempted to get her away from Jaidebpur.

Since then, Bibhabati had lived with her brother's family. No one had suggested that Satyendra Banerjee had deceived her or forced her to do anything against her will. "It should be remembered that a pardanashin lady in this country has to rely to a very great extent on some male person to manage her affairs, and the obvious person to rely on in the case of Bibhabati was her own brother." Throughout the trial, the plaintiff's side had attempted to abuse and vilify Satyendra Banerjee and the trial judge, felt Justice Lodge, had been "deeply impressed" with this campaign. It was suggested from some entries in Satyendra's diary that he gloated over the quarrels between Bibhabati's sisters-in-law. "It must, however, be realised that Satyendranath Banerjee at that stage was convinced that the people at Jaidebpur were determined to deceive Bibhabati, and by that deceipt to cheat her out of her property. Such being the case, it was not unnatural for him to rejoice in dissention among people whom he regarded as his enemies and the enemies of his sister. The fact that Satyendranath Banerjee rejoiced in the quarrels between the members of the Jaidebpur family does not suggest to me that he was in any way depraved."

As for the diary itself, Justice Lodge did not see anything in it "beyond a very natural resentment [of Satyendra] at what he considered the insulting attitude adopted to him by the servants of the Bhowal zemindars and by the zemindars in person, and a firm determination to get his sister out of the clutches of her deceased husband's people and to obtain possession and control of her estate" (572–78).

Rumors were said to have been circulating in Jaidebpur that the second kumar's body had not been cremated in Darjeeling and that he had been seen alive at various places in the company of sannyasis. "I am satisfied from the evidence on record that apart from the rumour in 1917, no definite information ever reached the family at Jaidebpur regarding the alleged survival of Ramendra Narayan Roy. . . . The rumour in 1917 is interesting in so far as it shows how ready the people of the locality were to believe that Ramendra Narayan Roy was alive. They were in a mood to accept a claimant, and if any one was inclined to put forward a claim, he must have realised from the experience of that year that an impostor bearing any resemblance to the late Ramendra Narayan Roy would have a reasonable chance of success" (586).

"Discussion and Agitation"

The plaintiff presented his memorial to the Board of Revenue in 1926. His story given there was different in many respects from the story offered at the trial. The trial judge thought the account given in the memorial was "nonsense and untrue" but disregarded it, since he accepted the plaintiff's explanation that he did not know what his lawyers had written.

I am unable to dismiss this solemn document in quite so airy a fashion. The memorial was not drawn up hurriedly, on the spur of the moment, by a man unacquainted with all the facts. It was drawn up after five years of discussion and agitation. The plaintiff was surrounded from the beginning by leading members of the Dacca Bar. . . . His supporters obtained the opinion of Sir Ashutosh Chaudhuri, who advised a suit in court, but they decided to adopt the memorial method first. They could not have rejected advice from such a source without anxious consideration and without the advice of other eminent lawyers. The memorial itself recited that Dwarkanath Chakravarty, a very eminent member of the Calcutta Bar, took an active part in drawing up the memorial. The memorial was presented by Langford James and argued by him before the Member of the Board of Revenue. It is inconceivable in my mind that a memorial drawn up in such circumstances could have been carelessly drafted. . . .

It seems clear to me that in 1926 the plaintiff believed that he would have the support of Jyotirmoyee Devi and her relatives for the version then given, and this single fact is sufficient to justify the court in regarding the evidence of these witnesses with the greatest suspicion. . . . We have been informed by Mr. Chatterjee in the course of his argument before us, that there was a change in advisers to the plaintiff between the date of institution of the suit and the date of the plaintiff's examination in the witness-box. . . . [I]t seems obvious to

me that the memorial version was dropped when the new director took charge
of the case. (587–88)

Recognition by Relatives

Justice Lodge then took up what for him was the crucial episode of the so-
called recognition of the plaintiff by Jyotirmayi Debi and her family. His
analysis of this evidence is central to his conclusion, so that we need to quote
him in some detail.

On their first meeting with the sadhu in Jaidebpur, Jyotirmayi and the
others in her family observed him carefully, "with the thought in their
minds that he might be Ramendra Narayan—and *did not recognise him.*" On
the second day, "after a long conversation in daylight, *there was still no recognition but a suspicion which had grown very strong.*" The sadhu then leaves
Jaidebpur and does not come back for a few days. On his second visit, Jyotirmayi has him examined for the marks on his body. Then comes the so-
called declaration of identity, when the sadhu breaks down under persistent
questioning and the showing of photographs.

> This conduct seems to me absolutely incredible. I find it impossible to believe
> that a devoted sister, who had been searching for years for her missing brother,
> would fail to recognise him at the first meeting even if it was dusk. The pic-
> ture of the second day's dinner party reads like a society novel; the well-bred
> hostess remarking to her guest that she saw a most remarkable likeness in him
> to her long lost brother, and then immediately changing the subject on re-
> ceiving a surly disclaimer from the sannyasi.
>
> The detail of Tebboo producing the photographs seems to me to have
> been invented by someone who had seen too many sentimental pictures from
> Hollywood.

It is unclear who Lodge meant as the inventor of the story. The incident of
the sadhu bursting into tears on being shown a photograph of the second
kumar was mentioned in Needham's report to Lindsay the following day,
so that if Lodge meant that the story had been invented by the inmates of
Jyotirmayi's house, he clearly overlooked the fact that in 1921 no one in
Jaidebpur was likely to have seen many Hollywood films, sentimental or
otherwise. But Lodge also had his own notion of a Bengali sentimentality
that did not need any American inspiration.

> The justification offered for Jyotirmoyee Devi's conduct is that she recognised
> from the beginning how much was at stake and how essential it was to be sure
> beyond all possibility of error. But why should she have thought like that? To
> her, the only thing that mattered was that her brother had come back. She was

not worried about the estate. I find it impossible to believe that she would have acted as she says she did. If the description of these days was a Bengali caricature of two cold-blooded reserved Englishmen meeting after a long absence, it might be good enough to raise a laugh; but as the description of a warmhearted sentimental Bengalee lady meeting the brother whom she had been longing to see for 12 long weary years, it seems to me to be utterly incredible. (598–99)

We might recall our discussion in an earlier chapter of Indian philosophical debates over recognition (*pratyabhijñā*), We had noticed there that most schools of philosophy regarded memory as inferior to perception (*pratyakṣa*) as a source of knowledge. It would be too much of an imaginative leap to infer from this a general cultural tendency in Bengal for people to be sceptical of spontaneous perceptions of sameness and to verify or corroborate them by tangible evidence such as marks or insignia (*abhijñāna*). But it is significant that whereas both Pannalal Basu and C. C. Biswas found the story of Jyotirmayi's recognition especially credible, Lodge thought the checking of bodily marks utterly unnatural and unconvincing.

The Declaration

If indeed the sadhu then decided to declare his identity, why did he have to do it in front of hundreds of people? Why couldn't he do it among his relatives? Why did he need to be questioned in public? "[I]t seems a fair inference to hold that he knew that such questions would be asked, and therefore, that he had been told about them."

> The success of the scheme was immediately apparent. The simple villagers, attracted by the rumour that Ramendra Narayan Roy had returned, had gathered in the courtyard. They were told that the sannyasi bore on his body all the identifying marks which Ramendra Narayan Roy bore. They were witnesses to this seemingly wonderful revelation of memory of details of the past. Then as they stood there gaping with astonishment, Jyotirmoyee Devi rushed out and welcomed the sannyasi as her brother. It is not surprising that these simple rustics were convinced. In half a day, a thousand converts were obtained, a thousand ardent eager missionaries to spread the new gospel throughout the length and breadth of Bhowal. These missionaries believed sincerely in the gospel they went out to preach, and by their obvious sincerity must have convinced others. And what an attractive gospel for the tenants! The plaintiff announced his intention of holding the estate for the benefit of the tenants, if he should succeed in recovering possession. As he so plausibly explained, of what use was great wealth to one who had adopted the life of an ascetic? But apart from the appeal to self-interest and the transparent sincerity of the

missionaries, the romance of the plaintiff's case, and the transformation of a
roué into a saint must have made a tremendous appeal to the tenants of the estate. That it did so is obvious. Crowds flocked into Jaidebpur daily simply to
have *darshan* of the plaintiff, and they did not come empty-handed. The astute
advisers of the plaintiff pressed home the advantage. A monster meeting was
arranged . . . by popular acclaim, the plaintiff was accepted as Ramendra Narayan Roy of Bhowal.[9]

The characterization here of peasants as simple, gullible, almost childlike
in their innocence and openness to manipulation, is so standard in official
discourse that it is hardly surprising when it comes from an ICS officer such
as Lodge. It was, one might say, an element in the colonial theory of Indian
society, because only such an axiom could make intelligible the colonial
desire to fulfil the role of the guardians of India's peasantry.[10] Strangely,
Lodge does not consider why, since the Bhawal tenants were being looked
after directly by the Court of Wards, they should be so keen to have a feck-
less, even if saintly, zamindar.

SUBSEQUENT MOVES

The plaintiff next sought an interview with Lindsay, the collector, and put
his case before him. "It must be conceded," said Justice Lodge, "that this
was a bold move—but audacity is a necessary quality of impostors." In actual fact, Lodge noted, there was little danger, because "the plaintiff was accompanied by two members of the Bar, who (inspite of J. H. Lindsay's recollection to the contrary) must have been present during the interview."
Further, Lindsay did not personally know the late second kumar. So the
plaintiff was not really taking a great risk.

Meanwhile in Calcutta, Satyendra Banerjee took steps to brief government officials on the facts regarding the second kumar's death and cremation in Darjeeling. His conduct "in going straight to the Secretariat for advice and not rushing off to Jaidebpur, showed common sense, not a guilty
conscience. I cannot imagine anything much more unwise in the circumstances, than for Satyendranath Banerjee to rush off to Jaidebpur to cate-
chise the plaintiff. . . . If he was of the opinion that members of the Jaidebpur family were deliberately supporting a man known to be an impostor,
and were procuring support for him, it was only natural that he should take
steps to secure evidence of Ramendra Narayan Roy's death and cremation
as soon as possible, and to have that evidence placed on record."

Lindsay soon went on to issue the "impostor notice." Lodge defended
the move to the hilt.

Lindsay was an Executive Officer, responsible for the administration of the
Bhowal estate. The pretender had launched a campaign of propaganda, and

tenants were being told that there was conclusive proof that the plaintiff was indeed Ramendra Narayan Roy. . . . In these circumstances, the tenants were withholding rent, and the administration of the estate was rendered extremely difficult. In my opinion, it was the Collector's duty to inform the tenantry at the earliest possible manner what the attitude of the Board of Revenue was to be. He was not a judge determining finally the rights of the parties; he could not afford to spend 2 or 3 years recording evidence, nor could he afford to listen to arguments for nearly a year as we have done. He had to act quickly. If instead of saying, "the Board of Revenue has got conclusive evidence", he had said, "the Board of Revenue has evidence which the Board considers conclusive," it would be difficult to criticise this notice. (607–13)

JYOTIRMAYI AS THE CHIEF CONSPIRATOR

The trial judge had accepted Jyotirmayi's honesty, because the possibility of her sponsoring, in the given circumstances, a Punjabi as her brother in order to lay claim to the Bhawal property was simply incredible. But what was the alternative to this incredible story? "It may be conceded," said Justice Lodge, "that it is most unusual for a Bengalee lady to put forward a Punjabee impostor as her brother; it is equally unusual for a Bengalee lady to deny her own husband." The alternative to the theory of conspiracy was a story of mistaken death, failed cremation, miraculous rescue, cremation of a substituted body, and loss of memory for eleven years, not counting such coincidences as an unrecorded storm and rain, the proximity of caves that were later found to be nonexistent, and so on. Which was the more improbable story? The trial judge did not compare the two sets of probabilities.

Moreover, Lodge felt that the trial judge had overestimated the difficulties faced by the conspirators. He had assumed that the plan had to be laid in the space of three days—between the sannyasi's first and second visits to Jyotirmayi's house in Jaidebpur. Although there was no evidence of any conspiracy before the sannyasi's arrival in Jaidebpur, one could not conclude from this that plans were not afoot. "The fact that steps recognisable as steps taken in furtherance of the conspiracy cannot be identified before the plaintiff's arrival in Jaidebpur does not mean that the conspiracy (if any) was conceived after his arrival."

The only two real difficulties in the path of the conspirators was to persuade people of the physical resemblance between the plaintiff and the kumar and the story of the loss of memory.

Once they found that people in general accepted the striking resemblance as a fact and swallowed the story of loss of memory, they ran no very great risk either of punishment or of censure—at least until they entered a witness box and commenced to give evidence on oath. There were some risks, it is true: but there was also prospect of great reward, and the risks were worth running. The learned counsel for the plaintiff has asked us to hold that because there was no evidence of any agreement between plaintiff and Jyotirmoyee Devi or others of her family, therefore Jyotirmoyee Devi would not profit by plaintiff's success. It is difficult to take such a submission seriously. The fact that an agreement has not been proved is not reason for supposing that no agreement can exist. . . .

In considering the question of conspiracy, one aspect of the case should be borne in mind. The plaintiff's conspiracy—if conspiracy there was—could have been hatched at any time before the 4th of May, 1921. The defendants' conspiracy to find a substituted body for cremation could not possibly have been conceived until 3 hours or so before it was successfully carried out. . . . (622–24)

Lodge clearly did not ask himself if the two events whose probabilities he was comparing were themselves comparable.

The Evidence on Recognition

The trial judge, thought Lodge, did not consider how much the evidence on recognition may have been influenced by the propaganda carried out on behalf of the plaintiff. "The very arguments which appealed so strongly to the learned trial judge must have occurred to many people—the improbability of a *purdanashin* Bengalee lady attempting to set up a Punjabee as her brother, the great probability that such an attempt would fail, and the opprobrium she would earn if it did." Many witnesses said that they had recognized the plaintiff after he had answered questions about the past or after he had recognized the witness. "With respect to those witnesses who could not accept the plaintiff until they were given instances of his memory of the past, it is clear that their supposed recognition has no value. They did not, in fact, recognise the plaintiff; they were convinced of his identity by evidence placed before them. The fact that the evidence convinced them is irrelevant; the question is whether the same evidence appeals to us as convincing."

Justice Lodge completely dismissed the evidence of recognition by Satyabhama Debi. The two letters written over her signature were "obviously not the unaided efforts of the old lady. They reveal clearly the cloven hoof of the legal adviser. In my opinion, they cannot be accepted as any indication of Satyabhama Devi's own feelings. They were merely moves in the campaign to get the plaintiff accepted." The performance by the plaintiff of the funerary rites of Satyabhama Debi was, once again, no evidence of honest recognition by the members of Satyabhama's family if in fact they were running an impostor. "Having set plaintiff up as her brother, Jyotirmoyee Devi could not avoid allowing him to perform these ceremonies. To have refused such permission would have been tantamount to public confession of conspiracy. If she had dishonestly supported his claim, she was bound to act as though she honestly believed him to be her brother." In other words, Justice Lodge seemed to be saying, since Jyotirmayi was running an impostor, every piece of evidence of her apparent honesty must actually be reckoned as proofs of her dishonesty.

It is true that large numbers of people in Bhawal accepted the plaintiff as the second kumar. "The tremendous influence of mass suggestion must be taken into consideration when examining the conduct of the persons concerned." We should, in fact, remember that Justice Lodge was writing his judgment in 1940, when the events of recent European politics and the unprecedented possibilities of mass manipulation by propaganda may have been playing on his mind. "Moreover, it may easily have happened that in the enthusiasm of the moment, some people accepted the plaintiff without question, but later when they came to consider the matter in the cold light of reason, they rejected him." Curiously, Lodge was here ignoring his own injunction that recognition, to be honest, had to be spontaneous, not requiring the weighing of evidence in the "cold light of reason."[11]

Reading Jyotirmoyee Devi's evidence, Justice Lodge thought "she was not frank, straightforward or truthful," that she "avoided giving a direct answer whenever possible. . . . [I]t shows that after three separate interviews followed by plaintiff's residence for three days as a guest in her house, she was still not fully convinced that he was her brother. The evidence of Jyotirmoyee Devi, therefore, considered as evidence of recognition, goes to show that plaintiff cannot possibly be Ramendra Narayan Roy."

One reason why the trial judge was persuaded that Jyotirmayi's recognition of the plaintiff was honest was that even Jogen Banerjee, the estate secretary who became a crucial person in the defense team, thought that her recognition was based on true belief. But this, commented Lodge, was not a good reason. Jogen Banerjee "must have known that many people would believe in a miraculous resurrection at the intervention of holy men like sannyasis. Therefore, unless he was already aware of suspicious conduct on her part, he had no reason for thinking at that time that Jyotirmoyee Devi was anything but honest."[12]

On the first rani Sarajubala Devi's evidence of recognition of the plaintiff, Lodge quoted two entire pages from her cross-examination, in which she was asked if she had already made up her mind before she actually saw the plaintiff. He then dismissed it with the single sentence: "This evidence does not, in my opinion, carry conviction."

This, in fact, was the standard manner of treatment by Justice Lodge of most of the plaintiff's witnesses on recognition—extracts from the evidence followed by a comment such as "This evidence seems to me unworthy of serious consideration" or "This story of recognition is simply incredible." Billoo Babu and Sagar Babu, for instance, are dismissed with the single sentence: "They have supported Jyotirmoyee Devi in every false story she has given." On Chandra Sekhar Banerjee, Lodge commented: "he was not able to recognise the plaintiff with certainty from his features but was convinced of the identity by the fact that plaintiff spoke Banua." He summed up the position with respect to the second kumar's relatives—an important feature of the case, as the puisne judge himself noted, in that, unlike in the Tichborne case, most of the relatives here had sided with the claimant—as follows. "The fact that the relatives of Ramendra Narayan Roy have almost all deposed in favour of the plaintiff is a circumstance in his favour: the evidence they have given is almost sufficient in my opinion to prove that he is an impostor. The conduct of all of them was unnatural; the evidence of most of them teems with falsehoods. When it is realised that many of them will profit appreciably if plaintiff succeeds, it is apparent that their evidence cannot carry conviction."[13]

For the Kumar's friends and acquaintances who deposed in favor of the plaintiff, Justice Lodge applied the criterion of whether their recognition was spontaneous. Most of them seemed to fail. Some, for instance, were "induced to accept plaintiff owing to his apparent knowledge of the past, and not owing to their recollection of his features." Another "was not wholly satisfied until he had examined plaintiff's feet." N. K. Nag, whose evidence had strongly persuaded Pannalal Basu, was doubtful about identity until the plaintiff told him the story of the kumar's visit to his house one night to ask his father for money. "I cannot believe," remarked Lodge, "that the most cautious of individuals who clearly recognised an old friend, would say when that friend offered proof of identity, 'some one might have told you I was coming.'" Nag may have been an honest witness, but there was no reason why the plaintiff could not have heard the story of the kumar's visit to his house from someone else. Besides, Nag was clearly exaggerating when he said that the plaintiff was fairer than the average Englishman— fair as a Norwegian, he had said. "The plaintiff was before us on many occasions; he is undoubtedly fair for a Bengalee, but there are many other Bengalees as fair; and to describe him as fairer than the average Englishman was a ridiculous exaggeration. In the circumstances, though I regard N. K. Nag as honest, I think it possible that his description of the meeting was highly coloured and inaccurate; and I regard his acceptance of plaintiff as no proof of recognition."

Justice Lodge's summary conclusion on the evidence of the kumar's friends is worth quoting for the wealth of cultural assumptions that lay buried under it.

Apparently, not a single one of his old friends and boon companions recognised him at sight and went up to him, slapped him on the back and exclaimed, "Hello, Ramendra, where have you been all this time, etc.?", or the Bengali equivalent for this. Even though they had learned (as they must have) that he had been recognised by Jyotirmoyee Devi and others, and bore the same marks as Ramendra, they could not recognise him at once. They had to look at him again and again and again, and persuade themselves that he was indeed Ramendra. This sort of recognition carries little weight. The Tichborne case in England showed that honest witnesses can be hopelessly wrong in identifying an old friend after the lapse of many years. In the present case, the evidence of recogniton is much more halting than in the Tichborne case.[14]

As far as the defense evidence on nonrecognition was concerned, Lodge admitted that it was "certainly not so strong as to prove conclusively that plaintiff is not Ramendra Narayan Roy." But, he said, "as the burden of proof is on the plaintiff, this is immaterial, if the plaintiff's evidence failed to prove affirmatively the fact of identity" (653).

PHYSICAL RESEMBLANCE

The lapse of time was a major consideration in the present case. It had a serious effect on the question of checking the physical resemblance between the plaintiff and the second kumar.

It is true that hundreds of witnesses have deposed from memory regarding his eyes, nose, ears, complexion, colour of hair, etc., and it is equally true that many of these witnesses were firmly convinced that they were speaking from memory of Ramendra Narayan Roy as they knew him in 1909 and earlier. But the fact remains that for 12 years or more after 1909 they lost sight of him; and their memories must have become dim and vague. Then they saw the plaintiff. An examination of the evidence of identification has shown, many of them accepted him without actual recognition, either on the evidence of his memory of persons and past events, or as a result of their confidence in Jyotirmoyee Devi, or even as a result of mass suggestion. These witnesses were many of them quite honest in their belief that plaintiff is Ramendra Narayan Roy. They had been seeing him continuously for 12 or 15 years before they gave evidence, and naturally the image of the plaintiff as he is, had supplanted in their minds the image of Ramendra Narayan Roy as he was. In other words, they had been refreshing their memory of Ramendra Narayan Roy for many years by looking at the plaintiff. Inevitably their description of Ramendra was affected by their inspection of plaintiff, and they gave the features of the plaintiff as those of Ramendra Narayan Roy.

It is unlikely that Lodge was aware of the Vaiśeṣika theory of the erasure of a memory trace (*saṃskāra*) following every act of memory and the creation of a new impression; otherwise, he would have jumped at it. For instance, when the plaintiff first appeared in Jaidebpur, the fact that his nose was wider than that of the second kumar was noticed and variously commented on. But later, many witnesses claimed unhesitatingly that there was no difference at all between the features of the plaintiff and those of the second kumar.

> From this it seems clear that the picture of the plaintiff has completely ousted the picture of Ramendra Narayan Roy from the minds of these witnesses.
>
> On the other hand, I suspect that people who saw the plaintiff, with their minds already made up that he was an impostor, immediately imagined differences in detail of which they had no clear recollection. Hence in attempting to compare the features of the plaintiff with those of Ramendra Narayan Roy, it is useless to consider features of the latter, of which we have no description dating from before the arrival of the plaintiff, or regarding which there is disagreement between the parties. (653–54)

There was, first, the color of the eyes. The plaintiff's eyes were light brown. "No Englishman would describe them as any other color than brown." Caddy's report had mentioned the Kumar's eyes as "grey" whereas Kali Prasanna Ghosh had stated that they were "rather brownish." The trial judge had concluded that Caddy had recorded the color as translated for him from *kaṭā* by the insurance agent Girish Chandra Sen. He had accepted Kali Prasanna's statement as more reliable. Lodge disagreed. "I should prefer to accept the report of Dr. Arnold Caddy. The opinion of an Englishman who is accustomed to thinking of the different shades of colour of the eye, noted down at the time he observed the colour, is more reliable than the opinion of a Bengalee gentleman who was not accustomed to noting the different shades of colour, and who did not make a note of his observation until a year or so after he had seen the eyes he was describing." But Justice Lodge had a further observation.

> Jyotirmoyee Devi appeared before us at the request of the learned counsel for the plaintiff that we should compare her eyes and her ankles with those of the plaintiff. Her eyes had a brown light in them, with a bluish or greenish tinge— the sort of eyes which are frequently described as hazel. In some lights the brown colour of her eyes is more noticeable, in other lights the green or blue shade predominates. I can well imagine anybody describing her eyes as "rather brownish" or as "hazel" or as "grey". It seems to me almost certain that the eyes of Ramendra Narayan Roy were rather like those of his sister Jyotirmoyee Devi, and had a definite blue or green or grey shade in them. On the other hand, the plaintiff's eyes are brown; and I cannot imagine any Englishman describing them as grey.

I am satisfied, therefore, that the colour of Ramendra Narayan Roy's eyes was not the same as the colour of the plaintiff's eyes.

The shape of the plaintiff's nose was obviously different from that of the second kumar. There was expert evidence suggesting that this may have been the result of a bony growth that was possibly syphilitic in origin. Justice Lodge, however, pointed out that the plaintiff never admitted that there was any change in the shape of his nose, and was supported in this by Jyotirmayi Debi. Hence, he could not accept that there was any "consistent explanation" offered by the plaintiff of the change.

On the scar near the plaintiff's ankle, the only reliable evidence about a similar scar on the kumar's body was Caddy's medical report. "The fact that the plaintiff has a similar scar in a similar place is a circumstance in his favour, but is by no means conclusive." Lodge himself suggested the possibility that it may have been deliberately caused in an attempt to replicate the mark.

Justice Lodge considered the evidence on syphilis at some length. Ramendra Narayan was known to be suffering from tertiary-stage syphilis. All experts were agreed that such patients are never cured. The doctors who examined the plaintiff differed on whether the marks found on his body were syphilitic in origin. Dr. K. K. Chatterjee was the one who was certain that they were. He, thought Lodge, "was less than frank with the other doctors and with the court. He went to find syphilis and interpreted almost everything he found as proof of syphilis. Whether he gave deliberately false evidence, or whether he was a bigoted enthusiast who found syphilis in every unexplained mark on the human body, may be arguable, but there is material on record to justify the less charitable of these views." But even if the marks on the plaintiff's body were syphilitic, they were trivial. Given the seriousness of the second kumar's disease, and given the plaintiff's claim that he was not treated for syphilis after 1909, it was impossible that these would be the only marks left on his body. "The evidence regarding syphilis is almost conclusive, in my opinion, to show that plaintiff is not Ramendra Narayan Roy."

The final conclusion of Justice Lodge on the issue of physical resemblance, which the trial judge had decided in favor of the plaintiff, was the following.

When it is realised that conspirators would not choose an impostor at random, but would look for a man of the right height and colouring, these particular details [of similarity] lose their significance. Irregular scars on the ankles of people who go about barefooted, cannot be uncommon. If the fact that Ramendra Narayan Roy had such a scar was notorious, this scar on the plaintiff might have been caused after he was selected and before he was put forward definitely as the Kumar.

The only really striking coincidence, therefore, is the scaly feet; and this is more than outweighed by the difference in the colour of the eyes and the extremely uncertain and trivial indications of syphilis on the person of the plaintiff.

. . . I hold that the comparison demonstrates almost conclusively that the two persons are not the same.[15]

MENTAL RESEMBLANCE

It was alleged that the defense did not seriously try to test the mind of the plaintiff on the ground that he had been tutored. Correspondingly, the plaintiff could also take the plea that his mysterious loss of memory prevented him from remembering a lot of things. In fact, Justice Lodge noted that the rival positions on any question of the plaintiff's memory were as follows:

[T]he plaintiff's counsel can and did argue:
1. If the answer is right, this proves memory;
2. If the answer is wrong, this proves there has been no tuition;
3. If the answer is "I don't know", this is explained by the loss of memory.
On the other hand, the defendants' counsel can and did argue:
1. If the answer is right, this shows tuition or acquired knowledge;
2. If the answer is wrong, this proves imposture;
3. If the answer is "I don't know", this is proof either of imposture or forget-fulness.

Whether the learned counsel for the defense was right or wrong in the attitude he adopted is of little consequence now. It may be that he missed opportunities of proving that plaintiff was an impostor: we are not entitled to assume that plaintiff would have given (if further cross-examined) additional proof of his identity. Plaintiff must convince the court of his identity from the evidence on record, not from the evidence which he might have given.

The evidence showed that even in 1933, twelve years after his appearance in Dhaka as a sannyasi and after twelve years of living in a Bengali family, the plaintiff was still speaking Bengali with a marked Hindi accent, forming sentences that were grammatically more Hindi than Bengali and mispronouncing the Bengali names of even his own friends and acquaintances. "Is it reasonable to suppose that the Englishman who went to Germany at the age of 25 and returned home after 12 years in that country, would continue throughout his life to pronounce William as Wilhelm?"

The plaintiff also claimed that he was unable to count, and witnesses were produced to establish that the second kumar could not count. Thus, one witness told a story of how the second kumar could read the value of cards but could not compute the value of the tricks. Yet in his own deposition, the plaintiff talked of fourteen or fifteen elephants, fifteen or sixteen pairs of peacocks, and forty or fifty horses. This showed, said Justice Lodge, "that he was familiar with the numbers and understood their meaning. It is perfectly clear that his statement that he could not count, even from 1 to 10, is untrue, and that he was avoiding the pronunciation of the numerals." The suggestion, one must say, was a little strange, considering that it was never disputed that the plaintiff spoke with a Hindustani accent, so that it is mysterious what would have been lost if he pronounced the numerals with the same accent.

Justice Lodge was also convinced from the evidence that the second kumar was familiar with the game of polo. "It is not unreasonable to suppose that during the years that elapsed between his supposed death and the examination of the plaintiff in the witness box, he would forget the lesser details of the game, the English terms and rules regarding fouls and crossing. But it is difficult to believe that his mind would become a perfect blank on the subject." On racing, the plaintiff's evidence "was that of a man entirely ignorant of racing, pretending to a knowledge he did not possess and making foolish guesses in answer to the questions asked. The evidence was essentially false evidence." On shooting, the evidence "revealed a complete ignorance of guns and shooting, and not merely ignorance of a few English terms. . . . I find it almost impossible to reconcile the ignorance displayed in this cross-examination with the known history of Ramendra Narayan Roy."[16]

As far as the evidence on handwriting was concerned, Justice Lodge thought it "in the highest degree undesirable" for the expert S. C. Chowdhury to agree to give his opinion to both the plaintiff and the defendants. This conduct was "so suspicious" that Lodge refused to consider his evidence given in court. But Chowdhury had also given his opinion earlier in 1932 to the Court of Wards, in which he had noted the differences between the two sets of signatures belonging to the second kumar and the plaintiff but had concluded that they were by the same person; the differences were caused by age or disease. Justice Lodge went into the differences himself, and concluded that Chowdhury's opinion was "guesswork of the wildest description." Lodge also thought that the fact that the plaintiff could only sign his name, with some resemblance to the signature of Ramendra Narayan, without being able to recognise or write the alphabet, showed that he had been taught to replicate the signature but not taught to write, since he was then likely to acquire a handwriting quite different from that of the Kumar. "[T]here is nothing in the handwriting of the plaintiff establishing his identity with Ramendra Narayan Roy, and there is one feature at least which suggests that the ability to write at all has been acquired since 1921."[17]

There were many witnesses who claimed the plaintiff had recognised them. "In the present case," argued Justice Lodge, "we have to consider the possibility of the plaintiff being an impostor assisted by a group of conspirators who were well aware of the imposture, and who were alert to assist plaintiff in his attempt to persuade people generally that he was Ramendra Narayan Roy. The evidence that plaintiff apparently recognised a large number of people would have no value, if it were shewn that the circumstances were such that he might have done so on instructions from a fellow conspirator." Examining the evidence, Lodge was "not satisfied that there was genuine recognition in any case." Continuing in his characteristic style of propounding his opinion without giving any reasons, he said: "Some of them were apparently convinced that there was no opportunity for other persons to inform plaintiff about their identity, but I am not satisfied that there was any sufficient reason for such conviction."

CONCLUSION ON IDENTITY

"I am satisfied," concluded Justice Lodge, "that the plaintiff is an impostor, supported by Jyotirmoyee Devi and others in the full knowledge that he is an impostor." The defendants had attempted to prove that the plaintiff was in actual fact a man called Mal Singh from Aujla village in Punjab. They presented a witness who claimed to be Dharamdas, the guru of the plaintiff. It was alleged by the plaintiff's side that he was not who he claimed to be, although it was significant, thought Lodge, that the plaintiff did not disown him in court. "Such a denial would have carried some weight, as a court would hesitate to believe that a *chela* would deny the identity of his own *guru*." It was also clear that the defendants produced a wrong photograph in court in place of the one that had been identified by the guru Dharamdas in Amritsar in 1921.

> I am inclined to hold, though with some hesitation, that the witness examined in court was the true Dharam Das, and was the same man who was examined by Lieut. Raghubir Singh in the Punjab in 1921. My hesitation is due to the fact that I find the evidence of the witness unconvincing in the extreme, but whether this unconvincing evidence proves the fact that the witness was not telling the truth, or merely that witness was a poor witness, I am not certain. The other evidence to prove that plaintiff is Mal Singh of Aujla is contradictory and unconvincing.
>
> The result is that I am inclined to the view that plaintiff is a Punjabee, but I am not satisfied that he was formerly Mal Singh of Aujla.

... In my opinion, the appeal should be allowed with costs: the judgment and decree of the original court should be set aside, and the suit dismissed with costs. (718–21)

BISWAS, J. AND LODGE, J. ON COSTELLO, J.

The special bench constituted for this case by Chief Justice Derbyshire consisted of three judges. The score was now 1–1 and Costello's judgment could break the tie. He had sent his judgment by mail. But would it count? The other two judges would have to decide that.

On August 29, 1940, Justice Biswas stated in court his views on the matter. He said that before he left for England, Justice Costello had been told by Biswas and Lodge what their conclusions were on the case. Costello had not formed a final opinion at that time. Lodge had finished writing his judgment and had sent a copy to Costello in England in December 1939. Biswas had taken longer to write his judgment, but had also sent it in instalments by air mail to Costello.

Before Costello, J. left for England, I placed him in full possession of the conclusion I had reached in the case as a whole, tentative, of course, as it was at the time, and equally did my learned brother Lodge, J. intimate to him the opinion he had formed. Our learned senior, however, did not indicate to us which way he was inclined or how he proposed to dispose of the appeal, and we broke up in this state of uncertainty, no *final* decision, whether by way of agreement or disagreement, having been reached as a result of our joint discussions.

This was unfortunate, as Lodge, J. and I happened to differ in our conclusions. . . .

Though no final decision was reached at a joint conference in the sense I have indicated, before Costello, J. left for England, I should perhaps be justified in saying, judging from the indications he had given while here, that his views, tentative as they were, were in accord with the conclusions I had come to and have since expressed in my judgment.

The fact that Lodge, J. and I have not found it possible to agree undoubtedly lends a special importance to the opinion of Costello, J., as it should have for this reason a determining effect on the result of the appeal. Not as a matter of form, but as a matter of substance, therefore, it is essential to consider if that opinion should not have been formed and expressed at a final conference with his colleagues.

Justice Biswas then described the principle that had been established in the Calcutta High Court that for a final judgment of the court, "there must have been a final meeting and consideration by all the judges who heard the case as to what their judgment was to be." The question now was: since there was no final discussion among the three judges on the conclusions they had individually reached, should the judgment of Costello be accepted as valid? Biswas stated his views: "if I am right in believing, as I do, that Costello, J.'s tentative views were in accord with those I have expressed, *and if it turns out now he has since revised his opinions,* the absence of an opportunity by further discussion and argument to have influenced his final judgment would indeed be a matter of consequence, affecting the final result of the appeal. In that case, . . . it would not be a matter to be brushed aside as a mere technicality, but be an objection striking at the foundation of the so-called judgment, or opinion, as I should prefer to call it." Biswas added that unlike Lodge or himself, Costello did not have with him in England the twenty-six volumes of evidence when he wrote his judgment.

It was true that to provide for a contingency such as this, the Calcutta High Court had recently framed a new rule that allowed a judge to pronounce the judgment of another judge if the latter was prevented from doing so himself by absence or any other reason. But the question, Justice Biswas reiterated, was not whether the judgment could be pronounced, but whether it would be a valid judgment, as distinct from a mere opinion. "Having considered the matter carefully, I should say, as at present advised, that the answer to this question should be in the negative. The opinion of Costello, J. should in that event be excluded from consideration, and . . . the present appeal should be disposed of on the basis of the opinions of the remaining members of the Bench."[18] If that were to happen, the two judges of the High Court having disagreed, the decision of the lower court would stand.

Lodge disagreed with Biswas's view. It was true, he said, that no final discussion was held between the three judges on their conclusions.

> But, on the other hand, throughout the long hearing of the appeal we had numerous opportunities of discussing the various points in issue. On each day of the hearing before the morning and afternoon sittings we discussed these matters again and again, and it was soon apparent which portions of the cases of the parties each of us could accept without difficulty, and which portions were more difficult of acceptance. I am unable to agree with my learned brother Biswas, J. that the views of our learned brother Costello, J., as tentatively expressed, were in accord with those expressed in the judgment already read out by my learned brother. . . .
>
> The impression left on my mind when our learned brother Costello, J. left for England was that if he could persuade himself to accept plaintiff's version and plaintiff's evidence on a few matters which we had discussed, he would have no difficulty in deciding the appeal in plaintiff's favour. If, on the other hand, he found these obstacles insuperable, he would have to decide against plaintiff.

On the question whether Costello's judgment should be accepted as valid, Lodge felt that the matter should be decided by the judge himself and not by the other judges.

> In the present case our learned brother Costello, J. has sent out his written judgment with instructions that it be read out on his behalf in his absence as his judgment in the case. Obviously, therefore, our learned brother has come to the conclusion that he is entitled to deliver his judgment in this manner. In my opinion, when one member of a bench of judges chooses a particular method of delivering his judgment, his colleagues on the bench are not entitled to sit in judgment on him and decide whether or not his method of delivering judgment is a proper one. We, as his colleagues on the bench, are bound, in my opinion, to treat a judgment so delivered as a valid judgment, unless and until a superior court should decide otherwise.
>
> If, however, I am called upon to express any opinion in the matter, I must hold that the judgment is a valid judgment.

The only serious point here was that there had been no final discussion among the three judges. But if this argument was accepted, Lodge observed, all three judgments would have to be considered null and void.

> In my opinon, it is for each judge to decide for himself whether he had discussed the matter sufficiently; and if one judge chooses to express a final decision, his brother is not entitled to insist on further discussion with the object of persuading the former to change his mind. . . .
>
> In the result, therefore, I hold that the judgment of Costello, J. which we are about to read is a valid judgment. If the conclusions arrived at in that judgment agree with those expressed by my learned brother Biswas, J., then, in my opinion, the appeal will stand dismissed. If, on the other hand, those conclusions agree with the conclusions expressed by me, the appeal will have to be allowed, with the suit dismissed.[19]

Chapter Eighteen

THE DECISION

Bᴇғᴏʀᴇ he was appointed to the Calcutta High Court in 1926, Sir Leonard Costello was a barrister in England. Like A. N. Chaudhuri, he had a law degree from Cambridge. Early in his career, he had earned some reputation for his knowledge of business law and was invited by the Society of Engineers in London to deliver a set of lectures on *The Law Relating to Engineering*.[1] He also authored a book on the Profiteering Act, and a particularly successful one, running into several editions, called *The Pocket Law Lexicon*.[2] Before coming to India, Costello was in 1923–1924 the Liberal member of Parliament from Huntingdownshire. In Calcutta, his reputation among nationalist Indian lawyers of the High Court was that of a die-hard of the old school who would not tolerate criticism of the government. A particularly celebrated case involved the application of the draconian Indian Press (Emergency Powers) Act 1931 to the *Ananda Bazar Patrika* of Calcutta. This was when Sir John Anderson was in Bengal, devoting his legendary administrative abilities to the task of putting down the "terrorist menace." The act empowered the administration to forfeit the deposit money of a vernacular newspaper for publishing material considered prejudicial to government. In the *Ananda Bazar* case, the two Indian judges—Sir Manmatha Nath Mukherjee and Sarat Kumar Ghosh—set aside the orders of forfeiture, but Costello strongly supported the executive action.[3]

On August 29, 1940, Justice Charu Chandra Biswas began to read out—with some anxiety, one imagines, given his differences with Justice Lodge—the judgment of Sir Leonard Costello on the case of the Bhawal sannyasi.

Gᴇɴᴇʀᴀʟ Rᴇᴍᴀʀᴋs ᴏɴ ᴛʜᴇ Cᴀsᴇ

This appeal arises out of a suit which, beyond doubt, is one of the most interesting and remarkable that ever came before a court of law in this country or indeed in any other. The strange and romantic story told by the plaintiff; the complexity and diversity of the facts to be investigated; the volume of the evidence; the number of witnesses examined; and the time occupied by the trial—all combined to make it a case which, it is no exaggeration to say, is unique in legal annals. (725)[4]

FIGURE 12. L.W.J. Costello

But there were several features of the case that were undesirable. There had clearly been an attempt by the Court of Wards administration to pressure witnesses within the jurisdiction of the Bhawal estate. Many crucial documents were not made available to the court, and in one instance in particular, a false photograph was produced. By the same token, documents belonging to the defendants "found their way into the possession of the plaintiff in a way both mysterious and unexplained." It was also obvious "that the case which was eventually made in the course of the hearing on behalf of the plaintiff was not fully prepared, or even in detail decided upon, before the actual trial began." The trial judge, thought Costello, was right in remarking that "the evidence was not shaping the case, but the case the evidence." As a result, there was much irrelevant matter introduced in the trial that had nothing to do with the case as it was ultimately argued. "[W]hat is far worse, in the course of the cross-examination of more than one of the witnesses, questions were put casting reflections upon their moral character and behaviour and making suggestions or insinuations with regard to their private lives, all of which questions were in the highest degree scandalous. . . . It ought never to have been permitted by the learned judge, for not only was it reprehensible in itself, but in all probability it had the effect of causing persons of some position and standing in life to evince a reluctance, or even refuse altogether, to come to court and give testimony in the witness box. (757)

However, Justice Costello observed, the strictures and criticisms made by A. N. Chaudhuri, counsel for the defendants, against the manner of the judgment of the lower court were "unjustifiable and regrettable." Judge Pannalal Basu, thought Costello, had "expressed himself throughout the judgment in clear, concise and unmistakable terms and in admirable language." Moreover, Chaudhuri was not inclined to read the judgment "in the way a book would normally be read, namely, by starting at the beginning and proceeding page by page to the end." He had preferred to pick out passages in isolation. If one read the judgment "in the same train of thought in which it was written," one would not find any of the defects Chaudhuri had complained about (760, 787).

Noting the differences with the Tichborne case, Justice Costello observed that in the Bhawal case, the plaintiff himself did not initially come forward to claim the property but was only persuaded to do so by others. Moreover, it was not a case of disappearance and presumed death; here a death was supposed to have occurred and the body said to have been cremated. Consequently, the identity question was inevitably tied up with the question of whether the second kumar had in fact died and his body been cremated. In other words, Costello was arguing that the issue was not just one of proving identity as sameness but something additional—establishing narrative identity through the period 1909 to 1921. That is to say, even if it was granted that most people had recognized the plaintiff and had come to accept him as Ramendra Narayan, it would still be necessary to explain the Darjeeling incidents and prove the plaintiff's story during the intervening years.

The story itself was "one of the most extraordinary, and indeed fantastic, that any court of law has been asked to accept and believe." And yet, on the whole, it was fairly cohesive and consistent, and the successive chapters might be called "macabre, mediaeval and romantic." But if the story was actually false, then it was "one which has been conceived, elaborated and invested with a wealth of imaginative detail and embroidery, and then supported with all appropriate evidence, concocted and collected with a foresight and skill which far transcend anything to be found in any of the ordinary run of false cases, which—one regrets to say—from time to time are brought before the courts in this country. In short, the plaintiff's story, if false, is one of the most gigantic impostures ever foisted upon a credulous and emotional public" (788).

Justice Costello, however, noted that the appellate court ought not to make sweeping judgments on the credibility of witnesses based only on the printed record. Perhaps alluding to the attitude of someone like Justice Lodge, Costello said: "in my opinion, a court of appeal should be very chary of interfering with the decision of a lower court upon a matter of the mere credibility of this witness or that, and still more chary of a wholesale discarding or disbelieving of large bodies of witnesses, however improbable the story they tell may seem to be" (787).

Like Lodge before him, Costello chose to reverse the order of treatment of the trial court's judgment and considered first the so-called Darjeeling chapter.

Illness and Supposed Death

Two crucial questions were: what was the kumar's illness in Darjeeling and what was the time of his alleged death? Of the evidence offered, Costello was quick to remark that "Crawford's certificate ought never to have been given." No one explained why Calvert should have taken the trouble to write in his own hand a lengthy condolence letter to Ranendra Narayan, a man he did not know. "It is a remarkable circumstance," commented Costello, "that the language of the letter is scarcely of the kind that one would expect from the pen of an English professional man." All Calvert could say in his examination was that he wrote the letter at the instance of someone from Step Aside. Calvert in his testimony also appeared to support the idea that he had treated the patient in Darjeeling for fourteen days when this was clearly not true.

The trial judge did not find evidence to support the plaintiff's charge that Satyendra Nath Banerjee and Ashutosh Dasgupta had conspired to poison him. Costello agreed: "it seems to me that upon the evidence which was before the court, the learned judge's conclusions are such that it is not possible for this court to hold that he was not right." Satyendra Banerjee was at the time "to all intents and purposes a mere hanger-on at Jaidebpur; a parasite on the estate whose interests lay wholly in keeping in the good graces of Ramendra Narayan Roy and his two brothers." He could hardly have foreseen that he might be able to lure his sister away from Jaidebpur and, following the rapid deaths of her brothers-in-law, gain control of her property.

Costello did not discuss at all the symptoms and cause of the kumar's illness. He fully accepted the trial judge's finding that it was not biliary colic, but possibly enteritis aggravated by accidental arsenical poisoning.

As far as the time of death was concerned, Justice Costello was not convinced that Calvert was present at Step Aside from the afternoon until midnight on the day the kumar died. In his letter to Lindsay, Calvert mentioned that "on my last visit," Dr. Nibaran Sen was present. "If, as Bibhabati Devi states, the doctor had been in the house for such a protracted period, the expression 'on my last visit' strikes me as being singularly inappropriate." Moreover, it was "in the highest degree unlikely" that an obscure doctor like Dr. B. B. Sarkar would be present at Step Aside for "several hours," as he mentions in his diary, if Dr. Calvert and Dr. Sen "were also in continuous attendance throughout the evening." Finally, there was the telegram of death that was never produced. After considering all the evidence, the trial judge had come to the conclusion that it was sent at night—possibly after midnight—and it said that the kumar had expired in the evening. The judge had also accepted the evidence of the Maitra group of witnesses: Justice Costello did not find "sufficient grounds for disagreeing with the learned judge in his general conclusions with regard to this evidence."[5]

Did it rain that night? The evidence, thought Costello, "was not sufficiently definite and unequivocal" to rule out the testimony of those witnesses who said they had attended the evening cremation and that it rained at the cremation ground. It was alleged that some witnesses claimed to have taken shelter in a building that did not exist in 1909. "It seems to me not unnatural that persons who were going to be witnesses in the case . . . should go up to Darjeeling and go over the ground to refresh their memory, and in that event they might quite honestly assume that some building they found near about the scene must have been the one in which they took shelter all those years before, not knowing that the particular building was not in existence at the material time. I do not think it can reasonably be held that because a witness or witnesses sheltered, or rather say they sheltered, in a building which had not come into existence at the time, that altogether refutes their evidence."

Justice Costello concluded that the trial judge's findings on the evening cremation were "quite reasonable, and certainly not so unwarranted as to require that we should characterise them as wrong." Costello, in fact, summarized the findings up to this point.

[T]he illness of which Ramendra Narayan Roy was suffering was not biliary colic, but an inflammatory condition of the intestines due to the introduction of a chemical irritant in the shape of arsenic, and that condition was such and the symptoms were of such a character that there were indications that "death" must have occurred at or about 7 P.M., in which event the body would certainly have been carried out for cremation the same evening. The direct evidence that the death was announced before dinner time, and that there was an evening cremation procession, was not displaced by any of the considerations put forward by the defendants and urged on their behalf as negativing these facts.[6]

THE MORNING CREMATION

The problem before the court, argued Costello, was as follows: "Was the positive evidence as to the morning proceedings and the identity of the corpse which was burnt on the 9th May sufficiently definite and reliable as to require a finding that it was none other than Ramendra Narayan Roy that was cremated on the 9th May, and so there never could have been an evening procession at all?" In other words, if there was reasonable evidence of an attempted evening cremation, then it would necessarily cast a shadow of suspicion on the morning cremation. Unless, therefore, the evidence was quite definite that the body cremated in the morning was that of the second kumar, the suspicion would remain and the plaintiff's story would not be disproved.

An important witness for the plaintiff was Ram Singh Subba. Costello saw no reason to suppose that the trial judge did not conscientiously examine the credibility of this witness. "It was urged on behalf of the appellants that the witness was a deliberate perjurer. I am unable to agree with that contention." On the other hand, given the other evidence on the morning procession, the trial judge was justified in deciding that R. N. Banerjee, witness for the defendants, was not present at all at the morning cremation. Examining the evidence as a whole, Judge Basu had come to the conclusion that the body which was taken out in the morning was lying in a room downstairs at the Step Aside. The significance of this fact was that if the body was not one brought down from the upper floor, then it added substance to the argument made by the plaintiff's side that it had been secretly brought into one of the lower rooms of the house in the course of the night. "On a review of all the relevant evidence," said Justice Costello, "I see no reason for disagreeing wih the finding of the learned judge."[7]

THE RESCUE

The crucial witness here was Darshandas, and the trial judge was clearly impressed by his credibility. The story was so improbable that it could scarcely have been invented, and if invented, it would not have withstood cross-examination in the witness box.

In my opinion, the fact that the bearing and demeanour of Darsan Das created so favourable an impression in the court below renders it extremely difficult for this court to take a view of his evidence contrary to that of the learned judge. No doubt, there is much in the circumstances of the rescue—as, for instance, the question of why the sannyasis did not make their presence known and restore the "dead" man to his friends when they returned to the cremation ground, and why did they retain control of the man they had rescued from an untimely death. Some explanation of all this was, however, given by Darsan Das, and having regard to the known peculiarities of sannyasis and their kind, it may perhaps be not altogether incredible.[8]

On the Darjeeling chapter as a whole, then, the trial judge had definitely found that the second kumar did not die but was in a comatose state, that his apparent death occurred in the early evening, that his body was taken to the cremation ground but not cremated, that the body cremated on May 9 was not that of the kumar but of someone else, and that the plaintiff's story of his rescue by sannyasis was substantially true. "[A]s in my opinion, the learned judge in no way misdirected himself or failed to give adequate and proper and independent consideration to the evidence, it would not be right for this court to interfere, whatever might have been our own view of the case, had we been trying it at first instance. It may perhaps be that time was on the side of the plaintiff, and that had the issues in controversy between the parties been adjudicated upon at an early stage, the result might have been different, but as to that, we cannot speculate. We can only adjudicate upon the matter upon the basis of the evidence on record" (821).

This was a rather extraordinary statement. What did Costello mean by it? Did he simply mean that since the judges of the High Court were not conducting the trial, and therefore did not have the advantage of watching and hearing the witnesses themselves, they should not second-guess the trial judge on the credibility of the witnesses and the relative importance he had assigned to the different testimonies? Costello clearly disapproved of the attitude taken by Lodge in this matter. The disapproval already represented quite a significant shift in position for a British judge of a colonial high court, for Costello was conceding to an Indian judge of a district court an autonomy of judgment and an awareness of his responsiblity that few others of his kind would have done. But perhaps Costello was also saying something else. How was it that "time was on the side of the plaintiff"? Was it just that because so many years had passed since the incidents in Darjeeling, it had now become difficult to disprove his admittedly fantastic story? Or did Costello mean that the conditions under which the trial had taken place and the appeal heard—in the middle and late 1930s—were a circumstance in the plaintiff's favor? Was Costello perhaps suggesting that had the case come to court, say, ten or fifteen years earlier, the trial judge might have treated the evidence differently, or responded differently to the conditions both within and outside the courtroom? We should not make too much of a single remark, even when it seems pregnant with mysterious meanings. But it is tempting to speculate that Costello, sitting at home in England in the middle of air raid sirens, the shriek of German bombers, and the crackle of anti-aircraft gunfire, could only think of an unseen courtroom in Dhaka as a rather distant place whose affairs were best left to the charge of the local man on the spot. Perhaps he was experiencing, we might say with a short leap of the historical imagination, a moment of decolonization. In that case, time was most definitely on the side of the plaintiff.

The Intervening Years

During the hearing of the appeal, I formed the impression that if the defendants-appellants could not succeed in satisfying the court that Ramendra Narayan Roy actually died and was cremated in Darjeeling, they would have great difficulty in displacing the evidence on record touching the question of identity, and that once the difficulty arising from the existence of the morning cremation had been surmounted, the path of the plaintiff would be comparatively easy, having regard to the overwhelming evidence he had been able to put before the court below on the matter of physical identity and the recognition by the relations and others.

An important feature of the plaintiff's story here was his alleged loss of memory. A mass of expert evidence was offered in the trial on "abstruse questions of psychology, morbid or otherwise," but Justice Costello did not think it was helpful. The only relevant question was whether one must rule out the story because it contradicted some law of nature, in the same way "as you can exclude his flying in the air by gravitation." The trial judge was entirely right in concluding that the story could not be ruled out on such grounds.

The plaintiff had apparently given on different occasions different accounts of his life from 1909 to 1920. This did not necessarily mean, thought Costello, that the main framework of the story was altogether untrue.

Was the mind of the plaintiff unrecognizably different from that of the second kumar? An attempt was made in the trial to set up Phani Bhusan Banerjee as a sort of gauge or measuring stick so that he could say, "What I know, Ramendra himself knew." Justice Costello was appalled by Phani Babu's "lesson book." "A more bare-faced and disgraceful exhibition of an attempt to coach a witness can rarely have been seen in any court of law. . . . One has only to compare the entries in Phani's book with some of the questions put in cross-examination of the plaintiff to understand how the design was intended to operate." The defendants repeatedly pointed to certain stupid and ridiculous answers given by the plaintiff on the subjects of racing and shooting. Costello thought that if anyone wanted to prepare an impostor for the part of the second kumar, they would have instructed him especially on racing and shooting, since those were the obvious areas where he was likely to be cross-examined. "To my mind, there is no doubt that the image of Ramendra Narayan Roy created or sought to be resurrected by the defendants' witnesses . . . was altogether exaggerated and embellished. . . . I am quite clear in my own mind that the plaintiff in the box displayed no greater ignorance and presented no more ridiculous a figure than one would expect Ramendra Narayan Roy to have done after years of wandering in the wilderness, if one may so put it, shut off from all ordinary contacts and social intercourse and amenities."

The case of the defendants was that after the arrival of the sadhu in Jaidebpur in 1921, a conspiracy was hatched by Jyotirmayi Debi and other members of her family to set up the plaintiff as the second kumar. This conspiracy, argued Justice Costello, "as far as one can see—there is not a scintilla of evidence to indicate anything else—must have been conceived and put into execution within the space of a few days at the uttermost, and when I pointed this out to Mr. Chaudhuri and suggested that the time factor was wholly against him, he was obviously embarrassed and indeed non-plussed, and quite unable to advance any theory, let alone facts, which would overcome this enormous obstacle."[9]

RECOGNITION

"One of the most outstanding of all the remarkable features in the case" was the defense insistence on the utter dissimilarity betweeen the plaintiff and the second kumar. "I have already pointed out how this theory of no resemblance militated against, if not indeed demolished, the idea of a conspiracy on the part of Jyotirmoyee Devi." The defendants tried to modify this extreme position in the later part of the trial and in the course of the appeal. "One suspects that the defendant-appellants had come to realise dimly, if not clearly, the dilemma which seemed likely to embarrass, if not to defeat, them entirely."

Jyotirmayi's evidence was crucial in establishing identity by recognition.

One aspect of the matter which in my mind weighs heavily in favour of the truth of Jyotirmoyee Devi's evidence is this: that if the plaintiff was merely an impostor dishonestly put forward, he did not, be it remembered, in the early stages push himself forward—it would have been just as easy to give one false tale as another, and if Jyotirmoyee Devi were indeed a conspirator, she or those associated with her might have invented a superficially more plausible and credible story of the events in the early days of May. As far as one can see, there is no reason why, if Jyotirmoyee Devi was dishonest, she should not have told a specious tale of instant and unhesitating recognition. In my view, the divergence from what one would expect as the normal tells rather in favour of than against the honesty of the witness.

As for the first rani, Sarajubala Debi, she was, Costello thought, "quite capable of blowing hot and cold as it suited her purpose at the moment." But he found her account of her first meeting with the plaintiff "reasonably convincing." Besides these two ladies, there were sixteen other close relations of Ramendra Narayan who swore to the identity of the plaintiff.

It seems hard to believe that all of these persons could either have deceived themselves into an honest supposed recognition of the plaintiff, or have deliberately brought themselves to give false evidence on his behalf. It is not sufficient, in my opinion, merely to brush their evidence aside, as it were, and stigmatise them either as fools or liars. The immediate circle of Jyotirmoyee Devi might conceivably have been beguiled or persuaded by her into supporting a nefarious scheme, whereby, directly or indirectly, Jyotirmoyee Devi might reap some advantage to herself, which she would be prepared to share with her confederates, but it is difficult to imagine what motive or inducement could so operate in the minds of the less intimate and more distant members of the family as to bring them on the witness box to lend support to a trumped-up case.

Costello also noted the other "truly remarkable feature" that apart from "the thoroughly discredited and rather despicable" Phani Banerjee, no one from the extended Bhawal Raj family came to give evidence against the plaintiff.

Another important witness on recognition was N. K. Nag. "I find myself at a loss to understand," said Costello, "how any outsider could ever have known the details of that particular story, or even if some one had contemporaneously known about it, it would have come back to mind at the crucial moment for the plaintiff to make use of it as a criterion of identity in a so timely and convincing way. I think it is in the highest degree improbable that the plaintiff could have been prepared and coached against the incursion of the doubting Nag." And in a scarcely disguised dig at his brother judge Lodge, Costello refused to accept that Nag could be regarded as an unreliable witness merely because he had described the second kumar as someone who was as fair as a Norwegian.[10]

BIBHABATI

Justice Costello carefully enunciated his assessment of the testimony of Bibhabati Debi. "Mr. Chaudhuri contended that it was unthinkable that an orthodox Brahmin lady would falsely deny her husband, and suggested in effect that widowhood was such an unenviable and almost shameful state that no Hindu woman would wish to remain in it, if there was a possibility of terminating it by acknowledging the lawful hisband, however undesirable and even repulsive a man he might happen to be." Costello did not deny that there was some substance in this argument. Nevertheless, "one has to ask oneself whether the circumstances of the present case were not such that the ordinary canons and obligations of a Hindu marital relationship might not have lost their force. Ramendra Narayan Roy was admittedly a man who in the days before Darjeeling paid little or no attention to his wife, but spent his time with low companions and loose women. He was suffering from a foul disease and was in every way a thoroughly undesirable and unpleasant young man."

Bibhabati was living in Calcutta in affluence and comfort. "She had made a life of her own with her brother and his family, and had long been accustomed to the routine and quietude of widowhood." If it was also argued that she was entirely under her brother's will, then one could easily understand why she would want to refuse to accept her husband.

> It is not necessary, in my opinion, to go so far as to attribute Bibhabati Devi's repudiation of the plaintiff to any deliberate dishonesty on her part. When one recalls the circumstances and facts of the kind of married life Bibhabati Devi had had with Ramendra Narayan Roy, and remembers that she was but a young girl at the time of the events of Darjeeling, it is quite possible to take the view that she may very well have been quite sincere in her belief that the man who in 1921 claimed to be Ramendra Narayan Roy was not her husband—possibly being stimulated to that belief by the attitude adopted by Satyendranath Banerjee towards the plaintiff or by subtle suggestion on his part.
>
> Whichever way one looks at the matter, it is manifest to my mind that both as regards Bibhabati Devi and Satyendranath Banerjee, there exists a motive for a denial of the plaintiff, whereas, as regards many, if not all, of the prominent witnesses on the other side, there was no motive or self-interest to induce them to acknowledge the plaintiff as Ramendra Narayan Roy. (834–36)

Physical Features

The two physical features of the plaintiff that Justice Costello thought were the "most significant pointers" were the scaly ankles and the scar on the left outer ankle. "Both of them are very difficult to account for on the mere basis of pure coincidence." Both the plaintiff and the second kumar had eyes that Bengalis would describe as *kaṭā*. There was a dispute on whether Dr. Caddy had been prompted by the insurance agent when he wrote in his report that the kumar's eyes were "grey." "the learned judge had the advantage of seeing the witnesses, and has drawn an inference which cannot be said to be incompatible with the evidence as recorded. It is, in my opinion, quite possible that as Dr. Caddy had seated himself to write down his opinon on the purely medical aspects of the examination, he was content to trust the observation of the agent for the supplying of the answers to the non-technical questions."

With regard to the marks on plaintiff's body, Justice Costello observed, once again with a possible allusion to Justice Lodge's views, that "it was nobody's case, and it was never suggested by the defendants, that any of the marks were fabricated or faked in any way whatever." It was Lodge who in his judgment had suggested, entirely of his own accord, that the scar on the plaintiff's ankle might have been deliberately produced. Both the second kumar and the plaintiff had a scar on the left ankle. "The coincidence is there, and it certainly tells in the plaintiff's favour."

The scaly feet, it was admitted, was a family peculiarity. It could not be artificially produced. "Taken in conjunction with the coincidence of the ankle scar, it does, in my opinion, carry the plaintiff a very long way indeed."

Another remarkable feature of the case was that the plaintiff actually admitted to having syphilis, "a position no one would willingly adopt unless it was absolutely essential to do so." Of the medical experts, Dr. K. K. Chatterjee was the most convinced that the plaintiff was an old syphilitic; the others were less definite. Costello thought that although Dr. Chatterjee was not quite truthful toward the other doctors examining the plaintiff, the trial judge was justified in placing greater reliance on his testimony because he was the specialist. Taking the medical evidence as a whole, "it certainly would be a fair conclusion to come to, that the medical evidence does not satisfactorily establish that there was no syphilis in the plaintiff."

Justice Costello concurred with the trial judge in his finding that the evidence of the physical features suggested that the plaintiff must be the second kumar himself.[11]

MENTAL IDENTITY

"Much more might have been done," thought Justice Costello, "than was, in fact, done to test the *bona fides* of the plaintiff." He agreed with the trial judge that even if there was tutoring, "the whole memory of the second Kumar" could not have been put into the mind of the plaintiff.

> It cannot be denied that in various respects this case has been mishandled on both sides, and it was no doubt a blunder in tactics as well as being ethically wrong to endeavour to further the plaintiff's case by calling evidence to lend support to the plaintiff's inability or apparent inability to count; but I do not

think the plaintiff's failure to answer the counting questions, put to him, is of any serious consequence. I think it is more than likely that he was being rather stubborn, and in a way aggressive, by way of reaction to the sort of catch questions which from time to time were put to him in cross-examination, and that his refusal to count was not due to ignorance. . . .

I think the learned judge was quite right in thinking that in judging the cross-examination of the plaintiff and the nature of the questions put to him— many of them might not unfairly be described as constituting a species of lo-gomachy rather than a searching of mind or memory—one has to endeavour to consider and appreciate how an illiterate and vacuous mind would be likely to respond to words not known or not familiar to it, or to words taken apart from any context. To put to such a man questions involving puns, or to pass from word to word, from meaning to meaning, would be almost certain to cause him to become confused and unimpressive. . . . I am unable to hold that the learned judges's findings regarding the mind of the plaintiff in relation to knowledge of English and English clothes, sports, billiards, polo and racing are not justified on the evidence before him.

Considering the judgment of the lower court as a whole, Justice Costello had much praise for the logical rigor of Pannalal Basu's presentation of his findings.

Despite the criticisms directed against the judgment of the trial court, it seems to me that the more one looks into it, the more one appreciates the logical working of the learned judge's mind. Throughout the judgment, he is en-deavouring to arrive at the truth, upon the evidence before him, by a series of stages whereby he, step by step, eliminates in turn aspects of the plaintiff's story, each of which might be sufficient to destroy him. . . . [Finally] he reaches the position that he is able to say, "Nothing, in my opinion, can displace the identity, unless it appears that the second Kumar died at Darjeeling, or that the plaintiff is Mal Singh of Aujla, or not a Bengalee at all."

The attempt was made at the trial to prove that the plaintiff was Mal Singh. The evidence of the Lahore witnesses on the description and an-tecedents of Mal Singh were quite inconsistent with those made before Raghubir Singh: "it is perhaps not surprising that the learned counsel for the defendants refrained from putting to the plaintiff, when in the box, that he was Mal Singh of Aujla." Then there was the substituted photograph and the false Dharamdas produced in court. The case that the plaintiff was Mal Singh was not proved. In fact, there was much to suggest that he was Ben-gali. "It seems to me extremely unlikely that if the plaintiff had been unable to speak Bengali, he would have made himself so prominent in May, 1921." Costello also remarked: "As far as my somewhat limited knowledge and experience goes, I should have said that, from my own observations of the plaintiff in court and in my chambers, there was nothing in his appearance that would suggest that he was other than a Bengalee."[12]

CONCLUSION

Justice Costello came to the conclusion "that no sufficient grounds have been made out by the appellants to justify a reversal by this court of the decision of the First Additional Judge of Dacca on the issue of fact." Once again with a thinly veiled reference to the views of his brother judge Lodge, he said: "I would emphasise again that in a case of this kind it is vitally important to guard against the possible influence on the mind of prejudice or instinctive ideas as to the probable merits of a claim of the kind made by the plaintiff. It would be altogether wrong to allow one's judgment to be influenced by any such considerations as—`The sadhu must be an impostor,' 'the plaintiff's story is too preposterous and too absurd to be believed,' 'the whole thing is impossible,' and so on. To do so would be to let suspicion run ahead of the evidence." The case of the defendants could have been better presented and, in general, they might have behaved better. "It may be that the defence was weakened by reason of over-zealousness, maladroitness and indiscretions." The "precipitate" impostor notice, the jāl sadhu order, deliberate intimidations of witnesses, Phani's diary, trying to influence the opinion of the handwriting expert S. C. Chowdhury, the juggling with photographs and putting forward a spurious Dharamdas—all of these detracted from the defense effort. "Moreover, it is possible, I think, that the general attitude of the Court of Wards and its officers in the course of the long years before the trial may have reacted on the minds of the people of Dacca in a way which created not only sympathy for the claimant, but augmented the number of adherents."

In the period between 1921 and 1930, there was, Costello thought, a "standstill war" between the two parties, each side waiting for the other to begin. For whatever reasons, the administration did not confront or prosecute the plaintiff. "As the result of their comparative inaction, the plaintiff was able to consolidate his position and to get his status recognised to such a degree that he was widely received in society, not only in Dacca but in Calcutta." The delay in instituting a suit could not be said to detract from the plaintiff's claim.

"I would add here that I have had the opportunity of reading the greater part of the comprehensive judgment written by my brother Biswas, and I am able to say that I agree with his reasoning generally, and with the conclusions at which he has in consequence arrived." Justice Costello's last pronouncement: "As Mr. Justice Biswas and myself are in agreement, the order of the court must be that the appeal is dismissed with costs" (864–68).

THE DECISION OF THE COURT

Leaving everyone on tenterhooks, the High Court adjourned for vacation without settling the question of whether Costello's text, read out in court, would count as a valid judgment. Biswas and Lodge had disagreed on this point. They announced that they would consider the matter in the light of Costello's stated views and come to a decision when the court reconvened.

More than two months later, on November 25, 1940, the matter was finally settled. Justice Biswas recalled that there were several discussions on the different issues of the appeal among the three judges, although there was no final conference before Costello left, because he had not yet come to a final decision. Biswas's views were that if Costello's decision agreed with his, as he thought it would on the basis of their discussions, then it should be considered a valid judgment. If it did not, then the lack of a final round of discussions would have a material bearing on the final decision of the court and in that event, in the opinion of Biswas, Costello's judgment ought not to be considered as valid. Now that it was known that Costello had come to the same conclusion as Biswas, the issue was clear: Costello's judgment was a valid one. Lodge had taken the position that in this matter, Costello's own views should prevail. Since he had chosen to announce his judgment in this particular form, the other judges should not express any views on the matter. Hence, in his opinion too, Costello's judgment was valid.

The final decision of the High Court was, therefore, that the appeal should be dismissed with costs.[13]

JUDGING THE JUDGES

Historians rarely have the opportunity to experiment with their material. Condemned by time to deal with events that have already happened, they are left with facts that are in principle irreversible and alterable only within the parameters of the historiographical—that is to say, as new narrative constructions of events based on previously unknown facts or on new interpretations of the facts. Beyond this, all that historians can do is speculate with counterfactuals: *if* things had happened not as they did but in some other way, how different would the event have been?

However, in the judicial trial, as the Italian historian Carlo Ginzburg has pointed out, one gets something quite close to "historical experimentation," because here the sources, the facts, the interpretations, the alternative narratives, are forced to confront one another, submit themselves to cross-examination and to the same tests of proof, and emerge as the adjudicated truth.[14] One could, therefore, in principle, take the entire mass of the evidence produced in a trial and, using the methods of the historian, "predict" the theoretically expected result for comparison, as in a laboratory experiment, with the actual judicial verdict.

But there are two different approaches one could take to such an "experiment." One would be to submit the evidence produced in court to tests of proof that are historically appropriate. If we were reconstructing a trial held during the Spanish Inquisition, it would be silly of us to predict its outcome on the basis of criteria of proof that we would expect from our courts today. We would have to "historicize" not only the evidence but the judicial process itself, using our knowledge of the history of Spanish society in that period to reconstruct the ways in which the judges would have reasoned in order to arrive at their decision. The truth we would find here would be, inescapably, a historically relative truth. In the case of the Bhawal sannyasi, then, the historian would have to tell the reader, on the basis of the historical knowledge of late colonial Bengal, how an Indian judge in a district court might be expected to judge the evidence produced before him and how, in turn, the judges of the High Court might look upon that judgment. All "predictions" here would be historically relative.

But is there not another kind of judgment that the historian is also obliged to make? Carlo Ginzburg, in particular, has made a strong plea against avoiding the question of truth in our historical reconstructions.[15] He would have us ask the further question: were the judges right in their conclusion? What can *we* say, on the basis of the evidence of the trial, about the truth of the event being adjudicated? It is a question which, I must confess, I could not resist asking myself during the whole time that I have worked on this book. It is also a question that I fully expect my readers to ask. Notwithstanding the judgments of the courts, they will say, what is our view of the evidence? Was the sannyasi *really* the second kumar of Bhawal?

Let us not shy away from our task. We will, in the remainder of this book, address both sets of questions. First, what were the specific historical conditions of late colonial Bengal that produced the judicial decision in the Bhawal sannyasi case? The answer to this question will have to be built around a political-cultural history of truth. Second, what *was* the truth of the Bhawal sannyasi? The answer here will have to affirm an idea of truth that is not limited by its own conditions of production.

POST-MORTEM

"The case of the defendants could have been better presented," thought Costello. If it was, could the result have been different? Quite probably. In the first place, there was the great blunder of the "utter dissimilarity" theory, commented upon by every judge, including Lodge. A. N. Chaudhuri said in the High Court that he did not want to concede anything to the judge in the mufassil, presumably implying that he did not believe that a subordinate judge of a district court would be capable of appreciating a more subtle argument. However, the strange fact is that, judging by the standards of the Tichborne case that was repeatedly alluded to as the most proximate legal precedent, it was not such a foolish argument after all. Jorge Luis Borges, in his retelling of the Tichborne story, describes thus the reasoning of Ebenezer Bogle, the man who, in a flash of divine inspiration one afternoon in Sydney, decided to put up Thomas Castro, alias Arthur Orton, as the long-lost Roger Tichborne: "Bogle knew that a perfect facsimile of the beloved Roger Charles Tichborne was impossible to find; he knew as well that any similarities he might achieve would only underscore certain inevitable differences. He therefore gave up the notion of likeness altogether. He sensed that the vast ineptitude of his pretense would be a convincing proof that this was no fraud, for no fraud would ever have so flagrantly flaunted features that might so easily have convinced. We should also not overlook the all-powerful collaboration of time: the vicissitudes of fortune, and fourteen years of antipodean life, can change a man."[16] Chaudhuri, we can be sure, knew all of the details of the Tichborne trial. If "utter dissimilarity" was a feature of the claimant in that case, could it not be the same here? If those who had put up Thomas Castro as Roger Tichborne could hope to get away with a flabby and dull claimant in place of the slim and cultured original, why couldn't those who had put up the plaintiff expect to fool people by displaying a bloated Punjabi wrestler in place of the well-polished Bengal aristocrat?

The difficulty was that it is only when one proceeds from the assumption, or at least a strongly held suspicion, that one is dealing with a case of fraud that one can perceive such a subtle and diabolical plot. Once the plot is perceived, every dissimilar feature becomes a proof of imposture. This is what happened at the Tichborne trials. This is what Chaudhuri must have expected to happen in Dhaka. Unfortunately, if one proceeds from the opposite assumption, the conditions of plausibility are reversed. If there is a strong suspicion that the man is the same, every item of similarity becomes evidence of identity. People begin to say, "No trickster could possibly produce a double who is so strikingly similar to the original. He must be the same man." Chaudhuri, Lodge, Borges (by another stroke of inexplicable coincidence, Borges wrote his story in Buenos Aires exactly when the Bhawal sannyasi trial began in Dhaka—in 1933–1934)—all of them were persuaded that they were dealing with an impostor. Hundreds of other people in Bhawal were not so persuaded; the similarities confirmed their suspicion that the second kumar had returned. If instead of the "utter dissimilarity" argument, the defendants had admitted that there was enough of a similarity to mislead a lot of people, they might have been able to avoid the impact of the mountain of evidence on superficial recognition and focused attention on the finer details of physical and mental identity.

Added to this was the refusal to examine the plaintiff on his memory. Admittedly, it was not an easy task to set tests of memory that would beat the efforts of the plaintiff's coaches (assuming, of course, that he had them). But by virtually not attempting the task at all, the impression was created that the defendants were shying away from the memory test because they were afraid the plaintiff would succeed.

The second failure was the futile attempt to prove that the plaintiff was Mal Singh, including the fiasco involving the false Dharamdas and the substituted photograph. In theory, the defendants did not need to show who the plaintiff really was, as long as they were able to disprove his claim to being Ramendra Narayan Roy. But having decided to use the police reports on the Punjab inquiry and then making a mess of the corroboration of the story in court, the defense certainly spoiled its own credibility.

The third major failure was the lack of evidence on the alleged conspiracy to put up an impostor. As it turned out, this was an irreducible gap in the defense story; as long as the gap was there, it was simply not credible why and how anyone would hatch such a seemingly impossible plan. Pannalal Basu in the lower court and Biswas and Costello in the High Court could not but be persuaded by the evidence on recognition by Jyotirmayi Debi and the others in and around her family because there was no evidence at all on how the plan to put up a total stranger could have been conceived and laid in the space of four or five days, and how all of the people who claimed to have recognized the plaintiff as the kumar could have profited from the success of the conspiracy. All that Lodge could say was that the absence of evidence of conspiracy was not reason enough to think that there was no conspiracy. But of course, such a crucial absence in the narrative chain was fatal for the plausibility of the story.

It is equally true, however, that there were weak links in the plaintiff's story, as well. The strongest part of the story, undoubtedly, was the evidence on identity—recognition by relatives and close acquaintances and the physical resemblance, including the distinguishing marks. Memory, which philosophers have claimed is the core of personal identity as constituted by psychological continuity, was the least amenable to examination. Lodge put it succinctly when he showed that irrespective of whether the plaintiff answered a memory question correctly or incorrectly or pleaded that he did not know, both sides could claim that it was an answer in their favor. Nevertheless, the correct answers tended to accumulate, and thereby to strengthen the impression that such mental continuity had to be genuine, because surely not all of the questions could have been anticipated and the answers supplied by others. Another point that was also made was that the plaintiff did not appear to be very clever or quickwitted (leading some witnesses to ask if one could expect a raja's son to be such an imbecile!); in that case, could he be expected to digest all the lessons he had been given and produce the right information at the right time?

If one were to take a reductionist view, one could say that once physical and mental identity was proved—either by the fact of social recognition or by an independent assessment of the material evidence—nothing else mattered, because there was no further fact that needed to be proved. The plaintiff had given a story of what happened in Darjeeling and had attempted to prove it. He could claim that this was the story as best as he knew it: clearly, he could have known nothing about the cremations—whether in the evening or in the morning—and recollected only dimly the details of his rescue by the sannyasis. Strictly speaking, therefore, it did not matter if his story of the Darjeeling episode was not fully corroborated, since it could not affect the fact of his identity.

But the reductionist view encounters a serious difficulty when it is faced with a contending narrative based on other facts which, if true, must by implication raise basic doubts about the fact of identity. Such is the narrative of the defendants describing the facts, corroborated by many, of a cremation in broad daylight of a body that they claimed was that of Kumar Ramendra Narayan. If identity proved by recognition and by the physical marks was true, the defendants' story of the morning cremation could not be true at the same time. But since the persuasiveness of the latter story lay in its *narrative* coherence, that was the ground on which it had to be disproved. In other words, faced with a contending narrative, the reductionist could not simply dismiss that story by logical inference from his finding on identity; he had to show that the story was unsustainable in its own terms. This was the thrust of A. N. Chaudhuri's argument against Pannalal Basu's judgment, although both Biswas and Costello thought that Basu was not guilty of this reductionist fallacy.

The point is worth considering a little further. Suppose there was physical evidence of an even more incontrovertible sort available on the sannyasi-kumar's identity. Let us imagine that the second kumar had left thumb impressions on certain documents and these were found to match those of the plaintiff. Or, since we are considering hypothetical situations anyway, imagine that methods of DNA testing were available in the 1930s and samples taken from Ramendra's relatives, or perhaps (why not?) from his own hair found on his durbar or shikar clothes, matched those of the plaintiff. Identity, we would have to say, was now established beyond reasonable doubt. But there was also the story of the cremation and, let us suppose, there was not a shred of evidence to suggest in any way that the body was not that of Ramendra Narayan. Would it not produce a deep mystery? The reductionist could say with justification that all of those who believed they had cremated the second kumar had been, in some unexplained way, misled, because, of course, the DNA test had to be conclusive. But those who had attended the cremation could also suggest that perhaps the test had not been done properly, that perhaps the samples were not correct, or even perhaps that some day science might discover that DNA tests are not conclusive after all, because how could they be asked to believe that they had cremated the wrong person?[17]

Faced with a contending narrative, therefore, even the reductionist will have to abandon the path of logical inference and propose a narrative that is consistent with his finding of identity. In other words, in order to persuade, he must construct a narrative of his own that explains how the processionists in Darjeeling could have carried and cremated, either by design or by genuine mistake, a body that was not of the second kumar. Were the plaintiff's lawyers able to do this? One curious feature of their witnesses was that no one who had claimed to have gone on the evening cremation was present at the morning one, so that no one, it seems, raised any question at the time as to why the same body should be cremated twice. The second gigantic gap was the lack of a credible explanation of how, and by whom, another body was produced within a couple of hours in the middle of the night to substitute for the missing body of the kumar. As Lodge pointed out, if there was a conspiracy here, no evidence had been produced to show who had planned it and how the plan was carried out, although he was wrong in going on to argue that the question was one of comparing the probability of success of one conspiracy with that of another. Clearly, without the cremation of a substituted body during the day on May 9, the *narrative identity* of the plaintiff could not be credibly established; yet the plaintiff's case finally was that this must be considered established by logical inference from the fact of identity.

If the defense case was imperfectly presented, its cause was served even less by the one judgment that went in its favor. Compared to the comprehensiveness and rigor of the judgments of Pannalal Basu and Charu Chandra Biswas, Lodge's judgment was sloppy, peremptory, and sometimes almost whimsical in its acceptance or rejection of this or that piece of evidence. Reading the judgments of the Indian judges, one cannot miss the sense of their being acutely aware of their interlocutors; they wrote as though they would have to answer for the slightest error of fact or slip of logic. Lodge wrote with the nonchalance of someone whose word was final; he did not appear to be used to having his judgment subjected to questioning.

An Excursus on Identity and Truth

It is clear that if a different set of lawyers had prepared a different case, if that case had come up before a different set of judges at a different time, the Bhawal sannyasi case might have been decided differently. In one sense, this point is trivial. Judicial truth, we know, is always produced within the limits of a particular judicial discourse. The British Indian judicial system, like all modern judicial systems, thought of itself as an objective process designed to produce the objective truth, in exactly the same way that the procedures of modern science are meant to produce objective knowledge. The truth, or so at least it is claimed, did not depend on the particular lawyer or judge in court, just as it did not depend on the particular experimenter in the laboratory. If the judgment was right, then anyone looking at the same evidence would have to come to the same conclusion, just as if a scientific theory was right, anyone repeating the same experiment would necessarily get the same results. Although this is the discursive foundation of law, however, the judicial truth, we know, is also produced within specific institutional boundaries. Here it is acknowledged, even within the judicial process, that individuals could make a difference, that judges have their biases and prejudices—that they could make mistakes. Hence the system of appeals to a higher court. But no such institutional procedure can be foolproof. Let us suppose that Henderson, district judge of Dacca, persuaded by the argument that no Indian judge could impartially decide on the Bhawal sannyasi case, had assigned it to be tried by a British member of the ICS—someone with the predispositions of Lodge, for instance. The judgment in the lower court could well have gone against the plaintiff, and even had he persisted with an appeal, who can tell that it would have succeeded?

But this is an undecidability that is no more or less than the intrinsic contingency of institutionally produced truth. Although the possibility seems more credible in a case that hung so tenuously on the balance as the Bhawal declaratory suit, one could, in principle, say this of any result of a judicial trial. There is, however, a more radical undecidability that is suggested by the Bhawal case. This has to do with establishing the truth of identity, especially where there has occurred a considerable lapse of time and, therefore, where memory has become a significant factor. Both A. N. Chaudhuri and R. F. Lodge seemed to come close to suggesting the problem, without actually saying it in so many words: in such cases, *whereas identity may be disproved by evidence, it can never be proved beyond doubt.* Consider once more our earlier imaginary example. If the DNA sample of the plaintiff did not match that of the second kumar, it would establish beyond doubt that the former was an impostor. But if it did match, would it still persuade someone who saw the kumar's body burn to ashes in front of his very eyes on a bright summer day in Darjeeling? Would he not be right in believing that there was some unresolved mystery in the whole thing?[18]

If this hypothesis is true, it would tend to go against those who argue for the freedom to fashion one's identity at will. For it would show that the systems of classification (ethnicity, race, religion, language, sex, caste, and so on) and the instruments of identification (photograph, signature, finger-print, registration, identity papers, school reports, medical records, and so on) by which modern governmental regimes operate, and which their legal apparatus upholds, will work relentlessly to fix and pin down certain in-variant features of identity that were likely to hold firm and remain visible over time. The liberal ideals of personal autonomy and freedom of choice can flourish only within the regulatory grid of such a legal-governmental system. If cultural practices are to continue that tolerate or encourage the crossing of boundaries, the absorption into the fold of strangers or the con-version to other ways of life, they must do so by either negotiating or evad-ing those legal-governmental regimes.

Indeed, one could go even further with this argument and point out an apparently paradoxical feature of all modern governmental systems that is revealed by the extraordinary material of the Bhawal sannyasi case. Colo-nial states, being later and peripheral manifestations of the modern state, sometimes disclose its anatomy in startlingly transparent ways. Or perhaps it was because the Bhawal case occurred at a point of transition from the dependent colonial to the sovereign postcolonial state that it proved by its exceptional judgment a general truth about the modern social order. That truth is the following: *modern governmental regimes must presume every indi-vidual to be an impostor until he or she is able to prove the contrary.*

The statement seems startlingly provocative, but I am not exaggerating. Yesterday, as I was entering the university library, I was stopped by a new security guard who did not know me. I had to produce my identity card with my photograph on it to prove that I was who I claimed to be—a member of the faculty. When I travel abroad, I have to produce my passport at every checkpoint. It is a test of identity that every passenger must pass. Some-times, in my case, the test is a little more exacting than usual. They pore over my passport, examine the watermarks and security seals, hold it under a machine emanating a mysterious ray, look suspiciously at my photograph. They have been told that brown-skinned men like me are given to forging their identity papers, so they have to be careful. They ask me what I do for a living and what is the purpose of my visit. I tell them I am a university professor on my way to a conference. They let me pass. I know that not everyone is as fortunate as I am. For some, a passport is not considered suf-ficient proof of identity; other tests have to be gone through. The authori-ties have the power to lay down what tests will satisfy them: the presump-tion always is that one is not who one claims to be until one is able to satisfy the authorities.[19] As a senior law enforcement official in the United States, summarizing the experience of professionals working in his agency, once put it: "Any time an individual walks up and presents an item of identifica-tion, that alone does not really give much assurance that he is who he says he is."[20]

It is not difficult to appreciate the concerns of all such officials. To the extent that they have to run a system of inclusions and exclusions, they must determine as unambiguously as possible who is or is not eligible. People will often try to fool them by claiming to be someone they are not, and the authorities have to be vigilant. There are those who seek to enter a country or to live there when they are not entitled to do so. Politicians often mobilize ineligible people to vote for them in elections. If there are welfare benefits to be obtained on the basis of age, sex, ethnicity, income, or some other social category, there will be an incentive for people to claim falsely to belong to that category. This could happen even in relatively innocent pursuits such as entering a sports competition with an age restriction or a subsidized or privileged facility by claiming to be a member. (I remember claiming to be a Muslim when visiting the great mosques of Cairo, because otherwise I would have had to pay somewhat hefty entry fees.) The most troubling problems arise, of course, from the criminal use of false identification. A criminal will secure counterfeit or stolen papers to hide from the law. He or she may even secure a dead infant's birth certificate and proceed to obtain travel documents, bank accounts, credit cards, licenses, and so on in someone else's name.[21] Curiously, in fighting the criminal use of false identification, the state itself will often employ undercover agents with false identities. Sometimes, to protect its agents and informers, it will even allow them to assume new lives under their new identities.

Even in the case of so-called voluntary disclosures of identity involving no criminal intent, the authorities may have reason to be sceptical about the information being offered. Census operations are meant to be based on information provided by citizens and other inhabitants, although many countries have laws that make it an offense to give false information to a census enumerator. But when I am asked to declare the facts of my identity, how far am I allowed to go to choose those that I like about myself? If I claimed that my mother-tongue was Swahili and my religion Atheism, would the enumerator accept it? I don't know. I have noticed, for instance, that in the 1981 census of Andhra Pradesh, there were people whose *religion* was entered as Australian, Chinese, French, Persian, Russian, or Viyatnami, whereas in the same census for West Bengal, the list of such religions outside the main classifications was extremely small. I can only conclude that the enumerators in Andhra were more willing to accept what they were told by their respondents, whereas those in West Bengal were more vigilant in sticking to the recognized classifications. I notice, for instance, that no more than twelve households in all of West Bengal were counted as being headed by individuals who declared themselves Atheists.[22] There is little doubt that a certain ethnographic orthodoxy has far greater hold over governmental classificatory systems than the recognition that identities can be fashioned.

There are also numerous instances in which the adoption of particular identities for the purposes of census enumeration is a hugely contested affair, and where state authorities are under pressure to verify the claims before accepting them. A general instruction in the Indian census, for instance, is to ask a person claiming to belong to the Scheduled Caste or Scheduled Tribe category to give the actual name of his or her caste or tribe (even though these names are not enumerated) and to check whether the name appears in the official list of Scheduled Castes and Tribes.[23] This is because there are certain special provisions of legislative representation, educational opportunities, employment, and so on, for these historically oppressed castes and tribes based on their demographic proportion, and there could be, or so it is believed, incentive to inflate the figures. The question of linguisitic or religious identification has also been hugely contentious, and census operations have been criticized, manipulated, and sometimes resisted in order to record the facts of identity in a particular manner.

If such are the procedures for verifying information on identity in a census, the rules of thumb for identifying people by class and ethnicity in situations involving criminal acts are, not surprisingly, even more summary and direct. A textbook widely used by Indian lawyers lists the following "physical peculiarities" by which a "Muhammadam male" may be identified.

(1) Circumcised. (2) Callosities on the centre of forehead, patella, tuberosity of left tibia and tip of left lateral (external) malleolus owing to special attitudes adopted during prayers. (3) Ear lobules not pierced, but left lobule may be pierced in a few cases. (4) Palm of left hand and tip of little finger sometimes stained with henna.

And "Hindu females" are supposed to display the following "noteworthy characteristics".

(1) Tattoo marks, between eyebrows, below crease of elbow, on dorsum of hand, and on chest, specially among low castes. (2) Nose-ring aperture in left nostril; in a few cases in septum as well. (3) A few openings along helix for earrings. (4) Vermilion painted in half parting on head and red mark on centre of forehead in woman having husbands alive. (5) Iron wristlet worn on left wrist in Bengal and ivory churis in Bombay and several glass bangles in U.P. *N.B.*— These are only worn by women whose husbands are alive. (6) Head shaved among class (Brahmin) widows. (7) Toes wide apart as usually no shoes are worn, but silver ornaments called Bichhawas are carried on the toes, especially among village women. (8) Trousers not worn except by Punjabi women.[24]

Behind all this concern over false identification is, of course, the assumption that for every person recognized by governmental authorities, there is a "true identity" that must be disclosed or found. It is not difficult to see that this is a requirement that emerges in its current ubiquity and anxious insistence only with the governmental regimes characteristic of the modern era. As pointed out most graphically by Michel Foucault, the humanization of the judicial and penal system, especially in the nineteenth century, was accompanied by a new concern that governments look after the physical and moral well-being of populations. This produced the plethora of agencies in modern society devoted to the collection, documentation, classification, and analysis of information about people. It is through such disciplinary and governmental systems that the "individual" was, in fact, produced as an entity that was identifiable at any given time, distinguishable from other individuals and describable in its changes over time.[25] Just as the anti-absolutist desire for individual liberty produced the dictum in the reformed criminal law that one must be presumed innocent until proved guilty, so we find the corresponding desire for the welfare of populations reflected in the dictum that one must be presumed to be an impostor until proved otherwise. The two maxims are not contradictory, but entirely consistent within the domain of modern governance. In the course of the twentieth century, in particular, as disciplinary regimes have broken out of the confines of specific institutions such as hospitals or prisons or schools and become immanent in practices of security and control that exist everywhere, the exercise of freedom too now requires the endlessly repeated demonstration of proofs of legitimate identity.[26] Now that the People have taken the place of the Prince, everyone is an impostor until the Prince-that-stands-for-the-People is satisfied to the contrary. The allegation against the Bhawal sannyasi was, if we look at it this way, actually typical of modern societies of control: in them, we are all princely impostors until we can prove otherwise.

Perhaps this is the reason why of all the cases of imposture that have come to court over the years, very few have ended with the alleged impostor being found to be who he or she claimed to be. (I have not found a single such case other than that of the Bhawal sannyasi; there cannot, I am sure, be too many others.) It is not without reason that the wise Montaigne, criticizing the judge in the famous trial of the false Martin Guerre in sixteenth-century Languedoc, said, "Let us have some form of judgment that shall say, 'The Court does not understand anything about it'—more freely and frankly than the Areopagites, who, finding themselves embarrassed with a case they could not unravel, ordered the parties to come again in a hundred years."[27] But this, we must also acknowledge, is a luxury enjoyed only by the historian—who, unlike the judge, does not necessarily have to pronounce on the truth of the case. In spite of this relative freedom, the historian's mistakes rarely have any immediate social consequences. The error of a judge could, however, have disastrous results on individual lives.

Are we then ready to pronounce our judgment on the Bhawal case? Not yet. We have to give the judges one more chance, because we have not yet exhausted the judicial process and its procedures for correcting itself.

Chapter Nineteen

TO LONDON AND BACK

Next Move

The decision of the High Court was a huge blow to the defendants in the Bhawal sannyasi case. Certainly, there was a keen expectation in official circles that the judges of the High Court would, as in the defamation suit of 1924–1925, overturn the judgment of the lower court. That C. C. Biswas would uphold the decision of Pannala Basu and that Lodge would reject it were no surprise. Even an impartial historian of the period, reading the emerging cultural-political trends in late colonial Bengal, would find those two judgments fairly predictable. But why did Costello decide the way he did? It remains one of the great mysteries of the Bhawal case. Biswas, it is true, claimed that he had been able, before Costello left for England, to persuade him toward his point of view. But so did Lodge, who was clearly surprised by the forthright support that Costello finally gave to Pannalal Basu's findings. Perhaps the answer lies, as I have suggested, in the phenomenological experience of distance suddenly brought to consciousness by the war, the exhaustion of endlessly waiting to resume his duties, and the growing awareness that he would never in fact go back to India. Or perhaps Costello, not being, like Lodge, a product of the colonial bureaucracy and not having been reared from youth in its values and prejudices, was able to see the evidence in a more neutral light, not as someone with a stake in the continuation of the system. Without more evidence on his reasonings or motivations, we cannot, unfortunately, say anything more to clarify the mystery of Costello's judgment.

We know, however, that the High Court decision left Satyendra Nath Banerjee utterly disconsolate. He clearly did not anticipate that the appeal would be defeated. Early in 1941, only a few months after the judgment, he died of a heart attack.[1]

In the meantime, World War II reached Calcutta. Within two months of the Japanese attack on Pearl Harbor, the British had to abandon Singapore. The retreat from Burma began in early 1942 and was completed by May. The Japanese were on the borders of Bengal, and an invasion was expected anytime after the rainy season. The port at Chittagong was repeatedly bombed, and the eastern districts were virtually abandoned by the British administration. Plans were finalized for an evacuation of Calcutta.

In December 1942, the city was bombed by the Japanese, causing panic on a scale never seen before. A British official reported later: "People were making frantic efforts to get away . . . and to get their valuables away. Large numbers of merchants and traders also left, and I was told that the ordinary shop commodities in Calcutta could be bought for next to nothing. That was towards the end of 1941. When I returned to Bengal myself in April, 1942, there was an atmosphere of tenseness and expectancy in Calcutta. . . . Houses were vacant. Bazar shops had very largely moved off and a great deal of the population had gone out. . . . [N]obody knew whether by the next cold weather, Calcutta would be in the possession of the Japanese"[2]

Along with thousands of other well-to-do residents of the city, the former sannyasi who had now been declared by two courts of law as Kumar Ramendra Narayan Roy of Bhawal left Calcutta. He was now under the care of Rani Sarajubala. Ever since the appeal in the High Court, the first rani had taken up the principal responsibility of financing and managing the plaintiff's case. She was a devoutly religious woman who had made large gifts to the Kalighat temple in Calcutta and the Jagannath temple in Puri. Secluded behind the mandatory purdah in her house on Ripon Street, she dealt with the lawyers and attorneys and approved their decisions. In 1942, she, along with her brother's family and her brother-in-law Ramendra, moved to Benaras.[3]

Until this time, the decree of the Dacca court had not been executed in favor of the plaintiff because an appeal had been filed against it in the High Court on behalf of Bibhabati Debi. This appeal was dismissed in February 1941. Ramendra Narayan had been allowed in the meantime to withdraw money from his share in the Bhawal estate against a security deposit of Rs.200,000. In May 1941, after he had won in the High Court, he obtained full possession of his one-third share.[4] The property was still managed by the Court of Wards: Ramendra Narayan signed a power of attorney to allow the manager of the estate to administer his property on his behalf. In fact, it was still not clear if he had crossed all the legal hurdles.

Rani Bibhabati refused to accept defeat. She was intent on making a further appeal—this time to the Privy Council in London, the final court of appeal in British India. During the entire period of the trial and the hearings in the High Court, she and her brother's family had been the targets of vicious attack in the popular press. They had been portrayed as the villains in the Bhawal sannyasi drama. Often there would be small crowds of people, usually from Dacca, in front of the house on Lansdowne Road, singing and chanting and shouting obscenities. At parties and on social occasions, people would point at them and whisper, "There, they are the ones who poisoned the kumar of Bhawal." But they also had a small group of loyal friends who supported them through the difficult days. There were the lawyers, of course, most notably P. B. Chakrabarti. Some people from Dacca also came periodically to pay their respects to the rani, including Ashutosh Dasgupta, befuddled by the unexpected complexity of life and utterly, even comically, deferential to her, a living proof of the ridiculousness of the popular canard about him and the rani. There were some influential people in Satyendra Banerjee's circle who also stood by the family. Saradindu Mukherjee was a zamindar and a member of the Legislative Council. He was convinced that the sadhu was a fraud and had testified against him in court. In 1937, he decided to make an even stronger statement of his faith in the Banerjee family; he arranged for the marriage of his daughter to Satyendra Banerjee's son. Many people advised him against the match, saying that the family was under a cloud and virtually ostracized. Saradindu Babu insisted that this would be the way to remove the unmerited social stigma.

Although Rani Bibhabati was eager to go ahead with an appeal to the Privy Council, the Board of Revenue was not keen to push matters any further. A. N. Chaudhuri, it appears, was so disappointed by the High Court result that immediately afterward he drove down to the riverfront at the Strand and tossed his brief into the waters of the Bhagirathi. He believed he had failed his clients and declined to have anything to do with a further appeal. P. B. Chakrabarti, who had assisted Chaudhuri in the High Court, was however convinced about the innate strength of the defendant's case and felt that an appeal to the Privy Council was worth a try. Bibhabati was only too willing.[5]

By then, it must have become obvious to all concerned that even if Kumar Ramendra finally managed to secure his rights to his property, his conjugal life with Bibhabati, for what it was worth, would not be restored. Sarajubala now laid out radical plans for her brother-in-law. In 1942–1943, she arranged for the marriage of the kumar with Dhara Mukherjee, a woman in her thirties from another Calcutta family that had come away to the north to escape the Japanese bombing. The wedding took place in Benaras with some pomp and ceremony.[6] (We must remind the reader that this was still a time when it was perfectly legal under British Indian law for a Hindu man to take a second wife.)

In Bengal, life was grim. In the west, the Quit India movement of the Congress found a major base in the district of Midnapore where, for a few months, the local administration in several police-station areas was effectively under the control of a rebel government.[7] In the east, having decided that there was no chance of defending the eastern districts, the British launched a scorched earth policy under which all means of local transportation, especially boats of all sizes and descriptions, were confiscated.

Apart from causing a huge dislocation to daily life in the riverine delta of coastal Bengal, the policy led to a total disruption of local trade, especially in foodgrains. Despite a bumper rice harvest, a famine of unprecedented proportions hit Bengal in 1943. Even conservative estimates put the mortality figure for the 1943 Bengal famine at around 1.5 million. The district of Dacca was one of the worst affected.[8]

B. C. Chatterjee, who had been counsel for the plaintiff in Dhaka and Calcutta, died in June 1943. By that time, a petition had been filed at the Privy Council in London on behalf of Bibhabati Debi for leave to appeal against the judgment of the Calcutta High Court. It was not usual for an appeal to be allowed when two lower courts had ruled in favor of the plaintiff. With the war raging in the skies and seas of Europe, it was unlikely that Bibhabati's petition would be heard soon.

The threat of an immediate Japanese invasion having receded, propertied and professional people began to return to Calcutta. Ramendra Narayan came back with his new wife, who settled down in a house owned by Rani Sarajubala on Vivekananda Road. It appears that Ramendra Narayan actually lived separately in a rented house on Dharmatala Street. Unfortunately, nothing is known of his life at this time.

THE PRIVY COUNCIL

The Judicial Committee of the Privy Council usually met in the Council Chamber in Westminster, overlooking Downing Street. It was a bizarre room, designed in a style supposedly called "romantic classicism" but in actual fact amounting to a hodgepodge of architectural motifs mixed up "in a singularly grotesque fashion."[9] Fortunately, bomb damage forced the council to move its sittings to the Palace of Westminster, and it was not until July 1946 that it had to come back to the much detested chamber. During the period of the war, the Indian division of the Judicial Committee sat in a committee room of the House of Lords. It was there that Bibhabati Debi's petition for special leave to appeal was heard in 1945.

Rani Bibhabati had expected Phani Bhusan Chakrabarti to organize her case in the Privy Council. But in early 1945, Chakrabarti was appointed a judge of the Calcutta High Court. It was a blow, and hit by one legal reverse after another, she suspected a conspiracy of some sort in the offer to P. B. Chakrabarti of the appointment exactly when he was about to leave for England with her brief.[10] Pankaj Coomar Ghose, son of Sasanka Coomar, who had been in the team of defense lawyers from the trial in Dhaka and knew the case in all its intricate details, now set off for London. He would, of course, only assist in the hearing. The petition would have to be argued before the Privy Council by a king's counsel. The one engaged was

W.W.K. Page, who had spent many years in Calcutta as a barrister at the High Court and had just returned to England to become king's counsel.

On the side of Ramendra Narayan Roy, the respondent, was a flamboyant lawyer. D. N. Pritt was both a prominent left-wing politician and a barrister with a substantial practice. He had been a Labour MP from 1935, and was well known as a sympathizer of the Soviet Union. He once defended Kishori Lal, a revolutionary, in the Privy Council. After India's independence, he would often be approached by zamindars to defend them against the new laws abolishing zamindari; he refused on political grounds. When he was asked in 1950 by the Government of East Pakistan to defend the Zamindari Abolition Act, he agreed "with pleasure, and success."[11] (This Act would abolish the Bhawal zamindari estate for ever.) In 1950, he would defend (without fee) the communist revolutionaries of the Telengana armed uprising in the Supreme Court of India, and in 1958 the controversial Education Bill of the Communist-led Kerala government.[12]

In 1945, however, he was attracted by the "Indian Tichborne case" for its legal complexity. He was assisted by a team of Indian lawyers—two barristers Upendranath Sen Gupta and R. K. Handoo and the Calcutta advocate Arabinda Guha, who had been on the plaintiff's team from Dhaka.

The immediate question before the Privy Council was whether or not to grant leave to appeal. Pritt strongly argued that the issues raised by the petitioner Bibhabati Debi were entirely questions of fact on which two courts had decided the same way. There were no justified reasons for the Privy Council to reopen the facts of the case. Page, on the other hand, argued that there were valid grounds to suggest that some evidence had been improperly admitted and other evidence improperly judged in the lower courts. After hearing the arguments, the Privy Council decided to grant special leave to the petitioner Bibhabati Debi to appeal.

Pritt said later that he faced a conflict of duty and interest that was "more acute than usual." His duty to his client was to fight hard to defeat the petition; "whereas, if I did not defeat the petition, I would then earn on the appeal, when it came forward, some very large fees. In fact, I earned about £15,000, a very high proportion of which went in taxation. . . . I failed to stop the judges granting special leave, and the appeal went on."[13]

The bench appointed to hear the appeal consisted of Lord Thankerton, Lord du Parcq, and Sir C. Madhavan Nair. William Watson, Baron Thankerton, a Scotsman, was at this time seventy-two years old, although he still had black hair and did not look his age. He had been appointed to the Privy Council in 1924 and became a lord of appeal in 1929. His opinions were said to be "masterpieces of concise and lucid statement." Outside court, however, he "enjoyed a good story, and had a considerable fund of after-dinner anecdotes with which he would delight the lawyers of Gray's Inn."[14] Herbert du Parcq, born on Jersey island, was a barrister of the Middle

Temple who became a member of the Court of Appeal and Privy Council in 1938. He was said to be "uniformly patient and courteous towards counsel and litigants alike," and was besides "a fine and accomplished speaker."[15] Sir Chettur Madhavan Nair was also a barrister from the Middle Temple, and had been a judge of the Madras High Court until 1939 before being appointed to the Privy Council.

William Page argued that the trial judge at the Dacca court had wrongly admitted the evidence of Satyendra Nath Maitra and the other professors staying at the Lowis Jubilee Sanitarium in May 1909. This evidence was crucial to the judge's finding that the kumar's death had occurred in the evening of May 8. But the evidence was inadmissible, since the man who is supposed to have carried the news of death to the Sanitarium was never identified or produced in court. It was merely a surmise that he was bringing word from Step Aside; no evidence had been produced to establish this. Therefore, the evidence of the Maitra group was based on nothing more than hearsay. There could have been a rumor afloat in Darjeeling that evening that the kumar had died, but this could not be evidence to justify a finding that death had actually occurred that evening.

Page also argued that the trial judge had wrongly disregarded the evidence of Dr. Andrew Caddy's medical report, in which it was clearly stated that the kumar's eyes were "grey" in color. It was obvious that Caddy could not have meant that the kumar's eyes were brown (which was the color of the plaintiff's eyes). But the judge had set aside this conclusive evidence and found that the kumar's eyes were brownish in color.

Third, Page argued that the kumar had numerous gummatous ulcers on his arms and legs, which were the result of tertiary-stage syphilis. The trial judge only found three scars on the plaintiff's elbows, which he took to be proof that the plaintiff was "an old syphilitic individual." Expert evidence was produced in court to establish that tertiary syphilis could not be cured, and that it was impossible for someone with the symptoms of syphilis that the kumar was known to have had to emerge twelve years later with the clear skin of the plaintiff.

Fourth, Page reminded the council that one judge of the High Court had upheld all of the points he was making, so that it could not be argued that there was a concurrent finding on all these points of fact.

Finally, Page sought to make a technical point that when Bibhabati Debi held her share of the estate after the presumed death of her husband, she was asserting a right that was adverse to that of her dead husband. The implication was that even if her husband was now found to be alive, he could not reclaim the property now in her possession.

Pritt later paid rich compliments to Page, "a lawyer for whom I have a great admiration." Years of practice in Calcutta had, of course, given him a knowledge of India, especially Bengal, which Pritt did not have. This, "coupled with his real understanding of the way cases should be conducted and his scrupulous fairness made it a pleasure to be in a case with him or against him."[16] Pritt made the argument that the trial judge was entitled, under the laws of evidence, to admit the evidence of the Maitra group and also to come to his findings based on his assessment of the entire body of evidence presented before him. The practice of the Privy Council was to decline to review the evidence when there were two concurrent judgments. There was no ground to depart from that practice.

THANKERTON'S JUDGMENT

The hearings went on for twenty-eight successive days, an extraordinarily long hearing by Privy Council standards. On July 30, 1946, Lord Thankerton read out his judgment with which Lord du Parcq and Sir Madhavan Nair were in agreement.

He noted, first, that the trial judge and the judges of the High Court had had the advantage of inspecting the plaintiff. That opportunity was not available to the board.

The practice of the board of not reviewing the evidence applied to concurrent findings of fact of two *courts*, and not to concurrent findings of the *judges*. Therefore, "a dissent by a member of the Appellate Court does not obviate the practice."

He also declared that "the Board will always be reluctant to depart from the practice in cases which involve questions of manners, customs or sentiments peculiar to the country or locality from which the case comes, whose significance is specifically within the knowledge of the Courts of that country." Thankerton noted especially that this was a case of "unusual magnitude and complication."

In this case, the concurrent finding of fact was that the plaintiff is Kumar Ramendra Narayan Roy. On this, the appellant had three contentions: one, concerning the admissibility of the evidence of the Maitra group; two, concerning the conclusive nature of the evidence of Dr. Caddy's report on the color of the Kumar's eyes; and three, concerning the signs of syphilis in the plaintiff.

On the evidence of the Maitra group regarding the man who brought the news of death to the Sanitarium in the evening, Thankerton said the following.

Their Lordships are of opinion that the statement and request made by this man was a fact within the meaning of ss. 3 and 59 of the Indian Evidence Act of 1872, and that it is proved by the direct evidence of witnesses who heard it, within the meaning of s. 60; but it was not a relevant fact unless the learned

Judge was entitled to make it a relevant fact by a presumption under the terms of s. 114. As regards the statement that the Kumar had just died, such a statement by itself would not justify any such presumption, as it might rest on mere rumour, but, in the opinion of their Lordships, the learned Judge was entitled to hold, in relation to the fact of the request for help to carry the body for cremation, that it was likely that the request was authorised by those in charge of Step Aside having regard to "the common course of natural events, human conduct and public and private business," and therefore, to presume the existence of such authority. Having made such presumption, the fact of such an authorised request thereby became a relevant fact, and the evidence of the Maitra group became admissible. Accordingly, this contention fails.

The lords of appeal were in effect saying that the trial judge was well within the law in making the presumption that the messenger appearing at the Sanitarium had been authorized by the people at Step Aside. Whether the presumption itself was correct was not something the Privy Council was prepared to examine, since this would require reopening the evidence.

The second contention was that Dr. Caddy's entry of the color of the kumar's eyes as "grey" must mean that he had distinguished grey from brown. This report should have been accepted as conclusive of the matter.

But this contention must fail, for not only was there conflicting evidence on the point, having regard to the statement in the affidavit dated March 6, 1910, given to the Insurance company by Kali Prasanna Vidyasagar, who had long been familiar with the Second Kumar and therein stated that the latter's eyes were rather brownish, but the witness Girish Chandra Sen stated that Dr. Caddy had asked him to look for any identification marks, and that he told the doctor "grey eyes", thereby meaning kata eyes. It follows that it was a question of value of evidence, and the learned Judge had before him evidence on which he was entitled to hold that the eyes of the Second Kumar were brownish, and therefore, similar to the eyes of the plaintiff.

The third contention concerned the sufficiency of the marks on the plaintiff's body to warrant a conclusion that he was syphilitic.

It is enough to say that the plaintiff has one scar on the left arm and two on the right arm, in each case about the elbow; these clearly, on the evidence, are a small proportion of the number of ulcers from which the Second Kumar was suffering in 1909, but there was evidence on which the learned Judge was entitled to hold that these three scars were the remains of some of the Second Kumar's ulcers. There was no definite evidence as to the permanency, or otherwise, of scars left by gummatous ulcers. There does not seem to have been any evidence which would enable the learned Judge to identify any scars on the legs of the plaintiff as corresponding in position with the position of the Second Kumar's ulcers on his legs.

Page had cited Dr. K. K. Chatterjee's evidence that if left untreated, the kumar's ulcers would have gone septic within three months and he would have died. "The plaintiff stated in his evidence that while with the Sannyasis, he had no treatment. But the doctor's evidence is a calculation of chances of recovery, which no doctor would maintain to be without exception, and it is not surprising that he later states that there is no normality in syphilis. The whole matter is one of the value of evidence, and this contention also fails."

Given their conclusions on the three contentions, their Lordships were of opinion "that the appellant has failed to establish any valid ground for departure from the practice of the Board."

In sum, the board held the following. First, in case of a concurrent judgment of two courts in India, on pure questions of law, the practice of the Privy Council was to decline the review of evidence for a third time, unless there were special circumstances. Their Lordships held that the appellant had failed to establish valid ground for departure from this practice. Second, regarding adverse possession by Bibhabati Debi against her presumably dead husband, under the Limitation Act IX of 1908, s. 144, their Lordships held that when a Hindu woman possessed an estate in the mistaken belief that her husband was dead, she could not claim that by possession she was asserting a right adverse to one whom she regarded as dead, that is, her husband. Third, on the admissibility of the evidence of the Maitra group, under the Evidence Act I of 1872, ss. 3, 59, 60 and 114, their Lordships held that the evidence was admissible.

The appeal was dismissed.[17]

The Secret History of Nationalism

Was decolonization already under way? The world war was won, negotiations were on about a quick transfer of power in India, an interim government of Indian political leaders was already in office in New Delhi—had the feeling become predominant among Britain's elites that Indian affairs were now best left to the judgment of Indians? It would be excessive if we tried to read the signs of an entire historical epoch in a single judgment of the Privy Council. So let us not make extravagant claims about the significance of the pronouncement by Lord Thankerton that, in the Privy Council's opinion, the trial judge in Dacca was well within his legal powers to decide as he did; the law lords in London would not intervene. Henderson, former district judge of Dacca and later a judge of the Calcutta High Court, thought it significant that "although there was no question of law in the case and it was not the practice of the Privy Council to dissent from a concurrent finding of fact, their Lordships gave the widow special leave to appeal."

Henderson came to the conclusion that "though they were not prepared to depart from their usual practice, [the Lordships'] judgment suggests that they agreed with Lodge J."[18] We may not all be able to read what Henderson read in Thankerton's prose; he seemed to think that the Privy Council would have been happy to overturn the judgment of the lower courts if only it had not been prevented by the usual practice. But then, someone else might suggest that the law lords thought it an inopportune time, given the political context, to choose to break the practice. Who knows? Maybe they were aware only of the strictly legal considerations in the case and utterly oblivious of the larger political picture. Maybe.

But there is no mistaking the nationalist location of the legal-political thinking of Pannalal Basu and Charu Chandra Biswas. They represented that generation of Indians who had—discursively, ideologically, often institutionally—prepared themselves for a transfer of power. By the late 1930s, this had happened in many institutions within and around the colonial state, and included men and women in several professions—teachers, doctors, scientists, journalists, bureaucrats, even soldiers and policemen. Among civil servants, there are many stories that circulate of heated debates in evening parties where Indian bureaucrats, enlivened by one whiskey too many, would lambaste their British colleagues for their imperialist crimes. One of them, when asked why he had chosen to serve such an oppressive power, is said to have retorted: "Only to keep one of you out."[19] It is clear that by the 1930s, the Indians entering the senior echelons of the colonial governmental services, including the armed forces, came from a middle class that had sufficiently absorbed the cultural influences of the modern West to be able to assert, without embarrassment or apology, and without the sense of cultural alienation from their own people that had afflicted the early generation of the so-called brown sahibs, a new national-modern cultural identity. "Never fully integrated with the British elements in these services," as one Indian member of the ICS describes the transition, the Indian members "had to retain their own identity which they asserted progressively as their numbers in the services grew. . . . They hoped for the attainment of independence by India though they could take no part in the movement to achieve it. They had the highest regard for the national leaders, though not many approved of the methods they adopted. . . . When independence came, they were happy."[20]

Nowhere was this more true than in the profession of the law. As is well known, the largest bulk of nationalist politicians in India were lawyers. Perhaps it was the perceived independence of the profession, and at the same time its close proximity to, indeed entanglement with, the workings of the colonial state, that allowed lawyers to engage wholeheartedly in anticolonial politics. (As A. N. Chaudhuri's father said, it was the only respectable profession in which one did not have to serve the British.) Reading the law, arguing their cases, debating about precedents, writing their judgments, Indian lawyers and judges thoroughly internalized the principles of modern English law and were deeply convinced that it represented the best values of enlightened and universal rationality. As a chief justice of the Calcutta High Court wrote fifteen years after Indian independence, "we owe to the British a deep debt of gratitude for the introduction of the Law-Courts and a system of dispensing justice based on the English pattern. Although our laws are moulded to our needs, they are inspired by the British system of jurisprudence, which fortunately happens to be one of the best systems that the world has ever produced."[21] At the same time, this generation of nationalists was also convinced that the law, based as it must be on universal principles of rational justice, should also be "moulded to our needs." The universal principles had to be interpreted, applied, elaborated, to suit the cultural and historical realities of India. This constituted for them their nationalist project—to construct a framework of modern laws for a modern state, perfectly consistent with the universal principles of rationality and modernity, but at the same time adapted to the particular cultural conditions of India. By the 1930s, this generation of nationalists had arrived at the conviction that only they could carry out that task. In fact, they believed that the colonial bureaucracy was now an active hindrance to the further progress of the institutions of the state in India toward a fully developed modern nation-state.

The texts of the judgments by Basu and Biswas are replete with the marks of this nationalist consciousness. We have seen this in their refusal to be overawed by the testimony of senior ICS officials, their energetic dissection and stinging condemnation of the roles played by Calvert, Crawford, Rankin, and Lindsay, and their scarcely concealed contempt for those Indians who were too close or too subservient to colonial officials. More fundamentally, we have seen this in their assumption of a certain interpretative position with respect to the cultural beliefs and practices of different types of Indians; this interpretative position, they were implicitly claiming, could not be open to Europeans because they could never have the necessary insider's knowledge that would make possible a correct assessment of, say, the value of evidence or the credibility of witnesses. It was, in one sense, an example of the classic nationalist move to claim sovereignty over a certain "inner" domain of national life—that of language, religion, family, women, spiritual culture—and to exclude the colonial ruler from that domain.[22] But the institutional site where this act of "sovereignty" was being exercised here was the judicial system, located at the very heart of the colonial state. It was from their positions as functionaries of the system that men like Basu or Biswas were virtually saying to their colonial masters: "We now know the universal principles of law as well as you do; we understand the cultural peculiarities of this country much better. Leave it to us to run the system."

It would not be too rash to speculate that had the Bhawal declaratory suit come up in the courts even ten years earlier, say at the time of the defamation suit, no Indian judge would have stood up to the organized assault of the official machinery to defend its prestige; even if he decided as Pannalal Basu did—going by what happened in the defamation case—the High Court was more than likely to overturn his judgment. A decade was a long time in the political history of the colonial world in the twentieth century. Between the 1920s and the 1930s, we could say from our account of the Bhawal case, a significant shift had taken place toward the dismantling of the structures of colonial rule from within the institutions of the colonial state. This was not a revolutionary overturning. On the contrary, it made possible, indeed ensured, a smooth transfer of power. After independence, even with a new republican constitution granting guaranteed fundamental rights and universal adult franchise, the institutions of the judicial system would remain virtually unaltered. Although the Supreme Court of India is now only fifty years old, the Calcutta High Court still calculates its age from 1862. The colonial judicial system, we now know, was actually taken over by nationalists from within. To answer the historical question about the Bhawal sannyasi case, therefore, we could say that its result is explained by the fact that it represented in microcosm the secret story of the transfer of power in late colonial India, carried out not so much in street demonstrations, prisons, and conference tables but within the interstices of the governmental apparatus itself—slowly, quietly, and in the end, decisively.

The nationalist critique of the colonial state was at the same time an affirmation of the universal principles of the modern state. Specifically, it identified the colonial bureaucracy as a power structure that was unlimited and unchecked. Instrinsically absolutist, it was a constant reminder of the fact that for all its modernity, colonial rule was ultimately based on the right of conquest. Such a conception of executive power was incompatible with a properly constituted modern state. Through the decades of the early twentieth century, as nationalist politicians in India fought against the attempts by the colonial bureaucracy to assert its dominance, lawyers and judges such as Pannalal Basu and C. C. Biswas were asserting what was in effect the principle of judicial independence. Quietly, almost imperceptibly, they were participating in the laying of the discursive foundations of the constitution of the independent nation-state. When the constituent assembly got down to business after 1947, the basic tenets of the Indian constitution had already been imagined into existence.

We should also remember that the lawyers on the plaintiff's side in this case included some of the stalwarts among nationalist lawyers of Calcutta—B. C. Chatterjee, Atul Gupta, Bankim Mukherjee, J. C. Gupta. Those on the side of the defendants were stamped by their proximity to the colonial government—Sir N. N. Sircar, Sir Binod Mitter, Sir B. L. Mitter, A. N. Chaudhuri of course, P. B. Chakrabarti, P. B. Mukharji. This distribution was reflected in the general perception of the Bhawal sannyasi case as a fight between the colonial government and the people.

An Excursus on the Subaltern

What about the people? Where did they stand in all this? We have met some of them at the trial—as we know, several hundred tenants appeared as witnesses on both sides. Some of their evidence was striking, as, for instance, of the one who said that he recognized the plaintiff as the second kumar when he lay down in front of him to touch his feet—the feet had the same scaly skin near the ankles that was a family trait of the kumars and their sisters. Or the evidence of the śolā artist who was locked up in a room at the Nalgola Rajbari and told that he would get no more orders if he did not sign a statement saying that the sannyasi had no resemblance with the second kumar. From all the available records, there is little doubt that the overwhelming mass of tenants on the estate were convinced that the plaintiff was indeed the kumar, and many were prepared, either because of a traditional sense of loyalty to their raja or because of their dislike for the Court of Wards, to face considerable hardship by making their loyalties public. At the time when the sadhu first appeared in Jaidebpur, the Khilafat and Non-cooperation movements had just taken off, and in the clamor of a broad anticolonial front led by virtually all Muslim and Hindu mass leaders, the Jaidebpur sadhu became a popular focus of anticolonial sentiments. But woven into the condemnation of the British attack on Islam and the Gandhian rhetoric of boycott of British institutions was a certain nebulous and utterly utopian ideal of a just kingship in which the raja protected and looked after the praja and the latter, in return, gave him unquestioned loyalty. The figure of the exiled raja as a sannyasi was without doubt a particularly appropriate one on which to hang such utopian sentiments.

An interesting question to ask is: how did such sentiments survive in the period of the rise of the Praja movement in east Bengal, which demanded the abolition of the zamindari system, and the growing communal animosities following repeated riots in Dhaka and its surrounding areas? It is hard to answer this question accurately merely on the basis of the material from the Bhawal sannyasi trial. The crucial ambiguity surrounding the figure of the sannyasi-kumar was that he was a zamindar who had not been allowed to sit on the gadi; he was a raja who should have ruled but never did. Not surprisingly, all of the complaints and grievances about real zamindars and real conditions of tenancy could be voiced by sympathizing with the wronged sannyasi-kumar as the embodiment of victimhood. The campaign to reinstate the second kumar was, in a curious way, perfectly consistent with the campaign to abolish zamindari.[23]

Most of the tenants of the Bhawal estate were Muslim. A majority of the talukdars were upper-caste Hindu. As far as one can tell from the evidence surrounding the trial, the communal politics of the 1930s and 1940s had no discernible impact on the support for or opposition to the plaintiff. Numerous Muslim tenants, including local leaders of the Praja movement, appeared for him as witnesses. Dozens of Muslim writers wrote enthusiastic pamphlets in his support, and Muslim poets composed ballads and songs. There was a shared idiom in eastern Bengal in which to talk about just kingship and social ethics—one that was easily translatable between an Islamic and a Hindu religious vocabulary. The popular literature on the Bhawal sannyasi flourished within this common idiom.

An argument has been sometimes made that the traditional framework of kingship, in which (contrary to Louis Dumont's theory of the caste system) the political was the guarantee for the religious, was crucial for the continuation of the delicate local structures of sectarian coexistence and tolerance built in many regions over many decades.[24] The decline of kingship, whether as zamindaris within British India or as principalities outside it, in the late colonial period, and their delegitimization in the face of the rising tide of democratic nationalism, coincided with the rapid growth of sectarian strife and violence. If this argument has any substance, it would go some way in explaining why, in a situation where the local zamindar was himself an idealized figure of the popular imagination, the growing specter of communal conflict should fail to cast its shadow on the popular desire to see him on the gadi.

Judged by the standards of modernity and progress, the social attitudes revealed in the popular literature on the Bhawal sannyasi affair were, without doubt, extremely conservative. Underneath the purple prose and witty rhyme, they show a distinct prejudice against the educated classes, portraying them as naturally inclined toward luxury, vanity, liquor, promiscuity, and irreligion. They also show a strong desire to restrict women to their traditional roles. There was an especially deep hostility to that threatening, even if spectral, figure—the educated woman. As such, this is not a surprising finding, because social historians of the nineteenth and twentieth centuries have noticed these characteristics of the "popular" domain in many other instances.[25] What is interesting in this case is that these attitudes coexisted in the same formation with others that had strong antifeudal and anticolonial elements, often within a single popular text.

Pannalal Basu, Charu Chandra Biswas, and Ronald Francis Lodge had something to say about women, too. Basu and Biswas were progressive nationalist men. Their views on women had been shaped by a hundred years of efforts by social reformers and nationalist educators in Bengal to change the conditions in which women lived. Despite their support for the legal rights of the plaintiff Ramendra Narayan Roy, both Basu and Biswas undoubtedly despised the lifestyle of the kumars and the decadent social and political morality it represented. They would have regarded it as a part of the colonial past, something that had no place in the modern future of the nation. It is equally certain that they regarded Bibhabati as a tragic victim of the oppression perpetrated on women in zamindari households, and later, after the supposed death of her husband, on widows in orthodox Brahmin families. Belonging to a generation whose sensibilities had been molded by the humanism of writers like Rabindranath Tagore and Saratchandra Chattopadhyay, Basu and Biswas would have been convinced of the need to abolish these cruel practices so that women in future would not have to suffer from them.[26]

Consistently with their progressive nationalism, however, they were unwilling to grant that Bibhabati herself might have shaped in any way the decisions that determined her life. At the time of the supposed death of her husband, she was a young girl, distraught, and she behaved, as the judges said, exactly as one would expect a Hindu widow to behave under the circumstances. She fell under the control of her brother, who took charge of her property and decided what she should say or do. Bibhabati, as a good Hindu woman, deserved to be under the protection of responsible and worthy men; her tragedy was, Basu or Biswas would have said, that she fell into the hands of a debauched husband and a scheming brother. If Satyendra Banerjee was the chief architect of the fight against the plaintiff, could Jyotirmayi Debi have been the chief conspirator in putting up an impostor? In the eyes of Basu and Biswas, if it was a question of comparing their qualifications for villainy, Satyen Banerjee would beat Jyotirmayi hands down. Already at the age of twenty-three, as one judge said, he had a head as shrewd and devious as that of a man of sixty. He had manipulated his sister, plotted with his associates and curried favor with officials, in order to get hold of her property and establish himself as a noted citizen of Calcutta. By comparison, Jyotirmayi was an elderly Brahmin widow born in a well-known landed family, orthodox in her lifestyle, with a religious bent of mind. She was someone utterly familiar to Basu or Biswas. It was not even conceivable, without tangible evidence, for them to believe that she could have plotted such a scheme with a view to deceiving the whole world. Lodge, by contrast, found it perfectly reasonable to think that Jyotirmayi was the chief conspirator who lied in court in order to instal a brother over whom she would have control. Despite a whole career as a judge in India, Lodge is unlikely even to have seen a woman of Jyotirmayi's description. Perhaps it was this ignorance that allowed him to go to the extent of arguing that even if there was no evidence of a conspiracy, it was still not impossible that Jyotirmayi had conspired.

The views of Basu and Biswas on women were also strongly marked by class and rank. They would not believe that Jyotirmayi was lying, but they were quite prepared to suspect that the nurse Jagat Mohini, being a woman of uncertain virtue, was capable of pretending that she was a Brahmin widow when in reality she was probably low-caste or a low-born Muslim. Jagat Mohini's cross-examination in court and the comments on her character in the judgments of both Pannalal Basu and C. C. Biswas are indicators of the class limits of progressive nationalism on the question of women. It has been suggested that the modern view of reformed Hindu society envisioned by Indian nationalist thinkers was a profoundly Brahminical sociology.[27] If so, the views of Basu and Biswas were very much in accordance with such a sociology.

If one considered the findings of all three courts on the Bhawal sannyasi case, one would not suspect that in actual fact the four most important characters who propelled the course of events in this affair were women. First, there was Jyotirmayi, whose determined interrogation of the sadhu led to the recognition of her brother. It was she who then became the chief support for the plaintiff, establishing him as Ramendra Narayan among her kin and acquaintances. She appeared in court and swayed the trial judge by the sincerity of her testimony. She appeared again before the High Court judges and allowed them to inspect her eyes and feet to check if they resembled those of the plaintiff. She was accused in court of having set up an impostor in order to gain control of the Bhawal property; none of the three courts accepted the allegation. Second, there was Sarajubala, the first rani. She decided to support the plaintiff sometime before the suit was filed in Dhaka. She financed the trial as well as the response to the appeal in the High Court. The bazaar gossip had it that she was having an affair with the plaintiff.[28] She certainly seemed to take charge of his life, including arranging his second marriage. Third, there was the little-discussed Ananda Kumari, the third rani. She had made a crucial place for herself in the whole story by successfully adopting a son in 1919, a little more than a year before the appearance of the sannyasi in Dacca, thereby destroying the claims of the sons of the Bhawal sisters. She was profoundly interested in defeating the plaintiff, because her adopted son was destined to inherit the entire Bhawal estate; if the plaintiff was confirmed as the second kumar, it could jeopardize the prospects of her son to even the one-third share to which she now had title. Ananda Kumari, therefore, energetically supported the second rani in her struggle. She lied through her teeth in court, often making exaggerated claims that embarrassed even the defense lawyers.

Finally, of course, there was Bibhabati. She had gone through a living nightmare. If there was foul play in Darjeeling, no one ever said that she had anything to do with it. After she came back as a widow from Darjeeling, she at first chose to stay on in Jaidebpur, despite her brother's warnings that her in-laws were plotting against her. Then she chose to leave. She made an entirely new life for herself in her brother's family. Following the sannyasi's appearance, she was resolute in her refusal to acknowledge him, never budging an inch. The judges preferred to portray her as a woman without a will of her own, a puppet in the hands of her brother, but none of them could deny that she was firm, unfazed, and supremely dignified in the face of a quite vicious cross-examination. She was the target of unrestrained vilification, including allegations of an extramarital affair, unwanted pregnancy, and incest.[29] After she lost in the High Court, she did not relent, even though her brother was dead. She pursued her lawyers and took her case all the way to the Privy Council, even though she no longer had the support of the government.

Now she had lost in the Privy Council too.

FINALE

News of the Privy Council judgment reached Calcutta by telegram on the following day, July 31, 1946. Kumar Ramendra Narayan had finally established in three courts of law that he was who he claimed to be—himself. As the news spread the next day, hundreds of people began to come to his house on Dharmatala Street to felicitate him. That evening, the kumar went to the Thanthania Kali temple on Cornwallis Street to offer a puja to the goddess. As he was leaving, he was seized by a stroke and fell down unconscious. He was brought back home, where he died two days later. He was sixty-three. In a short obituary note, the *Hindusthan Standard* wrote: "The deceased had been in indifferent health for some time, and had an attack of Haemoptysis since August 1. Many persons who went to his house to congratulate him on his success in the Privy Council appeal were shocked to learn of his death. It is stated that the Kumar had planned to go to Jaidevpur about the middle of this month to meet his friends and tenants."[30]

In Jaidebpur, the estate officials were in a fix. Under the orders of the High Court, the kumar had executed a power of attorney in the name of P. K. Ghosh, the manager, to administer his share of the estate until the Privy Council appeal was settled. The kumar was being paid a monthly allowance of Rs.1,100, and the rest of his income was being deposited in a separate account which, in two years since the High Court orders of 1944, now amounted to Rs.174,873–6as.–3p.[31] With the death of the kumar, the power of attorney had ceased, the manager could not operate the account, and the kumar's heirs had not been named.[32]

On August 10, 1946, the manager of the Bhawal estate received the following telegram from Dhara Debi in Calcutta: "Husband died Saturday third August Sradh on Tuesday thirteenth Please arrange Jaidebpur Brahmin feeding with Madhab's bhog distributing poors chiragur four annas each thirteenth positively in cooperation with all." The manager immediately wired back to say that he was unable to draw money from the late kumar's account and that consequently he would not be able to make arrangements for the ceremonial feeding of Brahmins and the poor on August 13.[33]

The kumar's śrāddha was held in Calcutta—his second after thirty-seven years—on August 13, 1946. Three days later, Calcutta sank into the worst sectarian violence in its history. Over the next four days, an estimated 4,000 people died in the Great Calcutta Killings. The late kumar's house on Dharmatala Street was in the epicentre of the violence. Dhara Debi, living in Maniktala, was at the edge of the worst-affected area.[34]

She persisted in trying to arrange for a ceremonial feast for Brahmins, the estate employees, and the poor in Jaidebpur. At the end of the month, she sent Prafulla Mukhuty, a lawyer, with money to Jaidebpur to organize a feast to mark the first month of the kumar's death. P. K. Ghosh, the estate manager, wrote to her, "as desired by you Prafulla Babu is being helped in making necessary arrangements for the feeding of the Jaidebpur Brahmins, officers etc tomorrow the 2nd Sept on the occasion of the first monthly sradh ceremony of the late lamented Kumar Ramendra Narayan Roy."[35]

Rani Bibhabati always insisted, until her death twenty years later, that although she had been defeated in every court of law on earth, she had won in the ultimate court of appeal. The man was trying to offer puja in the name of someone who was long dead. The goddess had punished him. She was not surprised by the Privy Council defeat; the astrologers of Benaras had told her she would lose. But they had also predicted that the other man would never be able to enjoy his property. They were right.[36]

In February 1950, the East Bengal Estates Acquisition and Tenancy Act was passed by the East Pakistan legislative assembly. It abolished the zamindari system and established a direct relation between tenants and the state. Zamindars were to be paid compensation for the loss of their proprietorship over the land and were allowed to keep a maximum of thirty-three acres of land in their direct possession for cultivation under their own supervision. Several zamindars went to court against the legislation, claiming it was a violation of the right of property and of the solemn pledge made to them by Lord Cornwallis in 1793. As we have mentioned, D. N. Pritt, who had successfully argued for the kumar of Bhawal in the Privy Council, now came to Dhaka to defend the Government of East Pakistan against the zamindars in the High Court.

Ram Narayan Roy, the adopted son of Ananda Kumari, the third rani, succeeded briefly to his share of the zamindari after the Privy Council judgment. When zamindari was abolished after 1950, his possessions were restricted to what he was allowed to hold directly. He moved with his mother to Calcutta in the mid-1950s, but it is known that he visited the estate periodically to collect his dues. These visits appear to have stopped in the 1960s.

As part of the settlement of the estate of Ramendra Narayan, the Court of Wards awarded Bibhabati Debi, as one of his widows, a sum of more than Rs.800,000. Her lawyers explained to her that it was her money, held back by the Court of Wards until the disposal of the appeal. Bibhabati said, "But are they not giving it to me because they think I am the widow of that man? If I take the money, will I not be accepting what I know to be false?" She refused to receive the payment.[37]

Of the two Indian judges who decided in favor of the plaintiff, Pannalal Basu was elected in 1952 to the West Bengal legislative assembly from Sealdah in Calcutta and joined the Congress government of Bidhan Chandra Roy as education minister. Two years later, as minister of land revenue, he moved the bill to abolish the zamindari system in West Bengal. Before the bill could be passed into the West Bengal Estates Acquisition Act, he died. Charu Chandra Biswas joined in 1946 the interim government of Jawaharlal Nehru as Union minister in charge of minorities, and from 1952 to 1957 was the Union law minister. In this capacity, he piloted through parliament the set of laws collectively called the Hindu Code bill—actually four separate pieces of legislation called the Hindu Marriage Act, the Hindu Succession Act, the Hindu Minority and Guardianship Act, and the Hindu Adoptions and Maintenance Act, all enacted in 1955. Among many fundamental changes brought about by these laws to the Hindu family and its rules of marriage, property, and inheritance, they legalized divorce, prohibited polygamy, and gave to the daughter the same rights of inheritance as the son. C. C. Biswas thus ensured that any future Bibhabati, faced with the prospect of having to live with an undesirable husband, would at least have a few more legal options.

Postscript

The Rajbari at Jaidebpur now houses several government establishments of Gazipur district. The Baro Dalan, once built for European visitors to the estate, is now the office of the deputy commissioner of Gazipur. The ground floor of Rajbilas, where the kumars had their living rooms, now houses the public works department. Upstairs, where the ranis lived, are the courtrooms of the various subordinate judges of Gazipur. The marble flooring has mostly disappeared, replaced by a plebian layer of cement. The tall doors with slatted shutters, made of fine old teak, are still magnificent. So is the Natmandir, recently repaired and painted. Behind the Natmandir is the office of the Bangladesh Election Commission. In front of the Rajbilas are innumerable ugly shacks where hundreds of deed writers sit every working day, writing letters, petitions, and legal documents for anxious clients who have had the misfortune of having to take recourse to the law courts.

Behind the Rajbilas is the Gazipur Town police station. The huge iron gates of the Rajbari still bear the coat of arms of the Bhawal estate. In front of the gates, what used to be the polo ground, where the sadhu of Jaidebpur once made his sensational public appearance on the back of an elephant before thousands of people, is now a football stadium.

On holidays, when the courts are closed, there are still groups of curious people who come to visit the Rajbari. Members of the local staff of the public works department are generous with their guidance. They proceed to narrate the story of the famous trial. The rani was having an affair with the doctor, they say. There, across the great tank, now filthy and covered with water hyacinth, was the doctor's house. Every morning, the doctor would stand there on the terrace of his house. Here the rani would stand on the upstairs balcony of the Rajbilas. They would exchange signs. Together, they plotted to poison the kumar and grab the property. Strangely, the popular imagination has now contracted the geographical range of the story to homely proportions. The kumar's body, the visitor is told, was taken to the sasan on the bank of the Chilai—there, no more than a mile in that direction. It was a stormy night, and the body disappeared. . . . The familiar story, told many times, is told again. Some elderly visitors claim to have heard it before: they had seen a *jatra* (play) once, or was it a film made in Calcutta?[38]

The Bhawal estate's house in Nalgola in Dhaka is on the bank of the Buriganga, a short distance away from Ahsan Manzil, the seat of the Dacca Nawabs, now restored and turned into a museum. The Nalgola house is occupied by squatters; the ceiling has collapsed on one side, and the rest is a godown for gunny bags and raw jute. Once again, it is only the massive teak doors that carry the memory of a more resplendent past.

Much of present-day Dhaka, the capital city of Bangladesh, is built on what was not long ago the estate of Bhawal. From Sonargaon Hotel, all along Maugbazar Road, and northward on both sides of the highway to Mymensingh, the new apartment blocks and residential areas were developed on lands that were once administered for decades by the Court of Wards on behalf of the ranis of Bhawal. Whoever has profited from the fruits of development, it was not the ranis.

In Calcutta, Nineteen Lansdowne Road is now the address of a huge block of luxury apartments. No trace remains of the house with the portico and the krishnachura tree. The grandchildren of Satyendra Nath Banerjee now live on a side street. They are fiercely protective of the memory of Bibhabati Debi, who they knew as the matriarch of the family. She was, they say, regal in her bearing, even as she always wore the coarse white cotton sari and close-cropped hair of the Brahmin widow. She was deeply affectionate, caring, and singularly honorable.

There is another story that has been handed down in the Banerjee family about the real identity of the plaintiff. He was brought up, they say, in the Rajbari at Jaidebpur as the son of a syce working in the stables. That is why he knew so much about the details of the family history. But he had been fathered—you know how it was in zamindari families in those days— by none other than Raja Rajendra Narayan himself. That explains the physical similarities with the second kumar. One more attempt, this, to establish a narrative identity of the plaintiff consistent with the story of the death of the second kumar in Darjeeling.

The house Step Aside is still a prominent location in Darjeeling. It is an elegant house, now owned by the government, and serves as a center for maternity care. It bears a large plaque memorializing the death in that house of Chitta Ranjan Das, the famous leader of Bengal. No one in Darjeeling knows anything any more about the second kumar of Bhawal.

NOTES

CHAPTER ONE
THE FACTS OF THE MATTER

1. Text of Satyabhama Debi's letter in Basu, *J*, p. 50.
2. Lodge, *J*, p. 586.
3. For a brief history of the Buckland Bund, see Muntassir Mamoon, *Ḍhākā: smṛti-bismṛtir nagarī*, pp. 178–81.
4. Basu, *J*, p. 61.
5. Ibid., p. 71.
6. Jyotirmayi Debi's evidence, cited ibid., p. 73.
7. Ibid., p. 74.
8. Ibid., pp. 74–75.
9. Ibid., p. 75.
10. Ibid., p. 80.
11. Lodge, *J*, pp. 601–2.
12. Basu, *J*, p. 101.
13. Quoted in Lodge, *J*, pp. 445–46.
14. Basu, *J*, pp. 107–8.
15. Ibid., p. 109.

CHAPTER TWO
AN ESTATE CALLED BHAWAL

1. B. C. Allen, *Eastern Bengal District Gazetteers: Dacca*, p. 3.
2. Ibid.
3. Nariaki Nakazato, *Agrarian System in Eastern Bengal, c.1870–1910*, p. 170.
4. The principal source for the history of the Bhawal estate is Nabinchandra Bhadra, *Bhāoyāler itihās*. Nabinchandra taught at the Jaidebpur School and wrote his history on the basis of "what could be known from stories still told by the people."
5. Jatindramohan Ray, *Ḍhākār itihās*, vol. 2, p. 618.
6. Jnanendranath Kumar, *Baṃśa paricay*, vol. 3, p. 96. The entry on the Bhawal Raj family on pp. 94–129 of this volume contains a detailed account of the family's history, largely based on Bhadra, *Bhāoyāler itihās*.
7. Jatindramohan Ray, *Ḍhākār itihās*, vol. 1, pp. 471–72.
8. M. I. Borah, ed., *Bahāristān-i-ghāybi* (in English).
9. Sudhindra Nath Bhattacharya, "State of Bengal under Jahangir" and "Conquests of Islam Khan (1608–1613)" in Jadunath Sarkar, ed., *The History of Bengal*, vol. 2, pp. 234–46 and 247–72.
10. Sudhindra Nath Bhattacharya, "Last Achievements of Islam Khan," ibid., pp. 273–88.

11. Apparently, there were sceptics who doubted that Kushadhwaj actually belonged to the lineage he claimed. They alleged that once he had attained a position of power and wealth, he got the Brahmins to invent a Bikrampur Brahmin lineage for him. See Kshitimohan Sen, *Jātibhed*, p. 165. I am grateful to Gautam Bhadra for this curious reference.

12. Nabinchandra Bhadra in *Bhāoyāler itihās* is eloquent in his condemnation of the cruel whims of the zamindars from the Ghazi family (though no individuals are mentioned by name). He gives two examples. The Ghazis, it seems, once decided to enact a boat disaster. They got some soldiers to line up on the riverbank, train their guns on a country boat packed with passengers crossing the river, and ordered them to fire. As dozens of panic-stricken men and women jumped into the water, the Ghazis gleefully watched the scene. They are also said to have ordered a pregnant woman to be brought in front of them and then had her stomach cut open, because they wanted to see the foetus inside her womb. "These depredations threatened the wealth of every rich man and the chastity of every beautiful woman in the country" (pp. 33–34). Curiously, exactly the same instances of cruelty—identical stories and identical phrases of condemnation—were used in the nineteenth century by Hindu writers to condemn Siraj-ud-daulah, the Nawab of Bengal, who was defeated by an English-inspired conspiracy in the infamous battle of Plassey in 1757. There is reason to suspect that Nabinchandra's indictment was framed more by a conventional rhetoric than by specific historical evidence.

13. Kedarnath Majumdar, *Ḍhākār bibaraṇ*, pp. 180–82.

14. F. D. Ascoli, *Final Report on the Survey and Settlement Operations in the District of Dacca, 1910 to 1917*, p. 59.

15. For clarifications on the identities of three prominent persons of Dacca, all called James Wise, see the Editor's Introduction by Muntassir Mamoon to James Wise, *Pūrbabaṅger bibhinna jāti, barṇa o peśār bibaraṇ*, especially p. 13.

16. Ascoli, *Report on Settlement in Dacca*, p. 103.

17. Ibid., p. 115.

18. For brief account of these movements, see Sekhar Bandyopadhyay, *Caste, Politics and the Raj: Bengal 1872–1937*, pp. 95–141.

19. The long poem called *Mager mulluk* was serialized in the Calcutta journal *Prākṛti* in 1892.

20. On the unhappy story of the relation between the two poets, see Brajendranath Bandyopadhyay, ed., *Sāhitya-sādhak-caritmālā, 74: Gobindacandra Dās;* Syed Abul Maqsud, *Gobindacandra dās;* Brajendranath Bandyopadhyay, *Sāhitya-sādhak-caritmālā, 66*, p. 55.

21. Surendramohan Mukhopadhyay, *Ḍhākār āśutoṣ dāsgupter jerā o bhāoyāl rājkāhinī*, p. 3.

22. Brajendranath Bandyopadhyay, *Sāhitya-sādhak-caritmālā 66*, p. 57.

23. Quoted in Tara Ali Baig, *The Moon in Rahu: An Account of the Bhowal Sannyasi Case*, pp. 110–11.

24. Ibid., p. 113.

25. See, in particular, Nakazato, *Agrarian System in Eastern Bengal*.

26. GB, Board of Revenue, Land Revenue, Proceedings. 56–57, January 1905, OIOC.

27. Ibid.

28. GB, Board of Revenue, Lower Provinces, Land Revenue, Wards Branch, Pro-

ceedings 101–105, January 1906, *Report on Administration of Wards' Estates for the Year 1904–1905* (hereafter GB, *Report on Wards' Estates*), WBSA.

29. Nakazato, *Agrarian System*, p. 300.

30. For an exhaustive and extraordinary list of *abwab*s, see Sasisekhar Ghosh, *Jamidārī-darpaṇ*.

31. Ascoli, *Report on Survey and Settlement in Dacca*, p. 42.

32. J. C. Jack, *Final Report on the Survey and Settlement Operations in the Bakarganj District*, p. 83.

33. Ascoli, *Report on Survey and Settlement in Dacca*, p. 44.

34. The classic literary depiction of zamindari oppression is the play by Mir Mosharaf Hosain, "Jamidār darpaṇ" (1873), in Kazi Abdul Mannan, ed., *Maśārraph racanā sambhār*, vol. 1.

35. For general surveys of agrarian relations in Bengal in the early twentieth century, see Sugata Bose, *Peasant Labour and Colonial Capital: Rural Bengal since 1770*; Partha Chatterjee, *Bengal 1920–1947: The Land Question*; Sugata Bose, *Agrarian Bengal: Economy, Social Structure and Politics, 1919–1947*; and specifically for east Bengal, Nakazato, *Agrarian System*.

36. GB, *Report on Wards' Estates*, WBSA.

CHAPTER THREE
ON HUNTING AND OTHER SPORTS

1. For a biography of Kitchener, see Philip Warner, *Kitchener: The Man Behind the Legend*. On the Curzon-Kitchener conflict, see Peter King, *The Viceroy's Fall: How Kitchener Destroyed Curzon*.

2. On Kitchener's kleptomania and alleged homosexuality, see King, *The Viceroy's Fall*, pp. 84, 3–37.

3. J. B. Rye and Horace A. Groser, *Kitchener in His Own Words*, p. 286.

4. Quoted in Basu, *J*, pp. 19–20.

5. The classic historical work on this subject is Sumit Sarkar, *The Swadeshi Movement in Bengal 1903–1908*.

6. Baig, *Moon in Rahu*, pp. 121–23.

7. The artist Paritosh Sen gives a vivid description of the procession as he remembers seeing it as a child. "Nowhere else in this subcontinent could one have seen such a gorgeous, immense and spectacular event. One could see in this procession the extraordinary artistry of those magic hands that had created the world-renowned muslin. For two days this intricate multi-coloured pageant, constantly shifting and changing, would pass before my eyes like a huge tapestry. It was like looking through a kaleidoscope. The active organizers were Hindu, but quite literally the procession was for all to join." Paritosh Sen, *Jindābāhār*, pp. 66–68. A more sceptical view is given by an English official: "Huge effigies, representations of gods and godesses, or grotesque figures of beasts and men in all the glory of tinsel and paint, are borne aloft, the wonder and admiration of the crowd. Some of the erections, lightly constructed of bamboo, stand fifty feet high, depicting whole stories in the glittering scenes and figures that adorn them. The subjects chosen for representation exhibit the widest catholicity of taste. The Fall of Port Arthur, a strongly modern and foreign incident to figure in this old-world festival, is shown in tier on

tier of one of the most significant structures, the designer's idea of war and of Russian and Japanese being quaint in the extreme." F. B. Bradley-Birt, *The Romance of an Eastern Capital*, p. 263.

8. Evidence of Girish Chandra Sen, life insurance agent. *ABP,* 7 February 1934.

9. Letters received by Bibhabati from her mother and sister were produced in court and appear in the evidence volumes in official English translations. I have used below the translations made by Tara Ali Baig.

10. Baig, *Moon in Rahu*, pp. 101–3.

11. Manoda Debi, "Janaikā gṛhabadhūr ḍāyeri," esp. p. 84.

12. Geraldine Forbes and Tapan Raychaudhuri, eds., *The Memoirs of Dr. Haimabati Sen: From Child Widow to Lady Doctor,* pp. 84–86.

13. Baig, *Moon in Rahu*, p. 108.

14. Ibid., pp. 125–26.

15. Ibid., pp. 134–35.

16. Ibid., pp. 135–36.

17. Ibid., pp. 160–62.

18. Ibid., pp. 162–64.

Chapter Four
What Happened in Darjeeling?

1. Durganath Chakrabarti, *Bhāoyāle mṛtyubāsī-darśan.*

2. Muhammad Fazlul Huq and Sultan Kabiraj, *Bhāoyāl kumār rahasya: nutan sambād* (Dhaka: Jahnabi Press, 1922).

3. Dineschandra De, *Bhāoyāler kathā o nabīn sannyāsī.*

4. Such as Niradchandra Chakrabarti, *Jaydebpurer yogī-prasaṅga.*

5. S. G. Hart, Collector to Commissioner, Dacca, 9 August 1919; and note of Commissioner, 18 August 1919, Bhawal Estate Papers, NAB.

6. Quoted in Lodge, *J,* pp. 602–3.

7. Quoted ibid., pp. 609–10.

8. Biswas, *J,* p. 31.

9. On the Khilafat and Non-cooperation movements in Bengal, see Rajat Kanta Ray, *Social Conflict and Political Unrest in Bengal 1875–1927,* pp. 225–310; and Chandiprasad Sarkar, *The Bengali Muslims: A Study in their Politicization 1912–1929,* pp. 102–44.

10. Fortnightly Report of the Government of Bengal on the Political Situation, first half of January 1922, WBSA.

11. Quoted in Lodge, *J,* pp. 606–7.

12. Quoted ibid., p. 458.

13. Niradchandra Chakrabarti, *Jaydebpurer yogī-prasaṅga,* p. 10.

14. Biswas, *J,* p. 49.

15. Costello, *J,* pp. 750–51.

16. In some sources, his name is mentioned as Surendra Mohan Mukherjee.

17. Niradchandra Chakrabarti, *Jaydebpurer yogī-prasaṅga.*

18. GB, Board of Revenue, Land Revenue, Proceedings A 52–53, July 1921; A 59–60, August 1921; A 11–12, August 1921, WBSA.

19. These documents are reproduced in Lodge, *J*, pp. 541–43.

20. Kedarnath Chakrabarti, *Bhāoyālī kāṇḍa*.

21. The story of the alleged impostor Pratapchand has passed into the modern folklore of Bengal largely as a result of Sanjibchandra Chattopadhyay's masterful narration in *Jāl pratāpcāṅd: bardhamān rājer galpa*. Strangely, it was only in the popular press that the Pratapchand affair was recalled as a precedent in the Bhawal sannyasi case. It was not mentioned even once in the voluminous proceedings in court, even though precedents from Britain, especially the Tichborne case, were frequently cited.

22. Full text of certificate in Lodge, *J*, p. 457.

23. Costello, *J*, p. 741.

24. Basu, *J*, p. 113.

25. Ibid., p. 116.

CHAPTER FIVE

FIRST BRUSH WITH THE LAW

1. Quoted in Brahmachari Brajendranath, *Bhāoyāl mānhānir rāy*.

2. Quoted in Basu, *J*, p. 88.

3. Details of Ashutosh Dasgupta's testimony are given in Surendramohan Mukhopadhyay, *Ḍhākār āśutoṣ dāsgupter jerā o bhāoyāl rājkāhinī*.

4. All the prescriptions served by Smith, Stanistreet and Co. are reproduced in Lodge, *J*, pp. 450–54.

5. The abbreviations used in the prescriptions mean: $\mathfrak{z}$ = dram; $\mathfrak{z}$ = ounce; ss = *semisse*, half; ad = up to; m = *misce*, mix; ft = *fiat*, make; Gr. = grain.

6. The testimonies are cited in Lodge, *J*, pp. 523–24.

7. The hearing in the High Court is described in detail in Surendramohan Mukhopadhyay, *Kalkātāy baḍa rāṇīr sahit bhāoyāl madhyam kumārer sākṣāt o bhāoyāl mānhāni: hāikorṭer rāy*.

8. *Emperor, appellant v. Purna Chandra Ghose, respondent*, in *Calcutta Weekly Notes*.

9. Mukhopadhyay, *Hāikorṭer rāy*, pp. 13–14.

10. Ibid, p. 15.

CHAPTER SIX

THE HOUSE ON LANSDOWNE ROAD

1. Surendranath Mukhopadhyay, *Hāikorṭer rāy*, p. 1.

2. Quoted in Nagendrakumar Chanda, *Bhāoyāler sannyāsī kumār*, p. 3.

3. Ibid, pp. 4–5.

4. Costello, *J*, p. 743.

5. Lodge, *J*, p. 480.

6. Cross-examination of Bibhabati Debi, reprinted in Chiranjib Sen, *Bhāoyāler mejakumār*, pp. 136–73.

7. Cross-examination of Rajkumari Jyotirmoyee Devi, reported in *ABP*, 12 July 1934.

8. Basu, *J*, pp. 113–14.

9. The history of these Hindu-Muslim clashes is described in Suranjan Das, *Communal Riots in Bengal 1905–1947.*

10. GB, Board of Revenue, *Report of the Administration of Wards' Estates for the year 1912–13*, p. 11, WBSA.

11. GB, Board of Revenue, Land Revenue, Proceedings, A22–23, August 1929, *Report of Administration of Wards', Attached and Trust Estates for 1334 BS (1927–28)*, Appendix I, WBSA.

12. J. M. Mitra and R. C. Chakravarty, eds., *The Bhowal Case*, Appendix A, pp. xvi–xxviii.

13. Ibid, pp. xxiii–xxiv.

14. GB, Board of Revenue, Land Revenue, Proceedings, A1–2, June 1931, *Report on Wards' Estates for 1336 BS (1929–30)*, p. 7, WBSA.

15. Evidence of Jogendra Nath Banerjee, *ABP*, 15 September 1935.

16. For details on the Chittagong armory raid, see Manini Chatterjee, *Do and Die: The Chittagong Uprising 1930–34*, and I. Mallikarjuna Sharma, *Easter Rebellion in India: The Chittagong Uprising.* There is also an important reminiscence literature on the subject; see, in particular, Ananta Singh, *Caṭṭagrām yuba bidroha*, and Kalpana Dutt, *Chittagong Armoury Raiders: Reminiscences.*

17. Statement of Dhirendra Ch. Ray, zamindar, Armanitola, Dacca, 19 June 1930, Dacca Riot Enquiry, GB Home Poll, Conf. File 444/30, WBSA.

18. See Suranjan Das, *Communal Riots in Bengal*, pp. 107–20. On the communalization of politics in this period, see Taj ul-Islam Hashmi, *Pakistan as a Peasant Utopia: The Communalization of Class Politics in East Bengal, 1920–1947.*

19. A. J. Dash, I.C.S., "A Fist in the Door," unpublished diary for the period 1927–1935, pp. 10–11, Mss. Eur. C.188/3, OIOC.

20. A. J. Dash, I.C.S., "The South District," ibid., p. 8.

21. Ibid., p. 11.

22. Ibid., p. 11.

23. Ibid., p. 9.

24. R. C. Dutt, *Imperialism to Socialism: Memoirs of an Indian Civil Servant*, p. 59.

25. David Washbrook, "Law, State and Agrarian Society in Colonial India."

26. "An Account of His Life": The Unpublished Reminiscences of Sir Alan Henderson, I.C.S., p. 114, Mss. Eur. D.1094, OIOC.

CHAPTER SEVEN
A FONDNESS FOR MIRACLES

1. I am immensely grateful to Professor Gautam Bhadra for his generous help in locating the sources and material for the writing of this chapter.

2. The classic here is Sanjibchandra Chattopadhyay, *Jāl pratāpcāṅd: bardhamān rājer galpa.* Gautam Bhadra's recent retelling of the history of this case, "Jāl rājār galpa" has been serialized in seven instalments in the weekly *Deś*, between August and October 1999.

3. The most comprehensive history of the Burdwan Raj in the eighteenth century is John R. McLane, *Land and Local Kingship in Eighteenth-century Bengal.*

4. This was the famous *patni* system, studied at length by agrarian historians. See, for instance, Ratnalekha Ray, *Change in Bengal Agrarian Society, c.1760–1850.*

5. *Jāl pratāpcāṅd*, pp. 16–17.

6. The report of W. M. Elliott, District Magistrate of Bankura, cited in McLane, *Land and Local Kingship*, p. 320.

7. Letter of A. Alexander, quoted in Sanjibchandra, *Jāl pratāpcāṅd*, p. 30.

8. Quoted ibid., p. 39.

9. Quoted ibid., p. 44.

10. Quoted ibid., pp. 97–98.

11. See William J. Herschel, *The Origin of Finger-printing*. Also see Francis Galton, *Finger Prints*.

12. Quoted ibid., pp. 47–48.

13. Quoted ibid., p. 51.

14. Quoted ibid., p. 86.

15. Quoted ibid., p. 101.

16. Ibid., p. 110.

17. McLane, *Land and Local Kingship*, p. 322.

18. Ibid., pp. 321–32.

19. The hearing of the appeal in the Sadar Dewani Adalat in Calcutta was reported in the periodical *Saṃbād pūrṇacandroday*, 9 Paus 1259 B.S. (22 December 1852). For further details on the Jalamutha estate, see Chitta Panda, *The Decline of the Bengal Zamindars: Midnapore 1870–1920*, p. 43.

20. Satischandra Bandyopadhyay, "Lyāṇḍorār jāl rājā."

21. *District Gazetteers of the United Provinces of Agra and Oudh*, vol. 2: *Saharanpur*, edited by H. R. Nevill.

22. Ibid, p. 121–22.

23. "Lyāṇḍorār jāl rājā."

24. Kedarnath Chakrabarti, *Bhāoyāli kāṇḍa*, p. 3.

25. Prabhatkumar Mukhopadhyay, *Ratna-dīp*.

26. The most detailed account of the Tichborne affair is Douglas Woodruff, *The Tichborne Claimant: A Victorian Mystery*.

27. Readers may also be aware of the retelling of the Tichborne story by Jorge Luis Borges in "Tom Castro, the Implausible Impostor" in Borges, *A Universal History of Infamy*, pp. 29–38. I am grateful to Arjun Mahey for reminding me of this story. When I had first read it in the 1970s, I had no clue that it had any connection with the story of the Bhawal sannyasi.

28. Reminiscences of Alan Henderson, p. 114.

29. Information was obtained from obituary notices on Pannalal Basu preserved by his son T. K. Basu. Interview with T. K. Basu, Calcutta, 9 August 1998.

CHAPTER EIGHT
THE IDENTITY PUZZLE

1. For a useful survey, see James Baillie, *Problems in Personal Identity*.

2. Parfit, *Reasons and Persons*, p. 202.

3. I have adapted this definition of the physical criterion from Baillie, *Problems in Personal Identity*, pp. 10–11.

4. John Locke, *An Essay Concerning Human Understanding* (1690), book 2, chap. 27, sec. 9.

5. Ibid., book 2, chap. 27, sec. 15.

6. Bernard Williams, *Problems of the Self,* pp. 46–63.

7. Some of the landmark works in this field, besides the ones already cited, are Sidney Shoemaker, "Persons and Their Pasts"; David Wiggins, *Sameness and Substance;* Robert Nozick, *Philosophical Explanations;* Richard Swinburne, *Personal Identity;* and Thomas Nagel, *The View from Nowhere.*

8. Peter Unger, *Identity, Consciousness and Value,* p. 276.

9. Parfit, *Reasons and Persons,* p. 281.

10. Ibid., p. 273; emphasis in the original. Also see, pp. 502–3. For a medley of examples showing the complexities involved in determining the "truth" of identity even within modern Western culture, see Hillel Schwartz, *The Culture of the Copy: Striking Likenesses, Unreasonable Facsimiles.*

11. See especially Paul Ricoeur, *Oneself as Another,* pp. 113–68.

12. Ibid., p. 119.

13. Ibid., p. 121.

14. Ibid., p. 168.

15. Jitendra Nath Mohanty, *Reason and Tradition in Indian Thought: An Essay on the Nature of Indian Philosophical Thinking,* p. 198.

16. Figure 4 is adapted from Satischandra Chatterjee, *The Nyāya Theory of Knowledge: A Critical Study of Some Problems of Logic and Metaphysics,* p. 22. I have changed some of the English terms to suit our usage here.

17. Mohanty, *Reason and Tradition,* p. 241. Mohanty himself makes an argument in this book for including within the domain of Indian thought memory as a form of true cognition and, by extension, history as a mode of true knowledge.

18. Narayan Chandra Goswami, ed., *Śrīmadannambhaṭṭa viracitah Tarkasaṃgrahah (saṭīkah) adhyāpanāsahitah,* p. 213.

19. For a brief overview of the treatment of pratyabhijñā by different philosophical schools, see Chatterjee, *Nyāya Theory,* pp. 205–8.

20. Jyoti Prasad Bhattacharya, "Pratyakṣa: Nyāyamat samīkṣā," pp. 261–2.

21. Jitendranath Mohanty, *Gaṅgeśa's Theory of Truth,* p. 54.

22. Wendy Doniger in her selection of stories of sexual masquerade, imposture, and doubling discusses several ways in which one might mistake one's lover for someone else, but includes only one reference to a story from India—a Telugu story in which a trickster notices a mole on a woman's leg when she is crossing a river and later cites the mole as proof that he was her husband. Wendy Doniger, *The Bedtrick: Tales of Sex and Masquerade,* p. 443 n86.

23. Mohanty, *Gaṅgeśa's Theory,* pp. 44–45.

24. Goswami, ed., *Tarkasaṃgrahah,* pp. 216–18.

25. For a summary discussion on the Nyāya theory of *śabda,* see Chatterjee, *Nyāya Theory,* pp. 318–57.

CHAPTER NINE
THE TRIAL BEGINS

1. B. C. Chatterjee, *The Betrayal of Britain and Bengal* (Calcutta: Brahmo Mission Press, 1933), in the Zetland Collection, Mss. Eur. D609/21(e), OIOC. Chatterjee

pointed out that C. R. Das was utterly heterodox in his lifestyle but was nevertheless the most revered public figure in Bengal. Brajen Seal and Meghnad Saha, although they belonged to castes from whom the Brahmins would not accept water, were universally acknowledged as intellectual giants.

2. B. C. Chatterjee, *An Appeal to the Lord Chairman and Members of the Joint Committee on Indian Constitutional Reform* (Calcutta: Brahmo Mission Press, 1933), Zetland Collection, Mss. Eur. D609/21(g), OIOC.

3. B. C. Chatterjee, *Supplementary Notes on the Premier's Award and the Poona Pact* (London: H. Smith, 1933), Zetland Collection, Mss. Eur. D609/21(f), OIOC.

4. See, for instance, Pradip Kumar Datta, *Carving Blocs: Communal Ideology in Early Twentieth-Century Bengal.*

5. Chatterjee, *An Appeal.*

6. One version of this story is given by his daughter Prasannamayi Debi in *Pūrbba kathā,* pp. 68–69.

7. "Statement of Facts" by J. Bignold, and Note by Sasanka Ghose, 1 July 1930, Bhawal Estate Papers, NAB.

8. Correspondence between P. J. Griffiths, manager of the Bhawal estate, Sasanka Ghose, and the Board of Revenue, August 1931, Bhawal Estate Papers, NAB.

9. Donald McPherson, Secretary, Board of Revenue to Commissioner, Dacca Division, 3 March 1931, Bhawal Estate Papers, NAB.

10. N.V.H. Symons, Secretary, Board of Revenue to Commissioner, Dacca Division, 15 December 1931, Bhawal Estate Papers, NAB.

11. Sarajubala Debi to Manager, Bhowal Court of Wards Estate, 17 May 1930, Bhawal Estate Papers. NAB.

12. Opinion of Sasanka Ghose, 29 May 1932, Bhawal Estate Papers, NAB.

13. Note from Commissioner's office, Dacca Division, 1 June 1932, Bhawal Estate Papers, NAB.

14. For a political history of this period, see Tanika Sarkar, *Bengal 1928–1934: The Politics of Protest.* Anderson rose higher after his stint in Bengal. As Viscount Waverley, he joined the War Cabinet, was given the charge of civil administration and atomic energy, and was nominated by Winston Churchill to the king as the next prime minister should he and Anthony Eden both perish on their way to Yalta. Anderson earned very high praise from Churchill: "He was, in the general judgement of Whitehall, the greatest administrator of his time, perhaps of any time in the country's history." *Dictionary of National Biography,* edited by Leslie Stephen and Sydney Lee.

15. *ABP,* 2 December 1933.

16. Ibid.; Basu, *J,* pp. 133–34; Lodge, *J,* pp. 626–28.

17. *ABP,* 2 December 1933.

18. *ABP,* 10 December 1933.

19. *ABP,* 14, 15, 16, 17, 19, 21 December 1933; Basu, *J,* p. 303.

20. *Dhākā prakāś,* 17 December 1933; *The Statesman,* 16 December 1933.

21. *The Statesman,* 16 December 1933; Lodge, *J,* p. 691.

22. *Dhākā prakāś,* 31 December 1933.

23. Basu, *J,* p. 264, 266.

24. *Dhākā prakāś,* 17 December 1933.

25. Ibid., 31 December 1933.

26. Ibid.
27. *ABP*, 5, 10, 13, 22 December 1933, 11 January, 2 February 1934.
28. *ABP*, 2 February 1934.
29. *ABP*, 26 January, 3, 9 February, 29 July 1934.
30. *ABP*, 11, 12 January, 16 February 1934.
31. *ABP*, 28, 30 January 1934.
32. *ABP*, 4, 5 December 1933, 19 January 1934.
33. *ABP*, 17 January 1934.
34. *ABP*, 26 January 1934.
35. *ABP*, 3 March 1934.
36. *ABP*, 11 March 1934.
37. *ABP*, 26 January 1934.
38. *ABP*, 4 January 1934.
39. *ABP*, 5 January, 2 February 1934.
40. *ABP*, 9, 26 January 1934.
41. *ABP*, 9, 26 January 1934.
42. *ABP*, 1 June 1934.
43. *ABP*, 27 May 1934.
44. *ABP*, 27 January 1934.
45. *ABP*, 3, 10, 11, 24 February 1934.
46. *ABP*, 25 February, 6 March 1934.
47. *ABP*, 28 February 1934.
48. *ABP*, 6, 10 April 1934.
49. *ABP*, 23 September 1934.
50. *ABP*, 3 March 1934.
51. *ABP*, 2 October 1934.
52. *ABP*, 22 March 1934.
53. *ABP*, 14 March 1934.
54. *ABP*, 13 May 1934; Basu, *J*, pp. 143–44.
55. *ABP*, 18 May 1934.
56. *ABP*, 20 September 1934.
57. *ABP*, 15 May 1934.
58. Basu, *J*, p. 95.
59. *ABP*, 25 December 1934.
60. *ABP*, 3, 4, 5, 6, 7, 8, 11, 12, 13, 14, 15, 17, 18 July 1934.
61. *ABP*, 23, 25 September, 6 October 1934.
62. *ABP*, 25, 27 November 1934.
63. *ABP*, 12, 15, 19, 22 December 1934; Basu, *J*, p. 253.
64. *ABP*, 3, 6 February 1935.
65. *Ḍhākā prakāś*, 8, 15 July 1934.

CHAPTER TEN
DARJEELING: THE PLAINTIFF'S CASE

1. Edmund Mitchell, *Thacker's Guide Book to Darjeeling and Its Neighbourhood*, pp. 77–79, 83.

2. *ABP*, 12 June 1934.

3. Basu, *J*, pp. 346–47.

4. *ABP*, 24 August 1934.

5. Mitchell, *Thacker's Guide Book*, p. 8.

6. Ibid, p. 90.

7. J. A. Keble, *Darjeeling Ditties and Other Poems*, p. 10.

8. A Pioneer Lady, *The Indian Alps* (London: Longmans, Green, 1876), quoted in Keble, *Darjeeling Ditties*, p. x.

9. *ABP*, 15 August 1934.

10. *ABP*, 25 August 1934.

11. *ABP*, 23 September 1934.

12. *ABP*, 14 December 1934.

13. *ABP*, 23 September 1934.

14. *ABP*, 2 October 1934.

15. *ABP*, 9 October 1934.

16. *ABP*, 4 December 1934.

17. *ABP*, 27 November 1934.

18. *ABP*, 21 August 1934.

19. *ABP*, 30 November, 4 December 1934.

20. *ABP*, 14 December 1934.

21. *ABP*, 16 June 1934.

22. *ABP*, 12, 13, 16 January 1935; Lodge, *J*, p. 530.

23. *ABP*, 18 January 1935.

CHAPTER ELEVEN
EXPERTS ON RECOGNITION

1. Basu, *J*, p. 8.

2. Ibid., p. 8.

3. Ibid., pp. 8–9.

4. *ABP*, 13, 16, 17 January 1934.

5. *The Statesman*, 22 May 1935.

6. *ABP*, 7, 9, 10 August 1935.

7. *ABP*, 10 August 1934; Basu, *J*, p. 211.

8. *ABP*, 1 June 1934; Basu, *J*, pp. 197, 210–11, 215.

9. Basu, *J*, p. 212.

10. Ibid., p. 213.

11. Ibid., p. 25.

12. *ABP*, 7, 8 February 1934.

13. Basu, *J*, p. 202.

14. Ibid., p. 186.

15. Major E. J. Somerset, IMS, "Reminiscence of an Indian Medical Service Officer," p. 129, Mss. Eur. D1023, OIOC.

16. Basu, *J*, p. 224.

17. Ibid., pp. 228–34; Lodge, *J*, p. 668.

18. Some of the abbreviations used in the prescriptions are as follows:

℥	dram
℥	ounce
aa	of each a like quantity
ad	up to
f. or ft.	*fiat*, make
Gr.	grain
m.	*misce*, mix
mist	mixture
ss.	*semisse*, half
T.D.S.	*ter die sumendus*, take thrice a day
p.c.	*post cibum or cibos*, after food or meals

Modern medicine in the early twentieth century, even in India, was, it seems, all Latin.

19. ABP, 22 February 1935; Basu, J, pp. 310, 316, 335; Biswas, J, p. 146; Lodge, J, p. 461.

20. ABP, 17, 19, 21 August 1934; Basu, J, p. 318; Biswas, J, p. 87.

21. Biswas, J, p. 88; Lodge, J, pp. 469–70.

22. Basu, J, pp. 318–19, 336–37; Biswas, J, p. 86.

23. Basu, J, pp. 319, 337.

24. Nagendranath Das, *Bhāoyāler rāṇī sannyāsīr laḍāi*, no. 1, pp. 3–12.

25. ABP, 10 October, 15, 17 November 1934.

26. ABP, 6 February 1935.

27. ABP, 7 February 1935.

28. Basu, J, p. 129.

29. Ibid., p. 8.

CHAPTER TWELVE
FOR THE DEFENSE

1. *ABP,* 15 February 1935.

2. *ABP,* 15 February 1935.

3. *ABP,* 31 July 1935.

4. *ABP,* 15 February 1935.

5. *The Statesman,* 2, 4, 10, 12 May 1935.

6. *ABP,* 27 July 1935.

7. *ABP,* 17 July 1935.

8. *ABP,* 20 July 1935.

9. *ABP,* 19 February 1935.

10. *ABP,* 30, 31 August, 1, 3 September 1935.

11. *The Statesman,* 2 April 1935; Basu, *J,* p. 360.

12. Basu, *J,* pp. 358–60.

13. *ABP,* 16, 17 February 1935.

14. Henderson, the district judge of Dacca, wrote about Rankin's death in his memoirs: "My old Comilla District Magistrate, Rankin, had been District Magistrate of Dacca for six years and knew the [Bhawal Raj] family well. Although he had

been retired for some years he was brought out to give evidence that the plaintiff was an impostor. Almost as soon as he had left the box he collapsed. It was found that he was suffering from cancer of the intestines, and he died a few days later. This made a tremendous impression on the Dacca Hindus, who were convinced to a man that he was the victim of divine vengeance for having given false evidence." A.G.R. Henderson, "An Account of his Life," p. 114, Mss. Eur. D.1094, OIOC.

15. A. J. Dash, I.S.C., "A Fist in the Door," unpublished diary for the period 1927–1935, p. 7, Mss. Eur. C.188/3, OIOC.

16. *ABP,* 21 February 1935; Lodge, *J,* p. 446.

17. Note from Commissioner's office, 12 September 1934, file 26/1936, Dacca Divisional Commissioner's Office Papers, NAB.

18. *ABP,* 23 February 1935; Basu, *J,* pp. 165–66.

19. *ABP,* 27 February 1935.

20. Basu, *J,* p. 279.

21. *Ḍhākā prakāś,* 28 April 1935; Basu, *J,* pp. 162–65.

22 *ABP,* 23, 24, 25 July 1935; Biswas, *J,* p. 409.

23. Government of India, Home Department, Intelligence Bureau, *Terrorism in India 1917–1936* (Simla: Government of India Press, 1937), p. 58.

24. *ABP,* 8, 13, 14, 15, 17, 20, 21 September 1935; Basu, *J,* p. 125.

25. Basu, *J,* p. 152.

26. Ibid., pp. 127–28.

27. Ibid., p. 298.

28. Chiranjib Sen [Amarendrakumar Sen], *Bhāoyāler mejakumār,* pp. 136–73; Basu, *J,* pp. 298–99.

29. *The Statesman,* 9, 18, 19, 20, 21, 22 June 1935; *Ḍhākā prakāś,* 30 June 1935.

30. Nagendranath Das, *Bhāoyāler rāṇī sannyāsīr laḍāi,* no. 2, *Bhāoyāler māmlā o rāyer kathā* pp. 1–3.

CHAPTER THIRTEEN
THE CLIMAX

1. Basu, *J,* pp. 184–85.

2. *The Statesman,* 22, 24 June 1935; Basu, *J,* pp. 29, 156, 247–49.

3. *ABP,* 10 July 1935.

4. *ABP,* 27 July 1935.

5. *ABP,* 29 August 1935.

6. *ABP,* 7 September 1935.

7. *ABP,* 7 September 1935.

8. *ABP,* 17 February 1934; Basu, *J,* pp. 159–62.

9. Nagendrakumar Das, *Bhāoyāler rāṇī sannyāsīr laḍāi,* no. 3, *Bhāoyāler dhūmketu,* pp. 6–12.

10. *ABP,* 22, 25, 26, 28 September, 31 October, 1, 3 November 1935; *The Statesman,* 28 September, 2, 4 November 1935.

11. *ABP,* 17 November 1935; Basu, *J,* p. 389.

12. *ABP,* 26, 27, 29 January 1936.

13. *ABP,* 3 February 1936.

14. Basu, *J*, pp. 390–91.

15. *The Statesman*, 21 November 1935; Basu, *J*, pp. 320–21, 332; Biswas, *J*, p. 92.

16. Basu, *J*, p. 345.

17. *ABP*, 8, 10, 11, 13, 14, 15, 18, 19, 21 December 1935; *The Statesman*, 12, 19 December 1935.

18. *ABP*, 10 January 1936.

19. Nagendranath Das, *Bhāoyāler rāṇī sannyāsīr laḍāi*, no. 4, *Bhāoyāler bijayī rājkumār*, pp. 1–2.

CHAPTER FOURTEEN
REASONINGS

1. Interview with T. K. Basu, Calcutta.

2. Figures in parentheses in this chapter indicate page numbers from Basu, *J*.

CHAPTER FIFTEEN
THE JUDGMENT

1. Figures in parentheses in this chapter indicate page numbers from Basu, *J*.

2. A. Guha, Pleader, Alipur to Commissioner, Dacca, 27 June 1936, Bhawal Estate Papers, NAB.

3. GB, Board of Revenue, *Report of Wards' Estates*, 1934–35, p. 11.

4. D. L. Stewart, Manager, Bhawal Estate to Nelson, Commissioner, 27 August 1935, File 11/1934, Dacca Divisional Commissioner's Office Papers, NAB.

5. Estate Manager's opinion on appeal for reconsideration of fees paid to Government Pleader, 15 February 1936; note by Collector, 21 February 1936; note by Commissioner, 28 February 1936, Bhawal Estate Papers, NAB.

6. A. N. Chaudhuri to Manager, Bhawal Court of Wards Estate, 16 June 1936; U. N. Ghosh, Manager, Bhawal Estate to Commissioner, Dacca, 19 June 1936; L. Fawcus to A. N. Chaudhuri, 29 July 1936, Bhawal Estate Papers, NAB.

7. Correspondence between U. N. Ghosh, Manager, S. P. Ghosh, Government Pleader, and Fawcus, Commissioner, June 1936, Bhawal Estate Papers, NAB.

8. Note by Commissioner, Dacca, 17 August 1936. Bhawal Estate Papers. NAB.

9. In a radio talk in 1966, Justice P. B. Mukharji mentioned that as many as four dailies appeared at the time, including one called *Dainik Bhawal*, that were exclusively dedicated to reports of the trial. Prasantabihari Mukhopadhyay, "Ekṭi bikhyāta māmlā" in Amit Chakrabarti and Krishnasarbari Dasgupta, eds., *Betār jagat serā prabandha saṃkalan*, pp. 31–34.

10. *Ḍhākā prakāś*, 30 August 1936.

11. Ibid.

12. *Netaji Collected Works*, vol. 7: *Letters to Emilie Schenkl 1934–1942*, edited by Sisir Kumar Bose and Sugata Bose, pp. 81–84.

13. On the many rumors concerning the reappearance of Subhas Chandra Bose

after World War II, see Leonard Gordon, *Brothers against the Raj: A Biography of Sarat & Subhas Chandra Bose*.

14. Henderson, "An Account of his Life," p. 114, Mss. Eur. D.1094, OIOC.

15. Commissioner, Dacca, to Collector, Dacca, 30 August 1936, Bhawal Estate Papers, NAB.

16. Notice (in Bengali) by W. H. Nelson, Commissioner, Dacca Division, 20 Bhadra 1343 B.S., Bhawal Estate Papers, NAB.

17. Agent, Imperial Bank of India, Dacca, to Manager, Bhawal Court of Wards Estate, 4 September 1936, File 11/1936, Dacca Divisional Commissioner's Office Papers, NAB.

18. U. N. Ghosh, Manager, Bhowal Estate to Commissioner, 29 September 1936; note by Commissioner, 3 October 1936, File 11/1936, Dacca Divisional Commissioner's Office Papers, NAB.

19. Commissioner, Dacca Division, to Collector, Dacca, 19 September 1936, File 26/1936, Dacca Divisional Commissioner's Office Papers, NAB.

20. A. Guha to Commissioner, Dacca, 30 September 1936. File 26/1936, Dacca Divisional Commissioner's Office Papers, NAB.

21. Board of Revenue, Bengal, *The Bengal Wards' Manual 1919*, section 51, p. 35.

22. S. Banerjee, Secretary, Board of Revenue, Bengal to First Additional District Judge, Dacca, 2 November 1936, File 26/1936, Dacca Divisional Commissioner's Office Papers, NAB.

23. A. K. Ghani Colombi, *Bhāoyāl yubarājer mṛtyu-līlā*, pp. 10–12.

Chapter Sixteen
The Appeal

1. Sachindra Bhusan Das Gupta, "The Curious Case of the Bhowal Sannyasi" in *The High Court at Calcutta: Centenary Souvenir 1862–1962*, pp. 180–86.

2. A. J. Dash, "Bengal Diary 1935–1937," unpublished memoirs. Mss. Eur. C.188/4, OIOC.

3. For an analysis, see Sugata Bose, *Agrarian Bengal: Economy, Social Structure and Politics, 1919–1947*. pp. 200–32.

4. Costello, *J*, p. 764.

5. A. N. Chaudhuri's arguments are summarized ibid., pp. 762–75.

6. The situation may be judged from the following piece of news in a letter written on 6 October 1940 by John Younie, district judge at Alipore, to his wife in Edinburgh: "You remember F. O. Bell who was SDO of Siliguri when you were in Darjeeling. News has come through that he has been torpedoed on his way out to India but he was picked up and is now back in England waiting for another boat." Letters from John to Dorothy Younie, Mss. Eur. D939/21, OIOC.

7. Figures in parentheses in this chapter indicate page numbers from Biswas, *J*.

8. The role of the administration is discussed ibid., pp. 24–42.

9. The issue of the diary is discussed ibid., pp. 53–67.

10. The condolence letter is discussed ibid., pp. 138–50.

11. The rainfall issue is discussed ibid., pp. 262–75.

12. Dr. Acharya's evidence is discussed ibid., pp. 279–87.

13. R. N. Banerjee's evidence is discussed ibid., pp. 305–15.

14. On the Jagadananda episode, see Sumanta Banerjee, *The Parlour and the Streets: Elite and Popular Culture in Nineteenth-Century Calcutta.*

15. Gita Debi's evidence is discussed in Biswas, *J*, pp. 315–22.

CHAPTER SEVENTEEN
RAZOR'S EDGE

1. *The Quarterly Civil List for Bengal*, 214, pp. 491–502.

2. Figures in parentheses in this chapter indicate page numbers from Lodge, *J*.

3. The time of death is discussed by Justice Lodge ibid., pp. 481–89.

4. This story is usually told of Principal Heramba Maitra of City College, Calcutta, who was held up as the model of Brahmo rectitude and disciplinarianism. B. C. Chatterjee took the liberty of transferring an apocryphal story to fit the equally credible figure of S. N. Maitra, the Brahmo college teacher.

5. The attempted evening cremation is discussed in Lodge, *J*, pp. 499–521.

6. The story of the rescue is discussed ibid., pp. 521–35.

7. The morning cremation is discussed ibid., pp. 545–51.

8. This body of evidence is discussed ibid., pp. 551–54.

9. The question of recognition by Jyotirmayi Debi is discussed ibid., pp. 591–600. Italics in original.

10. See in this connection, Ranajit Guha, "The Prose of Counter-Insurgency."

11. The criteria for assessing the evidence on recognition and Satybhama Debi's evidence is discussed in Lodge, *J*, pp. 613–21.

12. Jyotirmayi Debi's honesty is discussed ibid., pp. 624–26.

13. The evidence of the kumar's relatives is discussed ibid., pp. 628–37.

14. This part of the recognition evidence is discussed ibid., pp. 637–50.

15. Justice Lodge discusses the evidence on physical identity ibid., pp. 653–76.

16. The evidence on mental identity is discussed ibid., pp. 676–705.

17. The evidence on handwriting is discussed ibid., pp. 705–11.

18. Biswas, J.'s Supplementary Statement, in Biswas, *J*, pp. 430–33.

19. Reply to Biswas, J.'s Statement as to Validity of Costello, J.'s Judgment, in Lodge, *J*, pp. 721–23.

CHAPTER EIGHTEEN
THE DECISION

1. Leonard W. J. Costello, *The Law Relating to Engineering: A Course of Six Lectures delivered at Caxton Hall, Westminster.*

2. L. W. J. Costello and Richard O'Sullivan, *The Profiteering Act, 1919;* Costello, *The Pocket Law Lexicon explaining Technical Words, Phrases and Maxims of the English, Scotch and Roman Law.*

3. "The two judgments of these two eminent Judges, Sir Manmatha Nath and J. Costello, are typical of the two ways of interpretation of a statute—one by an In-

dian Judge nurtured and influenced by the noble ideas of freedom and democracy prevailing at the time and the other by the bureaucratic view of a European Judge dealing justice in a dependent country. Justice Costello, who will ever be remembered for the memorable judgment in the biggest civil case in India, belonged to the old school of 'die hards' who could not tolerate such criticism of the government by a dependent subject." Amarendra Nath Mukherjee, *Sentinels of Liberty*, pp. 85–86.

4. Figures in parentheses in this chapter indicate page numbers from Costello, *J.*

5. The illness and time of death are discussed ibid., pp. 790–802.

6. The evening cremation is discussed ibid., pp. 803–9.

7. The morning cremation is discussed ibid., pp. 809–17.

8. The story of the rescue is discussed ibid., pp. 817–20.

9. The intervening years are discussed ibid., pp. 822–26.

10. The evidence on recognition is discussed ibid., pp. 827–34.

11. The physical features are discussed ibid., pp. 836–49.

12. The evidence on mental identity is discussed ibid., pp. 850–64.

13. S. C. Das Gupta, ed., *The Bhowal Case: High Court Judgments*, pp. 869–72.

14. Carlo Ginzburg, *The Judge and the Historian: Marginal Notes on a Late-Twentieth-Century Miscarriage of Justice*, pp. 17–18.

15. Apart from *The Judge and the Historian*, some other writings of Ginzburg that address the question of truth in history are *History, Rhetoric, and Proof;* "Proofs and Possibilities: In the Margins of Natalie Zemon Davis' *The Return of Martin Guerre*"; "Morelli, Freud, and Sherlock Holmes: Clues and Scientific Method"; and *Clues, Myths, and the Historical Method*.

16. This quote is from a new translation of the Borges story: "The Improbable Impostor Tom Castro," in *The Universal History of Iniquity*, p. 13. In actual fact, Old Bogle did not have the determining role that Borges attributes to him in setting up Thomas Castro as Roger Tichborne.

17. New methods of DNA testing have recently overturned convictions secured earlier through methods of identification then considered reliable. One study lists twenty-eight such cases and argues that by subjecting DNA tests to "special admissibility rules," U.S. courts were being forced to rely on inferior types of evidence. E. Connors, T. Lundregan, N. Miller and T. McEwen, "Convicted by Juries, Exonerated by Science," The question inevitably arises: could not the results of today's DNA tests turn out in the future to be equally unreliable?

18. A committee in Britain suggested in 1974 that identification procedures could never satisfactorily establish identity and that in criminal cases, "whenever identity is truly in issue, no conviction should be permitted in law unless there is corroborative evidence of a different kind linking the accused with the offence." Lewis Hawser, *Evidence of Identity: Memorandum of Evidence to Lord Devlin's Committee*, p. 12. In India, there is no rule barring a judge from convicting an accused on the basis of identification evidence alone, although many judgments have stressed the importance of corroborative evidence. There appears to be a strong suspicion in the Indian judiciary that police procedures of identification are unreliable; the police have often been accused of being biased, corrupt, or incompetent in producing identification evidence. Vishnu Mitter, *V. Mitter's Law of Identification and Discovery*, pp. 5–10.

19. Even in the most liberal court decisions involving alleged illegal immigrants in Britain, the principle asserted is that for actual residents the burden was on the state to prove that one had entered the country on a false identity (since the state was seeking to deprive a resident of his or her freedom), but those seeking to enter the country must prove to the satisfaction of the immigration authorities that they were who they claimed to be. See the judgments in *R v Secretary of State for the Home Department, ex parte Okunuga*, Court of Appeal (Civil Division) [1999]; *R v Secretary of State for the Home Department, ex parte OBI* [1997] Imm AR 420; *R v Secretary of State for the Home Department, ex parte Mohammad Fazor Ali* [1987] Imm AR 471; *Ali v Secretary of State for the Home Department* [1984] Imm AR 23.

20. James B. Adams of the Federal Bureau of Investigation, 17 May 1977 U.S. Senate *False Identification: Hearings before the Committee of the Judiciary*, p. 34.

21. "The criminal use of deceased infant identities has reached major proportions today. The use of this technique is ever-increasing. Today's criminal feels exceedingly secure when cloaked in this type of documentation." Testimony of James B. Adams, ibid., p. 23. In this testimony, Adams mentioned the case of a person in New Jersey who had nearly three hundred different false identities and about a thousand credit cards.

22. *Census of India, 1981:* Series 2, Andhra Pradesh, Paper I of 1985, S. S. Jaya Rao, "Household Population by Religion of Head of Household"; Series 23, West Bengal, Paper I of 1984, S. N. Ghosh, "Household Population by Religion of Head of Household."

23. *Census of India, 1981:* "General Note" in "Special Tables for Schedules Castes and Scheduled Tribes" for each state and union territory.

24. Ram Lal Gupta, *Law of Identification*, p. 69.

25. See, in particular, Michel Foucault, *Discipline and Punish: The Birth of the Prison;* "Governmentality" in Graham Burchell, Colin Gordon, and Peter Miller, eds., *The Foucault Effect: Studies in Governmentality*, pp. 87–104; and "Politics and Reason" in Foucault, *Politics, Philosophy, Culture: Interviews and Other Writings 1977–84*, pp. 57–85. More generally, see Michel Foucault, *Power.*

26. For the extension of the Foucauldian idea of discipline to "societies of control" and its implications for questions of identity, see Nikolas Rose, *Powers of Freedom: Reframing Political Thought*, especially pp. 233–46.

27. Michel de Montaigne, "Of the Lame," quoted in Horace W. Fuller, *Noted French Trials: Impostors and Adventurers*, p. 26. The most well-known recent account of the Martin Guerre story is, of course, Natalie Zemon Davis, *The Return of Martin Guerre.*

CHAPTER NINETEEN
To LONDON AND BACK

1. Interview with Manjula Banerjee, Calcutta, 8 May 2000.

2. L. G. Pinnell, I.C.S., cited in Paul R. Greenough, *Prosperity and Misery in Modern Bengal: The Famine of 1943–44*, p. 88.

3. Interview with Sunil Mukherjee, Calcutta, 28 April 2000.

4. Chinmay Chaudhuri, *Meja bhāoyāl kumār,* pp. 225–27.

5. Interview with Manjula Banerjee.

6. Interview with Sunil Mukherjee.

7. Hitesranjan Sanyal, "The Quit India Movement in Medinipur District."

8. See Greenough, *Prosperity and Misery;* Amartya K. Sen, *Poverty and Famines: An Essay in Entitlement and Deprivation.* Asok Mitra, then a young ICS officer in Dacca, attributes the "denial policy" and the resultant famine to the cynicism and bloody-mindedness of the British administration, and in particular of the governor Herbert. Asok Mitra, *Towards Independence 1940–1947: Memoirs of an Indian Civil Servant,* pp. 101–15.

9. P. A. Howell, *The Judicial Committee of the Privy Council 1833–1876: Its Origins, Structure and Development,* p. 169.

10. Interview with Manjula Banerjee.

11. D. N. Pritt, *The Autobiography of D. N. Pritt,* Part One: *From Right to Left,* pp. 128–29.

12. Pritt, *Autobiography,* Part Three: *The Defence Accuses,* pp. 26–46, 171–76.

13. Pritt added: "When it became known that I had received a 'brief fee' of 10,000 guineas, I had so many requests from left-wing organisations for help in various good causes that some of my friends prepared a short statement to show that, after taking into account both the tax on the brief fee and the higher rate of tax incurred on the rest of my income by reason of the addition of the 10,000 guineas, my net gain out of the fee was about £780, for which I had done three months' work." *Autobiography,* Part Two: *Brasshats and Bureaucrats,* pp. 231–32.

14. *Dictionary of National Biography,* edited by Leslie Stephen and Sydney Lee. His gift of storytelling was not universally appreciated. Viscount Dunedin, a retired law lord, wrote to the Lord Chancellor in 1938: "Thankerton. Doing well as to work and law, but making himself a veritable nuisance by excessive talking. I was asked to speak to him, and did quite lately. He took it quite well, but I hear that instead of being better he is worse than ever." Viscount Dunedin to Lord Hailsham, cited in R. F. V. Heuston, *Lives of the Lord Chancellors 1885–1940,* p. 481.

15. *Dictionary of National Biography.*

16. Pritt, *Brasshats and Bureaucrats,* p. 232.

17. *Bibhabati Devi (Appellant) v. Ramendra Narayan Roy and Others (Respondents),* Privy Council, Appeal from the High Court of Judicature at Fort William in Bengal, Privy Council Appeal No. 17 of 1945, Bengal Appeal No. 15 of 1943, *Indian Cases* (Lahore), 227 (1946), part 3, pp. 177–85.

18. See Alan Henderson, "An Account of His Life," p. 114, Mss. Eur. D. 1094, OIOC.

19. Shaibal Kumar Gupta, *A Foot in the Door of the Indian Civil Service,* p. 33.

20. R. C. Dutt, *Imperialism to Socialism,* pp. 84–85. There are numerous autobiographical accounts of Indian professionals that document this transition. I have cited a few Bengal civilians here; there are many from other regions of India who tell similar stories, as, for example, C. D. Deshmukh, *The Course of My Life;* Y. D. Gundevia, *In the Districts of the Raj;* S. K. Kirpalani, *Fifty Years with the British,* S. Bhoothalingam, *Reflections on an Era: Memoirs of a Civil Servant;* B. K. Nehru, *Nice Guys Finish Second.* An informative and sensitive autobiography by a teacher in

government service in Bengal is Subodhchandra Sengupta, *Te hi no divasā gatāh*. A fictionalized account of the more traumatic transition in the Indian army is given in Amitav Ghosh, *The Glass Palace*.

21. D. N. Sinha, "The Last Hundred Years," in *The High Court: Centenary Souvenir*, pp. 6–27.

22. For extended discussions on this point, see Partha Chatterjee, *Nationalist Thought and the Colonial World: A Derivative Discourse?* and *The Nation and Its Fragments: Colonial and Postcolonial Histories*.

23. See in this connection, Taj ul-Islam Hashmi, *Pakistan as a Peasant Utopia*.

24. This particular criticism of Dumont was made by Nicholas B. Dirks, *The Hollow Crown: Ethnohistory of an Indian Kingdom*. Dumont's theory is set out most elaborately in his *Homo Hierarchicus: The Caste System and Its Implications*. Dirks has made the argument about the relation between traditional kingship and sectarian coexistence in his *Castes of Mind*.

25. See, for instance, Tanika Sarkar, "Talking about Scandals: Religion, Law and Love in Late Nineteenth Century Bengal."

26. For a discussion on the figure of the widow in modern social thought in Bengal, see Dipesh Chakrabarty, "Witness to Suffering: Domestic Cruelty and the Birth of the Modern Subject." More generally, on the private world of nationalist modernity in Bengal, see Dipesh Chakrabarty, *Provincializing Europe: Postcolonial Thought and Historical Difference*, especially pp. 117–236.

27. Dirks, *Castes of Mind*.

28. I have seen an unpublished novel by an American author that makes its central theme a romance between Sarajubala and Ramendra, based apparently on information supplied during an interview in the 1970s with Bipin, the second rani's "boy khansama."

29. Tara Ali Baig, in *The Moon in Rahu*, an astonishingly bad novel written after an interview with Bibhabati in 1960, refers explicitly to the incest theme. The chapbooks, by contrast, were much more muted.

30. *Hindusthan Standard*, 5 August 1946.

31. P. K. Ghosh, Manager, Bhowal Estate, to Commissioner, Dacca Division, 9 August 1946, File 84/1946 Dacca Divisional Commissioner's Office Papers, NAB.

32. G. C. Das, Officiating Government Pleader's opinion, 7 August 1946, File 84/1946, Dacca Divisional Commissioner's Office Papers, NAB.

33. P. K. Ghosh, Manager, to Dhara Debi, 12 August 1946, File 84/1946, Dacca Divisional Commissioner's Office Papers, NAB.

34. Suranjan Das, *Communal Riots in Bengal*, pp. 161–92.

35. P. K. Ghosh to Dhara Debi, 1 September, 1946. File 84/1946. Dacca Divisional Commissioner's Office Papers, NAB.

36. Interview with Manjula Banerjee.

37. Ibid.

38. A. K. Shahjahan, *Bhāoyāl sannyās (yātrābhinay); Sannyāsi rājā* (1975), directed by Piyush Bose, starring Uttam Kumar and Supriya Chaudhuri.

BIBLIOGRAPHY

ARCHIVAL RECORDS

National Archives of Bangladesh
  Bhawal Estate Papers
  Dacca Divisional Commissioner's Office Papers
Oriental and India Office Collections, British Library, London
  Manuscripts Collection: Papers of A. J. Dash, Alan Henderson, E. J. Somerset,
  John Younie
  Zetland Collection
  Government of Bengal, Revenue Proceedings
West Bengal State Archives, Calcutta
  Government of Bengal, Home (Political) Confidential
  Land Revenue Proceedings
  Reports on Wards' Estates

PUBLISHED GOVERNMENT RECORDS

Allen, B. C. *Eastern Bengal District Gazetteers: Dacca*. Allahabad: Pioneer Press, 1912.

Ascoli, F. D. *Final Report on the Survey and Settlement Operations in the District of Dacca, 1910 to 1917*. Calcutta: Bengal Secretariat Book Depot, 1917.

Bhawal Sannyasi Case: Full Text of the Judgment. Dhaka: Bosen, 1936.

Bibhabati Devi (Appellant) v. Ramendra Narayan Roy and Others (Respondents), Privy Council Appeal No. 17 of 1945. *Indian Cases* (Lahore), 227 (1946), part 3, pp. 177–85.

Board of Revenue, Bengal. *The Bengal Wards' Manual 1919*. (Calcutta: Bengal Secretariat Book Depot, 1920.

Census of India, 1981.

Das Gupta, S. C. ed. *The Bhowal Case: High Court Judgments*. Calcutta: S. C. Sarkar, 1941.

Emperor, appellant v. Purna Chandra Ghose, respondent. In *Calcutta Weekly Notes* 28 (January-July 1925), pp. 579–85.

Jack, J. C. *Final Report on the Survey and Settlement Operations in the Bakarganj District*. Calcutta: Bengal Secretariat Book Depot, 1915.

Mitra, J. M., and R. C. Chakravarty, eds. *The Bhowal Case*. Dhaka: Aligarh Library, 1990.

Nevill, H. R., ed. *District Gazetteers of the United Provinces of Agra and Oudh*. Vol. 2. *Saharanpur*. Allahabad: UP Government Press, 1909.

The Quarterly Civil List for Bengal, 214. Calcutta: Bengal Secretariat Book Depot, 1921.

Rizvi, S.N.H. *East Pakistan District Gazetteer*. Dhaka: East Pakistan Government Press, 1969.

U.S. Senate. Committee on the Judiciary. *False Identification: Hearings on S. 1096.* 95th Cong., 1st sess. Washington, D.C.: U.S. Government Printing Office, 1977.

NEWSPAPERS

Amrita Bazar Patrika, Calcutta
Ḍhākā prakāś, Dhaka
Hindusthan Standard, Calcutta
The Statesman, Calcutta

PRIMARY PUBLISHED SOURCES IN BENGALI

Bhadra, Nabinchandra. *Bhāoyāler itihās.* Dhaka: Sulabh Press, 1875.

Brajendranath, Brahmachari. *Bhāoyāl mānhānir rāy.* Bogura: Syndicate Machine Press, 1924.

Chakrabarti, Durganath. *Bhāoyāle mṛtyubāsī-darśan.* Dhaka: Victoria Press, 1921.

Chakrabarti, Kedarnath. *Bhāoyālī kāṇḍa.* Dhaka: Manomohan Library, 1921.

Chakrabarti, Niradchandra. *Jaydebpurer yogī-prasaṅga.* Dhaka: Gendaria Press, 1921.

Chanda, Nagendrakumar. *Bhāoyāler sannyāsī kumār.* Dhaka: no publisher, 1924.

Das, Nagendranath. *Bhāoyāler rāṇī sannyāsīr laḍāi.* Nos. 1–4. Calcutta: Saraswati Printing Works, 1936.

De, Dineschandra. *Bhāoyāler kathā o nabīn sannyāsī.* Dhaka: Narayan Press, 1921.

Fazlul Huq, Muhammad, and Sultan Kabiraj. *Bhāoyāl kumār rahasya: nūtan saṃbād.* Dhaka: Jahnabi Press, 1922.

Ghani Colombi, A. K. *Bhāoyāl yubarājer mṛtyu-līlā.* Dhaka: New India Printing Works, 1938.

Shahjahan, A. K. *Bhāoyāl sannyās (yātrābhinay).* Dhaka: Katha Prakash, 1962.

Mukhopadhyay, Surendramohan. *Ḍhākār āśutoṣ dāsgupter jerā o bhāoyāl rājkāhinī.* Dhaka: no publisher, 1923.

———. *Kalkātāy baḍa rāṇīr sahit bhāoyāl madhyam kumārer sākṣāt o bhāoyāl mānhāni: bāikorṭer rāy.* Dhaka: Associated Printing, 1925.

SECONDARY SOURCES IN BENGALI

Bandopadhyay, Brajendranath, ed. *Sāhitya-sādhak-caritmālā* 66, 74. Calcutta: Bangiya Sahitya Parishat, 1958, 1961.

Bandyopadhyay, Satischandra. "Lyānḍorār jāl rājā. *Prabāsī,* 2.1 (Baisakh 1309 B.S., April–May 1903): 26–30.

Bhattacharya, Jyoti Prasad. "Pratyakṣa: Nyāyamat samīkṣā." Ph. D. dissertation, Jadavpur University, Calcutta, 1990.

Chakrabarti, Amit, and Krishnasarbari Dasgupta, eds. *Betār jagat serā prabandha saṃkalan.* Calcutta: Mitra and Ghosh, 2000.

Chattopadhyay, Sanjibchandra. *Jāl pratāpcāṁd: bardhamān rājer galpa.* 1883; reprint, Calcutta: K. Ganguli, 1959.

Chaudhuri, Chinmay. *Meja bhāoyāl kumār.* Calcutta: Deep Prakashan, 1993.

Debi, Manoda. "Janaikā gṛhabadhūr ḍāyeri." *Ekṣaṇ* 15.3–4 (Monsoon 1982): 75–150.

Debi, Prasannamayi. *Pūrbba kathā.* 1917; reprint, Calcutta: Subarnarekha, 1982.

Ghosh, Sasisekhar. *Jamidārī-darpan.* Narail: Manager's Office, 1896.

Goswami, Narayan Chandra, ed. *Śrīmadannaṃbhaṭṭa viracitaḥ Tarkasaṃgrahaḥ (saṭī-kaḥ) adhyāpanāsahitaḥ.* Translated into Bengali. Calcutta: Sanskrita Pustak Bhandar, 1983.

Hosain, Mir Mosharaf. "Jamidār darpan," in *Maśārraph racanā sambhār,* edited by Kazi Abdul Mannan. Vol. 1. Dhaka: Bangla Academy, 1976.

Kumar, Jnanendranath. *Baṃśa paricay.* 3 vols. Calcutta: Gobardhan Press, 1923.

Majumdar, Kedarnath. *Ḍhākār bibaran.* Mymensingh: Research House, 1910.

Mamoon, Muntassir. *Ḍhākā: smṛti-bismṛtir nagarī.* Dhaka: Bangla Academy, 1993.

Maqsud, Syed Abdul. *Gobindacandra dās.* Dhaka: Bangla Academy, 1987.

Mukhopadhyay, Prabhatkumar. *Ratna-dīp.* In *Prabhāt granthābalī.* Vol. 3. Calcutta: Basumati Sahitya Mandir, n.d.

Ray, Jatindramohan. *Ḍhākār itihās.* 2 vols. 1912, 1915; reprint, Calcutta: Shaibya, 2000.

Sen, Chiranjib. *Bhāoyāler mejakumār.* Calcutta: Mandal Book House, 1965.

Sen, Kshitimohan. *Jātibhed.* Calcutta: Viswabharati, 1977.

Sen, Paritosh. *Jindābāhār.* Calcutta: Papyrus, 1979.

Sengupta, Subodhchandra. *Te hi no divasā gatāh.* Calcutta: Sahitya Samsad, 1984.

Singh, Ananta. *Caṭṭagrām yuba bidroha.* 2 vols. Calcutta: Sen and Co., 1968.

Wise, James. *Pūrbabaṅger bibhinna jāti, barṇa o peśār bibaran.* Translated by Fauzul Karim. Dhaka: Dhaka University Press, 1998.

Secondary Sources in English

Baig, Tara Ali. *The Moon in Rahu: An Account of the Bhowal Sannyasi Case.* Bombay: Asia Publishing House, 1968.

Baillie, James. *Problems in Personal Identity.* New York: Paragon, 1993.

Bandopadhyay, Sekhar. *Caste, Politics and the Raj: Bengal 1872–1937.* Calcutta: K. P. Bagchi, 1990.

Banerjee, Sumanta. *The Parlour and the Streets: Elite and Popular Culture in Nineteenth-Century Calcutta.* Calcutta: Seagull, 1989.

Bhoothalingam, S. *Reflections on an Era: Memoirs of a Civil Servant.* Delhi: Affiliated East-West Press, 1993.

Borah, M. I., ed. *Bahāristān-i-ghāybi.* 2 vols. Gauhati: Government of Assam, 1936.

Borges, Jorge Luis. *Collected Fictions.* Translated by Andrew Hurley. Harmondsworth: Penguin, 1999.

———. *A Universal History of Infamy.* Translated by Norman Thomas di Giovanni. New York: E. P. Dutton, 1972.

Bose, Sisir Kumar, and Sugata Bose, eds. *Netaji Collected Works.* Vol. 7: *Letters to Emilie Schenkl 1934–1942.* Delhi: Oxford University Press, 1994.

Bose, Sugata. *Agrarian Bengal: Economy, Social Structure and Politics, 1919–1947.* Cambridge: Cambridge University Press, 1986.

———. *Peasant Labour and Colonial Capital: Rural Bengal since 1770.* Cambridge: Cambridge University Press, 1993.

Bradley-Birt, F. B. *The Romance of an Eastern Capital.* London: Smith, Elder, 1906.

Burchell, Graham, Colin Gordon, and Peter Miller, eds. *The Foucault Effect: Studies in Governmentality.* Chicago: University of Chicago Press, 1991.

Chakrabarty, Dipesh. *Provincializing Europe: Postcolonial Thought and Historical Difference.* Princeton: Princeton University Press, 2000.

———. "Witness to Suffering: Domestic Cruelty and the Birth of the Modern Subject." In Timothy Mitchell, ed., *Questions of Moderntiy.* Minneapolis: University of Minnesota Press, 2000, pp. 49–86.

Chatterjee, Manini. *Do and Die: The Chittagong Uprising 1930–34.* New Delhi: Penguin, 1999.

Chatterjee, Partha. *Bengal 1920–1947: The Land Question.* Calcutta: K. P. Bagchi, 1984.

———. *The Nation and Its Fragments: Colonial and Postcolonial Histories.* Princeton: Princeton University Press, 1993.

———. *Nationalist Thought and the Colonial World: A Derivative Discourse?* London: Zed Books, 1986.

Chatterjee, Satischandra. *The Nyāya Theory of Knowledge: A Critical Study of Some Problems of Logic and Metaphysics.* Calcutta: University of Calcutta, 1978.

Connors, E., T. Lundregan, N. Miller, and T. McEwen. "Convicted by Juries, Exonerated by Science." *NIJ Research Report,* U.S. Department of Justice, June 1996.

Costello, Leonard W. J. *The Law Relating to Engineering: A Course of Six Lectures Delivered at Caxton Hall, Westminster.* London: Society of Engineers, 1911.

———. *The Pocket Law Lexicon Explaining Technical Words, Phrases and Maxims of the English, Scotch, and Roman Law.* London: Stevens and Sons, 1921.

Costello, Leonard W. J., and Richard O'Sullivan. *The Profiteering Act, 1919.* London: Stevens and Sons, 1919.

Das, Suranjan. *Communal Riots in Bengal 1905–1947.* Delhi: Oxford University Press, 1991.

Datta, Pradip Kumar. *Carving Blocs: Communal Ideology in Early Twentieth-Century Bengal.* Delhi: Oxford University Press, 1999.

Davis, Natalie Zemon. *The Return of Martin Guerre.* Cambridge: Harvard University Press, 1983.

Deshmukh, C. D. *The Course of My Life.* New Delhi: Orient Longman, 1974.

Dirks, Nicholas B. *Castes of Mind.* Princeton: Princeton University Press, 2001.

———. *The Hollow Crown: Ethnohistory of an Indian Kingdom.* Cambridge: Cambridge University Press, 1987.

Doniger, Wendy. *The Bedtrick: Tales of Sex and Masquerade.* Chicago: University of Chicago Press, 2000.

Dumont, Louis. *Homo Hierarchicus: The Caste System and Its Implications.* Chicago: University of Chicago Press, 1980.

Dutt, Kalpana. *Chittagong Armoury Raiders: Reminiscences.* New Delhi: People's Publishing House, 1979.

Dutt, R. C. *Imperialism to Socialism: Memoirs of an Indian Civil Servant.* New Delhi: Milind, 1985.

Forbes, Geraldine, and Tapan Raychaudhuri, eds. *The Memoirs of Dr. Haimabati Sen: From Child Widow to Lady Doctor.* Translated by Tapan Raychaudhuri. New Delhi: Roli Books, 2000.

Foucault, Michel. *Discipline and Punish: The Birth of the Prison.* Translated by Alan Sheridan. Harmondsworth: Penguin, 1979.

———. *Politics, Philosophy, Culture: Interviews and Other Writings 1977–84.* New York: Routledge, 1988.

———. *Power.* Edited by James D. Faubion. New York: New Press, 2000.

Fuller, Horace W. *Noted French Trials: Impostors and Adventurers.* Boston: Soule and Bugbie, 1882.

Galton, Francis. *Finger Prints.* 1892; reprint New York: Da Capo Press, 1965.

Ghosh, Amitav *The Glass Palace.* Delhi: Permanent Black, 2000.

Ginzburg, Carlo. *Clues, Myths, and the Historical Method.* Translated by John and Anne Tedeschi. Baltimore: Johns Hopkins University Press, 1989.

———. *History, Rhetoric, and Proof.* Hanover, N.H.: University Press of New England, 1999.

———. *The Judge and the Historian: Marginal Notes on a Late-Twentieth-Century Miscarriage of Justice.* Translated by Antony Shugaar. London: Verso, 1999.

———. "Morelli, Freud, and Sherlock Holmes: Clues and Scientific Method." In Umberto Eco and Thomas A. Sebeok, eds., *The Sign of Three: Dupin, Holmes, Peirce.* Bloomington: Indiana University Press, 1983, pp. 81–118.

———. "Proofs and Possibilities: In the Margins of Natalie Zemon Davis' *The Return of Martin Guerre.*" *Yearbook of Comparative and General Literature* (1988), pp. 113–27.

Gordon, Leonard. *Brothers Against the Raj: A Biography of Indian Nationalist Sarat and Subhas Chandra Bose.* New York: Columbia University Press, 1990.

Greenough, Paul. *Prosperity and Misery in Modern Bengal: The Famine of 1943–44.* New York: Oxford University Press, 1982.

Guha, Ranajit. "The Prose of Counter-Insurgency." In Guha, ed., *Subaltern Studies II.* Delhi: Oxford University Press, 1983), pp. 1–42.

Gundevia, Y. D. *In the Districts of the Raj.* Hyderabad: Orient Longman, 1992.

Gupta, Ram Lal. *Law of Identification.* Lucknow: Eastern Book Company, 1963.

Gupta, Shaibal Kumar. *A Foot in the Door of the Indian Civil Service.* Calcutta: Papyrus, 1996.

Hashmi, Taj ul-Islam. *Pakistan as a Peasant Utopia: The Communalization of Class Politics in East Bengal, 1920–1947.* Boulder, Colorado: Westview Press, 1992.

Hawser, Lewis. *Evidence of Identity: Memorandum of Evidence to Lord Devlin's Committee.* London: Justice Educational and Resarch Trust, 1974.

Herschel, William J. *The Origin of Finger-printing.* 1916; reprint, New York: AMS Press, 1974.

Heuston, R.F.V. *Lives of the Lord Chancellors 1885–1940.* Oxford: Clarendon Press, 1964.

The High Court at Calcutta: Centenary Souvenir 1862–1962. Calcutta: High Court Buildings, 1963.

Howell, P. A. *The Judicial Committee of the Privy Council 1833–1876: Its Origins, Structure and Development.* Cambridge: Cambridge University Press, 1979.

Keble, J. A. *Darjeeling Ditties and Other Poems.* Calcutta: Calcutta General Printing, 1917.

King, Peter. *The Viceroy's Fall: How Kitchener Destroyed Curzon.* London: Sidgwick and Jackson, 1986.

Kirpalani, S. K. *Fifty Years with the British.* Hyderabad: Orient Longman, 1993.

Locke, John. *An Essay Concerning Human Understanding*. 1690; Oxford: Clarendon Press, 1979.

McLane, John R. *Land and Local Kingship in Eighteenth-Century Bengal*. Cambridge: Cambridge University Press, 1993.

Mitchell, Edmund. *Thacker's Guide Book to Darjeeling and Its Neighbourhood*. Calcutta: Thacker, Spink, 1899.

Mitra, Asok. *Towards Independence 1940–1947: Memoirs of an Indian Civil Servant*. Bombay: Popular Prakashan, 1991.

Mitter, Vishnu. *V. Mitter's Law of Identification and Discovery*. Allahabad: Law Book Company, 1978.

Mohanty, Jitendra Nath. *Gaṅgeśa's Theory of Truth*. Santiniketan: Centre of Advanced Study in Philosophy, Viswabharati, 1966.

————. *Reason and Tradition in Indian Thought: An Essay on the Nature of Indian Philosophical Thinking*. Oxford: Clarendon Press, 1992.

Mukherjee, Amarendra Nath. *Sentinels of Liberty*. Calcutta: Nalanda's, 1966.

Nagel, Thomas. *The View from Nowhere*. New York: Oxford University Press, 1986.

Nakazato, Nariaki. *Agrarian System in Eastern Bengal, c.1870–1910*. Calcutta: K. P. Bagchi, 1994.

Nehru, B. K. *Nice Guys Finish Second*. New Delhi: Viking, 1997.

Nozick, Robert. *Philosophical Explanations*. Cambridge: Harvard University Press, 1981.

Panda, Chitta. *The Decline of the Bengal Zamindars: Midnapore 1870–1920*. Delhi: Oxford University Press, 1996.

Parfit, Derek. *Reasons and Persons*. Oxford: Clarendon Press, 1984.

Pritt, D. N. *The Autobiography of D. N. Pritt*. 3 vols. London: Lawrence and Wishart, 1965–1966.

Ray, Rajat Kanta. *Social Conflict and Political Unrest in Bengal 1875–1927*. Delhi: Oxford University Pres, 1984.

Ray, Ratnalekha. *Change in Bengal Agrarian Society, c.1760–1850*. New Delhi: Manohar, 1979.

Ricoeur, Paul. *Oneself as Another*. Translated by Kathleen Blamey. Chicago: University of Chicago Press, 1992.

Rose, Nikolas. *Powers of Freedom: Reframing Political Thought*. Cambridge: Cambridge University Press, 1999.

Rye, J. B. and Horace A. Groser. *Kitchener in His Own Words*. New York: Frederick A. Stokes, n.d.

Sanyal, Hitesranjan. "The Quit India Movement in Medinipur District." In Gyanendra Pandey, ed., *The Indian Nation in 1942*. Calcutta: K. P. Bagchi, 1988, pp. 19–76.

Sarkar, Chandiprasad. *The Bengal Muslims: A Study in Their Politicization 1912–1929*. Calcutta: K. P. Bagchi, 1991.

Sarkar, Jadunath, ed. *The History of Bengal*. Vol. 2. Dhaka: University of Dacca, 1948.

Sarkar, Sumit. *The Swadeshi Movement in Bengal 1903–1908*. New Delhi: People's Publishing House, 1973.

Sarkar, Tanika. *Bengal 1928–1934: The Politics of Protest*. Delhi: Oxford University Press, 1987.

————. "Talking about Scandals: Religion, Law and Love in Late Nineteenth Century Bengal." *Studies in History* 13.1 (1997): 63–95.

Schwartz, Hillel. *The Culture of the Copy: Striking Likenesses, Unreasonable Facsimiles.* New York: Zone Books, 1996.

Sen, Amartya K. *Poverty and Famines: An Essay in Entitlement and Deprivation.* Oxford: Clarendon Press, 1981.

Sharma, I. Mallikarjuna. *Easter Rebellion in India: The Chittagong Uprising.* Hyderabad: Marxist Study Forum, 1993.

Shoemaker, Sidney. "Persons and Their Pasts." *American Philosophical Quarterly* 7.4 (October 1970): 269–85.

Stephen, Lesley, and Sydney Lee, eds. *Dictionary of National Biography.* 5 vols. London: Oxford University Press, 1949–1950.

Swinburne, Richard. *Personal Identity.* Oxford: Blackwell, 1984.

Unger, Peter. *Identity, Consciousness and Value.* New York: Oxford University Press, 1990.

Warner, Philip. *Kitchener: The Man behind the Legend.* London: Hamish Hamilton, 1985.

Washbrook, David. "Law, State and Agrarian Society in Colonial India." *Modern Asian Studies* 15.3 (1981): 649–721.

Wiggins, David. *Sameness and Substance.* New York: Oxford Unievrsity Press, 1980.

Williams, Bernard. *Problems of the Self.* Cambridge: Cambridge University Press, 1973.

Woodruff, Douglas. *The Tichborne Claimant: A Victorian Mystery.* London: Hollis and Carter, 1957.

INDEX